Advanced Oracle SQL Tuning
The Definitive Reference

Oracle In-Focus Series

Donald K. Burleson

To Janet, whose love and support helped to make this book a reality.

Advanced Oracle SQL Tuning
The Definitive Reference

By Donald K. Burleson

Copyright © 2014 by Rampant TechPress. All rights reserved.
Printed in the United States of America.
Published in Kittrell, North Carolina, USA.

Oracle In-Focus Series: Book #37
Series Editor: Donald K. Burleson
Production Manager: Janet Burleson
Editors: Janet Burleson, Robin Rademacher
Production Editor: Janet Burleson
Cover Design: Janet Burleson
Printing History: June 2011, December 2011, October 2012, March 2014
Oracle, Oracle8, Oracle8i, Oracle9i, Oracle10g, Oracle11g and Oracle 12c are trademarks of Oracle Corporation.

ISBN-13: 978-0-9916386-0-4
Library of Congress: 2014904248

Table of Contents

Using the Online Code Depot

Purchase of this book provides complete access to the online code depot that contains sample code scripts. Any code depot scripts in this book are located at the following URL in zip format and ready to load and use:

rampant.cc/adv-sql_tuning.htm

If technical assistance is needed with downloading or accessing the scripts, please contact Rampant TechPress at rtp@rampant.cc.

Preface

At its most basic level, an Oracle database can be thought of as nothing more than a SQL processing engine. The Oracle instance is simply a vehicle for storing and retrieving data, and almost all database operations are via some SQL and DML.

The idea of a standardized structured query language (SQL) was a cornerstone of the original relational database manifesto. To relational database purists, all relational algebra and relational set theory revolves around SQL syntax.

While relational theory is interesting, a working professional must understand the practical tools and techniques for tuning real-world SQL in a real-world production environment. Hence, I have deliberately skipped over the theory and focused on the practical aspects of Oracle SQL tuning.

Back in the early days of Data Processing, before it was renamed Information Technology, SQL was a revolution because it relieved the programmer of the cumbersome navigational database access. Thus, SQL became wildly popular as an end-user tool for accessing data.

But along with these ease of use came great under-the-covers complexity! Oracle SQL was expected to be able to always generate the best execution plan, a problematic challenge to any relational database.

Oracle rose to become the world's most robust and flexible database because their dialect of SQL is infinitely extensible via built-in functions.. These SQL extensions make SQL almost a true procedural language as evidenced by Oracle analytic functions.

I wrote this book because Oracle SQL tuning is an indispensible skill for every Oracle professional, not just the DBA. Every Oracle developer learns SQL syntax, but they are not done with a query simply because it returns the correct answer.

Rather, developers are now required to ensure that their SQL runs at peak performance, and this requires knowledge on how to rip under-the-covers and understand the machinations of Oracle's internal execution plans.

However, I am deliberately resisting the temptation to recommend SQL as a replacement for a procedural language. The latest incarnations of Oracle SQL contain advanced analytics that can be used to solve complex information processing without using a procedural language.

In my experience, using SQL as a replacement for PL/SQL is a mistake.   It was never designed as a replacement for procedural language, and super-complex SQL statements are incredibly hard to understand, maintain and tune.

Lastly, this is a pragmatic book, based upon my 25 years as a working DBA. If you are looking for theory and proofs, this is the wrong book for you.

I have designed this book to avoid "theory" and focus on explaining the internals of SQL tuning in plain English.   For a complete understanding of the theoretical foundations of SQL, see Vadim Tropashko's great book *"SQL Design Patterns"*. For a treatment of advanced SQL programming techniques, I also recommend Laurent Schneider's book *"Advanced Oracle SQL Programming"*.

Introduction to Oracle SQL Tuning

"I think we need to tune your SQL"

Introduction to Oracle SQL

Many Oracle professionals do not know that databases existed decades before the advent of Oracle. Since the 1970's, commercial databases have thrived and database administrators have managed large online systems and written queries to extract their data.

While SQL has become the de-facto standard for data access in relational databases, it is important to note that the acronym "SQL" is a bit of a misnomer. It can be argued that SQL is neither structured, query-only nor a real language:

- **Structured:** Like any other procedural tool, SQL can be written in an unstructured fashion. As of 2009, many people were using Oracle SQL as a full-blown procedural language as noted in Oracle ACE Laurent Schneider's book *"Advanced Oracle SQL Programming"*.

- **Query:** SQL is not query-only, and a subset of SQL called DML (Data Manipulation Language) performs updates, inserts and deletes.

- **Language:** SQL is not a true language per-se. SQL is embedded inside languages. As a data access method, SQL does not support all of the traditional language constructs (Boolean logic, looping); hence, Oracle SQL is embedded into existing languages such as C++ with the Pro*C pre-compiler, Java, PL/SQL and COBOL.

Even though it was never designed to process data, SQL is becoming more like a programming language, especially after the introduction of the ISO SQL99 enhancements. As implemented by Oracle, Oracle 9i ISO enhancements include the following new table join syntax:

- ***with* clause:** It is now possible to pre-materialize complex subqueries in-line, just like with global temporary tables.

- ***natural* join:** This useful Oracle syntax feature improves the readability of SQL by removing join criteria from the *where* clause.

- **The *using* clause:** This allows the specification the join key by name.

- **The *on* clause:** This syntax allows specification the column names for join keys in both tables.

There have also been programmatic enhancements to SQL that allow the simulation of Boolean branching in the form of the *if* statement. Oracle SQL allows the addition of Boolean logic and branching using the *decode* and *case* clauses. The *case* statement is a more flexible extension of the *decode* statement. In its simplest form the Oracle *case* function is used to return a value when a match is found:

```
select
   last_name,
   commission_pct,
  (case commission_pct
    when 0.1 then 'Low'
    when 0.15 then 'Average'
    when 0.2 then 'High'
    else 'N/A'
  end ) Commission
from employees;
```

The SQL *case* statement allows if-then-else processing, just like PL/SQL. The following is a more complex version of a *case* expression where a comparison expression is used to find a match:

```
select
   last_name,
   job_id,
```

```
   salary,
   (case
     when job_id LIKE 'SA_MAN' and salary < 12000 then '10%'
     when job_id LIKE 'SA_MAN' and salary >= 12000 then '15%'
     when job_id LIKE 'IT_PROG' and salary < 9000 then '8%'
     when job_id LIKE 'IT_PROG' and salary >= 9000 then '12%'
     else 'NOT APPLICABLE'
   end ) Raise
from
   employees;
```

Oracle SQL continues to evolve from a data extraction-only access method into a full-blown procedural language; however, this is not always a good thing. SQL was never designed to be a procedural interface, and procedural SQL can be very difficult to optimize.

SQL is everywhere, even on candy wrapper as shown with this printing error below:

SQL code accidentally printed onto a candy wrapper

Despite its ubiquitous nature, SQL tuning remains a huge challenge. The following section will provide a closer look at the evolution of Oracle SQL and illustrate how tuning SQL is critical to all Oracle databases.

The origin of relational SQL

Back in the 1970's, I was a junior programmer and DBA, and I remember the pre-relational data access methods used by the non-relational predecessors to Oracle, namely the Hierarchical IMS and the IDMS Network database engines. Back then, extracting data was not for beginners, and end-users were required to attend three-day classes in pre-relational data extraction tool such as the Cullinet *"Culprit"* access language.

The standard for Network databases was determined by the Committee On Development of Applied Symbolic Languages (CODASYL), specifically their DataBase Task group, the DBTG.

The following is an example of the cumbersome navigational queries in the CODASYL DBTG Network database. The code below navigates, record-by-record through the database:

```
    MOVE 'JONES' TO CUST-DESC.
    OBTAIN CALC CUSTOMER.
    MOVE CUSTOMER-ADDRESS TO OUT-REC.
    WRITE OUT-REC.
    FIND FIRST ORDER WITHIN CUSTOMER-ORDER.
        PERFORM ORDER-LOOP UNTIL END-OF-SET.

**************
 ORDER-LOOP.
**************

    OBTAIN FIRST ORDER-LINE-REC WITHIN ORDER-LINE.
    PERFORM ORDER-LINE-LOOP UNTIL END-OF-SET.
    FIND NEXT ORDER WITHIN CUSTOMER-ORDER.

    **************
    ORDER-LINE-LOOP.
    **************

        OBTAIN NEXT ORDER-LINE-REC WITHIN ORDER-LINE.
        MOVE QUANTITY-ORDERED TO OUT-REC.
        WRITE OUT-REC.
        OBTAIN OWNER WITHIN ORDER-LINE-PRODUCT
        MOVE PRODUCT-NAME TO OUT-REC.
        WRITE OUT-REC.
```

Figure 1.1: *An example of navigational data access in IDMS*

Thus, navigational data access requires a computer program to navigate, record by record, through the database, chasing pointers to retrieve related records as shown in Figure 1.2:

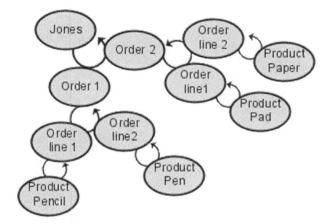

Figure 1.2: *Navigational data access*

Clearly, something needed to be done in order to make easy data access available to the end-user community. Early attempts focused on natural language interfaces to databases, such as Excalibur Corporations "Savvy" tool, which attempted to translate a free-form query into a structured form that a database could understand.

Dr. Ted Codd and Chris Date first introduced the concept of the Structured Query Language (SQL) in 1979 as a replacement for record-by-record data access.

As noted in the introduction to this chapter, SQL is technically not just a query language. SQL performs much more than queries in that it allows updates, deletes and inserts. Remember, SQL is also not a language. Instead, SQL is embedded within procedural languages such as Java or C++. Consequently, the name of Structured Query Language seemed logical for Dr. Codd's new tool.

In theory, SQL offers three classes of operators: select; project; and join.

The *select* operator

The *select* operator serves to shrink the table vertically by eliminating unwanted rows. To make relational theory more impressive, Codd and Date used regal verbiage. For example, rows were dubbed "instantiations of tuples" (tuples rhymes with "couples"), and the select operator was used to reduce the number of tuples from a table as shown in Figure 1.3:

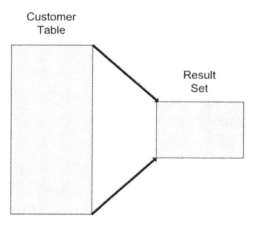

Figure 1.3: *The select operator filters out unwanted rows*

The *project* operator

The *project* operator (pronounced like a film projector, not like project management) serves to shrink the table horizontally by removing unwanted columns as shown in Figure 1.4.

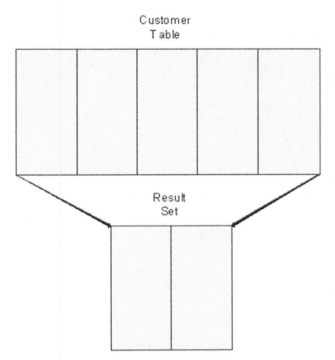

Figure 1.4: *The project operator eliminates unwanted columns*

Most commercial implementations of SQL do not directly support the *project* operation, and projections are achieved by specifying the list of columns desired in *SELECT* clause of the SQL statement.

The *join* operator

The *join* operator allows the dynamic linking of two tables that share a common column value. The *join* operation can be achieved by stating the selection criteria for two tables and equating them with their common columns as shown in Figure 1.5 below, but in practice there are many types of joins including the *cross join* that produces a Cartesian product of the rows in both tables.

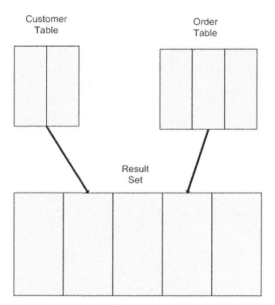

Figure 1.5: *A join makes a wide fat set from two thin sets*

There are also *outer joins* that allow the inclusion of rows that are missing in one of the joined tables.

Now that the theory has been covered, it is time to delve into the declarative nature of SQL and see how this is a double-edged sword for the SQL tuning expert.

The declarative nature of SQL

Because SQL is a declarative language, it is possible to write the same query in many forms, each getting the same result but with vastly different execution plans and performance. Re-writing SQL for faster performance is an important tuning technique:

- **Rewrite SQL to remove subqueries:** Subqueries can be very problematic from a performance perspective.

- **Rewriting the SQL in PL/SQL:** For certain types of SQL queries, rewriting complex SQL in PL/SQL can result in more than a 20x performance improvement.

- **Rewrite SQL to simplify query:** Decomposing a query into multiple queries using the *with* clause or global temporary tables greatly aids performance.

The following example illustrates how the same query can be written many ways. In this example, the goal is to see all books that do not have any sales.

💾 **Code depot password = sqltune**

This query below has a sub-query, a non-correlated sub-query to be specific. From a reader's perspective, this SQL is straightforward, and it is easy to understand the meaning "show me books without any sales":

```
select
   book_key
from
   book
where
   book_key not in
      (select book_key from sales);
```

In later chapters, it will become clearer why there are serious problems with subqueries that might return *null* values. It is a good idea to discourage the use of the NOT IN clause, which invokes a sub-query, and to prefer NOT EXISTS, which invokes a correlated sub-query, since the query returns no rows if any rows returned by the sub-query contain *null* values.

```
select
   book_key
from
   book
where
   not exists (select book_key from sales);
```

Subqueries can often be re-written to use a standard outer join, resulting in faster performance. How an outer join uses the plus sign (+) operator to tell the database to return all non-matching rows with *null* values will be covered later in this book. Hence, combining the outer join with a *null* test in the *where* clause to reproduce the result set without using a sub-query looks like the following:

```
select
   b.book_key
from
   book  b,
   sales s
where
   b.book_key = s.book_key(+)
and
   s.book_key IS null;
```

When SQL sucks

Because SQL is so flexible, any given query may have a dozen solutions, each with varying readability and performance. It is the developer's job to use the SQL best practices from this book to write SQL that is both maintainable and optimized

The following is an actual example of a poorly written SQL query. Take a quick look and it should be clear that it is hard to read, and the internal execution plan is horrible:

🖫 convoluted.sql

```
SELECT ART.DEMO_MEMBER DEMO_MEMBER,
       (SELECT PARAMETER_VALUE
        FROM   PPM_CIA_PREMIUM_VAL CIA_VAL
        WHERE  CIA_VAL.PRD_DEMO_CHRSTC_MEMBER = ART.DEMO_MEMBER
           AND CIA_NAME IN ('Baseline')
           AND PRMA_MKT_MEMBER = ?
           AND INVOICE_TYPE_NAME IN ('Weekly')
           AND GROUP_TYPE_CODE = 'C'
       ) WEEKLY_VALS,
       (SELECT PARAMETER_VALUE
        FROM   PPM_CIA_PREMIUM_VAL CIA_VAL
        WHERE  CIA_VAL.PRD_DEMO_CHRSTC_MEMBER = ART.DEMO_MEMBER
           AND CIA_NAME IN ('Baseline')
           AND PRMA_MKT_MEMBER = ?
           AND INVOICE_TYPE_NAME IN ('Monthly')
           AND GROUP_TYPE_CODE = 'C'
       ) MONTHLY_VALS,
       (SELECT PARAMETER_VALUE
        FROM   PPM_CIA_PREMIUM_VAL CIA_VAL
        WHERE  CIA_VAL.PRD_DEMO_CHRSTC_MEMBER = ART.DEMO_MEMBER
           AND CIA_NAME IN ('Baseline')
           AND PRMA_MKT_MEMBER = ?
           AND INVOICE_TYPE_NAME IN ('90Day')
           AND GROUP_TYPE_CODE = 'C'
       ) NINETYDAY_VALS,
       (SELECT PARAMETER_VALUE
        FROM   PPM_CIA_PREMIUM_VAL CIA_VAL
        WHERE  CIA_VAL.PRD_DEMO_CHRSTC_MEMBER = ART.DEMO_MEMBER
           AND CIA_NAME IN ('Baseline')
           AND PRMA_MKT_MEMBER = ?
           AND INVOICE_TYPE_NAME IN ('Annual')
           AND GROUP_TYPE_CODE = 'C'
       )      ANNUAL_VALS,
       'C' AS GROUP_TYPE_CODE
FROM
       (SELECT DISTINCT PRD_DEMO_CHRSTC_MEMBER DEMO_MEMBER
        FROM            PPM_CIA_PREMIUM_VAL
        WHERE           CIA_NAME IN ('Baseline')
                    AND PRMA_MKT_MEMBER = ?
                    AND INVOICE_TYPE_NAME IN ('Weekly' ,
                                              'Monthly',
                                              'Annual' ,
                                              '90Day')
                    AND GROUP_TYPE_CODE = 'C'
        GROUP BY        PRD_DEMO_CHRSTC_MEMBER
       ) ART

UNION ALL
SELECT     ART.DEMO_MEMBER DEMO_MEMBER,
           (SELECT PARAMETER_VALUE
            FROM   PPM_CIA_PREMIUM_VAL CIA_VAL
            WHERE  CIA_VAL.PRD_DEMO_CHRSTC_MEMBER = ART.DEMO_MEMBER
               AND CIA_NAME IN ('Baseline')
               AND PRMA_MKT_MEMBER = ?
               AND INVOICE_TYPE_NAME IN ('Weekly')
               AND GROUP_TYPE_CODE = 'T'
```

```
        ) WEEKLY_VALS,
        (SELECT PARAMETER_VALUE
        FROM    PPM_CIA_PREMIUM_VAL CIA_VAL
        WHERE   CIA_VAL.PRD_DEMO_CHRSTC_MEMBER = ART.DEMO_MEMBER
            AND CIA_NAME IN ('Baseline')
            AND PRMA_MKT_MEMBER = ?
            AND INVOICE_TYPE_NAME IN ('Monthly')
            AND GROUP_TYPE_CODE = 'T'
        ) MONTHLY_VALS,
        (SELECT PARAMETER_VALUE
        FROM    PPM_CIA_PREMIUM_VAL CIA_VAL
        WHERE   CIA_VAL.PRD_DEMO_CHRSTC_MEMBER = ART.DEMO_MEMBER
            AND CIA_NAME IN ('Baseline')
            AND PRMA_MKT_MEMBER = ?
            AND INVOICE_TYPE_NAME IN ('90Day')
            AND GROUP_TYPE_CODE = 'T'
        ) NINETYDAY_VALS,
        (SELECT PARAMETER_VALUE
        FROM    PPM_CIA_PREMIUM_VAL CIA_VAL
        WHERE   CIA_VAL.PRD_DEMO_CHRSTC_MEMBER = ART.DEMO_MEMBER
            AND CIA_NAME IN ('Baseline')
            AND PRMA_MKT_MEMBER = ?
            AND INVOICE_TYPE_NAME IN ('Annual')
            AND GROUP_TYPE_CODE = 'T'
        )       ANNUAL_VALS,
        'T' AS GROUP_TYPE_CODE
FROM
        (SELECT DISTINCT PRD_DEMO_CHRSTC_MEMBER DEMO_MEMBER
        FROM            PPM_CIA_PREMIUM_VAL
        WHERE           CIA_NAME IN ('Baseline')
                    AND PRMA_MKT_MEMBER = ?
                    AND INVOICE_TYPE_NAME IN ('Weekly' ,
                                              'Monthly',
                                              'Annual' ,
                                              '90Day')
                    AND GROUP_TYPE_CODE = 'T'
        GROUP BY        PRD_DEMO_CHRSTC_MEMBER
        ) ART
ORDER BY GROUP_TYPE_CODE
```

Look like Greek? It is never a good practice, to write convoluted SQL! The following paragraphs show the same query, rewritten for clarity and faster performance.

The above convoluted query can be completely rewritten for faster performance and easier maintainability. Take a minute to compare these two SQL statements, and it should become clear why the SQL below runs faster and is easier to understand and maintain.

```
select
    art.prd_demo_chrstc_member demo_member,
    sum(decode(art.invoice_type_name,'weekly',art.parameter_value))   weekly_vals,
    sum(decode(art.invoice_type_name,'monthly',art.parameter_value))  monthly_vals,
    sum(decode(art.invoice_type_name,'90day',art.parameter_value))    ninetyday_vals,
    sum(decode(art.invoice_type_name,'annual',art.parameter_value))   annual_vals,
    art.group_type_code
from
    ppm_cia_premium_val art
where CIA_NAME IN ('Baseline')
and
    prma_mkt_member = ?
and
    invoice_type_name in ('Weekly' ,
                          'Monthly',
                          'Annual' ,
                          '90Day')
and
    group_type_code in ('C','T')
```

```
group by art.prd_demo_chrstc_member,art.group_type_code
order by art.group_type_code, art.prd_demo_chrstc_member;
```

SQL is very flexible, and an equivalent query can be written in many ways with each giving the same result but with radically different readability and execution response time.

Because any given problem can be solved in SQL with many different syntax combinations, it is critical that a good SQL developer understand SQL best practices to ensure that their SQL is easy to maintain, and most importantly, that it has an optimal execution plan.

Who tunes SQL?

I have worked in database shops since 1983, and there remains a sharp division of opinions about who is responsible for tuning SQL:

- **Developers:** Many programmers are not interested in SQL, and all they care about is getting the right results.

- **DBAs:** Many DBAs do not have access to the production source code, so it can be very difficult for you to tune individual SQL statements.

Many Oracle professionals believe that their job is finished as soon as they get their SQL to give the correct results. After all, the general assumption is that the DBA can tune the SQL later, after it goes into production!

Sadly, many developers do not care about SQL performance. When developers are not judged on the performance of their coding outside of simply getting the right result, they focus on getting their code done quickly without any regard for overall performance.

This programming problem is not confined to Oracle, and many IT managers are more concerned with programmer productivity than execution speed.

In the 21st century, programming competitions are judged by the coder who can solve the problem the fastest. This was not always the case. Back in the days when "Information Systems" was called "Data Processing", programming competitions were judged by who could write the code at performed the most efficiently.

It is sad that very few Oracle shops require that their SQL be vetted for performance, and they only look at SQL tuning when they have a system-wide performance crisis! It is scary that many Oracle developers do not know how to create an execution plan, much less read a explain plan.

I believe that DBAs and developers alike need to understand the internal machinations of SQL so they can get the data that they need with a minimum amount of work. The following section will provide a closer look at SQL tuning.

Understanding SQL Tuning

Before relational databases were introduced, database queries required knowledge of the internal structures, and developers needed to build in their tuning as they wrote their query. This all changed when the SQL standard imposed a declarative solution to database queries.

Now, instead of the developer coding for optimal performance, the SQL optimizer is relied upon to do the tuning, determining the important data access methods such as what indexes to use and the optimal sequence to join multiple tables together. This is not always a good thing, as it makes it insanely easy for a beginner to write SQL that performs poorly.

Today, it is not enough for a developer to write an SQL statement that provides the correct answer; they must write the query to return the rows as quickly as possible.

Watch SQL performance!

The SQL is only have done when the correct output is returned. It is also necessary to ensure optimal performance! Because SQL is declarative, there are many ways to formulate a query, each with identical results but with different response time.

This remainder of this book provides a complete review the following areas of SQL tuning:

- The goals of SQL tuning
- Simplifying complex SQL
- SQL Optimization instance parameters
- Statistics and SQL optimization
- Oracle and CBO statistics
- Oracle tuning with hints
- Oracle SQL profiles

- AWR and SQL tuning

- ADDM and SQL tuning

The first three sections referenced above will be an overview of general Oracle tuning concepts, so that the basic tools and techniques for tuning SQL optimization are clearly introduced. The focus will then shift to an exploration of the new Oracle SQL Profiles, and will eventually delve into the internals of AWR and explore how the SQLTuning and SQLAccess advisor use time-series metadata.

The following section provides a quick, simple review of the goals of SQL tuning.

The top-down approach to Oracle tuning

In all types of Oracle tuning, a top-down approach is critical because some components impose constraints on their own components. For example, no amount of Oracle tuning is going to help when the server is experiencing problems. Since the server encompasses the Oracle instance environment, inspection of the server is the first step in any tuning engagement as show in Figure 1.6:

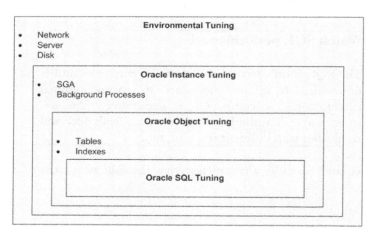

Figure 1.6: *The nested nature of Oracle tuning*

It is a huge mistake to tune the SQL before the DBA has tuned the database instance. For example, hundreds of hours can be spent tuning SQL only to find all of the hard work wiped out when the DBA changes any of the hundreds of "silver bullet" instance parameters. These are called silver bullets because a single change to a silver bullet parameter (e.g. *optimizer_mode*) will result in system-wide changes to the SQL workload.

It is also important to note that SQL tuning is only one of many tuning activities within Oracle. The most important tuning activity is a proper system design, which effects system-wide performance more than any other factor as shown in Figure 1.7:

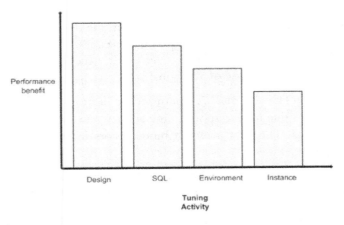

Figure 1.7: *The relative benefits of different Oracle tuning activities*

Also, while environmental tuning activities such as disk and network optimization can help Oracle performance, it is the optimization of the SQL queries that is the driving force behind Oracle tuning activities. For more complete information on how SQL tuning fits in to an overall Oracle tuning strategy, see my *book Oracle Tuning: The Definitive Reference* now available in an updated Third Edition.

It is time to dig a bit deeper and learn about the goals within the SQL tuning step.

The Goals of SQL Tuning

There are many approaches to SQL tuning and this section describes a fast, holistic method of SQL tuning where the SGA are optimized, the all-important optimizer parameters are evaluated and the CBO statistics are collected, all based on current system load. Once the best overall optimization is achieved, the next step is to drill down into the specific cases of sub-optimal SQL and change their execution plans with SQL profiles, specialized CBO stats or hints.

In Oracle, there are two goals for SQL tuning, and the DBA will choose one of these optimizer goals by setting the silver bullet optimizer_mode parameter. The optimizer_mode is called a silver bullet because changing this single parameter will have a profound impact on the SQL workload, radically changing the underlying execution plans.

There are two choices for the best SQL plan, the one that minimizes response time versus the plan that minimizes resource consumption.

Choose one:

- **Minimize resource consumption:** The *all_rows* optimizer, the default, is set to fetch the rows with a minimum amount of computing resources. The *all_rows* mode favors less expensive full-scan operations over index, access, which may return the rows faster, but at the expense of additional I/O.

- **Minimize response time:** The *first_rows_n* optimizer_mode (e.g. *first_rows_1*, *first_rows_10*) is designed to minimize response time latency and start returning rows as quickly as possible. The first_rows_n mode favors index access for faster SQL execution speed.

As noted earlier in this chapter, it is not unusual to find SQL that is less than optimal due to the push to get the right result at the expense of overall system performance.

This is a big shift in attitude from the days when coding contests were won by the developer getting the correct result using the least amount of resources.

This change in attitude is directly attributable to the shifting economics. In the early days, hardware was expensive, and it made sense to pay a programmer to carefully optimizer a program.

Today, hardware costs make up a much smaller percentage of the IT budget, and SQL optimization is not as important to an IT manager as high productivity. This change in attitude over time is represented by the graph in Figure 1.8:

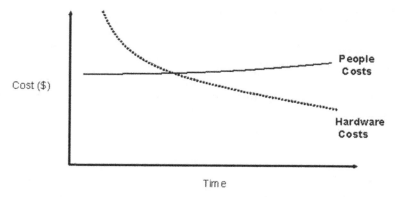

Figure 1.8: *The shifting costs of programmers vs. hardware*

Even though human costs now outweigh computing costs, SQL tuning remains critical, especially for SQL that executes thousands of times per hour. Hence, it is important to ensure that SQL programmers understand the importance of writing efficient SQL, right out of the gate. It costs time and money to go back and tune inefficient SQL after it has been written and implemented. Bad performing SQL can also result in customer relationship problems.

Despite the inherent complexity of tuning SQL, there are general guidelines that every Oracle DBA follows in order to improve the overall performance of their Oracle systems. The goals of SQL tuning are simple:

- Replace unnecessary large-table full-table scans with index scans
- Cache small-table full table scans
- Ensure optimal table join order
- Verify optimal index usage
- Verify optimal join techniques
- Tune complex subqueries to remove redundant access

These goals may seem deceptively simple, but these tasks comprise 90 percent of SQL tuning as shown in the pyramid in Figure 1.9:

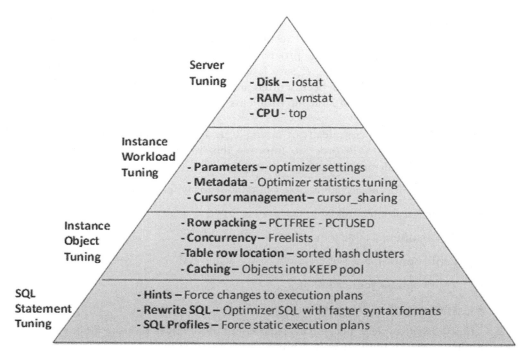

Figure 1.9: *The SQL tuning hierarchy*

In a nutshell, SQL tuning has some decision rules and follows a top-down approach. The following section will reveal some successful SQL tuning methods.

Roadblocks to SQL Tuning

Companies using vendor packages with Oracle can end up being one of thousands of shops struggling with optimizing and tuning vendor systems that they did not write and cannot change. Oracle shops are now using giant enterprise resource planning (ERP) solutions such as Oracle Applications, SAP and PeopleSoft, plus there are thousands of independent application vendors that are using Oracle as their database.

From small departmental applications to giant ERP packages, customers are now asserting their right to be provided with reliable documentation about the proper configuration for Oracle. This is especially true for vendors of departmental applications that are growing their client base and moving from small simple databases such as MySQL and SQL Server to a robust database such as Oracle.

Oracle SQL tuning is not always easy, and many managerial and technical limitations impose barriers to SQL optimization:

- **Vendor packages:** Many vendor packages have highly inefficient SQL because their SQL is designed to run on any relational database. It is not optimized for Oracle, yet the vendor rules prohibit customer changes to their source code. Fortunately, SQL that cannot be touched can still be tuned by altering the plans directly from the library cache, using special tricks like swapping execution plans in stored outlines or swapping SQL profiles.

- **Ad-hoc SQL:** Many systems offer ad-hoc query facilities with tools such as Crystal Reports to facilitate one-off SQL, written by inexperienced end users. As noted with vendor packages, Oracle SQL tuning becomes more difficult when it is not possible to get your hands on the SQL source code.

- **Resistance from management:** SQL "ownership" is a big deal in many IT infrastructures. It can often be hard for a DBA to tune a bad SQL statement because the SQL is "owned" by a development group.

- **Diminishing marginal returns:** It makes sense to always tune the SQL first that has the highest impact on the instance, also known as the low-hanging fruit. With this approach, there comes a point where the work involved in tuning seldom run SQL statements outweighs the cost of the time invested as shown in Figure 1.10:

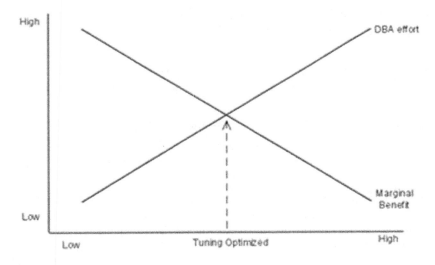

Figure 1.10: *The diminishing marginal returns of SQL tuning*

Barriers aside, SQL tuning is possible in almost every case, and the best place to start by working to understand all of the different SQL tuning options.

Successful SQL Tuning Methods

Oracle SQL tuning experts use an endless number of techniques, but there are some common techniques that can be used to optimize the most important SQL in any database.

Every experienced Oracle professional has developed their own method for identifying and tuning sub-optimal SQL, and they all work! Oracle is not a science, it is an art. There are an infinite number of valid ways to tune SQL, all of which achieve the goal of ensuring fast response time and minimum resource consumption.

Even though there are many SQL tuning methods, they all share some common techniques. The following is a short list of common SQL tuning tips and tricks:

- **Tune the workload first:** Always tune the workload as a whole before attempting to tune any individual SQL statements. Holistic tuning is achieved by finding the best settings for the SQL optimizer parameters, such as *optimizer_mode*, *optimizer_index_cost_adj* and *db_file_multiblock_read_count*, before tuning individual SQL statements. Once the global settings have been tuned, the "outlier" SQL statements that require manual tuning will have to be minimized.

- **Avoid re-parsing of SQL statements:** The library cache is intended to make SQL re-entrant. The savvy DBA will be sure to use *cursor_sharing* when appropriate.

- **Never assume that CBO statistics are correct:** Using the Garbage In/Garbage Out (GIGO) principle, the DBA should not hesitate to re-analyze tables and indexes with *dbms_stats*.

- **Use histograms for tuning:** Many common SQL problems, such as sub-optimal table join order, are caused by poor cardinality estimates. We apply histograms to help the optimizer estimate the size of intermediate rowset operations.

- **Use function-based indexes**: In almost all cases, the use of a built-in function like *to_char, decode, substr*, etc. in an SQL query may cause a full-table scan of the target table. To avoid this problem, many Oracle DBAs will create corresponding indexes that make use of function-based indexes. If a corresponding function-based index matches the built-in function of the query, Oracle will be able to service the query with an index range scan thereby avoiding a potentially expensive full-table scan.

- **Use materialized views:** Materialized views can pre-summarize aggregations and pre-join tables, making SQL run super fast in systems with low volume update activity.

- **Decompose complex SQL:** The *with* clause and global temporary tables can be used to flatten out complex subqueries and make execution times **faster.**

- **Avoid subqueries:** Many types of subqueries, such as those using *exists, in* or *not in*, can be rewritten as a standard join with faster performance.

- **Watch out for counterintuitive tips:** Tricks such as using *where rownum=1* can be dangerous.

- **Use views sparingly:** Views were designed to assist end users. Plus, they can make complex queries appear as if they were a discrete table. Hence, running production queries against views can cause a host of optimization problems.

- **Watch out for the *having* clause:** It is often possible to decompose a complex query using the *with* clause to avoid the use of the expensive *having* clause.

- **Use UNION ALL whenever possible:** The UNION clause removes duplicates, and it must perform an expensive sort to remove duplicate rows. Instead, using the UNION ALL clause is faster because it does not sort to remove duplicate rows.

- **Always reference an indexed column:** SQL with a WHERE clause that does not reference any indexed columns can result in an unnecessary large-table full-table scan.

- **Avoid using BIF's in *where* clause predicates:** It is best not to invalidate columns by changing the left-hand side of a WHERE clause predicate (*where substr(last_name,1,3) = 'Jon'; where trunc(my_date) = trunc(sysdate)*).

- **Test with the *rule* hint:** The *rule* hint is fantastic for testing whether a sub-optimal SQL query is failing because of a missing index or bad CBO statistics. In many cases, the *rule* hint's simplicity can help tune SQL statements faster.

Again, these are just a few of the common SQL tuning tricks. There are many, many more.

These tricks will be expanded upon in subsequent chapters. Now it is time to move on and explore the root causes of poor Oracle performance.

Tuning by Simplifying SQL Syntax

There are several methods for simplifying complex SQL statements, and Oracle will sometimes automatically rewrite SQL to make it more efficient.

- Rewrite the query into a more efficient form
- Use the *with* clause
- Use Global Temporary Tables

- Use Materialized Views

The following example shows how SQL can be rewritten. For a simple example of SQL syntax and execution speed, the following queries can be used. All of these SQL statements produce the same results, but they have widely varying execution plans and execution performance.

A non-correlated sub-query

```
select
  book_title
from
  book
where
  book_key not in (select book_key from sales);

Execution Plan
----------------------------------------------------------
   0      SELECT STATEMENT Optimizer=CHOOSE (Cost=1 Card=1 Bytes=64)
   1    0   FILTER
   2    1    TABLE ACCESS (FULL) OF 'BOOK' (Cost=1 Card=1 Bytes=64)
   3    1    TABLE ACCESS (FULL) OF 'SALES' (Cost=1 Card=5 Bytes=25)
```

An outer join

```
select
  book_title
from
  book   b,
  sales  s
where
  b.book_key = s.book_key(+)
and
  quantity is null;


Execution Plan
----------------------------------------------------------
0    SELECT STATEMENT Optimizer=CHOOSE (Cost=3 Card=100 Bytes=8200)

1   0 FILTER
2   1   FILTER
3   2    HASH JOIN (OUTER)
4   3     TABLE ACCESS (FULL) OF 'BOOK' (Cost=1 Card=20 Bytes=1280)
5   3     TABLE ACCESS (FULL) OF 'SALES' (Cost=1 Card=100 Bytes=1800)
```

A Correlated sub-query

```
select
  book_title
from
  book
where
  book_title not in (
```

```
            select
            distinct
              book_title
            from
              book,
              sales
            where
              book.book_key = sales.book_key
            and
              quantity > 0);
```

```
Execution Plan
----------------------------------------------------------
0   SELECT STATEMENT Optimizer=CHOOSE (Cost=1 Card=1 Bytes=59)
1   0  FILTER
2   1   TABLE ACCESS (FULL) OF 'BOOK' (Cost=1 Card=1 Bytes=59)
3   1   FILTER
4   3     NESTED LOOPS (Cost=6 Card=1 Bytes=82)
5   4       TABLE ACCESS (FULL) OF 'SALES' (Cost=1 Card=5 Bytes=90)
6   4       TABLE ACCESS (BY INDEX ROWID) OF 'BOOK' (Cost=1 Card=1)
7   6         INDEX (UNIQUE SCAN) OF 'PK_BOOK' (UNIQUE)
```

As illustrated here, the formulation of a SQL query has a dramatic impact on the execution plan for the SQL, and the order of the *WHERE* clause predicates can make a difference. Savvy Oracle developers know the most efficient way to code Oracle SQL for optimal execution plans, and the best Oracle shops train and expect their developers to formulate efficient SQL.

Causes of poor Oracle performance

What are the most common root-causes of poor Oracle performance? Every Oracle tuning expert will give a different opinion, but I've prepared my list, based upon my decades of experience tuning large and complex Oracle databases:

- **Bad Database Design:** The number one offender to poor performance is over-normalization of Oracle tables, excessive or unused indexes and 15-way table joins for what should be a simple fetch.

- **Poor server optimization:** Setting the server kernel parameters and I/O configuration (e.g. direct I/O) is critical to Oracle performance.

- **Bad disk I/O configuration:** This can be the result of inappropriate use of RAID5, disk channel bottlenecks and poor disk striping.

- **Poor Optimizer Statistics:** Prior to Oracle 10g's introduction of automatic statistics, a common cause of poor SQL performance was missing/stale CBO statistics and missing histograms. Even in Oracle 11g, the optimizer cannot always be trusted to choose the right statistics for every situation

---

- **Object contention:** Failure to set ASSM, *freelists* or *freelist_groups* for DML-active tables and indexes can cause very slow DML performance.

- **Under-allocated RAM regions:** Not allocating enough RAM for *shared_pool_size*, *pga_aggregate_target* and *db_cache_size* can cause an I/O-bound database.

- **Non-reentrant SQL:** All SQL should use bind variables, preferably in the code or via *cursor_sharing=force*, to make SQL reusable within the library cache.

- **Unset initialization parameters:** Many of the initialization parameters are made to be set by the DBA, such as *db_file_multiblock_read_count* before 10gr2 and *optimizer_index_caching*, and failing to set these parameters properly results in poorly optimized execution plans.

- **Excessive nested loop joins:** In 64-bit Oracle systems, there are gigabytes available for RAM sorts and hash joins. Failing to set *pga_aggregate_target* to allow the CBO to choose hash joins can result in very slow SQL performance.

- **Human Misfeasance:** The DBA's failure to monitor their database via STATSPACK/AWR, set-up exception reporting alerts via OEM and adjusting the instance to match changing workloads is a major cause of poor performance.

These are just some general guidelines for SQL tuning. The following section will provide a deeper look into the specific steps for optimizing SQL statements.

Optimizing Oracle SQL Execution

The key to success with the Oracle Cost-based Optimizer (CBO) is stability, and ensuring success with the CBO involves the consideration of several important infrastructure issues.

- **Ensure viable execution plans:** Whenever an object is re-analyzed, the execution plan for thousands of SQL statements may be changed. Most successful Oracle sites will choose to lock down their SQL execution plans by carefully controlling CBO statistics, using stored outlines (optimizer plan stability), adding detailed hints to their SQL or by using Oracle SQL Profiles. Again, there are exceptions to this rule. Ad-hoc systems such as Laboratory databases (LIMS) are one exception. For these databases, the DBA will choose to use dynamic sampling and allow the SQL execution plans to change as the data changes.

- **Reanalyze statistics only when necessary:** One of the most common mistakes made by Oracle DBAs is to frequently re-analyze the schema. The sole purpose of doing that is to change the execution plans for its SQL, and if it isn't broken, don't fix it. If the DBA is satisfied with current SQL performance, re-analyzing a schema could cause significant performance problems and undo any tuning efforts of the development staff. In practice, very few shops are sufficiently dynamic to require periodic schema re-analysis.

- **Pre-tune the SQL before deploying:** Many Oracle systems developers assume that their sole goal is to write SQL statements that deliver the correct data from Oracle. In reality, writing the SQL is only half the job and successful Oracle sites require all developers to ensure that their SQL accesses Oracle in an optimal fashion. Many DBAs will export their production CBO statistics into their test databases so that their developers can see how their SQL will execute when it is placed into the production system. DBAs and staff should be trained to use the autotrace and TKPROF utilities and to interpret SQL execution results.

- **Manage schema statistics:** All Oracle DBAs should carefully manage the CBO statistics to ensure that the CBO works the same in their test and production environments. A savvy DBA knows how to collect high quality statistics and then migrate production statistics into their test environments. This approach ensures that all SQL migrating into production has the same execution plan as it did in the test database.

- **Tune the overall system first:** The CBO parameters are very powerful because a single parameter change could improve the performance of thousands of SQL statements. Changes to critical CBO parameters such as *optimizer_mode*, *optimizer_index_cost_adj* and *optimizer_index_caching* should be done before tuning individual SQL statements. This reduces the number of sub-optimal statements that require manual tuning.

- **Determining the optimal table join order:** One of the most common problems with complex SQL is that the tables are not joined in the optimal order. Oracle tries to make the first table join (the "driving" table), produce the smallest number of rows, to reduce the intermediate row baggage that must be input to later table joins. Oracle 11g extended optimizer statistics, histograms and the *ordered* or *leading* hints are great ways to verify optimal table join order.

- **Remove unnecessary large-table full table scans:** Unnecessary full table scans (FTS) are an important symptom of sub-optimal SQL and cause unnecessary I/O that can drag down an entire database. The tuning expert first evaluates the SQL based on the number of rows returned by the query.

- **Cache small-table full table scans:** For cases in which a full table scan is the fastest access method, the tuning professional should ensure that a dedicated data buffer is available for the rows. In Oracle7, an *alter table xxx cache* command can be issued. In Oracle8 and beyond, the small-table can be cached by forcing it into the *keep* cache. Logical reads (consistent gets) are often 100x faster than a disk read and small, frequently referenced objects such as tables, clusters and indexes should be fully cached in the *keep* cache. Most DBAs check the *x$bh* view

---

periodically and move any table that has 80% or more of its blocks in the buffer into the *keep* cache. In addition, *dba_hist_sqlstat* should be checked for tables that experience frequent small-table full-table scans.

Prior to Oracle10g, it was an important job of the Oracle DBA to properly gather and distribute statistics for the CBO. The goal of the DBA was to keep the most accurate production statistics for the current processing. In some cases, there may be more than one set of optimal statistics.

For example, the best statistics for OLTP processing may not be the best statistics for the data warehouse processing that occurs each evening. In this case, the DBA will keep two sets of statistics and import them into the schema when processing modes change.

Of course, the SQL can be tuned until your heart's content, but if the optimizer is not fed with the correct statistics, the optimizer may not make the correct decisions. Before tuning, it is important to ensure that statistics are available and that they are current.

The following section will provide a closer look at the goals listed above as well as how they simplify SQL tuning. The following section will provide a closer look at one of my favorite SQL tuning techniques, tuning SQL by altering the predicate sequence within the *where* clause.

Watching the SQL *where* clause

Many people believe that the Oracle cost-based SQL optimizer does not consider the order that the Boolean predicates appear in the *where* clause. However, there is some indication that this is not completely true, as evidenced by the *ordered_predicates* SQL hint, which was created specifically to keep the optimizer from rearranging the predicates in the *where* clause.

The *ordered_predicates* hint is specified in the *where* clause of a query and is used to specify the order in which Boolean predicates should be evaluated, but the *ordered_predicates* hint was deprecated starting in Oracle 10g.

In the absence of *ordered_predicates*, Oracle uses the following steps to evaluate the order of SQL predicates:

- Subqueries are evaluated before the outer Boolean conditions in the *where* clause.

- All Boolean conditions without built-in functions or subqueries are evaluated in reverse from the order they are found in the *where* clause, with the last predicate being evaluated first.

- Boolean predicates with built-in functions of each predicate are evaluated in increasing order of their estimated evaluation costs.

The problem is that the Oracle SQL optimizer might rearrange the order of the *where* clause predicates, causing sub-optimal execution plans.

Oracle also suggests that the predicate order in the *where* can be very important when CPU costing is turned-on and system statistics (*dbms_stats.gather_system_stats*) have not been collected. Their view is that the Oracle optimizer keeps an internal reference list showing the estimated CPU costs for each SQL operation, and this list is calibrated at pare time against the *cpuspeed* metric from the *dbms_stats* metadata.

Again, the behavior of Oracle SQL optimization changes radically with each new release, and no standard rules apply, so your mileage may vary.

When testing SQL performance, my preference is to test different execution plans by placing the most restrictive Boolean predicate first after the *where* keyword. It does not always work, put it is still a good SQL best practice.

The next section will cover the idea of removing unnecessary large-table full-table scans. This will only be mentioned here briefly, as complete details are provided in Chapter 5, *Tuning Oracle full table scans*.

Remove unnecessary large-table full table scans

Oracle says that if the query returns less than 40 percent of the table rows in an ordered table or seven percent of the rows in an unordered table, based on the index key value described by *clustering_factor* in *dba_indexes*, the query can be tuned to use an index in lieu of the full-table scan.

However, it is rarely that simple. The speed of a full-table scan versus an index scan depends on many factors:

- Missing indexes, especially function-based indexes
- Bad/stale CBO statistics
- Missing CBO Histograms
- Clustering of the table rows to the used index
- System ability to optimize multiblock I/O (*db_file_multiblock_read_count*)

The most common tuning tool for addressing unnecessary full table scans is the addition of indexes, especially function-based indexes. The decision about removing a

---

full-table scan should be based on a careful examination of the amount of logical I/O (consistent gets) of the index scan versus the costs of the full table scan.

This decision should be made while factoring in the multiblock reads and possible parallel full-table scan execution. In some cases, an unnecessary full-table scan can be forced to use an index by adding an index hint to the SQL statement.

Setting SQL Optimization Goals

The characteristics of the SQL query workload determine the overall SQL optimization goal, which, in turn, translates into your choice of *optimizer_mode*, the most important SQL tuning parameter of all.

Some Oracle professionals have SQL that never needs to change as their data changes. And for these shops; For any SQL, there exists one, and only one, optimal execution plan.

While this is not true for every database, those with static data systems can greatly simplify SQL tuning. Once this optimal execution plan is determined, it should be made persistent with optimizer plan stability. In contrast, other shops want their SQL to change execution plans whenever there has been a significant change to the CBO statistics.

Stable shops where the table statistics rarely change will want to employ optimizer plan stability to make execution plans persistent, while shops where the CBO statistics frequently change will tune their queries without optimizer plan stability so that the run-time optimizer is free to choose the most appropriate execution plan based on the CBO statistics.

The choice of SQL philosophy has a dramatic impact on the required approach to SQL tuning and statistics maintenance. The following areas need to be taken into consideration when making a decision on you specific approach:

- **Table and index statistics**: The dynamic philosophy relies heavily on the table and index statistics, and these statistics must be recomputed each time that a table has a significant change. In contrast, the static philosophy does not rely on statistics.

- **SQL Profiles**: The use of SQL profiles and Optimizer Plan stability to "freeze" SQL execution plans depends heavily of the type of workload. The dynamic shop does not use optimizer plan stability because it wants the freedom for the execution plan to change whenever there is a major change to the data inside the tables. Conversely, the static shop relies on optimizer plan stability to make its tuning changes permanent and to improve SQL execution time by avoiding reparsing of SQL statements.

- **Adaptive Cursor sharing**: The dynamic shop often has SQL that is generated by ad-hoc query tools with hard-coded literal values embedded within the SQL. Hard-coded literal values make the SQL statements non-reusable unless *cursor_sharing=force* is set in the Oracle initialization file. Shops that are plagued with non-reusable SQL can adopt either the persistent or the dynamic philosophy. To use optimizer plan stability with non-reusable SQL, the DBA will set *cursor_sharing=force* and then extract the transformed SQL from the library cache and use optimizer plan stability to make the execution plan persistent.

- **Adaptive statistics collection**: Starting in Oracle 12c, Oracle now evaluates cardinality estimates, learning from mistakes and adaptive statistics can be disabled with *optimizer_adaptive_reporting_only=true*.

The next sections will provide a closer look at these competing SQL philosophies in order to help make the determination of which one best fits your organization.

The Persistent SQL Workload

In a shop with relatively static tables and indexes, it may be desirable to adopt the persistent SQL philosophy that states that there exists only one optimal execution plan for any SQL statement. Shops that subscribe to this philosophy are characterized by stable applications that have been tuned to use host variables rather than literal values in all SQL queries.

Persistent shops also have tables and indexes whose recomputed statistics rarely change the execution plan for their SQL queries, regardless of how often the statistics are recomputed. Many persistent shops have all of their SQL embedded inside PL/SQL packages, and the applications will call their SQL using a standard PL/SQL function of a stored procedure call. This insulates all of the SQL from the application programs and ensures that all applications execute identical SQL. It also ensures that all of the SQL has been properly tuned.

Choosing the persistent approach means that all tuned SQL will utilize optimizer plan stability and that the CBO statistics will be used only for ad-hoc queries and new queries that have not yet been tuned.

Of course, there is also a performance benefit to using optimizer plan stability because the SQL statements are pre-parsed and ready to run. This approach is generally used in shops where experience has found that the execution plans for SQL rarely change after the CBO statistics have been reanalyzed.

The persistent SQL philosophy requires the DBA to write scripts to detect all SQL statements that do not possess stored outlines and to tune these queries on behalf of the developers. The persistent SQL philosophy also requires less reliance on CBO statistics, and the DBA generally analyzes tables only when they are first migrated into the production environment. Since optimizer plan stability does not rely on statistics, the server overhead of periodically re-computing statistics for the CBO is avoided.

The Dynamic SQL Workload

The dynamic SQL philosophy subscribes to the belief that Oracle SQL should change execution plans in accordance with the changes to the CBO statistics. Shops that subscribe to the dynamic SQL philosophy are characterized by highly volatile environments where tables and indexes change radically and frequently. These shops frequently reanalyze their CBO statistics and allow the CBO to choose the execution plan based upon the current status of their CBO statistics.

A good example of a shop that uses the dynamic SQL philosophy would be one where tables grow over a specified period of time and then are purged before new data is reloaded. In these types of environments, the *num_rows* and *avg_row_len* for the tables are frequently changing, as are the distributions of index values. This change in statistics, in turn, causes the CBO to choose a different execution plan for the SQL queries.

Decision-support environments and scientific databases often adopt this philosophy because entirely new subsets of data are loaded into tables, the data is analyzed, the tables truncated, and a wholly different set of data is loaded into the table structures.

Another common characteristic of dynamic shops is that the SQL cannot be easily tuned. Oracle databases that are accessed by casual users via ODBC and third-party tools such as Crystal Reports or Microsoft Access are often forced into the dynamic philosophy because the incoming SQL is always different.

However, it is very important to note that the use of third-party application suites, such as SAP and PeopleSoft, does not always require the adoption of the dynamic philosophy. The SQL from these types of application suites can be captured in the library cache, and optimizer plan stability can be used to make the execution plan persistent.

These shops require a very different approach to SQL tuning than do persistent SQL shops. Each time new data is loaded or the data changes, the affected tables and indexes must be reanalyzed. These shops often incorporate the *dbms_stats* package directly into their load routines.

In Oracle, the DBA for dynamic shops must be vigilant for changes to the distribution of index column values. When column values for any index become skewed, the DBA must create column histograms for the index so the optimizer can choose between a full-table scan and an index range scan to service queries.

Many companies adopt a philosophy without completely realizing the ramifications of their chosen approach. In practice, most shops begin with a dynamic philosophy and then undertake to migrate to the static approach after experience indicates that their execution plans rarely change after a reanalysis of the tables and indexes.

Holistic Oracle Tuning

Oracle professionals must always undertake the performance of holistic tuning before delving into the tuning of specific SQL statements. Holistic tuning is an approach that has been the bread and butter of successful corporate DBAs since the earliest days of Oracle6.

In Oracle 11g, this holistic approach has been codified in the SQL Performance Analyzer (SPA), a new tool for simplifying the setting of optimizer statistics and initialization parameters. In SPA, the DBA chooses a representative workload and runs it, comparing the overall SQL execution plans with different sets of CBO statistics and settings for the silver bullet initialization parameters.

Prior to Oracle 10g, adjusting the optimizer_index_cost_adj parameter was the only cost-effective way for large shops to compensate for sampling issues in dbms_stats. As of 10g, the use of dbms_stats.gather_system_stats and improved sampling within dbms_stats has made adjustments to these parameters far less important. Today, the savvy DBA always optimizes their CBO statistics before adjusting their silver bullet parameters.

Dealing with Time Constraints

In a busy Oracle shop, the DBA often does not have the luxury of undertaking the time consuming task of reorganizing fragmented tables with dbms_redefinition and manually gathering optimal CBO statistics, especially the tedious task identifying columns that require histograms.

Hence, some DBA managers want a quick fix and undertake optimizing their workload by lowering their value for *optimizer_index_cost_adj* or by adjusting other broad-brush optimizer parameters.

Maintaining SQL Infrastructure

It is the job of the DBA to collect CBO statistics and ensure that the test and development databases have optimizer statistics that represent the production database. In this example, the current CBO statistics are exported into a table called *stats_table_oltp*:

```
dbms_stats.export_system_stats('stats_table_oltp');
```

When the information is captured, the table can be moved to other instances and the *import_system_stats* procedure in *dbms_stats* used to overlay the CBO statistics when processing modes change:

```
dbms_stats.import_system_stats('stats_table_oltp');

dbms_stats.import_system_stats('stats_table_dss');
```

CBO parameters should be optimized to the workload and then left alone. Many Oracle shops change the fundamental characteristics of their CBO by changing the global CBO parameters. Especially dangerous are changes to optimizer_mode and optimizer_index_cost_adj, and these changes should only be made when a sound reason exists.

Other CBO parameters such as *pga_aggregate_target* (*hash_area_size* and *sort_area_size*) are less dangerous and can be set at the individual session level to change how the CBO evaluates a query.

Some shops try to ensure consistency of SQL execution with static execution plans. Remember, reanalyzing a schema could cause thousands of SQL statements to change execution plans. Many Oracle shops have implemented standards that require that all SQL, when tested and approved in their test environment, function identically in production.

Some techniques for assisting developers in tuning their SQL include:

- Training them to use the autotrace and TKPROF utilities and to interpret SQL execution results.

- Forcing all SQL that is migrating into production to have verification that the SQL has been tuned.

- Making performance an evaluation criterion. Instead of noting that the best developer is the developer who writes SQL the fastest, add the mandate that a good developer also writes SQL that performs efficiently.

One way to help developers achieve their SQL tuning mandate is to migrate the statistics that were used in SQL testing into the production environment when the SQL is migrated. However, the DBA must ensure that a migration of statistics from test into production does not adversely affect the execution plans of other SQL that touch the target table. Hence, the DBA will carefully manage the CBO statistics, ensuring that no SQL changes execution plans after it is migrated into production.

Encapsulating SQL for Fast Performance

As application code moves away from external programs and into the database engine, DBAs need to understand the related memory requirements for Oracle stored procedures and know how to manage Oracle stored procedures for optimal database performance.

Oracle stored procedures and triggers are becoming more popular, and more application code will move away from external programs and into the database engine. However, Oracle DBAs must be conscious of the increasing memory demands of Oracle stored procedures and carefully plan for the days when all of the database access code (PL/SQL) resides within the database.

Today, most Oracle Server databases have only a small amount of code in Oracle stored procedures, but this is rapidly changing. There are many compelling benefits for putting all Oracle SQL inside Oracle stored procedures, including:

- **Faster performance**: Oracle stored procedures load once into the shared pool and remain there unless they become paged out. Subsequent executions of the Oracle stored procedure are far faster than executions of external code.

- **Coupling of data with behavior**: DBAs can use naming conventions to couple relational tables with the behaviors associated with a table using Oracle stored procedures as *methods*. This is the same technique used in object-oriented programming, where member *methods* are tightly coupled to each object instantiation.

- **Isolation of SQL code**: Since all SQL is moved out of the external programs and into the Oracle stored procedures, the application programs become nothing more than calls to Oracle stored procedures. As such, it becomes very simple to swap out one database and swap in another one. Moving all SQL into the data dictionary also allows SQL to be tuned via rewriting the SQL or adding hints without directly touching the application layer.

One of the foremost reasons Oracle stored procedures and triggers function faster than traditional code is related to caching in the Oracle System Global Area (SGA). After an Oracle stored procedure has been loaded into the shared pool of the SGA, it remains there until it is paged out of memory to make room for other Oracle stored procedures.

Within the library cache, SQL is paged out based on a least recently used (LRU) algorithm. Once loaded into the RAM memory of the shared pool, procedures will execute very quickly, and the trick is to prevent pool thrashing as many procedures compete for a limited amount of shared-pool memory.

Pinning SQL into Packages

For frequently-referenced SQL, the SQL can be encapsulated into a stored procedure, the stored procedure placed into a package and then the package pinned into the Oracle SGA RAM area.

Some shops require all programmers to encapsulate their SQL into Oracle stored procedures, so that the SQL moves out of the external programs and the application program becomes independent of the database layer.

When using stored procedure calls, there is no SQL in the application and the application data requests are nothing more than a series of calls to Oracle stored procedures. This makes the application programs completely portable, while at the same time offering the benefit of using the Oracle dictionary as a central repository for all SQL.

Once the SQL is inside a package, the packages can be marked as non-swappable, telling the database that after their initial load they must always remain in memory. This is called *pinning* or memory fencing. Oracle provides the procedure *dbms_shared_pool.keep* procedure for pinning a package in SGA RAM.

The next section will delve more into an important principle, how hardware technology drives Oracle software and how changing technology changes the way SQL is tuned.

How Hardware Affects SQL Tuning Techniques

When I teach SQL tuning, I make the point that hardware advances always precede Oracle advances, and the rapid advances in data storage hardware are driving a complete reworking of the Oracle SQL optimizer. Disk I/O cost is the single slowest factor in Oracle SQL, which was a driving factor in the way that the CBO was originally designed.

For examples, the cost figures seen in execution plans are based on the obsolete idea that an average disk read takes 10 milliseconds. When using spinning platter disks, average I/O numbers can be meaningless because disks are notorious for widely varied response times.

A disk may fetch a block in five milliseconds and 10 minutes later, fetch a block in 30 milliseconds. This is why it is an exercise in futility to use science and equations to predict the performance of SQL. Oracle has acknowledged this with their exciting new SQL tuning tools that reply on empirical timings rather than abstract theory.

Hardware becomes better and cheaper ever year, and this is especially true for data storage hardware. When I wrote the first officially authorized Oracle Press book on Oracle SQL tuning back in 1992, RAM was ten times more expensive than it is today, and disk costs were substantial. The following section will cover how SQL tuning changes over time.

The changing landscape of Oracle SQL Tuning

Hardware technology is driven by economics, and Oracle is driven by hardware technology:

- When SMP servers with many CPUs were introduced, Oracle was ready with parallel query.

- When 64-bit servers leaped over the 2 gig RAM limit, Oracle was ready with onboard software that allowed multi-terabyte SGA regions.

- When disk prices fell, it became feasible to introduce redundancy into third-normal form (3NF) schemas, and Oracle was ready with tools like advanced replication, Oracle Streams and materialized views.

- When NUMA became available, Oracle leveraged on the super-fast T1 RAM.

- As SSD become popular, Oracle introduces tools like the *flash_cache* to allow leveraging of this super-fast RAM disk storage.

Oracle's response to hardware technology changes are driven directly by Larry Ellison, a true genius and visionary who is almost clairvoyant in anticipating the future needs for data storage. For example, Larry developed his "database appliance", a diskless PC with only a Java-enabled web browser almost a decade before the market was ready. Now in 2010, there is a glimpse of the infrastructure for the return of the 3270-style dumb terminal PC's, an infrastructure where all software, such as word processing, e-mail and spreadsheets, are managed and controlled in a "cloud" somewhere on the Interweb.

When a new hardware technology is released, vendors struggle over how to leverage the new technology, and this has been true since the earliest days of data processing:

When the first personal computers were introduced in the early 1980's, knowledge of assembler language was needed to do anything with them, and the old Altair computers were worthless to American industry. It was not until the advent of software tools like VisiCalc, an early spreadsheet, that computers were widely adopted. The same principle holds true today!

Gordon Moore, Director of the Research and Development Laboratories at Fairchild Semiconductor, published a research paper titled "Cramming more components into integrated circuits" in 1965. This landmark paper gave birth to "Moore's Law," which postulated that CPU power gets four times faster every three years as shown in Figure 1.11:

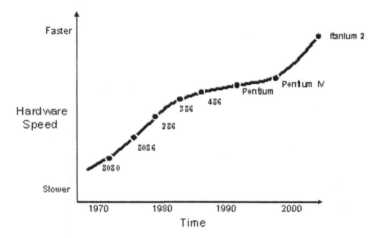

Figure 1.11: *Moore's Law: (Source: Fairchild Semiconductor)*

Moore's law has held true over the three decades since it was first published, and it has been extended to cover RAM and disk storage costs as well.

However, the "real" Moore's Law cannot be boiled down into a one-size fits-all statement that all hardware gets faster and cheaper. Prices are always falling, but there are important exceptions to Moore's Law. This is especially true with regard to disk and RAM technology, the most important hardware components for any Oracle database as shown in Figure 1.12:

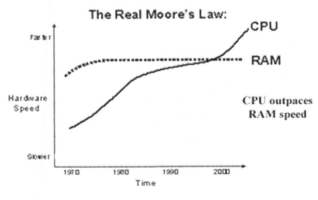

Figure 1.12: *Changes in speed over time for CPU, Disk and RAM*

These curves are not linear and this trend has a profound impact on the performance of Oracle databases. It is interesting to note that RAM speed has remained fixed for nearly 30 years!

Because CPU speed continues to outpace memory speed, RAM subsystems must be localized to keep the CPUs running at full capacity, and this heralded the advent of Non-Uniform Memory Access (NUMA) and the localization of RAM being placed physically close to the CPU's.

So, how does this change the way that SQL is tuned? Any greybeard Oracle professional will say that SQL tuning was very different twenty years ago when RAM was super-expensive:

- **Circa 1990 SQL Tuning**: Almost all databases were I/O bound, and SQL tuning focused on reducing physical reads.

- **Circa 2010 SQL Tuning:** Most mission critical systems use SSD or large buffers, and SQL tuning is focused on reducing other system bottlenecks like CPU, SQL parsing and latch contention.

The next section will reveal how holistic workload tuning has changed within each release of Oracle.

A Release-centric Approach to SQL Optimization

Each release of Oracle brings enhancements and changes to the way that the Oracle DBA optimizes their system-wide workloads. In general, these approaches to global SQL optimization are highly dependent on the release of Oracle:

- **Oracle6 - Oracle7:** In Oracle7, there were significant shortcomings to the cost-based optimizer, and many Oracle professionals were forced to tweak the CBO throttles to achieve the largest amount of optimized SQL. These techniques include setting *optimizer_mode=rule*, and adjusting *optimizer_index_cost_adj*. This period also heralded the introduction of the CBO histogram, an important feature for SQL optimization.

- **Oracle8 - Oracle8i:** In the Oracle8 series of releases, the cost-based optimizer was ready for prime time, and materialized views and enhanced CBO statistics collection were introduced. The introduction of function-based indexes to alleviate unnecessary full-table scans also occurred during this period, and the *dbms_stats* package was introduced to allow better collection of schema metadata, to help the CBO make more intelligent optimization decisions. The rule-based optimizer (RBO) remained a popular tuning tool for simple databases, and the adjustment of SQL workload optimization relied on changing *optimizer_mode*, *optimizer_index_cost_adj* and *optimizer_index_caching*. This was also the time of the use of global temporary tables for optimizing multi-step SQL queries. Best of all, the BSTAT-ESTAT utility was enhanced with the STATSPACK tool to allow for the historical storage of tuning information, indispensable for proactive workload tuning.

- **Oracle9i:** With Oracle9i came the new *v$sql_plan* view to help tune SQL proactively and the *dbms_stats* package was enhanced to be more intelligent. Still, the DBA was frequently forced to optimize their SQL by adjusting the optimizer parameters. This was also the beginning of the ability to collect a "deep" sample with *dbms_stats* and save it, a tool that is especially useful for large shops where production CBO statistics can be exported and imported into test and development instances, allowing developers to optimize their SQL before it is introduced into production. This period also yielded the *dbms_redefinition* package to allow online reorganization of fragmented tables.

- **Oracle 10g:** Oracle 10g greatly aided the optimization of large SQL workloads with the introduction of dynamic sampling and root-cause optimization with *dbms_stats*. Oracle acknowledged that the root cause of sub-optimal SQL execution plan related to the quality of CBO statistics. Additionally, they introduced enhancements to *dbms_stats* to allow for automatic histogram creation and the *gather_system_stats* procedure for collecting all-important external information, most notably the average disk access timings for index access (sequential reads) and full-scan access (scattered reads). This changed the landscape for SQL tuning, as it was now possible to address the root cause of suboptimal execution plans. However, many DBAs who were under time constraints were unable to undertake the time consuming analysis required to verify that they have optimal statistics and they resorted to the quick fix of adjusting the optimizer parameters.

- **Oracle 10g Release 2:** Starting in Oracle 10g release 2, Oracle recommends not setting the *db_file_multiblock_read_count* parameter, allowing Oracle to empirically determine the optimal setting.

- **Oracle 11g:** With Oracle 11g there comes the promise of a greatly improved *dbms_stats* package, running 2x faster and automatically collecting a statistically significant sample size. There is also the promise of better detection of columns for histograms. Oracle technical support claims that adjusting the CBO statistics addresses the root cause of sub-optimal execution and that changes to the *optimizer_index_cost_adj* are "rarely" required. However, the DBA still needs to set the optimal *optimizer_mode* and *optimizer_index_caching*. It is possible to run scripts to intelligently set an appropriate value for *optimizer_index_caching*.

- **Oracle12c:** Oracle 12c introduces dynamic statistics sampling, a new method for improving execution statistics by sampling SQL results sets in real-time.

In sum, the techniques for holistic SQL optimization change radically by release level, and in Oracle10g and Oracle11g it is now less time consuming to fix the root cause of CBO issues by adjusting the CBO statistics.

The general holistic SQL optimization steps for 9i, 10g and 11g include addressing the root cause (bad statistics) whenever feasible. The starting point is the verification of a correct sample size using *dbms_stats* followed by the determination of an intelligent threshold for re-analyzing statistics.

Next, the low-hanging fruit, high-impact sub-optimal SQL, are identified. The next step is to add histograms to improve access for queries against skewed and out-of-bounds queries. Also, this is the time to add histograms where necessary and if applicable to improve the CBO's ability to determine the optimal table join order.

1. Run *dbms_stats.gather_system_stats* to get external I/O tuning for full-scan vs. index I/O.

2. Intelligently set *optimizer_mode* and *optimizer_index_caching*, testing with a representative workload in a real-world environment.

3. Optimize the silver bullet parameters (*db_cache_size, db_file_multiblock_read_count*, etc.)

4. Set *optimizer_index_cost_adj*, if required, to fix any remaining suboptimal execution plans.

5. Finally, tune individual SQL statements using SQL profiles.

The following section will reveal how Oracle Database 11g SQL tuning tools are addressing hardware advances and how that continues to affect the way SQL is tuned.

11g SQL Tuning Enhancements

After the Apollo moon landing systems used solid-state data storage, everybody assumed that computers with moving parts would soon be obsolete. Nobody would have guessed that spinning platters storage would still be in use in the 21st century. In 2010, it is amazing that state-of-the-art database systems still have hardware that contains moving parts!

Instead of measuring I/O in milliseconds with a wide range of average response time, today's solid-state disks (SSD or flash disk) can fetch data in microseconds. Plus, they can do it with uniform response time! These changes have profound impact on the way that Oracle optimizes SQL statements.

In theory, the difference between disk milliseconds (thousandths of a second) and RAM microseconds (millionths of a second) suggest RAM is 10,000 times faster than disk. But in practice, SSD fetches Oracle data anywhere from 50 to 600 times faster than the old-fashioned spinning platters.

Oracle has invested zillions of dollars in developing their SQL optimizer, and many Oracle professionals do not appreciate the software engineering challenge of writing a program that always chooses the best execution plan for any given SQL statement.

In order to get the simplicity of automatic SQL optimization, the Oracle engineers must code for phenomenal complexity. The Oracle optimizer is truly one of the world's most complex software programs, a tool of exceptional flexibility.

The following sections will explore the evolution of Oracle SQL enhancements in Oracle 11g and show how the optimizer continues to become more intelligent with each new release. Each new release brings changes to the Oracle optimizer, but many are in terms of bug fixes and optimizer improvements. Oracle 11g has over 480 new enhancements, and it can be challenging to tease out the important new SQL features, but list that follows is a good start.

The enhancements below are largely transparent, which means that the only sign that they are working is that SQL runs faster; however, this list demonstrates Oracle's commitment to continuing to make the optimizer more intelligent with each new release of Oracle:

- **View join elimination:** Oracle continues to advance intelligent view processing and now only joins tables in a view that are needed for the final result set. For example, a view may join five tables, but a query using the view many only require that two tables be joined.

- **Extended optimizer statistics:** One of the most exciting new features of Oracle 11g is improvement to the *dbms_stats* package, specifically the ability to aid complex queries by providing extended statistics to the cost-based optimizer. The 11g extended optimizer statistics are intended to improve the optimizer's guesses for the cardinality of combined columns and columns that are modified by a built-in or user-defined function.

- **Better statistics collections:** The *dbms_stats* package has been greatly enhanced in 11g, running twice as fast as in 10g. Plus the 11g *dbms_stats auto_sample_size* now collects a statistically significant sample, even for highly skewed data distributions.

- **Improved function-based index statistics:** In 11g, statistics for function-based indexes can be collected automatically. For example, if there is a function-based index on a *compute_total* function, the following *dbms_stats* invocation could be used:

```
dbms_stats.gather_table_stats
   (ownname => SCOTT,
    tabname => 'SALES',
    method_opt => 'FOR ALL COLUMNS FOR COLUMNS
   (compute_total(cust_sales))' );
```

Operational SQL enhancements in 11g

Oracle introduced two new tools in 11g, the SQL Performance Analyzer (SPA) and the oddly named Real Application Testing (RAT) framework. These are milestone tools in Oracle SQL tuning because they finally codify the holistic tuning approach that embrace global SQL optimization. With RAT and SPA, we it has become possible to optimize our environment (optimizer parameter settings, metadata statistics) using real-world workloads, tuning the entire workload.

While Oracle professionals have been doing this manually for years, this new approach is revolutionary because it discourages the bottom-up approach whereby individual SQL statements are tuned first, only to have the changed undone by changes to global parameters.

The following section provides a peek at the new 11g plan baselines and shows how Oracle now tracks changes to SQL execution plans.

Automating 11g SQL Tuning with Plan Baselines

One great way to tune SQL in 11g is to allow Oracle to test the run-time SQL performance and change execution plans whenever a SQL statements runs more than three times faster than an old plan! This empirical tuning method is a radical departure from the ineffective "scientific" approach of attempting to compute the costs of different execution plans.

No theory, no complex SQL tuning methodologies to memorize, just a real-world pragmatic approach to SQL tuning that removes the guesswork and justifies all changes before they are rolled into production.

Oracle 11g now enhances SQL profiles with SQL Plan baselines, a new tool that lets you automatically capture execution plans. It is as simple as setting the parameter *optimizer_capture_sql_plan_baselines=true* and Oracle will begin collecting and storing SQL execution plans.

Once the execution plans have been captured for the most popular SQL, the 11g SQL Plan Management tool, implemented via the *dbms_spm* package, can be used. Next real-world SQL workloads (a.k.a SQL tuning sets) are evaluated, and compared to yield their before-and-after SQL performance. Then, execution plans are only changed for SQL that runs at least 3x faster.

Oracle12c adaptive execution plans

The Oracle12c adaptive execution plans are a add-on to Oracle dynamic sampling, a new feature of dynamic statistics.

Oracle is striving to get over an ongoing issue with always having enough detail in the metadata to always choose the "best" execution plan, and Oracle is now working towards an adaptive, "self-learning" optimizer. In this new approach, "real-time" statistics collection is done at query execution time, and the optimizer has the option of changing a tables join methods between a hash join to a nested loops join, well after the original plan was generated! Join statistics are now monitored for executing SQL statements and a new *v$sql* column *is_reoptimizable* has been added to indicate when a query will benefit from dynamic statistics.

This funky new functionality is controlled by a parameter *optimizer_adaptive_reporting_only=false*, and it can be disabled with *optimizer_adaptive_reporting_only=true*.

In a sense, the dynamic sampling feature has been replaced by a dynamic statistics feature. You can see information about these last-minute changes to SQL execution plans with the dbms_xplan package, using the format of "*+all_dyn_plan +adaptive*". Oracle also introduces SQL plan directives, and there is a new DBMS package *dbms_spd* to manage these sub-components of an execution plan.

One of the most common "problems" with a sub-optimal execution plan is when the optimizer cannot guess the proper cardinality for a table join result or a filtering condition. The 12c optimizer has been enhanced to "peek" into the query results to see if the query cardinality estimate corresponds to the initial guess from the optimizer. If the optimizer notices that he came up with a sub-optimal SQL execution plan, the optimizer will:

- Store the "real" stats in the data dictionary as "adaptive statistics".

- Take the change into consideration for later queries, using the "real" cardinality in lieu of the cardinality estimate.

- Note a new step called a "STATISTICS COLLECTOR" in a tkprof (SQL Trace).

- The resulting stats are cached as shared dynamic stats specific for the statement, including the bind values. This information can be used by any session using the same SQL query.

Oracle has implemented this new adaptive statistics collection within Oracle dynamic sampling, such that whenever the existing statistics (or 12c "extended statistics") fail to generate an optimal plan, the output from the dynamic sampling will be made persistent within the data dictionary.

Oracle 12c Improved histogram buckets

Starting in Oracle 12, Oracle now automatically invokes dbms_stats for (insert into tablename (select. . .) statements and CTAS statements. Oracle also introduces hybrid histograms. When the number of distinct values in a histogram is greater than 254, some "almost popular" values can get "lost" in the bucket, resulting in sub-optimal index usage.

A single bucket can now store the popularity of than value, effectively increasing the number of buckets, without actually increasing it. Also, the maximum number of buckets can be increased using a new histogram parameter argument.

Next, let's move on and take a look at how to tune SQL that cannot be touched.

Tuning When the SQL Cannot Be Touched

Ad-Hoc query tools that generate SQL (e.g. Crystal Reports) and Vendor controlled packages have SQL where the source code cannot be touched.

One important 11g enhancement is with SQL profiles, a replacement for stored outlines (plan stability), both of which allow us to "freeze" parts of execution plans. SQL profiles allow capture and storage of the execution plan for SQL statements such that a good execution plan can be swapped out for a bad one, without ever touching the application SQL!

This swapping of SQL profiles is a Godsend for tuning vendor applications and ad-hoc SQL tools like Crystal Reports, where it is not possible to directly change the SQL statement.

Changing the SQL that hides in a pre-compiled program is impossible without access to the source code. In other cases, the software vendor may explicitly prohibit any changes to the source code. It them becomes necessary to come up with a creative way to tune the SQL without touching the source code.

The central idea behind "swapping" SQL profiles is simple. Define a SQL profile that specifies the SQL statement to be tuned as well as an alternative execution plan, in the form of hints. When this SQL is executed and hits the library cache, Oracle detects that a SQL profile exists for this statement and automatically applies the hints to change the execution plan.

Oracle 11g also has an extremely cool technique for adding a hint to a stored SQL profile using the *dbms_sqltune.import_sql_profile* procedure. In the following example, the optimizer mode is easily changed from *first_rows_10* to *all_rows*:

```
begin
  dbms_sqltune.import_sql_profile(
    name      => 'test',
    category  => 'default',
    sql_text  => 'select /*+ first_rows(10) */ * from emp order by emp_id',
    profile   => sqlprof_attr('all_rows','ignore_optim_embedded_hints')
  );
end;
/
```

Combining the above tools yields a powerful arsenal for tuning SQL statements without ever touching the SQL statement. The *dbms_sqltune* package has an *import_sql_profile* procedure which allows hints to be swapped from one SQL profile into another SQL profile as shown here:

```
dbms_sqltune.import_sql_profile(
    sql_text => 'select * from emp',
    profile => sqlprof_attr('ALL_ROWS','IGNORE_OPTIM_EMBEDDED_HINTS')
    category => 'DEFAULT',
    name => 'change_emp',
    force_match => &&6
);
```

Working examples of swapping SQL profiles are available through a simple online search for the *dbms_sqltune* package and the *import_sql_profile* procedure.

The Flash Cache and SQL tuning

There is no question that I/O is the single most important part of SQL tuning. As RAM prices fall below $1,000.00 per GB, many shops are moving to solid-state storage, using solid-state disks or giant data buffer regions to fully cache their important data.

Today, a millisecond is an eternity, and the ancient spinning platter disks that have been in use since the 1970's are finally becoming obsolete. Oracle 11gR2 includes a feature called *flash_cache*, a table and index argument that resembles the assignment of high use objects to the KEEP pool. However, unlike the KEEP pool which uses volatile RAM disk, the *flash_cache* is used for tertiary storage on solid-state disk (SSD).

The flash cache features is only for Exadata servers and Linux, but a quick online search for Guy Harrison and *flash_cache* will yield a web page where he describes a special patch that allows the use of Oracle *flash_cache* without requiring the purchase of a million dollar Exadata server.

In plain English, Oracle *flash_cache* is recognizing a hierarchy of storage hardware, organized by access speed:

- **Data Buffer RAM:** The KEEP pool can cache objects for super-fast access at RAM speeds. Of course, this data is not persistent.

- **Solid-state disk:** SSD is not as fast as native RAM, but it remains hundreds of times faster than platter disks. However, all SSD suffers from a severe write penalty and is not ideal for high DML data.

- **Disk spindles:** The old magnetic-coated spinning platters from the 1960's comprise the bulk of Oracle data storage, with stone-age access speeds expressed in milliseconds.

The docs suggest that the *flash_cache* refers to "flash" SSD memory, but it appears that this approach is using SSD as a temporary cache and not as permanent home for the data, as seen with SSD flash memory.

Many people misunderstand that the flash memory is very different from the rack-mounted industrial strength solid-state disk.

In traditional SSD, the flash memory is an external rack mount device and it looks like just a bunch of disks (JBOD), and the Oracle data files are allocated directly onto the flash media. Conversely, in Oracle's approach, the flash_cache refers to internal flash SSD, and the flash_cache syntax treats it like temporary caching instead of permanent storage.

The Oracle documentation suggests enabling the *flash_cache* when the data buffer advisor suggests that Oracle wants more RAM, which is almost always the case, when the system is disk I/O bound and when there are spare CPU cycles. They mention CPU because moving to solid-state flash storage removes disk I/O, but it changes the workload bottleneck to CPU in many cases.

The main point is that the hardware advances always precede Oracle advances, and that the rapidly falling costs of RAM are changing the way SQL is tuned.

With that introduction to the access method for internal tables, it is time to take a look at yet another kind of table, the Oracle external table.

External Tables and SQL

One of the most exciting advances introduced back with Oracle9i was the ability to access non-Oracle files with Oracle SQL. This functionality, called external tables, still has important ramifications for systems where external files need to be available for non-database applications and appear to be a table within Oracle.

External tables allows users to define the structure of almost any flat file on their server and have it appear to Oracle as if it were a real table. This process is diagrammed in Figure 1.13:

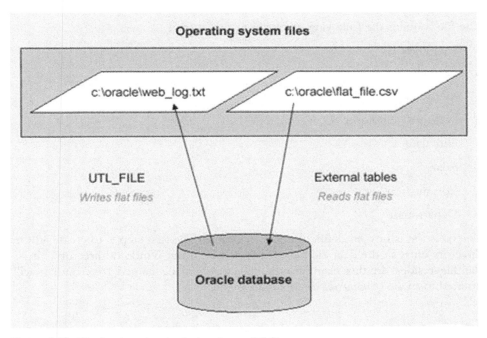

Figure 1.13: *The Oracle read and write interfaces to OS files*

Oracle lets a database program write to flat files using the *utl_file* utility. Combined with external table's read ability, the introduction of this topology removed the requirement that all Oracle data reside inside Oracle tables, opening new applications for Oracle. The next section will provide a closer look at how this feature works.

Defining an External Table

The goal is to have Oracle to refer to this comma-delimited flat file:

```
7369,SMITH,CLERK,7902,17-DEC-80,800,20
7499,ALLEN,SALESMAN,7698,20-FEB-81,1600,300,30
7521,WARD,SALESMAN,7698,22-FEB-81,1250,500,30
7566,JONES,MANAGER,7839,02-APR-81,2975,,20
7654,MARTIN,SALESMAN,7698,28-SEP-81,1250,1400,30
7698,BLAKE,MANAGER,7839,01-MAY-81,2850,,30
7782,CLARK,MANAGER,7839,09-JUN-81,2450,,10
7788,SCOTT,ANALYST,7566,19-APR-87,3000,,20
7839,KING,PRESIDENT,,17-NOV-81,5000,,10
7844,TURNER,SALESMAN,7698,08-SEP-81,1500,0,30
7876,ADAMS,CLERK,7788,23-MAY-87,1100,,20
```

The file contains the following employee information:

- Employee ID
- Last name
- Job description
- Manager's employee ID
- Hire date
- Salary
- Commission
- Department

The question is how to define this file to Oracle? The first step is to create an Oracle directory entry in the data dictionary that points to the Windows directory where the flat file resides. In this example, the directory will be named *testdir* and it will be pointed to *c:\docs\pubsdb\queries* as shown below:

```
create directory testdir as 'c:\docs\pubsdb\queries';
```

Now that the directory has been created, the structure of the external file can be defined to Oracle as follows:

```
create table
   emp_ext
(
   empno     number(4),
   ename     varchar2(10),
```

```
   job      varchar2(9),
   mgr      number(4),
   hiredate date,
   sal      number(7,2),
   comm     number(7,2),
   deptno   number(2)
)
organization external
(
   type oracle_loader
   default directory testdir
   access parameters
   (
      records delimited by newline
      fields terminated by ','
   )
location ('emp_ext.csv')
)
reject limit 1000;
```

In this syntax, the column of the external table is defined in much the same way as an internal Oracle table. The external definitions occur in the organization external clause:

- **default directory testdir** : The directory where the file resides

- **records delimited by newline** : The new line character

- **fields terminated by ','** : The column termination character

- **location ('emp_ext.csv')** : The name of the external file

External Definitions for the Comma-delimited File

Now the external table has been defined, reports can be run against the external table using SQL, just as if the table resided inside the database. In the query below, note the use of the sophisticated *rollup* parameter to summarize salaries by both department and job title.

```
ttitle 'Employee Salary|Cubic Rollup'

col deptno   heading 'Department|Number'
col job      heading 'Job|Title'
col num_emps heading 'Number of|Employees' format 9,999
col sum_sal  heading 'Total|Salary'        format $99,999

select
   deptno,
   job,
   count(*)  num_emps,
   sum(sal)  sum_sal
from
   emp_ext
```

```
group by
  rollup
  (
    deptno,
    job
  );
```

```
Wed Jun 12                                page    1
                    Employee Salary
                     Cubic Rollup

Department Job       Number of    Total
  Number Title       Employees    Salary
---------- --------- --------- --------
      10 MANAGER            1    $2,450
      10 PRESIDENT          1    $5,000
      10                    2    $7,450
      20 ANALYST            1    $3,000
      20 CLERK              1    $1,100
      20 MANAGER            1    $2,975
      20                    3    $7,075
      30 MANAGER            1    $2,850
      30 SALESMAN           4    $5,600
      30                    5    $8,450
                          10   $22,975
```

Limitations on External Tables

Because external tables are fairly new, Oracle has not yet perfected their use. This feature has several limitations, including:

- **No support for DML**: External tables are read-only, but the base data can be edited in any text editor.

- **Poor response for high-volume queries**: External tables have a processing overhead, perform full scans, and are not suitable for large tables.

It is also possible to define spreadsheets to Oracle. This technique has had important ramifications for shops where users control system-wide parameters inside desktop spreadsheets and Oracle knows immediately about changes. Some key tips regarding defining spreadsheets to Oracle are:

- The external file must be comma-delimited and stored on the server as a file with a *.csv* extension.

- External spreadsheets are not good for large files because the entire file must be reread into Oracle whenever a change is saved to the spreadsheet.

- End users must never reformat the data columns inside the spreadsheet environment.

It is important to remember, when defining the flat file as an external table, the file remains on the operating system as a flat file, where it can be read and updated with a variety of tools, including spreadsheets. Using Microsoft's Excel spreadsheets, the external table data can be read just as if it were standard spreadsheet data as shown in Figure 1.14:

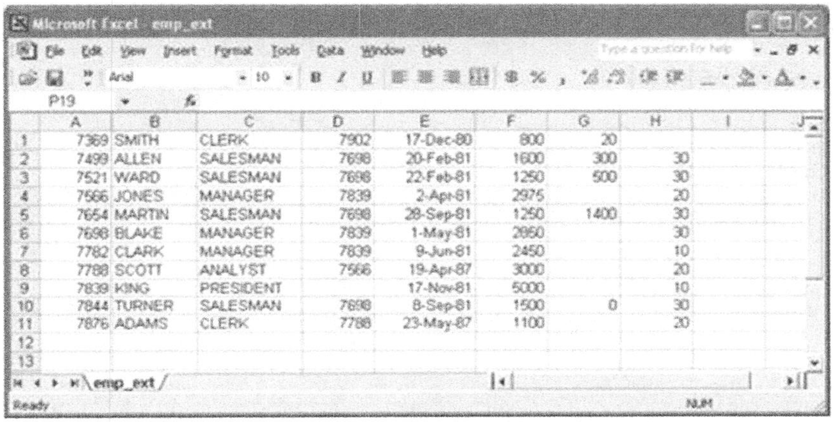

Figure 1.14: *An external table inside an Excel spreadsheet*

End users can now manage critical tables inside easy-to-use spreadsheets. Oracle immediately notices whenever a change is made to the spreadsheet. However, there are important limitations to using spreadsheets as Oracle tables, the foremost being excessive disk I/O whenever the spreadsheet has changed.

The next section will provide a deeper look into the use of spreadsheets as Oracle tables.

Internals of External Table SQL

It is important to recognize that Oracle data inside spreadsheets will not be accessible as quickly as internal row data. Oracle cannot maintain row-level locking because the operating system, not Oracle, is in command. When a spreadsheet is defined as an external table, Oracle has no way of knowing when individual row data changes. The operating system will only tell Oracle that the entire spreadsheet has changed.

In addition, data blocks that are read from an external table are not placed inside the Oracle data buffers. The dictionary query below demonstrates that Oracle does not read the external table rows into the RAM data cache.

```
select
```

```
        bp.name              pool_name,
        ob.name              object,
        ob.subname     sub_name,
        sum(buf_count) buffer_blocks
from
        (select set_ds, obj, count(*) buf_count
        from x$bh group by set_ds, obj)     bh,
        obj$                                ob,
        x$kcbwds                            ws,
        v$buffer_pool                       bp
where
   ob.dataobj# = bh.obj
and
   ob.owner# > 0
and
   bh.set_ds = ws.addr
and
   ws.set_id between bp.lo_setid and bp.hi_setid
group by
        bp.name,
        ob.name,
        ob.subname
order by
        bp.name,
        ob.name,
        ob.subname;
```

The listing below shows that selections from the table do not reside in the data
buffers following a SQL query.

```
SQL> select ename from pubs.emp_ext;

SQL> @buf_data

POOL_NAME OBJECT                  SUB_NAME                   BLOCKS
--------- ----------------------- ------------------------- --------
DEFAULT   PUBLISHER                                              2
          REPCAT$_REPPROP                                        1
          SNS$BINDINGS$                                          2
          SNS$INODE$                                             2
          SNS$NODE_INDEX                                         1
          SNS$REFADDR$                                           3
          SNS$REFADDR_INDEX                                      3
          SYS_C001042                                            1
          SYS_C001414                                            1
```

Oracle does not clarify whether a separate buffering mechanism is used for external
tables. With this lack of buffering, Oracle must reread the entire spreadsheet for each
SQL invocation that accesses the external table.

To maintain data integrity, Oracle must detect when the spreadsheet data has
changed, but there is no way to discover when specific spreadsheet values have
changed. When Oracle detects that the flat file has been updated, all data in the RAM
data buffers becomes invalid, and the entire spreadsheet must be reread. This is the
primary reason external tables are not efficient for large volumes of data.

Because Oracle reads operating system files in data blocks, the amount of disk I/O can be computed by determining the number of spreadsheet blocks with a simple shell script. In this script, the Oracle database has 8-KB block sizes:

```
bytes=`ls -al|grep emp_ext.csv|awk '{ print $5 }'`
num_bytes=`expr $bytes`
blocks=`expr $num_bytes / 8192`
echo $blocks
```

This script will tell exactly how many disk reads are required to access the Oracle external table whenever a change is made.

Limitations of Comma-delimited Spreadsheet Files

In order for Oracle to successfully read comma-delimited (csv) files, it is important to avoid making spreadsheet-specific changes because Excel will change the internal storage of the column to accommodate the formatting. For example, assume that a manager reformats the *salary* column for comma display, as shown in Figure 1.15:

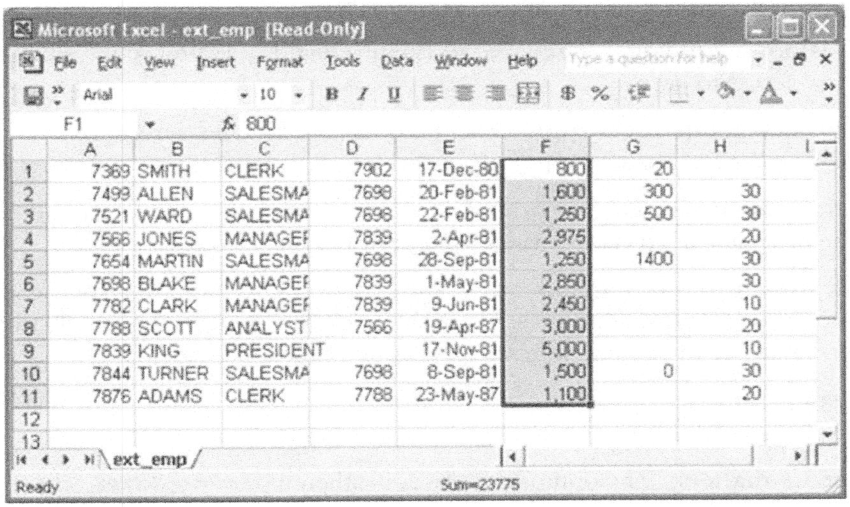

Figure 1.15: *Reformatting a comma-delimited (csv) spreadsheet*

Once the file has been saved, Oracle can no longer read the *salary* column because the column has been stored in quotes. To Oracle, this defines the column as a character:

```
7369,SMITH,CLERK,7902,17-Dec-80,800,20,
7499,ALLEN,SALESMAN,7698,20-Feb-81,"1,600",300,30
```

```
7521,WARD,SALESMAN,7698,22-Feb-81,"1,250",500,30
7566,JONES,MANAGER,7839,2-Apr-81,"2,975",,20
7654,MARTIN,SALESMAN,7698,28-Sep-81,"1,250",1400,30
7698,BLAKE,MANAGER,7839,1-May-81,"2,850",,30
7782,CLARK,MANAGER,7839,9-Jun-81,"2,450",,10
7788,SCOTT,ANALYST,7566,19-Apr-87,"3,000",,20
7839,KING,PRESIDENT,,17-Nov-81,"5,000",,10
7844,TURNER,SALESMAN,7698,8-Sep-81,"1,500",0,30
7876,ADAMS,CLERK,7788,23-May-87,"1,100",,20
```

The accidental reformatting of the file makes it unreadable by Oracle. Special care must be taken to instruct end users to never change the spreadsheet formatting once it is defined to Oracle.

Conclusion

This chapter covered the basic history of SQL and examined the general principles of Oracle SQL tuning. The main points of this chapter include:

- **SQL is a standard**: SQL was proposed as part of the relational database manifesto, and SQL is an ANSI standard data access language.

- **SQL is declarative:** There are many ways to write the same SQL statement, all with identical results but with varying performance.

- **SQL is not a language:** Rather, SQL is embedded inside procedural languages to allow access to data.

- **Always take a top-down approach:** It is critical to tune the server environment and workloads first, before optimizing individual SQL statements.

- **Oracle version matters:** Oracle SQL is constantly being improved and each release of Oracle has its own nuances and quirks.

- **Know your optimizer goal:** Some shops tune SQL for fast response time (*optimizer_mode=first_rows_n*) while other shops choose to tune their SQL to run with a minimum of computing resources (*optimizer_mode=all_rows*).

- **Holistic settings:** Oracle has super powerful optimizer parameters whereby a single change can change the entire performance landscape.

- **Metadata matters:** The optimizer statistics gathered by *dbms_stats* are critical to fast SQL execution plans.

The next chapter will cover the cost-based Oracle SQL optimizer and show how the optimizer always attempts to choose the best execution plan for any SQL statement.

The Oracle Cost-based SQL Optimizer

The cost-based optimizer can be very mysterious

The core component of Oracle SQL tuning is the software known as the cost-based optimizer, or CBO for short.

Inside the SQL optimizer

Oracle has spent zillions of dollars developing their SQL optimizer, and the CBO is truly one of the world's most sophisticated software engineering feats. The optimizer has the weighty challenge of *always* coming-up with the *best* execution plan for any query.

However, it is critical to understand that while the optimizer developers are distinguished scientists, with many hailing from MIT and other top-notch Engineering Colleges, the process of SQL optimization is not scientific. In other words, understanding optimizer theory (e.g. decision tree theory) and algorithms will not help SQL run faster.

The Oracle optimizer is a software program, written by people.

- The optimizer has nuances and quirks, and its behavior changes radically between releases of Oracle.

- Theory will not help in SQL tuning. SQL tuning is all about experimentation and testing.

While it is tempting to apply scientific theory to how a SQL optimizer should work, it is important to remember that Oracle's implementation of the CBO is highly proprietary and the internal machinations are highly confidential.

The CBO is a giant computer program, written by humans, and keeping this fact in mind will greatly aid in the overall understanding of SQL optimization.

Tuning with the rule-based SQL optimizer

Oracle's first implementation of SQL used a rule-based optimizer as opposed to today's cost-based optimizer. Oracle Corporation recognizes that their SQL optimizer is the core of their database engine, and they have invested heavily in improving their SQL optimizer with each release, making the Oracle optimizer one of the world's most expensive and complex software programs.

Appreciate the Complexity!

To truly appreciate the SQL optimizer, consider how difficult it is to engineer a software program that always generates an optimal execution plans for any query. Oracle's optimizer is one of the world's most sophisticated software engineering feats.

But Oracle's evolution from rule-based into cost-based optimization was not without pitfalls. Oracle quickly realized that the rule-based optimizer (RBO) could do a better job if it had information about the detailed characteristics of the tables and columns, "cost" information that was to be incorporated into the new CBO.

However, the phenomenal complexity of gathering and using table and column metadata for SQL optimization cannot be underestimated. It took many years before

---

the CBO would reliably generate the best execution plan for any giver query. News about the future of rule-based optimization has been an integral part of each release of Oracle since version 7:

- **Oracle 7:** Oracle announced that the RBO would not be available in Oracle 8 and requested that Oracle customers migrate to cost-based optimization.

- **Oracle 8:** Oracle announced that the RBO would be retired in Oracle 8i. During this time, Oracle continued to use rule-based optimization for the Oracle Applications products.

- **Oracle8i:** Oracle announced that the RBO would be retired in Oracle 9i.

- **Oracle9i:** Oracle announced that RBO was to be removed in Oracle 10g. During this time, Oracle Applications 11i was introduced, using cost-based optimization. However, many of the SQL statements in 11i had *rule* hints embedded inside the source code.

- **Oracle 10g:** Oracle suggested that the rule-based optimizer will be returned in Oracle 11g.

The RBO is very elegant for its simplicity and has often made faster execution choices than the early implementations of Oracle's cost-based optimizer.

In fact, Oracle Applications products used the RBO until 2001 when the Oracle Apps 11i product was introduced. It was with the release of Oracle8i (8.1.6) that the CBO became faster than the RBO in all cases as shown in Figure 2.1:

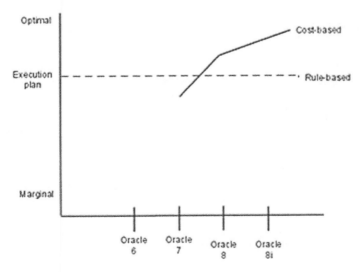

Figure 2.1: *The evolution of the CBO and RBO*

Today in Oracle11g, both the CBO and the RBO are commonly used to derive the execution plan for Oracle SQL statements. Even though Oracle announced plan to retire the RBO as early as the 1990's, it remains today as an important tool for optimizing Oracle SQL.

While it is very tempting to go into the relative advantages of the RBO and CBO within each successive release of Oracle, there are some general observations to be made about the characteristics of the rule-based optimizer:

- **Always use the Index**: If an index can be used to access a table, choose the index. Indexes are always preferred over a full-table scan of a sort merge join. A sort merge join does not require an index.

- **Always starts with the driving table**: The last table in the *from* clause will be the driving table. For the RBO, this should be the table that chooses the least amount of rows. The RBO uses this driving table as the first table when performing nested loop join operations.

- **Full-table scans as a last resort**: The RBO is not aware of Oracle parallel query and multi-block reads and does not consider the size of the table. Hence, the RBO dislikes full-table scans and will only use them when no index exists.

- **Any index will do**: The RBO will sometimes choose a less than ideal index to service a query. This is because the RBO does not have access to statistics that show the selectivity of indexed columns.

- **Simple is sometimes better**: Prior to Oracle8i, the RBO often provided a better overall execution plan for some databases.

The biggest shortcoming of the RBO is that it will common choose the wrong index to access a table. This is because the RBO does not have statistics to tell it the relative selectivity and cardinality of the indexes column.

Why the *rule* hint is still popular in Oracle 12c

Since the release of Oracle8, Oracle has threatened to phase out the rule-based optimizer (RBO). For Oracle Applications, it was ironic that Oracle Apps used the RBO, and Oracle made a big deal out of announcing that Oracle Applications 11i eBusiness suite was moving to the cost-based SQL optimizer (CBO).

Of course, when the actual SQL in *v$sql* is carefully examined, it becomes clear that literally hundreds of their SQL statements have the *rule* hint!

The *rule* hint is a trick used by many SQL tuning professionals, and it is the first thing that experts try when tuning a SQL statement since it points to problems with optimizer statistics (see *dbms_stats* and CBO histograms).

Also see MetaLink note 375386 where Oracle notes sub-optimal execution plans for RMAN in 10g release 2! The solution is to forget about fixing the CBO statistics. Oracle recommends this fix, added to the RMAN script:

```
alter session set optimizer_mode=rule;
```

The next section will show how Oracle determines the cost of internal SQL access methods.

Costs and the CBO

It is called the cost-based optimizer because Oracle builds a decision tree and applies costs figures to the operations within a SQL statement.

There are two types of factors that influence the CBO: those factors that are immutable and thus cannot be changed; and those for which there is some control. The immutable factors in a SQL statement include basic issues such as the number of rows returned by the query. But far and away, variable factors influence the costing decisions made by the optimizer:

- **Disk I/O speed**: The cost of disk I/O is the single most important factor in SQL optimization. Disk I/O is measured in thousandths of a second, an eternity for a database, and something that needs to be avoided whenever possible.

- **Available RAM:** The DBA configures the Oracle instance RAM resources, and the optimizer will be severely limited if there is not enough RAM for hash joins (via *pga_aggregate_target*, *sort_area_size* and *hash_area_size*).

- **Object metadata:** The DBA controls the quality of the metadata via the dbms_stats package. This data includes the number of rows in a table, the distribution of values within a column and other critical information about the state of the tables and indexes.

- **Server metadata:** The DBA controls the gathering of server-side metadata via *dbms_stats.gather_system_stats*. This measures CPU speed, single probe disk read speed (db file sequential reads) and multi-block reads (db file scattered reads).

There are many other factors, but this gives the general idea of how the costing decisions of the optimizer can be influenced.

Default disk speed!

If you forget to analyze server statistics with *dbms_stats.gather_system_stats*, Oracle uses a default disk I/O speed of ten milliseconds.

To better understand the process of SQL costing and optimization, it is a good idea to start by examining the process of transforming a SQL statement from its raw syntax into a finished executable.

The steps for executing a SQL statement

There are many intermediate steps between submitting a SQL statement and viewing the result set. Most SQL developers only see syntax and semantic errors and results, while the rest of the internal machinations are hidden from view. Figure 2.2 shows an overview of the steps involved in optimizing a SQL statement:

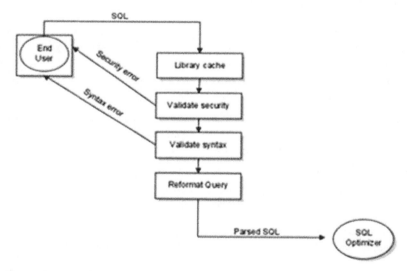

Figure 2.2: The steps in optimizing a SQL statement

This process warrants a closer look to see how an Oracle SQL statement is transformed after it enters the Oracle library cache.

1. **Parse phase:** During parsing, Oracle loads the SQL into the RAM heap of the library cache. Oracle then searches for an identical statement in library cache, and if not found, it checks the syntax

2. **Semantic phase:** Once the SQL statement has been validated for syntax, all table and column names are checked against the data dictionary to ensure that they exist.

3. **Security check phase:** This phase validates the security rules to ensure that the requestor is authorized to view the data. This involves comparing the privileges of the user against the names of the tables in the SQL. Valid privileges may exist via grants, virtual private database rules (row-level security) or via the "grant execute" model.

4. **Query rewrite phase:** Oracle is intelligent, and the optimizer may decide to rewrite a query into an equivalent, but faster, form. For example, Oracle may rewrite subqueries into standard joins with a not null test. It is not unusual to see query rewrite when the SQL can use a materialized view.

5. **Costing phase:** In this phase, Oracle determines all possible ways to service the query and generates a decision tree, adding costs to each leaf, and choosing the plan with the best cost. (Note: The cost figures that are displayed in a SQL execution plan are not the real costs used by the optimizer, and Oracle may chose a plan with a higher cost, depending upon the *optimizer_mode* (e.g. *first_rows_n* vs. *all_rows*)).

6. **Generate phase:** In this phase, Oracle takes its chosen plan and translates it into native calls to the Oracle data files. If SQL is being embedded inside a procedural language such as C or Cobol, the SQL pre-compiler will comment-out the SQL source statements and replace them with native language calls.

7. **Bind phase:** The executable is now bound to the Oracle database and all variable values are assigned real values for execution.

8. **Execution phase:** The executable code is now run against the Oracle data files.

9. **Transform phase:** After execution the SQL query, Oracle may sort the result set and apply function-based transformations to the rowset.

10. **Fetch phase:** After completion of the query, the result rows are fetched back into the calling program. (e.g. PL/SQL, C program, SQL*Plus).

There is a lot of internal processing involved. The next section will provide a close look at each of these steps and see how the pieces fit together.

SQL Parsing and the library cache

The very first step of SQL execution is to see if the SQL statement already exists in the library cache. Just as a data buffer serves to prevent re-accessing frequently referenced data blocks, the library cache piece of the shared pool exists to store frequently referenced SQL statements for fast reuse.

When a SQL statement is received into Oracle from an external program, the first step is to check if the statement already exists. This is done with a hashing algorithm which generates a unique address number within the library cache.

This hash value indicates a SQL's address, its place in the RAM heap.

If an existing statement is found at this address, Oracle can load-and-go very quickly, but when it is not found, Oracle loads the SQL into this address and begins processing the SQL from scratch. This is known as a hard parse as shown in Figure 2.3:

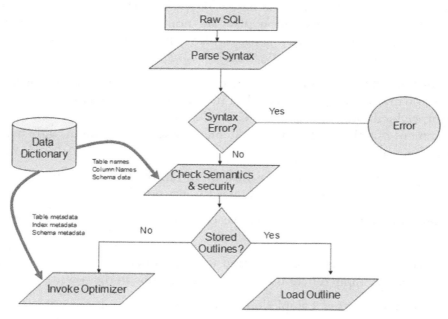

Figure 2.3: *The steps for parsing a SQL statement*

Because Oracle uses a hash to determine the address for a SQL statement, it important that all SQL be identical to be re-used. For example, a hashing algorithm would indicate that the following SQL statements are different, when they really only differ by capitalization and spacing:

```
select  * from emp;

Select * from Emp;

SELECT * FROM EMP;
```

Note: Depending on your release of Oracle, case insensitivity has been implemented and uppercase/lowercase does not matter to hashing a SQL statement.

One tip for SQL tuning experts is to always look at the executions column of *v$sql* and *dba_hist_sql* because it indicates how many times a SQL statement has been reused.

If there is much SQL where executions=1, then the system may have excessive overhead from hard parsing. So, how is it possible to ensure that all forms of a SQL statement are identical and thereby reduce the expensive hard parsing? Here are few common techniques:

- **Place all SQL inside stored procedures:** This encapsulation of SQL has several major benefits. In addition to ensuring that all forms of the SQL are identical to reduce hard parsing, it also has the benefit of allowing the stored procedure to be cached in the shared pool using *dbms_shared_pool.keep*.

- **Avoid numeric literals in SQL:** It always a good idea to use host variable inside SQL and avoid literal values. For example, the SQL in the form (select stuff from emp where emp_name= ':var1) can be reused, where SQL with literal values (select stuff from emp where emp_name='JONES') is unlikely to ever be reused by another statement. For end-user query tools that generate ad-hoc SQL with literal values embedded inside the SQL (e.g. Crystal Reports), Oracle gives us the *cursor_sharing=force* and cursor_sharing=similar features to make SQL reentrant.

See chapter 16, *SQL Tuning & the Library Cache* for more details on these technique for making SQL reentrant and reusable.

Now, it is time to take a closer look at how Oracle transforms a SQL statement into working executable machine code.

Creating a SQL executable

Oracle provides the *shared_pool_size* parameter to cache SQL so that it is not necessary to parse, over and over again. However, SQL can age-out if the *shared_pool_size* is too small or if it is cluttered with non-reusable SQL (i.e. SQL that has literals *"where name = "fred"*) in the source.

What is the difference between a hard parse and a soft parse in Oracle? In plain English, a brand new SQL statement goes through the entire parsing process from scratch, while a previously parsed SQL may experience a soft parse. Hence, a soft parse does not require a shared pool reload and the associated RAM memory allocation.

Check your parse calls!

A high value for "parse call" (> 10/sec.) indicates that the system has many incoming unique SQL statements, or that the SQL is not reentrant (i.e. not using bind variables).

A hard parse is when SQL must be reloaded into the shared pool. A hard parse is worse than a soft parse because of the overhead involved in shared pool RAM allocation and memory management. Once loaded, the SQL must then be completely re-checked for syntax as well as semantics and an executable generated.

Excessive hard parsing can occur when the *shared_pool_size* is too small and reentrant SQL is paged out, or when there are non-reusable SQL statements without host variables.

The *cursor_sharing* parameter offers an easy way to make SQL reentrant, and remember that host variables should always be used in SQL so that they can be reentrant.

Optimizer behavior and parameters

The CBO is influenced by many configuration settings. Settings for important CBO parameters can have a dramatic impact of CBO performance. These settings provide a place to start when exploring the CBO.

Choosing the CBO *optimizer_mode* is the first step. After that, other important CBO parameters can be examined.

The *optimizer_mode* parameter

In Oracle 11g there are several optimizer modes, all set by the value of the *optimizer_mode* parameter. The values can include: *all_rows*; *first_rows_1*; *first_rows_10*; and *first_rows_100*. Plus, there is the most important optimizer mode of all for SQL testing, the *rule* mode. The *rule* optimizer mode reflects the obsolete RBO, but using a *rule* hint is a valuable Oracle tuning tool.

The *all_rows* optimizer mode is designed to minimize computing resources and it favors full-table scans. Index access (*first_rows*) adds additional I/O overhead, but they return rows faster, back to the originating query as shown in Figure 2.4:

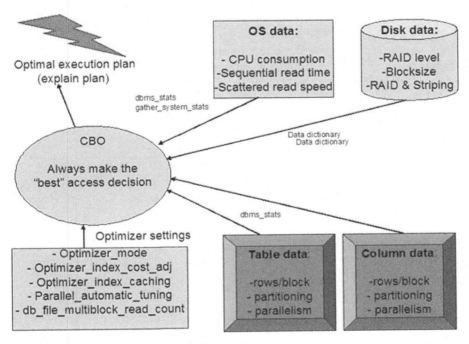

Figure 2.4: *The factors that influence SQL execution*

While the *optimizer_mode* is a system-wide parameter, the *optimizer_mode* can be set at the system-wide level, for an individual session or for a specific SQL statement:

```
alter system set optimizer_mode=first_rows_10;
```

```
alter session set optimizer_mode = all_rows;
```

```
select /*+ first_rows(100) */ from student;
```

To understand the best optimizer mode for us, start by asking "What is the best execution plan for a SQL statement"?

Is the best execution plan the one that begins to return rows the fastest, or is the best execution plan the one that executes with the smallest amount of computing resources? Of course, the answer depends on the processing needs of the database.

The new *opt_param* SQL hint can be used to quickly test the effect of another optimizer parameter value without using an alter session command:

```
select /*+ opt_param('optimizer_mode','first_rows_10') */ col1,

select /*+ opt_param('optimizer_index_cost_adj',20) */ col1,
```

The *all_rows* optimizer mode is designed to minimize computing resources, and it favors full-table scans. Indexes add additional I/O overhead, but they return rows faster, back to the originating query:

The following is a simple query :

```
select
    customer_name
from
    customer
where
    region = 'south'
order by
    customer_name;
```

If the best execution plan is the one that starts to return rows the fastest, a concatenated index on region and *customer_name* could be used to immediately start delivering table rows in their proper order, even though excess I/O will be required to read the nonadjacent data blocks as shown in Figure 2.5.

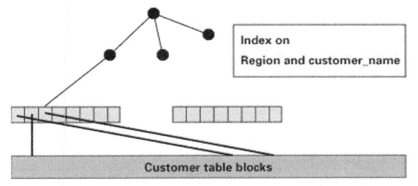

Figure 2.5: *Fetching data blocks from an un-clustered index*

Assume that this execution plan starts delivering results in .0001 seconds and requires 10,000 *db_block_gets*. But what if the goal is to minimize computing resources? If this SQL is inside a batch program, then it is not important to start returning rows quickly, and a different execution plan would take fewer computing resources.

In this example, a parallel full-table scan followed by a back-end sort will require less machine resources and less I/O because blocks do not have to be reread to pull the data in sorted order as shown in Figure 2.6 below.

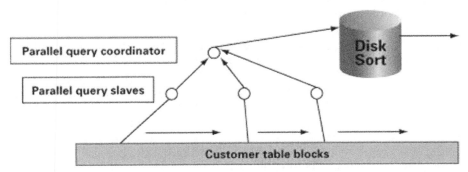

Figure 2.6: *Speeding up a SQL query with parallel processing*

In this example, the result is expected to take longer to deliver (no rows until the sort is complete), but there will be far less I/O because blocks will not have to be re-accessed to deliver the rows in presorted order.

Next, assume that this execution plan delivers the result in 10 seconds with 5,000 *db_block_gets*.

The optimizer and *where* clause order

When the optimizer begins its work, the items in the *where* clause are of primary importance because they govern the tables joining and rows filtering for the result set. In SQL that involves many tables, the cardinality, or the estimated number of rows returned, is critical to making a good optimization decision.

Some of the things that influence the order of application of the predicates include:

- Their position in the *where* clause.

- The kind of operators involved

- Automatic datatype conversion.

- The presence or absence of bind variables (*cursor_sharing*)

- The optimizer mode (*all_rows or first_rows_n*)

- The *_optimizer_cost_model* setting (IO or CPU)

- The use of *query_rewrite_enabled*

- Hints (e.g. ordered, *use_hash*)

Many people believe that the Oracle cost-based SQL optimizer does not consider the order that the Boolean predicates appear in the *where* clause.

However, there is some evidence that this is not complete true, as evidenced by the *ordered_predicates* SQL hint.

The *ordered_predicates* hint is specified in the *where* clause of a query and is used to specify the order in which Boolean predicates should be evaluated. In the absence of *ordered_predicates*, Oracle uses the following steps to evaluate the order of SQL predicates:

- Subqueries are evaluated before the outer Boolean conditions in the *where* clause.

- All Boolean conditions without built-in functions or subqueries are evaluated in reverse from the order they are found in the *where* clause, with the last predicate being evaluated first.

- Boolean predicates with built-in functions of each predicate are evaluated in increasing order of their estimated evaluation costs.

It is also important to note the bug in Oracle9i where adjusting *optimizer_index_cost_adj* will cause CPU costs to be considered in execution plans. More important, setting the SQL optimizer cost model (CPU or IO) will also affect the way that the optimizer evaluates predicate.

The next section will delve into the main SQL optimization goals, minimizing response time vs. minimizing computing resources.

High throughput vs. fast response time

Many people assume that the defaults for the Oracle parameters are just right for their systems, not realizing the incompatible goals of optimizing for throughput vs. optimizing for fast response time.

The default in Oracle 11g for the *optimizer_mode* is *all_rows*, an optimizer mode that has the goal of maximizing total throughout by choosing SQL access plans that minimize server resources. While this is a worthy goal, optimizing for maximum system throughout is not the same as optimizing for the fastest response time.

- **Optimize SQL for fast response time:** This is a "selfish" goal; minimizing response time for individual queries, regardless of the expense to other tasks on the system. Fast response time is often associated with index access.

- **Optimize SQL for efficient throughput:** This is a holistic system-wide optimizer goal that is concerned with optimizing your entire workload to maximize total throughout as a whole. High throughput is often associated with parallelized large-table full-table scans.

To get the fastest response time is it often necessary to use the *first_rows optimizer_mode*, a setting that directs the SQL optimizer to choose plans that start returning rows back to the calling application as quickly as possible. Optimizing for the fastest response time often involves using indexes, an access technique that returns rows quickly but incurs more I/O operations.

Are optimizing for fast response time and optimal throughout totally incompatible? The answer lies with the utilization of server resources. In a perfect world with unlimited server resources, it would be reasonable to accept any burden associated with the overhead of index processing, but that would not help batch jobs where the goal is manipulating zillions of rows, often using parallel query.

Optimizing SQL for multiple workloads

In the real world, shops frequently have bi-modal workloads, processing online transactions during the day and running batch jobs at night. A day mode would have parameter setting that enables fast response time, such as *optimizer_mode=first_rows_10*. A night mode would be optimized for throughput, adjusting the system parameters to maximize parallelism and full scan activity, an approach favored by *optimizer_mode=all_rows*.

For these systems past historical workload trends can be analyzed and used to predict when a workload changes and what type of configuration it requires. I discuss a complete method for this in my book "Oracle Tuning: The Definitive Reference", but in a nutshell, it involves running historical queries against performance data from AWR or STATSPACK, or by using trend analysis tools such as Ion for Oracle as shown in Figure 2.7:

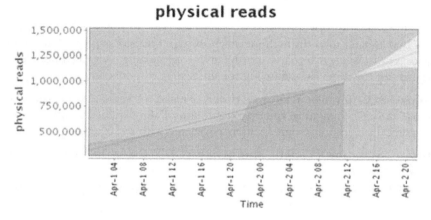

Figure 2.7: *Using Ion for Oracle to predict workload trends*

The following are the steps to analyze workloads for a self-tuning architecture:

- The first step in understand Oracle workloads in any system is to analyze their characteristics, using the historical database provided in STATSPACK or AWR.

- Once the workload has been identified and their goals set (response time or high throughout), *alter system* commands can be used to adjust the configuration of the instance to accommodate the changes in workload.

Because this approach is proactive, the system never suffers a slow-down. The approach is unlike Oracle automation tools like Automatic Memory Management (AMM), which are reactive, and wait until a problem occurs before changing the SGA pool sizes.

The effect of *optimizer_mode* on SQL execution plans

There are several silver bullet optimizer parameters, system-wide settings that have a profound impact on system-wide performance, most important being *optimizer_mode*, *optimizer_index_caching* and *optimizer_index_cost_adj*.

The *optimizer_mode* is the most powerful of these silver bullet parameters and a change can radically alter the characteristics of the SQL execution workload.

Oracle recommends that the best *optimizer_mode* be determined based upon the user's specific optimizer goals, to minimize response times (*first_rows_n*), or to minimize resource consumption (*all_rows*) for each unique SQL workload as shown in Figure 2.8.

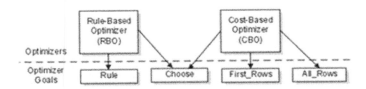

Figure 2.8: *Oracle offers several optimizer goals*

To see which global *optimizer_mode* is best for a particular SQL workload, Oracle offers the 11g Real Application Testing (RAT) tool, in addition to traditional benchmarking techniques for testing the performance of a workload as a whole.

Oracle offers several optimizer modes that allows the DBA to choose their definition of the best execution plan for them:

- ***optimizer_mode=all_rows***: This is the default optimizer mode with the goal of ensuring that overall computing resources are minimized, even if no rows are available until the entire query has completed. The *all_rows* access method often favors a parallel full-table scan over a full-index scan and sorting over presorted retrieval via an index. Because the *all_rows* mode favors full-table scans, it is best suited for data warehouses, decision-support systems and batch-oriented databases where intermediate rows are not required for real-time viewing.

- ***optimizer_mode=first_rows_n***: This *first_rows* optimizer mode enhancement optimizes queries for a small, expected return set. The values are *first_rows_1*, *first_rows_10*, *first_rows_100* and *first_rows_1000*. The CBO uses the *n* in *first_rows_n* as an important driver in determining cardinalities for query result sets. By telling the CBO, a priori, that only a certain number of rows are expected back from the query, the CBO will be able to make a better decision about whether to use an index to access the table rows.

- ***optimizer_mode=rule***. The rule-based optimizer (RBO) is the archaic optimizer mode from the earliest releases of Oracle Database. The rule-based optimizer has not been updated in nearly a decade and is not recommended for production use because the RBO does not support any new features of Oracle since 1994, including bitmap indexes, table partitions and function-based indexes. However, Oracle Corporation still uses the *rule* hint in their own SQL within Oracle eBusiness suite, and the *rule* hint remains a great way to test SQL execution speed.

To see how important the *optimizer_mode* is to SQL execution, consider the following time consuming query. This is a three-way table join that returns 100,000 rows and performs tens of thousands of logical I/O operations:

```
set autotrace on;

select
    p.pat_first_name,
    p.Pat_last_name,
    v.arrive_dt_tm,
    v.depart_dt_tm,
    r.test_name,
    r.result_val,
    r.result_dt_tm
from
    patient p,
    pat_visit v,
    pat_result r
where
    p.pat_id=v.pat_id
and
    v.visit_id=r.visit_id;
```

To observe the changes to the execution plans and SQL response times, the query will be run with several different optimizer_mode values:

optimizer_mode=all_rows

With the default optimizer_mode of all_rows, this query performs two full-scan operations against the target tables and feeds these into a hash join. This is consistent with the optimizer goal of all_rows, which is to minimize computing resources. Remember, index access involves additional I/O:

```
alter session set optimizer_mode=all_rows;
```

ID	PID	Operation	Name	Rows	Bytes	Cost	CPU Cost	IO Cost	Temp space

ID	PID	Operation	Name	Rows	Bytes	Cost	CPU Cost	IO Cost	
0		SELECT STATEMENT		29M	2432M	153683	19G	152495	
1	0	HASH JOIN		29M	2432M	153683	19G	152495	309M
2	1	HASH JOIN		4990K	252M	16033	2G	15874	43M
3	2	TABLE ACCESS FULL	PATIENT	1000K	32M	1754	235M	1740	
4	2	TABLE ACCESS FULL	PAT_VISIT	5000K	90M	4705	1G	4635	
5	1	TABLE ACCESS FULL	PAT_RESULT	30M	944M	58074	9G	57500	

```
Statistics
-----------------------------------------------------------
     149 recursive calls
       0 db block gets
   30841 consistent gets
   10988 physical reads
       0 redo size
 3848972 bytes sent via SQL*Net to client
   73672 bytes received via SQL*Net from client
    6668 SQL*Net roundtrips to/from client
       0 sorts (memory)
       0 sorts (disk)
  100000 rows processed
```

optimizer_mode=first_rows

This optimizer mode became obsolete as of the release of version 10g; however, it is important to see how its use affects performance in earlier versions. When the *optimizer_mode* is changed to *first_rows*, the execution plan changes, where the hash join is replaced by a nested loops join operation, and the full table scans are replaced by index range scans. The *first_rows* access incurs additional I/O, more than the full scans in the *all_rows* plan, but the index access ensures the fastest possible response time:

```
alter session set optimizer_mode=first_rows;
```

ID	PID	Operation	Name	Rows	Bytes	Cost	CPU Cost	IO Cost
0		SELECT STATEMENT		29M	2432M	46M	355G	46M
1	0	NESTED LOOPS						
2	1	NESTED LOOPS		29M	2432M	46M	355G	46M
3	2	NESTED LOOPS		4990K	252M	7004942	52G	7001775
4	3	TABLE ACCESS FULL	PATIENT	1000K	32M	1754	235M	1740
5	3	TABLE ACCESS BY INDEX ROWID	PAT_VISIT	5	95	7	52750	7
6	5	INDEX RANGE SCAN	XIE1PAT_VISIT	5		2	16093	2
7	2	INDEX RANGE SCAN	XIE1PAT_RESULT	6		2	16293	2
8	1	TABLE ACCESS BY INDEX ROWID	PAT_RESULT	6	198	8	60642	8

```
Statistics
-----------------------------------------------------------
       0 recursive calls
       0 db block gets
  177164 consistent gets
       0 physical reads
       0 redo size
 3589015 bytes sent via SQL*Net to client
   73672 bytes received via SQL*Net from client
    6668 SQL*Net roundtrips to/from client
       0 sorts (memory)
       0 sorts (disk)
```

```
100000   rows processed
```

optimizer_mode=first_rows_100

When the *optimizer_mode* is changed to *first_rows_100*, the plan changes again, to a plan identical to the *all_rows optimizer_mode*.

```
alter session set optimizer_mode=first_rows_100;
```

ID	PID	Operation	Name	Rows	Bytes	Cost	CPU Cost	IO Cost
0		SELECT STATEMENT		29M	2432M	153683	19G	152495
1	0	HASH JOIN		29M	2432M	153683	19G	152495
2	1	HASH JOIN		4990K	252M	16033	2G	15874
3	2	TABLE ACCESS FULL	PATIENT	1000K	32M	1754	235M	1740
4	2	TABLE ACCESS FULL	PAT_VISIT	5000K	90M	4705	1G	4635
5	1	TABLE ACCESS FULL	PAT_RESULT	30M	944M	58074	9G	57500

```
Statistics
----------------------------------------------------------
        0   recursive calls
        0   db block gets
   177164   consistent gets
        0   physical reads
        0   redo size
  3589015   bytes sent via SQL*Net to client
    73672   bytes received via SQL*Net from client
     6668   SQL*Net roundtrips to/from client
        0   sorts (memory)
        0   sorts (disk)
   100000   rows processed
```

optimizer_mode=rule

Using the oldest optimizer_mode, the RULE hint, the optimizer has chosen a different index from the first_rows plan. This is because the rule-based optimizer (the RBO) does not have access to metadata statistics from dbms_stats and commonly chooses a sub-optimal index, an index with less selectivity.

```
alter session set optimizer_mode=rule;
```

ID	PID	Operation	Name
0		SELECT STATEMENT	
1	0	NESTED LOOPS	
2	1	NESTED LOOPS	
3	2	NESTED LOOPS	
4	3	TABLE ACCESS FULL	PAT_RESULT
5	3	TABLE ACCESS BY INDEX ROWID	PAT_VISIT
6	5	INDEX UNIQUE SCAN	XPKPAT_VISIT
7	2	INDEX UNIQUE SCAN	XPKPATIENT
8	1	TABLE ACCESS BY INDEX ROWID	PATIENT

```
Statistics
----------------------------------------------------------
        0   recursive calls
        0   db block gets
```

```
247417   consistent gets
   874   physical reads
     0   redo size
3769059  bytes sent via SQL*Net to client
 73672   bytes received via SQL*Net from client
  6668   SQL*Net roundtrips to/from client
     0   sorts (memory)
     0   sorts (disk)
100000   rows processed
```

optimizer_mode=choose

Using the obsolete *optimizer_mode=choose*, the execution plan returns to the *all_rows* plan. This is because the choose mode switches between *rule* and *choose* depending upon the presence of optimizer statistics (from *dbms_stats*).

```
alter session set optimizer_mode=choose;
```

ID	PID	Operation	Name	Rows	Bytes	Cost	CPU Cost	IO Cost
0		SELECT STATEMENT		29M	2432M	153683	19G	152495
1	0	HASH JOIN		29M	2432M	153683	19G	152495
2	1	HASH JOIN		4990K	252M	16033	2G	15874
3	2	TABLE ACCESS FULL	PATIENT	1000K	32M	1754	235M	1740
4	2	TABLE ACCESS FULL	PAT_VISIT	5000K	90M	4705	1G	4635
5	1	TABLE ACCESS FULL	PAT_RESULT	30M	944M	58074	9G	57500

```
Statistics
----------------------------------------------------------
       149   recursive calls
         0   db block gets
     30841   consistent gets
     10988   physical reads
         0   redo size
   3848972   bytes sent via SQL*Net to client
     73672   bytes received via SQL*Net from client
      6668   SQL*Net roundtrips to/from client
         0   sorts (memory)
         0   sorts (disk)
    100000   rows processed
```

It becomes apparent that the choice of the proper *optimizer_mode* for our SQL workload is one of the most important decisions to be made. The next section provides a closer look at how *optimizer_mode* affects SQL response time performance.

Optimizer mode and query performance

Begin by reviewing the amount of consistent gets that were required to service this query. Remember, a consistent get is a logical I/O, a buffer read, and a well-tuned SQL statement will fetch the desired rows with a minimum amount of consistent gets. In the above test, there are vastly different execution plans and vastly different counts for consistent gets as shown in Table 2.1 below:

Optimizer Mode	Consistent gets
all_rows	30,841
first_rows	177,164
first_rows_100	177,164
rule	247,417

Table 2.1: *Optimizer mode and resulting Consistent gets*

It should now be apparent that the value for *optimizer_mode* has a profound impact on the resulting SQL execution plans. Hence, the best *optimizer_mode* for a specific workload should be tested and chosen prior to performing any specific tuning of SQL statements.

While the optimizer_mode is the single most important factor in invoking the cost-based optimizer, there are other parameters that influence the CBO behavior. The next section will provide a quick look at these parameters.

Oracle parameters that influence the CBO

While the optimizer_mode parameter governs the global behavior of the CBO, there are many other Oracle parameters that have a great impact on CBO behavior. Because of the power of the CBO, Oracle provides several system-level parameters that can adjust the overall behavior of the CBO. These adjustment parameters generally involve the choice of using an index versus doing a full-table scan, and the CBO's choice of table join methods.

However, Oracle does not recommend changing the default values for many of these CBO setting because the changes can affect the execution plans for thousands of SQL statements. The following are the major optimizer parameters:

- *optimizer_mode:* The most powerful parameter of all, the optimizer_mode dictates the overall goal for the optimizer, such as whether to optimizer for response time (first_rows_n) or for minimizing resource consumption (all_rows).

- *optimizer_index_cost_adj:* This parameter alters the costing algorithm for access paths involving indexes. The smaller the value, the lower the cost of index access.

- **optimizer_index_caching:** This parameter tells Oracle how much of your index is likely to be in the RAM data buffer cache. The setting for optimizer_index_caching affects the CBO's decision to use an index for a table join (nested loops) or to favor a full-table scan.

- **db_file_multiblock_read_count** (Prior to Oracle 10g release 2): When this parameter is set to a high value, the CBO recognizes that scattered (multiblock) reads may be less expensive than sequential reads. This makes the CBO friendlier to full-table scans. The *db_file_multiblock_read_count* value is automated in 10gr2 and beyond.

- **hash_area_size (if not using** *pga_aggregate_target*): The setting for hash_area_size parameter governs the propensity of the CBO to favor hash joins over nested loop and sort merge table joins.

- **sort_area_size (if not using** *pga_aggregate_target*): The sort_area_size influences the CBO when deciding whether to perform an index access or a sort of the result set. The higher the value for sort_area_size, the more likely that a sort will be performed in RAM, and the more likely that the CBO will favor a sort over presorted index retrieval.

The idea optimizer settings depend on the environment and are heavily influenced by the system's costs for scattered disk reads versus sequential disk reads.

The *opt_param* hint

Starting in Oracle 10g release 2, Oracle introduced the *opt_param* SQL hint, without documentation. It appears that the *opt_param* hint is very similar to the alter session method for changing parameters, but it only applies to that specific SQL statement.

Remember that for testing, the effect of another optimizer parameter value at the query level can be quickly tested without using an *alter session* command, using the new *opt_param* SQL hint:

```
Syntax: opt_param(<parameter_name> [,] <parameter_value>).
```

For example, the effect of different optimizer modes in SQL can be tested directly with hints:

```
select /*+ opt_param('optimizer_mode','first_rows_10') */ col1, col2
select /*+ opt_param('optimizer_index_cost_adj',20) */ col1, col2
```

For another example, the SQL below turn-off *hash_join_enabled* (to force a nested loop, usually), but only for that SQL statement:

```
select /*+ opt_param('hash_join_enabled','false') */
    dept_no,
    emp_name,
    empno
from
    emp e,
```

```
    dept d
where
    e.ename=d.dname;
```

The *opt_param* hint is also useful for testing the effect of global parameters such as *optimizer_mode* and *optimizer_cost_model*.

```
select /*+ opt_param('optimizer_mode','first_rows_10') */
```

```
select /*+ opt_param('_optimizer_cost_model','io') */
```

```
select /*+ opt_param('optimizer_index_cost_adj',20) */
```

```
select /*+ opt_param('optimizer_index_caching',20) */
```

Next, it is time to examine one of the most powerful (and dangerous) Oracle SQL tuning knobs, the *optimizer_index_cost_adj* throttle.

Using *optimizer_index_cost_adj*

The *optimizer_index_cost_adj* parameter was created to allow users to change the relative costs of full-scan versus index operations.

The *optimizer_index_cost_adj* can be thought of as a throttle, adjusting the relative costs of a full-table scan:

- A small value for *optimizer_index_cost_adj(10 to 30)*, and index access becomes less costly.

- A higher value for *optimizer_index_cost_adj* makes full scans more attractive.

The *optimizer_index_cost_adj* parameter is the most important optimizer parameter of all, and the default setting of 100 may not be optimal for a particular SQL workload. For some OLTP systems, re-setting this parameter to a smaller value (between 10- to 30) may result in huge performance gains!

Tip! Try workload statistics first!

In Oracle 10g and beyond, a similar result to *optimizer_index_cost_adj* can be achieved by analyzing workload statistics with *dbms_stats.gather_system_stats*.

Also note that for database that are CPU-bound, as per the top-5 timed events in a STATSPACK or AWR report, deploying CPU costing (_optimizer_cost_model) may have a similar affect as does lower values for optimizer_index_cost_adj.

Remember, the all_rows optimizer mode is designed to minimize computing resources, and it favors full-table scans. Index access (first_rows_n) adds additional I/O overhead but returns rows faster, back to the originating query.

Prior to Oracle 10g, adjusting the optimizer parameters was often the only way to compensate for sample size issues with dbms_stats. As of 10g, the use of dbms_stats.gather_system_stats and improved sampling within dbms_stats had made adjustments to these parameters far less important. Ceteris Parabus, always adjust the CBO statistics before adjusting any optimizer parameters.

In systems experiencing slow performance because the CBO first_rows_n optimizer_mode is favoring too many full-table scans, the value of the optimizer_index_cost_adj parameter can be reduced to immediately tune all of the SQL in the database to favor index scans over full-table scans.

Changing optimizer_index_cost_adj is sometimes a silver bullet in the sense that a lower value may improve the performance of an entire database workload, especially in cases where the database is OLTP and it has been verified that the full-table scan costing is too low for the user's specific needs.

The optimizer_index_cost_adj parameter is an initialization parameter that can be very useful for SQL tuning. It is a numeric parameter with values from zero to 10,000 and a default value of 100. It can also be enabled at the session level by using the alter session set optimizer_index_cost_adj = nn syntax. This parameter allows tuning of the optimizer behavior for access path selection to be more or less index friendly, and it is very useful when it is felt that the default behavior for the CBO favors full-table scans over index scans.

If response time is critical, it is necessary to ensure that Oracle always uses index access to fetch rows as quickly as possible, but on some servers, a full-table scan may be faster than index access. Essentially, the CBO's choice about index vs. full-scan access depends on the relative costs of each type of operation.

The default value for optimizer_index_cost_adj is 100, and any value less than 100 makes the CBO view indexes as less expensive. If you do not like the propensity of the CBO to choose optimizer_mode parameter to favor full-table scans, the value of optimizer_index_cost_adj can be lowered to 20, thereby telling the CBO to give a lower cost to index scans over full-table scans.

Even in Oracle9i, the CBO sometimes falsely determines that the cost of full-table scan is less than the cost of an index access. The *optimizer_index_cost_adj* parameter is a great approach to whole-system SQL tuning, but it will be important to evaluate the overall effect by slowly resetting the value down from 100 and observing the percentage of full-tale scans.

Another approach is to slowly bump down the value of *optimizer_index_cost_adj* when the database is bounced and then either use the *access.sql* or *plan9i.sql* scripts (available via a Google search for "plan9i.sql") or reexamine SQL from the STATSPACK *stats$sql_summary* table to see the net effect of index scans on the whole database.

Is re-setting *optimizer_index_cost_adj* required after 9i?

There is some debate on whether optimizer_index_cost_adj needs to be changed in 10g and 11g, with conflicting reports from the end-user community. Remember, only change *optimizer_index_cost_adj* as a last resort.

Alternatives to optimizer_index_cost_adj!

In 10g and beyond, the same effect can be achieved with *dbms_stats.gather_system_stats*. This samples the relative costs of full scans vs. index scan and adjusted the costs accordingly.

Some claim that adding specialized CBO statistics (i.e. histograms) will alleviate the need to change the default values for *optimizer_index_cost_adj*, while others note that numerous bugs and other issues require that *optimizer_index_cost_adj* be changed in order for all relevant indexes to be invoked.

Changing CBO SQL Optimizer Parameters

An emergency involving an Oracle 11g client from Phoenix who was experiencing steadily degrading performance involved a large number of large-table full-table scans which were suspected to being unnecessary. This suspicious information was found by a quick look into *v$sql_plan* view using the *plan10g.sql* script that is found earlier in this chapter.

The top SQL was extracted from v$sql and timed as-is with an index hint. While it was unclear why the CBO was not choosing the index, the query with the index hint ran almost 20x faster. After acting quickly and running a script against v$bh and user_indexes, the DBA discovered that approximately 65 percent of the indexes were currently inside the data buffer cache.

Based on similar systems, the next step was to lower *optimizer_index_cost_adj* to a value of 20 in hopes of forcing the CBO to lower the relative costs of index access.

```
optimizer_index_cost_adj=20

optimizer_index_caching=65
```

This change relieved the problem and made it such that the table indexes were being used. The next section will cover techniques for changing optimizer parameters values at the user level.

Changing Optimizer Parameters at the User Level

In the previous examples, global changes were made which will affect the entire system. It is also possible to re-set the optimizer parameters at the session level, changing the optimizer settings for a particular user. This is especially useful for changing the optimizer characteristics for batch jobs when the goal might be to change the default *first_rows* optimization to *all_rows*, and change the optimizer weights for full-scan access and index caching:

```
create or replace trigger
   logon_batch
after logon on database
declare pragma autonomous_transaction;
begin
if user = 'scott' then
execute immediate 'ALTER SESSION SET optimizer_mode=all_rows';
execute immediate 'ALTER SESSION SET optimizer_index_cost_adj=90';
execute immediate 'ALTER SESSION SET optimizer_index_caching=25';
end if;
end;
/
```

As a result of these actions, the execution plans for over 350 SQL statements were changed, and the overall system response time was cut in half.

Next let's look at how to measure I/O costs for disk reads.

Measuring I/O Costs for Scattered and Sequential Reads

Remember, optimizer_index_cost_adj depends upon the relative costs of index access (a *db file sequential read*) vs. full-scan access (a *db file scattered read*). Hence, measuring the relative costs of these operations can give insights into the optimal value for optimizer_index_cost_adj for a specific SQL workload.

For Oracle9i and before, the script below can be used to measure these I/O costs on the database and get a recommended starting value for *optimizer_index_cost_adj*. This scripts show the difference between scattered read times and sequential read times, but the best solution is to always remember to run *dbms_stats.gather_system_stats*):

💾 optimizer_index_cost_adj.sql

```
col c1 heading 'Average Waits|forFull| Scan Read I/O'     format 9999.999
col c2 heading 'Average Waits|for Index|Read I/O'         format 9999.999
col c3 heading 'Percent of| I/O Waits|for Full Scans'     format 9.99
col c4 heading 'Percent of| I/O Waits|for Index Scans'    format 9.99
col c5 heading 'Starting|Value|for|optimizer|index|cost|adj' format 999

select
   a.average_wait                                  c1,
   b.average_wait                                  c2,
   a.total_waits /(a.total_waits + b.total_waits)  c3,
   b.total_waits /(a.total_waits + b.total_waits)  c4,
   (b.average_wait / a.average_wait)*100           c5
from
   v$system_event a,
   v$system_event b
where
   a.event = 'db file scattered read'
and
   b.event = 'db file sequential read'
;
```

The following is the output from the script.

Average waits for full scan read I/O	Average waits for index read I/O	Percent of I/O waits for full scans	Percent of I/O waits for index scans	Starting Value for optimizer index cost adj
1.473	.289	.02	.98	20

In this example, the suggested starting value of 20 for *optimizer_index_cost_adj* may be too high because 98 percent of the data waits are on index (sequential) block access. Weighting this starting value for *optimizer_index_cost_adj* to reflect the reality that this system has only two percent waits on full-table scan reads, a typical OLTP system with few full-table scans, is a practical matter. It is not desirable to have an automated value for *optimizer_index_cost_adj* to be less than one or more than 100.

This same script may give a very different result at a different time of the day because these values change constantly, as the I/O waits accumulate and access patterns change. Oracle has the *dba_hist_sysmetric_summary* table for time-series analysis of this behavior.

Hypercharge SQL with system stats!

Instead of changing optimizer_index_cost_adj, a better solution is to sample the disk speed with *dbms_stats.gather_system_stats*. This helps the CBO understand the costs of disk I/O.

Again, remember that *optimizer_index_cost_adj* should not be changed until after trying root cause remedies such as gathering disk I/O tunings with *dbms_stats.gather_system_stats*.

Now that the CBO parameters have been covered, it is time to take a look at how to help the CBO make good execution-plan decisions by providing the CBO with information about the schema.

Understanding CBO Statistics

The most important key to success with the CBO is to carefully define and manage statistics. In order for the CBO to make an intelligent decision about the best execution plan for the SQL, it must have information about the table and indexes that participate in the query. When the CBO knows the size of the tables and the distribution, cardinality, and selectivity of column values, the CBO can make an informed decision and almost always generates the best execution plan.

In 10g and beyond, Oracle automatically collects CBO statistics. However, there are cases when additional schema information helps tune SQL statements. See the section later in this book on tuning with histograms for the full story.

As a review, the CBO gathers information from many sources, and it has the lofty goal of using DBA-provided metadata to always make the best execution plan decision.

The next section will address areas of CBO statistics and show how to gather top-quality statistics for the CBO and how to create an appropriate CBO environment for your database.

Extended Optimizer Statistics

One of the most exciting new features of Oracle 11g is improvement to the *dbms_stats* package, specifically the ability to aid complex queries by providing extended statistics to the cost-based optimizer (CBO).

The 11g extended optimizer statistics are intended to improve the optimizer's guesses for the cardinality of combined columns and columns that are modified by a built-in or user-defined function.

In Oracle 10g, it was clear that dynamic sampling can be used to provide inter-table cardinality estimates, but dynamic sampling has important limitations. However, the 11g extended statistics in *dbms_stats* relieves much of the problem of sub-optimal table join orders.

In the absence of column histograms and extended statistics, the Oracle CBO must be able to guess the size of complex result sets information, and it sometimes gets it wrong. This is one reason why the *ordered* hint is one of the most popular SQL tuning hints; using the *ordered* hint allows the user to specify that the tables be joined together in the same order that they appear in the *from* clause.

This is a good time to take a closer look and understand how the 11g extended *dbms_stats* data helps the optimizer make better guesses of result set sizes.

The new 11g *dbms_stats* package has several new procedures to aid in supplementing histogram data, and the state of these extended histograms can be seen in the user_tab_col_statistics view:

- *dbms_stats.create_extended_stats*

- *dbms_stats.show_extended_stats_name*

- *dbms_stats.drop_extended_stats*

It is easy to invoke extended statistics with *dbms_stats*, specialty histogram analysis using function-based columnar data:

```
begin
  dbms_stats.gather_table_stats (
    ownname   => 'SCOTT',
    tabname   => 'CUSTOMER',
    method_opt => 'for all columns size skewonly for columns
(upper(cust_name))'
  );
end;
```

Another way of invoking extended statistics is to use the new *for columns* option with the *method_opt*. In the example below, the columns (*cust_id* and *cust_category*) are specified directly within the *method_opt* call:

```
begin
   dbms_stats.gather_table_stats (
      ownname          => 'SCOTT',
      tabname          => 'CUSTOMER',
      estimate_percent=> 100,
      method_opt  => 'FOR ALL COLUMNS SIZE SKEWONLY FOR
COLUMNS(CUST_ID,CUST_CATEGORY)',
      cascade          => true
```

The Oracle 10g default value for *dbms_stats method_opt* is for all columns size auto.

Using *for all columns size auto* directs Oracle to decide automatically which will get histograms. Oracle examines the skew of column values and also examines the workload associated with the columns, querying v$sql for current SQL. However, the overhead of creating and managing zillions of histograms can easily outweigh the performance benefits of having the histograms.

There is a perpetual trade-off between sub-optimal plans and unneeded overhead of superfluous or un-referenced histograms. An exploration of intelligent histogram creation, is needed, a method that uses AWR to correlate the SQL to the objects, avoiding histograms that are never used, and develop a method to only create histograms that make a difference.

Some believe in the practice of running statistics by schedule such as weekly. Some believe in just calculating statistics when the data changes. Still others believe that statistics are only needed to fix a poor access path, and once things are good; they should not be touched. It is difficult to say who is correct.

Oracle automatically reanalyzes schema statistics based on the number of changes to row in the table, but it may be sub-optimal, and many senior Oracle DBAs use more sophisticated methods for determining when to re-analyze CBO statistics.

Although the Oracle CBO is one of the world's most sophisticated software achievements, it is still the job of the Oracle professional to provide valid statistics for the schema and understand how Oracle parameters affect the overall performance of the SQL optimizer.

Keep in mind, suboptimal SQL execution plans are a major reason for poorly performing Oracle databases, and because the CBO determines the execution plans, it is a critical component in Oracle optimization.

The *dbms_stats* utility is a great way to improve SQL execution speed. By using *dbms_stats* to collect top quality statistics, the CBO will usually make an intelligent decision about the fastest way to execute any SQL query. The *dbms_stats* utility continues to improve and the exciting new features of automatic sample size and automatic histogram generation greatly simplify the job of the Oracle professional.

Oracle Optimizer Costing

There is a cost column in the execution plan, which yields a number that estimates the number of single-block disk reads that the optimizer thinks will be required to serve the query. Oracle does their cost in terms of disk reads because disk reads are the single most expensive operation for any SQL statement, thousands of times slower than any other operation.

The Oracle CBO displays cost figures, but these are very misleading because a low cost value does not always indicate the real lowest cost that is select by the optimizer. In other words, Oracle does not always choose the lowest real cost value, and Oracle does not disclose the exact behavior of their optimizer, a prized competitive edge over other competing databases.

While Oracle does not publish the internal machinations of their proprietary optimizer costing model, many Oracle experts have reverse engineered the software and developed equations for estimating the cost.

Some Oracle experts may overcome costing issues by adjusting the *optimizer_index_cost_adj* parameter for a specific user and deciding that the best action for changing the execution plan for a query, changing the query with a hint, is impossible because of code access limitations. This limitation imposed by not being able to change the SQL is common with seeded ad-hoc SQL or with vendor packages.

In this case, you could use a login trigger to set *optimizer_index_cost_adj* to a higher value, thereby increasing the probability that the Oracle optimizer would choose a full scan operation.

Some Oracle experts have tried to replicate the optimizer's costing algorithm, deriving the internal costing of index scan costs and table scan costs:

- **Index Cost** = Blevel+ceil(leaf_blocks*ix_selectivity)

- **Table Scan cost** = ceil(clustering_factor*table_selectivity)

- **Nested loops Cost** = Cost of an Outer Table + (Cost of Inner Table * Cardinality of Outer Table)

- **Nested Loops Table Scan Cost** = (Current Cost of Inner Table Scan * Outer Table Card)*OICA/100

Again, beware that Oracle does not publishing their costing internals, and that the cost values in an execution plan are misleading because they do not always reflect the real best access plan for an SQL statement.

In sum, while the cost columns in an explain plan are interesting to see, Oracle's estimate of the number of disk reads for a query is likely not reliable enough to be used when tuning most production SQL statements.

Oracle Dynamic Sampling

One of the greatest problems with the Oracle CBO was the inability of the Oracle DBA to gather accurate schema statistics. Even with the dbms_stats package, the schema statistics were often stale and the DBA did not always create histograms for skewed data columns and data columns that are used to estimate the size of SQL intermediate result sets.

For example, assume there is a motor vehicle database with a low-cardinality column like *region*, which has only four values as shown in Figure 2.9:

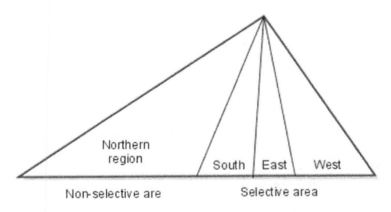

Figure 2.9: *The popularity of a column values influences the execution plan*

In this case, it makes sense to invoke an index scan on the unpopular values (*south, east* and *west*), but because the *northern* region comprises most of the rows values, a full-table scan may be more effective than using an index.

The DBA's failure to create histograms for skewed values has resulted in an underserved bad reputation for the Oracle's CBO. Novice DBAs often falsely accuse the CBO of failing to generate optimal execution plans when the real cause of the suboptimal execution plan was their own failure to collect complete schema statistics that would detect skewed values.

Oracle has automated the collection and refreshing of schema statistics in Oracle. This automates the DBA's task and ensures that Oracle will always gather good statistics and choose the best execution plan for any query. Using the enhanced dbms_stats package, Oracle will automatically estimate the sample size, detect skewed columns that would benefit from histograms, and refresh the schema statistics when they become stale.

This automates a very important DBA task and ensures that Oracle always has the statistics that it needs to make good execution plan choices. The following is an example using the dbms_stats package:

```
begin
    dbms_stats.gather_schema_stats(
        ownname          => 'SCOTT',
        estimate_percent => dbms_stats.auto_sample_size,
        method_opt => 'for all columns size repeat',
        degree           => 7
    );
end;
/
```

By default, Oracle collects statistics for the SQL optimizer via the default of autostats_target = auto. Sadly, this is confusing because this command appears to be similar in function to this command to disable statistics collection:

```
exec dbms_scheduler.disable('sys.gather_stats_job');
```

It astonishes me how many shops prohibit any unapproved production changes and yet re-analyze schema stats weekly. Evidently, they do not understand that the purpose of schema re-analysis is to change production SQL execution plans, and they act surprised when performance changes!

Me, I don't like surprises, and when schema statistics are reanalyzed automatically, the optimizer can force thousands of SQL statements to change execution plans. Setting *autostats_target* to oracle turns off automatic statistics collection in 10g:

```
exec dbms_stats.set_param('autostats_target','oracle');
```

This is a good move if CBO statistics are optimal and there is no need to risk changing the SQL execution plans.

The Dynamic Sampling Hint

The use of the *dynamic_sampling* hint is very useful for highly volatile tables and global temporary tables.

In 10g, the *dynamic_sampling* hint to can be used to direct Oracle to estimate the cardinality of highly volatile tables.

The dynamic sampling hint is also useful for estimating the size of dynamically created objects such as global temporary tables (GTT's).

```
select /*+ dynamic_sampling(customer 4) */
   pol_no,
   sales_id,
   sum_assured,
   premium
from
   customer;
```

Sub-Optimal Table Join Order

Historically, there was always a nagging problem with the CBO. Even with good statistics, the CBO would sometimes determine a suboptimal table join order, causing unnecessarily large intermediate result sets. For example, consider the complex *where* clause in the query below.

Even with the best schema statistics it can be impossible to predict the optimal table join order. The table join order that has the smallest intermediate baggage. As one might expect, reducing the size of the intermediate row sets can greatly improve the speed of the query.

```
select
   stuff
from
   customer
natural join
   orders
natural join
   item
```

```
natural join
   product
where
   credit_rating * extended_credit > .07
and
   (qty_in_stock * velocity) /.075 < 30
or
   (sku_price / 47) * (qty_in_stock / velocity) > 47;
```

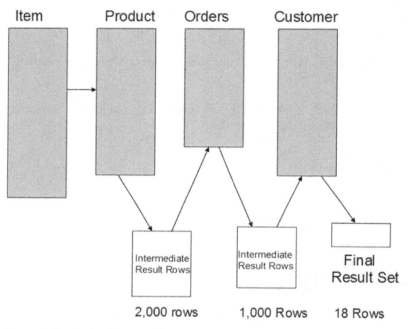

Figure 2.10: *Optimal intermediate row sets*

For the following example, there is a three-way table join against tables that all contain over 10,000 rows each. This database has 50,000 student rows, 10,000 course rows and 5,000 professor rows.

If the number of rows in the table determined the best table join order, one would expect that any 3-way table join would start by joining the *professor* and *course* tables, and then join the *result* set to the *student* table.

However, whenever there is a *where* clause, the total number of rows in each table does not matter if index access is being used. The following is a sample query:

```
select
   student_name
from
```

```
   professor
natural join
   course
natural join
   student
where
   professor = 'jones'
and
   course = 'anthropology 610';
```

```
Stan Nowakowski
Bob Crane
James Bakke
Patty O'Furniture
```

Despite the huge numbers of rows in each table, the final result set will only be four rows. If the CBO can guess the size of the final result, sampling techniques can be used to examine the *where* clause of the query and determine which two tables should be joined together first.

There are only two table join choices in the simplified example:

- Join student to course and result to professor

- Join professor to course and result to student

Which is better? The best solution will be the one where *result* is smallest. Because the query is filtered with a *where* clause, the number of rows in each table is incidental, and the real concern is the number of rows where professor = 'jones' and "where course = 'Anthropology 610'.

If the specific output goal is known, the best table join order becomes obvious. Assume that Professor Jones is very popular and teaches 50 courses, and that Anthropology 610 has a total of eight students. With this knowledge, it is clear that the size of the intermediate row baggage is very different. Figure 2.11 shows the following join of *professor* to *course* and *result* to *student*.

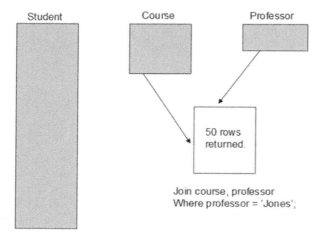

Figure 2.11: *A suboptimal intermediate row size*

If the CBO were to join the *student* table to the *course* table first, the intermediate result set would only be eight rows, far less baggage to carry over to the final join as shown in Figure 2.12 which demonstrates the following join of *student* to *course* and *result* to *professor*.

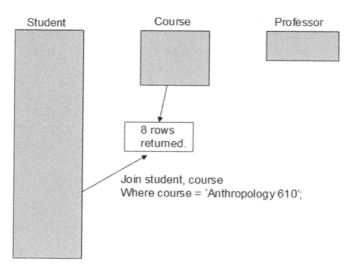

Figure 2.12: *An optimal intermediate row size*

Now that there are only eight rows returned from the first query, it is easy to join the tiny eight row result set into the PROFESSOR table to get the final answer.

Managing Schema Statistics with *dbms_stats*

When a SQL statement is executed, the database must convert the query into an execution plan and choose the best way to retrieve the data. For Oracle, each SQL query has many choices for execution plans, including which index to use to retrieve table row, what order in which to join multiple tables together, and which internal join methods to use (Oracle has nested loop joins, hash joins, star joins, and sort merge join methods). These execution plans are computed by the CBO.

The choice of executions plans made by the Oracle SQL optimizer is only as good as the Oracle statistics. To always choose the best execution plan for a SQL query, Oracle relies on information about the tables and indexes in the query.

Starting with the introduction of the *dbms_stats* package, Oracle provides a simple way for the Oracle professional to collect statistics for the CBO. The old-fashioned analyze table and *dbms_utility* methods for generating CBO statistics are obsolete and somewhat dangerous to SQL performance because they do not always capture high quality information about tables and indexes. The CBO uses object statistics to choose the best execution plan for all SQL statements.

The *dbms_stats* utility does a far better job in estimating statistics, especially for large partitioned tables, and the better stats result in faster SQL execution plans. Andrew Holdsworth of Oracle Corporation notes that dbms_stats is essential to good SQL performance, and it should always be used before adjusting any of the Oracle optimizer initialization parameters:

> *"The payback from good statistics management and execution plans will exceed any benefit of init.ora tuning by orders of magnitude"*

Most experts agree that the majority of common SQL problems can be avoided if statistics are carefully defined and managed. In order for the CBO to make an intelligent decision about the best execution plan for SQL, the CBO must have information about the table and indexes that participate in the query. This information includes:

- The size of the tables
- The indexes on the tables
- The distribution of column values
- The cardinality of intermediate result sets

Given this information, the CBO can make an informed decision and almost always generates the best execution plan. The following section will cover how to gather top quality statistics for the CBO, as well as how to create an appropriate CBO environment for the database.

Getting top-quality statistics for the CBO

The choices of executions plans made by the CBO are only as good as the statistics available to it. The old-fashioned analyze table and dbms_utility methods for generating CBO statistics are obsolete and somewhat dangerous to SQL performance. The CBO uses object statistics to choose the best execution plan for all SQL statements.

The dbms_stats utility does a far better job in estimating statistics, especially for large partitioned tables, and the better statistics result in faster SQL execution plans. The following is a sample execution of dbms_stats with the options clause:

```
exec dbms_stats.gather_schema_stats( -
   ownname          => 'SCOTT', -
   options          => 'GATHER AUTO', -
   estimate_percent => dbms_stats.auto_sample_size, -
   method_opt       => 'for all columns size repeat', -
   degree           => 34 -
   )
```

Here is another *dbms_stats* example that creates histograms on all indexes columns:

```
begin
dbms_stats.gather_schema_stats(
ownname=>'TPCC',
method_opt=>'FOR ALL INDEXED COLUMNS SIZE SKEWONLY',
cascade=>true,
estimate_percent=>100);
end;
/
```

There are several values for the options parameter that we need to know about:

- **gather:** This option re-analyzes the whole schema.

- **gather empty:** This option only analyzes objects that have no statistics,

- **gather stale:** This option is used with the monitoring feature and only re-analyzes tables with more than 10 percent modifications (inserts, updates, deletes).

- **gather auto:** This option will re-analyze objects that currently have no statistics and objects with stale statistics (objects with more than 10% row changes). Using the gather auto option is like combining gather stale and gather empty options.

Both gather stale and gather auto require monitoring. Issuing the alter table xxx monitoring command causes Oracle to track changed tables with the dba_tab_modifications view. The following shows that the exact number of inserts, updates and deletes are tracked since the last analysis of statistics:

```
SQL> desc dba_tab_modifications;

Name                  Type
---------------------------------
TABLE_OWNER           VARCHAR2(30)
TABLE_NAME            VARCHAR2(30)
PARTITION_NAME        VARCHAR2(30)
SUBPARTITION_NAME     VARCHAR2(30)
INSERTS               NUMBER
UPDATES               NUMBER
DELETES               NUMBER
TIMESTAMP             DATE
TRUNCATED             VARCHAR2(3)
```

The most interesting of the above listed options is the *gather stale* option. Since all statistics will become stale quickly in a robust OLTP database, it is important to remember that the rule for *gather stale* is > 10% row change based on num_rows at statistics collection time.

As a result, almost every table except read-only tables will be reanalyzed with the *gather stale* option, making the *gather stale* option best for systems that are largely read-only. For example, if only five percent of the database tables get significant updates, then only five percent of the tables will be reanalyzed with the *gather stale* option.

To aid in intelligent histogram generation, Oracle uses the method_opt parameter of dbms_stats. There are also important options within the method_opt clause, namely *skewonly*, *repeat* and *auto*:

```
=>'for all columns size skewonly'

=>'for all columns size repeat'

=>'for all columns size auto'
```

The *skewonly* option is very time intensive because it examines the distribution of values for every column within every index.

If *dbms_stats* finds an index whose columns are unevenly distributed, it will create a histogram for that index to aid the cost-based SQL optimizer in making a decision about index versus full-table scan access. For example, if an index has one column that is in 50 percent of the rows, a full-table scan is faster than an index scan to retrieve these rows.

```
-- ****************************************************************
-- SKEWONLY option—Detailed analysis
--
-- Use this method for a first-time analysis for skewed indexes
-- This runs a long time because all indexes are examined
-- ****************************************************************
begin
   dbms_stats.gather_schema_stats(
      ownname          => 'SCOTT',
      estimate_percent => dbms_stats.auto_sample_size,
      method_opt       => 'for all columns size skewonly',
       degree          => 7
    );
end;
```

If the statistics need to be reanalyzed, the reanalyze task will be less resource intensive with the *repeat* option. Using the *repeat* option, Oracle will only reanalyze indexes with existing histograms and will not search for other histogram opportunities. This is statistics should be reanalyzed on a regular basis.

```
-- ****************************************************************
-- REPEAT OPTION - Only reanalyze histograms for indexes
-- that have histograms
--
-- Following the initial analysis, the weekly analysis
-- job will use the "repeat" option. The repeat option
-- tells dbms_stats that no indexes have changed, and
-- it will only reanalyze histograms for
-- indexes that have histograms.
-- ****************************************************************
begin
   dbms_stats.gather_schema_stats(
      ownname          => 'SCOTT',
      estimate_percent => dbms_stats.auto_sample_size,
      method_opt       => 'for all columns size repeat',
      degree           => 7
    );
end;
```

The dbms_stats procedure can be made to analyze schema statistics very quickly on SMP servers with multiple CPU's. Oracle allows for parallelism when collecting CBO statistics, which can greatly speed up the time required to collect statistics. A parallel statistics collection requires an SMP server with multiple CPUs.

Statistics Enhancements for Oracle 10g and Beyond

Each new release of Oracle brings enhancements, and 10g radically changed some important defaults for Oracle statistics collection using *dbms_stats*.

The one-size-fits-all approach is a great baseline, but the automatic 10g statistics collection may not be just right for every database.

Oracle 10g does automatic statistics collection and any original customized *dbms_stats* job with customized parameters will be overlaid.

There may also be a statistics deficiency (i.e. not enough histograms) causing performance issues. In these cases you can re-analyze object statistics using *dbms_stats* and make sure to collect system statistics.

```
execute dbms_stats.gather_system_stats('start');

-- wait an hour or so

execute dbms_stats.gather_system_stats('stop');
```

There are also cases where it is necessary to disable the automatic statistics collection on Oracle10g because of the high expense of the 10g default arguments for *dbms_stats* *method_opt* which is *for all columns size auto*. This default causes lots of work as Oracle examines all columns to determine if they may benefit from having histograms.

Starting with Oracle Database 10g, there are some new arguments available for the *dbms_stats* package subprograms. Those parameters are *granularity* and *degree*.

Granularity

This parameter is used in subprograms such as *gather_table_stats* and *gather_schema_stats*. This parameter indicates the granularity of the statistics for collection, particularly for partitioned tables. As an example, the global statistics can be gathered on a partitioned table, or global and partition-level statistics can be gathered. It has two options. They are: *auto;* and *global* and *partition*.

When the *auto* option is specified, the procedure determines the granularity based on the partitioning type. Oracle collects global, partition-level, and sub-partition level statistics if sub-partition method is *list*. For other partitioned tables, only the global and partition level statistics are generated.

When the *global* and *partition* option is specified, Oracle gathers the global and partition level statistics. No sub-partition level statistics are gathered even it is composite partitioned object.

Degree

With this parameter, it is possible to specify the *degree* of parallelism. In general, the *degree* parameter allows the DBA to parallelize the statistics gathering process. The degree parameter can take the value of *auto_degree*.

When the *auto_degree* is specified, Oracle will determine the degree of parallelism automatically. It will be either 1 (serial execution) or *default_degree* (the system default value based on number of CPUs and initialization parameters), according to the size of the object. Take care if Hyper Threading is used, as the DBA will have less computational power than Oracle assumes.

DML Table Monitoring

With Oracle Database 10g and beyond, the *statistics_level* initialization parameter functions as a global option for the table monitoring mechanism. This mechanism overrides the table level *monitoring* clause. In other words, the *[no] monitoring* clauses are now obsolete. The statistics_level parameter was available in 9i.

If the *statistics_level* parameter is set to *basic*, the monitoring feature is disabled. When it is set to *typical* (which is the default setting) or ALL, then the global table monitoring is enabled.

These changes are aimed at simplifying operations and also making them consistent with other related statistics. The modification monitoring mechanism is now enabled by default, and users of the *gather auto* or *stale* feature of *dbms_stats* no longer have to enable monitoring explicitly for every table under the default settings.

The following section will introduce the importance of estimating the optimal sample size when gathering schema statistics.

Automating Statistics Sample Size with *dbms_stats*

The higher the quality of the schema statistics will result in higher probability that CBO will choose the optimal execution plan. Unfortunately, doing a complete analysis of every row of every table in a schema could take days and most shops must sample their database to get CBO statistics.

The goal of estimating the sample size is to take a large enough sample of the database to provide top quality data for the CBO while not adversely impacting server resources. Now that how the *dbms_stats* option works has been introduced, it will be useful see how to specify an adequate sample size for *dbms_stats*.

In earlier releases, the DBA had to guess what percentage of the database provided the best sample size and sometimes under analyzed the schema. Starting with Oracle9i, the *estimate_percent* argument was added to *dbms_stats* to allow Oracle to automatically estimate the best percentage of a segment to sample when gathering statistics. A sample invocation follows below:

```
estimate_percent => dbms_stats.auto_sample_size
```

After collecting statistics with an automatic sample size, the accuracy of the automatic statistics sampling can be verified by looking at the sample_size column on any of these data dictionary views:

- *dba_object_tables*
- *dba_tab_col_statistics*
- *dba_tab_partitions*
- *dba_tab_subpartitions*
- *dba_part_col_statistics*
- *dba_subpart_col_statistics*
- *dba_tables*
- *dba_tab_cols*
- *dba_tab_columns*
- *dba_all_tables*
- *dba_indexes*
- *dba_ind_partitions*
- *dba_ind_subpartitions*

In practice, the auto_sample_size option of dbms_stats generally chooses a sample_size from five to 20 percent when using automatic sampling, depending on the size of the tables and the distribution of column values.

A sample that is too small can impact the CBO, so it is important to always take a statistically significant sample size for every object in the schema. The next section will introduce some methods DBAs use to ensure that their SQL optimizer always has great schema statistics.

Testing New CBO Statistics

It is always a best practice run *dbms_stats* intelligently. The default in Oracle 10g with the table monitoring feature is to re-analyze after 10% of the table rows change, but the old adage "if it ain't broke don't fix it" applies here.

Within the world of Oracle SQL optimization there are two main optimizer philosophies. There are those who believe that there is one and only one optimal execution plan for their SQL versus those with dynamic environments that want their execution plans to change as optimizer statistics and parameters change.

It all depends on the volatility of the data. The Oracle optimizer has always been sensitive to changes to alterations in metadata statistics with dbms_stats. Some scientific applications (e.g. Clintrial) have highly volatile data. Tables are huge one minute and small the next. In most cases, the DBA thinks the execution plans should change along with the data. However, in my experience, over 70% of Oracle shops will not benefit from changes to SQL execution plans.

Avoiding Monday Morning Mayhem

Many shops make the mistake of scheduling a re-analyze of their schema every Sunday, leading to the phenomenon called "Monday Morning Mayhem", as thousands of execution plans change! The only reason CBO statistics are re-analyzed is to alter execution plans, so there should be no surprise when Mondays do not go so well after a Sunday re-analyze!

As previously noted, changes to the CBO statistics are a silver bullet, a single action that has a profound impact on the entire workload landscape. Obviously, proper testing is required.

To aid in pre-testing silver bullet changes such as parameters, CBO stats, etc., Oracle 11g provides the SQL Performance Manager (SPM). It also has the *optimizer_use_pending_statistics* parameter, whereby the following command can be used to test the SQL workload:

```
alter session set optimizer_use_pending_statistics=true;
```

However, a more practical way to test new CBO statistics is to create a representative SQL tuning set (STS) and test the workload using the production statistics, which are migrated to test from production.

The following section will cover how specialized statistics such as histograms assist with SQL tuning.

Tuning SQL with Histograms

Histograms are an add-on feature to the *dbms_stats* procedure that store the distribution of column values in either height-balanced or weight-balanced buckets. Histograms may help the Oracle optimizer in two ways:

- **Index vs. full-scan access**: Histograms are important when the column value requires the CBO to decide whether to use an index vs. a full-table scan.

- **Table join order**: Histograms can reveal the expected number of rows returned from a table query (i.e. *select * from customer where state = 'NC';*), thereby helping the optimizer determine the fastest table join order.

A skewed index column distribution can happen whenever the column referenced within a SQL query *where* clause has a non-uniform distribution of values, making a full-table scan faster than index access.

By default, Oracle assumes that all columns have evenly distributed values, and dbms_stats is used to create histograms when it is necessary to tip-off the SQL optimizer that Oracle has a column with an uneven distribution of values.

In a perfect world, every skewed column should have histograms, but that is not practical because histograms add significant overhead:

- **Creating Histogram**: Analyzing a large column that has many distinct values in a multi-zillion row table could take many hours. The cost to build a histogram is a direct function of *num_rows* and the number of distinct column values.

- **Using Histogram**: The presence of histograms adds additional processing overhead to SQL statements at optimization time.

Since skewed column values affect SQL performance, histograms should only be used when they are required for a faster CBO execution plan. Histograms incur additional overhead during the parsing phase of an SQL query and can be used effectively only when:

- A column's values cause the CBO to make an incorrect guess: If the CBO makes a wrong assumption about the size of an intermediate result set, it may choose a sub-optimal execution plan. A histogram added to the column often provides the additional information required for the CBO to choose the best plan.

- Significant skewing exists in the distribution of a column's data values: The skew must be important enough to make the CBO choose another execution plan.

- A table column is referenced in one or more queries: Never create histograms if queries do not reference the column. Novice DBAs may mistakenly create histograms on a skewed column, even if it is not referenced in a query.

The ability to seek columns that should have histograms, and then automatically create the histograms was a new Oracle9i feature of the dbms_stats package.

Before Oracle9i, the DBA had to manually detect those data columns that needed histograms and manually create them using these guidelines:

- Create a histogram whenever a column is referenced by many SQL *where* clauses and when the data is heavily skewed, such that the optimal execution plan would change depending on the value in the *where* clause.

- Create histograms when the optimizer cannot accurately predict the size of intermediate result sets in n-way table joins.

Figure 2.13 below shows an example of skewed and non-skewed data columns.

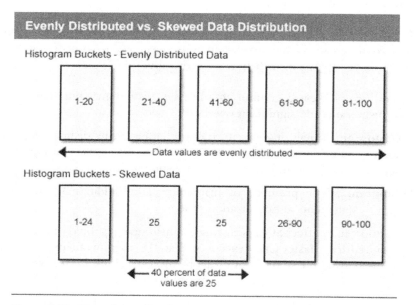

Figure 2.13: *Skewed data distribution vs. evenly distributed data.*

By using the *repeat* option, histograms are collected only on the columns that already have histograms. Like any other CBO statistic, histograms are static and need to be refreshed when column value distributions change. When refreshing statistics, the *repeat* option would be used as in the example below:

```
execute dbms_stats.gather_schema_stats(
  ownname          => 'SCOTT',
  estimate_percent => DBMS_STATS.AUTO_SAMPLE_SIZE,
  method_opt => 'for all columns size repeat',
  degree           => DBMS_STATS.DEFAULT_DEGREE);
```

Since it examines the data distribution of values for every column within every index, the *skewonly* option introduces a very time consuming build process. The dbms_stats package creates histograms to help the CBO make a table access decision; i.e., index versus a full-table scan when it finds an index whose column values are distributed unevenly. From the vehicle_type example, if an index has one column value (e.g., CAR) that exists in 65 percent of the rows, a full-table scan will be faster than an index scan to access those rows, as in this example:

```
execute dbms_stats.gather_schema_stats(
  ownname          => 'SCOTT',
  estimate_percent => DBMS_STATS.AUTO_SAMPLE_SIZE,
  method_opt       => 'for all columns size skewonly',
  degree           => DBMS_STATS.DEFAULT_DEGREE);
```

Histograms are also effective with queries that have bind variables and queries with cursor_sharing enabled. In these cases, the CBO decides if the column value could affect the execution plan, and if it does, it substitutes a literal for the bind variable and proceeds to perform a hard parse.

Watch your histograms!

Histograms impose an additional execution overhead and histograms should not be used arbitrarily. They should be used only when they allow the CBO to significantly improve query speed.

Look Out!

The following section will provide a look at an exciting SQL optimization feature, Dynamic Sampling, which was first introduced in Oracle 10g.

Automating Histogram Creation with *dbms_stats*

One exciting feature of *dbms_stats* is the ability to automatically look for columns that should have histograms, and create the histograms. Multi-bucket histograms add a huge parsing overhead to SQL statements, and histograms should ONLY be used when the SQL will choose a different execution plan based upon the column value.

As a review, there are histogram-related options within the *method_opt* clause, namely *skewonly*, *repeat* and *auto*.

```
method_opt=>'for all columns size skewonly'

method_opt=>'for all columns size repeat'

method_opt=>'for all columns size auto'
```

In practice, there is a specific order to use the different options of *dbms_stats*. Remember, analyzing for histograms is time-consuming, and histograms are used under two conditions:

- **Table join order:** The CBO must know the size of the intermediate result sets (cardinality) to properly determine the correct join order the multi-table joins.

- **Table access method:** The CBO needs to know about columns in SQL where clauses, where the column value is skewed such that a full-table scan might be faster than an index range scan. Oracle uses this skew information in conjunction with the *clustering_factor* columns of the *dba_indexes* view.

Hence, the following is the proper order for using the *dbms_stats* package to locate proper columns for histograms:

> 1. **Skewonly option:** Use *skewonly* only to do histograms for skewed columns, for cases where the value will make a difference between a full-table scan and an index scan.

> 2. **Monitor:** Next, turn-on monitoring. Issue an *"alter table xx monitoring"* and *"alter index yyy monitoring"* command for all segments in the schema.

> 3. **Auto option:** Once monitoring is in-place, it will be necessary to re-analyze with the auto option to create histograms for join columns within tables. This is critical for the CBO to determine the proper join order for finding the driving table in multi-table joins.

> 4. **Repeat option:** Finally, use the *repeat* option to re-analyze only the existing histograms.

Periodically, it will be desirable to re-run the *skewonly* and *auto* option to identify any new columns that require histograms. Once located, the repeat option will ensure that they are refreshed with current values.

A low cardinality column with less than 254 distinct values will create a frequency histogram, and if there are more than 254 distinct column values, Oracle will create a height-balanced Histogram. The DBA can also specify the number of histogram buckets in *dbms_stats*, and this creates a height-balanced histogram.

Histogram Improvements

Oracle Corporation performed a representative test of the Oracle11g enhancements to the *dbms_stats* package, correctly noting that *skewed* data distributions were problematic in 10g because the *dbms_stats* package did not manage skew and out of range values in an optimal fashion. Their test also demonstrated several exciting improvements to *dbms_stats*:

- **Faster collection**: The *dbms_stats* package is approximately 2x faster when collecting statistics. Of course, the recommended procedure with *dbms_stats* is to collect a single, deep sample and save the statistics, but this performance feature is welcome, especially for very large shops.

- **Refined automatic sample size**: Rahn notes that the 11g *dbms_stats auto_sample_size* now collects a statistically significant sample, even for highly skewed data distributions.

Overall, the design of Oracle 11g has taken great strides towards improving the automated collection of CBO statistics, ensuring that SQL will be optimized with much less manual intervention.

	You can still use the *monitoring* clauses as well as the *alter_schema_tab_monitoring* and *alter_database_tab_monitoring*, but these clauses and procedures are now considered as no operation. They execute without giving any error, but have no effect.
Hot Tip!	

dbms_stats.gather_fixed_objects_stats tips

Starting in Oracle 10g there is a new procedure called *dbms_stats.gather_fixed_objects_stats* for analyzing the dictionary fixed structures (the *x$* tables). The docs note that fixed objects should be analyzed only once, unless the

---

workload footprint changes and it is necessary to be connected a *sys* (or a user with *sysdba*) to invoke *dbms_stats.gather_fixed_object_stats*.

Just as with the workload statistics, Oracle recommends that the *x$* tables be analyzed only once and during a typical database workload.

```
exec dbms_stats.gather_schema_stats('SYS',gather_fixed=>TRUE)

exec dbms_stats.gather_fixed_objects_stats('ALL');
```

Oracle 10g also brought *dbms_stats.export_fixed_objects_stats* and *dbms_stats.import_fixed_objects_stats* for migrating production workload statistics into test and development instances.

Re-analyzing Optimizer Statistics

It astonishes me how many shops prohibit any un-approved production changes and yet re-analyze schema stats weekly. Evidently, they do not understand that the purpose of schema re-analysis is to change their production SQL execution plans, and they act surprised when performance changes!

Most Oracle experts only recommend scheduled re-analysis for highly dynamic databases, and most shops save one very deep sample with histograms, storing the statistic with the *dbms_stats.export_schema_stats* procedure. The only exceptions are highly-volatile systems (i.e. lab research systems) where a table is huge one day and small the next.

For periodic re-analysis, many shops us the table monitoring option and also *method_opt=auto* after they are confident that all histograms are in place.

Saving and Re-using Statistics

For data warehouses and database using the *all_rows optimizer_mode*, Oracle9iR2 and beyond have the ability to collect the external *cpu_cost* and *io_cost* metrics. The ability to save and re-use schema statistics is important for several types of Oracle shops:

- **Bi-Modal shops**: Many shops get huge benefits from using two sets of stats, one for OLTP (daytime) and another for batch (evening jobs).

- **Test databases**: Many Oracle professionals will export their production statistics into the development instances so that the test execution plans more closely resemble the production database.

Getting Top Quality Optimizer Statistics

Because Oracle schema statistics work best with external system load, my preferences is to schedule a valid sample (using *dbms_stats.auto_sample_size*) during regular working hours. In the following example, statistics are refreshed using the *auto* option which works with the table monitoring facility to only re-analyze those Oracle tables that have experienced more than a 10% change in row content:

```
begin
   dbms_stats.gather_schema_stats(
      ownname          => 'SCOTT',
      estimate_percent => dbms_stats.auto_sample_size,
      method_opt       => 'for all columns size auto',
      degree           => 7
   );
end;
/
```

Tips for Optimizing the CBO with Statistics

There are several tips for optimizing your CBO with good statistics:

- **Find skewed columns that are referenced in SQL**: Many shops do not use *method_opt=skewonly* and suffer from poor execution plans on skewed column access.

- **Find histograms for foreign key columns:** Many DBAs forget that the CBO must have foreign-key histograms in order to determine the optimal table join order (i.e. the *ordered* hint).

- **Fix the cause, not the symptom**: For example, whenever I see a sub-optimal order for table joins, I resist the temptation to add the *ordered* hint, and instead create histograms on the foreign keys of the join to force the CBO to make the best decision.

For new features, explore the Oracle11g automatic histogram collection mechanism that interrogates *v$sql_plan* to see where the foreign keys are used. It claims to generate histograms when appropriate, all automatically.

Oracle Workload Statistics and SQL Performance

Everyone knows that the external environment has a profound impact on SQL performance, and the Oracle cost-based optimizer now has the ability to consider real-world timings for multiblock reads (*mreadtim*) and sequential read I/O times (*sreadtim*) within the *dbms_stats.gather_system_stats* procedure.

Oracle has two types of CBO statistics for estimating disk read times workload and noworkload statistics. The noworkload statistics gather data by submitting random reads against all data files, while the workload statistics increments internal counters to measure database I/O activity.

- **Noworkload statistics:** These include *cpuspeednw*, *ioseektim* and *iotfrspeed*.

- **Workload statistics**: These are gathered by *dbms_stats.gather_system_stats* and include *sreadtim*, *mreadtim*, *cpuspeed*, *mbrc*, *maxthr* and *slavethr*.

If both workload and noworkload statistics are available, the optimizer uses the workload statistics in hopes of getting the best execution plan for the SQL. The output from *dbms_stats.gather_system_stats* is stored in the *aux_stats$* table and it can be queried as follows to see the current values for the database:

```
select
   sname,
   pname,
   pval1
from
   sys.aux_stats$;
```

SNAME	PNAME	PVAL1
SYSSTATS_INFO	STATUS	
SYSSTATS_INFO	DSTART	
SYSSTATS_INFO	DSTOP	
SYSSTATS_INFO	FLAGS	1
SYSSTATS_MAIN	CPUSPEEDNW	502.005
SYSSTATS_MAIN	IOSEEKTIM	10
SYSSTATS_MAIN	IOTFRSPEED	4096
SYSSTATS_MAIN	SREADTIM	7.618
SYSSTATS_MAIN	MREADTIM	14.348
SYSSTATS_MAIN	CPUSPEED	507
SYSSTATS_MAIN	MBRC	6
SYSSTATS_MAIN	MAXTHR	32768
SYSSTATS_MAIN	SLAVETHR	

Oracle workload statistics that are gathered with *dbms_stats.gather_system_stats* now gather real-workload I/O performance metrics:

- **sreadtim:** Single block read time in milliseconds

- **mreadtim:** Multiblock read time in ms

- **cpuspeed:** CPU speed

- **mbrc:** Average blocks read per multiblock read (see *db_file_multiblock_read_count*)

- **maxthr:** Maximum I/O throughput (for OPQ only)

- **slavethr:** OPQ Factotum (slave) throughput (OPQ only)

Advanced Oracle SQL Tuning

The *dbms_stats.gather_system_stats* procedure measures important timings within the database and adjusts the optimizers' propensity to choose indexes vs. full-scans.

The Oracle 11g Performance Tuning Guide notes that the timing of the workload sample is important and that samples should be run during a time when legitimate multiblock reads are performed or during a staged workload that performs full-table scans. The docs also note that bad timing of a system statistics sample can cause less than optimal estimates for the timings of full-table scan I/O.

The *dbms_stats.gather_system_stats* procedure is especially useful for multi-mode Oracle shops that run OLTP during the day and DSS at night. The *dbms_stats.gather_system_stats* procedure is invoked as an elapsed time capture, making sure to collect the statistics during a representative heavy workload:

```
execute dbms_stats.gather_system_stats('Start');

-- one hour delay during high workload

execute dbms_stats.gather_system_stats('Stop');
```

The data collection mechanism of the *dbms_stats.gather_system_stats* procedure works in a similar fashion to my script that measures I/O times to optimizer the *optimizer_index_cost_adj* parameter. The *dbms_stats.gather_system_stats* also relates to the undocumented *_optimizer_cost_model* parameter and the *db_file_multiblock_read_count* setting.

disk_read_wait.sql below compare the relative costs of sequential and scattered read times:

💾 disk_read_waits.sql

```sql
select
   sum(a.time_waited_micro)/sum(a.total_waits)/1000000 c1,
   sum(b.time_waited_micro)/sum(b.total_waits)/1000000 c2,
   (
      sum(a.total_waits) /
      sum(a.total_waits + b.total_waits)
   ) * 100 c3,
   (
      sum(b.total_waits) /
      sum(a.total_waits + b.total_waits)
   ) * 100 c4,
   (
      sum(b.time_waited_micro) /
      sum(b.total_waits)) /
      (sum(a.time_waited_micro)/sum(a.total_waits))
   ) * 100 c5
from
   dba_hist_system_event a,
```

```
   dba_hist_system_event b
where
   a.snap_id = b.snap_id
and
   a.event_name = 'db file scattered read'
and
   b.event_name = 'db file sequential read';
```

The following is sample output from a real system showing an empirical test of disk I/O speed. Scattered reads (full-table scans) are always expected to be far faster than sequential reads (index probes) because of Oracle sequential prefetch according to the setting for *db_file_multiblock_read_count*, which is now obsolete as of Oracle 10gR2.

The listing below shows a starting value for *optimizer_index_cost_adj* based on the relative I/O costs, very similar to *dbms_stats.gather_system_stats:*

- scattered read (full table scans) are fast at 13ms (c3)

- sequential reads (index probes) take much longer 86ms (c4)

- starting setting for *optimizer_index_cost_adj* at 36:

C1	C2	C3	C4	C5
13,824	5,072	13	86	36

In OLTP databases it is very rare for the fundamental nature of a schema to change. Large tables remain large, and index columns rarely change distribution, cardinality, and skew. The DBA should only consider periodically re-analyzing the total schema statistics if the database matches the following criteria:

- **CPU-intensive databases:** Many scientific systems load a small set of experimental data, analyze the data, produce reports, and then truncate and reload a new set of experiments. There are also Oracle databases with super large data buffer caches, with reduce physical I/O at the expense of higher CPU consumption. For these types of systems, it may be necessary to re-analyze the schema each time the database is reloaded.

- **Highly volatile databases:** In these rare cases, the size of tables and the characteristics of index column data changes radically. For example, Laboratory Information Management Systems (LIMS) load, analyze, and purge experimental data so frequently that it is very difficult to always have optimal CBO statistics. If a database has a table that has 100 rows one week and 10,000 rows the next week, the DBA may want to consider using Oracle dynamic sampling or a periodic reanalysis of statistics.

The following section will show how Oracle SQL optimization can be adjusted to evaluate I/O costs of CPU costs.

External Costing with the Optimizer

Over the past decade, Oracle has been enhanced to consider external influences when determining the best execution plan. Because the Oracle Database does not run in a vacuum, the optimizer must be able to factor in the costs of external disk I/O and the cost of CPU cycles for each SQL operation. This process is especially critical for queries running all_rows optimization, where minimizing server resources is a primary goal.

- ***cpu_cost:*** The Oracle SQL optimizer can now estimate the number of machine cycles required for an operation and factors this cost into the execution plan calculation. The CPU costs associated with servicing an Oracle query depends upon the current server configuration, which Oracle cannot see.

- ***io_cost:*** The CBO had been enhanced to estimate the number of physical block reads required for an operation. The I/O cost is proportional to the number of physical data blocks read by the operation.

Internally, Oracle uses both the CPU and I/O cost estimations in evaluating the execution plans, but these factors can be weighted according to the stress on the server. If the top 5 timed events include CPU, then the SQL may need to be optimized to minimize CPU resources. This equation becomes even more complex when parallel query is factored in, where many concurrent processes are servicing the query.

The best benefit for using CPU costing is for all_rows execution plans where cost is more important than with first_rows_n optimization.

CPU consumption tip!

On a 64-bit server with a large data cache or if solid-state disks are in use, minimizing CPU consumption could be important. These are the types of databases that benefit from cpu_cost.

Fixing CBO Statistics

A client had just moved their system into production and was experiencing a serious performance problem. The emergency support DBA found that the optimizer_mode=first_rows, and there was only one table with statistics. The

---

database was running cost-based but seemed completely unaware of the necessity to analyze the schema for CBO statistics.

The trouble began when the DBA wanted to know the average row length for a table. After using a Google search to determine that the location of that information was the dba_tables.avg_row_len column, it was determined that the values were NULL. The DBA then went to MetaLink and learned gathering statistics with *dbms_stats* would fill in the avg_row_len column.

CBO will dynamically estimate statistics for all tables with missing statistics, and when using optimizer_mode=first_rows with only one table analyzed, any SQL that touches the table will be optimized as a cost-based query. In this case, a multi-step silver bullet did the trick:

```
exec dbms_stats.delete_table_stats('username', 'tablename');_
exec dbms_stats.gather_table_stats('username', 'tablename');
```

When the system immediately returned to an acceptable performance level, the DBA realized the importance of providing complete and timely statistics for the CBO using the dbms_stats utility.

Repairing Obsolete CBO Statistics Gathering

A client called and expressed confusion as to why their system was grinding to a halt. There was a serious degradation in SQL performance after the implementation of partitioned tablespaces in a 16-CPU Solaris 64-bit Oracle 11.1.0.7 system. The changes in the development and QA instances had been thoroughly tested.

As it turned out, analyze table and analyze index commands had been used to gather the CBO statistics. The dbms_stats utility gathers partition-wise statistics. There was not time to pull a deep sample collection, so a dbms_stats was issued with a ten percent sample size. It is parallelized with 15 parallel processes to speed-up the statistics collection:

```
exec dbms_stats.gather_schema_stats( -
    ownname          => 'SAPR4', -
    options          => 'GATHER AUTO', -
    estimate_percent => 10, -
    method_opt       => 'for all columns size repeat', -
    degree           => 15 -
)
```

In less than 30 minutes, the improved CBO statistics tripled the performance of the entire database.

Setting the SQL Optimizer Cost Model

Starting with Oracle9i, DBAs have the ability to view the estimated CPU, TEMP and I/O costs for every SQL execution plan step. Oracle Corporation has noted that typical OLTP databases are becomingly increasingly CPU-bound and has provided the ability for the DBA to make the optimizer consider the CPU costs associated with each SQL execution step.

The developers of Oracle10g recognized this trend toward CPU-based optimization by providing the ability to choose CPU-based or I/O-based costing during SQL optimization with the 10g default being CPU-costing. In Oracle10g, system stats are gathered by default, and in Oracle9i the DBA must manually execute the *dbms_stat.gather_system_stats* package to get CBO statistics.

```
alter session set "_optimizer_cost_model"=choose;

alter session set "_optimizer_cost_model"=io;

alter session set "_optimizer_cost_model"=cpu;
```

This parameter can be used to choose the best optimizer costing model for a particular database, based on the I/O and CPU load.

The choice of relative weighting for these factors depends upon the existing state of the database. Databases using 32-bit technology and the corresponding 1.7 gigabyte limit on SGA RAM size tend to be I/O-bound with the top timed events being those performing disk reads:

```
Top 5 Timed Events
~~~~~~~~~~~~~~~~~~                                    % Total
Event                              Waits   Time (s) Ela Time
--------------------------------  -------- --------- -------
db file sequential read            xxxx     xxxx       30
db file scattered read             xxxx     xxxx       40
```

Once 64-bit became popular, Oracle SGA sizes increased, more frequently referenced data was cached, and databases became increasingly CPU-bound. Also, solid-state disk (RAM SAN) has removed disk I/O as a source of waits:

```
Top 5 Timed Events
~~~~~~~~~~~~~~~~~~                                    % Total
Event                              Waits   Time (s) Ela Time
```

```
-------------------------------- ------------ ----------- --------
CPU time                                  xxxx        xxxx       55.76
db file sequential read                   xxxx        xxxx       27.55
```

The gathered statistics are captured via the dbms_stats package in 9.2 and above, and the following CPU statistics are captured automatically in 10g and beyond are stored in the *sys.aux_stat$* view.

- single block disk read time, in microseconds

- multiblock disk read-time, in microseconds

- CPU speed in mhz

- average *db_file_multiblock_read_count* in number of blocks

A database where CPU is the top timed event may benefit from a change in the SQL optimizer to consider the CPU costs associated with each execution plan.

Using CPU costing may not be good for databases that are I/O-bound. Also, changing to CPU-based optimizer costing will change the predicate evaluation order of the query. My Oracle Support Community (MOSC) bulletin 276877.1 provides additional information on this.

Turning on CPU Costing

According to the documentation, CPU costs are considered when SQL optimizer schema statistics are gathered with the *dbms_stat.gather_system_stats* package, which is the default behavior in Oracle10g and beyond, and CPU costs will be considered in all SQL optimization.

To ensure that CPU costing is in use, just set the undocumented parameter "*_optimizer_cost_model*"=*cpu*;

I/O-bound databases, especially 32-bit databases, may want to utilize I/O-based SQL costing. The default optimizer costing in Oracle11g is CPU, and it can be changed to IO costing by using these techniques:

- Ensure that *optimizer_index_cost_adj* is set to the default value (Oracle9i bug 2820066)

- Add a *no_cpu_costing* hint in the SQL

- *alter session set "_optimizer_cost_model"=io;*

- Set init.ora hidden parameter _optimizer_cost_model=io

In sum, CPU cost is always computed regardless of optimizer mode when *optimizer_index_cost_adj* is set in unpatched Oracle versions less than 10.1.0.2.

The following section shows how to change from CPU-based to I/O-based SQL optimization when the processing characteristics of the database change on a regular basis.

Bi-modal System Configuration

It is not uncommon for databases to be bi-modal, operating OLTP during the day (CPU-intensive) and doing aggregations and rollups (I/O-intensive) at night.

The CPU and I/O statistics can now be captured using *dbms_stats* and then swapping them in as the processing mode changes. Most shops do this with the dbms_scheduler (*dbms_job*) package so that the statistics are swapped at the proper time.

Solid State Oracle and SQL tuning

One guiding principle of Information Technology is that hardware advances always precede software advances, and Oracle is no exception. At this point in time, hardware advances are changing the way SQL is tuned.

As Oracle entered the hardware market through their acquisition of Sun Microsystems in 2009, Oracle became a soup-to-nuts vendor, another IBM with the ability to control and manage the entire IT stack from hardware up to the front-end application.

This has profound ramifications for Oracle, especially now with 12c features that directly address hardware, such as the *flash_cache* feature, which leverages on the flash SSD that now resides in most new server from Sun, HP and IBM. Today's expandable server (like the Sun Fire X4640 Server, with 12 to 48 processors and 512 goig RAM) have onboard SSD, and external SSD now approaches $1,000 per gigabyte.

the million dollar Exadata server X3 is capable of performing at blistering speeds with its solid-state disks:

- **OLTP speed:** Exadata X3 can process over 1.5 million SQL random reads/sec.

- **Warehouse speed:** Over 100 Gigabytes per second for full-table scans

While Oracle makes inroads into "big data", numerous other vendors are offering-up SSD solutions for their server, changing the landscape of Oracle performance tuning.

So, how does the advent of SSD impact Oracle SQL tuning? First, note that SSD fundamentaly changes the landscape of an Oracle instance:

- **Uniform access speed:** Oracle systems statistics (*dbms_stats.gather_system_stats*) are designed to measure the relative speeds of sequential vs. scattered reads on disk, and everyone remembers from school that the read-write head movement occurs less for full-scans, making *db file scattered reads* have less latency than index access via *db file scattered reads* events.

- **Wide bandwidth:** Platter disks faced contention within disk controllers, an issue not seen with SSD which has much higher concurrent access to the data blocks.

- **No data buffers:** The question will become whether the *db_cache_size* will eventually become redundant when the media is also solid-state. In my benchmark tests, the fastest throughput comes with a tiny *db_cache_size* with SSD back-ends

In traditional SQL tuning for both fast response time and high throughput, the primary goal has been to tweak the SQL so that it retrieves the requested rows with a minimum of touches to the database files, thereby minimizing *consistent gets*.

Conclusion

This chapter has introduced the Oracle optimizer software and explained how Oracle determines the execution plans for queries. The main points of this chapter include:

- Oracle estimates costs in terms of executed disk reads, and they are of very limited value.

- The *optimizer_mode* is the single most important choice for tuning the SQL workload.

- *dbms_stats.gather_system_stats* can be used to determine the relative costs of sequential vs. scattered disk reads.

- The *dbms_stats* package is critical for providing the optimizer with valid metadata.

The next chapter will explore the internal machinations with an Oracle SQL execution plan.

Oracle SQL Execution Plans

Execution plans reveal the magic of database access

Inside SQL Execution Details

Many developers are uneducated about the internals of SQL processing, and the place to start learning is by revealing the access plan for a SQL statement using the *explain plan*, or execution plan.

The education will start with an overview of the standard relational model and the *explain plan* utility.

Because SQL has declarative syntax, what you ask for is what you get, many people never see the execution internals for a SQL statement. This was deliberately hidden in the original relational database manifesto because Codd and Date postulated that revealing the execution internals would never be necessary because the SQL optimizer would always choose the best execution plan.

But what is an execution plan, and how what is the process for seeing one?

117

When an SQL statement is passed to Oracle, the cost based optimizer (CBO) uses database statistics, such as information about table such as the number of rows or distribution of column values, to create an execution plan which it uses to retrieve the data in the most efficient matter.

The Obsolete Explain Plan Syntax

To see the internal execution steps on a SQL statement, the relational model provides for entering the words *explain plan for* to reveal the execution plan for that SQL statement. This is true for Oracle as well as all relational databases including SQL Server, DB2, Sybase, MySQL and Informix databases.

Explain plan is elderly!

DO NOT use explain plan syntax in Oracle, it can give incorrect results! Instead, use the SQL*Plus *autotrace* or the *dbms_xplan* utility!

To use the obsolete explain plan utility, first create a plan table. Oracle provides a script in *$ORACLE_HOME/rdbms/admin* called *utlxplan.sql*. Execute *utlxplan.sql* and create a public synonym for the *plan_table*.

```
SQL> CONN sys/password AS SYSDBA

Connected

SQL> @$ORACLE_HOME/rdbms/admin/utlxplan.sql

Table created.

SQL> GRANT ALL ON sys.plan_table TO public;

Grant succeeded.

SQL> CREATE PUBLIC SYNONYM plan_table FOR sys.plan_table;

Synonym created.
```

With the plan table present, execution plans using the *autotrace* feature of SQL*Plus can then be generated.

All relational databases use an *explain plan* utility that takes the SQL statement as input, runs the SQL optimizer and outputs the access path information into a *plan_table*, which can then be interrogated to see the access methods.

```
explain plan
   set statement_id = 'test1'
for
   set statement_id = 'run1'
into
   plan_table
for
   select stuff from mytable;
```

Again, we NEVER use the standard explain plan for syntax with Oracle to see execution plans. The following section will explain why this is so.

Why the Explain Plan Gives Wrong Details!

It is possible that the standard relational *explain plan for* syntax show a plan that is incorrect, and the execution plan that is actually being implemented may not be what is revealed.

This commonly happens when the query has a bind variable. This happens because the *explain plan* utility does not consider the value of a host variable, while the Oracle optimizer may consider a host variable, when bind variable peeking is enabled with the 11g adaptive cursor sharing feature.

As a remedy, always use the *dbms_xplan* utility and avoid using the Oracle implementation of the ANSI standard *explain plan for querylist* syntax.

Wrong Plans When Not Using *explain plan*

The CBO is extremely sophisticated proprietary software, and Oracle does not release details of its internal machinations. In general, the execution plan will match the fetch, but sometimes the explain plan does not match the real-time execution, even when not using *explain plan*. Some possible explanations for an incorrect explain plan may include:

- Using the obsolete *explain plan* for syntax

- An older execution plan is cached in the library cache

- Dynamic sampling is altering the execution plan

- A bind variable influence runtime execution by using query rewrite (via setting *cursor_sharing=force* or *cursor_sharing=similar*), prior to the 11g adaptive cursor sharing enhancement.

- Your materialized view rewrite has a bug.

Explain plan has limited value!

While the internal machinations of the optimizer are fascinating, there is far more benefit in ensuring that the SQL is well-structured and that all indexes exist.

The next section will show how to display execution plans with the SQL*Plus *set autotrace* command.

Using the SQL*Plus *autotrace* Utility

The simplest way to get an execution plan is to use the autotrace feature of SQL*Plus. The autotrace utility is an underutilized feature of SQL*Plus. It offers statement tracing and instant feedback on any successful *select, insert, update* or *delete* statement. The utility requires a plan table (for the Explain Plan) under the current user's schema. In addition, it requires the *plustrace* or DBA role for the user executing the trace. The source for the *plustrace* role can be found in *$ORACLE_HOME/sqlplus/admin/plustrce.sql*.

Tracing is enabled via the set autotrace command in SQL*Plus:

```
SQL> set autotrace on

SQL> select ename from emp where empno = 1122;

no rows selected


Execution Plan
----------------------------------------------------------
0 SELECT STATEMENT Optimizer=CHOOSE
1 0 TABLE ACCESS (BY INDEX ROWID) OF 'EMP'
2 1 INDEX (UNIQUE SCAN) OF 'PK_EMP' (UNIQUE)


Statistics
----------------------------------------------------------
83 recursive calls
0 db block gets
21 consistent gets
3 physical reads
0 redo size
221 bytes sent via SQL*Net to client
```

```
368 bytes received via SQL*Net from client
1 SQL*Net roundtrips to/from client
0 sorts (memory)
0 sorts (disk)
0 rows processed
```

Oracle's *autotrace* provides instantaneous feedback including the returned rows, execution plan and statistics. The user does not need to be concerned about trace file locations and formatting since the output is displayed instantly on the screen. This is important data that can be used to tune the SQL statement.

The SQL*Plus autotrace command has the following options:

- **on**: The set autotrace on command will provide detailed statistics for the Oracle SQL and show the amount of time spent parsing, executing and fetching rows. The parse phase is the time spent by the query determining the optimal execution plan, and this phase can be quite high for queries with more than five tables unless the *ordered* or *rule* hints are used. The execution phase is the time spent executing the query, and the fetch phase is the time spent returning the rows to the query.

- **on explain**: Displays returned rows and the explain plan, but it does not execute the SQL query. Running this SQL*Plus directive will execute the SQL query and also provide the execution plan for the SQL statement.

- **on statistics**: Displays returned rows and statistics

- **trace explain**: Displays the execution plan for a select statement without actually executing it. For example: set autotrace trace explain

- **traceonly:** Displays execution plan and statistics without displaying the returned rows. This option should be used when a large result set is expected.

These SQL*Plus directives can make it easy for the Oracle professional to ensure that their SQL statements are properly tuned. Remember, the hallmark of a good developer is someone who can not only make SQL statements, but make SQL that executes quickly as well.

The SQL*Plus *autotrace* is so easy to use that it should be the first tracing utility used for most SQL performance tuning issues. Oracle has the *tkprof* utility that can be used for more detailed analysis.

For DBAs requiring the lowest level debugging, *oradebug*, will do the job.

By switching this feature on, an execution plan is displayed for all suitable statement runes by SQL*Plus, as shown below.

It is important to notice the execution statistics at the bottom of this listing. The metrics for *consistent gets*, *physical reads*, *SQL*Net activity* and *disk sorts* can quickly reveal if the SQL is optimized.

```
SQL> set autotrace on

SQL> select *
  2  from     emp e, dept d
  3  where    e.deptno = d.deptno
  4  and      e.ename  = 'SMITH';


    EMPNO ENAME      JOB          MGR HIREDATE      SAL    COMM
---------- ---------- --------- ---------- --------- ---------- ------
    DEPTNO     DEPTNO DNAME        LOC
---------- ---------- --------- ---------- --------------
     7369 SMITH      CLERK       7902 17-DEC-80      800
       20         20 RESEARCH     DALLAS


Execution Plan
----------------------------------------------------------
   0      SELECT STATEMENT Optimizer=CHOOSE
   1    0   NESTED LOOPS
   2    1     TABLE ACCESS (FULL) OF 'EMP'
   3    1     TABLE ACCESS (BY INDEX ROWID) OF 'DEPT'
   4    3       INDEX (UNIQUE SCAN) OF 'PK_DEPT' (UNIQUE)


Statistics
----------------------------------------------------------
      81  recursive calls
       4  db block gets
      27  consistent gets
       0  physical reads
       0  redo size
     941  bytes sent via SQL*Net to client
     425  bytes received via SQL*Net from client
       2  SQL*Net roundtrips to/from client
       0  sorts (memory)
       0  sorts (disk)
       1  rows processed
```

Fast SQL evaluation trick!

In the *autotrace* statistics, compare the "*rows processed*" with the "*consistent gets*". This will give an idea about how many trips (disk block reads) were required to fetch the returned rows.

Using *autotrace* is a relatively easy way to get the execution plan, but it requires that the statement run to completion. If the query is particularly inefficient or returns many rows, this may take considerable time. A better option is to run the explain plan statement manually, which is shown in the next section.

Using Explain Plan

The explain plan statement generates the execution plan for a query without executing the query itself, allowing the execution plan for poorly performing queries to be displayed without impacting the database. The following example shows how the explain plan statement is used to generate an execution plan.

```
SQL> explain plan for
  2  select *
  3  from    emp e, dept d
  4  where   e.deptno = d.deptno
  5  and     e.ename  = 'SMITH';
```

Explained.

If multiple people are accessing the same plan table, or a history of the execution plans is to be saved, the *statement_id* clause of the explain plan statement should be used. This associates a user specified identifier with each plan, which can be used when retrieving the data.

The following example shows how the *statement_id* is set using the explain plan statement.

```
SQL> explain plan set statement_id = 'TIM' for
  2  select *
  3  from    emp e, dept d
  4  where   e.deptno = d.deptno
  5  and     e.ename  = 'SMITH';
```

Explained.

At this point the execution plan data is present in the *plan_table*, which can be queried using several methods to display the execution plan.

Using *utlxpls.sql* to See SQL Explain Plans

Prior to Oracle 9i Release 2, the utlxpls.sql script or the *utlxplp.sql* script for parallel queries was used to query the *plan_table* and display execution plan. The example below shows the expected output from the script.

```
SQL> explain plan for
  2  select *
  3  from    emp e, dept d
  4  where   e.deptno = d.deptno
```

```
    5    and     e.ename   = 'SMITH';

Explained.

SQL> @$ORACLE_HOME/rdbms/admin/utlxpls.sql

Plan Table
--------------------------------------------------------------------------------
| Operation                      | Name    | Rows | Bytes| Cost  | Pstart| Pstop |
--------------------------------------------------------------------------------
| SELECT STATEMENT               |         |      |      |       |       |       |
|  NESTED LOOPS                  |         |      |      |       |       |       |
|   TABLE ACCESS FULL            |EMP      |      |      |       |       |       |
|   TABLE ACCESS BY INDEX RO     |DEPT     |      |      |       |       |       |
|    INDEX UNIQUE SCAN           |PK_DEPT  |      |      |       |       |       |
--------------------------------------------------------------------------------
8 rows selected.
```

By default, the Oracle scripts do not accept a statement_id parameter, but they can be modified to create a personal script, like the *explain.sql* script shown below.

💾 explain.sql

```
-- *********************************************************************
-- Parameters:
--   1) Statement ID
-- *********************************************************************
SET PAGESIZE 100
SET LINESIZE 200
SET VERIFY OFF
COLUMN plan             FORMAT A50
COLUMN object_name      FORMAT A30
COLUMN object_type      FORMAT A15
COLUMN bytes            FORMAT 9999999999
COLUMN cost             FORMAT 9999999
COLUMN partition_start  FORMAT A20
COLUMN partition_stop   FORMAT A20
select LPAD(' ', 2 * (level - 1)) ||
       DECODE (level,1,NULL,level-1 || '.' || pt.position || ' ') ||
       INITCAP(pt.operation) ||
       DECODE(pt.options,NULL,'',' (' || INITCAP(pt.options) || ')') plan,
       pt.object_name,
       pt.object_type,
       pt.bytes,
       pt.cost,
       pt.partition_start,
       pt.partition_stop
from   plan_table pt
start with pt.id = 0
  and pt.statement_id = '&1'
connect by prior pt.id = pt.parent_id
  and pt.statement_id = '&1';
```

The following example shows the output from the *explain.sql* script.

```
SQL> explain plan set statement_id = 'TIM' for
  2  select *
  3  from    emp e, dept d
  4  where   e.deptno = d.deptno
  5  and     e.ename  = 'SMITH';

Explained.

SQL> @explain.sql
```

The *utlxpls.sql* script is still present in later versions of Oracle, but it now displays the execution plan using the *dbms_xplan* package.

The Oracle *dbms_xplan* Utility

The *dbms_xplan* package was introduced in Oracle 9i Release 2 as a standard server-based method for displaying execution plans. It was intended as a replacement for the *utlxpls.sql* script which is now implemented using the *dbms_xplan* package. The package contains a table function called display, which can be queried to display an execution plan, as shown below.

```
|SQL> explain plan for
  2  select *
  3  from    emp e, dept d
  4  where   e.deptno = d.deptno
  5  and     e.ename  = 'SMITH';
Explained.

SQL> SET LINESIZE 130
SQL> SET PAGESIZE 0
SQL> SELECT *
  2  FROM    TABLE(DBMS_XPLAN.display);
```

```
Plan hash value: 1863486531
-----------------------------------------------------------------------------
| Id  | Operation                   | Name    | Rows | Bytes | Cost (%CPU)| Time     |
-----------------------------------------------------------------------------
|   0 | SELECT STATEMENT            |         |    1 |    57 |    4   (0)| 00:00:01 |
|   1 |  NESTED LOOPS               |         |    1 |    57 |    4   (0)| 00:00:01 |
|*  2 |   TABLE ACCESS FULL         | EMP     |    1 |    37 |    3   (0)| 00:00:01 |
|   3 |   TABLE ACCESS BY INDEX ROWID| DEPT   |    1 |    20 |    1   (0)| 00:00:01 |
|*  4 |    INDEX UNIQUE SCAN        | PK_DEPT |    1 |       |    0   (0)| 00:00:01 |
-----------------------------------------------------------------------------
Predicate Information (identified by operation id):
-----------------------------------------------------------------------------
   2 - filter("E"."ENAME"='SMITH')
   4 - access("E"."DEPTNO"="D"."DEPTNO")
```

The display function can accept three parameters which affect the output displayed:

- **table_name:** The name of plan table to be queried. The default value is *plan_table*.

- **statement_id**: The *statement_id* of the plan to be displayed. The default value is NULL.

- **format**: This controls the level of detail displayed. The default value is *typical*. Other values include *basic, all* and *serial*.

The following example shows the usage of these parameters with *dbms_xplan*.

```
SQL> explain plan set statment_id='TSH' for
  2  select *
  3  from    emp e, dept d
  4  where   e.deptno = d.deptno
  5  and     e.ename  = 'SMITH';

Explained.

SQL> SET LINESIZE 130
SQL> SET PAGESIZE 0
SQL> select *
  2  from    TABLE(DBMS_XPLAN.DISPLAY('PLAN_TABLE','TSH','BASIC'));

Plan hash value: 1863486531
-------------------------------------------------
| Id  | Operation                    | Name    |
-------------------------------------------------
|   0 | SELECT STATEMENT             |         |
|   1 |  NESTED LOOPS                |         |
|   2 |   TABLE ACCESS FULL          | EMP     |
|   3 |   TABLE ACCESS BY INDEX ROWID| DEPT    |
|   4 |    INDEX UNIQUE SCAN         | PK_DEPT |
-------------------------------------------------
```

The *dbms_xplan.display_awr* procedure can be very helpful in diagnosing Oracle performance issues. Using the Automatic Session History (ASH) tables, it is possible to go through different times of day and compare reports from times where performance has been good, with those times when performance has been bad.

The ASH components allow comparison of *SQL_IDs* between different times of day to see which queries seemed to be going through dramatic changes. Once a *SQL_ID* was found that experienced such a dramatic change *dbms_xplan.display_awr* can be used to find all the different iterations of the query.

The *dbms_xplan.display_awr* is quite useful. It allows the user to input only a SQL_ID, and Oracle will show the explain plans for that SQL_ID as recorded in the AWR. The following is an example of such a statement:

```
select * from TABLE(dbms_xplan.display_awr('93djdy6ss3'));
```

The next step is to look through the results to identify any inconsistencies large enough to result in huge differences in performance.

The DBA or developer first needs to create the plan table. The DDL for this table is in the *$ORACLE_HOME/rdbms/admin/utllxplan.sql* file.

Thus the *dbms_xplan.display_awr* procedure can be a big help in diagnosing Oracle performance issues.

Introduction to SQL Tracing

There are times when more diagnostics than those shown in an execution plan or to wit the autotrace utility are needed. For these rare cases, Oracle provides several SQL tracing tools:

- **Oracle trace analyzer**: The *trcanlzr* utility provides detailed trace information about SQL execution.

- **Oracle session trace:** The *trcsess* utility consolidates trace information from selected trace file.

- **Oracle SQL trace:** The *tkprof* utility is designed to provide SQL execution details.

Beware, these detailed tracing tools use system resources to capture the detailed statistics and it is important to be very careful that diagnostics do not cause a performance problem. The following are cases where additional tracing might be useful.

- **Incorrect results**: When a SQL statement produces inconsistent results, it is necessary to trace the I/O path to see exactly how the results are being formulated.

- **I/O details:** While the simple autotrace shows consistent gets and disk reads, sometimes the types of I/O being done by the SQL must be identified. The *db file scattered read* indicates a full-table scan, while *db file sequential read* events are associated with index access.

Again, detailed tracing is only needed in rare occasions, and most of the time, an execution plan and *autotrace* details are sufficient to diagnose a SQL problem. The next section will provide a review of the trace analyzer utility.

Using Trace Analyzer to Trace SQL

The Oracle Trace Analyzer (*trcanlzr*) is an application from Oracle with much the same purpose as *tkprof*. It is also designed to help analyze the trace files generated by

---

SQL tracing. Trace Analyzer offers enhancements over *tkprof* in a number of areas. Several of the key improvements are as follows:

- Trace Analyzer provides a more detailed list of wait events for every SQL statement that is part of the trace file. Only in recent versions has *tkprof* provided at least limited wait information. Older versions provide no information on wait events regardless of the trace data.

- Trace Analyzer reports totals for statements that execute multiple times; whereas *tkprof* would report each execution separately. This is important when tracing a process that is updating many records, but doing it one row at a time. Identifying this with *tkprof* requires more manual effort.

- Trace Analyzer provides the values used by bind variables, as long as the trace file was generated at a level that includes bind variables; whereas this feature is not available with *tkprof*.

Installation of Trace Analyzer is fairly straightforward as long as the instructions are followed completely. Metalink document 224270.1 provides an adequate explanation for finding the files to accomplish a trace analyzer the installation as well as how to install and use it. It is important to follow the instructions exactly.

Executing Trace Analyzer

The first step is to ensure tracing us enabled at the appropriate level. For example, to provide maximum trace data, a Level 12 trace can be started for the current session:

```
ALTER SESSION SET EVENTS '10046 TRACE NAME CONTEXT FOREVER, LEVEL 12';
```

After the session executes for enough time to gain needed data, the *trcanlzr.sql* script can be executed. It requires the name of the directory object. This object points to the physical operating system directory for the *user_dump_dest*. The installation of the utility will automatically create the directory object required, named UDUMP.

```
@d:\trcanlzr.sql UDUMP asg920xr_ora_13033.trc
```

Once executed, the output will be displayed on the screen and a spool file is created in the current directory. It is possible to change the output spool file by modifying the *trcanlzr.sql* script.

Using the *trcsess* Utility

When solving tuning problems, session traces are very useful and offer vital information. Traces are simple and straightforward for dedicated server sessions, but for shared server sessions, many processes are involved. The trace pertaining to the user session is scattered across different trace files belonging to different processes. This makes it difficult to get a complete picture of the life cycle of a session.

The *trcsess* command-line utility consolidates trace information from selected trace files based on specified criteria. The criteria include *session id*, *client id*, *service name*, action name and module name. This allows the compilation of multiple trace files into a single output file.

The syntax for the *trcsess* utility is:

```
trcsess [output=output_file_name]
[session=session_Id]
[clientid=client_Id]
[service=service_name]
[action=action_name]
[module=module_name]
[trace_files]
```

Where:

- **output:** This specifies the file where the output is generated. When this option is not specified, the standard output is used for the output.

- **session:** This consolidates the trace information for the session specified. The session ID is a combination of session index and session serial number.

- **clientid:** This consolidates the trace information given client ID.

- **service:** This consolidates the trace information for the given service name.

- **action:** This consolidates the trace information for the given action name.

- **module:** This consolidates the trace information for the given module name.

- ***trace_files***: This is a list of all trace file names, separated by spaces, in which *trcsess* will look for trace information. The wild card character * can be used to specify the trace file names. If trace files are not specified, all the files in the current directory are checked by *trcsess*.

Activating trace on multiple sessions means that trace information is spread throughout many trace files. For this reason, Oracle 10g introduced the *trcsess* utility, allowing trace information from multiple trace files to be identified and consolidated into a single trace file. The *trcsess* usage is listed below.

```
trcsess [output=<output file name >]   [session=<session ID>]
[clientid=<clientid>] [service=<service name>] [action=<action name>]
[module=<module name>]

<trace file names>
```

```
output=<output file name> output destination default being standard output.

session=<session Id> session to be traced.
Session id is a combination of session Index & session serial number e.g.
8.13.

clientid=<clientid> clientid to be traced.

service=<service name> service to be traced.

action=<action name> action to be traced.

module=<module name> module to be traced.

<trace_file_names> Space separated list of trace files with wild card '*'
supported.
```

Use Oracle's *trcsess* command-line utility to consolidate the information from all the trace files into a single output file.

```
trcsess output="hr_report.trc" service="APPS1"
module="PAYROLL" action="bulk load"
```

Then run *tkprof* against the consolidated trace file to generate a report. It is recommended that some experimentation be done with *tkprof* to become familiarized with the options available in this useful utility.

```
..\udump> tkprof hr_report.trc
output=hr_trc_report SORT=(EXEELA, PRSELA,FCHELA)
```

Using *tkprof* to Trace SQL

The Oracle *tkprof* utility is a less detailed SQL tracing utility that provides information on SQL execution. Even though it is called *tkprof*, the *tkprof* component is only the formatting utility, and the real trace is collected by executing the *dbms_system.set_sql_trace_in_session* procedure.

Using *tkprof* involves these steps:

Step 1: Set the environment

Before *tkprof* tracing can be enabled, the environment must first be configured by performing the following steps:

- **Enable Timed Statistics**: This parameter enables the collection of certain vital statistics such as CPU execution time, wait events, and elapsed times. The resulting trace output is more meaningful with these statistics. The command to enable timed statistics is:

```
alter system set timed_statistics = true;
```

- **Set the User Dump Destination Directory:** The trace files generated by Oracle are placed in the *user_dump_dest* directory as specified in the init.ora deck (spfile). The user dump destination can also be specified for a single session using the *alter session* command. Make sure that enough space exists on the device to support the number of trace files that are expected to be generated.

```
alter session set user_dump_dest='/u01/app/oracle/.mysid/udump";
```

Step 2: Turn Tracing On

The next step for *tkprof* is to enable tracing. By default, tracing is disabled due to the burden (5-10%) it places on the database. Tracing can be defined at the session level:

```
alter session set sql_trace = true;

dbms_session.set_sql_trace(true);
```

It is also possible enable tracing for another user's session by using the *set_sql_trace_in_session* command:

```
dbms_system.set_sql_trace_in_session(sid,serial#,true);
```

The *sid* (Session ID) and *serial#* for any SQL statement can be obtained by querying the *v$session* view. Once tracing with Oracle *tkprof* is enabled, Oracle generates and stores the statistics in the trace file. The trace file name is version specific.

Because of the resources required to collect the detailed execution information, Oracle *tkprof* tracing should be enabled only on those sessions that are having problems that cannot be diagnosed with the SQL*Plus *autotrace* utility.

- Explain Plan is not as useful when used in conjunction with *tkprof* since the trace file contains the actual execution path of the SQL statement. Use Explain Plan

---

when anticipated execution statistics are desired without actually executing the statement.

- When tracing a session, remember that nothing in *v$session* indicates that a session is being traced. Therefore, trace with caution and remember to disable tracing after an adequate amount of trace data has been generated.

- *The tkprof* utility does not control the contents of a trace file, it simply formats them. Oracle provides multiple ways to actually generate the trace file. *tkprof* is valuable for detailed trace file analysis. For those DBAs that prefer a simpler tracing mechanism with instant feedback, the *autotrace* utility should be used.

Costs and the Cost-based Optimizer

One of the most common questions asked by beginning SQL tuning professionals is *"What does the cost column in a SQL execution plan mean?"*

The answer is not simple, largely because the costing figures are not fully documented, but roughly, they correspond to the cost of a single block disk I/O, like a *db file sequential read.*

Hence, the cost column in an execution plan is not a reliable way to judge the real costs of a SQL statements response time. The cost column is supposed to be a guess of the number of single block disk reads required, but it's not very useful for SQL tuning.

The costing is done via a mathematical model that builds a decision tree, and Oracle always chooses the plan with the lowest cost, but not always the plan with the fastest response time, as this depends on the *optimizer_mode.* However, this algorithm is constantly changing as Oracle refines their software and it is possible to only make very general statements about its behavior.

The cost-based optimizer (CBO) was originally developed back when disk was super-expensive and minimizing disk I/O was a major goal in SQL tuning. Today, of course, many systems use super-fast flash memory (solid-state disks), and I/O is not so much of an issue. Nonetheless, estimated disk costs are the motivating factor behind the optimizer's estimates of cost.

In the example below, the optimizer estimates four physical disk reads to service a nested loops join, and hence there is a cost=4:

```
--------------------------------------------------------------------
| Id  | Operation        | Name  | Rows  | Bytes | Cost (%CPU)| Time     |
--------------------------------------------------------------------
|   0 | SELECT STATEMENT |       |     1 |    57 |     4   (0)| 00:00:01 |
```

```
|   1 |   NESTED LOOPS                     |         |    1 |    57 |    4   (0)| 00:00:01 |
| * 2 |     TABLE ACCESS FULL              | EMP     |    1 |    37 |    3   (0)| 00:00:01 |
|   3 |     TABLE ACCESS BY INDEX ROWID    | DEPT    |    1 |    20 |    1   (0)| 00:00:01 |
| * 4 |       INDEX UNIQUE SCAN            | PK_DEPT |    1 |       |    0   (0)| 00:00:01 |
----------------------------------------------------------------------------------------
```

If this cost is estimated based on the average sampled I/O latency gathered by *dbms_stats.gather_system_stats*, it might be possible to estimate the run-time for a query. In this example, assume that the average disk I/O delay is 15 milliseconds. A cost of 4 would mean that the optimizer expects the query to take roughly 60 milliseconds to complete.

This feature of the optimizer to analyze and express costing in terms of physical disk reads is one reason why the optimizer buffering parameters like *optimizer_index_caching* are important when tuning a SQL workload.

The best vs. the cheapest plan

The cost figures that are displayed in a SQL execution plan do not always reflect the real costs of a query. Oracle may choose a plan with a higher cost, depending upon the optimizer's goal (e.g. first_rows_n vs. all_rows).

Remember, the cost figures can be quite misleading and should not be used as guidelines for SQL tuning for several reasons:

- The optimizers costing can be wrong because of stale or missing metadata, especially histograms.

- The lowest cost value does not always indicate the real lowest cost that is select by the optimizer.

- In *first_rows_n* optimization, extra I/O is required to access the data via indexes and get the row back quickly. Hence, the optimizer may choose a more expensive plan because it will return rows faster than a cheaper plan that uses less machine resources.

Even with complete metadata it is impossible for any optimizer to always guess the accurate size of a result set, especially when the where clause has complex column calculations.

In other words, Oracle does not always choose the lowest cost value, and Oracle does not disclose the exact behavior of their optimizer, which allows them a prized competitive edge over other competing databases.

For example, consider a million row table that takes 30 seconds to full scan. Now, consider a SQL that returns 10,000 rows in sorted order via an index where *clustering_factor* approaches *num_rows*, and two possible execution plans:

- **Index scan:** More I/O (and cost) to traverse the index top pull the rows in sorted order, but the query starts delivering rows immediately

- **Full table scan and back-end sort:** This may involve far less work (and less cost), but we will not see any results for 30 seconds.

Remember, sorting a result set does not always require a back-end sort, and Oracle can use an index to retrieve the rows in pre-sorted order as shown in Figure 3.1:

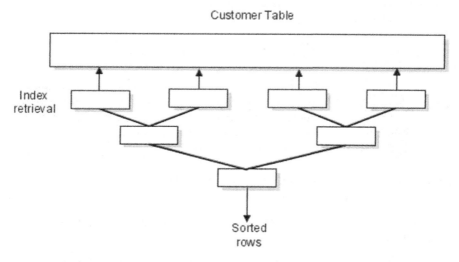

Figure 3.1: *Using an index to retrieve rows in pre-sorted order*

In this example, the optimizer cannot always assume that the least cost plan is the best plan when optimizing for fast response time.

Remember, the job of the CBO is to always choose the best execution plan for any SQL statement, and this is no small challenge.

According to the Oracle documentation, the I/O and CPU costs are evaluated as shown below:

```
       (#SRds * sreadtim) + (#MRds * mreadtim) + (#CPUCycles/cpuspeed)
Cost = ---------------------------------------------------------------
                              sreadtim
```

where:

- #SRds: number of single block reads

- #MRds: number of multi block reads

- #CPUCycles: number of CPU Cycles

And the following values, gathered in the aux_stats$ table from db*ms_stats.gather_system_stats*:

- *M*readtim: multi block read time

- *S*readtim: single block read time

- *C*puspeed: CPU cycles per second

Note that the external costing is heavily influenced by the estimated cost of disk reads, as measured by the v$ tables, and the estimated CPU costs associated with each internal operation.

dbms_stats can be run over a one hour period to gather timing for some of these parameters:

```
dbms_stats.gather_system_stats('INTERVAL', interval=> 60)
```

Once collected, the system statistics values are shown in the *aux_stats$* fixed view as represented below in *display_system_stats.sql*:

🖫 display_system_stats.sql

```
select ¶
   pname,
   pval1
from
   sys.aux_stats$
where
   pname IN ('SREADTIM', 'MREADTIM', 'MBRC', 'CPUSPEED');


PNAME          PVAL1
------------ ----------
SREADTIM          3
MREADTIM          8
CPUSPEED       2032
MBRC             16
```

Oracle keeps details about the costs of many components of SQL execution and uses these average costs to influence the choices made by the cost-based SQL optimizer. Here are some examples:

- **Hash join costs:** Oracle knows the average amount of RAM memory consumed by a hash join.

- **Sort costs:** Oracle keeps track of the RAM required for sorting and aggregation operations.

- **Table scan costs:** Oracle keeps information about the time required to perform a multiblock read (db file scatter reads).

- **Index block access costs:** Oracle knows the average time required to fetch a single block (db file sequential reads).

Remember that these costs are weighted differently depending on the choice of Oracle *optimizer_mode*. With an OLTP system with the *first_rows_n* optimizer mode, the CBO makes it more important to return rows quickly than to minimize resource costs.

On the other hand, if the *all_rows* optimizer mode is in use for a data warehouse, the CBO will be heavily influenced by these external factors because the *all_rows* mode is designed to minimize resource consumption.

The *all_rows* optimizer mode is designed to minimize computing resources and it favors full-table scans. Index access (*first_rows_n*) adds additional I/O overhead but they returns rows faster back to the originating query:

The cost figures that are displayed in a SQL execution plan are not described in any Oracle documentation, and it has been demonstrated that the plan with the lowest cost number is not always the plan chosen by the optimizer.

Further, the cost figures do not always indicate the best execution plan for a query, given the divergent optimizer goals of *First_rows_n* (optimizer for response time) and *all_rows* (optimize for minimizing computing resources).

The CBO costs can either be based on estimated I/O costs or estimated CPU costs.

- **Object statistics:** The table and index analyze with *dbms_stats*.

- **Object histograms:** Histograms are used to guess the cardinality of result set sizes.

In general, the lower the CBO-calculated cost, the faster the query will run, but the costs used by the CBO are only estimates. The CBO creates these estimates based on many variables:

- **System statistics**: External resources usage statistics gathered from *dbms_stats.gather_system_stats*) have an impact of the CBO cost estimates.

- **Optimizer parameters**: The settings for important CBO parameters (hash_area_size, db_file_multiblock_read_count, optimizer_index_caching, optimizer_index_cost_adj, etc.) affect the costs.

However, if there are sub-optimal statistics, the CBO can misjudge the costs. The most common causes for inaccurate CBO costing estimates may include:

- **Bad table join order:** Sub-optimal table join order can be caused by missing histograms.

- **Inaccurate I/O estimates:** Oracle uses the estimate of single block read time which can be inaccurate if system statistics (i.e. dbms_stats.gather_system_stats) are missing.

- **Buffer caching estimates:** If optimizer_index_caching is not set or if the contents of the data buffers vary greatly, the optimizer can mis-estimate the I/O costs for a query optimization.

Starting with Oracle9i, the user has been given the ability to view the estimated CPU, TEMP tablespace usage and I/O costs for every SQL execution plan step. Oracle Corporation has noted that typical OLTP databases are becomingly increasingly CPU-bound and has provided the ability for the DBA to make the optimizer consider the CPU costs associated with each SQL execution step.

As a review, the CBO gathers information from many sources and has the lofty goal of using DBA-provided metadata to always make the best execution plan decision.

Oracle uses both the CPU and I/O cost estimations in evaluating the execution plans. This equation becomes even more complex when parallel query is factored in, where many concurrent processes are servicing the query.

The best benefit from using CPU costing is for *all_rows* execution plans, where cost is more important than with first_rows_n optimization.

Oracle 10g addressed this trend toward considering CPU consumption by providing the ability to choose CPU-and-I/O based or exclusively I/O-based costing during SQL optimization. The 10g default is CPU-costing.

In Oracle10g, system stats are gathered by default, and in Oracle9i the DBA must manually execute the *dbms_stats.gather_system_stats* package to get CBO statistics:

```
alter session set "_optimizer_cost_model"=choose; -- default value

alter session set "_optimizer_cost_model"=io;

alter session set "_optimizer_cost_model"=cpu;
```

The *dbms_stats.gather_system_stats* procedure measures important timings within the database and adjusts the optimizers' propensity to choose indexes vs. full-scans.

SQL Tuning and Execution Statistics

One mistake commonly made by SQL tuning people is neglecting to empirically test the speed of their query.

When tuning SQL, many Oracle professionals only focus on the execution plans and the associated cost figures. The reason why the cost figures in a SQL execution plan do not always reflect the fastest execution plan has already been covered. That failure to necessarily reflect the fastest execution plan is why is is critical to always set timing on and time the query's actual execution speed and the number of logical I/O's (consistent gets).

Many people analyze their execution plans, and choose the one that they believe has the best execution plan, without actually timing the SQL for execution speed.

Without checking the time and the plan, it is possible to end up using expensive new features unintentionally.

Consider this simple SQL by Oracle ACE Laurent Schneider to find out the best paid employees in each department:

```
create table
   lsc_emp
as
   select * from emp;

create index lsc_i on lsc_emp(deptno,sal);

exec dbms_stats.gather_table_stats(user,'LSC_EMP',cascade=>true)
```

Before Oracle introduced analytic functions, one way to find the highest paid employees in a department is to use an exists subquery. The subquery would compute the max salary and serve as the value against which the outer query measured salaries:

```
select
   *
from
   lsc_emp e1
where
```

```
    exists (
        select
            1
        from
            lsc_emp e2
        where
            e1.deptno=e2.deptno
            having e1.sal=max(e2.sal)
);
```

Notice here that the subquery causes multiple index range scans to be invoked inside of the full table scan of the emp table:

```
Execution Plan
----------------------------------------------------------
Plan hash value: 2224773357

-------------------------------------------------------------------------------
| Id | Operation          | Name    | Rows | Bytes | Cost (%CPU)| Time     |
-------------------------------------------------------------------------------
|  0 | SELECT STATEMENT   |         |    1 |    68 |   56   (0)| 00:00:01 |
|* 1 |  FILTER            |         |      |       |           |          |
|  2 |   TABLE ACCESS FULL| LSC_EMP |  107 |  7276 |    2   (0)| 00:00:01 |
|* 3 |   FILTER           |         |      |       |           |          |
|  4 |    SORT AGGREGATE   |         |    1 |     7 |           |          |
|* 5 |     INDEX RANGE SCAN| LSC_I  |   10 |    70 |    1   (0)| 00:00:01 |
-------------------------------------------------------------------------------

Predicate Information (identified by operation id):
---------------------------------------------------

   1 - filter( EXISTS (SELECT MAX("E2"."SALARY") FROM "LSC_EMP" "E2"
              WHERE "E2"."DEPARTMENT_ID"=:B1 HAVING MAX("E2"."SALARY")=:B2))
   3 - filter(MAX("E2"."SALARY")=:B1)
   5 - access("E2"."DEPARTMENT_ID"=:B1)
```

Finally, note that this query required 79 consistent gets:

```
Statistics
----------------------------------------------------------
          1  recursive calls
          0  db block gets
         79  consistent gets
          0  physical reads
          0  redo size
       1991  bytes sent via SQL*Net to client
        520  bytes received via SQL*Net from client
          2  SQL*Net roundtrips to/from client
          0  sorts (memory)
          0  sorts (disk)
         11  rows processed
```

For the next case, the query will be run using the Oracle analytic functions. In this example, the exists subquery is replaced with an in-line view, a select inside the from clause, and the rank analytic function is used to determine the highest salaried employees:

```
select
    *
from
    (
    select
        e.*,
        rank()
    over
        (partition by deptno order by sal desc) r
    from
        lsc_emp e)
where
    r=1
and
    deptno is NOT NULL;
```

Note: While this query runs much faster than the original exists clause, it is much harder to understand, and consequently, much harder to maintain.

Why does this form of the query runs faster? The very different execution plan below shows a window sort pushed rank execution plan operation.

```
Execution Plan
-----------------------------------------------------------
Plan hash value: 151729177

---------------------------------------------------------------------------------
| Id  | Operation                | Name    | Rows  | Bytes | Cost (%CPU)| Time     |
---------------------------------------------------------------------------------
|   0 | SELECT STATEMENT         |         |   107 | 15622 |     3  (34)| 00:00:01 |
|*  1 |  VIEW                    |         |   107 | 15622 |     3  (34)| 00:00:01 |
|*  2 |   WINDOW SORT PUSHED RANK|         |   107 |  7276 |     3  (34)| 00:00:01 |
|   3 |    TABLE ACCESS FULL     | LSC_EMP |   107 |  7276 |     2   (0)| 00:00:01 |
---------------------------------------------------------------------------------

Predicate Information (identified by operation id):
-----------------------------------------------------------

   1 - filter("R"=1)
   2 - filter(RANK() OVER ( PARTITION BY "DEPARTMENT_ID" ORDER BY
               INTERNAL_FUNCTION("SALARY") DESC )<=1)
```

But more importantly, note that the Statistics show only 4 consistent gets, as opposed to 79 consistent gets in the original query. While a reduction in consistent gets does not always correlate to faster execution time, it is fair to say that this form of the query does 19 times less I/O to retrieve the desired rows!

```
Statistics
-----------------------------------------------------------
          1  recursive calls
          0  db block gets
          4  consistent gets
          0  physical reads
          0  redo size
       2151  bytes sent via SQL*Net to client
        520  bytes received via SQL*Net from client
          2  SQL*Net roundtrips to/from client
          1  sorts (memory)
```

```
 0  sorts (disk)
12  rows processed
```

Now, some may believe the analytic query runs faster because it scans the table only once, but even though it does less I/O, the analytics operation is quite expensive. Remember, the best way to judge the speed of a query is to measure it, using the SQL*Plus *set timing on* command.

Again, always remember that execution plans costs and consistent gets may not always yield the fastest execution speed, and what appears to be the fastest execution plan may run slower than other alternative forms of the same query.

Learning the Sequence of Explain Plan Steps

When Codd and Date created the relational data model, the execution plan was an afterthought, largely because the SQL optimizer was always supposed to generate the best execution plan; hence, there was no real need to understand the internal machinations of Oracle execution plans.

However, in the real world, all SQL tuning experts must be proficient in reading Oracle execution plans and understanding the steps within explain plans and the sequence in which the steps are executed.

Reading an explain plan is important for many reasons, and Oracle SQL tuning experts reveal the explain plans to check many things:

- Ensure that the tables will be joined in optimal order.

- Determine the most restrictive indexes to fetch the rows.

- Determine the best internal join method to use (e.g. nested loops, hash join).

- Determine that the SQL is executing the steps in the optimal order.

Reading SQL execution plans has always been difficult, but there are some tricks to help determine the correct order that the explain plan steps are executed.

Ordering the Sequence of Execution Plan Steps

SQL execution plans are interpreted using a preorder (reverse) transversal algorithm. This is a fancy way of saying that to read an execution plan, look for the innermost indented statement. That is generally the first statement executed, but there are exceptions as shown below in the 3-way table join.

The following are some general rules for reading an explain plan:

1. The first statement executed is the one that has the most indentation.

2. If two statements appear at the same level of indentation, the top statement is executed first.

To see how this works, take a look at this plan. Which operation is first to execute?

```
-----------------------------------------------------------------
| Id | Operation          | Name | Rows | Bytes | Cost (%CPU)| Time     |
-----------------------------------------------------------------
|  0 | SELECT STATEMENT   |      |  10  |  650  |  7   (15)| 00:00:01 |
|* 1 |  HASH JOIN         |      |  10  |  650  |  7   (15)| 00:00:01 |
|  2 |   TABLE ACCESS FULL| JOB  |   4  |  160  |  3    (0)| 00:00:01 |
|  3 |   TABLE ACCESS FULL| EMP  |  10  |  250  |  3    (0)| 00:00:01 |
-----------------------------------------------------------------
```

The answer is that the full table scan operation on the job table will execute first. The following is another example plan. Try to read this one:

```
ID  Par Operation
 0      SELECT STATEMENT Optimizer=CHOOSE
 1    0   TABLE ACCESS (BY INDEX ROWID) OF 'EMP'
 2    1     NESTED LOOPS
 3    2       TABLE ACCESS (FULL) OF 'DEPT'
 4    2       INDEX (RANGE SCAN) OF 'IX_EMP_01' (NON-UNIQUE)
```

Complex SQL explain plans can be hard to read, so sometimes I like to graph them. Here is the graph for this execution plan:

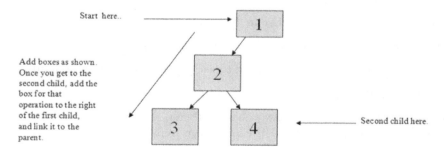

To see how this query executes, the tree is traversed in reverse order, a method termed preorder traversal. From the left most, deepest child, we traverse the tree moving up, and to the right through each branch.

Start here..

Follow the left most branch to the last child. This child executes first. This is an full scan of a table.

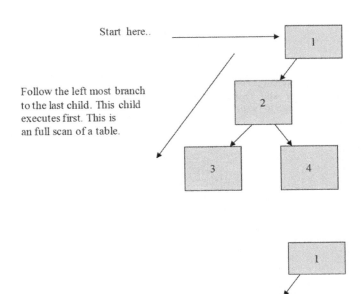

Now, traverse up the tree to the next operation, which is operation 2. Operation 2 is a nested loop.

Now, go all the way down this tree to the deepest child operation.

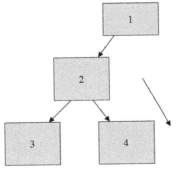

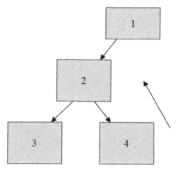

This deepest child executes. In this case it is a index lookup. Oracle will traverse the tree in reverse to the next operation.

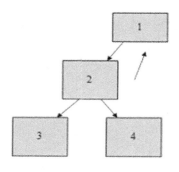

Step 2, the parent of steps 3 and 4, now process the row sets returned by 3 and 4. Step 2, in this case, is a join operation known as a nested loop. It passes it's resulting row set up the tree to it's parent operation.

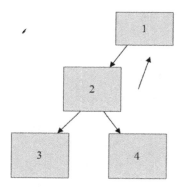

Finally, step one executes, which is an index lookup. It's row set is combined with the row set from step two, and the query result set is returned to the calling program.

By reviewing this hierarchy of SQL execution steps, the order of operations is 3, 4, 2, 1:

```
SEQ  ID  Par Operation
         0    SELECT STATEMENT Optimizer=CHOOSE
3    1   0    TABLE ACCESS (BY INDEX ROWID) OF 'EMP'
4    2   1      NESTED LOOPS
```

```
2    3    2        TABLE ACCESS (FULL) OF 'DEPT'
1    4    2        INDEX (RANGE SCAN) OF 'IX_EMP_01' (NON-UNIQUE)
```

Understanding the sequence of SQL execution plan steps is a critical skill, so some more examples follow.

Consider this SQL query:

```
select
   a.empid,
   a.ename,
   b.dname
from
   emp a,
   dept b
where
   a.deptno=b.deptno;
```

The execution plan is:

```
Execution Plan
----------------------------------------------------------
   0         SELECT STATEMENT Optimizer=CHOOSE (Cost=40 Card=150000
   1    0      HASH JOIN (Cost=40 Card=150000 Bytes=3300000)
   2    1        TABLE ACCESS (FULL) OF 'DEPT' (Cost=2 Card=1 Bytes=10)
   3    1        TABLE ACCESS (FULL) OF 'EMP' (Cost=37 Card=150000 Bytes=
```

What is the order of operations for this execution plan?

Answer: Execution plan steps are 2, 3, 1

Consider this query:

```
select
   a.empid,
   a.ename,
   b.dname
from
   emp a,
   dept b
where
   a.deptno=b.deptno;
```

The execution plan is:

```
Execution Plan
----------------------------------------------------------
   0         SELECT STATEMENT Optimizer=CHOOSE (Cost=864 Card=150000
   1    0      HASH JOIN (Cost=864 Card=150000 Bytes=3300000)
   2    1        TABLE ACCESS (BY INDEX ROWID) OF 'DEPT' (Cost=826 Card=1
   3    2          INDEX (FULL SCAN) OF 'IX_DEPT_01' (NON-UNIQUE) (Cost=26
   4    1        TABLE ACCESS (FULL) OF 'EMP' (Cost=37 Card=150000
```

What is the order of operations for this execution plan?

Answer: Execution plans steps are 3, 2, 4, 1

Here is the same query, but slightly different plan:

```
select
    a.empid,
    a.ename,
    b.dname
from
    emp a,
    dept b
where
    a.deptno=b.deptno;
```

The execution plan is:

```
Execution Plan
----------------------------------------------------------
    0        SELECT STATEMENT Optimizer=CHOOSE
    1     0  NESTED LOOPS (Cost=39 Card=150000 Bytes=3300000)
    2     1    TABLE ACCESS (FULL) OF 'DEPT' (Cost=2 Card=1 Bytes=10)
    3     1    TABLE ACCESS (FULL) OF 'EMP'
```

What is the order of operations for this execution plan?

Answer: Execution plans steps are 2, 3, 1

The next example will show how to find the SQL execution steps for a three table join:

```
select
    a.ename,
    a.salary,
    b.dname,
    c.bonus_amount,
    a.salary*c.bonus_amount
from
    emp a,
    dept b,
    bonus c
where
    a.deptno=b.deptno
and
    a.empid=c.empid;
```

What is the order of operations for the resulting execution plan?

```
Execution Plan
----------------------------------------------------------
   0      SELECT STATEMENT Optimizer=CHOOSE (Cost=168 Card=82 Bytes=3936)
   1    0   TABLE ACCESS (BY INDEX ROWID) OF 'EMP' (Cost=2 Card=1 Bytes=12)
   2    1  ·  NESTED LOOPS (Cost=168 Card=82 Bytes=3936)
   3    2     MERGE JOIN (CARTESIAN) (Cost=4 Card=82 Bytes=2952)
   4    3       TABLE ACCESS (FULL) OF 'DEPT' (Cost=2 Card=1 Bytes=10)
   5    3       BUFFER (SORT) (Cost=2 Card=82 Bytes=2132)
   6    5         TABLE ACCESS (FULL) OF 'BONUS' (Cost=2 Card=82
   7    2       INDEX (RANGE SCAN) OF 'IX_EMP_01' (NON-UNIQUE) (Cost=1
                   Card=1)
```

This is a little tougher, especially since the innermost step (Step 6) is not the first step executed. Using the mapping method, it is clear that step 2 has two children, three and seven, and step 3 has two children, four and five. Step 5 has a lone child, step 6.

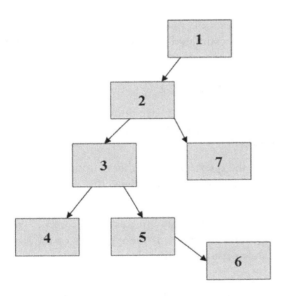

With the map, it is possible to follow the established rules for preorder traversal and see that the execution plan steps start at step 4, followed by step 6. In this case, the execution order is 4,6,5,3,7,2,1.

The following is a more challenging SQL statement. What are the steps for this execution plan?

```
Execution Plan
----------------------------------------------------------
   0      SELECT STATEMENT Optimizer=CHOOSE (Cost=2871 Card=2 Bytes=143)
   1    0   UNION-ALL
```

```
2    1      SORT (GROUP BY) (Cost=2003 Card=1 Bytes=59)
3    2        FILTER
4    3          HASH JOIN (Cost=1999 Card=1 Bytes=59)
5    4            INDEX (FAST FULL SCAN) OF 'XIN8OPS_FLT_LEG' (UNIQUE)
6    4            INDEX (RANGE SCAN) OF 'XIN3BAG_TAG_FLT_LEG' (UNIQUE)
7    1      SORT (GROUP BY) (Cost=868 Card=1 Bytes=84)
8    7        FILTER
9    8          NESTED LOOPS (Cost=864 Card=1 Bytes=84)
10   9            HASH JOIN (Cost=862 Card=1 Bytes=57)
11   10             INDEX (FAST FULL SCAN) OF 'XIN1SCHED_FLT_LEG' (UNIQUE)
12   10             INDEX (FAST FULL SCAN) OF 'XIN8OPS_FLT_LEG' (UNIQUE)
13   9            INDEX (RANGE SCAN) OF 'XIN2BAG_TAG_FLT_LEG' (UNIQUE)
```

Remember, start by drawing a map of the steps. The order of operations is 5, 6, 4, 3, 2, 11, 12, 10, 13, 9, 8, 7, 1.

With that look into how to sequence the steps of SQL execution, it is time to move on to the supplemental information that Oracle provides about SQL execution.

Explain Plan Supplemental Information

The following notations may appear in execution plans, where the execution plan reveals estimates for the cardinality, cost and estimated number of bytes for each plan step:

Optimizer=first_rows_10 (Cost=168 Card=82 Bytes=3936)

- **Optimizer=*first_rows_10:*** indicates that the cost based optimizer is being used. Remember, when optimizing for response time, *first_rows_n* is a better choice than the *all_rows* optimizer mode.

- **Cost:** The Oracle calculated cost for the query. This number is usually ignored because it is an internal number and it does not relate to the actual costing that is used by the optimizer.

- **Card:** This is the number of rows that the optimizer guesses it will return. The cardinality estimate is especially important because it is these guesses of the size of the result set that drives important decisions such as the optimal table join order.

- **Bytes:** This is the number of bytes that might be returned, a rough idea of the total baggage that must be passed to any subsequent steps.

A common mistake for beginners is to place too much importance on the cost information.

> ### Tip! Ignore the cost information!
>
> Many SQL tuning experts have noted that the cost item in an explain plan does not always correspond with the rea" costs used in the CBO decision tree.

Now that how to generate an execution plan and the sequencing rules for each step of execution have been covered, it is time to take a closer look at the types of SQL access methods:

Table scan types:

- Full table scan (large table)
- Full table scan (small table)
- Fast Full scan
- Parallel full table scan

Logical table Join types:

- Nested loops
- Sort merge joins
- Hash joins
- STAR transformation

Index access types:

- Index range scan
- Index unique scan
- Bitmap index conversions of symbolic keys to ROWID's

The next section will provide a closer look at how SQL handles these types of plan steps.

Inside SQL Table Joining

Many people are surprised to learn that there are two distinct types of table join methods in SQL. The logical join and the physical join are quite different:

- **Logical join types:** These logical join types include the *outer join, inner join, right outer join,* and *left outer join*

- **Physical join types**: The physical join types include the *nested loops, hash join, sort merge join,* and the *STAR transformation*

Some queries will perform faster with *nested loop* joins, some with *hash* joins, while others favor sort-merge joins. It is difficult to predict what join technique will be fastest a priori, so many Oracle tuning experts will test run the SQL with each different table join method.

These goals may seem deceptively simple, but these tasks comprise 90 percent of SQL tuning, and they do not require a thorough understanding of the internals of Oracle SQL. It does, however, require an understanding of how the SQL optimizers work. The key is knowing that feeding the optimizer incorrect statistics may cause it to make incorrect decisions.

To get the best plan, the statistics must be present, and they must be current.

Some believe in the practice of running statistics on a schedule, such as weekly. Some believe in just calculating statistics when the data changes. Still others believe that statistics should only be run to fix a poor access path, and once things are good they should not be touched again.

Now that we have covered basic joins types, let's go to the next section where we delve into the table join methods.

The Nested Loops Join

The nested loops join method is the most common table join type.

There are two sides to a nested loops join. In a nested loop join, rows are accessed from a driving table. Usually, is it easy to spot the driving table because it uses the *table access full* or *index range scan* access method. Plus, the driving table result set is always nested within a probe of the second table, which is normally using an *index unique scan* method.

To understand the nested loops method, consider this simple query that performs a logical equi-join against two tables.

```
select
    ename,
    dname
from
    dept,
    emp
where
    emp.deptno = dept.deptno;
```

In this example. the SQL is selecting all employees. When an explain plan for a nested loops join is read, the driving table will be the first table specified after the *nested loops* table access method.

```
OPERATION
-----------------------------------------------------------------
OPTIONS                          OBJECT_NAME              POSITION
-------------------------------- ------------------------ ----------

SELECT STATEMENT
  NESTED LOOPS
                                                               1
    TABLE ACCESS
FULL                             EMP                           1
    TABLE ACCESS
BY INDEX ROWID                   DEPT                          2
      INDEX
RANGE SCAN                       DEPT_DEPTNO                   1
```

When Oracle joins two tables with a nested loop, only one of the indexes may be accessed as a range. The optimizer always performs an index range scan on one index, gathers the *rowid* values, and does fetch by *rowid* on the matching rows in the other table. For example:

```
select
    customer_name,
    order_date
from
    customer
    orders
where
    customer.cust_key = orders.cust_key;
```

The Oracle documentation notes the internals of nested loops joins:

"In a nested loop join, for every row in the outer row set, the inner row set is accessed to find all the matching rows to join.

Therefore, in a nested loop join, the inner row set is accessed as many times as the number of rows in the outer row set."

Oracle will only scan one index, build a set of keys, and then probe the rows from the other table as shown in Figure 3.2.

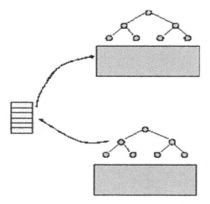

Figure 3.2: *Table joins include index range scans and index unique scans*

So, if this nested loop never uses the customer index, why is it there? The answer is, for index unique scans. In an index unique scan, a single row is accessed within the index, as seen in this query:

```
select
    customer_last_name,
    customer_address
from
    customer
where
    cust_key = 123;
```

Tracking index range scans

It is possible to identify those indexes with the most index range scans with the following simple AWR script.

💾 awr_sql_index_freq.sql

```
col c1 heading 'Object|Name'         format a30
col c2 heading 'Option'              format a15
col c3 heading 'Index|Usage|Count'   format 999,999

select
  p.object_name c1,
  p.options      c2,
  count(1)       c3
from
```

```
    dba_hist_sql_plan    p,
    dba_hist_sqlstat   s
where
    p.object_owner <> 'SYS'
and
    p.options like '%RANGE SCAN%'
and

    p.operation like '%INDEX%'
and
    p.sql_id = s.sql_id
group by
    p.object_name,
    p.operation,
    p.options
order by
    1,2,3;
```

The following is the output showing overall total counts for each object and table access method.

Object Name	Option	Index Usage Count
CUSTOMER_CHECK	RANGE SCAN	4,232
AVAILABILITY_PRIMARY_KEY	RANGE SCAN	1,783
CON_UK	RANGE SCAN	473
CURRENT_SEVERITY	RANGE SCAN	323
CWM$CUBEDIMENSIONUSE_IDX	RANGE SCAN	72
ORDERS_FK	RANGE SCAN	20

This will quickly identify indexes that will benefit the most from a 32k blocksize.

This index list can be double verified by using the AWR to identify indexes with high disk reads during each AWR snapshot period. The sample script below, *awr_top_tables_phyrd.sql*, exposes the top five tables accessed mostly heavily by physical disk reads for every snapshot interval:

🖫 awr_top_tables_phyrd.sql

```
col c0 heading 'Begin|Interval|time'  format a8
col c1 heading 'Table|Name'           format a20
col c2 heading 'Disk|Reads'           format 99,999,999
col c3 heading 'Rows|Processed'       format 99,999,999

select
*
from (
select
    to_char(s.begin_interval_time,'mm-dd hh24') c0,
    p.object_name c1,
```

```
       sum(t.disk_reads_total) c2,
       sum(t.rows_processed_total) c3,
       DENSE_RANK() OVER (PARTITION BY to_char(s.begin_interval_time,'mm-dd
hh24') ORDER BY SUM(t.disk_reads_total) desc) AS rnk
from
   dba_hist_sql_plan    p,
   dba_hist_sqlstat t,
   dba_hist_snapshot s
where
   p.sql_id = t.sql_id
and
   t.snap_id = s.snap_id
and
   p.object_type like '%TABLE%'
group by
   to_char(s.begin_interval_time,'mm-dd hh24'),
   p.object_name
order by
c0 desc, rnk
)
where rnk <= 5;
```

The following is the sample output from the above script:

Begin Interval time	Table Name	Disk Reads	Rows Processed	RNK
10-29 15	CUSTOMER_CHECK	55,732	498,056	1
10-29 15	CON_UK	18,368	166,172	2
10-29 15	CURRENT_SEVERITY	11,727	102,545	3
10-29 15	ORDERS_FK	5,876	86,671	4
10-29 15	SYN$	2,624	23,674	5
10-29 14	CUSTOMER_CHECK	47,756	427,762	1
10-29 14	CON_UK	15,939	142,878	2
10-29 14	CURRENT_SEVERITY	6,976	113,649	3
10-29 14	X$KZSRO	4,772	119,417	4
10-29 14	ORDERS_FK	2,274	20,292	5
10-29 13	CUSTOMER_CHECK	25,704	213,786	1
10-29 13	CON_UK	8,568	71,382	2
10-29 13	OBJ$	3,672	30,474	3
10-29 13	X$KZSRO	2,448	20,328	4
10-29 13	SYN$	1,224	10,146	5

This report shows the tables with the highest disk reads, very important information for disk tuning.

The *dba_hist_sql_plan* table can also be used to gather counts about the frequency of participation of objects inside queries. This is a great query to quickly see what is going on between the tables and the SQL that accesses them.

awr_sql_object_freq.sql

```
col c1 heading 'Object|Name'      format a30
col c2 heading 'Operation'        format a15
col c3 heading 'Option'           format a15
col c4 heading 'Object|Count'     format 999,999

break on c1 skip 2
break on c2 skip 2

select
  p.object_name c1,
  p.operation   c2,
  p.options     c3,
  count(1)      c4
from
  dba_hist_sql_plan p,
  dba_hist_sqlstat  s
where
  p.object_owner <> 'SYS'
and
  p.sql_id = s.sql_id
group by
  p.object_name,
  p.operation,
  p.options
order by
  1,2,3;
```

The following output shows overall total counts for each object and table access method.

Object Name	Operation	Option	Object Count
CUSTOMER	TABLE ACCESS	FULL	305
CUSTOMER _CHECK	INDEX	RANGE SCAN	2
CUSTOMER_ORDERS	TABLE ACCESS	BY INDEX ROWID	311
CUSTOMER_ORDERS		FULL	1
CUSTOMER_ORDERS_PRIMARY	INDEX	FULL SCAN	2
CUSTOMER_ORDERS_PRIMARY		UNIQUE SCAN	311
AVAILABILITY_PRIMARY_KEY		RANGE SCAN	4
CON_UK		RANGE SCAN	3
CURRENT_SEVERITY_PRIMARY_KEY		RANGE SCAN	1
CWM$CUBE	TABLE ACCESS	BY INDEX ROWID	2
CWM$CUBEDIMENSIONUSE		BY INDEX ROWID	2
CWM$CUBEDIMENSIONUSE_IDX	INDEX	RANGE SCAN	2
CWM$CUBE_PK		UNIQUE SCAN	2
CWM$DIMENSION_PK		FULL SCAN	2
MGMT_INV_VERSIONED_PATCH	TABLE ACCESS	BY INDEX ROWID	3
MGMT_JOB		BY INDEX ROWID	458
MGMT_JOB_EMD_STATUS_QUEUE		FULL	181
MGMT_JOB_EXECUTION		BY INDEX ROWID	456
MGMT_JOB_EXEC_IDX01	INDEX	RANGE SCAN	456

```
MGMT_JOB_EXEC_SUMMARY          TABLE ACCESS     BY INDEX ROWID     180

MGMT_JOB_EXEC_SUMM_IDX04       INDEX            RANGE SCAN         180

MGMT_JOB_HISTORY               TABLE ACCESS     BY INDEX ROWID       1

MGMT_JOB_HIST_IDX01            INDEX            RANGE SCAN           1
MGMT_JOB_PK                                     UNIQUE SCAN        458

MGMT_METRICS                   TABLE ACCESS     BY INDEX ROWID     180
```

Using the output above, it is easy to monitor object participation, especially indexes, in the SQL queries and the mode with which an object was accessed by Oracle.

While it's important to tune individual SQL statements, the most important method is the holistic tuning whereby the SQL workload is optimized by adjusting init.ora parameters and CBO statistics.

The next section will provide a look at holistic SQL tuning methods that involve aggregating of historical execution plan information.

Interrogating SQL Execution Plans

The first script below examines the execution plans of *plan9i.sql* and reports on the frequency of every type of table and index access including full-table scans, index range scans, index unique scans and index full scans. The script goes to the appropriate view, *v$sql_plan* in *plan9i.sql* and *dba_hist_sql_plan* in *plan10g.sql*, and parses the output, counting the frequency of execution for each type of access.

The following *plan9i.sql* script will show the SQL that is currently inside the library cache.

🖫 plan9i.sql

```
set echo off;
set feedback on

set pages 999;
column nbr_FTS   format 999,999
column num_rows  format 999,999,999
column blocks    format 999,999
column owner     format a14;
column name      format a24;
column ch        format a1;

column object_owner heading "Owner"              format a12;
column ct             heading "# of SQL selects" format 999,999;

select
```

```
   object_owner,
   count(*)    ct
from
   v$sql_plan
where
   object_owner is not null
group by
   object_owner
order by
   ct desc
;
--spool access.lst;

set heading off;
set feedback off;

set heading on;
set feedback on;
ttitle 'full table scans and counts|  |The "K" indicates that the table is
in the KEEP Pool (Oracle8).'
select
   p.owner,
   p.name,
   t.num_rows,
--   ltrim(t.cache) ch,
   decode(t.buffer_pool,'KEEP','Y','DEFAULT','N') K,
   s.blocks blocks,
   sum(a.executions) nbr_FTS
from
   dba_tables   t,
   dba_segments s,
   v$sqlarea a,
   (select distinct
     address,
     object_owner owner,
     object_name name
   from
     v$sql_plan
   where
     operation = 'TABLE ACCESS'
     and
     options = 'FULL') p
where
   a.address = p.address
   and
   t.owner = s.owner
   and
   t.table_name = s.segment_name
   and
   t.table_name = p.name
   and
   t.owner = p.owner
   and
   t.owner not in ('SYS','SYSTEM')
having
   sum(a.executions) > 9
group by
   p.owner, p.name, t.num_rows, t.cache, t.buffer_pool, s.blocks
order by
```

```
      sum(a.executions) desc;

column nbr_RID   format 999,999,999
column num_rows  format 999,999,999
column owner     format a15;
column name      format a25;

ttitle 'Table access by ROWID and counts'
select
   p.owner,
   p.name,
   t.num_rows,
   sum(s.executions) nbr_RID
from
   dba_tables t,
   v$sqlarea s,
   (select distinct
      address,
      object_owner owner,
      object_name name
   from
      v$sql_plan
   where
      operation = 'TABLE ACCESS'
      and
      options = 'BY ROWID') p
where
   s.address = p.address
   and
   t.table_name = p.name
   and
   t.owner = p.owner
having
   sum(s.executions) > 9
group by
   p.owner, p.name, t.num_rows
order by
   sum(s.executions) desc;

--~*************************************************
--   Index Report Section
--~*************************************************

column nbr_scans  format 999,999,999
column num_rows   format 999,999,999
column tbl_blocks format 999,999,999
column owner      format a9;
column table_name format a20;
column index_name format a20;

ttitle 'Index full scans and counts'
select
   p.owner,
   d.table_name,
   p.name index_name,
   seg.blocks tbl_blocks,
   sum(s.executions) nbr_scans
from
   dba_segments seg,
```

```
      v$sqlarea s,
      dba_indexes d,
    (select distinct
        address,
        object_owner owner,
        object_name name
      from
        v$sql_plan
      where
        operation = 'INDEX'
        and
        options = 'FULL SCAN') p
where
    d.index_name = p.name
    and
    s.address = p.address
    and
    d.table_name = seg.segment_name
    and
    seg.owner = p.owner
having
    sum(s.executions) > 9
group by
    p.owner, d.table_name, p.name, seg.blocks
order by
    sum(s.executions) desc;


ttitle 'Index range scans and counts'
select
    p.owner,
    d.table_name,
    p.name index_name,
    seg.blocks tbl_blocks,
    sum(s.executions) nbr_scans
from
    dba_segments seg,
    v$sqlarea s,
    dba_indexes d,
    (select distinct
        address,
        object_owner owner,
        object_name name
      from
        v$sql_plan
      where
        operation = 'INDEX'
        and
        options = 'RANGE SCAN') p
where
    d.index_name = p.name
    and
    s.address = p.address
    and
    d.table_name = seg.segment_name
    and
    seg.owner = p.owner
having
    sum(s.executions) > 9
```

```
group by
   p.owner, d.table_name, p.name, seg.blocks
order by
   sum(s.executions) desc;


ttitle 'Index unique scans and counts'
select
   p.owner,
   d.table_name,
   p.name index_name,
   sum(s.executions) nbr_scans
from
   v$sqlarean s,
   dba_indexes d,
   (select distinct
     address,
     object_owner owner,
     object_name name
   from
     v$sql_plan
   where
     operation = 'INDEX'
     and
     options = 'UNIQUE SCAN') p
where
   d.index_name = p.name
   and
   s.address = p.address
having
   sum(s.executions) > 9
group by
   p.owner, d.table_name, p.name
order by
   sum(s.executions) desc;
```

Below is the AWR version of the SQL execution plan script. Unlike the *plan9i.sql* script that only extracts current SQL from the library cache, the *plan10g.sql* script accesses the AWR *dba_hist_sqlplan* table and yields a time-series view of the ways that Oracle is accessing tables and indexes.

💾 plan10g.sql

```
spool plan.lst

set echo off
set feedback on

set pages 999;
column nbr_FTS   format 99,999
column num_rows  format 999,999
column blocks    format 9,999
column owner     format a10;
column name      format a30;
column ch        format a1;
```

```
column time        heading "Snapshot Time"         format a15

column object_owner heading "Owner"                 format a12;
column ct           heading "# of SQL selects" format 999,999;

break on time

select
   object_owner,
   count(*)    ct
from
   dba_hist_sql_plan
where
   object_owner is not null
group by
   object_owner
order by
   ct desc
;


--spool access.lst;

set heading on;
set feedback on;

ttitle 'full table scans and counts|  |The "K" indicates that the table is
in the KEEP Pool (Oracle8).'
select
   to_char(sn.end_interval_time,'mm/dd/rr hh24') time,
   p.owner,
   p.name,
   t.num_rows,
--    ltrim(t.cache) ch,
   decode(t.buffer_pool,'KEEP','Y','DEFAULT','N') K,
   s.blocks blocks,
   sum(a.executions_delta) nbr_FTS
from
   dba_tables  t,
   dba_segments s,
   dba_hist_sqlstat a,
   dba_hist_snapshot sn,
   (select distinct
     p1.sql_id,
     object_owner owner,
     object_name name
   from
     dba_hist_sql_plan p1
   where
     operation = 'TABLE ACCESS'
     and
     options = 'FULL') p
where
   a.snap_id = sn.snap_id
   and
   a.sql_id = p.sql_id
   and
   t.owner = s.owner
   and
```

```
      t.table_name = s.segment_name
      and
      t.table_name = p.name
      and
      t.owner = p.owner
      and
      t.owner not in ('SYS','SYSTEM')
having
      sum(a.executions_delta) > 1
group by
      to_char(sn.end_interval_time,'mm/dd/rr hh24'),p.owner, p.name,
t.num_rows, t.cache, t.buffer_pool, s.blocks
order by
      1 asc;


column nbr_RID  format 999,999,999
column num_rows format 999,999,999
column owner     format a15;
column name      format a25;

ttitle 'Table access by ROWID and counts'
select
      to_char(sn.end_interval_time,'mm/dd/rr hh24') time,
      p.owner,
      p.name,
      t.num_rows,
      sum(a.executions_delta) nbr_RID
from
      dba_tables t,
      dba_hist_sqlstat  a,
      dba_hist_snapshot sn,
    (select distinct
        pl.sql_id,
        object_owner owner,
        object_name name
      from
         dba_hist_sql_plan pl
      where
         operation = 'TABLE ACCESS'
         and
         options = 'BY USER ROWID') p
where
      a.snap_id = sn.snap_id
      and
      a.sql_id = p.sql_id
      and
      t.table_name = p.name
      and
      t.owner = p.owner
having
      sum(a.executions_delta) > 9
group by
      to_char(sn.end_interval_time,'mm/dd/rr hh24'),p.owner, p.name, t.num_rows
order by
      1 asc;

--************************************************
--  Index Report Section
```

```
--***************************************************

column nbr_scans   format 999,999,999
column num_rows    format 999,999,999
column tbl_blocks  format 999,999,999
column owner       format a9;
column table_name  format a20;
column index_name  format a20;

ttitle 'Index full scans and counts'
select
   to_char(sn.end_interval_time,'mm/dd/rr hh24') time,
   p.owner,
   d.table_name,
   p.name index_name,
   seg.blocks tbl_blocks,
   sum(s.executions_delta) nbr_scans
from
   dba_segments seg,
   dba_indexes d,
   dba_hist_sqlstat    s,
   dba_hist_snapshot sn,
   (select distinct
      pl.sql_id,
      object_owner owner,
      object_name name
   from
      dba_hist_sql_plan pl
   where
      operation = 'INDEX'
      and
      options = 'FULL SCAN') p
where
   d.index_name = p.name
   and
   s.snap_id = sn.snap_id
   and
   s.sql_id = p.sql_id
   and
   d.table_name = seg.segment_name
   and
   seg.owner = p.owner
having
   sum(s.executions_delta) > 9
group by
   to_char(sn.end_interval_time,'mm/dd/rr hh24'),p.owner, d.table_name,
p.name, seg.blocks
order by
   1 asc;


ttitle 'Index range scans and counts'
select
   to_char(sn.end_interval_time,'mm/dd/rr hh24') time,
   p.owner,
   d.table_name,
   p.name index_name,
   seg.blocks tbl_blocks,
   sum(s.executions_delta) nbr_scans
```

```
from
   dba_segments seg,
   dba_hist_sqlstat s,
   dba_hist_snapshot sn,
   dba_indexes d,
   (select distinct
      pl.sql_id,
      object_owner owner,
      object_name name
   from
      dba_hist_sql_plan pl
   where
      operation = 'INDEX'
      and
      options = 'RANGE SCAN') p
where
   d.index_name = p.name
   and
   s.snap_id = sn.snap_id
   and
   s.sql_id = p.sql_id
   and
   d.table_name = seg.segment_name
   and
   seg.owner = p.owner
having
   sum(s.executions_delta) > 9
group by
   to_char(sn.end_interval_time,'mm/dd/rr hh24'),p.owner, d.table_name,
p.name, seg.blocks
order by
   1 asc;

ttitle 'Index unique scans and counts'
select
   to_char(sn.end_interval_time,'mm/dd/rr hh24') time,
   p.owner,
   d.table_name,
   p.name index_name,
   sum(s.executions_delta) nbr_scans
from
   dba_hist_sqlstat s,
   dba_hist_snapshot sn,
   dba_indexes d,
   (select distinct
      pl.sql_id,
      object_owner owner,
      object_name name
   from
      dba_hist_sql_plan pl
   where
      operation = 'INDEX'
      and
      options = 'UNIQUE SCAN') p
where
   d.index_name = p.name
   and
   s.snap_id = sn.snap_id
   and
```

```
   s.sql_id = p.sql_id
having
   sum(s.executions_delta) > 9
group by
   to_char(sn.end_interval_time,'mm/dd/rr hh24'),p.owner, d.table_name,
p.name
order by
   1 asc;

spool off
```

The output is shown below, and it is the same in 9i and 10g. A good way to start the review of the results is by looking at the counts of full-table scans for each AWR snapshot period. This report gives all the information needed to select candidate tables for the *keep* pool.

The database will benefit from placing small tables, less than two percent of *db_cache_size*, that are subject to frequent full-table scans in the *keep* pool. The report from an Oracle Applications database below shows full-table scans on both large and small tables.

The goal is to use the *recycle* pool for segregating large tables involved in frequent full-table scans. To locate these large-table full-table scans, the *plan9i.sql* full-table scan report for a 9i and beyond database:

```
                full table scans and counts
Snapshot Time   OWNER       NAME                      NUM_ROWS C K   BLOCKS  NBR_FTS
-------------   ---------   ----------------------    -------- - -   ------- ------   12/08/12 14
APPLSYS     FND_CONC_RELEASE_DISJS          39 N K      2   98,864
            APPLSYS     FND_CONC_RELEASE_PERIODS      39 N K      2   98,864
            APPLSYS     FND_CONC_RELEASE_STATES        1 N K      2   98,864
            SYS         DUAL                             N K      2   63,466
            APPLSYS     FND_CONC_PP_ACTIONS        7,021 N K  1,262   52,036
            APPLSYS     FND_CONC_REL_CONJ_MEMBER       0 N K     22   50,174

12/08/12 15 APPLSYS     FND_CONC_RELEASE_DISJS        39 N K      2   33,811
            APPLSYS     FND_CONC_RELEASE_PERIODS      39 N K      2    2,864
            APPLSYS     FND_CONC_RELEASE_STATES        1 N K      2   32,864
            SYS         DUAL                             N K      2   63,466
            APPLSYS     FND_CONC_PP_ACTIONS        7,021 N     1,262   12,033
            APPLSYS     FND_CONC_REL_CONJ_MEMBER       0 N K     22   50,174
```

One table in the listing is a clear candidate for inclusion in the *recycle* pool. The *fnd_conc_pp_actions* table contains 1,262 blocks and has experienced many full-table scans.

Examining this report, it is easy to quickly identify three files that should be moved to the *keep* pool by selecting the tables with less than 50 blocks that have no "K" designation.

Oracle developed the *keep* pool to fully cache blocks from frequently accessed tables and indexes in a separate buffer. When determining the size of the *keep* pool, the

---

Tracking index range scans   **165**

number of bytes comprising all tables that will reside in the *keep* area must be summed. This will insure that the *keep cache* buffer is large enough to fully cache all the tables that have been assigned to it.

Oracle requires that a table only reside in a tablespace of the same blocksize as the buffer assigned to the table. For example, if the *default* buffer is set at 32K, the alter command below would not work if the customer table resides in a 16K tablespace. The default *keep*, and *recycle* designations only apply to the default blocksize; *keep* and *recycle* buffers cannot be assigned different sizes than that of the default *db_block_size*.

```
alter table CUSTOMER storage (buffer_pool KEEP);
```

The whole reason for the existence of the *keep* pool is to always have a data buffer hit ratio of 100 percent. The blocksize of the *keep* pool is not important because all blocks, once loaded, will remain in RAM memory. A *keep* pool might be defined as a 32K blocksize because a large *recycle* buffer was needed to improve the performance of full-table scans.

Monitor the KEEP pool!

Selecting tables for the *keep* pool requires inspecting the data cache over time. These reports include only SQL that happens to be in the library cache at the time the report is run.

Look Out!

Since the goal for the *data buffer hit ratio* of the *keep* pool is 100 percent, each time a table is added to *keep*, the number of blocks in that table must also be added to the *keep* pool parameter in the Oracle file.

These scripts can also show counts for indexes that are accessed via *rowid*, indicative of non-range scan access. The result is shown below.

```
Table access by ROWID and counts
Wed Dec 22
```

Snapshot	Time	OWNER	NAME	NUM_ROWS	NBR_RID
12/16/11	19	SYSMAN	MGMT_TARGET_ROLLUP_TIMES	110	10
12/17/11	06	SYSMAN	MGMT_TARGET_ROLLUP_TIMES	110	10
12/17/11	07	SYSMAN	MGMT_TARGET_ROLLUP_TIMES	110	10
12/17/11	08	SYSMAN	MGMT_TARGET_ROLLUP_TIMES	110	10
12/17/11	12	SYSMAN	MGMT_TARGET_ROLLUP_TIMES	110	10
12/17/11	13	SYSMAN	MGMT_TARGET_ROLLUP_TIMES	110	10
12/17/11	14	SYS	VIEW$	2,583	84
		SYSMAN	MGMT_TARGET_ROLLUP_TIMES	110	10
12/17/11	17	SYS	VIEW$	2,583	82
12/17/11	18	SYSMAN	MGMT_TARGET_ROLLUP_TIMES	110	10

Advanced Oracle SQL Tuning

```
12/17/11 20    SYSMAN    MGMT_TARGET_ROLLUP_TIMES          110    10
12/17/11 21    SYSMAN    MGMT_TARGET_ROLLUP_TIMES          110    10
12/17/11 22    SYSMAN    MGMT_TARGET_ROLLUP_TIMES          110    10
12/17/11 23    SYSMAN    MGMT_TARGET_ROLLUP_TIMES          110    10
12/18/11 00    SYSMAN    MGMT_TARGET_ROLLUP_TIMES          110    10
12/18/11 01    SYSMAN    MGMT_TARGET_ROLLUP_TIMES          110    20
12/18/11 02    SYSMAN    MGMT_TARGET_ROLLUP_TIMES          110    10
12/18/11 03    SYSMAN    MGMT_TARGET_ROLLUP_TIMES          110    10
12/18/11 04    SYSMAN    MGMT_TARGET_ROLLUP_TIMES          110    10
12/18/11 05    SYSMAN    MGMT_TARGET_ROLLUP_TIMES          110    10
12/18/11 09    SYSMAN    MGMT_TARGET_ROLLUP_TIMES          110    20
12/18/11 11    SYSMAN    MGMT_TARGET_ROLLUP_TIMES          110    20
```

Counts of index full scans and index range scans can also be acquired, and this data is very useful for locating those indexes that might benefit from segregation onto a larger blocksize.

```
Index full scans and counts

Snapshot Time   OWNER     TABLE_NAME              INDEX_NAME                 TBL_BLOCKS  NBR_SCANS
--------------- --------- ----------------------- -------------------------- ---------- ---------
12/08/04 14     SYSMAN    MGMT_FAILOVER_TABLE     PK_MGMT_FAILOVER                    8         59
12/08/04 15     SYSMAN    MGMT_FAILOVER_TABLE     PK_MGMT_FAILOVER                    8         58
12/08/04 16     SYS       WRH$_TEMPFILE           WRH$_TEMPFILE_PK                    8         16
                SYSMAN    MGMT_FAILOVER_TABLE     PK_MGMT_FAILOVER                    8         59
12/08/04 17     SYS       WRH$_STAT_NAME          WRH$_STAT_NAME_P                    8        483
                SYSMAN    MGMT_FAILOVER_TABLE     PK_MGMT_FAILOVER                    8         58
12/08/04 18     SYSMAN    MGMT_FAILOVER_TABLE     PK_MGMT_FAILOVER                    8         59
12/08/04 19     SYSMAN    MGMT_FAILOVER_TABLE     PK_MGMT_FAILOVER                    8         58
12/08/04 20     SYSMAN    MGMT_FAILOVER_TABLE     PK_MGMT_FAILOVER                    8         59
12/08/04 21     SYSMAN    MGMT_FAILOVER_TABLE     PK_MGMT_FAILOVER                    8         58
12/08/04 22     SYSMAN    MGMT_FAILOVER_TABLE     PK_MGMT_FAILOVER                    8         58
12/08/04 23     SYSMAN    MGMT_FAILOVER_TABLE     PK_MGMT_FAILOVER                    8         59
12/09/04 00     SYSMAN    MGMT_FAILOVER_TABLE     PK_MGMT_FAILOVER                    8         58
12/09/04 01     SYSMAN    MGMT_FAILOVER_TABLE     PK_MGMT_FAILOVER                    8         59
12/09/04 02     SYSMAN    MGMT_FAILOVER_TABLE     PK_MGMT_FAILOVER                    8         59
12/09/04 03     SYSMAN    MGMT_FAILOVER_TABLE     PK_MGMT_FAILOVER                    8         59
12/09/04 04     SYSMAN    MGMT_FAILOVER_TABLE     PK_MGMT_FAILOVER                    8         58
12/09/04 05     SYSMAN    MGMT_FAILOVER_TABLE     PK_MGMT_FAILOVER                    8         59
12/09/04 06     SYSMAN    MGMT_FAILOVER_TABLE     PK_MGMT_FAILOVER                    8         58
12/09/04 07     SYSMAN    MGMT_FAILOVER_TABLE     PK_MGMT_FAILOVER                    8         59
12/09/04 08     SYSMAN    MGMT_FAILOVER_TABLE     PK_MGMT_FAILOVER                    8         58
12/09/04 09     SYSMAN    MGMT_FAILOVER_TABLE     PK_MGMT_FAILOVER                    8         59

Index range scans and counts

Snapshot Time   OWNER     TABLE_NAME              INDEX_NAME                 TBL_BLOCKS  NBR_SCANS
--------------- --------- ----------------------- -------------------------- ---------- ---------
12/08/04 14     SYS       SYSAUTH$                I_SYSAUTH1                          8        345
                SYSMAN    MGMT_JOB_EXECUTION      MGMT_JOB_EXEC_IDX01                 8       1373
                SYSMAN    MGMT_JOB_EXEC_SUMMARY   MGMT_JOB_EXEC_SUMM_IDX04            8         59
                SYSMAN    MGMT_METRICS            MGMT_METRICS_IDX_01                80         59
                SYSMAN    MGMT_PARAMETERS         MGMT_PARAMETERS_IDX_01              8        179
                SYSMAN    MGMT_TARGETS            MGMT_TARGETS_IDX_02                 8         61
12/08/04 15     SYS       SYSAUTH$                I_SYSAUTH1                          8        273
                SYSMAN    MGMT_JOB_EXECUTION      MGMT_JOB_EXEC_IDX01                 8       1423
                SYSMAN    MGMT_JOB_EXEC_SUMMARY   MGMT_JOB_EXEC_SUMM_IDX04            8         58
```

Now that the use of the *v$sql_plan* view to see how tables and indexes are used by our SQL has been introduced, it is time to investigate techniques for finding the most resource intensive SQL for tuning.

Tracing SQL Execution History

Shops that want static SQL execution plans can use a variety of methods to track when execution plans change over time, as a result of *dynamic_sampling* or a re-analyze of the optimizer statistics.

SQL Plan history analysis is not an easy chore. As the world's most robust and complex database, Oracle offers something for everyone, and it can be confusing to optimize Oracle because of the plethora of features.

One wonderful feature of Oracle is the ability to have SQL execution plans change when the characteristics of the underlying table changes. For shops where a table is huge one day and small the next, of shops where column distribution vary wildly, dynamic SQL is a Godsend.

However, dynamic SQL changes are not so great for stable shops where there exists one, and only one optimal execution plan for any given SQL statement.

Because SQL plans will change whenever changes are made to the instance, any SQL statement will have a history of execution plans. Here are some common acts that will change execution plans:

- Enabling dynamic sampling

- Re-analyze the schema statistics (done automatically, starting in 10g)

- Changing an optimizer parameter (optimizer_mode, optimizer_index_cost_adj)

- Enabling parallelism

This execution plan history can be seen by running scripts against the STATSPACK (*stats$sql_plan and stats$sql_plan_usage*) or the AWR (*dba_hist_sql_plan*) tables.

Once the SQL_ID for a statement has been acquired, the built-in *dbms_xplan.display_awr* procedure can be used to see all the different execution plans for the query.

The *dbms_xplan.display_awr* allows the input of only a SQL_ID, for Oracle to reveal the explain plans for that SQL_ID, as recorded in the AWR. This simple query will show changes to SQL explain plan history. This requires the purchase of the extra cost licenses for AWR.

```
select * from table(dbms_xplan.display_awr('&sqlid'));
```

Oracle 11g has introduced a wealth of new tools to help freeze optimal SQL execution plans, so that they do not change when the data changes These are tools such as the 11g SQL Performance Analyzer which uses a scientific approach to run real-world workloads and only change the SQL execution plans when they are at least 3x faster.

Also, the Oracle CBO group coined the term plan regression for changes that result in a sub-optimal execution plan. While Oracle 11g has tools for tracking explain plans, manual methods can still be used, such as gathering changes to execution plans from STATSPACK or the extra-cost AWR tables.

Using SQL Profiles

One inherent problem in SQL is related to the dynamic nature of SQL performance. SQL was designed to be very sensitive to external influences, and any number of routine changes, such as adding an index or re-analyzing statistics, can make changes to SQL execution plans.

This instability of SQL is a blessing for some shops and a nightmare for others. Many shops want to freeze SQL execution plans after tuning to ensure that they do not have any unplanned performance problems.

The Oracle SQL Tuning advisor allowed the implementation of tuning suggestions in the form of SQL profiles that will improve performance, and SQL profiles can be used the same way as stored outlines (optimizer plan stability). The SQL Profile is a collection of the historical information of prior runs of the SQL statement, comparison details of the actual and estimated cardinality and predicate selectivity, etc.

A SQL Profile is stored persistently in the data dictionary, so it does not require any application code changes.

A SQL profile helps generate a better execution plan than the normal optimization because it is tested against a real-world workload in the SQL Tuning Set (STS). Additional tasks like checking for advanced predicate selectivity, correlation between columns, join skews, and complex predicates such as functions, help in profiling the SQL statement. Once a SQL statement is profiled and stored, differing execution plans can be invoked at will.

> "SQL profiles will soon officially deprecate the old-fashioned stored outlines (a.k.a. optimizer plan stability)" Source: Oracle Corporation

- "Stored outlines will be desupported in a future release in favor of SQL plan management. In Oracle Database 11g Release 1 (11.1), stored outlines continue to function as in past releases."

- However, Oracle strongly recommends the use of SQL plan management for new applications.

- SQL plan management creates SQL plan baselines, which offer superior SQL performance and stability compared with stored outlines."

As a review, stored outlines (optimizer plan stability) allow the DBA to freeze SQL execution plans and more importantly, change execution plans without touching the SQL source, a critical tool for tuning third-party vendor systems where the source code is inaccessible.

In earlier release of Oracle, the storing of plan outlines for SQL statements was known as optimizer plan stability and insured that changes in the Oracle environment do not affect the way a SQL statement is optimized by the cost based optimizer.

Swapping execution plans

Any of the thousands of shops using a vendor package with Oracle may struggle with optimizing and tuning vendor systems that they did not write and cannot change. So, how is it possible to tune SQL when it is not possible to access the SQL source code?

In traditional SQL tuning, changes are made by rewriting the SQL statement into a more efficient form or by changing the execution plan by adding hints to the *select* clause. With SQL that hides inside a compiled program, changing the SQL is impossible. In other cases, the software vendor may explicitly prohibit any changes to the source code and users must come up with a creative way to tune the SQL without touching the source code.

Oracle provides a trick technique for tuning SQL when it is not possible to touch the source code, such as dynamically generated SQL, SQL inside 3rd party vendor packages and compiled programs with embedded SQL.

Before SQL profiles were introduced, stored outlines were swapped to make changes to SQL in cases where the user cannot touch the statement.

Prior to Oracle10g, MetaLink note 92202.1 described a procedure to tune untouchable SQL by performing these steps:

- Identify the sub-optimal SQL and create a stored outline.

- Tune an equivalent query with a faster execution plan and create a stored outline.

- Swap the bad stored outline for the tuned stored outline.

As of Oracle 10g and beyond, the swapping of stored outlines has been superseded by a similar technique for swapping the new SQL profiles.

The following section will address the swapping of SQL profiles in more detail.

Swapping SQL Profiles

The central idea behind swapping SQL profiles is simple. Define a SQL profile that specifies the SQL statement to be tuned along with an alternative execution plan, in the form of hints. When this SQL is executed and hits the library cache, Oracle detects that a SQL profile exists for this statement and automatically applies the hints to change the execution plan.

Hence, it is possible tune SQL statements without ever touching the SQL statement itself. This is accomplished using the *dbms_sqltune* package which has an *import_sql_profile* procedure which allows the swapping of hints from one SQL profile into another SQL profile.

```
dbms_sqltune.import_sql_profile(
    sql_text => 'select * from emp',
    profile => sqlprof_attr('ALL_ROWS','IGNORE_OPTIM_EMBEDDED_HINTS')
    category => 'DEFAULT',
    name => 'change_emp',
    force_match => &&6
);
```

To see how to swap out SQL profiles, start by examining the *dbms_sqltune* package and the *import_sql_profile* procedure.

The example below forces a query that specifies *first_rows_10* to change to *all_rows*.

Execute *dbms_sqltune.import_sql_profile* with the profile to add the hint whenever a matching SQL statement is detected in the library cache.

The first step is to execute the query and displays the execution plan which shows an index full scan:

```
SQL> select /*+ first_rows(10) */ * from sh.customers order by cust_id;

-----------------------------------------------------
| Id | Operation              | Name         |
-----------------------------------------------------
```

```
|   0 | SELECT STATEMENT              |            |
|   1 |   TABLE ACCESS BY INDEX ROWID| CUSTOMERS    |
|   2 |    INDEX FULL SCAN            | CUSTOMERS_PK |
---------------------------------------------------
```

The next step is to import the all_rows hint into any query that matches the original query:

```
begin
  dbms_sqltune.import_sql_profile(
    name     => 'test',
    category => 'DEFAULT',
    sql_text => 'select /*+ first_rows(10) */ * from sh.customers order by
cust_id',
    profile  => sqlprof_attr('ALL_ROWS','IGNORE_OPTIM_EMBEDDED_HINTS')
  );
end;
/
```

The final step is to re-execute the original query and see that the plan has changed:

```
SQL> select /*+ first_rows(10) */ * from sh.customers order by cust_id;

-------------------------------------------------
| Id  | Operation          | Name      |
-------------------------------------------------
|   0 | SELECT STATEMENT    |           |
|   1 |   SORT ORDER BY      |           |
|   2 |    TABLE ACCESS FULL| CUSTOMERS |
-------------------------------------------------
```

Internally, SQL profiles are stored in the data dictionary with the SQL profile name, an attribute name and the attribute value, which is the hint that is to be applied to the SQL.

The following is a query to display the hints within a SQL profile:

```
select
   attr_val          hint_name
from
   dba_sql_profiles prof,
   sqlprof$attr     hnt
where
   prof.signature = hnt.signature
and
   name like ('&profile_name')
order by
   attr#;
```

It should be apparent that SQL profiles are a great way of freezing SQL execution plans, and it is also possible to swap out a bad plan for a good plan without ever touching the SQL source code.

Changing SQL Execution Plans with Hints

In the relational database manifesto as written by Codd and Date, the optimizer is supposed to take care of all optimization without intervention. However, in the real world, it is sometimes necessary to override the optimizer, and that is why hints were created.

Because there is no slot for hints in the ANSI standard for SQL, hints must be placed within comments, right after the select statement as shown below:

```
select /*+ first_rows_10 */
from
    emp;

select -- first_rows_10
from
    emp;
```

Thus, there are two ways to specify comments in SQL, and most SQL developers use the "C" language style of hints the /*+ *my_hint* */ comment that is used in many procedural languages.

Beware of Misspelled Hints!

Because hints are embedded into comments, a spelling error will cause the hint to be treated as a comment and ignored!

Oracle has hundreds of hints, and prior to more in depth information about hinting, the two very important points should be carefully considered:

- **Good hints vs. bad hints:** There are good hints that help the optimizer make a better decision and bad hints, which may cause problems.

- **Hints are rarely a root cause solution:** In the retail industry, they say *"The customer is always right"*, and the same should be held true that *"The optimizer is always right"*. If the optimizer is making a bad decision, it is important to investigate the root cause with can be stake or missing metadata (via *dbms_stats*), sub-optimal global optimizer parameter settings (e.g. *optimizer_mode*, *optimizer_index_cost_adj*) or an Oracle bug. Remember, only good hints should be used as a final solution.

When the optimizer makes a mistake, it can be very tempting to add a hint and move the SQL into production. However, it is important to notify the DBA of the sub-optimal SQL and insist that the issue be investigated, escalating the issue to management if the DBA does not treat the issue as an emergency.

In practice, while sub-optimal SQL is not a huge issue, it is a symptom of a much larger issue, and fixing a problem execution plan may also have the side effect of improving the execution plans of thousands of other SQL statements!

In theory, the optimizer is always right, but in reality, Oracle offers hundreds of hints as shown in Table 3.1:

all_rows	index_join	ordered
and_equal	index_rrs	ordered_predicates
antijoin	index_ss	overflow_nomove
append	index_ss_asc	parallel
bitmap	index_ss	parallel_index
buffer	index	piv_gb
bypass_recursive_check	leading	piv_ssf
bypass_ujvc	like_expand	pq_distribute
cache	local_indexesmaterialize	pq_map
cache_cb	merge	pq_nomap
cache_temp_table	merge_aj	push_pred
cardinality	merge_sj	push_subq
choose	mv_merge	remote_mapped
civ_gb	nested_table_get_refs	restore_as_intervals
collections_get_refs	nested_table_set_refs	rewrite
cpu_costing	nested_table_set_setid	rule
cube_gb	nl_aj	save_as_intervals
cursor_sharing_exact	nl_sj	scn_ascending
defref_no_rewrite	no_access	selectivity
dml_update	no_buffer	semijoin
domain_index_no_sort	no_expand	semijoin_driver
domain_index_sort	no_expand_gset_to_union	skip_ext_optimizer
driving_site	no_fact	sqlldr
dynamic_sampling	no_filtering	star
dynamic_sampling_est_cdn	no_index	star_transformation
expand_gset_to_union	no_merge	swap_join_inputs
fact	no_monitoring	sys_dl_cursor
first_rows	no_order_rollups	sys_parallel_txn
force_sample_block	no_prune_gsets	sys_rid_order
full	no_push_pred	tiv_gb
gby_conc_rollup	no_push_subq	tiv_ssf
global_table_hints	no_qkn_buff	unnest
hash	no_semijoin	use_anti
hash_aj	no_stats_gsets	use_concat
hash_sj	no_unnest	use_hash
hwm_brokered	noappend	use_merge
ignore_on_clause	nocache	use_nl
ignore_where_clause	nocpu_costing	use_semi
index_asc	noparallel	use_ttt_for_gsets
index_combine	noparallel_index	
index_desc	norewrite	
index_ffs	or_expand	

Table 3.1: *Common documented Oracle hints*

There are also undocumented hints, as shown below in Table 3.2, meaning that they should only be used with caution and only in a test environment:

bypass_recursive_check	ignore_on_clause	no_unnest
bypass_ujvc	ignore_where_clause	nocpu_costing
cache_cb	index_rrs	overflow_nomove
cache_temp_table	index_ss	piv_gb
civ_gb	index_ss_asc	piv_ssf
collections_get_refs	index_ss_desc	pq_map
cube_gb	like_expand	pq_nomap
cursor_sharing_exact	local_indexes	remote_mapped
deref_no_rewrite	materialize	restore_as_intervals
dml_update	mv_merge	save_as_intervals
domain_index_no_sort	nested_table_get_refs	scn_ascending
domain_index_sort	nested_table_set_refs	skip_ext_optimizer
dynamic_sampling	nested_table_setid	sqlldr
dynamic_sampling_est_cdn	no_expand_gset_to_union	sys_dl_cursor
expand_gset_to_union	no_fact	sys_parallel_txn
force_sample_block	no_filtering	sys_rid_order
gby_conc_rollup	no_order_rollups	tiv_gb
global_table_hints	no_prune_gsets	tiv_ssf
hwm_brokered	no_stats_gsets	unnest
		use_ttt_for_gsets

Table 3.2: *Undocumented Oracle hints*

The sheer complexity of the Oracle hints can be overwhelming. The following section will provide information on when it is best to use hints to tune SQL.

Good hints vs. bad hints

If the Oracle optimizer always made correct guesses about the size of internal result sets, hints would be far less common, but make no mistake, it's impossible for any software product to always make the correct guess, based on the limited information in the data dictionary.

I have the *ordered* hint on my good hint list because there are times when I know better than the optimizer about the future state of the tables, and in cases where the is one, and only one optimal table join order, the ordered hint is a good hint because it can save the optimizer a huge amount of processing at parse time, especially for SQL that joins more than 10 tables.

Good hint or bad hint, hints as a last-resort and your should always try to find the rot cause of your suboptimal plan (stale/missing statistics, wrong optimizer_mode), etc.

When the optimizer makes a mistake, it's very tempting to add a "good" hint, and move the SQL into production. In practice, while your sub-optimal SQL is not a huge issue, it is a symptom of a much larger issue, and fixing your execution plan may also have the side effect of improving the execution plans of thousands of other SQL statements!

There are "good" hints, those that help the optimizer make a better decision.

The global optimizer mode hints (*all_rows, first_rows_1, first_rows_10, first_rows_100, first_rows_1000*) are good hints because they are used when the majority of the SQL workload is optimal, but there are "outlier" SQL that needs a different optimizer mode.

The only exceptions are hints that give "a priori" information to the CBO like these good hints:

append
(no)append
parallel
(no)parallel
rewrite
(no)rewrite
all_rows
cardinality
cpu_costing
cursor_sharing_exact
driving_site
dynamic_sampling
first_rows_1
first_rows_10
first_rows_100
first_rows_1000
opt_param
ordered
ordered_predicates
selectivity
skip_ext_optimizer

Of course, you could argue that the CBO would not need some good hints (e.g. number of rows returned by query, table join order, etc.), but sometimes there is no substitute for a-priori knowledge.

When to Use an Oracle Hint

Although some hints are bad, it is important to understand that hints remain a powerful SQL tuning tool. Just because hints are bad in production SQL, this does not minimize their importance as a tuning tool when developing a SQL statement. The following is my good hint list:

- *all_rows*

- *append*

- *cardinality*

- *cpu_costing*

- *cursor_sharing_exact*

- *driving_site*

- *dynamic_sampling*

- *first_rows_1*

- *first_rows_10*

- *first_rows_100*

- *first_rows_1000*

- *noappend*

- *noparallel*

- *norewrite*

- *ordered*

- *ordered_predicates*

- *parallel*

- *rewrite*

- *selectivity*

- *skip_ext_optimizer*

I have the *ordered* hint on my good hint list because there are times when I know better than the optimizer about the future state of the tables, and in cases where there is one and only one optimal table join order, the ordered hint is good because it can save the optimizer a huge amount of processing at parse time, especially for SQL that joins more than 10 tables.

The global optimizer mode hints, *all_rows, first_rows_1, first_rows_10, first_rows_100, first_rows_1000,* are good hints because they are used when the majority of the SQL workload is optimal, but there are outlier SQL that needs a different optimizer mode.

Oracle makes the cost-based SQL optimizer more intelligent with each release. With each new release, Oracle provides an increasing number of methods for changing the execution plans for SQL statements. While hints are used for tuning as well as documentation, the most common use for Oracle hints is as a debugging tool. The hints can be used to determine the optimal execution plan, and then by working backwards, adjust the statistics to make the vanilla SQL simulate the hinted query.

The following is a list of common hints that are used to change the execution plan in the cost-based optimizer:

- **all_rows :** This is the cost-based approach designed to provide the best overall throughput and minimum resource consumption.

- **and_equal(table_name index_name1) :** This hint causes merge scans of 2 to 5 single column indexes.

- **cluster(table_name) :** This hint requests a cluster scan of the table_name.

- **first_rows :** This is the cost-based approach designed to provide the best response time.

- **full :** This hint requests the bypassing of indexes, doing a full-table scan.

- **hash(table_name) :** This hint causes a hash scan of table_name.

- **hash_aj :** This hint is placed in a *not in* sub-query to perform a hash anti-join.

- **index(table_name index_name) :** This hint requests the use of the specified index against the table. If no index is specified, Oracle will choose the best index.

- **index_asc(table_name index_name) :** This hint requests to use the ascending index on a range scan operation.

- **index_combine(table_name index_name) :** This hint requests that the specified bitmapped index be used.

- **index_desc(table_name index_name) :** This hint requests to use the descending index on a range scan operation.

- **merge_aj:** This hint is placed in a *not in* sub-query to perform an anti-join

- **no_expand:** The NO_EXPAND hint prevents the cost-based optimizer from considering OR-expansion for queries having OR conditions or IN-lists in the WHERE clause. Usually, the optimizer considers using OR expansion and uses this method if it decides the cost is lower than not using it. This OR expansion is related to optimizer internals and does not mean that the logic itself will be changed and return a different result set.

- **no_merge:** This hint is used in a view to prevent it from being merged into a parent query.

- **nocache:** This hint causes the table cache option to be bypassed.

- **noparallel:** This hint turns off the parallel query option.

- **ordered:** This hint requests that the tables should be joined in the order that they are specified (left to right).

- **parallel(table_name degree) :** For full table scans, this hint requests that the table_name query be executed in parallel mode with degree processes servicing the table access.

- **push_subq:** This hint causes all sub-queries in the query block to be executed at the earliest possible time.

- **rowid:** This hint requests a ROWID scan of the specified table.

- **rule:** This hint indicates that the rule-based optimizer should be invoked, sometimes due to the absence of table statistics.

- **Star:** This hint forces the use of a star query plan, provided that there are at least three tables in the query and a concatenated index exists on the fact table.

- **use_concat :** This hint requests that a union all be used for all or conditions

- **use_hash(table_name1 table_name2) :** This hint requests a hash join against the specified tables.

- **use_merge:** This hint requests a sort merge operation.

- **use_nl(table_name) :** This hint requests a nested loop operation with the specified table as the driving table.

Using Oracle hints can be very complicated, and Oracle developers only use hints as a last resort, preferring to alter the statistics to change the execution plan. Oracle contains more than 124 hints, and many of them are not found in the Oracle documentation.

Covered in more detail in chapter 14, *Tuning SQL subqueries*, Oracle will often detect an inefficient query form and automatically rewrite it into a more efficient form. It is also possible to accomplish this with hints. The next hint is illustrative because it shows how an Oracle hint can make the optimizer rewrite a complex query into multiple, simpler queries.

Automatic Query Rewrite with Hints

The *use_concat* hint is used in complex queries with multiple OR conditions, and it directs Oracle to rewrite the query into multiple queries. This hint is often used when a query has many OR conditions in the *where* clause.

Consider the following example query. *Deptno, job,* and *sal* all have B-tree indexes. It is important to point out that if these indexes were bitmap indexes, the execution plan would not use a full-table scan. Oracle automatically uses bitmap indexes for queries with multiple *or* conditions on bitmap index columns.

```
select
   ename
from
   emp
where
   deptno = 10
or
   sal < 5000
or
   job = 'CLERK';
```

There are two options with this scenario. The first option is to create three bitmap indexes on *deptno, sal,* and *clerk*. This can be done because the index columns are low cardinality and would result in a bitmap merge execution plan.

The second option is the use the *use_concat* hint to separate the query into three B-tree index scans. The result sets from these indexes are then combined using the *union* operator.

Below is the example of the execution plan with the B-tree indexes. A full-table scan must be used to satisfy the several OR conditions:

```
OPERATION
---------------------------------------------------------------------
OPTIONS                       OBJECT_NAME                 POSITION
---------------------------   -------------------------   ----------
  SELECT STATEMENT
                                                                1
    TABLE ACCESS
FULL                          EMP                               1
```

If the indexes were bitmap indexes, the execution plan would have been much faster:

```
OPERATION
---------------------------------------------------------------------
OPTIONS                       OBJECT_NAME                 POSITION
---------------------------   -------------------------   ----------
  SELECT STATEMENT
                                                                4
```

```
     TABLE ACCESS
BY INDEX ROWID                 EMP                              1
     BITMAP CONVERSION
TO ROWIDS                                                       1
       BITMAP OR
                                                                1
         BITMAP INDEX
SINGLE VALUE                   EMP_DEPTNO_BIT                   1
         BITMAP MERGE
                                                                2
           BITMAP INDEX
RANGE SCAN                     EMP_SAL_BIT                      1
         BITMAP INDEX
SINGLE VALUE                   EMP_JOB_BIT                      3
```

Once again using the three B-tree indexes, the *use_concat* hint can be evoked to change the execution plan:

```
select /*+ use_concat */
    ename
from
    emp
where
    deptno = 10
or
    sal < 5000
or
    job = 'CLERK';
```

The full-table scan has been replaced with the result of the union of the three queries. Each of these used the B-tree index for the singe columns and a *concatenation* plan to union the results together, as shown below:

```
OPERATION
---------------------------------------------------------------------
OPTIONS                    OBJECT_NAME                    POSITION
-------------------------  ---------------------------- ----------
SELECT STATEMENT
                                                             3
  CONCATENATION
    TABLE ACCESS
BY INDEX ROWID             EMP                                1
    INDEX
RANGE SCAN                 EMP_JOB                            1
    TABLE ACCESS
BY INDEX ROWID             EMP                                2
    INDEX
RANGE SCAN                 EMP_SAL                            1
    TABLE ACCESS
BY INDEX ROWID             EMP                                3
    INDEX
RANGE SCAN                 EMP_DEPT                           1
```

When Hints Are Ignored

Hints are optimizer directives, used for altering optimizer execution plans. Remember, an optimizer hint is a directive that is placed inside comments inside the

---

SQL statement and used in those rare cases where the optimizer makes an incorrect decision about the execution plan. Since hints are inside comments, it is important to ensure that the hint name is spelled correctly and that the hint is appropriate to the query.

For example, the following hint is invalid because *first_rows* access and parallel access are mutually exclusive. That is because parallel access always assumes a full-table scan and *first_rows* favors index access.

```
-- An invalid hint
select /*+ first_rows parallel(emp,8)*/
   emp_name
from
   emp
order by
   ename;
```

Some Oracle professionals will place hints together to reinforce their wishes. For example, if there is a SMP server with eight or more CPUs, it might be desirable to use Oracle Parallel Query to speed up legitimate full-table scans. Some hints and when they are ignored are included in Table 3.3 below:

Hint	When Ignored
cluster	When used with a noncluster table
hash	When used with a noncluster table
hash_aj	When no subquery exists
index	When the specified index does not exist
index_combine	When no bitmapped indexes exist
merge_aj	When no subquery exists
parallel	When a plan other than *table access full* is invoked
push_subq	When no subquery exists
star	When improper indexes exists on the fact table
use_concat	When no multiple *or* conditions exist in the *where* clause
use_nl	When indexes do not exist on the tables

Table 3.3: *Oracle hints and when they are ignored*

When using parallel query, one should seldom turn on parallelism at the table level (for instance, with *alter table customer parallel 35)* because the setting of parallelism for a table influences the optimizer. This causes the optimizer to see that the full-table scan is inexpensive.

Hence, most Oracle professionals specify parallel query on a query-by-query basis, combining the full hint with the parallel hint to ensure a fast parallel full-table scan:

```
-- A valid hint
select /*+ full parallel(emp,35)*/
   emp_name
from
   emp
order by
   ename;
```

Why is My Hint Ignored?

It is advisable to only use the good hints like ordered and ordered_predicates. A SQL hint is an optimizer directive and cannot be ignored, but there are at least two reasons why it appears that a hint is being ignored. Some of these reasons are covered in the following sections.

Syntax Error Hints are Ignored

Oracle does not report when a hint is misspelled, and because hints are embedded into comments, errors will appear as if the hint is being ignored. If table name or index name is spelled incorrectly, the hint will not be used. The following query shows a hint with a misspelled table name:

```
select /*+ index(erp, dept_idx) */ * from emp;
```

A hint will also be ignored if it is specified improperly. For example, the table name is mandatory for an index hint. The following hint will be ignored because the table name is not specified in the query:

```
select /*+ index(dept_idx) */ * from emp;
```

Incompatible Hints are Ignored

Incongruent hints, such as those that do not make sense to Oracle, are ignored. In the context of the query an incompatible hint is indeed ignored, such as a query that specifies incompatible access plans. For example, the following hints are inconsistent and one will be ignored:

- Ignored: Parallel hint with index hint

- Ignored: Full hint with index hint

Hints With Bad Parameters are Ignored

It is possible to have a valid hint, with correct syntax and semantics, that is ignored because of a lack of server resources. For example, the use_hash hint is dependent upon there being enough RAM as defined by pga_aggregate_target or hash_area_size. If these settings prohibit the optimizer from invoking a hash join, the use_hash hint will be ignored.

```
select /*+ use_hash(e,b) parallel(b, 15) */
   e.ename,
   hiredate,
   b.comm
from
   smalltab e,
   largetab b
where
   e.ename = b.ename;
```

Oracle 11g now has a feature to silently allow *insert* SQL to accept duplicates with the *ignore_row_on_dupkey_index* hint. When *ignore_row_on_dupkey_index* hint is used in a SQL insert on a table with a unique key index, all duplicates will be silently ignored, rather than causing the traditional error, *ORA-00001 unique constraint violated.*

The Oracle docs note that the *ignore_row_on_dupkey_index* are unlike any other hints because they have an effect on the semantics of the SQL statement, actually changing the functionality of the DML statement.

The *ignore_row_on_dupkey_index* hint is also unique because unlike a regular hint embedded inside comments, an error will result. In traditional SQL hints, hints with syntax, semantic or resource errors will cause the hint to be ignored.

However, this hint will cause an ORA-38912 error if the correct arguments are not passed. Note that the *ignore_row_on_dupkey_index* hint requires two arguments, the table name and index name. If the index name is omitted, the ORA-38912 error is thrown as shown in the example below:

```
insert /*+ ignore_row_on_dupley_index(unique_cust) */
into
   unique_cust
(select * from non_unique_cust);
```

```
ORA-38912:  An index must be specified in the index hint
```

Cause: Index specification was missing in an ignore_row_on_dupkey_index or change_dupkey_error_index hint.

Action: In the hint, specify a unique index that exists on the table.

Functionally, the *ignore_row_on_dupkey_index* hint is somewhat similar to the SQL merge statement because it ignores duplicates on insert.

Examples of using the ignore_row_on_dupkey_index hint

The following is an example of using this hint to load a unique table from a non-unique table, while preventing aborts due to duplicate values:

```
insert /*+ ignore_row_on_dupley_index(unique_cust, unique_cust_pk_idx) */
into
   unique_cust
(select * from non_unique_cust);
```

When tuning SQL, Oracle hints are a common and useful tool. To use these tools effectively, you must understand how these hints are used individually, together and with different table access methods. Below are some important points to remember:

- Hints are ignored when they are incompatible with the execution plan or when incorrectly formatted. It is critical to be careful to use the correct syntax.

- When using the CBO, suspect SQL statements can be tuned by adding the *first _rows* or *rule* hint.

- When hints are applied to both outer queries and subqueries. When a hint is in the outer query, it does not apply to the inner query.

Conclusion

The SQL execution plan is the tool for revealing the internal machinations of a statement and Oracle offers many ways to change the execution steps and internals. The main points of this chapter include:

- The *plan9i.sql* and *plan10g.sql* scripts can be used to identify possible tuning issues, by locating large-table full-table scans.

- You can swap execution plans with optimizer plan stability and with SQL profiles.

Advanced Oracle SQL Tuning

- Hints are optimizer directives that can be used to facilitate the changing of execution plans.

- Oracle offer good hints that provide additional information to the optimizer, and bad hints which constrain a query from using a new access method.

It is time to move on to the subject of Oracle join internals and see how tables are joined from an internal perspective.

Oracle SQL Join Internals

It's not a hardware problem so let's try tuning the SQL

The principles of relational normalization dictate that like-minded data be grouped together in tables, and an important function of SQL is to retrieve data from multiple tables in the most efficient way.

Oracle Table Join Types

Understanding SQL join tuning requires a start with examining the logical table join forms and then moves on to investigation into the physical ways that Oracle gathers rows from multiple tables.

The previous chapters have provided information on how to make the distinction between the logical form of a SQL query and the internal machinations that make the optimizer return the desired rows. This chapter will examine the interface layer between the logical and physical layers of Oracle SQL to assist in gaining an understanding of the transformations.

When looking at advanced SQL tuning, readers probably already know the different logical types of joins that Oracle allows with a SQL statement. These logical join types include *inner* joins, *outer* joins, *natural* joins, *cross* joins and *equi-joins*, but these are very different from the physical join types. Internally, Oracle has a whole other set of join types, with names like *nested loops* joins, *hash* joins and *merge* joins as shown in Figure 4.1 below:

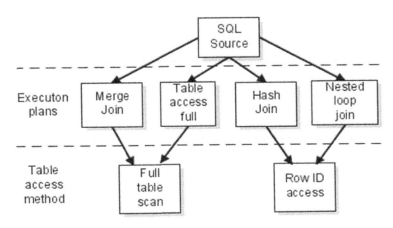

Figure 4.1: *Physical join types and table access methods*

Remember that the internal join method has nothing to do with the logical join, and the type of physical join is a function of Oracle constructs. For example, joining two tables that have indexes will result in *nested loops* join, while tables with missing indexes may experience a *sort merge* join. Also, the Oracle *hash* join is directly influenced by the DBA's setting for the optimizer parameters *pga_aggregate_target* and/or *hash_area_size*.

Before bridging the gap between logical and physical joins, the following sections offer a review the following types of logical joins in SQL:

The Equi-Join

The *equi-join* is the standard equality join that is used to merge two tables based on matching key values. For example, the following is an *equi-join* for displaying all employees and their bonuses:

```
select
    emp.ename,
    emp.deptno
    bonus.comm
from
    emp,
```

```
    bonus
where
    emp.ename = bonus.ename
;
```

Here, note that the employee name serves as the join key (*where emp.ename = bonus.ename*) yet *ename* does not need to be displayed in the result set:

```
ENAME          DEPTNO        COMM
----------  ----------  ----------
ALLEN              30         300
WARD               30         500
MARTIN             30        1400
```

The *equi-join* is the most straightforward and common of all of the relational join operators. Internally, Oracle may service an *equi-join* with *nested loops*, *hash* join or a *sort merge* join, the choice of physical join method depends on the characteristics of the underlying Oracle database.

The *equi-join* query above has a sort merge execution plan:

```
---------------------------------------------------------------------------------
| Id  | Operation                    | Name    | Rows  | Bytes | Cost (%CPU)| Time     |
---------------------------------------------------------------------------------
|   0 | SELECT STATEMENT             |         |    14 |   280 |     6  (17)| 00:00:01 |
|   1 |  MERGE JOIN                  |         |    14 |   280 |     6  (17)| 00:00:01 |
|   2 |   TABLE ACCESS BY INDEX ROWID| DEPT    |     4 |    44 |     2   (0)| 00:00:01 |
|   3 |    INDEX FULL SCAN           | PK_DEPT |     4 |       |     1   (0)| 00:00:01 |
|*  4 |   SORT JOIN                  |         |    14 |   126 |     4  (25)| 00:00:01 |
|   5 |    TABLE ACCESS FULL         | EMP     |    14 |   126 |     3   (0)| 00:00:01 |
---------------------------------------------------------------------------------

Predicate Information (identified by operation id):
---------------------------------------------------

   4 - access("E"."DEPTNO"="D"."DEPTNO")
       filter("E"."DEPTNO"="D"."DEPTNO")
```

Internally, Oracle joins the tables based upon the pre-defined primary-key, foreign-key relationships, joining the matching rows based on matching key values as shown in Figure 4.2.

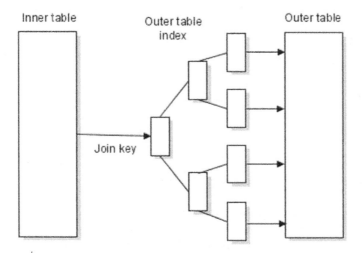

Figure 4.2: *Joining a table based on matching keys*

The next section will provide a look into the *outer* join.

The *Outer* Join Operator

Oracle allows the inclusion of non-matching rows in a join by specifying an *outer* join. In the pre SQL-99 syntax, the outer join is specified by placing a plus-sign (+) in the *where* clause. In SQL-99 syntax, there are separate keywords for a *left outer* join and a *right outer* join, and there is also a *full outer* join, which includes non-matching rows from both tables.

```
select
    emp.ename,
    emp.deptno,
    bonus.comm
from
    emp,
    bonus
where
    emp.ename = bonus.ename(+);
```

When running this query, the plus sign (+) tells Oracle to include *emp* rows, even where there was no matching value in the *bonus* table (e.g. employees who got no bonus):

```
ENAME        DEPTNO      COMM
----------  ----------  ----------
ALLEN            30         300
WARD             30         500
```

Oracle Table Join Types

```
MARTIN           30        1400
FORD             20
SCOTT            20
JAMES            30
KING             10
BLAKE            30
MILLER           10
TURNER           30
CLARK            10
JONES            20
ADAMS            20
SMITH            20
```

Internally, the *nested loops outer* access method may service *outer* joins.

A *left* or *right* outer join is where rows in one table that do not have a matching row in the second table are selected with null values for the unknown columns. In this case the above example can be changed by moving the plus sign to the other side of the equality, directing Oracle to display *bonus* rows that do not have a match in the *emp* table:

```
select
    e.ename,
    d.deptno,
    d.loc
from
    emp e,
    dept d
where
    e.deptno(+)=d.deptno;
```

```
ENAME          DEPTNO LOC
----------     ---------- -------------
SMITH              20 DALLAS
ALLEN              30 CHICAGO
```

Id	Operation	Name	Rows	Bytes	Cost (%CPU)	Time
0	SELECT STATEMENT		14	280	6 (17)	00:00:01
1	MERGE JOIN OUTER		14	280	6 (17)	00:00:01
2	TABLE ACCESS BY INDEX ROWID	DEPT	4	44	2 (0)	00:00:01
3	INDEX FULL SCAN	PK_DEPT	4		1 (0)	00:00:01
* 4	SORT JOIN		14	126	4 (25)	00:00:01
5	TABLE ACCESS FULL	EMP	14	126	3 (0)	00:00:01

The results is a *merge* join outer physical execution plan. The next section will cover the logical *full outer* join.

The Oracle Full Outer Join

The *full outer* join, and the related *full hash join* in Oracle 11g, has no direct equivalent in Oracle8i and earlier releases, but it is very handy for find missing rows in both tables.

Oracle author John Garmany notes that there are no standard Oracle formats for a *full outer* join in Oracle8i and earlier. Instead, a *left* and *right outer* join with a *union* must be used to get the same results.

```
select
  author_last_name,
  book_key
from
  author,
  book_author
where
  author.author_key = book_author.author_key(+)
union
 select
   author_last_name,
   book_key
 from
   author,
   book_author
 where
   author.author_key(+) = book_author.author_key
 order by author_last_name;
```

```
AUTHOR_LAST_NAME                             BOOK_K
------------------------------------------   ------
clark
hester                                       B101
hester                                       B109
hester                                       B116
jeckle                                       B102
```

Notice that the union removed duplicate rows, and the results set was ordered once at the end of the query.

Using the ANSI format, it is also possible to *outer* join multiple tables with multiple *outer* joins. That was not allowed in the standard Oracle format.

```
select
  author_last_name c1,
  book_title       c2
from
  author full outer join book_author using (author_key)
         full outer join book using (book_key)
order by author_last_name;
```

```
Author                         Title
------------------------------  ----------------------------
clark
hester                         windows success
hester                         pay no taxes and go to jail
hester                         oracle12c sql tuning
```

In the example above, three tables were joined using *full outer* joins. This allows the inclusion of both books without authors and the authors without books in the resulting report.

Another correct equivalence for a full outer join in Oracle8i would be using a *union all* operator:

```
select
    stuff
from
    a,
    b
where
    a.x=b.x(+)
union all
select
    stuff
from
    a,
    b
where
    a.x(+)=b.x
and
a.x is null;
```

Laurent Schneider notes that the *full outer* join syntax can be very usable in the real world when looking for the differences between two tables:

```
SQL> create table t1(id number);

Table created.

SQL> insert into t1(id) values (1);

1 row created.

SQL> insert into t1(id) values (2);

1 row created.

SQL> create table t2(id number);

Table created.

SQL> insert into t2(id) values (1);

1 row created.

SQL> insert into t2(id) values (3);

1 row created.
```

```
SQL> commit;

Commit complete.

SQL> select t1.id, t2.id
  2    from t1 full join t2
  3    on (t1.id=t2.id)
  4    where t1.id is null or t2.id is null;

        ID         ID
---------- ----------
         2          3
```

This shows the full outer join is very useful in cases where we want to see the differences between two related tables. The next section will delve into the *union all* logical join type.

The *union all* Operator

The *union all* is quite simple. In essence, the *union all* is used to paste together the rows from several queries into a common result set:

```
select
   1 n
from
   dual
union all
select
   2 n
from
   dual
union all
select
   2 n
from dual;
```

```
         N
----------
         1
         2
         2
```

```
-------------------------------------------------------------------------
| Id | Operation       .  | Name | Rows | Cost (%CPU) | Time     |
-------------------------------------------------------------------------
|  0 | SELECT STATEMENT  |      |    3 |    6  (67) | 00:00:01 |
|  1 |  UNION-ALL        |      |      |            |          |
|  2 |   FAST DUAL       |      |    1 |    2   (0) | 00:00:01 |
|  3 |   FAST DUAL       |      |    1 |    2   (0) | 00:00:01 |
|  4 |   FAST DUAL       |      |    1 |    2   (0) | 00:00:01 |
-------------------------------------------------------------------------
```

To use *union all* to paste together multiple SQL queries, each query must have the same number of columns and the datatypes must be the same or compatible.

The *union* Operator

Just like the *union all* operator, *union* pastes together the output from multiple queries, but with *union* all duplicate rows are removed:

```
select 1 n
from
   dual
union
select 2 n
from
   dual
union
select 2 n
from
   dual;
```

```
         N
----------
         1
         2
```

```
--------------------------------------------------------------------
| Id | Operation        | Name | Rows  | Cost (%CPU)| Time     |
--------------------------------------------------------------------
|  0 | SELECT STATEMENT |      |    3  |    9  (78)| 00:00:01 |
|  1 |  SORT UNIQUE     |      |    3  |    9  (78)| 00:00:01 |
|  2 |   UNION-ALL      |      |       |           |          |
|  3 |    FAST DUAL     |      |    1  |    2   (0)| 00:00:01 |
|  4 |    FAST DUAL     |      |    1  |    2   (0)| 00:00:01 |
|  5 |    FAST DUAL     |      |    1  |    2   (0)| 00:00:01 |
--------------------------------------------------------------------
```

Note that internally, a *union all* plan is executed, fetching all unique rows, but there is an additional operation to remove the duplicates rows with the *sort unique* operation. Due to the overhead of the back-end sort, *union all* performs better than a simple *union*, especially if the result set is large and has to executed on slow disk storage in the *temp* tablespace.

The *minus* operator

The *minus* operator is essentially the opposite of the *union* operator. While the *union* operator pastes in the results of a second query, the *minus* operator subtracts any rows that are present in the first query, removing all duplicate rows.

Use *minus* instead of *not in* operators!

When filtering away rows, beginners are often tempted to use a *not in* subquery. Even though the results of the two might be the same, the *minus* operator is far more efficient.

The following code selects all department numbers and then uses *minus* to remove all department numbers that appear in the *emp* table:

```
select
    deptno
from
    dept
minus
select
    deptno
from
    emp;
```

```
     DEPTNO
- - - - - - - - - -
         40
```

```
-----------------------------------------------------------------------
| Id | Operation          | Name    | Rows | Bytes | Cost (%CPU)| Time     |
-----------------------------------------------------------------------
|  0 | SELECT STATEMENT   |         |    4 |    54 |    5  (80)| 00:00:01 |
|  1 |  MINUS             |         |      |       |           |          |
|  2 |   SORT UNIQUE NOSORT|        |    4 |    12 |    2  (50)| 00:00:01 |
|  3 |    INDEX FULL SCAN | PK_DEPT |    4 |    12 |    1   (0)| 00:00:01 |
|  4 |   SORT UNIQUE      |         |   14 |    42 |    3  (34)| 00:00:01 |
|  5 |    TABLE ACCESS FULL| EMP    |   14 |    42 |    2   (0)| 00:00:01 |
-----------------------------------------------------------------------
```

The results show that only department 40 remains because the other department numbers exist in the *emp* table already.

The *intersect* operator

The *intersect* operator does exactly what the name implies; it filters out the intersection of two result sets. The *intersect* operator selects the only the matching rows that are present in two separate queries.

The following only department numbers that appear in both the *dept* and the *emp* tables:

```
select
   deptno
from
   emp
intersect
select
   deptno
from
   dept;

   DEPTNO
----------
        10
        20
        30
```

```
--------------------------------------------------------------------------------
| Id | Operation           | Name    | Rows | Bytes | Cost (%CPU)| Time     |
--------------------------------------------------------------------------------
|  0 | SELECT STATEMENT    |         |    4 |    54 |    5  (60) | 00:00:01 |
|  1 |  INTERSECTION       |         |      |       |            |          |
|  2 |   SORT UNIQUE       |         |   14 |    42 |    3  (34) | 00:00:01 |
|  3 |    TABLE ACCESS FULL| EMP     |   14 |    42 |    2   (0) | 00:00:01 |
|  4 |   SORT UNIQUE NOSORT|         |    4 |    12 |    2  (50) | 00:00:01 |
|  5 |    INDEX FULL SCAN  | PK_DEPT |    4 |    12 |    1   (0) | 00:00:01 |
--------------------------------------------------------------------------------
```

The results show that departments 10, 20 and 30 are present in both tables. Using *intersect* is particularly useful when we have a very large number of columns that must be compared.

Why not use a standard equi-join, which will give the exact same result, only showing matching rows:

```
select
   deptno
from
   emp   e,
   dept  d
where
   d.deptno = e.deptno;

   DEPTNO
----------
        10
        20
        30
```

Using the *intersect* operator, the SQL optimizer does not have to figure out how to join the tables and the pre-execution parsing can be quicker.

SQL programmers are faced with these choices all the time, especially when using advanced SQL analytic functions. Remember, the best choice is the one executes fastest (*first_rows_n*) or with the least resources (*all_rows*).

In some cases, complex problems are not appropriate for SQL, and a solution will run faster if broken down into many separate queries and placed inside PL/SQL.

The anti-join operator

An *anti-join* is seen when a subquery contains a *not in* or a *not exists* clause. Essentially, an *anti-join* is a type of subquery where any rows found in the subquery are explicitly not included in the result set.

Internally, an *anti-join* returns rows from the left side of the predicate, the outer query, for which there is no corresponding row on the right side of the predicate.

The following is a simple anti-join, a *not in*, non-correlated subquery to display authors who have not yet written a book:

```
select
   author_last_name
from
   author
where
   author_key not in
       (select author_key from book_author);
```

This same query can also be specified with an anti-join that uses the *not exists* operator:

```
select
   author_last_name
from
   author a
where not exists
   (select 1 from book_author ba
   where ba.author_key = a.author_key);
```

The following is the execution plan for this anti-join. When there is a query within a query, the subquery is treated as a separate query, and the results are then passed to the outer query. The optimizer recognizes that there is no *where* clause for this subquery and properly invokes a full-table scan because all of the rows in both tables are required to satisfy the query.

Note that the two equivalent anti-joins have identical execution plans:

```
-------------------------------------------------------------------------
| Id | Operation          | Name        | Rows | Bytes | Cost (%CPU)| Time     |
-------------------------------------------------------------------------
|  0 | SELECT STATEMENT   |             |    2 |    34 |    3   (0)| 00:00:01 |
|  1 |  NESTED LOOPS ANTI |             |    2 |    34 |    3   (0)| 00:00:01 |
|  2 |   TABLE ACCESS FULL| AUTHOR      |   10 |   120 |    2   (0)| 00:00:01 |
|* 3 |   INDEX RANGE SCAN | SYS_C004000 |   20 |   100 |    1   (0)| 00:00:01 |
-------------------------------------------------------------------------
```

It is interesting to note that an anti-join has many equivalent forms, each returning the exact same results, but with vastly different execution plans and run-time performance.

Beware of anti-join equivalents!

In some cases, a *not in* or *not exists* anti-join can be rewritten to use an outer join with a *not null* test or an *in* subquery with the *minus* operator.

For example, each of the queries below are equivalent to the anti-join examples from above.

Note the very different execution plans for these equivalent forms of anti-join queries:

```
--********************************************
--   Outer join
--********************************************

select
   author_last_name
from
   author          a
full outer join
   book_author     ba
on
   a.author_key = ba.author_key
where
   royalty is NULL;
```

Id	Operation	Name	Rows	Bytes	Cost (%CPU)	Time
0	SELECT STATEMENT		26	572	6 (0)	00:00:01
1	VIEW		26	572	6 (0)	00:00:01
2	UNION-ALL					
* 3	FILTER					
4	NESTED LOOPS OUTER		25	1225	4 (0)	00:00:01
5	TABLE ACCESS FULL	AUTHOR	10	360	2 (0)	00:00:01
6	TABLE ACCESS BY INDEX ROWID	BOOK_AUTHOR	3	39	2 (0)	00:00:01
* 7	INDEX RANGE SCAN	SYS_C004000	3		1 (0)	00:00:01
8	NESTED LOOPS ANTI		1	13	2 (0)	00:00:01
* 9	TABLE ACCESS FULL	BOOK_AUTHOR	1	8	2 (0)	00:00:01
* 10	INDEX UNIQUE SCAN	SYS_C003994	10	50	0 (0)	00:00:01

```
--********************************************
--   IN with minus
--********************************************

select
   author_last_name
from
```

```
   author
where
   author_key in
       (select author_key from author minus select author_key from
book_author);
```

```
---------------------------------------------------------------------------
| Id  | Operation                    | Name        | Rows | Bytes | Cost (%CPU)| Time     |
---------------------------------------------------------------------------
|   0 | SELECT STATEMENT             |             |   10 |   190 |    5  (40)| 00:00:01 |
|   1 |  NESTED LOOPS                |             |   10 |   190 |    5  (40)| 00:00:01 |
|   2 |   VIEW                       | VW_NSO_1    |   10 |    70 |    4  (50)| 00:00:01 |
|   3 |    MINUS                     |             |      |       |           |          |
|   4 |     SORT UNIQUE              |             |   10 |    50 |           |          |
|   5 |      INDEX FULL SCAN         | SYS_C003994 |   10 |    50 |    1   (0)| 00:00:01 |
|   6 |     SORT UNIQUE              |             |   25 |   125 |           |          |
|   7 |      INDEX FULL SCAN         | SYS_C004000 |   25 |   125 |    1   (0)| 00:00:01 |
|   8 |   TABLE ACCESS BY INDEX ROWID| AUTHOR      |    1 |    12 |    1   (0)| 00:00:01 |
|*  9 |    INDEX UNIQUE SCAN         | SYS_C003994 |    1 |       |    0   (0)| 00:00:01 |
---------------------------------------------------------------------------
```

The Oracle Semi-Join

A semi-join is a SQL query that uses *exists* clause, a special type of join that omits duplicate rows in the subquery. The following simple example shows the use of the *exists* clause with a subquery to show all books that have had sales.

```
select
   book_key
from
   book
where
   exists (select book_key from sales);
```

These types of join are called semi-joins because they are not full joins and there is not a one-for-one match in the joined table rows.

Note that the number of rows in the *exists* subquery does not change the number of rows processes in the outer query. In other words, even if a book has 100 rows in the *sales* table, only one match will appear in the outer query. The entire subquery is processed first, and the results are then passed back to the outer query.

If the purpose of this semi join is to display all books that have had sales, it is clear that this query could be written in many other ways. This same query could be written with the *in* clause and also with a standard join.

```
--*************************************************
-- Two equivalent forms of an "exists" semi-join
--*************************************************

select
   book_key
from
   book
```

```
where
    book_key in
        (select book_key from sales)
;

select distinct
    book_key
from
    book  b,
    sales s
where
    b.book_key = s.book_key;
```

The Oracle optimizer takes into consideration that there are many ways to write a semi-join using the *exists* clause, and depending on the release level in use, Oracle may rewrite a query automatically to use a more efficient form. This "query rewrite" mechanism is much the same as when Oracle re-writes queries to use materialized views.

Prior to Oracle10g, there was a bug that caused a huge execution difference between *exists* and *in*. Starting in 10g release 2, Oracle will automatically rewrite an *in* subquery to use the *exists* clause.

Hot Tip!

Rewrite *exists* semi-joins!

It is often possible to rewrite *exists* subqueries with a standard join using the select distinct to remove duplicate rows.

By now, your head is probably swimming with the plethora of ways to select data from tables. But wait, there's more! The next section will cover even more SQL options, those introduced by the ISO SQL 99 standard.

Oracle ISO 99 Table Syntax

Starting back in version 9i, Oracle has made some important enhancements to include support for the ISO 99 SQL standard. As implemented by Oracle, this includes the following new table join syntax:

- **Cross join**: This is a join that creates a Cartesian product of the rows in both tables, just like in a standard join when the *where* clause does not specify the join criteria for many tables.

- **Natural join**: This is a useful Oracle syntax feature that improves the readability of SQL by removing join criteria from the *where* clause.

- **The *using* clause**: This allows the user to specify the join key by name.

- **The *on* clause**: This syntax allows the user to specify the column names for join keys in both tables.

- **Left outer join**: This returns all the rows from the table on the left side of the join, along with the values from the right-hand side or nulls if a matching row does not exist.

- **Right outer join**: This returns all the rows from the table on the right side of the join, along with the values from the left-hand side or nulls if a matching row does not exist.

- **Full outer join**: This returns all rows from both tables, filling in any blanks with nulls. There is no equivalent for this in Oracle8i.

Most of these enhancements were introduced to allow non-Oracle applications to quickly port onto an Oracle database, and it is important to remember that these are just syntax differences.

The ISO 99 standard does not bring any new functionality to Oracle SQL, it just adds new syntax. The following section will cover the cross join, something that is only useful in super-rare cases. This join should send up alarm signals.

The *cross* join

In Oracle, the *cross* join syntax produces a Cartesian product, very much the same as forgetting to add a *where* clause when joining two tables:

```
select
   last_name,
   dept_id
from
   emp,
   dept;
```

In Oracle9i and beyond, the *cross join* syntax can be used to achieve the same Cartesian product of the rows from both tables:

```
select
   last_name,
   dept_id
from
   emp
cross join
   dept;
```

A *cross* join computes the cartesian product of all rows from the one table to the rows of the other table. The cross join is an extremely poor choice and is rarely if ever used because of the Cartesian product. For example, if you were to join a 1,000 row table with a 5,000 row table, the result set would be 5,000,000 rows, far too large to have any practical use, except for the rare exception noted below, using the *with* clause.

Cross joins are usually errors!

The *cross* join is normally seen when the developer forgets to include the join criteria for several tables, and it is almost always an error.

The following example shows the cross join because the user has forgotten to specify a *where* clause to join the *dept* table with itself, thereby producing a cartesian product of all possible combinations of values:

```
select
    d1.dname,
    d2.dname
from
    dept d1,
    dept d2;
```

```
DNAME            DNAME
--------------   --------------
ACCOUNTING       ACCOUNTING
ACCOUNTING       OPERATIONS
ACCOUNTING       RESEARCH
ACCOUNTING       SALES
OPERATIONS       ACCOUNTING
OPERATIONS       RESEARCH
OPERATIONS       SALES
RESEARCH         ACCOUNTING
RESEARCH         RESEARCH
RESEARCH         SALES
SALES            ACCOUNTING
SALES            OPERATIONS
SALES            RESEARCH
SALES            SALES
```

Id	Operation	Name	Rows	Bytes	Cost (%CPU)	Time
0	SELECT STATEMENT		16	320	5 (0)	00:00:01
1	MERGE JOIN CARTESIAN		16	320	5 (0)	00:00:01
2	TABLE ACCESS FULL	DEPT	4	40	2 (0)	00:00:01
3	BUFFER SORT		4	40	3 (0)	00:00:01
4	TABLE ACCESS FULL	DEPT	4	40	1 (0)	00:00:01

The following example shows one of the very rare cases where a cartesian product might be useful. For specialized queries like this one, the *cross* join can be useful when combined with other joins:

```
with
   jobs
as
(
   select
   distinct
      job
   from
      emp
)
select
   jobs.job,
   dept.deptno,
   count(emp.empno)
from
   emp
right join
(
   jobs
cross join
   dept
)
on
(
   jobs.job=emp.job
   and
   dept.deptno=emp.deptno
)
group by
   jobs.job,
   dept.deptno;
```

JOB	DEPTNO	COUNT(EMP.EMPNO)
ANALYST	10	0
ANALYST	20	2
ANALYST	30	0
ANALYST	40	0
CLERK	10	1
CLERK	20	2
CLERK	30	1
CLERK	40	0
MANAGER	10	1
MANAGER	20	1
MANAGER	30	1
MANAGER	40	0
PRESIDENT	10	1
PRESIDENT	20	0
PRESIDENT	30	0
PRESIDENT	40	0
SALESMAN	10	0
SALESMAN	20	0
SALESMAN	30	4
SALESMAN	40	0

```
-----------------------------------------------------------------------
| Id  | Operation       | Name   | Rows  | Bytes | Cost (%CPU)| Time   |
-----------------------------------------------------------------------
```

Oracle ISO 99 Table Syntax

205

```
|   0 | SELECT STATEMENT        |         |   | 15 |  555 | 10  (30) | 00:00:01 |
|   1 |  HASH GROUP BY          |         |   | 15 |  555 | 10  (30) | 00:00:01 |
|*  2 |   HASH JOIN OUTER       |         |   | 20 |  740 |  9  (23) | 00:00:01 |
|   3 |    VIEW                 |         |   | 20 |  440 |  6  (17) | 00:00:01 |
|   4 |     MERGE JOIN CARTESIAN|         |   | 20 |  180 |  6  (17) | 00:00:01 |
|   5 |      VIEW               |         |   |  5 |   30 |  3  (34) | 00:00:01 |
|   6 |       HASH UNIQUE       |         |   |  5 |   40 |  3  (34) | 00:00:01 |
|   7 |        TABLE ACCESS FULL| EMP     |   | 14 |  112 |  2   (0) | 00:00:01 |
|   8 |      BUFFER SORT        |         |   |  4 |   12 |  6  (17) | 00:00:01 |
|   9 |       INDEX FAST FULL SCAN| PK_DEPT |  |  4 |   12 |  1   (0) | 00:00:01 |
|  10 |    TABLE ACCESS FULL    | EMP     |   | 14 |  210 |  2   (0) | 00:00:01 |

  2 - access("DEPT"."DEPTNO"="EMP"."DEPTNO"(+) AND
             "JOBS"."JOB"="EMP"."JOB"(+))
```

To understand the performance problems caused by Cartesian joins, consider this query that has an execution cost of 18 quadrillion!

```
select
    *
from
    dba_objects,
    dba_users,
    dba_tab_columns,
    dba_indexes,
    dba_tables,
    dba_tablespaces,
    dba_segments;
```

```
Execution Plan
--------------------------------------------------------

--------------------------------------------------------
| Id | Operation       | Name  | Rows | Bytes | Cost (%CPU)
--------------------------------------------------------
|  0 | SELECT STATEMENT |      |  18E |  15E |   939P  (32)
```

Running this query might consume computing resources for many hours, a huge waste of scarce processing cycles. The next section will cover the natural join.

The *natural join*

The natural join is a SQL-99 standard whereby the tables are joined without specifying the criteria in the *where* clause:

```
select
    stuff
from
    emp
natural join
    dept;
```

Functionally, the natural join is great because the where clause will only contain actual filtering conditions, making the SQL easier to understand and maintain.

I like the *natural join* because it removes the join clutter in the *where* clause so that the *where* clause only contains the actual filtering conditions for the final rowset.

Of course, the use of *natural* join requires that both columns have identical names in each table. It is interesting to note that this feature works even without primary or foreign key referential integrity.

Oracle8i:

```
select
    book_title,
    sum(quantity)
from
    book,
    sales
where
    book.book_id = sales.book_id
group by
    book_title;
```

Oracle9i and beyond:

```
select
    book_title,
    sum(quantity)
from
    book
natural join
    sales
group by book_title;
```

The *natural join* simplifies Oracle SQL because the *where* clause will only contain filtering predicates, making the SQL easier to read and maintain.

The *using* Clause

The *using* clause is used if several columns share the same name but the goal is not to join using all of these common columns. The columns listed in the *using* clause cannot have any qualifiers in the statement, including the *where* clause:

```
select
    dept_id,
    city
from
    departments,
    locations
where
    departments.location_id = location.location_id;
```

In Oracle9i and beyond, the *using* clause can be invoked as follows:

```
select
   department_name,
   city
from
   departments
join
   locations
using (location_id);
```

The *on* Clause

The *on* clause is used to join tables where the column names do not match in both tables. The join conditions are removed from the filter conditions in the *where* clause:

Oracle8i:

```
select
   department_name,
   city
from
   department,
   location
where
   department.location_id = location.loc_id;
```

In Oracle9i and beyond, the *on* clause can be invoked:

```
select
   department_name,
   city
from
   department d
join
   location l
on
   (d.location_id = l.loc_id);
```

Oracle Mutable Joins

Mutable joins are those where more than two tables are joined. The ISO SQL 1999 standard always assumes the tables are joined from the left to the right, with the join conditions only being able to reference columns relating to the current join and any previous joins to the left:

Oracle8i:

```
select
   emp_id,
   city_name,
```

```
   dept_name
from
   location l,
   department d,
   emp e
where
   d.location_id = l.location_id
and
   d.department_id = e.department_id;
```

In Oracle9i and beyond, a mutable join can be used:

```
select
   emp_id,
   city_name,
   dept_name
from
   locations l
join
   departments d
on
   (d.location_id = l.location_id)
join
   employees e
on
   (d.department_id = e.department_id);
```

ISO 99 *outer* join Syntax

The ISO 99 standard removes the onerous plus sign (+) from Oracle outer joins and makes outer join SQL easier to understand.

Left Outer Join

In a left outer join, all rows in the left-hand table are returned, even if there is no matching column in the joined tables. In this example, all employee last names are returned, even those employees who are not yet assigned to a department:

```
select
   last_name,
   d.department_id
from
   emp  e,
   dept d
where
   e.department_id = d.department_id(+);
```

In Oracle9i and beyond, the left outer join is supported:

```
select
   last_name,
```

```
    d.department_id
from
    emp e
left outer join
    dept d
on
    e.department_id = d.department_id;
```

Right Outer Join

In a right outer join, all rows in the right-hand table are returned, even if there is no matching column in the joined tables. In this example, all department IDs are returned, even for those departments without any employees:

```
select
    last_name,
    d.department_id
from
    employees e,
    departments d
where
    e.department_id(+) = d.department_id;
```

In Oracle9i and beyond, a right outer join can be used:

```
select
    last_name,
    d.department_id
from
    employees e
right outer join
    departments d
on
    (e.department_id = d.department_id);
```

The ISO 99 standard is another example of Oracle's commitment to enhancing its implementation of SQL. The most popular of these enhancements will be the *natural* join, which simplifies SQL syntax, and the *left outer* join and *right outer* join, which eliminate the need for the clumsy (+) syntax.

Starting with Oracle9i, the confusing outer join syntax using the (+) notation has been superseded by ISO 99 outer join syntax. There are three types of outer joins; left, right and full outer joins. The purpose of an outer join is to include non-matching rows, and the outer join returns these missing columns as NULL values. The following examples illustrate the syntax differences between these variations in join syntax:

Left outer join: Oracle8i

```
select
   last_name,
   department_name
from
   employees e,
   departments d
where
   e.department_id = d.department_id(+);
```

Left outer join: Oracle9i

```
select
   last_name,
   department_name
from
   employees e
left outer join
   departments d
on
   e.department_id = d.department_id;
```

Now it is time to move on and look at a non-traditional table type, external tables, and see how SQL is optimized for querying data outside Oracle.

When queries are written using logical join techniques, the Oracle optimizer uses a different set of algorithms for executing the joins.

Oracle Internal Machinations for SQL

Oracle has invested zillions of dollars in the cost-based optimizer (CBO), and it is legitimately ranked among the world's most sophisticated software programs.

The following code will return different internal operations for processing SQL statements within Oracle:

```
select distinct
   operation   c1,
   options     c2
from
   dba_hist_sql_plan
order by c1, c2;
```

The results of this query reveal many of Oracle's execution plan options:

```
Oracle                     Oracle
Operation                  option
------------------------   ------------------------
BUFFER                     SORT
COLLECTION ITERATOR        PICKLER FETCH
CONCATENATION
```

CONNECT BY	WITH FILTERING
CONNECT BY PUMP	
COUNT	STOPKEY
COUNT	
CREATE TABLE STATEMENT	
DDL STATEMENT	
DELETE	
DELETE STATEMENT	
FAST DUAL	
FILTER	
FIRST ROW	
FIXED TABLE	FIXED INDEX
FIXED TABLE	FULL
FOR UPDATE	
HASH	GROUP BY
HASH	UNIQUE
HASH JOIN	OUTER
HASH JOIN	RIGHT ANTI
HASH JOIN	RIGHT OUTER
HASH JOIN	SEMI
HASH JOIN	
INDEX	FULL SCAN
INDEX	RANGE SCAN
INDEX	RANGE SCAN (MIN/MAX)
INDEX	SKIP SCAN
INDEX	UNIQUE SCAN
INLIST ITERATOR	
INSERT STATEMENT	
LOAD AS SELECT	
MERGE	
MERGE JOIN	CARTESIAN
MERGE JOIN	OUTER
MERGE JOIN	
MERGE STATEMENT	
MINUS	
NESTED LOOPS	ANTI
NESTED LOOPS	OUTER
NESTED LOOPS	
PARTITION RANGE	ALL
PARTITION RANGE	ITERATOR
PARTITION RANGE	SINGLE
SELECT STATEMENT	
SEQUENCE	
SORT	AGGREGATE
SORT	GROUP BY
SORT	GROUP BY NOSORT
SORT	JOIN
SORT	ORDER BY
SORT	ORDER BY STOPKEY
SORT	UNIQUE
TABLE ACCESS	BY INDEX ROWID
TABLE ACCESS	BY LOCAL INDEX ROWID
TABLE ACCESS	BY USER ROWID
TABLE ACCESS	CLUSTER
TABLE ACCESS	FULL
TABLE ACCESS	SAMPLE
TEMP TABLE TRANSFORMATION	
UNION-ALL	PARTITION
UNION-ALL	

```
UPDATE
UPDATE STATEMENT
VIEW
WINDOW                          SORT
```

There is a vast array of internal algorithms including several types of nested loops and merge joins, plus six types of hash joins. There are also numerous data access methods, including many types of internal sorts and table access methods. The following section will start by covering the main Oracle table join types.

Oracle Physical Join Types

When examining an execution plan for a SQL statement, there may be the physical join implementations, with names like *nested loops*, *sort merge* and *hash join*.

The following section provides a quick look at these physical join types.

The *sort merge* join

The sort merge join is one of the oldest physical join types, and it is frequently seen when a SQL statement specifies a join on columns that do not possess an index.

```
select /*+ first_rows_10 */
    ename,
    dname
from
    dept,
    emp
where
    emp.deptno = dept.deptno
and
    emp.deptno = 10
;
```

Here is the execution plan, showing the full scans and the subsequent sort operation:

```
OPERATION
-------------------------------------------------------------------
OPTIONS                     OBJECT_NAME               POSITION
-------------------------    ------------------------   ----------
SELECT STATEMENT
  MERGE JOIN
                                                           1
    SORT
JOIN                                                       1
      TABLE ACCESS
FULL                         EMP                           1
    SORT
JOIN                                                       2
      TABLE ACCESS
FULL                         DEPT                          1
```

In this case, Oracle must perform expensive full-table scans against both tables, sort the results and then deliver back the matching rows as shown in Figure 4.3:

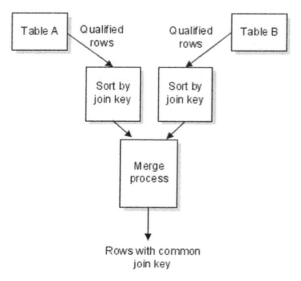

Figure 4.3: *A sort merge join*

However, a merge join is not always a bad plan. Sometimes performing a full-table scan and a back-end sort is preferable because it uses less computing resources than index access. This is congruent with the *all_rows* optimizer mode where the goal is not the fastest response time but to minimize computing resources. A sort merge join is frequently used in data warehouses where the full-scan operations are parallelized for fast access to both tables.

In the following example, a parallel query is run against a 64 CPU server, hence *parallel degree* of *cpu_count*-1, and force the sort merge join with the *use_merge* hint:

```
select /*+ use_merge(e,b) parallel(e, 63) parallel(b, 63) */
   e.ename,
   hiredate,
   b.comm
from
   emp e,
   bonus b
where
   e.ename = b.ename;
```

The execution plan for this sort merge join is included below. Note that the logical equi-join in the *where* clause *(where e.ename = b.ename)* does not produce a common *nested loops* or *hash* join because of the *use_merge* hint. Also, the *parallel* hint tells the

Oracle optimizer to bypass indexes and invoke parallel full-table scans against both tables.

```
OPERATION
-----------------------------------------------------------------
OPTIONS                      OBJECT_NAME                POSITION
---------------------------  -------------------------  ---------
  SELECT STATEMENT
                                                            5
   MERGE JOIN
                                                            1
PARALLEL_TO_SERIAL
     SORT
JOIN                                                        1
PARALLEL_COMBINED_WITH_PARENT
       TABLE ACCESS
FULL                         EMP                           1
PARALLEL_TO_PARALLEL

     SORT
JOIN                                                        2
PARALLEL_COMBINED_WITH_PARENT
       TABLE ACCESS
FULL                         BONUS                         1
PARALLEL_TO_PARALLEL
```

The optimizer may invoke a sort merge join under the following circumstances:

- When no indexes exist to join the table columns and the *hash_area_size* or *pga_aggregate_target* does not offer enough RAM for a *hash* join.

- When the optimizer cardinality estimates indicate that the SQL will require visiting the majority of data blocks from both tables.

- When the *all_rows optimizer_mode* determines that a full-table scan is less resource intensive than an index access

Because a sort merge join often indicates a problem, such as missing join criteria of a missing index, SQL tuning professionals run specialized scripts to see when these join types occur.

Again, a sort merge join may indicate missing indexes, a good clue when performing SQL tuning.

🖫 find_merge_joins.sql

```
col c1 heading 'Date'               format a20
col c2 heading 'Hash|Join|Count'    format 99,999,999
col c3 heading 'Rows|Processed'     format 99,999,999
col c4 heading 'Disk|Reads'         format 99,999,999
col c5 heading 'CPU|Time'           format 99,999,999


ttitle 'Merge Joins over time'

select
  to_char(
```

```
     sn.begin_interval_time,
     'yy-mm-dd hh24'
  )                                       snap_time,
  count(*)                                ct,
  sum(st.rows_processed_delta)            row_ct,
  sum(st.disk_reads_delta)                disk,
  sum(st.cpu_time_delta)                  cpu
from
   dba_hist_snapshot      sn,
   dba_hist_sqlstat       st,
   dba_hist_sql_plan      sp
where
-- Additional cost licenses are required to access the dba_hist tables.
   st.snap_id = sn.snap_id
and
   st.dbid = sn.dbid
and
   st.instance_number = sn.instance_number
and
   sp.sql_id = st.sql_id
and
   sp.dbid = st.dbid
and
   sp.plan_hash_value = st.plan_hash_value
and
   sp.operation = 'MERGE JOIN'
group by
   to_char(sn.begin_interval_time,'yy-mm-dd hh24');
```

The sort merge join can be the best execution plan for batch oriented queries that are tuned to minimize server resources. Hence, OLTP and transaction-oriented systems should always be on the lookout for *sort merge* joins.   Now let's examine *nested loops* joins.

Oracle *nested loops* joins

The *nested loops* table join is one of the original table join plans and it remains the most common. In a *nested loops* join, we have two tables a driving table and a secondary table.

The rows are usually accessed from a driving table *index range scan*, and the driving table result set is then nested within a probe of the second table, normally using an *index range scan* method.

To see how nested loops works, consider this theoretical query:

```
select
   employee_name,
   department_name
from
```

```
   employees    e,
   departments d
where
   e.department_id = d.department_id;
```

Here we see that we are doing a standard equi-join. If we assume that we have the standard primary-key, foreign-key relationship for *department_id* (i..e an index on these columns, then Oracle may choose a *nested loops* approach to join this table, performing a full-scan on the department table (the driving table), and looping through the *emp.dept_ix* to access the matching rows in the employee table.

```
for each department loop
   for each employee in that department loop
     show employees in department
   end loop
end loop
```

We can re-write this pseudocode in PL/SQL to see the nested loop structure:

```
begin
   for deptrow in
    (select department_id, department_name from departments) loop
     for emprow in
        (select employee_name from employees where department_id =
        deptrow.department_id) loop
           dbms_output.put_line(emprow.employee_name || ' - ' ||
           deptrow.department_name);
     end loop;
   end loop;
end;
/
```

As a review, nested loop joins are the most common method for Oracle to match rows in multiple tables. Nested loop joins always invoke an index and hence, they cannot be parallelized.

Driving table and nested loops

When performing a *nested loops* join, the SQL optimizer will always make the smallest table the driving table, or a table without an index.

While the *nested loops* table join method is very common, it cannot scale as well as *hash* joins and *sort merge* joins because it cannot be parallelized. On large SMP servers with 32 or 64 processors, the full-scans that occur in *hash* joins and *sort merge* joins can be parallelized, up to the number of processors-1, for super-fast full scan operations.

However, most online transactions only retrieve a tiny percentage of the table rows, the optimizer rightfully chooses to invoke the *nested loops* join method for OLTP queries.

Next, let's see what happens when the SQL optimizer fails to generate nested loops joins.

When the optimizer fails to choose nested loops joins

When tuning SQL we must always remember that the optimizer can sometimes fail to choose the "best" table join method. This is especially true for cases where a *hash* join is wrongly chosen over *nested loops*.

This is frequently the case when we have sub-optimal schema statistics (especially column histograms) can lead to cases where the optimizer makes an incorrect guess about the cardinality of a result set and wrongly invokes a join that requires a full-table scan, not choosing nested loops. For example, consider this query:

```
select
   sales_stuff
from
   sales
natural join
   stores
where
   state = 'idaho';
```

If we assume that Idaho has less than 1% of the rows in the sales table, we would want to force the optimizer to invoke a *nested loops* join, so that we may use an index for the join. This can be accomplished in several ways:

- **Analyze a column histogram on the *state* column**: This will address the root cause of the issue since the optimizer will now recognize that Idaho is a low cardinality query.

- **Use a hint**: Hints are a last resort because of unintended side-effects, but the *use_nl_with_index* hint can be used to force the query to choose a nested loops join method.

- **Invoke dynamic sampling**: The *opt_estimate* hint or the *dynamic_sampling* hint can be used to force the *nested loops* join:

```
-- *****************************************
-- Nested loops hint
-- *****************************************
select /*+ use_nl_with_index */
```

```
      sales_stuff
from
      sales
natural join
      stores
where
      state = 'idaho';

--************************************
-- Dynamic sampling
--************************************
select /*+ dynamic_sampling(sales,10)
      sales_stuff
from
      sales
natural join
      stores
where
      state = 'idaho';

--************************************
-- opt_estimate hint
--************************************
select /*+ opt_estimate(table,sales,scale_rows=.001)
      sales_stuff
from
      sales
natural join
      stores
where
      state = 'idaho';
```

Be careful with the *use_nl* hint!

Using the *use_nl* hint can force a query to use a *nested loops* join, but the use of join hints can create a problem, especially with nested loops indexes which reply on indexes.

If the index were dropped, the result would be a horrific join plan. To alleviate this issue, the *use_nl_with_index* hint can be used. This hint will only direct a *nested loops* join if the suitable index is present. The next section will cover how to do holistic SQL tuning by tracking the nested loop joins.

Tracking SQL Nested Loop Joins

A competent SQL tuning expert will track the characteristics of their SQL workloads, and they always track the various join types over time. The following *awr_nested_join_alert.sql* script to count nested loop joins per hour.

This script will only track SQL that Oracle has been directed to capture via threshold settings in AWR or STATSPACK, and STATSPACK and AWR will not collect transient SQL that did not appear in *v$sql* at snapshot time. Hence, not all SQL will appear in these reports.

🖫 **awr_nested_join_alert.sql**

```
col c1 heading 'Date'                  format a20
col c2 heading 'Nested|Loops|Count'    format 99,999,999
col c3 heading 'Rows|Processed'        format 99,999,999
col c4 heading 'Disk|Reads'            format 99,999,999
col c5 heading 'CPU|Time'              format 99,999,999

accept nested_thr char prompt 'Enter Nested Join Threshold: '

ttitle 'Nested Join Threshold|&nested_thr'

select
  to_char(
    sn.begin_interval_time,
    'yy-mm-dd hh24'
  )                                    snap_time,
  count(*)                             ct,
  sum(st.rows_processed_delta)         row_ct,
  sum(st.disk_reads_delta)             disk,
  sum(st.cpu_time_delta)               cpu
from
  dba_hist_snapshot    sn,
  dba_hist_sqlstat     st,
  dba_hist_sql_plan    sp
-- make sure that you are licensed to read the AWR tables
where
  st.snap_id = sn.snap_id
and
  st.dbid = sn.dbid
and
  st.instance_number = sn.instance_number
and
  sp.sql_id = st.sql_id
and
  sp.dbid = st.dbid
and
  sp.plan_hash_value = st.plan_hash_value
and
  sp.operation = 'NESTED LOOPS'
group by
  to_char(sn.begin_interval_time,'yy-mm-dd hh24')
having
      count(*) > &nested_thr;
```

The output below shows the number of total nested loop joins during the snapshot period along with a count of the rows processed and the associated disk I/O. This report is useful where the DBA wants to know if increasing pga_aggregate_target will improve performance.

```
                 Nested Loop Join Thresholds

              Nested
              Loops        Rows         Disk        CPU
Date          Count     Processed      Reads        Time
-----------   ------    ----------   ----------   ----------
04-10-10 16      22          750          796    4,017,301
04-10-10 17      25          846            6    3,903,560
04-10-10 19      26          751        1,430    4,165,270
04-10-10 20      24          920            3    3,940,002
04-10-10 21      25          782            5    3,816,152
04-10-11 02      26          905            0    3,935,547
04-10-11 03      22        1,001            0    3,918,891
```

Now that nested loops joins have been covered, it is time to look at the second most common physical join type, the hash join.

The Oracle *hash* Join

The *hash* join was introduced in Oracle7 release 3 as a new physical table join option that was ideally suited to cases where a small table is joined to a large table. In a *hash* join, the Oracle database does a full-scan of the driving table, builds a RAM hash table, and then probes for matching rows in the other table. For certain types of SQL, the hash join will execute faster than a nested loop join, but the *hash* join uses more RAM resources.

The propensity of the SQL optimizer to invoke a hash join is heavily controlled by the setting for the *hash_area_size* and *pga_aggregate_target* Oracle parameter. The larger the value for *hash_area_size*, the more hash joins the optimizer will invoke. In some releases of Oracle, the *hash_area_size* defaults to double the value of the *sort_area_size* parameter, but it is highly dependent upon parameter settings and the release level. Here is how to see these values on your Oracle database:

```
SQL> show parameters area_size

NAME                                 TYPE        VALUE
-----------------------------------  ----------  -------------------
bitmap_merge_area_size               integer     1048576
create_bitmap_area_size              integer     8388608
hash_area_size                       integer     1048576
sort_area_size                       integer     524288
workarea_size_policy                 string      MANUAL
```

Pay special attention to the readings on sort operations, and see that Oracle first attempts to sort row results sets inside the RAM memory of the SGA or PGA. Sorting can occur whenever an SQL statement contains an order by or group by clause.

You control the hash joins in your system!

The DBA directly controls the invocation of hash joins by setting *hash_area_size* and *pga_aggregate_target* parameters. If they are too small, no hash joins occur.

If there is no room in the RAM memory region to sort the results set quickly, Oracle will go to the temporary tablespace and complete the sort operation using disk storage. The management of sorting is a very critical part of SQL tuning because RAM memory sorts are many thousands of times faster than sorts that have to be done inside the temporary table space.

The idea behind a hash join is to use PGA RAM to build an in-memory hash table from the smaller driving table. Rows in the RAM hash table are then used as build input row sources, providing the ROWID required to probe into the larger table as shown in Figure 4.4 below:

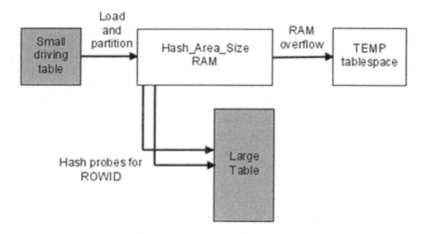

Figure 4.4: *The internals of an Oracle hash join*

Note that the hash join is highly dependent on the RAM that the DBA allocates to the PGA, and specifically, the *hash_area_size*. Ideally, the entire smaller table should fit into the RAM hash area, but it can be paged out to disk using the TEMP tablespace.

Know when to invoke hash joins!

As a rule of thumb, whenever the driving table will fit into the *hash_area_size ([pga_aggregate_target)* RAM, a hash join may run faster than a nested loops join.

One great feature of Oracle is the ability to see the amount of RAM used for different stages of SQL execution. The next section will cover a tool that can be used to see how much RAM is required by Oracle hash joins.

Displaying Hash RAM usage for execution plan steps

Oracle has the ability to display RAM memory usage along with execution plan information using the *v$sql_plan* view.

See the chapter 7 section *Viewing RAM usage for hash joins in SQL* for complete details and a script to reveal the RAM usage for the hash joins in any specific SQL statement.

The *v$sql_workarea* view can be queried to see memory usage for each step of an SQL execution plan, but it requires the address of the SQL statement:

```
select
   address
from
   v$sql
where
   sql_text like '%NEW_CUSTOMER%';
```

The resulting SQL address inside the SGA is:

```
88BB460C
```

Now that the SQL address has been identified, just plug the SQL address into the query below.

This query uses *v$sql_workarea* to see the RAM usage associated with each execution plan step:

```
select
   operation,
   options,
   object_name                     name,
   trunc(bytes/1024/1024)          "input(MB)",
   trunc(last_memory_used/1024)    last_mem,
   trunc(estimated_optimal_size/1024)  opt_mem,
   trunc(estimated_onepass_size/1024)  onepass_mem,
   decode(optimal_executions, null, null,
          optimal_executions||'/'||onepass_executions||'/'||
          multipasses_exections)    "O/1/M"
from
   v$sql_plan      p,
   v$sql_workarea  w
where
   p.address=w.address(+)
and
   p.hash_value=w.hash_value(+)
and
   p.id=w.operation_id(+)
and
   p.address='88BB460C';
```

Now, via *v$sql_workarea,* it is easy to see the memory usage associated with each execution plan step:

```
OPERATION      OPTIONS  NAME   input(MB) LAST_MEM OPT_MEM ONEPASS_MEM O/1/M
-----------    -------- ----   --------- -------- ------- ----------- ---
SELECT STATE
SORT           GROUP BY             4582       8      16          16 26/0/0
HASH JOIN      SEMI                 4582    5976    5194        2187 16/0/0
TABLE ACCESS   FULL     ORDERS        51
TABLE ACCESS   FULL     LINEITEM
```

The next section will cover how partitioning factors into the physical hash join.

Hash Partitioning and Hash Joining

Internally, a large hash join involves two steps, a partition phase and a join phase. In the partition phase, a large driving table, too big to fit into the hash area RAM, is segmented into partitions inside the TEMP tablespace.

Once the driving table is chunked into manageable pieces thehash join can treat each one independently. Because the last chunk must be completed before the query can end, partitioning the driving table into equal chunks is critical. Oracle relies on histogram statistics to guess the cardinality of the driving tables and uses secret bit-vector filtering techniques to partition the driving table for the hash join. A partition hash join is shown in Figure 4.5:

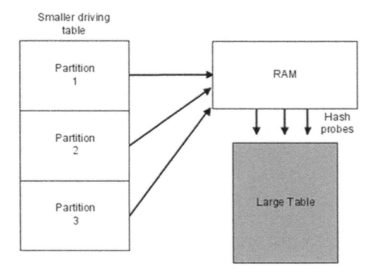

Figure 4.5: *A partitioned hash join*

After the partitioning is done, the hash table is built from the partitions. If the driving table is larger than the size of the hash memory available, the hash table overflow is dealt with by performing a *nested-loops hash join*.

Once the hash table is created, the join phase, which involves probing from the hash table into the other table to be joined, can be started.

The actual hash join is called a *grace* join where the ROWID values in the hash table are matched with the other table via a full-table scan.

Partitioned Outer Join

The partitioned outer join was first introduced in Oracle 10g and allows the use of *partition by* syntax to select the partition key of the outer table even where there are no matching rows in the other table:

```
select
   d.deptno,
   e.job,
   count(e.empno)
from
   emp e
partition by
   (e.job)
right join
   dept d
```

```
on
    (e.deptno=d.deptno)
group by
    d.deptno,
    e.job
order by
    d.deptno,
    e.job;
```

DEPTNO	JOB	COUNT(E.EMPNO)
10	ANALYST	0
10	CLERK	1
10	MANAGER	1
10	PRESIDENT	1
10	SALESMAN	0
20	ANALYST	2
20	CLERK	2
20	MANAGER	1
20	PRESIDENT	0
20	SALESMAN	0
30	ANALYST	0
30	CLERK	1
30	MANAGER	1
30	PRESIDENT	0
30	SALESMAN	4
40	ANALYST	0
40	CLERK	0
40	MANAGER	0
40	PRESIDENT	0
40	SALESMAN	0

Id	Operation	Name	Rows	Bytes	Cost (%CPU)	Time
0	SELECT STATEMENT		11	682	11 (28)	00:00:01
1	SORT GROUP BY		11	682	11 (28)	00:00:01
2	VIEW		20	1240	10 (20)	00:00:01
3	MERGE JOIN PARTITION OUTER		20	360	10 (20)	00:00:01
4	SORT JOIN		4	12	2 (50)	00:00:01
5	INDEX FULL SCAN	PK_DEPT	4	12	1 (0)	00:00:01
* 6	SORT PARTITION JOIN		14	210	3 (34)	00:00:01
7	TABLE ACCESS FULL	EMP	14	210	2 (0)	00:00:01

```
  6 - access("E"."DEPTNO"="D"."DEPTNO")
      filter("E"."DEPTNO"="D"."DEPTNO")
```

For each job of *emp* and for each department of *dept*, there will be a matching row. This looks like a cross join query, but it is much more efficient here because the employee table is selected only once. The job is a column of *emp* and is selected even when there is no matching row in *emp*. Only left and right partitioned joins are supported to date.

Now that the basics of hash joins have been covered, it is time to look at specific techniques for optimizing Oracle hash joins.

Tuning Oracle Hash Joins

As previously noted, the DBA has direct control over the propensity for the optimizer to choose a hash join, via the settings for *hash_area_size* and/or *pga_aggregate_target*. The following are some general tips for tuning hash joins:

- **Use lots of RAM**: To avoid disk partitioning of the hash table in the TEMP tablespace, it is important to ensure that the hash area in RAM is at least 1.6 times as large as the driving table.
- **Check column skew:** Check for an even distribution of values for the hash join key and if it is skewed, create a column histogram using *dbms_stats*.
- **Parallelize the full-table scans**: As typical Oracle servers have anywhere from 16 to 64 CPUs, the full-table scans can be parallelized for faster performance.
- **Try nested loops joins:** From the section on nested loops joins, recall that the optimizer may have stale statistics and invoke a *hash* join when a *nested loops* join is faster. Make sure to try the *use_nl_with_index* hint with set timing on to try both join types.

Look Out!

Hash Join tuning is tricky!

In some cases, no single task may consume more than 5% of the *pga_aggregate_target* region before the sort pages out to the TEMP tablespace for a disk sort.

The following script, *hash_area.sql,* can be used to dynamically allocate the proper *hash_area_size* for the SQL query in terms of the size of the target table.

🖫 hash_area.sql

```
set heading off;
set feedback off;
set verify off;
set pages 999;

spool run_hash.sql

select
   'alter session set hash_area_size='||trunc(sum(bytes)*1.6)||';'
from
   dba_segments
where
   segment_name = upper('&1');

spool off;
```

```
@run_hash
```

Below is the output from this script. The script above passes the driving table name as an argument and the script generates the appropriate alter session command to ensure that there is enough space in hash_area_size RAM to hold the driving table.

```
SQL> @hash_area customer

alter session set hash_area_size=3774873;
```

On large SMP servers with Oracle parallel query, it is also possible to use the parallel hint with a hash join to speed up the full-table scans that are involved in a hash join.

Always use the *parallel* hint!

When parallelizing full-table scans, always use the *parallel* hint, and avoid setting parallelism at the table or system level. This is because it will make the optimizer falsely chose full scans.

Parallelizing Hash Joins

Setting the degree of parallelism will dramatically speed up the full-table scans in large table hash joins, and the *use_hash* and *parallel* hints can be combined to improve join performance.

The *use_hash* hint directs the optimizer to invoke a hash join against the specified tables, and the parallel query has been manually specified:

```
select /*+ use_hash(e,b) parallel(e, 63) parallel(b, 63) */
   e.ename,
   hiredate,
   b.comm
from
   emp e,
   bonus b
where
   e.ename = b.ename;
```

Here is the execution plan for the hash join. Note that both tables in this join are using parallel query to obtain their rows.

```
OPERATION
- - - - - - - - - - - - - - - - - - - - - - - - - - - - - - - - - - - - - - - - - - - - - -
OPTIONS                        OBJECT_NAME              POSITION
- - - - - - - - - - - - - - - - - - - - - - - - - - - - - - - - - - - - - - - - - - - - - -
 SELECT STATEMENT
                                                               3
  HASH JOIN
                                                               1
 PARALLEL_TO_SERIAL
   TABLE ACCESS
 FULL                          EMP                             1
 PARALLEL_TO_PARALLEL
   TABLE ACCESS
 FULL                          BONUS                           2
```

Watch the high water mark!

Remember that full-table scans always run up to a table's high-water mark. If a table has lots of deleted rows, full scans will run faster after being coalesced and reorganized.

The next section covers a new physical join type in version 11g, the full hash join.

The Oracle 11g Full Hash Join

The new Oracle 11g *hash join full* execution plan uses RAM to create results that use less than 50% of the logical I/O (consistent gets) than a traditional full join.

A full hash join is used just like a standard full join, to join two tables together and include non-matching rows from each table, but the only difference is internal.

Instead of performing I/O to the temp tablespace, Oracle builds RAM structures in the PGA to perform the detailed internal processing faster than ordinary full joins as shown in Figure 4.6.

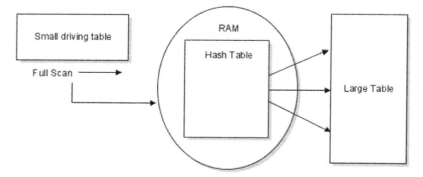

Figure 4:6: *A hash join uses RAM to speed up row matching*

In the example below, the desire is to include employees with departments as well as departments without employees. A full outer join retrieves rows from both tables, whether or not they have a matching row, and is used in cases where non-matching rows from both tables are needes. There are many ways to formulate a full join, and here is an example using the *with* clause:

```
with
    emp
as
(
    select
        'joel' ename,
        40 deptno
    from
        dual
    union all
    select
        'mary' ename,
        50 deptno
    from
        dual
)
select
    e.ename,
    d.dname
from
    emp e
full join
    dept d
using
(
    deptno
);


ENAM  DNAME
----  --------------
```

```
JOEL    OPERATIONS
MARY
        SALES
        RESEARCH
        ACCOUNTING
```

```
------------------------------------------------------------------------
| Id  | Operation            | Name    | Rows | Bytes | Cost (%CPU)| Time     |
------------------------------------------------------------------------
|   0 | SELECT STATEMENT     |         |    8 |   120 |    8  (13) | 00:00:01 |
|   1 |  VIEW                | VW_FOJ_0|    8 |   120 |    8  (13) | 00:00:01 |
| * 2 |   HASH JOIN FULL OUTER|        |    8 |   176 |    8  (13) | 00:00:01 |
|   3 |    VIEW              |         |    2 |    18 |    4   (0) | 00:00:01 |
|   4 |     UNION-ALL        |         |      |       |            |          |
|   5 |      FAST DUAL       |         |    1 |       |    2   (0) | 00:00:01 |
|   6 |      FAST DUAL       |         |    1 |       |    2   (0) | 00:00:01 |
|   7 |     TABLE ACCESS FULL| DEPT    |    4 |    52 |    3   (0) | 00:00:01 |
------------------------------------------------------------------------

Predicate Information (identified by operation id):
---------------------------------------------------

   2 - access("E"."DEPTNO"="D"."DEPTNO")
```

For more details on using the 11g full hash join, see chapter 7, "*RAM and SQL Tuning*". The following section will cover a technique for interrogating SQL table join methods.

Interrogating SQL Table Join Methods

The choice between a *hash* join and a *nested loops* join depends on several factors:

- The relative number of rows in each table

- The presence of indexes on the key values

- The settings for static parameters such as *index_caching* and *cpu_costing*

- The current setting and available memory in *pga_aggregate_target*

Hash joins do not use indexes and perform full-table scans often using parallel query. Hence, the use of hash joins with parallel full-table scans tend to drive up CPU consumption.

Also, PGA memory consumption becomes higher when hash joins are used, but if AMM is enabled, it is not usually a problem.

The following query produces a report alerting the DBA when hash join operations count exceeds some threshold:

💾 hash_join_alert.sql

```
col c1 heading 'Date'               format a20
col c2 heading 'Hash|Join|Count'    format 99,999,999
col c3 heading 'Rows|Processed'     format 99,999,999
```

```
col c4 heading 'Disk|Reads'           format 99,999,999
col c5 heading 'CPU|Time'             format 99,999,999


accept hash_thr char prompt 'Enter Hash Join Threshold: '

ttitle 'Hash Join Threshold|&hash_thr'

select
   to_char(sn.begin_interval_time,'yy-mm-dd hh24')   c1,
   count(*)                                          c2,
   sum(st.rows_processed_delta)                      c3,
   sum(st.disk_reads_delta)                          c4,
   sum(st.cpu_time_delta)                            c5
from
   dba_hist_snapshot sn,
   dba_hist_sql_plan  p,
   dba_hist_sqlstat   st
where
   st.sql_id = p.sql_id
and
   sn.snap_id = st.snap_id
and
   p.operation = 'HASH JOIN'
having
   count(*) > &hash_thr
group by
   begin_interval_time;
```

The sample output might look the following, showing the number of hash joins during the snapshot period along with the relative I/O and CPU associated with the processing.

The values for *rows_processed* are generally higher for hash joins which do full-table scans as opposed to nested loop joins with generally involved a very small set of returned rows.

Hash Join Thresholds

Date	Hash Join Count	Rows Processed	Disk Reads	CPU Time
04-10-12 17	22	4,646	887	39,990,515
04-10-13 16	25	2,128	827	54,746,653
04-10-14 11	21	17,368	3,049	77,297,578
04-10-21 15	60	2,805	3,299	5,041,064
04-10-22 10	25	6,864	941	4,077,524
04-10-22 13	31	11,261	2,950	46,207,733
04-10-25 16	35	46,269	1,504	6,364,414

Now that we have seen how Oracle chooses join types, it is time to explore how Oracle chooses the order in which to join tables.

Verifying optimal Join techniques

Some queries will perform faster with *nested loop*s joins, some with *hash* joins, while others favor sort-merge joins. It is difficult to predict what join technique will be fastest, so many Oracle tuning experts will test run the SQL with each different table join method. The optimizer has many join methods available including a merge join, a nested loop join, hash join and a star join. To choose the best join method, the optimizer must guess at the size of the intermediate result sets from multi-way table joins.

To make this guess, the optimizer has incomplete information. Even if histograms are present, the optimizer cannot know for certain the exact number of rows that will be returned from a join. The most common remedy is to use hints to change the join type (*use_nl, use_hash*), re-size *hash_area_size* or *pga_aggregate_target*, or re-analyze the statistics and histograms on the target tables.

Evaluating Oracle Physical Join Performance

While the sort merge join and the hash join are very similar in terms of function, the nested loops join is quite different from the other join techniques as shown in Table 4.1:

Join Type	Advantages	Sorting	Large Row Subsets
Sort merge join Hash join	Faster throughput	Yes	Fast
Nested loop join	Faster response time	No	Slow

Table 4.1: *The relative advantages of physical join types*

These goals may seem deceptively simple, but these tasks comprise 90 percent of SQL tuning, and they do not require a thorough understanding of the internals of Oracle SQL.

Of course, you can tune the SQL all you want, but if you do not feed the optimizer with the correct statistics, the optimizer may not make the correct decisions. It is important to ensure that statistics are present and that they are current.

Some believe in the practice of running statistics by schedule such as weekly, some believe in just calculating statistics when the data changes, still others believe that statistics are only run to fix a poor access path, and once things are good should not be touched. It is difficult to say who is correct.

Next, let's take a look at table join optimization.

Oracle Table Join Optimization

One of the most important jobs of the optimizer is determining the best order in which to join the tables together, and if the DBA has intimate knowledge of the data, it is possible to inspect the *where* clause of the query to infer the optimal join order.

When a query always has a fixed optimal join order, some developers will add an *ordered* or *leading* hint. The problem with forcing the sequence of table joins with the *ordered* hint is that it can be impossible to predict a priori the optimal table-join order, with optimal being the one that has the smallest intermediate baggage.

When large tables are joined and the result set is small, it is critical that Oracle know the number of rows in each table after the queries *where* clause is considered, and adding histograms to the join columns can help give the optimizer this information.

If the cardinality of the table is too-high, meaning the intermediate row sizes are larger than they have to be, then histograms on the most selective column in the *where* clause will tip off the optimizer and change the table join order.

Histograms are also used to predict cardinality and the number of rows returned, an important factor in determining the fastest table join order.

Consider a situation where there is a *vehicle_type* index and 65 percent of the values are for the CAR type, when a query with *where vehicle_type = 'CAR'* is specified, a full-table scan would be the fastest execution plan. However, a query with *where vehicle_type = 'TRUCK'* would be faster when using access via an index.

Reducing the size of the intermediate row-sets can greatly improve the speed of the query.

```
select
  stuff
```

```
from
  customer
natural join
  orders
natural join
  item
natural join
  product
where
  credit_rating * extended_credit > .07
and
  (qty_in_stock * velocity) /.075 < 30
or
  (sku_price / 47) * (qty_in_stock / velocity) > 47;
```

In this example, the four-way table join only returns 18 rows, but the query carries 9,000 rows in intermediate result sets, slowing-down the SQL execution speed as shown in Figure 4.7:

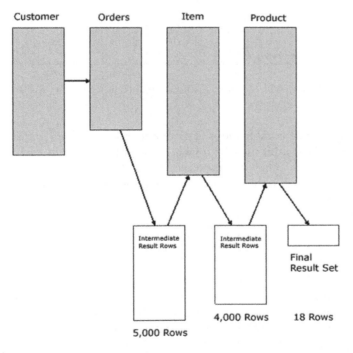

Figure 4.7: *Sub-optimal intermediate row sets*

If it were somehow possible to predict the sizes of the intermediate results, it would be possible to re-sequence the table-join order to carry less intermediate baggage during the four-way table join, in this example carrying only 3,000 intermediate rows between the table joins as shown in Figure 4.8:

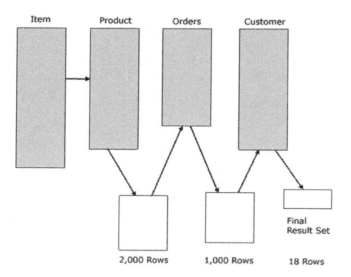

Figure 4.8: *Optimal intermediate row sets*

In Oracle, the number of possible paths a join can take is based on the number of tables participating in the join.

The raw number of possible combinations is determined using the n! (factorial) of the number of tables. For those a bit rusty with what a factorial is, basically each integer is taken up to "n" times each other, for example, 4!=(1*2*3*4) which is equal to 24. This does not seem too bad, until there are 8 and above tables. The value for 8! is 40,320 possible join paths.

The parameter for setting the maximum allowed number of paths for the optimizer to consider is *optimizer_max_permutations,* and it is set to 80,000 by default.

Changing the default value of the *optimizer_max_permutations* setting to a value less than the original setting results in join orders being evaluated first. For example just reducing the setting by one in 8i to 79,999 improves the consideration of join orders. In 9i and beyond, setting it to 1,999 has similar results. So this leads to the second tip: Set the *optimizer_max_permutations* parameter to slightly less than the default value to improve join order consideration.

Another parameter of interest is the *optimizer_search_limit.* The *optimizer_search_limit* parameter defaults to 5. If the number of tables returning more than a single row in the query is less than *optimizer_search_limit* then the full factorial number of possible joins will be used in determining the path.

If the number of tables returning more than a single row is greater than the *optimizer_search_limit* then Cartesian products are eliminated from the possible joins considered. Therefore the maximum number of joins considered for a given query with less than *optimizer_search_limit+1* of involved tables can be expressed by either the value of *optimizer_max_permutations* or the *optimizer_search_limit_factorial*, whichever is larger.

If the number of non-single row tables in a query is greater than *optimizer_search_limit*, then the maximum number of permutations to consider is the larger of:

```
(optimizer_max_permutations or optimizer_search_limit factorial)
-------------------------------------------------------------
(number of possible start tables + 1)
```

Usually the setting of the *optimizer_search_limit* is not touched. However, the setting of 5 for *optimizer_search_limit* is the default setting and it can be set to any integer value. It is unlikely that resetting this value will have much effect unless there is a significantly number of large joins such as in a DSS or data warehouse. If the star join is enabled, the *optimizer_search_limit* sets the threshold above which the STAR algorithm will be considered for tables joins.

In 10g and beyond both the optimizer_max_permutations and *optimizer_search_limit* are being deprecated and made into undocumented settings defaulting to 2000 and 5 respectively.

In the absence of column histograms, the Oracle CBO must be able to guess the result set size and it sometimes gets it wrong. This is one reason why the *ordered* hint is one of the most popular SQL tuning hints, because using the *ordered* hint allows the user to specify that the tables be joined together in the same order that they appear in the *from* clause, like this:

```
select /+ ORDERED */
   product_name
from
   item
natural join
   product
natural join
   orders
natural join
   customers;
```

Remember, if the values for the professor and course table columns are not skewed, it is unlikely that the 10g automatic statistics would have created histograms buckets in the *dba_histograms* view for these columns.

The Oracle CBO needs to be able to accurately estimate the final number of rows returned by each step of the query and then use schema metadata from running *dbms_stats* to choose the table join order that results in the least amount of baggage (intermediate rows) from each of the table join operations.

But this is a daunting task. When a SQL query has a complex *where* clause it can be very difficult to estimate the size of the intermediate result sets, especially when the *where* clause transforms column values with mathematical functions.

Optimal Table Join Order and Transitive Closure

One important technique in Oracle SQL tuning is ensuring that Oracle joins tables together in the proper order, a critical tuning task. One common techniques for tuning SQL is to add redundant SQL join conditions to give the SQL optimizer additional information about the nature of the query.

Formally, this is called transitive closure, the idea that given two equals, a third condition exists:

```
if a=b and a=c, therefore b=c
```

With this in mind, how does transitive closure apply to Oracle SQL and determining the optimal table join order? Consider the following query that joins three tables.

When joining two tables with the SQL99 natural join syntax, the where clause predicates are normally chained, indicating that a=b and b=c:

```
select *
from
   a,
   b,
   c
where
   a.id = b.id
and
   b.id = c.id;
```

Now, transitive closure dictates that when a=b and b=c that therefore a=c, and this predicate can be added to the SQL without changing the logic or the results:

```
select *
from
    a,
    b,
    c
where
    a.id = b.id
an
    b.id = c.id
and
    a.id = c.id;
```

It only makes sense that the more information given to the optimizer, the better the resulting decision. Plus, the Oracle 11g optimizer is not always conscious of transitive closure.

There are confirmed cases where adding the transitive closure rules result in the optimizer making better cardinality estimates and thereby choosing a better execution plan.

Add redundant join criteria!

When tuning complex n-way table joins, testing with redundant join criteria will give the CBO for cardinality information, sometimes resulting in better execution plans.

For complete coverage of transitive closure in Oracle SQL, see Vadim Tropashko's book *SQL Design Patterns*.

SQL Tuning with the *ordered* Hint

The ordered hint orders ensures that tables are joined in the order specified in the from clause, with the first table serving as the driving table. This hint is often used in cases where four or more tables need to be joined in a specific order, like when tuning data warehouse queries.

The ordered hint determines the driving table for the query execution and also specifies the order that tables are joined together. The ordered hint requests that the tables should be joined in the order that they are specified in the *from* clause, with the first table in the *from* clause specifying the driving table. Using the ordered hint can save a huge amount of parse time and speed SQL execution because the optimizer is given the best order to join the tables.

The *ordered* hint can save time and shorten the lengthy process of parsing SQL when doing large n-way table joins. These join operations can often take 30 minutes or more to parse SQL. For instance, an 8 table join requires Oracle to examine 40,320 (8!) potential join operations. Skilled DBAs can use the ordered hint to bypass this time-consuming SQL operation.

The following example query demonstrates how the *ordered* hint can join tables together in a specific order, as specified in the *from* clause.

This example requires that the tables be joined in a specific order (*emp, dept, sal, bonus*). The SQL also allows different join methods to be specified. In this example, *emp* and *dept* will be joined with a hash join, and *sal* and *bonus* will use a *nested loops* join, as specified below:

```
select /*+ ordered use_hash (emp, dept) use_nl (sal, bonus) */
from
    emp,
    dept,
    sal,
    bonus
where . . .
```

Of course, the *ordered* hint is most commonly used in data warehouse queries or in SQL that joins more than five tables.

SQL execution is dynamic, and tuning a SQL statement for the current data may not be optimal at a future date. The following section provides more information on tuning SQL with hints.

SQL Tuning with the *ordered_predicates* Hint

The next hint is the *ordered_predicates* hint. This hint is used in the *where* clause to direct the order that the Boolean predicates are evaluated. To better demonstrate how this hint is used, it is a good idea to review how the CBO typically evaluates SQL predicates. The three rules are as follows:

- Subqueries are evaluated before the outer Boolean conditions.

- Boolean conditions lacking subqueries or built-in functions are evaluated in their order in the *where* clause.

- Boolean predicates using built-in functions are ordered according to their costs. The optimizer compares the costs for each predicate and then places them in an increasing order.

The *ordered_predicates* hint overrides these rules, allowing the *where* clause items to be evaluated in the order that they appear in the query.

How is SQL join cardinality estimated?

In the absence of column histograms, the Oracle CBO must be able to guess on information, Sometimes the guess is right, and sometimes the guess is wrong. This is one reason why the *ordered* hint is one of the most popular SQL tuning hints, because using the *ordered* hint allows the DBA to specify that the tables be joined in the same order that they appear in the *from* clause, like this:

```
select /+ ordered */
   student_name
from
   student
natural join
   course
natural join
   professor
where
   professor = 'jones'
and
   course = 'anthropology 610';
```

If the values for the *professor* and *course* table columns are not skewed, it is unlikely that the 10g automatic statistics would have created histograms buckets in the *dba_histograms* view for these columns.

The Oracle CBO needs to be able to accurately estimate the final number of rows returned by each step of the query and then use schema metadata from running *dbms_stats* to choose the table join order that results in the least amount of baggage, in the form of intermediate rows, from each of the table join operations.

This is a daunting task. When an SQL query has a complex *where* clause, it can be very difficult to estimate the size of the intermediate result sets, especially when the *where* clause transforms column values with mathematical functions. Oracle has made a commitment to making the CBO infallible, even when incomplete information exists.

Tuning with the *cardinality* hint

The use of the cardinality hint compensates for the optimizer's inability to estimate the inter-table join result set. This is NOT a problem with the optimizer, as no

---

amount of metadata will help when joining tables with complex, multi-column where clauses.

The cardinality hint is used in two general cases, complex joins and dynamically created tables like global temporary tables (and possibly using materializations using the *with* clause):

```
select /*+ cardinality( gtt 500 ) */
   stuff
from
   global_temp_table gtt;
```

Oracle 9i first introduced the new dynamic sampling method for gathering run-time schema statistics, and it is now enabled by default in Oracle10g and beyond.

However, dynamic sampling is not for every database. The following section will reveal why this is the case.

Enabling Dynamic Sampling of Statistics

The main objective of dynamic sampling is to create more accurate selectivity and cardinality estimates, which in turn helps the CBO generate faster execution plans. Dynamic sampling is normally used to estimate single-table predicate selectivity when collected statistics cannot be used or are likely to lead to significant errors in estimation. It is also used to estimate table cardinality for tables without statistics or for tables whose statistics are too out of date to trust.

The *optimizer_dynamic_sampling* initialization parameter controls the number of blocks read by the dynamic sampling query. The parameter can be set to a value from zero to 10. In Oracle version 10g, the default for this parameter is set to two, automatically enabling dynamic sampling. The *optimizer_features_enable* parameter will turn OFF dynamic sampling if it is set to a version earlier than 9.2.0.

A value of zero means dynamic sampling will not be performed. Increasing the value of the parameter results in more aggressive dynamic sampling in terms of both the type of tables sampled, analyzed or unanalyzed, and the amount of I/O spent on sampling.

By default, Oracle will sample 32 random blocks. It is also important to know that dynamic sampling does not occur on tables that contain less than 32 blocks.

There is also a new dynamic sampling hint, *dynamic_sampling(tablename level)*, where *tablename* is the name of the table to be dynamically sampled and *level* is the same setting from zero to ten. The default value for the *level* is two, which will only sample tables that have not been analyzed with *dbms_stats*.

```
select /*+ dynamic_sampling (customer 4) */
    customer_name, . . . .
```

The following are the level descriptions, and remember, the higher the level, the deeper the sampling. The sampling levels are cumulative and each level contains all of the sampling of the prior level:

- **Level 1**: Samples tables that appear in join or subquery conditions that have no indexes and have more blocks than 32, the default for dynamic sampling.

- **Level 2 (default)**: Samples all unanalyzed tables that have more than 32 blocks.

- **Level 3**: Samples tables using a single column that applies selectivity to the table being sampled.

- **Level 4**: Samples tables using two or more columns that apply selectivity to the table being sampled.

- **Level 5**: Doubles the dynamic sample size and samples 64 blocks on tables.

- **Level 6**: Quadruples the dynamic sample size and samples 128 blocks on tables.

- **Level 7**: Samples 256 blocks on tables.

- **Level 8**: Samples 1,024 blocks on tables.

- **Level 9**: Samples 4,096 blocks on tables.

- **Level 10**: Samples all of the block in the tables.

 **Dynamic sampling is not for everyone!**

Beware, that dynamic sampling can cause SQL performance problems in some cases!

When *dynamic_sampling* was first introduced back in Oracle9i, it was used primarily for data warehouse systems with complex queries. Because it is enabled by default in Oracle10g and beyond, the DBA may want to turn off *dynamic_sampling* to remove unnecessary overhead if any of the following are true:

- The system utilizes an online transaction processing (OLTP) database with small, single-table queries.

- Queries are not frequently re-executed as determined by the *executions* column in *v$sql* and *executions_delta* in *dba_hist_sqlstat*.

- Multi-table joins have simple *where* clause predicates with single-column values and no built-in or mathematical functions.

Dynamic sampling is ideal whenever a query is going to execute multiple times, because the sample time is small compared to the overall query execution time.

By sampling data from the table at runtime, Oracle can quickly evaluate complex *where* clause predicates and determine the selectivity of each predicate, using this information to determine the optimal table join order. The following section will cover the sample table scan.

Sampling Table Scans

A sample table scan retrieves a random sample of data of a selected size. The sample can be from a simple table or a complex *select* statement, such as a statement involving multiple joins and complex views.

To peek inside dynamic sampling, some simple SQL queries can be run. The following SQL statement uses a sample block and sample rows scan on the *customer* table. There are 50,000 rows in this table. The first statement shows a sample *block scan* and the last SQL statement shows a sample *row scan*.

```
select
   count(*)
from
   customer
   sample block(20);


COUNT(*)
----------
   12268


select
   pol_no,
   sales_id,
   sum_assured,
   premium
from
   customer
```

```
sample (0.02);
```

```
  POL_NO   SALES_ID SUM_ASSURED    PREMIUM
---------- ---------- ----------- ---------- --
     2895         10        2525          2
     3176         10        2525          2
     9228         10        2525          2
    11294         11        2535          4
    19846         11        2535          4
    25547         12        2545          6
    29583         12        2545          6
    40042         13        2555          8
    47331         14        2565         10
    45283         14        2565         10
```

Just as the data can be sampled with SQL, the Oracle CBO can sample the data prior to formulating the execution plan. For example, the new *dynamic_sampling* SQL hint can be used to sample rows from the table:

```
select /*+ dynamic_sampling (customer 10) */
   pol_no,
   sales_id,
   sum_assured,
   premium
from
   customer;
```

```
  POL_NO   SALES_ID SUM_ASSURED    PREMIUM
---------- ---------- ----------- ---------- --
     2895         10        2525          2
     3176         10        2525          2
     9228         10        2525          2
    11294         11        2535          4
    19846         11        2535          4
    25547         12        2545          6
    29583         12        2545          6
    40042         13        2555          8
    47331         14        2565         10
    45283         14        2565         10
```

Dynamic sampling addresses an innate problem in SQL, and this issue is common to all relational databases. Estimating the optimal join order involves guessing the sequence that results in the smallest amount of intermediate row sets, and it is impossible to collect every possible combination of *where* clauses.

Dynamic sampling is almost a miracle for databases that have large n-way table joins that execute frequently. By sampling a tiny subset of the data, the Oracle CBO gleans clues as to the fastest table join order.

Fortunately, *dynamic_sampling* does not take a long time to execute, but it can cause unnecessary overhead for all Oracle databases. Dynamic sampling is just another example of Oracle's commitment to making Oracle an intelligent, self-optimizing database.

SQL Tuning with the *dynamic_sampling* hint

The use of the *dynamic_sampling* hint is useful for highly volatile tables and global temporary tables cases where ad-hoc metadata statistics will improve the SQL execution plans.

In Oracle versions 10g and beyond, the *dynamic_sampling* hint can be used to direct Oracle to estimate the cardinality of highly volatile tables.

The dynamic_sampling hint is also useful for estimating the size of dynamically created objects such as global temporary tables (GTT's).

```
select /*+ dynamic_sampling(customer 4) */
   pol_no,
   sales_id,
   sum_assured,
   premium
from
   customer;
```

The next section will cover a very specialized join technique, the star transformation, a specialty join used in super-large data warehouse environments.

The *star transformation* join

In a typical *star* schema, the super-large full-table scans can never be cached, but it is important to be able to control the caching of the dimension tables and indexes.

The basic principle behind the *star* schema is to introduce highly redundant data for performance reasons. Essentially, a fact table is a first normal form representation of the database, with a very high degree of redundancy being added into the tables. This de-normalized design greatly improves the simplicity of the design, but at the expense of redundant data.

By pre-joining the tables, the central fact table consist primarily of rows with a single data item, also known as the fact, while the rest of the columns contain foreign keys into the dimension tables, which contain detains about the fact as shown in Figure 4.9:

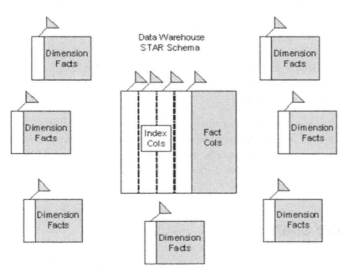

Figure 4.9: *A star schema*

For queries of a fact table or a dimension table, the *star* hint can greatly improve the join speed of data warehouse queries. A permutation of the hash join, the star join techniques builds a hash index on the fact table indexes.

Requirements Star Transformation Join

The star join can be a very fast way to join a fact table to dimension tables but to invoke the star join, the following prerequisites must be present:

- There must be at least three tables being joined

- Starting with Oracle8i, bitmap index structures must be present on the fact and dimension tables for any database version of Oracle 8i and higher

- An explain plan must be used to verify that the *nested loops* table access operation is being used to perform the join.

The following section will provide an overview of Oracle index access methods.

Types of Index Access Methods

There are several ways that Oracle can use an index:

- **Index unique scan**: This is a vertical use of the index whereby Oracle drops through the index to get the ROWID for a given symbolic key.

- **Index range scan**: This is where a range of logically contiguous keys are read from the index nodes.

- **Index fast full scan (Index FFS)**: This is a horizontal index access method whereby the index is read sideways, reading data block by data block, instead of dropping down through the tree nodes.

- **And-equal filter**: This is an index access method that gathers multiple sets of ROWIDs from the *where* clause of a query (e.g., *select person_name from person where status = 'SINGLE' and age < 66;*). The *and-equal* will build two sets of ROWIDs, remove duplicates and return the intersection of the ROWIS lists.

The following sections will delve a little deeper into these access methods.

Inside the index range scan

In an index range scan Oracle traverses a section of the index tree, grabbing related rows. This can be for a non-unique index:

```
select stuff from cust where cust_status = "A";
```

It is also possible to see a range scan for a constrained condition:

```
select stuff from cust where cust_rating > 3 and cust_rating < 26;
```

The speed of an index range scan depends largely on the physical co-location of the key values. In the example above, if the *cust* rows are sequenced in *cust_rating* order (as evidenced where the *cust_rating's dba_indexes.clustering_factor* approximates the number of data blocks in the cust table), then Oracle will be able to grab many related rows with each disk read.

Conversely, a table where the cust_rating values are scattered willy-nilly through the table (and *cust_rating's dba_indexes.clustering_factor* approaches *num_rows*) then a request for 50 keys may result in 50 separate disk accesses.

Row sequence maters!

If 95% of your table access is via a single index range scan, re-sequencing the rows (or using sorted hash clusters) can greatly reduce run-time I/O.

Remember, Oracle's *clustering_factor* in the *dba_indexes* view will tell you how synchronized your table rows are with your index. When the *clustering_factor* is close to the *dba_tables.blocks*, the table rows are synchronized with the index. As the *clustering_factor* approaches the *dba_tables.num_rows*, the rows are out of synchronization with the index key values.

Inside the index fast full scan

The index fast full scan is Oracle's answer to a full table scan, except for indexes. In an index fast full scan, Oracle does not access the index via the keys, and instead sucks the index into RAM using a multi-block read, just like a full table scan.

Index fast full scans are great when Oracle recognized that a SQL query can be satisfied without even having to touch a table row:

```
select count(*) from cust where status > 3 and status < 26;
```

Oracle might invoke an index fast full scan under these conditions:

- **A bounded count operation**: Where you are counting index key values, the index fast full scan is ideal.

- **Everything is in the index:** When Oracle notes that all select and where clause components are in the index, the base table does not need to be touched.

Like all access methods, Oracle uses your CBO statistics to determine if an index fast-full scan is the "best" access method, given your specific optimizer goal.

Size does matter!

The index fast-full scan is faster than a full-table scan primarily because indexes are usually smaller than the base table.

In the real-world, it's not obvious when the index fast-full scan will produce a result set the fastest because the speed of an index fast-full scan depends on these external parameters:

- **Proper statistics for the cost-based optimizer:** The schema should have been recently analyzed, and the *optimizer_mode* parameter must not be set to RULE.

- **The degree of parallelism on the index:** Note that the parallel degree of the index is set independently; the index does *not* inherit the degree of parallelism of the table.

- **The setting for *optimizer_index_cost_adj:*** This controls the relative cost of index access. The smaller the value, the less expensive index access becomes, relative to full scans.

- **The setting for *db_file_multiblock_read_count:*** This parameter factors in the cost of the full-index scan. The higher the value, the "cheaper" the full-index scan will appear.

- **The presence of histograms on the index:** For skewed indexes, this helps the cost-based optimizer evaluate the number of rows returned by the query.

For testing, is is possible to force an index fast full-index scan by specifying the *index_ffs* hint, and on SMP servers with multiple processors, and the *index_ffs* hint should be combined with a *parallel_index* hint to improve response time:

```
select distinct /*+ index_ffs(c color_idx) parallel_index(c color_idx)
    color,
    count(*)
from
    car c
group by
    color;
```

Test time your queries!

It is nearly impossible to guess if an *index_ffs* is going to be the fastest execution plan. Hence, a savvy Oracle DBA will test run the queries and see the elapsed time!

Conclusion

This chapter has covered various access methods and the relative advantages of each. The main points of this chapter include:

- Oracle has both "logical" access methods, and "physical" methods

- Logical join methods include equi-joins and outer joins

- Physical access methods include *nested loops* and *hash joins*

- The type of physical access method depends heavily on external factors and environmental parameter settings

- When testing the response time for physical join types, it is nearly impossible to make predictions. Instead, query response times should be tested with set timing on in SQL*Plus.

The next chapter will provide a look at full scan operations and why they are critical to SQL tuning.

Tuning Oracle
Full Table Scans

Watching full table scans is an important monitoring task.

As the Oracle optimizer evolved, access plans became more sophisticated and the optimizer became more intelligent about when to punt and read the entire table, front-to-back. A full table scan is frequently the best way to access a table, and it depends on many factors.

Inside the Full-table Scan

In a nutshell, Oracle faces two decisions when deciding how to read a table:

- **Invoke an index**: Oracle can read an index to collect specific ROWIDs.

- **Full table scan**: Oracle can read all of the data blocks for a table.

Internally, a full table scan manifests itself in an execution plan as *table access full*, and it is one of the most interesting features in all of SQL tuning for several reasons. It is common for beginners to assume that just because an index exists on a table, that index access is always the fastest way to access the data. This is not always the case.

The Types of Full Scan Operations

While most Oracle professionals only see the common *table access full* execution plan and the associated *db file scattered read* events, there are several types of full scan operations, some for table and others for index access. There are also parallel full scans, depending on whether Oracle is running on an SMP-enable server Figure 5.1:

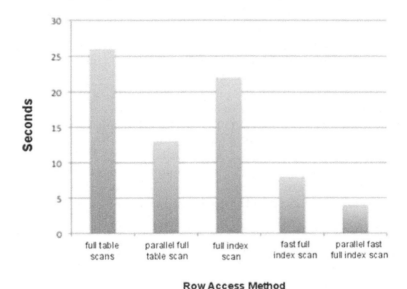

Figure 5.1: *The relative speeds of full scan operations*

The number of processors on the database server can help speed up full table scans with parallel query, a powerful tuning feature that uses the extra CPUs to fire off parallel processes to divide and conquer, a large table by breaking it into equal chunks and reading the chunks simultaneously. This is covered in more detail in Chapter 9, *Tuning Parallel SQL Execution.*

Why Full Scan I/O is Cheaper than Index I/O

When Oracle reads a table front to back, a great deal of disk latency is saved. Remember, 95% of the disk latency is the time required for the read-write head to move itself under the proper cylinder. Once there, the read-write head sits idle and the platter spins beneath it, and Oracle can read in data blocks as fast as the disk platter can spin, a process called the *db file scattered read.*

Oracle data files that are using Automatic Storage Management (ASM) have implemented the strip and mirror everywhere (SAME) principle, a RAID-10 combination of disk striping and mirroring. Even though a data file is striped across many disk spindles, it is the *stripe size* that mandates how many adjacent data block reside on disk, and the average latency for full-scan I/O will be noticeably faster than index access, which Oracle calls *db file sequential read* operations.

Look Out! Oracle samples the relative speed of full-scan and index access when the DBA runs the *dbms_stats.gather_system_stats* procedure. Running this job is very important for the Oracle optimizer to make an intelligent decision about when to invoke a full scan.

Nothing in Oracle SQL tuning is ever black or white; there are always shades of gray, and there are times when a full scan operation is invoked as a last resort, when the optimizer cannot figure out whether to use an index.

It is critical to understand that a full-table scan is a symptom of a possible sub-optimal SQL plan. While not all full scans are evil to performance, full table scans are a symptom of other common tuning problems like missing indexes and sub-optimal schema statistics (*dbms_stats*).

Remember, for small tables, a full-table scan is better than a full-scan, but a large-table full-table scan should always be examined as a possible problem. The following section will show cases where a large-table full-table scan is indeed evil.

When a Large-table Full-table Scan is Evil

While full-table scans are not necessarily evil, they do indeed signal a possible tuning opportunity. Unnecessary large table full-table scans can cause a huge amount of unnecessary I/O, placing a processing burden on the entire database.

But how to we tell when a large-table full-table scan is evil? One measure is to compare the number of data block touches (*consistent_gets*) with the number of rows returned by the SQL.

Whenever a SQL has a small number of rows are returned, compare the number of rows in the table to the number of rows returned to get a general idea of the efficiency of a query. Anytime there is a large-table full-table scan that fetches less than 20% of the rows in the table, there should be further investigation to determine whether the full-scan is legitimate or if there is a missing index.

Call in the FBI!

Hot Tip!

One of the most common cases for bad full-scans is a missing function-based index (FBI). Remember, anything that is in there *where* clause of a SQL statement can be indexed.

Now it is time for a closer look at how to examine full-scan operations and determine how to tune for possible sub-optimal full table scans.

First, it must be completely clear that index access comes at a price. When using the *first_rows_n optimizer mode*, a conscious decision has been made to use indexes.

In fact, the term *first rows* refers to an indexes ability to quickly start retuning rows to a SQL query, deliberately invoking the extra I/O required to use an index. When *first_rows_n* is used to optimize SQL for fast response time, it is important to understand that the less expensive full scan operations are being forsaken for index access.

When using the default *optimizer_mode* of *all_rows*, Oracle attempts to optimizer SQL to fetch the desired rows with a minimum amount of resource consumption.

For a simple example, consider the following query:

```
select
    stuff
from
    emp
where
    deptno = 'MARKETING'
order by
    empno;
```

For the sake of illustration, assume that the table consumes 10,000 data block and the index has 4,000 data blocks. The following list includes several choices of access plans:

- **Minimize computing resources (*all_rows*)**: The *emp* table could be read front-to-back with a full-table scan, and then the Marketing rows could be filtered out and sorted. Because the data blocks are contiguous on disk, only a single movement of the read-write head is required (about 10 milliseconds), and the table is quickly read. Because result sets are commonly sequenced with the *order by* clause, all rows sorted before the rows are displayed, and the entire query must be completed before the rows can be presented back to the calling query.

■ **Minimize response time (*first_rows_n*)**: The rows are fetched using an index on *deptno* and *empno*. Traversing the index and randomly accessing the target rows might require 1,000 read-write movements, far more expensive than a full scan. However, it is possible to start passing back the result set to the calling SQL almost immediately because the index serves to pre-filter and pre-sort the results.

In systems that run non-interactive SQL in batch jobs, fast response time is not important and the SQL will be optimized using *all_rows optimizer_mode* which favors full-table scans to minimizing computing resources. Conversely, shops that have online transaction processing (OLTP) wish to optimize their SQL to deliver the rows back quickly using *first_rows_n* optimization which favors index access.

Small table scans can be cached!

Small-table full-table scans are often legitimate, and frequently-scanned small tables should be cached into the KEEP pool.

Now that the fundamental trade-off between indexed versus full-table scan access has been covered, it is a good time to take a look at how Oracle makes the decision to invoke full-scan operations.

Full Table Scans and Stripe Size

In these days when most Oracle databases adopt either the ASM or RAID-10 SAME approach, every table is physically mapped across many physical disk drives as shown in Figure 5.2:

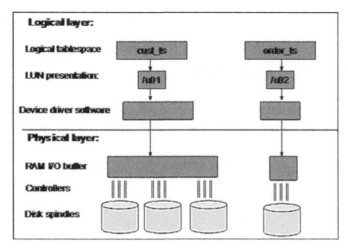

Figure 5.2: *The mapping between logical tables and physical disks*

Estimating the cost of a full-table scan on a table with contiguous data blocks on a single disk is easy, it is the cost of moving the read-write head under the cylinder, plus the rotational delay as Oracle reads-in the data blocks. However, in the real world, Automatic Storage Management (ASM) and RAID make the calculation of the cost of a full-table scan more challenging.

It is the stripe size that matters most, because the stripe size dictates the number of contiguous blocks on each disk, which factors directly into the cost of the *db file scattered read* that are required to service the full-table scan.

In ASM, the *x$kffxp* fixed table contains the mapping between files, extents and allocation units and this fixed table can be used to track the stripe allocations across all of the disks for the table, assuming that the large table has been allocated into a separate data file, which is an Oracle best practice for large tables that span many disk spindles:

```
select
   *
from
   x$kffxp
where
   number_kffxp=
   (select file_number from v$asm_alias
    where name='mytablefile.dbf');
```

But the stripe size is only one factor in weighing the costs of a full-table scan. It is also necessary to consider the number of rows returned by the query. For example, if

---

the query returns over half of the table rows, the full-table scan is almost always the fastest execution plan.

SQL Result Set Size and Full Table Scans

As previously noted, full-scan queries that return a small number of rows might indicate a missing index opportunity, but what can be said about the threshold for invoking a full-table scan?

To visit 90% of the table rows, a full-scan is clearly the most efficient access plan, but what about queries that want 60% of the table rows? What about queries that access 40%? Do they run faster with a full-scan? The answer is the same as it is for most Oracle questions "It Depends".

Consider a query that only returns 20% of the table rows, yet the optimizer bypasses an appropriate index in favor of a full-table scan. In cases like this, many internal factors influence the decision to invoke a full scan.

- **Disk I/O speed**: On average, full scan I/O is significantly faster than index access. All of this changes when the database files are on solid-state RAM disk (SSD) where access speed is uniform, regardless of the type of I/O.

- **Multiblock reads count:** The *db_file_multiblock_read_count* parameter controls is a sequential prefetch mechanism that reduces disk latency for multiblock reads. Starting in 10g release 2, Oracle automatically computes the optimal value for the db_file_multiblock_read_count parameter, an important factor in the cost of a full-scan operation.

- **Parallel server resources:** Full scan operations on large SMP servers with (8, 16, 32 or 64 CPU's) can be far cheaper because Oracle parallel query can be used to create multiple processes to simultaneously read chunks of the table. Oracle parallel query scales linearly, and a full-scan with parallel degree 63 would return the rows approximately 60 times faster than a single process.

- **Table size:** Reading a small table front to back may be cheaper than index access when the table is tiny. For example, it is almost always cheaper to read a 20 block table with a full-scan than to use an index because the full-scan would involve only one movement of the disk read-write head.

- **Block size and *avg_row_len*:** The number of rows that are read in a single I/O is a very important factor in the decision to invoke a full-table scan. Reading a table with 32k blocks requires less time than reading the same data file in 2k blocksizes. This factor is usually negligible, but in some cases it makes a big difference, especially when the table contains large object data types (BLOB, CLOB).

- **Row sequencing to the best index:** If the rows are physically placed on disk in the same sequence as the index (using tools like sorted hash cluster tables), then the clustering_factor in dba_indexes is near the value of the blocks column in dba_segments. This means that index access will require lees disk I/O, because a single block read of the target table might return many related rows. In an un-sequenced table, the clustering factor is much higher than blocks, it asymptotically approaches the value of num_rows in the dba_tables view.

- **Index statistics:** The optimizer evaluates the selectivity of the index and the depth of the index tree. It then computes the number of I/O operations that are required to service the query via the index. In some cases, the presence of optional index statistics, called histograms, also makes a difference.

- **The high-water mark for the table:** The high-water mark for a table reflects the highest point for row occupancy. In cases where a significant number of rows have been deleted from a table, the high-water mark remains at the original level, and a full-table scan will often read many dead blocks below the high-water mark. This causes full-scan operations to incur excessive I/O, until the high-water mark is lowered by reorganizing or coalescing the table.

- **Stripe size:** We use RAID-10 and Automatic storage management (ASM), to randomize data across all disks to avoid hot spots and reduce disk enqueues. When a table is striped, the table blocks are randomized across many disk spindles, making full-scan operations more expensive. This is because the read-write heads must relocate under another cylinder whenever a stripe on a disk has relocated.

Of course, these are only general factors and it will be necessary for each DBA to empirically test their own query to see whether index access of full-scan access is best for that specific query.

When comparing index access to full-scan access, the bottom line is that the goals is to use the access method that returns the rows fastest, and no amount of theory beats an old-fashioned *set timing on* with a timing benchmark in SQL*Plus. I have seen queries that are fastest with a full-table scan accessing as little as 30% of the table rows.

For example, for a server with 64 CPUs and using an index where *dba_indexes clustering_factor* approaches *num_rows*, indicating an unclustered index, the threshold for a full-table scan might be as low as 20% of the table rows.

Conversely, a query on a server with 4 CPUs with a large blocksize and a *clustering_factor* approaching *dba_tables blocks*, indicating a well clustered index, might have a full-table scan threshold as high as 70% of the table rows.

Again, the *plan9i.sql* script can be used to indicate the full-table scans, and then they can be evaluates manually to determine whether or not Oracle is choosing an optimal plan. The following section will cover situation where large-table full-table scans might be called mistakenly.

Unnecessary Large-table Full-table Scans

One common symptom of a sub-optimal SQL query is a full-table scan. Full table scans are wrongly invoked in several cases:

- **Missing indexes**: If the DBA forgets to create a key index, a full-table scan may be the only option.

- **Super-complex queries**: Queries with super complicated where clauses are often associated with full table scans. This is an Oracle punt, a smart way to avoid a super-long time parsing complex *where* clause predicates. When the optimizer encounters a complex query, it can often take longer to determine the fastest plan than it would to run the query with a full scan. Hence, the optimizer might decide to save parsing time by quickly invoking a full-table scan.

- **Bad statistics:** If the optimizer statistics are not reflective of the actual state of the table data, a full-table scan might be invoked.

- **Optimizing to min*imize* resource consumption:** When using the all_rows optimizer_mode, Oracle's goal is to create a SQL plan that minimizes computing resources and not necessarily the plan that returns the rows the fastest. Hence, Oracle might choose a full-scan because it involves less I/O than accessing the table via an index.

These conditions have given full-table scans a bad reputation as being evil. This is nonsense, of course, but many people fail to understand the fundamental nature of SQL access operations, and when it makes sense for the optimizer to invoke a full table scan.

NULL Values and Index Access

One challenge with all relational databases is having the optional ability to index on a NULL column. By default, relational databases ignore NULL values because the relational model says that NULL means not present. Hence, Oracle indexes will not include NULL values.

For example, the index definition in the following example would not index on open positions any new employee positions that are stored with a NULL employee name:

```
create index
    emp_ename_idx
on
   emp
   (ename);
```

Whenever a SQL query asks for the open position employee slots *where ename is NULL*, there will be no index entries for NULLS in *emp_name_idx* and Oracle would perform an unnecessary large-table full-table scan.

```
Execution Plan
-----------------------------------------------------------
0 SELECT STATEMENT Optimizer=CHOOSE (Cost=1 Card=1 Bytes=6)
1 0 TABLE ACCESS (FULL) OF 'EMP' (Cost=1 Card=1 Bytes=6)
```

To get around the optimization of SQL queries that choose NULL column values, a function-based index can be created using the null value built-in SQL function to index only on the NULL columns.

Note that the null value (NVL) function replaces NULL values with the character string null, a real value that can participate in an index as shown below:

```
-- ************************************************
-- create an FBI on ename column with NULL values
-- ************************************************

create index
    emp_null_ename_idx
on
   emp
   (nvl(ename,'null'));

exec dbms_stats.gather_table_stats(emp,'t',cascade=>true);
```

This technique can also be used with NULL numeric values. This syntax replaces NULL values with a zero as shown below:

```
-- ************************************************
-- create an FBI on emp_nbr column with NULL values
-- ************************************************
create index
    emp_null_emp_nbr_idx
on
   emp
   (nvl(ename,o));
```

```
exec dbms_stats.gather_table_stats(emp,'t',cascade=>true);
```

Now, the index can be used and the speed of any queries that require access to the NULL columns will be greatly improved. One of the two following changes must be made to accomplish this:

- Add a hint to force the index

- Change the *where* predicate to match the function

The following is an example of using an index on NULL column values:

```
-- ************************
-- insert a NULL row
-- ************************
insert into emp (empno) values (999);
set autotrace traceonly explain;

-- **********************************************************
-- test the index access (change predicate to use FBI)
-- **********************************************************
select /*+ index(emp_null_ename_idx) */
   ename
from
   emp e
where
   nvl(ename,'null') = 'null';
```

Another option is the following technique, which includes building an index with an arbitrary numeric column value to trick Oracle into using an index:

```
SQL> select count(1) from t where n is null;


COUNT(1)
----------
      334


Execution Plan
----------------------------------------------------------
   0      SELECT STATEMENT Optimizer=CHOOSE (Cost=3 Card=1 Bytes=3)
   1    0    SORT (AGGREGATE)
   2    1      TABLE ACCESS (FULL) OF 'T' (Cost=3 Card=334 Bytes=1002)


SQL> create index tind on t(n, 1);  ----> 1 is any arbitrary value.

Index created.
```

```
SQL> exec dbms_stats.gather_table_stats(user,'t',cascade=>true);

PL/SQL procedure successfully completed.

SQL> select count(1) from t where n is null;

 COUNT(1)
----------
      334

Execution Plan
----------------------------------------------------------
   0      SELECT STATEMENT Optimizer=CHOOSE (Cost=2 Card=1 Bytes=4)
   1    0   SORT (AGGREGATE)
   2    1     INDEX (RANGE SCAN) OF 'TIND' (NON-UNIQUE) (Cost=2 Card=3
          34 Bytes=1336)
```

Now let's take a look at how NULL values effect SQL execution and hoiw queries can be re-written for faster execution speeds.

Never Replace a NULL Value for Index Access

In a standard Oracle index, NULL values cannot participate in the index; however, some developers might be tempted to circumvent this issue by replacing all NULL in the table values with a literal value, such as N/A, thereby allowing the index to be used as shown:

```
update
   emp
set
   middle_name to 'N/A'
where
   middle_name IS NULL;

select
   emp_name
from
   emp
where
   middle_name = 'N/A';
```

Of course, this is not recommended because there is a real distinction between a missing NULL value and a value of blanks or zero.

There are several real life horror stories where NULL values have been replaced with literals:

One fellow chose a vanity license plate for his car with the value of "XXXXXX". Several months later, he received thousands of traffic tickets where the officer had noted the license plate number as XXXXXX.

In another funny case, a similar situation happened when a motorist chose a license plate that said NO PLATE and got forwarded thousands of parking tickets where the meter maid had listed "no plate" on the ticket!

The lesson is clear: Never violate the rules of relational NULLS just to force index access.

Avoiding Full Scans on SQL with a not equals Clause

Due to the declarative nature of SQL, any statement can be formed many ways. Consider the three ways that a *not equal* can be written:

```
select ename from emp where job <> 'MANAGER';
```

```
select ename from emp where job != 'MANAGER';
```

```
select ename from emp where job not in ('MANAGER');
```

The *not equals* operator, or a *not in* operator, will always use a full-table scan unless the column values are skewed and column histograms specifically indicate that index access is better.

For example, consider a query with a *region* index where 90 percent of the values are for the Southern region. The following query would rightly choose a full-table scan because the index is very non-selective:

```
select
   name,
   status
from
   cust
where
   region <> 'Northern';
```

However, the following SQL would run faster with index access because only a tiny number of region values are not in the Southern region.

```
select
   name,
   status
from
   cust
where
   region <> 'Southern';
```

The next section will show how to use the like clause to remove unnecessary large-table full-table scans.

Full Table Scans and the like Clause

Indexing when using the SQL *like* clause can be tricky because the wildcard (%) operator can invalidate the index. Search for something in the beginning of the string as follows:

```
where x like 'abc%'
```

The optimizer will be able to translate this into this form:

```
where x >= 'abc' and x < 'abd'
```

In this case, the index range scan is obvious.

But the *like* clause can cause expensive full-table scans. For example a *last_name* index would be okay with a *like 'SMI%'* query, but unusable with *like '%SMI%'*.

Queries that use the *like* clause will commonly invoke a full-table scan, especially when the percent sign is used in the leading side of the SQL.

For example, the following SQL would use an index because the like mask begins with characters and the existing index will be able to service the query.

```
select
   ename
```

```
   job,
   hiredate
from
   emp
where
   ename like 'BURLE%';
```

In this case, the *ename_idx* is used instead of a full table scan.

```
OPERATION
------------------------------------------------------------------------
OPTIONS                          OBJECT_NAME                 POSITION
-------------------------------  -------------------------   ----------
SELECT STATEMENT
                                                                    1


   INDEX
RANGE SCAN                       ENAME_IDX                         1
```

However, when the *like* mask has the percent sign in the beginning of the mask, the index cannot be used:

```
select
   ename
   job,
   hiredate
from
   emp
where
   ename like '%SON';
```

In this case, a full-table scan is invoked:

```
OPERATION
------------------------------------------------------------------------
OPTIONS                          OBJECT_NAME                 POSITION
-------------------------------  -------------------------   ----------
SELECT STATEMENT
                                                                   26

   INDEX
FULL SCAN                        ENAME_IDX                         1
```

So, how can unnecessary full scans be prevented when using the *like* clause? There are various solutions to this issue of a leading wildcard:

- **Context indexes**: For read-only tables, Oracle*Text indexes can be used to remove full-table scans when using the *like* operator.

- **Index hint**: You can use an index hint to replace the full-table scan with an index fast full scan.

- **Case insensitive searching:** This 10g R2 feature allows for case insensitive searches without using a *upper* or *lower* case BIF transformation of the target column as shown below:

```
alter session set NLS_COMP=ANSI;

alter session set NLS_SORT=GENERIC_BASELETTER;

select * from customer where full_name = 'Don Burleson'
```

The next section will delve more deeply into one of the most important SQL tuning techniques for text-based searches. These are tools that allow searching inside text columns with indexes, thereby avoiding the dreaded unnecessary large-table full-table scan.

Oracle case insensitive searches

Oracle allows a case insensitive search method for SQL that avoids index invalidation and unnecessary full-table scans. It is also possible to employ Oracle*Text indexes to remove full-table scans when using the *like* operator. Prior to Oracle10g release 2, case insensitive queries required special planning, and the following were some techniques for insuring index usage for text-based queries:

1. **Function-based index (FBI):** Transform data in the query to make it case insensitive. NOTE: This can invalidate indexes without a function-based index.

```
create index
   upper_full_name
on
   customer ( upper(full_name));

select
   full_name
from
   customer
where
   upper(full_name) = 'DON BURLESON';
```

2. **Triggers**: One clumsy approach involves using a trigger to transform the data to make it case insensitive or store the data with the *lower* or *upper* BIF.

3. **Use *generic_baseletter*:** Case insensitive searches can be conducted with SQL*Plus *alter session* commands as shown below:

```
alter session set NLS_COMP=ANSI;
```

```
alter session set NLS_SORT=GENERIC_BASELETTER;

select * from customer where full_name = 'Don Burleson'
```

4. **Use *binary_ci*.** In Oracle 10 release 2 and beyond, the *binary_ci* parameter can be used for case insensitive searches in SQL. The following is another example of using case insensitive searches to speed up SQL by removing index access using the Oracle 10g release 2 *binary_ci* feature:

Initialization parameters:

```
NLS_SORT=binary_ci

NLS_COMP=ansi
```

Sample index create:

```
create index
   caseless_name_index
on
   customer
(
   nlssort( full_name, 'NLS_SORT=BINARY_CI')
);

alter session set nls_sort=binary_ci;

select * from customer where full_name = 'Don Burleson';
```

The next section will illustrate how to use the Oracle Context utility to speed up text searches on read-only tables.

Using Oracle*Text Indexes with the SQL like Clause

One serious SQL performance problem occurs when the SQL *like* clause operator is used to find a string within a large Oracle table column (e.g. *varchar(2000)*, *clob*, *blob*):

```
select stuff from bigtab where text_column like '%ipod%';
select stuff from bigtab where full_name like '%JONES';
```

Due to the fact standard Oracle cannot index into a large column, these *like* queries cause full-table scans, and Oracle must examine every row in the table, even when the result set is very small. These unnecessary full-table scans are a problem for a couple of reasons:

- Unnecessary large-table full-table scans increase the load on the disk I/O subsystem, reading block that are not needed to fetch the result set.

- Small table full table scans in the data buffer can cause high *consistent gets* and drive up CPU consumption.

The *Oracle*Text* utility, formerly called *Oracle ConText* and *Oracle Intermedia,* allows parsing through a large text column and index on the words within the column.

Unlike ordinary b-tree or bitmap indexes, Oracle *context, ctxcat* and *ctxrule* indexes can be set not to update as content is changed. Since most standard Oracle databases will use the *ctxcat* index with standard relational tables, the DBA must decide on a refresh interval. To help with this decision, Oracle provides the *sync* operator. The default is *sync=manual* and the index must manually be synchronized with *ctx_ddl.sync_index* as shown:

```
SYNC (MANUAL | EVERY "interval-string" | ON COMMIT)]
```

Hence, Oracle*Text indexes are only useful for removing full-table scans when the tables are largely read-only and/or the end-users do not mind not having 100% search recall in situations where:

- the target table is relatively static (e.g. nightly batch updates)

- end-users would not mind missing the latest row data

Oracle*Text works with traditional data columns and also with XML, MS-Word docs and Adobe PDF files that are stored within Oracle.

Oracle*Text has several index types:

- **ctxcat Indexes**: A *ctxcat* index is best for smaller text fragments that must be indexed along with other standard relational data (*varchar2*).

```
where catsearch(text_column, 'ipod')> 0;
```

- **context Indexes**: The *context* index type is used to index large amounts of text such as *word, pdf, xml, html* or plain text documents.

```
where contains(test_column, 'ipod', 1) > 0
```

- ***ctxrule* Indexes**: A *ctxrule* index can be used to build document classification applications.

These types of indexes allow the old-fashioned SQL *like* syntax to be replaced with *contains* or *catsearch* SQL syntax.

When the query is executed with the new index, the full-table scan is replaced with a index scan, greatly reducing execution speed and improving hardware stress as shown below:

```
Execution Plan
-------------------------------------------------------
   0          SELECT STATEMENT Optimizer=FIRST_ROWS
   1    0     SORT (ORDER BY)
   2    1       TABLE ACCESS (BY INDEX ROWID) OF 'BIGTAB'
   3    2         DOMAIN INDEX OF 'TEXT-COLUMN_IDX'
```

Since *Oracle*Text* indexes are intended for read-only applications, there must also be rules developed for when to resynchronize the indexes.

Index Resynchronization

Since rebuilding an *Oracle*Text* index (*context, ctxcat, ctxrule*) requires a full-table scan and a generous amount of internal parsing, it is not practical to use triggers for instantaneous index updates.

Updating Oracle*Text indexes is easy, and they can be scheduled using *dbms_job* or the Oracle 10g *dbms_scheduler* utility package. Oracle*Text provides a *ctx_ddl* package with the *sync_index* and *optimize_index* procedures:

```
SQL> exec ctx_ddl.sync_index('text_column_idx');

SQL> exec ctx_ddl.optimize_index('text_column_idx','FULL');
```

For example, if a nightly *dbms_scheduler* job is created to call *sync_index*, the index will be refreshed, but the structure will become sub-optimal over time. Oracle recommends periodic use of the *optimize_index* package to periodically rebuild the whole index from scratch. Index optimization can be performed in three modes (*fast, full* or *token*).

In summary, the *Oracle*Text* indexes are great for removing unnecessary full-table scans from static Oracle tables, and they can reduce I/O by several orders of magnitude, greatly improving overall SQL performance.

It should now be a bit more clear how to force Oracle to use indexes for specific SQL, so it should now be more apparent that an important tuning task is to identify unnecessary large-table full-table scans.

Be vigilant for full-table scans!

While not all large-table full-table scans are inappropriate, the full-table scan is a common symptom of missing indexes, bad optimizer statistics and other issues.

Look Out!

The question now is how to go about seeking and validating full-table scans. Oracle provides several tools to make this easy.

Remove Unnecessary Large-table Full-table Scans

While not all large-table full-table scans are problematic, a large-table full-table scan is a common symptom of a SQL execution problem. Large-table full-table scans in an explain plan (TABLE ACCESS FULL) should always be examined to verify that it is not due to a database problem, such as a missing index.

Unnecessary large-table full-table scans are an important symptom of sub-optimal SQL and cause unnecessary I/O that can drag down an entire database.

The first step in validating a full-table scan is evaluating the SQL based on the number of rows returned by the query and a best guess about the number of trips to the data blocks that would be needed to fetch the rows.

Oracle indicates that in situations where the query returns less than 40 percent of the table rows in an ordered table or seven percent of the rows in an unordered table, the query can be tuned to use an index in lieu of the full-table scan; however, in reality there is no fixed number because it depends on many factors like the *db_block_size* and *db_file_multiblock_read_count*.

This decision is partly based on the index key value described by *clustering_factor* in the *dba_indexes* view. However, it is not a simple process.

The choice between a full table scan and index access as the best access plan for a SQL statement depends on many factors. The most common cause of unnecessary full-table scans is an *optimizer_mode* that favors full-table scans, like *all_rows*, or a missing index, especially a function-based indexes.

These factors are listed in their order of importance:

- **Sub-optimal *optimizer_mode*:** The *all_rows* mode minimizes computing resources and favors full-table scans, while the *first_rows_n* (e.g. *first_rows_10*, *first_rows_100*) mode favors index access.

- **Missing indexes:** Missing indexes, especially missing function-based indexes, will cause unnecessary large-table full-table scans.

- **Bad CBO statistics:** Missing or stale SQL optimizer statistics, gathered via *dbms_stats*, will cause Oracle to misjudge the execution plan for a SQL query.

- **Missing CPU and disk statistics:** Missing system statistics, gathered with *dbms_stats.gather_system_stats*, will prevent the optimizer from making a smart decision about invoking multi-block I/O.

- **Histograms:** For skewed data columns, missing column histograms will influence the choice of index versus full-table scan access.

- **Index clustering:** The physical row order on the data blocks is important to know when choosing an index as is the clustering of the table rows to the desired index, as displayed in *dba_indexes* clustering factor.

- **Sub-optimal setting for *db_file_multiblock_read_count*:** The optimization of *db_file_multiblock_read_count* has been automated in Oracle 10g R2 and beyond to prevent errors.

- **Sub-optimal setting for *optimizer_index_cost_adj*:** This is a throttle that makes index access more attractive to the optimizer, and lowering the value of *optimizer_index_cost_adj* will cause the SQL optimizer to favor indexes.

- **Sub-optimal setting for *optimizer_index_caching*:** The *optimizer_index_caching* parameter is set by the DBA to help the optimizer know, on average, how much of an index resides inside the data buffer.

- **Parallel query:** Enabling Oracle parallel query (OPQ) will influence the optimizer that full-scans are less expensive, and it may change the execution plans for hundreds of SQL statements. On an SMP server with dozens of CPUs, a full-table scan can be parallelized for faster execution. However, a data block should never be read unless it is needed to get rows for the SQL result set. Remember, parallel query only affects full-table scans, and it has no effect when performing index access.

- **Disk blocksize:** The number of rows that resides on each disk data block influences the choice between a full-table scan of an index scan. This is especially true when using RAID with a smaller stripe size, and reading a table with a 2k block size would take significantly more I/O and reading a table with a 32k block size.

Fix the root cause, not the symptom!

Hot Tip!

Do not doink with *optimizer_index_cost_adj* until checking for the right *optimizer_mode* and insuring that fresh table and system statistics are available. Fix the problem, not the symptom.

In sum, the decision about removing a full-table scan should be based on a careful examination of the amount of logical I/O (consistent gets) of the index scan versus the costs of the full-table scan, based on the number of rows returned by the query.

With this general idea behind examining large-table full-table scans, it is time to take a look at how to locate full-scan operations.

Locating Full-scan Operations

I have several free scripts on the w eb at www.dba-oracle.com that can be used to find SQL that invokes full-scans. The most commonly used script is called *plan9i.sql*, and this script can be used to display all operations that have full-table scans. The name *plan9i.sql* only refers to the release where it first worked, it works great on Oracle 12c.

I also have a time-series version of this script called *plan10g.sql*, for those who have purchased a pack license to query the *dba_hist_sqlstat* table. Unlike *plan91.sql*, the *plan10g.sql* shows the SQL over time, for each snapshot period.

The result is a very important full table scan report:

```
                  Full table scans and counts

OWNER          NAME                  NUM_ROWS C K    BLOCKS   NBR_FTS
-------------  -------------------- --------- - - -------- ---------
SYS            DUAL                            N              2    97,237
SYSTEM         SQLPLUS_PRODUCT_PRO             N K            2    16,178
DONALD         PAGE                 3,450,209 N        932,120     9,999
DONALD         RWU_PAGE                   434 N              8     7,355
DONALD         PAGE_IMAGE              18,067 N          1,104     5,368
DONALD         SUBSCRIPTION              476 N K          192     2,087
DONALD         PRINT_PAGE_RANGE          10 N K           32       874
ARSD           JANET_BOOKS               20 N              8        64
PERFSTAT       STATS$TAB_STATS            N               65        10
```

Moving from left to right the following columns are displayed:

- **Table owner and table name**

- **num_rows:** This is the current number of rows as per the last analyze with *dbms_stats*.

- **C:** This is the old Oracle7 cache utility, now obsolete.

- **K:** This flag indicates whether the table resides in the KEEP pool. This is important for small tables that experience frequent full-scan operations, to ensure that they are kept on the RAM data buffers for fast repeated access.

- **blocks:** This is the number of blocks in the table. This is an important column because it is the number of blocks in the table, not necessarily the number of rows, which determines whether afull-scan is appropriate.

- **nbr_fts:** This is the number of full-tab le scans, as reported by *v$sql_plan* of *dba_hist_sql_plan* respectively.

In the report above, there are several tables that have a large number of full-scan operations.

Tuning Large-table Full-table Scans

This report can also be used to identify large tables that experience full-table scans. While full-table scans may be legitimate, full-scans are an indicator of possible sub-optimal execution as highlighted below:

Full table scans and counts

OWNER	NAME	NUM_ROWS	C	K	BLOCKS	NBR_FTS
SYS	DUAL		N		2	97,237
SYSTEM	SQLPLUS_PRODUCT_PRO		N	K	2	16,178
DONALD	PAGE	3,450,209	N		932,120	9,999
DONALD	RWU_PAGE	434	N		8	7,355
DONALD	PAGE_IMAGE	18,067	N		1,104	5,368
DONALD	SUBSCRIPTION	476	N	K	192	2,087
DONALD	PRINT_PAGE_RANGE	10	N	K	32	874
ARSD	JANET_BOOKS	20	N		8	64
PERFSTAT	STATS$TAB_STATS		N		65	10

Of course, not all large-table full-table scans are evil, but they warrant inspection. Also, this report is useful for identifying large-table full-table scans that can be parallelized. Parallel scans are covered in a later chapter, but it is important to note that legitimate large-table full-table scans can be parallelized with a degree of cpu_count-1. For non-warehouse databases, it is also a good idea to turn-on parallel query at the query level using a parallel hint.

This report shows the table name, and it is simple to run a quick query to display all SQL that accesses this table. Then it is possible to gather an explain plan for these statement to inspect the access plans:

```
select
    sql_text
from
    v$sql
where
    upper(sql_text) like("%TABLENAME%)':
```

For SQL statements that invoke full-scan operations, the DBA must inspect the *where* clause to see if there is an indexing opportunity. \

Next, let's see how seeking small-table full-table scans is important.

Tuning Small-table Full-table Scans

The report listing from plan91.sql shows both large and small table scans. The blocks column to identify small tables with small-table full-table scans:

```
                          Full table scans and counts

OWNER          NAME                   NUM_ROWS C K    BLOCKS   NBR_FTS
-------------- ---------------------- -------- - - -------- --------
SYS            DUAL                            N              2   97,237
SYSTEM         SQLPLUS_PRODUCT_PRO            N K             2   16,178
DONALD         PAGE                  3,450,209 N        932,120    9,999
DONALD         RWU_PAGE                    434 N              8    7,355
DONALD         PAGE_IMAGE             18,067 N           1,104    5,368
DONALD         SUBSCRIPTION               476 N K         192    2,087
DONALD         PRINT_PAGE_RANGE           10 N K          32      874
ARSD           JANET_BOOKS                20 N              8       64
PERFSTAT       STATS$TAB_STATS               N             65       10
```

The above result indicates that the rwu_page table resides on only 8 data blocks and has experienced 7,355 full-scan operations. For any legitimate small-table full-table scans, the table can be quickly cached into the KEEP pool with the following syntax:

```
alter table
    rwu_page
storage (buffer_pool keep);
```

In most cases, small tables will self cache themselves because the table will ping itself to the most recently used (MRU) end of the data buffer each time that the table is referenced, but placing these tables into the KEEP area is a best practice because of having applied an intelligent criteria to this assignment.

KEEP Pool Assignment Rules

Since the idea of the KEEP is to fully cache the object, the goal is to locate those objects that are small and experience a disproportional amount of I/O activity. The Oracle documentation states one possible rule for KEEP pool assignment:

A good candidate for a segment to put into the KEEP pool is a segment that is smaller than 10% of the size of the DEFAULT buffer pool and has incurred at least 1% of the total I/Os in the system.

It is easy to locate segments that are less than 10% of the size of their data buffer, but Oracle does not have a mechanism to track I/O at the segment level. To get around this issue, some DBAs place each segment into an isolated tablespace, so that the AWR can show the total I/O. However, this is not a practical solution for complex schemas with hundreds of segments.

 **The KEEP pool is only for large databases!**

The default behavior of the Oracle data buffer will serve to cache most small-tables without using the KEEP pool. The KEEP pool is only for VLDB systems to segregate I/O.

Using this guideline, there are many approaches which can be completely automated. For the buf_keep_pool.sql query, the rules are simple, and adjustable, depending upon each individual workload:

- KEEP where the table is small (<50 blocks) and the table experiences frequent full-table scans.

- KEEP any objects that consume more than 10% of the size of their data buffer.

- KEEP if the object consumes more than 10% of the total size of the data buffer.

- KEEP if more than 50% of the objects blocks already reside in the data buffer.

- KEEP if a segment that is smaller than 10% of the size of the DEFAULT buffer pool and has incurred at least 1% of the total I/Os in the system.

- KEEP segments that average over five buffer touches and occupy over twenty blocks in the cache.

The assignment of high use object into the KEEP pool can be automated. The following section provides a deeper look at this process.

Scripts for Automating KEEP Pool Assignment

Another method for identifying tables and indexes for the KEEP pool involves the examination of the percentage current blocks in the data buffer.

It is highly unlikely that an undeserving table or index would meet this criteria. Of course, any such script would need to be run at numerous times during the day because the buffer contents change very rapidly.

Keep an eye on your KEEP pool size!

Obviously, the KEEP pool must be large enough to hold all objects that are assigned to the KEEP pool, and the KEEP pool size will have to be periodically inspected and adjusted accordingly.

The following script can be run every hour via *dbms_scheduler* and will automate the monitoring of KEEP pool candidates. Every time it finds a candidate, the DBA will execute the syntax and adjust the total KEEP pool size to accommodate the new object.

💾 buf_keep_pool.sql

```
set pages 999

set lines 92


spool keep_syn.lst

drop table t1;

create table t1 as
select
   o.owner          owner,
   o.object_name    object_name,
   o.subobject_name subobject_name,
   o.object_type    object_type,
   count(distinct file# || block#)        num_blocks
from
   dba_objects  o,
   v$bh         bh
where
   o.data_object_id = bh.objd
and
   o.owner not in ('SYS','SYSTEM')
and
   bh.status != 'free'
group by
   o.owner,
```

```
    o.object_name,
    o.subobject_name,
    o.object_type
order by
    count(distinct file# || block#) desc
;

select
    'alter '||s.segment_type||' '||t1.owner||'.'||s.segment_name||' storage
(buffer_pool keep);'
from
    t1,
    dba_segments s
where
    s.segment_name = t1.object_name
and
    s.owner = t1.owner
and
    s.segment_type = t1.object_type
and
    nvl(s.partition_name,'-') = nvl(t1.subobject_name,'-')
and
    buffer_pool <> 'KEEP'
and
    object_type in ('TABLE','INDEX')
group by
    s.segment_type,
    t1.owner,
    s.segment_name
having
    (sum(num_blocks)/greatest(sum(blocks), .001))*100 > 80
;


spool off;
```

The following is sample of the output from this script.

```
alter TABLE BOM.BOM_DELETE_SUB_ENTITIES storage (buffer_pool keep);
alter TABLE BOM.BOM_OPERATIONAL_ROUTINGS storage (buffer_pool keep);
alter INDEX BOM.CST_ITEM_COSTS_U1 storage (buffer_pool keep);
```

Another KEEP Pool Script Approach

As previously noted, it is possible for DBAs to choose their own rules for KEEP pool assignment, based on the unique characteristics of their own workload. Once it has been empirically verified that correct rule set is in use for the workload, this automation of KEEP pool assignments serves as a self-documenting feature.

The query shown below utilizes the *x$bh* view to identify all the objects that reside in blocks averaging over five touches and occupying over twenty blocks in the cache.

The script finds tables and indexes that are referenced frequently and are good candidates for inclusion in the KEEP pool.

🖫 buf_keep_pool_5_tch_20_blks.sql

```
-- ************************************************
-- You MUST connect as SYS to run this script
-- ************************************************
connect sys/manager;

set lines 80;
set pages 999;

column avg_touches            format 999
column myname heading 'Name'  format a30
column mytype heading 'Type'  format a10
column buffers                format 999,999

SELECT
   object_type  mytype,
   object_name    myname,
   blocks,
   COUNT(1) buffers,
   AVG(tch) avg_touches
FROM
   sys.x$bh     a,
   dba_objects b,
   dba_segments s
WHERE
   a.obj = b.object_id
and
   b.object_name = s.segment_name
and
   b.owner not in ('SYS','SYSTEM')
GROUP BY
   object_name,
   object_type,
   blocks,
   obj
having
   avg(tch) > 5
and
   count(1) > 20;
```

The following is the output where the active objects within the data buffers based on the number of data blocks and the number of touches are shown:

Type	Name	BLOCKS	BUFFERS	AVG_TOUCHES
TABLE	PAGE	104	107	44
TABLE	SUBSCRIPTION	192	22	52
INDEX	SEQ_KEY_IDX	40	34	47
TABLE	SEC_SESSIONS	80	172	70
TABLE	SEC_BROWSER_PROPERTIES	80	81	58

TABLE	EC_USER_SESSIONS	96	97	77

The DBA must now decide whether the hot objects are to be segregated into the KEEP pool.

The results from this script will differ every time it is executed because the data buffers are dynamic, and data storage is transient. Some DBAs schedule this script as often as every minute, if they need to see exactly what is occurring inside the data buffers.

Sizing the KEEP Pool

Once the tables and indexes have been loaded into the KEEP buffer pool, the *buffer_pool keep* syntax must be increased by the total number of blocks in the migrated tables.

The following script will total the number of blocks that the KEEP pool requires, insuring 100 percent data caching. The script adds 20 percent to the total to allow for growth in the cached objects. The DBA should run this script frequently to make sure the KEEP pool always has a DBHR of 100 percent.

🖫 size_keep_pool.sql

```
prompt The following will size your init.ora KEEP POOL,
prompt based on Oracle8 KEEP Pool assignment values
prompt

select
'BUFFER_POOL_KEEP = ('||trunc(sum(s.blocks)*1.2)||',2)'
from
   dba_segments s
where
   s.buffer_pool = 'KEEP';
```

This script outputs the Oracle parameter that resizes the KEEP pool for the next restart of the Oracle instance. The parameter is placed in the init.ora file. Oracle10g deprecates *buffer_pool keep* and it cannot be modified with an *alter system* command.

```
BUFFER_POOL_KEEP=(1456, 3)
```

Now, the database can be bounced and the parameter change will take effect.

Conclusion

This chapter has been dedicated to evaluating Oracle full-scan operations for effective SQL execution. The main points of this chapter include:

- Large-table full-table scans can be the most effective execution plan, but they can indicate missing indexes, missing materialized views and stale CBO statistics.

- Full-scan operations are favored by the *all_rows* optimizer goal, while index access is favored by *first_rows_n optimizer_mode*.

- It is not uncommon to find unnecessary full-scans when the SQL uses the *like* clause. It is possible to create specialized index techniques to allow for indexes to be invoked with the *like* clause.

- Not all large-table full-table scans are evil. Each query must be evaluated independently to determine whether the full-scan is better than index access.

- The caching of small-table full-table scans can be fully automated by using the KEEP pool and customized scripts.

With this information, it is now time to move on and explore more indexing techniques that will ensure that all SQL statements are running that peak performance.

Oracle SQL Tuning with Indexes

You must ensure that your SQL has the right indexes

Introduction

When discussing Oracle indexes it is important to understand that indexes have several functions. Indexes are used to maintain referential integrity and to remove full-table scans, but their most critical purpose is to speed up SQL by providing a direct path to matching table rows. An Oracle database can run without any indexes at all, but it is the tuning professional's job to create and maintain the optimal set of indexes for the SQL workload.

SQL Tuning with Indexes

Oracle is the world's most powerful and flexible database and it has numerous index types to improve the speed of Oracle SQL queries. Disk storage has become unbelievably inexpensive and Oracle leverages upon cheap storage with new indexing types, based upon algorithms that dramatically increase the speed with which Oracle queries are serviced.

This chapter explores the internals of Oracle indexing by reviewing the standard b-tree index, bitmap indexes, function-based indexes, and index-only tables (IOTs). It also covers how these indexes may dramatically increase the speed of Oracle SQL queries.

Because indexes are such an important component to SQL tuning, this chapter is quite large and covers these important topics:

- Types of Oracle Indexes
    - Single-column b-tree indexes
    - Multi-column b-tree indexes
    - Bitmap indexes
    - Bitmap join indexes
- Tuning SQL with function-based indexes
- Tuning SQL with the CASE statement
- Tuning SQL with regular expressions
- Using Index-only tables
- Removing superfluous indexes
- Removing un-used indexes
- Index usage and clustering
- Forcing index usage
- Index maintenance
- Index monitoring
- Rebuilding indexes for SQL performance

With respect to SQL optimization, Oracle uses indexes to alleviate the need for large-table, full-table scans and disk sorts. In the absence of an index, the SQL optimizer may not be able to find an efficient way to service the SQL query and invoke an expensive full table scan.

Not all full-scans are bad!

Hot Tip!

If your SQL *optimizer_mode is* set to minimize computing resources (*all_rows*), a full-scan on a small table may be more efficient than index access.

In addition to speeding up SQL, Oracle indexes are also used to enforce the uniqueness of columns and to maintain one-to-many and many-to many data relationships, as defined by primary and foreign keys constraints.

When a user creates a primary or unique foreign key, Oracle builds indexes on their behalf and then uses these indexes to enforce the data relationships between all parent and child rows.

For example, in a one-to-many relationship, Oracle will not allow a child row to exist without a matching parent row, and every insert of a row to the child table will cause Oracle to lookup the parent key to ensure that the logical data relationship is maintained.

Be careful when disabling referential integrity!

Look Out!

While Oracle does not recommend it, some database independent ERP applications such as SAP will turn off primary and foreign key constraints in order to improve DML performance and reduce overhead.

While some trustworthy applications will deliberately disable indexes for primary and foreign keys, this techniques only works in systems where the end-user cannot access the database with any ad-hoc interfaces such as SQL*Plus or ODBC.

Turning-off referential integrity is risky, but it has been done successfully for applications that require high performance data loading. In some applications, referential integrity is temporarily disabled and re-enabled after batch data loads.

The Types of Oracle indexes

Oracle offers a wealth of index structures, each with their own benefits and drawbacks. Here are some of the most common:

- **Single-column B-tree indexes**: This is the standard tree index that Oracle has been using since the earliest releases.

- **Multi-column b-tree indexes:** Multiple columns can be defined to match any SQL *where* clause, providing super-fast access to the desired rows. These *concatenated* indexes allow many table columns to be combined into a single index.

- **Bitmap indexes:** Bitmap indexes are commonly used where an index column has a relatively small number of distinct values, low cardinality. Bitmap indexes are common in data warehouses, and they are suitable for tables that experience frequent updates.

- **Bitmap join indexes:** This is an index structure whereby data columns from other tables appear in a multi-column index of a junction table. This is the only create index syntax to employ a SQL-like *from* clause and *where* clause.

- **Index-only tables**: In cases where every column in the table is needed by a multi-column index, the table itself becomes redundant, and the table rows can be maintained within the index tree.

- **Reverse key indexes:** To improve SQL *insert* performance, an index can be built with the *reverse* keyword, internally reversing the keys. The reverse key index behaves like an ordinary b-tree index, but it performs faster in RAC systems. See Chapter 18, **Oracle DML Tuning** for details on using reverse key indexes.

Except in rare exceptions, Oracle will only use one index to access any given table. In complex n-way table joins, however, there may be many index types in the plan, including bitmap indexes, a single-column b-tree index or multi-column b-tree indexes.

The following sections will provide a deeper look into each type of Oracle index and show how they are used to speed up SQL queries by reviewing standard Oracle b-tree indexes.

The Oracle b-tree Index

The oldest and most popular type of Oracle index is the tried and true b-tree index, a basic index type that has not changed since the earliest releases of Oracle and remains the most widely used index type within a typical Oracle database. Conceptually, Oracle uses a rows location as a pointer to a row. Just as a home address uniquely identifies where an individual lives, an Oracle ROWID uniquely identified where an index rows resides.

A b-tree index can be conceptualized as a long list of key and ROWID pairs, organized in a tree form for fast lookup of a symbolic key. However, in reality, the higher level index nodes will have start and end key values, while the lowest level tree nodes contain the actual ROWID and key pairs. The amount of key pairs in the lowest level nodes depends upon the key length and the index blocksize.

Oracle can read an index sideways via the index fast full scan, but the most common access method is traversing an index via dropping-down into the index using the key value as illustrated in Figure 6.1 below:

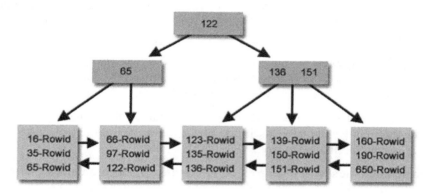

Figure 6.1: *An Oracle b-tree index*

In addition to speeding access to table rows, b-tree indexes are also used to avoid large sorting operations. In most queries with an *order by* clause, Oracle will retrieve the rows and then sort them in RAM.

However, the optimizer can also choose to use the index to fetch the rows in pre-sorted order. For example, a SQL query requiring 10,000 rows to be presented in sorted order will often use a b-tree index to avoid the very large sort required to deliver the data to the end user.

It is then possible to drop quickly through the tree to find the symbolic key, and once the corresponding ROWID has been located, the rows can be fetched directly as shown in Figure 6.2:

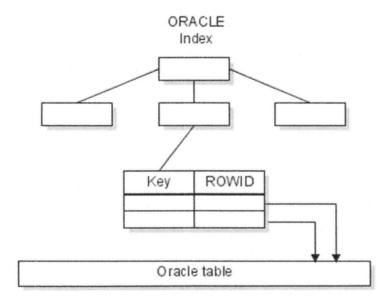

Figure 6.2: *Index traversal for a b-tree index*

Oracle offers several options when creating an index using the default b-tree structure. A *concatenated* index can be created on multiple columns to improve access speeds for queries with multiple *where* clause predicates. It is also possible to specify that different columns be sorted in different orders with one column sorted *ascending* and the next column in *descending* order. This is very an index can be forced to match the sort order of a report and fetch the report rows quickly, in pre-sorted order.

For example, the following code would create a b-tree index on a column called *last_name* in ascending order and have a second column within the index that displays the salary column in descending order:

```
create index
   name_salary_idx
on
   person
(
   last_name   asc,
   salary      desc
);
```

While b-tree indexes are great for simple queries, they are not very good for low-cardinality columns. These are columns with a relatively low number of distinct values and do not have the selectivity required in order to benefit from standard b-tree index structures.

In order to properly manage the blocks, Oracle controls the allocation of pointers within each data block. As an Oracle tree grows via the insertion of rows into the table, Oracle fills the block. Then the block is full, it splits, creating new index nodes (data blocks) to manage the symbolic keys within the index. Hence, an Oracle index block may contain two types of pointers:

- Pointers to other index nodes (data blocks)
- ROWID pointers to specific table rows

Oracle manages the allocation of pointers within index blocks, and this is the reason why a *pctused* value, the freelist re-link threshold, cannot be specified for indexes. When an index block structure is examined closely, the number of entries within each index node is a function of two values:

- The length of the symbolic key
- The blocksize for the index tablespace

Each data block within the index contains nodes in the index tree, with the bottom nodes, leaf blocks, containing pairs of symbolic keys and ROWID values.

A single task inserts rows into an empty Oracle b-tree until the block is logically full, based on the specification of the *pctfree* parameter for the index. At that point, inserts of more rows will cause the index tree to split, creating a new index node on a new data block to manage the symbolic keys within the index. Hence, an Oracle index block may contain pointers to other index nodes or ROWID/Symbolic-key pairs.

Creating a b-tree Index

Conceptually a b-tree index can be thought of as a set of symbolic keys and ROWID pairs that allow the SQL to lookup the symbolic key and quickly find the matching ROWID. Once the SQL has the ROWID, it can proceed directly to the desired data block and fetch the row.

When an index has been created, it is important to note that Oracle b-tree indexes have two layers, a logical layer, consisting of the key and ROWID pairs, and a physical layer, consisting of the disk data blocks. Because Oracle's software engineers chose to map the boundary of a logical index node to a disk data block, the blocksize impacts the structure of the index tree.

The Oracle block size serves as the boundaries for each index node, *(inode)* for short, and the index blocksize determines how many pairs of symbolic keys and ROWIDs may fit on each index node.

As an index grows, there are two types of expansion operations:

- **Splitting:** As the data block become logically full according to the setting for the *pctfree* index parameter, each index block is marked as full and the disk data block removed from the index freelist. Subsequent index growth will require Oracle to fetch a new data block from the freelist, thereby adding a new node to the index tree.

- **Spawning:** At predetermined size threshold, Oracle will decide to spawn the b-tree to create a new level. The number of levels for any given index can be viewed in the *blevel* column of the *dba_indexes* view. The most common height of an index is three levels, but large data warehouses will see indexes spawn into four tree levels.

Now that how the logical tree nodes are tied to the physical disk blocks has been covered, let's examine how the size of the disk data block impacts the b-tree structure.

Index behavior and Oracle blocksize

Because the blocksize affects the number of keys within each index node, it follows that the blocksize will have an effect on the structure of the index tree. All else being equal, large 32k blocksizes will have more keys per data block, resulting in a flatter index than the same index created in a 2k tablespace. A large blocksize will also reduce the number of consistent gets during index access, improving performance for scattered reads and range scan access.

While most Oracle databases will not see any appreciable benefit from multiple blocksizes, mission-critical applications can see a real benefit. In very large, high-activity databases, some Oracle tuning experts utilize the multiple blocksize feature of Oracle because it provides buffer segregation and the ability to place objects with the most appropriate blocksize to reduce buffer waste.

Because the index block size is directly tied to the index node structure, an index in a 2k blocksize with have less index keys per node than an index that uses a 32k blocksize, and an index in a 2k blocksize will also spawn into more levels than an index in a 32k blocksize.

According to Christopher Foot, author of the OCP Instructors Guide for Oracle DBA Certification, larger index block sizes might improve the key density and improve the run-time index performance, with less tree levels to traverse in order to fetch the required ROWID:

> *"A bigger block size means more space for key storage in the branch nodes of B-tree indexes, which reduces index height and improves the performance of indexed queries."*

While in most cases the index blocksize does not have an appreciable effect on SQL performance, very large mission critical databases with frequently deploy multiple blocksizes for indexes under these conditions:

- **Preventing index key fragmentation**: Indexes on large column datatypes (e.g. *varchar(2000)*, *clob*, *long*) should have a large enough blocksize to hold multiple rows on a single data block. For example, an 8k blocksize would not be appropriate for an index on a 10k symbolic key.

- **Small blocksizes and RAC**: Oracle Real Application Clusters (RAC) system can reduce pinging if indexes are placed in a smaller blocksize. This minimizes the overhead of block transfers across the cache fusion layer.

- **Small blocksizes to reduce contention**: In cases of super-high concurrent DML, placing an index into a smaller blocksize can increase throughout. In some high-performance systems, high-DML indexes will be segregated into non-standard blocksizes with smaller data buffers, thereby improving DML performance by reducing the amount of data buffer block to scan when seeking dirty blocks.

- **Large blocksize for large reads:** In certain cases, you will place an index that experiences lots of multi-block range scans, index fast full scans into a larger blocksize, thereby increasing the amount of data retrieved in a single read operation.

Today, most large corporate Oracle systems will deploy the multiple blocksize feature of Oracle because it provides buffer segregation and the ability to place objects with the most appropriate blocksize to reduce buffer waste. Some of the world record TPC Oracle benchmarks use very large data buffers and multiple blocksizes, see www.tpc.org for details.

Look Out!

Multiple blocksizes are not for everyone!

Deploying multiple index blocksizes requires considerable experience and skill, and it should only be attempted on very large corporate databases by a seasoned Oracle DBA. Again, multiple blocksizes are only for high-activity VLDB systems.

Now that what happens when a b-tree index grows has been covered, it is a good time to examine what happens when an index contracts. Whenever possible, Oracle attempts to keep the index data blocks evenly balanced, but when rows are deleted en-masse, Oracle deliberately chooses not to incur the runtime overhead of re-balancing the index disk data block.

It would take considerable overhead to move rows around to evenly balance the tree entries across the data blocks, and the Oracle engineers wisely chose to include a logical delete feature. As rows are deleted, Oracle maintains an internal threshold, similar to the *pctused* threshold for tables, where Oracle marks a data block as empty without physically taking the overhead to wipe the disk block clean.

In cases where large batch jobs delete millions of rows from tables, massive empty spaces appears on the data block, leading to an index fragmentation condition called *index browning*. Just as a lightning strike can cause a section of a tree to become dead, Oracle indexes will have large numbers of near-empty data blocks that cause index scan operations to take longer than required.

If the extra-cost Oracle Segment Advisor software has been purchased, Oracle can be configured to make notifications about this condition.

The next section will delve into how bitmap indexes are used in read-only database for super-fast access to low cardinality columns.

Tuning SQL with Bitmapped Indexes

Oracle bitmap indexes are very different from standard b-tree indexes. Bitmap structures can be conceptualized as a two-dimensional array with one column for every row in the table being indexed. Each column represents a distinct value within the bitmapped index. This two-dimensional array represents each value within the index multiplied by the number of rows in the table.

At row retrieval time, Oracle decompresses the bitmap into the RAM data buffers so it can be rapidly scanned for matching values. These matching values are delivered to Oracle in the form of a ROWID list, and these ROWID values may directly access the required information.

It is very easy for a beginner to forget that bitmap indexes are only for low-cardinality columns, meaning columns with only a few unique values like *gender, color, year of birth* or *ethnicity*, and bitmap indexes are effective in read-only tables only where new rows are loaded at night and the bitmaps rebuilt.

Distinct Key Values and Bitmap Indexes!

The maximum cardinality for bitmap indexes is a function of the number of distinct values and the size of the key, but far and away it is the number of distinct values that

---

is the largest contributing factor to the maximum number of distinct values possible in a bitmap index.

As the number of distinct values increases, the number of rows in the bitmap increases linearly, such that a bitmap index with 100 values may thousands of times smaller than a bitmap index on 10,000 distinct column values.

Benchmarks have shown these trends in SQL performance and the number of distinct bitmap index values, as a percentage of total table rows, and the clustering factor for the index column. All else being equal, cardinality is one of the most important factors in deciding to use a bitmap index, but there are rare cases where a bitmap on a column with 10,000 key values might be appropriate.

So, what is the maximum threshold for unique values in a bitmap index? The answer, as with all Oracle tuning questions, is "It depends". To understand how a bitmap works, remember that a bitmap is a two dimensional matrix with two axis. The number of rows in the table is one axis, and the number of distinct key values is the other axis as illustrated in Figure 6.3:

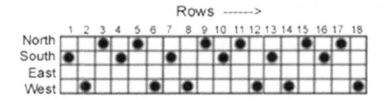

Figure 6.3: *A bitmap index is a two dimensional array*

Hence, a bitmap index on a million row table with ten distinct values in the index column will have ten million cells in the bitmap. Conversely, a bitmap on a million rows table with an index column with 1,000 distinct values will be much larger, with a billion cells.

The *clustering_factor* is important because Oracle performs bitmap index compression.

If a bitmap index column has a good *clustering factor* , meaning that it is close to the number of blocks in the table, the index values are adjacent, and Oracle will be able to compress the index far better than a bitmap on an unclustered column.

Bitmap Compression, Row Clustering, and Column Cardinality

It should be clear that it is not exclusively the number of distinct values in the index that governs the choice of using a bitmap, it is also a function of the percentage the distinct values as a percentage of rows in the table and the clustering of the column values, as per the *clustering_factor* column in the *dba_indexes* view. Hence, a decision for a bitmap is a function of these criteria:

- **The ratio of rows to distinct values**: A more accurate estimate of the suitability of a bitmap index is the ratio of distinct rows to the number of total rows in a table.

- **Clustering factor**: The clustering of the index keys to the physical data blocks has an influence on bitmap indexes.

In a table where the bitmap columns appear in the same physical order as the rows, related column values will be adjacent on each data block.

The *clustering_factor* will be close to the value of the *blocks* column in *dba_data_files*, and Oracle will be able to compress the bitmap index.

When a bitmap index sees repeating column values, the matching rows can be omitted from the bitmap. As a bitmap is being created or updated, Oracle looks to the previous index entry.

If it is the same, Oracle replaces the bitmap entry with a SAME AS PRIOR flag and continues until a new key value is detected.

As an extreme case, consider a million rows table where the column has 100,000 distinct values and *clustering_factor* ~= blocks.

Because all adjacent columns values are grouped together, the bitmap axis goes from 1,000,000 rows down to 100,000, making for a highly compressed bitmap.

In the compressed example below, all East rows appear adjacent in rows 1-5, all North values reside on rows 6-13, all South values are in rows 14-15, and all West rows reside on rows 16-18 as shown in Figure 6.4:

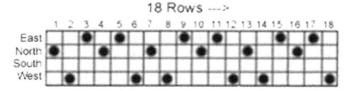

An unclustered bitmap

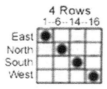

A clustered bitmap

Figure 6.4: *A bitmap index compresses adjacent key value*

Again, in most cases, there will not be a lot of adjacent index values, so it quite rare to see extensive compression.

Exceptions to the Rule! High Cardinality Bitmap Indexes

Oracle is not an exact science, and for every rule there are exceptions!

At first glance, the Oracle 11g documentation can appear contradictory. In some places, there are excellent rules-of-thumb for bitmap index cardinality:

> *"You typically want to use bitmap indexes on low degree of cardinality columns and B-tree indexes on high degree of cardinality columns.*
>
> *As a general rule, a cardinality of under 1% makes a good candidate for a bitmap index."*

However, there are rare cases where high cardinality columns can be used in bitmap indexes, and Oracle suggests that these conditions are acceptable for a bitmap index:

- If the number of distinct values of a column is less than 1% of the number of rows in the table.

- If the values in a column are repeated more than 100 times, then the column is a candidate for a bitmap index.

Now that bitmap index compression has been explained, it should be clear that there are rare cases where high cardinality columns might be candidates for bitmap indexes.

So, which are the right maximum values for a bitmap index? Who knows? Running performance benchmarks on each unique database will be required to find the answer!

The only way to know for sure is to perform real-world benchmark testing real SQL workloads. The *dbms_workload_capture* procedure can be used to grab a representative SQL workload from the production database and replay the workload in a test instance using the new bitmap index.

Now that the fundamental issues surrounding bitmap indexes have been addressed, it is a good time to examine how they are used by the SQL optimizer to fetch rows with a minimum of buffer touches.

Combining Bitmaps: The Bitmap Merge Operation

Bitmap indexes are normally used with static tables and materialized views which are updated at night and rebuilt after batch row loading.

Beware of bitmap on high DML tables!

Bitmap indexes are best for tables that are read-only during query time. The DML overhead of maintaining bitmap indexes can be huge, and while bitmap index update speed is improved in 11g, updates are still quite expensive.

Because bitmap columns are generally low cardinality, they have very little value by themselves, and the power comes when Oracle combines multiple bitmaps in a bitmap merge operation. Remember, the real benefit of bitmapped indexing occurs when one table includes multiple bitmapped indexes.

Alone, each individual column has low cardinality is not very selective, but the creation of multiple bitmapped indexes provides a very powerful method for rapidly answering difficult SQL queries as illustrated in Figure 6.5:

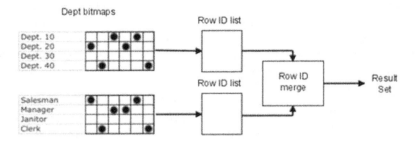

Figure 6.5: *A bitmap merge operation*

Consider a case where there are multiple columns with low cardinality values, such as *car_color*, *car_make*, *car_model* and *car_year*. Each column contains less than 100 distinct values on their own, and a b-tree index would be fairly useless in a database of 20 million vehicles.

However, combining these indexes in a query can provide response times that are a lot faster than the traditional method of reading each one of the 20 million rows in the base table. For example, assume the goal is to find the license plate numbers of maroon Fords manufactured in 2011:

```
-- ***************************************************
-- SQL will multiple low-cardinality specifications
-- ***************************************************

select
   license_plat_nbr
from
   vehicle
where
   color = 'maroon'
and
   make = 'ford'
and
   year = 2011;
```

Oracle uses a specialized optimizer method called a bitmapped index merge to service this query. In a bitmapped index merge, each Row ID, or RID, list is built independently by using the bitmaps, and a special merge routine is used in order to compare the RID lists and find the intersecting values. Using this methodology, Oracle can provide sub-second response time when working against multiple low-cardinality columns as shown in Figure 6.6:

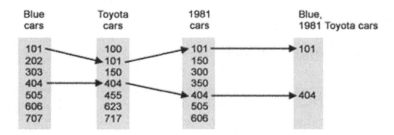

Figure 6.6: *Oracle bitmap merge join*

When using bitmapped indexes, it is important to remember several very important points:

- **Tables are commonly be read-only:** The run-time overhead for updating a bitmap is huge, and bitmapped indexes are designed for databases where data is loaded in batch mode, and the bitmaps recreated after each data load.

- **Columns are usually low cardinality:** Each unique value of a bitmap index increases the size of an index, and as a general rule, and column with more than a few hundred distinct values will not perform well with a bitmap index.

- **Combinatorial SQL is best for bitmaps:** Any single bitmap index is of very limited value, and the real power of a bitmap index happens when a SQL query has predicates from multiple low-cardinality columns.

This section has given some insight into the power of bitmap indexes, so it makes sense to now move on and look at a cousin of the bitmapped index, the bitmap join index, a novel way of pre-joining related table columns for fast row retrieval.

SQL Tuning with Bitmap Join Indexes

Oracle9*i* first added the bitmap join index to its mind-boggling array of table join methods. This new table access method required the creation of an index that performs the join at index creation time and that creates a bitmap index of the keys used in the join. But unlike most relational database indexes, the indexed columns do not reside in the table.

Oracle revolutionized index creation by allowing a *where* clause to be included in the index creation syntax. This feature revolutionized the way relational tables are accessed via SQL.

The bitmap join index is extremely useful for table joins that involve low-cardinality columns, but bitmap join indexes are not useful in all cases. They should not be used for OLTP databases due to the high overhead associated with updating bitmap indexes. The next section will provide a closer look at how this type of index works.

How Bitmap Join Indexes Work

The following is a simple example for illustrating bitmap join indexes. It consists of a many-to-many relationship where there are parts and suppliers with an inventory table serving as the junction for the many-to-many relationship. Each part has many suppliers and each supplier provides many parts as illustrated in Figure 6.7:

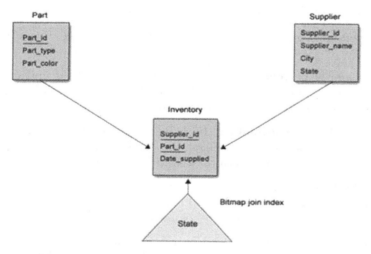

Figure 6.7: *A bitmap join index on a many-to-many relationship*

This bitmap join index specified the join criteria for the three tables and created a bitmap index on the junction table (Inventory) with the *part_type* and *state* keys.

For this example, assume the database has 300 types of parts and the suppliers provide parts in all 50 states. So there are 50 distinct values in the *state* column and 300 distinct values in the *part_type* column.

Note that an index was created on the Inventory table using columns contained in the *Supplier* and *Part* tables. The idea behind a bitmap join index is to pre-join the low cardinality columns, making the overall join faster.

It is well known that bitmap indexes can improve the performance of Oracle queries where the predicates involve the low cardinality columns, but this technique has never been employed in cases where the low cardinality columns reside in a foreign table.

To create a bitmap join index, issue the following Oracle DDL, noting the inclusion of the *from* and *where* clauses inside the *create index* syntax:

```
create bitmap index
   part_suppliers_state
on
   inventory(
      parts.part_type,
      supplier.state)
from
   inventory i,
   parts p,
   supplier s
where
   i.part_id=p.part_id
and
   i.supplier_id=p.supplier_id;
```

This is a fascinating idea: the concept of placing a SQL *where* clause in a *create index* statement! The bitmap join index syntax borrows the ANSI *from* clause and *where* clause from SQL.

Bitmap Join Index Example

The following example uses a SQL query to illustrate how bitmap join indexes work. To get a list of all suppliers of pistons in North Carolina, this query would be used:

```
select
   supplier_name
from
   parts
natural join
   inventory
natural join
   suppliers
where
   part_type = 'piston' and state='nc';
```

Prior to Oracle9i, this form of SQL query would be serviced by a *nested loops* join or *hash* join of all three tables. With a bitmap join index, the index has pre-joined the tables, and the query can quickly retrieve a row ID list of matching table rows in all three tables.

Oracle benchmarks claim that bitmap join indexes can run a query more than eight times faster than traditional indexing methods. However, this speed improvement is dependent upon many factors, and the bitmap join is not a panacea. Some restrictions on using the bitmap join index include:

- The indexed columns must be of low cardinality, usually with less than 100 distinct values.

- The query must not have any references in the *where* clause to data columns that are not contained in the index.

- The overhead when updating bitmap join indexes is substantial. For practical use, bitmap join indexes are dropped and rebuilt each evening about the daily batch load jobs. This means that bitmap join indexes are useful only for Oracle data warehouses that remain read-only during the processing day.

Remember: Bitmap join indexes can tremendously speed up specific data warehouse queries but at the expense of pre-joining the tables at bitmap index creation time. It makes sense to also be concerned about high-volume updates. Bitmap indexes are notoriously slow to change when the table data changes, and this can severely slow down *insert* and *update* DML against the target tables.

Exclusions for Bitmap Join Indexes

Oracle imposes restrictions on when the SQL optimizer is allowed to invoke a bitmap join index. For queries that have additional criteria in the *where* clause that does not appear in the bitmap join index, Oracle will be unable to use this index to service the query. For example, the following query will not use the bitmap join index:

```
select
   supplier_name
from
   parts
natural join
   inventory
natural join
   suppliers
where
   part_type = 'piston'
and
   state = 'nc' and part_color = 'yellow';
```

Oracle has introduced extremely sophisticated execution plan features that can dramatically improve query performance, but these features cannot be used automatically. The Oracle professional's challenge is to understand these new indexing features, analyze the trade-offs of additional indexing, and judge when the new features can be used to speed queries.

When Oracle SQL Chooses the Wrong Index

Back in the day when Oracle used the rule-based optimizer, up until 2007 in Oracle apps, the rule-based optimizer would commonly choose an index with poor selectivity.

If the goal for SQL tuning is fast response time, the point is simply to get the desired rows with a minimum of data block touches. With respect to indexes, one sure sign of Oracle choosing a wrong index, one with less that optimal selectivity, is excessive *db file sequential read*, the type of disk read that indicates index access. The Oracle *tkprof* utility can easily be run to see the I/O details for any SQL statement.

Oracle SQL has metadata that shows the selectivity of the index, and it is rare to see Oracle choose a less than stellar index, unless, of course, there is a missing index. However, there are cases where Oracle SQL chooses the wrong index, even in Oracle 11g.

Hot Tip!

Beware of high sequential reads!

Oracle can tell you if you are using a wrong index. One sure sign of a sub-optimal index are cases where you see too many *db file sequential read* events to justify fetching the row set.

Beware of the Fast Fix

If a sub-optimal index bug is reported to Oracle technical support, it is important to resist the temptation to set the *optimizer_features_enable* parameter. This is a fast fix workaround approach that fixes the issue but does not address the root cause issue that caused the optimizer to choose the wrong index. Instead of downgrading the optimizer functionality to an earlier release, insist that Oracle resolve the root cause issue and issue a patch for the problem.

What are the best techniques for forcing the optimizer to use an index? While this technique is rarely used in production environments, it is a great SQL tuning tool, allowing query execution time to be tested with different indexes.

Forcing Index Usage

One of the most common question that I hear is *"Why is Oracle not using my index?"* Usually, this is because the table is so small that full-scan access is always faster and

---

cheaper; however, there are cases when the execution of a SQL statement is deliberately altered to change index access. Here are some common techniques:

- Changing optimizer parameters (*optimizer_mode*, *optimizer_index_cost_adj*)

- Adding column histograms with *dbms_stats*

- Changing index attributes: unique vs nonunique

- Using an index hint

In general, index access usually starts returning rows faster than full-scan activity, but there are exceptions. Remember, it is the cost of the read-write head movement time on an I/O that takes up most of the latency, and a multi-block read from a full scan that scan a dozen data blocks will always take less time than a dozen individual disk reads on discontiguous block.

Obviously, if I only want a dozen rows from a million row table, using an index would be the best access method, but what about a query that reads 30% of the table rows? What about a query that reads 60% of the table rows?

What is the threshold for using an index? The answer depends primarily upon the number of rows requested and the density of the rows per block, which, in turn, are a function of *avg_row_len* and *db_xxk_block_size*. But in the real world it is not that simple, since there are many other intervening factors such as how much if an index is cached in RAM (see the *optimizer_index_caching* parameter), and the selectivity of the target index.

Look Out!

Are you under-indexed?

When I evaluate an OLTP database, I check how much space is used for indexes vs. data. A properly indexed OLTP database will have at least 30% of space dedicated to indexes, often as much as 60%.

Oracle Does Not Use My Index

Oracle not using an index can be due to:

- **Bad/incomplete statistics**: Make sure to re-analyze the table and index with *dbms_stats* to ensure that the optimizer has good metadata.

- **Wrong optimizer_mode**: The *first_rows_n* optimizer mode is to minimize response time, and it is more likely to use an index than the default *all_rows* mode.

Advanced Oracle SQL Tuning

- **Bugs**: There are a variety of optimizer changes in recent releases of the database that cause Oracle not to use an index.

- **Cost adjustment**: In some cases, the optimizer will still not use an index, and the *optimizer_index_cost_adj* must be decreased.

Try a rule hint!

For testing unnecessary large table full table scans, try a *rule* hint (*select /*+ RULE */ col1*). If the query uses the index with a *rule* hint, you have an issue with the CBO statistics.

The Oracle cost-based optimizer (CBO) carefully evaluates every query when making the decision whether to invoke a full-table scan or index access, and index usage can be forced with in index hint. The goal of the SQL optimizer is to only force an index when it is the best access plan for any given optimization goals. As a review, we repeat Figure 6.8, showing a number of factors that can influence Oracle's choice of index:

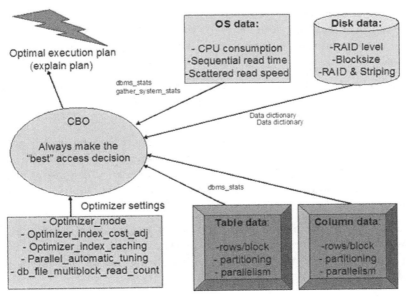

Figure 6.8: *Many factors influence Oracle's choice of index*

Some of the variables that influence the decision to force or ignore an index include:

- **The numbers of blocks in the table:** Small tables are accessed faster with a full scan and forcing index usage may hurt performance.

- **System statistics:** the *dbms_stats.gather_system_stats* procedure measures external timing for index access (sequential reads) and full-scan access (scattered reads). If Oracle sees expensive index disk reads, it may ignore an index.

- **System parameters:** There are several initialization parameters that can impact the propensity of the optimizer to choose an index:

  - ***db_file_multiblock_read_count:*** Prior to this setting becoming automating in Oracle 10.2, this parameter helped govern the relative costs of full-scan vs. index costs.

  - ***sort_area_size*** (if not using *pga_aggregate_target*): The *sort_area_size* influences the CBO when deciding whether to perform an index access or a sort of the result set. The higher the value for *sort_area_size*, the more likely that a sort will be performed in RAM, and the more likely that the CBO will favor a sort over presorted index retrieval.

- **Optimizer parameter values:** Several optimizer parameters can be adjusted to force Oracle to use an index:

  - ***optimizer_mode:*** The *all_rows* access method often favors a parallel full-table scan over an index scan. The *first_rows_n optimizer_mode* will often stop Oracle from ignoring an index because it favors index access over computing resources.

  - ***optimizer_index_cost_adj:*** This parameter alters the costing algorithm for access paths involving indexes. The smaller the value, the lower the cost of index access.

  - ***optimizer_index_caching:*** The *optimizer_index_caching* parameter is set by the DBA to help the optimizer know, on average, how much of an index resides inside the data buffer. The setting for *optimizer_index_caching* affects the CBO's decision to use an index for a table join (nested loops) or to favor a full-table scan.

For an example of how parameters can effect index usage, a developer may be tempted to switch to the *all_rows optimizer_mode* or add an *all_rows* hint to their SQL, believing that it will improve throughput, while not realizing that *all_rows* favors full-scans over index usage.

In a similar example, some developers will mistakenly add a *parallel* hint to a SQL statement to improve performance, not realizing that Oracle parallel query only works with full-scans.

The Oracle SQL optimizer is obviously very intelligent, and he will often bypass an index whenever a full-scan or a more selective index can be used.

The next section will explore the most powerful indexing tool of all, the function-based index. The FBI is the single most frequently overlooked of all of the SQL tuning tools.

Using *nls_date_format* with Date Indexes

One of the single most common SQL coding errors is a developer specifying a date check in their *where* clause that invalidates the data, index causing a sub-optimal SQL execution plan. In more serious cases, improperly specific date references in a SQL *where* clause can cause production crashes, especially when the SQL only fails with specific date values.

Hence, properly specifying date values is critical to proper SQL coding, and many SQL experts advise explicitly specifying the date conversion to that the predicate compares values, date to date:

```
select
   stuff
from
   mytab
where
   order_date > to_date('14-MAY-2009','DD-MON-YYYY');
```

As a best practice, the left-hand side column should be free of any built-in functions that will make the index unusable.

Function-based indexes can be used to make an index match the *where* clause exactly, but in many cases the index can be used with a few adjustments to the syntax of the data statement and adjusting the *nls_date_format* parameter.

One maddening feature of relational databases is the implicit *date* datatypes and the problems associated with making the SQL use a generic index upon a *date* column.

In SQL, there is always an implicit type conversion when a SQL statement does a date check. To understand this issue, consider these queries:

```
--*********************************************************
-- This will use the index because nls_date_format matches
--*********************************************************
alter session set nls_date_format= 'DD-MON-YYYY';
select stuff from mytab where order_date > '14-MAY-2009';

alter session set nls_date_format = 'MON';
select stuff from mytab where order_date = 'MAR';
```

```
alter session set nls_date_format = 'DAY';
select stuff from mytab where order_date = 'TUESDAY';
```

```
-- ********************************************************
-- These may not use the order_date index because of
-- the nls_date_format mismatch
-- ********************************************************
alter session set nls_date_format= 'DD-MON-RR';
select stuff from mytab where order_date > '14-MAY-2009';

alter session set nls_date_format = 'DAY';
select stuff from mytab where order_date = 'APRIL';

alter session set nls_date_format = 'MON';
select stuff from mytab where order_date = 'TUESDAY';
```

Why does the second set of queries fail to use an index? This is because Oracle always does an implicit conversion of the right-hand side of the query to change the predicate into a date datatype.

Problems occur when the system's default *nls_date_format* does not match the database where the original query was written and tested. This can lead to super-serious production problems, especially when the implicit conversion makes the SQL work with some dates and not others.

The setting for *nls_territory* and *nls_date* can affect the *nls_date_format*, such that SQL may not use an index when moved onto another platform. This is why it is important to always test the SQL to ensure that the date index is being used.

These cases are rare, but when problems occur, the results can be devastating. As a developer best practice, many shops require the SQL coder to explicitly perform the conversion using the *to_date* built-in function. This also has the side benefit of not requiring careful monitoring of the current value for *nls_date_format*:

```
-- ********************************************************************
-- To be safe, match the data datatypes and specify the date format:
-- ********************************************************************
select stuff from mytab
where
   order_date > to_date('14-MAY-2009','DD-MON-YYYY');

select stuff from mytab
where
   order_date = to_date('APRIL','MON');

select stuff from mytab
where
   order_date = to_date('TUESDAY','DAY');
```

This is how the *nls_date_format* can help Oracle use indexes. Taking it to the next level involves information on how to write the correct syntax for complex date manipulation in SQL.

Managing Complex Date Comparisons in SQL

It is fairly easy to put a date check in SQL, but it is not so easy to ensure that the SQL uses the matching date index. To aid in specifying complex date predicates, Oracle offers a host of powerful functions for comparing date column values.

For example, assume a query to is needed display data from the first Monday of each quarter year. In this case, the *add_months* function can elegantly be used to return the answer, while ensuring that the query is able to use the data index:

```
select
   stuff
from
   mytab
where
   'next_day(add_months(trunc(sysdate, ''q''), 3), ''monday'')'
```

The next few sections will show some more examples of using date BIF's for complex SQL *where* clause specifications.

Using the *months_between* Date Function

This Oracle date function returns the months between two dates. For example, to figure out how many months an employee has worked for the company, the *months_between* Oracle date function can be used:

```
select
  months_between(sysdate,emp_date_of_hire)
from
  emp;
```

```
MONTHS_BETWEEN(SYSDATE,EMP_DATE_OF_HIRE)
----------------------------------------
                              58.7710805
                              70.7710805
                              34.7710805
```

This Oracle date function returns the fraction of a month. Trunc or round could be used to make the results more readable.

Using the *add_months* Date Function

The *add_months* Oracle date function gives the same day, n number of months away. Note that the n can be positive or negative, so it is possible to go backwards in time.

```
select
  sysdate,
  add_months(sysdate,1),
  add_months(sysdate,2),
  add_months(sysdate,3),
  add_months(sysdate,4),
  add_months(sysdate,5),
  add_months(sysdate,6)
from
  dual;
```

```
SYSDATE    ADD_MONTH ADD_MONTH ADD_MONTH ADD_MONTH ADD_MONTH ADD_MONTH
--------- --------- --------- --------- --------- --------- ---------
24-JAN-05 24-FEB-05 24-MAR-05 24-APR-05 24-MAY-05 24-JUN-05 24-JUL-05
```

```
select
  sysdate,
  add_months(sysdate,-1),
  add_months(sysdate,-2),
  add_months(sysdate,-3),
  add_months(sysdate,-4),
  add_months(sysdate,-5),
  add_months(sysdate,-6)
from
  dual;
```

```
SYSDATE    ADD_MONTH ADD_MONTH ADD_MONTH ADD_MONTH ADD_MONTH ADD_MONTH
--------- --------- --------- --------- --------- --------- ---------
24-JAN-05 24-DEC-04 24-NOV-04 24-OCT-04 24-SEP-04 24-AUG-04 24-JUL-04
```

Using the *last_day* Date Function

The *last_day* Oracle date function returns the last day of the month of the input date. To find the first day of the next month, one can be added to the *last_day* results.

```
select
  sysdate,
  last_day(sysdate)    eom,
  last_day(sysdate)+1 fom
from dual;
```

```
SYSDATE    EOM       FOM
--------- --------- ---------
24-JAN-05 31-JAN-05 01-FEB-05
```

Using the *next_day* Date Function

The *next_day* Oracle date function returns the date of the *day_of_week* after date d. *day_of_week* can be the full name or abbreviation.

Below, *next_day()* is used to get the date for the next Monday, next Friday, and the first Tuesday of next month.

```
select
  sysdate,
  next_day(sysdate,'monday') "next mon",
  next_day(sysdate,'friday') "next fri",
  next_day(last_day(sysdate)+1,'tuesday') "first tue"
from dual;
```

```
SYSDATE    Next Mon  Next Fri  First Tue
---------  --------- --------- ---------
24-JAN-05 31-JAN-05 28-JAN-05 08-FEB-05
```

Using the *round* Date Function

The *round* function is commonly used to round-off numbers, but *round()* can also be used with dates. The *round()* function returns the date rounded to the format.

In this example, the current date (24 January 2005) is rounded to the closest month and year:

```
select
  sysdate,
  round(sysdate,'month') month,
  round(sysdate,'year')  year
from
  dual;
```

```
SYSDATE   MONTH     YEAR
--------- --------- ---------
24-JAN-05 01-FEB-05 01-JAN-05
```

Notice that *sysdate* is past midmonth so the month was rounded to the next month. The example is not past midyear, however, so the year was rounded to the beginning of the current year.

Using the *trunc* Date Function

As with the numeric *trunc* function, the date version simply truncates the date to the level specified in the format. The *trunc* function is often used to chop-off unwanted

---

parts of a date. IN the example, below *trunc* is used to convert the data to the first day of the current month, and the first day of the current year:

```
select
  sysdate,
  trunc(sysdate,'month') month,
  trunc(sysdate,'year')  year
from
  dual;


SYSDATE    MONTH      YEAR
---------  ---------  ---------
24-JAN-05  01-JAN-05  01-JAN-05
```

Now that the process for how to specify dates in SQL to ensure index usage has been introduced, it is a good time to look at cases where it has been necessary to create a function-based index to match a complex *where* clause specification.

Index Usage and Built-in Functions

It should be obvious by now that Oracle provides many built-in functions (BIFs) that can be used to transform table column data. The BIF feature can save developers and programmers a great deal of time, automating the cumbersome task of translating incoming column values into Oracle (e.g. *update customer set date_of_birth = to_date('03-25-1956','MM-DD-YYYY');*). BIFs can also be used to format non-displayable native datatypes. For example, one BIF formats the *date* datatype into a readable format.

Here are some common BIFs that can be used to simplify SQL queries:

- **decode:** This function is used to translate values in a SQL statement from an abbreviation into a readable value. One example is using this function to translate a state abbreviation into the full state name.

- **to_char:** This function is used to convert numeric columns into character representations. This is often used with the *date* datatype.

- **upper:** This function is used to ensure that the retrieval of case-sensitive data is properly serviced.

- **lower:** This function is used to convert text to lower case. This is particularly useful when searching for lines of text.

- **substr:** This function is used to extract sub-strings from larger datatype columns, for instance the area code of a phone number.

With regard to Oracle tuning, it is important to note that using BIFs will often cause the SQL optimizer to perform a full-table scan because the BIF in the *where* clause has not been matched with a function-based index. This can be avoided by creating a function-based index to match the BIF used.

One common use of an Oracle BIF is the use of the *to_char* function to translate a column containing the *date* datatype. The following query displays the number of STATSPACK snapshots occurring in the month of January.

```
select
   count(*)
from
   perfstat.stats$snapshot
where
   to_char(snap_time,'Mon') = 'Jan;
```

When using a generic index in the *snap_time* column, the *to_char* function is not able to use the *date* index. With the use of BIFs however, an index can be created on *to_char(snap_time,'Mon')*, thereby avoiding a full-table scan for the SQL query.

Finding BIFs

When performing system-wide tuning, it is important to remember that an invalidated index column might not always invoke a full-table scan, and instead, the SQL might just choose a less selective index instead.

Always be on the lookout for BIFs in the *where* clause of SQL statements. The following SQL can be run against the *v$sqlarea* view to quickly identify SQL statements that might have a BIF in their *where* clause:

🖫 **find_bif.sql**

```
set lines 2000;

select
   sql_text,
   disk_reads,
   executions,
   parse_calls
from
   v$sqlarea
where
   lower(sql_text) like '% substr%'
or
   lower(sql_text) like '% to_char%'
or
   lower(sql_text) like '% decode%'
order by
   disk_reads desc
;
```

With each release of Oracle, there are dozens of new features, and it can be a challenge determining which tuning features are right for any particular system. For SQL tuning, the FBI ranks among one of the most powerful Oracle features.

Tuning SQL with FBIs

Even though FBIs were quietly introduced way back in Oracle 8i, many Oracle professional still fail to fully utilize them as one of the single most powerful Oracle tuning tools. FBIs allow the creation of indexes on expressions, internal functions and user-written functions in PL/SQL and Java.

Prior to the advent of the FBI, using a built-in function would often invalidate the index and cause an expensive full table scan. Examples of SQL with function-based queries might include the following:

```
select * from customer where substr(cust_name,1,4) = 'BURL';

select * from customer where to_char(order_date,'MM') = '01';

select * from customer where upper(cust_name) = 'JONES';

select * from customer where initcap(first_name) = 'Mike';
```

Oracle always seems to interrogate the *where* clause of the SQL statement to see if a matching index exists. By using function-based indexes, the Oracle designer can create a matching index that exactly matches the predicates within the SQL *where* clause. This ensures that the query is retrieved with a minimal amount of disk I/O and the fastest possible speed.

Oracle DBAs have long known that there are many silver bullet tuning techniques, single changes that have a profound impact on the entire SQL workload. These include any global setting that affects the execution plans of SQL statements such as:

- Parameter settings (*optimizer_mode*, *optimizer_index_cost_adj*)
- New CBO statistics
- New patchsets/ new releases
- Indexes (especially function-based indexes)
- Materialized views

Out of these powerful tools, the most readily available is the addition of a missing index, especially a function-based index.

If the goal of an index is to fetch the desired row-set with a minimum of databases touches (e.g. *consistent_gets*), a function-based index is a Godsend because anything that in the *where* clause of a SQL statement may have a matching function-based index.

In almost all cases, the use of a built-in function like *to_char, decode, substr*, etc. in an SQL query may cause a full-table scan of the target table. For example, consider this query:

```
-- ********************
-- select March sales
-- ********************

select
   sum(sales)
from
   mysales
where
   to_char(order_date, 'MON') = 'MARCH';
```

In this case, without a specific index on (*to_char(order_date,'MON'*), the above query will be forced to read every row in the *sales* table, even though an index already exists on the *order_date* column.

To avoid this problem, many Oracle DBAs will create corresponding indexes that make use of FBIs. If a corresponding function-based index matches the built-in function of the query, Oracle will be able to service the query with an index range scan thereby avoiding a potentially expensive full-table scan.

The following is a simple example. Suppose a SQL statement has been identified that has hundreds of full-table scans against a large table with a built-in function (BIF) in the *where* clause of the query. After examining the SQL, it is simple to see that it is accessing a customer by converting the customer name to uppercase using the upper BIF.

```
select
   c.customer_name,
   o.order_date
from
   customer c,
   order    o
where
  upper(c.customer_name) = upper(:v1)
and
   c.cust_nbr = o.cust_nbr;
```

Running the explain plan utility confirms suspicions that the upper BIF is responsible for an unnecessary large-table full-table scan.

```
OPTIONS                       OBJECT_NAME                       POSITION
----------------------------  --------------------------------  ----------
```

```
SELECT STATEMENT
                                                                    4
    NESTED LOOPS
                                                                    1
      TABLE ACCESS
FULL                            CUSTOMER                            1
      TABLE ACCESS
BY INDEX ROWID                  ORDER                               2
        INDEX
RANGE SCAN                      CUST_NBR_IDX                        1
```

The TABLE ACCESS FULL CUSTOMER option confirms that this BIF is not using the existing index on the *customer_name* column. Since a matching function-based index may change the execution plan, a function-based index can be added on *upper(customer_name)*.

It can be risky to add indexes to a table because the execution plans of many queries may change as a result. This is not a problem with a function-based index because Oracle will only use this type of index when the query uses a matching BIF.

```
create index
    upper_cust_name_idx
on
    customer
      (upper(customer_name))
   tablespace
      customer_idx
;

exec dbms_stats.gather_index_stats('scott', ' upper_cust_name_idx');
```

Now, the SQL can be re-explained to show that the full-table scan has been replaced by an index range scan on the new function-based index.

For this query, the execution time has been decreased from 45 seconds to less than two seconds.

```
OPERATION
-----------------------------------------------------------------------
OPTIONS                         OBJECT_NAME                    POSITION
-----------------------------   -----------------------------  ---------
SELECT STATEMENT
                                                                    5
    NESTED LOOPS
                                                                    1
      TABLE ACCESS
BY INDEX ROWID                  CUSTOMER                            1
        INDEX
RANGE SCAN                      CUST_NBR_IDX                        1
      TABLE ACCESS
BY INDEX ROWID                  ORDER                               2
        INDEX
RANGE SCAN                      UPPER_CUST_NAME_IDX                 1
```

This simple example serves to illustrate the foremost SQL tuning rule for BIFs. Whenever a BIF is used in a SQL statement, a function-based index must be created.

However, it is important to always carefully examine the *where* clause of a query to see if there are alternatives to using a function-based index.

For example, at first glance these *where* clause predicates might be candidates for a function-based index:

```
-- ******************************
-- Will not use ship_date index
-- ******************************
where trunc(ship_date) > trunc(sysdate-7);


-- ******************************
-- Will not use ship_date index
-- ******************************
where to_char(ship_date,'YYYY-MM-DD') = '2004-01-04';
```

Even though the *ship_date* column has an index, the *trunc* and *to_char* built-in functions will invalidate the index, causing sub-optimal execution with unnecessary I/O. However, in these cases the *where* clause can be reformulated to make the *ship_date* index work, without having to create a function-based index:

```
-- *********************
-- Uses ship_date index
-- *********************
where ship_date >= trunc(sysdate-7) + 1;

-- *********************
-- Uses ship_date index
-- *********************
where ship_date = to_date('2004-01-04','YYYY-MM-DD');
```

Whenever possible, it is preferable to use an existing index before creating a function-based index.

The next section will show how a function-based index can be used with a *case* statement, a powerful tuning tool for complex queries.

Using *case* Statements with an FBI

Using FBIs makes it possible to create an index on any built-in function, including a *case* expression. The following example uses a *case* within the create index syntax:

```
create index
   case_index
as
```

```
    (case SOURCE_TRAN
    when 'PO' then PO_ID
    when 'VOUCHER' then voucher_id
    ELSE journal_id
    end = '0000000001'
end);
```

Once created, CBO statistics will need to be created, but beware that there are numerous bugs and issues when analyzing a function-based index.

```
exec dbms_stats.gather_index_stats('OWNER', 'CASE_INDEX');

exec dbms_stats.gather_table_stats(
   ownname=>null,
   tabname=> 'CASE_TAB,
   estimate_percent=>null,
   cascade=>true,
   method_opt=> 'FOR ALL HIDDEN COLUMNS SIZE 1'
);

exec dbms_stats.gather_table_stats(
ownname => 'OWNER',
tabname => 'CASE_TAB',
cascade => TRUE);
```

As a final step, execution plan for the query should be run and checked to ensure that the SQL with *case* is using the appropriate index.

Tip! Index on *decode* statements!

You can use a function-based index with a *decode* statement! This is an important feature, being able to transform column data and index upon the transformation.

Now, it is time to move on and take a look at how to manage indexes on complex functions.

Indexing on Complex Functions

After considering the power of the function-based index, it would be normal to wonder if there is any limit to the ability to index into complex expressions. Jonathan Gennick shows a great example where Oracle regular expressions are used to extract acreage references from inside a text string, ignoring important factors such as case sensitivity and words stems (acre, acres, acreage):

```
column park_name format a30
column acres     format a13
```

```
select
  park_name,
  REGEXP_SUBSTR(description,'[^ ]+[- ]acres?',1,1,'i') acres
from
   michigan_park
where
   REGEXP_LIKE(description, '[^ ]+[- ]acres?','i');
```

The output shows that the regular expression has parsed out the acreage figures, just as if they were a discrete data column with the table:

PARK_NAME	ACRES
Mackinac Island State Park	1800 acres
Muskallonge Lake State Park	217-acre
Porcupine Mountains State Park	60,000 acres
Tahquamenon Falls State Park	40,000+ acres

The only problem with this query is that it will always perform a large-table full-table scan on the *michigan_park* table, causing unnecessary overhead for Oracle.

However, using the powerful function-based indexes could eliminate the unnecessary overhead by using the regular expression directly in the index:

```
create index
   parks_acreage
on
   michigan_parks
 (REGEXP_LIKE(description, '[^ ]+[- ]acres?','i'));
```

The rules for choosing an FBI on a complex expression (regular expression, decode) is a trade-off between several factors:

- **The number of blocks in the table**: A full-table scan of a super-large table can cause I/O contention.

- **The percentage of rows returned**: If the regular expression returns only a small percentage of the total table rows, a regular expression index will greatly reduce I/O.

- **The frequency of the query**: If the query is executed frequently, Oracle may do millions of unnecessary full-table scans.

- **The tolerance for slower row inserts**: Parsing the text column at insert time to add the row to the regular expression index will slow-down inserts.

This trade-off represents an age-old quandary. If the regular expression is built once at insert time, it can be used over-and-over again with little overhead. Conversely, using regular expressions in SQL without a supporting index will cause repeated full-table scans.

Optimizer Statistics and FBIs

Based on the fact that an FBI applies a function to a data column, special steps must be taken for the optimizer to be able to utilize the FBI. The Oracle documentation notes that collecting statistics and histograms are important prerequisites:

> *"You should analyze the table after creating a function-based index, to allow Oracle to collect column statistics equivalent information for the expression.*
>
> *Optionally, you can collect histograms for the index expressions by specifying for all hidden columns size number_of_buckets in the method_opt argument to the dbms_stats procedures."*

Look Out!

Be careful with automatic analysis!

The Oracle documentation says that in 10g and beyond it is not necessary to analyze an index after it is created. However, the smart DBAs will analyze manually.

The following are some methods for analyzing a function-based index, but beware that they may not work on all releases of Oracle.

```
--  Gather index stats for function-based index

exec dbms_stats.gather_index_stats('OWNER', 'CASE_INDEX');


--  Gather table stats for function-based index exec
dbms_stats.gather_table_stats(
   ownname=>null,
   tabname=> 'CASE_TAB,
   estimate_percent=>null,
   cascade=>true,
   method_opt=> 'FOR ALL HIDDEN COLUMNS SIZE 1'
);

exec dbms_stats.gather_table_stats(
ownname => 'OWNER',
tabname => 'CASE_TAB',
cascade => TRUE);
```

Function-based indexes can be tricky to get working, and SQL execution plans must be verified to ensure that they are working before they are migrated into production.

Conclusions on FBIs

In sum, function-based indexes are one of the true Silver Bullet techniques, proving that a single action can have a profound impact on an entire SQL workload. There are several points to remember about function-based indexes:

- A single FBI might optimizer hundreds of SQL statements, reducing system-wide I/O.

- Function-based indexes can match anything in a *where* clause, even derived data like that from a decode statement.

- It important to collect CBO stats and possibly histograms to ensure that the FBI is used properly by the optimizer.

Even though using a function-based index is tricky, it is well worth the effort since the function-based indexes create a direct path to the target data blocks that contain the desired rows.

The next section will provide insight into tuning with Oracle regular expressions.

SQL tuning with Regular Expression Indexes

Oracle regular expression syntax has profound implications for Oracle tuning. This is especially true in the area of indexing where indexes can be created on regular expressions, eliminating expensive full-table scans in-favor of fast index access. Regular expressions, especially the regexp_like syntax, are extremely powerful for extracting facts from large text columns.

Regular expression indexes are a type of function-based index, and they can dramatically reduce database overhead for pattern-matching queries.

The following are some little known facts about regular expressions:

- They can be used with bind variables

- They can be included in function-based indexes

The use of indexing on regular expressions will covered in more detail in the following section.

Indexing on Regular Expressions

In parsing with regular expressions such as *regexp_like* as shown in , the Jonathan Gennick's example that was previously presented in the section on Indexing on Complex Functions, Oracle regular expressions were to extract acreage references from inside a test string. Also included in that section was the corresponding SQL showing how to take advantage of function-based indexes in order to eliminate the costly overhead of the full-table scan resulting from the use of the regular expressions.

However, Oracle Guru Laurent Schneider notes that it is illegal to have an index on a Boolean function, but there could be an index on a case expression returning 1. Note the *where* clause in this *create index* syntax:

```
create index
    i
on
   michigan_parks
   (case when
      description like '_% acre%'
   or
      description like '_%-acre%'
   then 1 end);
```

```
select
   *
from
   michigan_parks
where
   (case when
      description like '_% acre%'
   or
      description like '_%-acre%' then 1 end)
is not null;
```

This simple index definition would create a yes/no index on all park records that contain a reference to the values : acre; acres; or acreage. The database would experience the overhead once, when each rows is added to the table, and not over-and-over again when queries are executed.

Case Sensitive Searches with Indexes

Oracle 10g release 2 introduced a case insensitive search method for SQL that avoids index invalidation and unnecessary full-table scans. Oracle*Text indexes can also be employed in order to remove full-table scans when using the *like* operator. Prior to Oracle10g R2, case insensitive queries required special planning:

Step 1 - Transform data in the query to make it case insensitive. This can invalidate indexes without a function-based index:

```
create index
   upper_full_name
on
   customer (upper(full_name));

select
   full_name
from
   customer
where
   upper(full_name) = 'DON BURLESON';
```

Step 2 - Use a trigger to transform the data to make it case insensitive or store the data with the *to_lower* or *to_upper* BIF.

Step 3 - Use ALTER SESSION commands:

```
alter session set nls_comp=ansi;
alter session set nls_sort=generic_baseletter;
select * from customer where full_name = 'Don Burleson'
```

In Oracle10g R2 and beyond, there is the following fresher approach to case insensitive searches. Set the following initialization parameters:

- nls_sort=binary_ci

- nls_comp=ansi

Next, create a sample index:

```
create index
   caseless_name_index
on
   customer
(
   nlssort( full_name, 'NLS_SORT=BINARY_CI')
);

alter session set nls_sort=binary_ci;

select * from customer where full_name = 'Don Burleson';
```

The next section will cover Oracle*Text indexes, a specialized index for read-only data.

SQL Tuning with Oracle*Text Indexes

One serious SQL performance problem occurs when the SQL *like* clause operator is used to find a string within a large Oracle table column (e.g. *varchar(2000)*, *clob*, *blob*):

```
select stuff from bigtab where text_column like '%ipod%';

select
   stuff
from
   bigtab
where
   full_name like '%JONES';
```

Because standard Oracle cannot index into a large column, the like queries cause full-table scans, and Oracle must examine every row in the table, even when the result set is very small. These unnecessary full-table scans are a problem:

- Large-table full-table scans increase the load on the disk I/O sub-system

- Small table full table scans in the data buffer cause high consistent gets and drive up CPU consumption

The Oracle*Text utility (formerly called Oracle Con*Text and Oracle Intermedia) allows parsing through a large text column and index on the words within the column.

Unlike ordinary b-tree or bitmap indexes, Oracle *context*, *ctxcat* and *ctxrule* indexes are not updated as content is changed. Since most standard Oracle databases will use the *ctxcat* index with standard relational tables, the DBA has to decide on a refresh interval.

Hence, Oracle*Text indexes are only useful for removing full-table scans when the tables are largely read-only and/or the end-users do not mind not having 100% search recall:

- The target table is relatively static (e.g. nightly batch updates)

- End-users would not mind missing the latest row data

Oracle*Text works with traditional data columns and also with XML, MS-Word docs and Adobe PDF files that are stored within Oracle. Oracle*Text has several index types:

- ***ctxcat* Indexes**: A *ctxcat* index is best for smaller text fragments that must be indexed along with other standard relational data (VARCHAR2).

  ```
  where catsearch(text_column, 'ipod') > 0;
  ```

Advanced Oracle SQL Tuning

- **context Indexes**: The *context* index type is used to index large amounts of text such as Word, PDF, XML, HTML or plain text documents.

  ```
  where contains(test_column, 'ipod', 1) > 0
  ```

- **ctxrule Indexes**: A *ctxrule* index can be used to build document classification applications.

These types of indexes allow the old-fashioned SQL "*like*" syntax to be replaced with *contains* or *catsearch* SQL syntax.

When the query is executed with the new index, the full-table scan is replaced with an index scan, greatly reducing execution speed and improving hardware stress:

```
Execution Plan
-----------------------------------------------------------
   0        SELECT STATEMENT Optimizer=FIRST_ROWS
   1    0     SORT (ORDER BY)
   2    1       TABLE ACCESS (BY INDEX ROWID) OF 'BIGTAB'
   3    2         DOMAIN INDEX OF 'TEXT-COLUMN_IDX'
```

Next let's look at how to resynchronize Oracle*Text indexes after an update.

Oracle*Text Index Resynchronization

Because rebuilding an Oracle*Text index, such as *context, ctxcat* or *ctxrule* requires a full-table scan and lots of internal parsing, it is not practical to use triggers for instantaneous index updates.

Updating Oracle*Text indexes is easy and they can be scheduled using *dbms_job* or the Oracle 10g *dbms_scheduler* utility package. Oracle*Text provides a *ctx_ddl* package with the *sync_index* and *optimize_index* procedures:

```
exec ctx_ddl.sync_index('text_column_idx');

exec ctx_ddl.optimize_index('text_column_idx','full');
```

For example, if nightly dbms_scheduler job is created to call *sync_index*, the index will be refreshed, but the structure will become sub-optimal over time. Oracle recommends that the *optimize_index* package be used periodically to rebuild the whole index from scratch. Index optimization can be performed in three modes: *fast; full;* or *token.*

In sum, the Oracle*Text indexes are great for removing unnecessary full-table scans from static Oracle tables and they can reduce I/O by several orders of magnitude, greatly improving overall SQL performance.

Tuning SQL with Index Organized Tables

Starting back in the days of Oracle8, Oracle recognized that a table with an index on every column did not require table rows. In other words, Oracle recognized that by using a special table access method called an index fast full scan, the index could be queried without actually touching the data itself.

Oracle codified this idea with its use of Index Organized Table (IOT) structure. When using an IOT, Oracle does not create the actual table but instead keeps all of the required information inside the Oracle index.

At query time, the Oracle SQL optimizer recognizes that all of the values necessary to service the query exist within the index tree, at which time the Oracle cost-based optimizer has a choice of either reading through the index tree nodes to pull the information in sorted order or invoke an index fast full scan, which will read the table in the same fashion as a full table scan, using sequential prefetch, as defined by the *db_file_multiblock_read_count* parameter.

The multiblock read facility allows Oracle to very quickly scan index blocks in linear order, quickly reading every block within the index tablespace. Here is an example of the syntax to create an IOT.

```
create table
   emp_iot
(
   emp_id     number,
   ename      varchar2(20),
   sal        number(9,2),
   deptno     number,
   constraint
      pk_emp_iot_index
   primary key
      (emp_id)
)
organization
   index
tablespace
   demo_ts_01
pcthreshold
   20
including
   ename;
```

In sum, the index-only tablespace is perfect for queries where all of the column data can be contained within the index tree, alleviating the need for a traditional table.

Testing New Oracle Indexes

Adding a missing index is a powerful silver bullet for Oracle tuning because a single new index can affect the performance of thousands of SQL queries. But remember, the changes are not guaranteed to always be good. Silver bullets can work both ways. While a silver bullet causes a profound change to a workload, the change might also be a bad one, and careful testing is always required.

While the Oracle optimizer is not likely to choose a sub-optimal plan when a new index is added, it can happen, and when testing a new index for migration to production, complete workload testing is de-rigueur.

In Oracle 11g, there is a new *init.ora* parameter to assist with index testing. This is the *optimizer_use_invisible_indexes* parameter. While the default for *optimizer_use_invisible_indexes* is false, the setting can be changed for the session to allow testing oft new indexes:

```
alter session set optimizer_use_invisible_indexes=true;
```

When setting optimizer_use_invisible_indexes=true, Oracle will allow the testing of the effect of new indexes solely within the session without effecting any other SQL. If the DBA sees that the new index has the desired effect, the index can be altered to make it visible to the optimizer:

```
alter index myindex visible;
```

Don't do this in production!

The *optimizer_use_invisible_indexes* parameter should never be used on a production database. A test or QA database is the place to test new indexes, never production!

Hot Tip!

In the real world, any new indexes would be tested in a QA database, by capturing a representative SQL workload and testing the workload using the Oracle 11g SQL Performance Manager (SPM) with the new index. Only then, can the new index be confidently migrated into the production environment.

Testing SQL Workloads with Invisible Indexes

Testing workloads is critical to ensure the positive impacts of changes outweigh the negatives. During an observation period, the new index is created in an QA environment and some SQL tuning Sets (STS) are used to monitor the database performance to determine whether or not to keep the new index. If performance is negatively affected, the index would need to be rebuilt before it could be used again.

Another potential use for invisible indexes is in situations where specific applications require an index temporarily. For example, an index can be created as invisible to allow specific SQL statements to use the index while leaving the rest of the database unaffected. Creating a visible index for this same purpose would cause the optimizer to consider the new index for all execution plans on that object.

Consider the introduction of a reporting application into a large production database. Shortly after the go-live, a query in the application is found to be running slowly. The query is consuming excessive amounts of resources due to a full-table scan on a large, highly referenced table, *order_lines*.

After identifying this query, there is a realization that creating an index on column *order_lines.attribute7* would immediately resolve this particular issue. This issue needs to be resolved as soon as possible without impacting any other processes that use this object.

In this situation, creating an invisible index as a temporary solution until the application code can be reviewed would be an ideal solution. This method would alleviate the immediate problem without potentially affecting other users and processes that use the *order_lines* table.

Below, an invisible index was created on *order_lines.attribute7*:

```
create index
   order_lines_inv
on
   order_lines(attribute7) invisible;
```

This one query can be modified to explicitly use the invisible index with an *index* hint:

```
select /*+ index (order_lines order_lines_inv) */
   id
from
   order_lines
where
   attribute7 = 11001;
```

If the application code cannot be modified, it is possible to instruct the optimizer to include invisible indexes at the session level:

```
alter session set optimizer_use_invisible_indexes = true;
```

Keep in mind that rebuilding an invisible index will make it visible.

Invisible indexes are an attractive feature for the process of dropping an index. They are also useful when a specific application needs the benefit of a temporary index without impacting the database on a wider scale.

Be prudent with invisible indexes!

Since the database must still maintain an invisible index for all DML operations, invisible indexes should not be used unless absolutely necessary.

Once the indexes are in place, there has to be a way to monitor them. The following section will provide some guidance on how to perform index monitoring.

Monitoring Index Usage

STATSPACK and AWR are perfect for holistic tuning because it is possible not only to monitor the usage of specific indexes, but it is also possible to see how indexes are being used for the entire SQL workload, which is super-valuable information for SQL tuning.

For specific time periods, index access by snapshot period can be summarized with the following SQL:

🖫 awr_sql_index_access.sql

```
col c1  heading 'Begin|Interval|Time'    format a20
col c2  heading 'Index|Range|Scans' format 999,999
col c3  heading 'Index|Unique|Scans' format 999,999
col c4  heading 'Index|Full|Scans' format 999,999

select
  r.c1   c1,
  r.c2   c2,
  u.c2   c3,
  f.c2   c4
from
(
select
  to_char(sn.begin_interval_time,'yy-mm-dd hh24')  c1,
  count(1)                            c2
from
   dba_hist_sql_plan p,
   dba_hist_sqlstat   s,
   dba_hist_snapshot sn
where
   p.object_owner <> 'SYS'
and
```

```
    p.operation like '%INDEX%'
and
    p.options like '%RANGE%'
and
    p.sql_id = s.sql_id
and
    s.snap_id = sn.snap_id
group by
  to_char(sn.begin_interval_time,'yy-mm-dd hh24')
order by
1 ) r,
(
select
  to_char(sn.begin_interval_time,'yy-mm-dd hh24')   c1,
  count(1)                          c2
from
    dba_hist_sql_plan p,
    dba_hist_sqlstat  s,
    dba_hist_snapshot sn
where
    p.object_owner <> 'SYS'
and
    p.operation like '%INDEX%'
and
    p.options like '%UNIQUE%'
and
    p.sql_id = s.sql_id
and
    s.snap_id = sn.snap_id
group by
  to_char(sn.begin_interval_time,'yy-mm-dd hh24')
order by
1 ) u,
(
select
  to_char(sn.begin_interval_time,'yy-mm-dd hh24')   c1,
  count(1)                          c2
from
    dba_hist_sql_plan p,
    dba_hist_sqlstat  s,
    dba_hist_snapshot sn
where
    p.object_owner <> 'SYS'
and
    p.operation like '%INDEX%'
and
    p.options like '%FULL%'
and
    p.sql_id = s.sql_id
and
    s.snap_id = sn.snap_id
group by
  to_char(sn.begin_interval_time,'yy-mm-dd hh24')
order by
1 ) f
where
      r.c1 = u.c1
  and
      r.c1 = f.c1;
```

The sample output below shows those specific times when the database performs unique scans, index range scans and index fast full scans:

```
Begin                 Index     Index     Index
Interval              Range     Unique    Full
Time                  Scans     Scans     Scans
-----------------     --------  --------  --------
12-10-21 15              36        35         2
12-10-21 19              10         8         2
12-10-21 20                         8         2
12-10-21 21                         8         2
12-10-21 22              11         8         3
12-10-21 23              16        11         3
12-10-22 00              10         9         1
12-10-22 01              11         8         3
12-10-22 02              12         8         1
```

In Oracle10g and beyond, it is easy to see what indexes are used, when they are used and the context in which they are used. The following is a simple AWR query that can be used see index usage for a specific index over time. Note how it shows the number of times that an index is used each hour:

🖫 awr_count_index_details.sql

```
col c1 heading 'Begin|Interval|time'  format a20
col c2 heading 'Search Columns'       format 999
col c3 heading 'Invocation|Count'     format 99,999,999


break on c1 skip 2

accept idxname char prompt 'Enter Index Name: '

ttitle 'Invocation Counts for index|&idxname'

select
   to_char(sn.begin_interval_time,'yy-mm-dd hh24')  c1,
   p.search_columns                                 c2,
   count(*)                                         c3
from
   dba_hist_snapshot  sn,
   dba_hist_sql_plan  p,
   dba_hist_sqlstat   st
where
   st.sql_id = p.sql_id
and
   sn.snap_id = st.snap_id
and
   p.object_name = '&idxname'
group by
   begin_interval_time,search_columns;
```

The query will accept an index name and produce an output showing a summary count of the index specified during the snapshot interval. This can be compared to the number of times that a table was invoked from SQL.

Here is a sample of the output from this index usage script:

```
Invocation Counts for cust_index

Begin
Interval                              Invocation
time             Search Columns         Count
------------------  --------------   ----------
12-10-21 15              1                3
12-10-10 16              0                1
12-10-10 19              1                1
12-10-11 02              0                2
12-10-11 04              2                1
12-10-11 06              3                1
12-10-11 11              0                1
12-10-11 12              0                2
12-10-11 13              2                1
12-10-11 15              0                3
12-10-11 17              0               14
12-10-11 18              4                1
12-10-11 19              0                1
12-10-11 20              3                7
12-10-11 21              0                1
```

Watch for seldom-used indexes!

Using the query above, seek out seldom-used indexes that may be associated with weekly or monthly jobs. For these, consider building the index specifically for the infrequent job and then dropping the index until the next invocation.

Monitoring for Index Range Scans

When deciding to segregate indexes into larger blocksizes, it is important to understand that those indexes that are subject to frequent index range scans and fast-full scans will benefit the most from a larger blocksize.

When Oracle joins two tables with a nested loop, only one of the indexes may be accessed as a range. The optimizer always performs an index range scan on one index, gathers the *rowid* values and does fetch by *rowid* on the matching rows in the other table. For example:

```
select
   customer_name,
   order_date
from
   customer
   orders
where
   customer.cust_key = orders.cust_key;
```

The Oracle documentation notes that a nested loop involves two loops:

> *"In a nested loop join, for every row in the outer row set, the inner row set is accessed to find all the matching rows to join.*
>
> *Therefore, in a nested loop join, the inner row set is accessed as many times as the number of rows in the outer row set."*

Oracle will only scan one index, build a set of keys, and then probe the rows from the other table as illustrated in Figure 6.9.

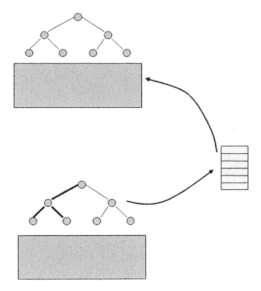

Figure 6.9: *Table joins include index range scans and index unique scans*

So, if this nested loop never uses the customer index, why is it there? The answer is, for index unique scans. In an index unique scan, a single row is accessed within the index, as seen in this query:

```
select
```

```
    customer_last_name,
    customer_address
from
    customer
where
    cust_key = 123;
```

In sum, the DBA must find out how their indexes are being used by the SQL. An index that never experiences range scans would not benefit from a larger blocksize. The question becomes one of finding those indexes that experience lots of range scans, and AWR can help.

It is possible to identify those indexes with the most index range scans with the following simple AWR script.

🖫 index_range_scans.sql

```
col c1 heading 'Object|Name'         format a30
col c2 heading 'Option'              format a15
col c3 heading 'Index|Usage|Count'   format 999,999

select
  p.object_name c1,
  p.options      c2,
  count(1)       c3
from
   dba_hist_sql_plan p,
   dba_hist_sqlstat  s
where
   p.object_owner <> 'SYS'
and
   p.options like '%RANGE SCAN%'
and

   p.operation like '%INDEX%'
and
   p.sql_id = s.sql_id
group by
   p.object_name,
   p.operation,
   p.options
order by
   1,2,3;
```

The following is the output showing overall total counts for each object and table access method.

```
                                              Index
Object                                        Usage
Name                       Option             Count
-------------------------- ---------------    --------
CUSTOMER_CHECK             RANGE SCAN          4,232
AVAILABILITY_PRIMARY_KEY   RANGE SCAN          1,783
CON_UK                     RANGE SCAN            473
CURRENT_SEVERITY           RANGE SCAN            323
```

```
CWM$CUBEDIMENSIONUSE_IDX      RANGE SCAN      72
ORDERS_FK                     RANGE SCAN      20
```

This will quickly identify indexes that will benefit the most from a 32k blocksize.

This index list can be double verified by using the AWR to identify indexes with high disk reads during each AWR snapshot period. The sample script below exposes the top five tables accessed mostly heavily by physical disk reads for every snapshot interval:

🖫 busy_table_io.sql

```
col c0   heading  'Begin|Interval|time'  format a8
col c1   heading  'Table|Name'           format a20
col c2   heading  'Disk|Reads'           format 99,999,999
col c3   heading  'Rows|Processed'       format 99,999,999

select
*
from (
select
    to_char(s.begin_interval_time,'mm-dd hh24') c0,
    p.object_name c1,
    sum(t.disk_reads_total) c2,
    sum(t.rows_processed_total) c3,
    DENSE_RANK() OVER (PARTITION BY to_char(s.begin_interval_time,'mm-dd
hh24') ORDER BY SUM(t.disk_reads_total) desc) AS rnk
from
  dba_hist_sql_plan p,
  dba_hist_sqlstat t,
  dba_hist_snapshot s
where
  p.sql_id = t.sql_id
and
  t.snap_id = s.snap_id
and
  p.object_type like '%TABLE%'
group by
  to_char(s.begin_interval_time,'mm-dd hh24'),
  p.object_name
order by
c0 desc, rnk
)
where rnk <= 5;
```

The following is the sample output from the above script:

```
Begin
Interval  Table                   Disk        Rows
time      Name                    Reads    Processed       RNK
--------  --------------------  --------  -----------  ----------
10-29 15  CUSTOMER_CHECK          55,732      498,056           1
10-29 15  CON_UK                  18,368      166,172           2
10-29 15  CURRENT_SEVERITY        11,727      102,545           3
10-29 15  ORDERS_FK                5,876       86,671           4
10-29 15  SYN$                     2,624       23,674           5

10-29 14  CUSTOMER_CHECK          47,756      427,762           1
```

```
10-29 14 CON_UK                    15,939      142,878      2
10-29 14 CURRENT_SEVERITY           6,976      113,649      3
10-29 14 X$KZSRO                    4,772      119,417      4
10-29 14 ORDERS_FK                  2,274       20,292      5

10-29 13 CUSTOMER_CHECK            25,704      213,786      1
10-29 13 CON_UK                     8,568       71,382      2
10-29 13 OBJ$                       3,672       30,474      3
10-29 13 X$KZSRO                    2,448       20,328      4
10-29 13 SYN$                       1,224       10,146      5
```

This report shows the tables with the highest disk reads which is very important
information for disk tuning.

The *dba_hist_sql_plan* table can also be used to gather counts about the frequency of
participation of objects inside queries. This is a great query to quickly see what is
going on between the tables and the SQL that accesses them:

🖫 count_table_access.sql

```
col c1  heading 'Object|Name'       format a30
col c2  heading 'Operation'         format a15
col c3  heading 'Option'            format a15
col c4  heading 'Object|Count'      format 999,999

break on c1 skip 2
break on c2 skip 2

select
   p.object_name  c1,
   p.operation    c2,
   p.options      c3,
   count(1)       c4
from
   dba_hist_sql_plan p,
   dba_hist_sqlstat  s
where
   p.object_owner <> 'SYS'
and
   p.sql_id = s.sql_id
group by
   p.object_name,
   p.operation,
   p.options
order by
   1,2,3;
```

The following output shows overall total counts for each object and table access
method.

Object Name	Operation	Option	Object Count
CUSTOMER	TABLE ACCESS	FULL	305
CUSTOMER _CHECK	INDEX	RANGE SCAN	2

```
CUSTOMER_ORDERS                  TABLE ACCESS      BY INDEX ROWID        311
CUSTOMER_ORDERS                                    FULL                    1


CUSTOMER_ORDERS_PRIMARY          INDEX             FULL SCAN               2
CUSTOMER_ORDERS_PRIMARY                            UNIQUE SCAN           311
AVAILABILITY_PRIMARY_KEY                           RANGE SCAN              4
CON_UK                                             RANGE SCAN              3
CURRENT_SEVERITY_PRIMARY_KEY                       RANGE SCAN              1


CWM$CUBE                         TABLE ACCESS      BY INDEX ROWID          2
CWM$CUBEDIMENSIONUSE                               BY INDEX ROWID          2


CWM$CUBEDIMENSIONUSE_IDX         INDEX             RANGE SCAN              2
CWM$CUBE_PK                                        UNIQUE SCAN             2
CWM$DIMENSION_PK                                   FULL SCAN               2

MGMT_INV_VERSIONED_PATCH         TABLE ACCESS      BY INDEX ROWID          3
MGMT_JOB                                           BY INDEX ROWID        458
MGMT_JOB_EMD_STATUS_QUEUE                          FULL                  181
MGMT_JOB_EXECUTION                                 BY INDEX ROWID        456

MGMT_JOB_EXEC_IDX01              INDEX             RANGE SCAN            456


MGMT_JOB_EXEC_SUMMARY            TABLE ACCESS      BY INDEX ROWID        180


MGMT_JOB_EXEC_SUMM_IDX04         INDEX             RANGE SCAN            180


MGMT_JOB_HISTORY                 TABLE ACCESS      BY INDEX ROWID          1


MGMT_JOB_HIST_IDX01              INDEX             RANGE SCAN              1
MGMT_JOB_PK                                        UNIQUE SCAN           458

MGMT_METRICS                     TABLE ACCESS      BY INDEX ROWID        180
```

Using the output above, it is easy to monitor object participation, especially indexes, in the SQL queries and the mode with which an object was accessed by Oracle.

Why is it important to know how tables and indexes are accessed? Objects that experience multi-block reads may perform faster in a larger blocksize and also reduce SGA overhead as shown in Figure 6.10.

Figure 6.10: *Using Ion to find the most popular indexes*

The problem has always been that it is very difficult to know what indexes are the most popular. In Oracle10g, it is easy to see what indexes are used, when they are used and the context in which they are used. Here is a simple AWR query to plot index usage:

🖫 index_usage_hr.sql

```
col c1 heading 'Begin|Interval|time'  format a20
col c2 heading 'Search Columns'       format 999
col c3 heading 'Invocation|Count'     format 99,999,999
```

```
break on cl skip 2

accept idxname char prompt 'Enter Index Name: '

ttitle 'Invocation Counts for index|&idxname'

select
   to_char(sn.begin_interval_time,'yy-mm-dd hh24')   c1,
   p.search_columns                                  c2,
   count(*)                                          c3
from
   dba_hist_snapshot   sn,
   dba_hist_sql_plan   p,
   dba_hist_sqlstat    st
where
   st.sql_id = p.sql_id
and
   sn.snap_id = st.snap_id
and
   p.object_name = '&idxname'
group by
   begin_interval_time,search_columns;
```

This will produce an output like following, showing a summary count of the index specified during the snapshot interval. This can be compared to the number of times that a table was invoked from SQL.

```
Invocation Counts for cust_index
```

Begin Interval time	Search Columns	Invocation Count
04-10-21 15	1	3
04-10-10 16	0	1
04-10-10 19	1	1
04-10-11 02	0	2
04-10-11 04	2	1
04-10-11 06	3	1
04-10-11 11	0	1
04-10-11 12	0	2
04-10-11 13	2	1
04-10-11 15	0	3
04-10-11 17	0	14
04-10-11 18	4	1
04-10-11 19	0	1
04-10-11 20	3	7
04-10-11 21	0	1

Figure 6.11 shows a sample screenshot of output produced by the Ion tool for index access:

SQL tuning with Regular Expression Indexes

Most Used Indexes

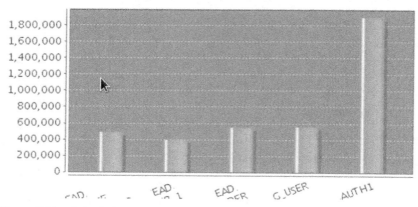

Figure 6.11: *Index Invocation Count in Ion Tool*

It quickly becomes clear that the AWR SQL tuning tables offer a wealth of important time metrics:

💾 awr_sql_index_freq.sql

```
col c1 heading 'Object|Name'         format a30
col c2 heading 'Operation'           format a15
col c3 heading 'Option'              format a15
col c4 heading 'Index|Usage|Count'   format 999,999

break on c1 skip 2
break on c2 skip 2

select
  p.object_name c1,
  p.operation   c2,
  p.options     c3,
  count(1)      c4
from
  dba_hist_sql_plan p,
  dba_hist_sqlstat  s
where
  p.object_owner <> 'SYS'
and
  p.operation like '%INDEX%'
and
  p.sql_id = s.sql_id
```

```
group by
   p.object_name,
   p.operation,
   p.options
order by
  1,2,3;
```

The following output shows the overall total counts for each object and table access method:

Object Name	Operation	Option	Index Usage Count
CUSTOMER _CHECK	INDEX	RANGE SCAN	4
CUSTOMER _PRIMARY		UNIQUE SCAN	1
CUSTOMER_ORDERS_PRIMARY		FULL SCAN	1
CUSTOMER_ORDERS_PRIMARY		UNIQUE SCAN	247
AVAILABILITY_PRIMARY_KEY		RANGE SCAN	4
CON_UK		RANGE SCAN	3
CURRENT_SEVERITY_PRIMARY_KEY		RANGE SCAN	2
CWM$CUBEDIMENSIONUSE_IDX		RANGE SCAN	2
CWM$CUBE_PK		UNIQUE SCAN	2
CWM$DIMENSION_PK		FULL SCAN	2
CWM$MODEL_PK		UNIQUE SCAN	2
LOGMNR_LOG$_PK		FULL SCAN	3
LOGMNR_SESSION_PK		UNIQUE SCAN	1
MBAB_PK		UNIQUE SCAN	1
MBAP_PK		UNIQUE SCAN	1
MBA_PK		UNIQUE SCAN	1
MBFAC_PK		RANGE SCAN	1
MBPFB_PK		RANGE SCAN	1
MGMT_ARU_OP_PK		UNIQUE SCAN	1
MGMT_ARU_PRD_PK		UNIQUE SCAN	1
MGMT_ARU_RLS_PK		UNIQUE SCAN	1
MGMT_BUG_FIX_APPLIC_CL_IDX		RANGE SCAN	1
MGMT_CURRENT_METRICS_PK		RANGE SCAN	20
MGMT_CURRENT_METRICS_PK		UNIQUE SCAN	156
MGMT_ECM_SNAP_IDX		RANGE SCAN	3
MGMT_EMD_PING_PK		UNIQUE SCAN	1
MGMT_INV_COMPONENT_IDX		FAST FULL SCAN	2
MGMT_INV_COM_CONT_IDX		RANGE SCAN	1
MGMT_INV_PATCH_CONT_IDX		RANGE SCAN	1
MGMT_JOB_EXEC_IDX01		RANGE SCAN	921
MGMT_JOB_EXEC_SUMM_IDX04		RANGE SCAN	364
MGMT_JOB_HIST_IDX01		RANGE SCAN	3
MGMT_JOB_PK		UNIQUE SCAN	923

This data can be summed up by snapshot period yielding an overall view of how Oracle is accessing the table data.

🖫 awr_access_counts.sql

```
ttitle 'Table Access|Operation Counts|Per Snapshot Period'

col c1 heading 'Begin|Interval|time'    format a20
col c2 heading 'Operation'              format a15
```

```
col c3 heading 'Option'                    format a15
col c4 heading 'Object|Count'              format 999,999

break on c1 skip 2
break on c2 skip 2

select
  to_char(sn.begin_interval_time,'yy-mm-dd hh24')   c1,
  p.operation    c2,
  p.options      c3,
  count(1)       c4
from
  dba_hist_sql_plan p,
  dba_hist_sqlstat  s,
  dba_hist_snapshot sn
where
  p.object_owner <> 'SYS'
and
  p.sql_id = s.sql_id
and
  s.snap_id = sn.snap_id
group by
  to_char(sn.begin_interval_time,'yy-mm-dd hh24'),
  p.operation,
  p.options
order by
  1,2,3;
```

This output shows the overall total counts for each object and table access method:

```
Begin
Interval                                          Object
time                Operation      Option          Count
------------------  -------------  --------------  -------
12-10-15 16         INDEX          UNIQUE SCAN          1

12-10-15 16         TABLE ACCESS   BY INDEX ROWID       1
12-10-15 16                        FULL                 2

12-10-15 17         INDEX          UNIQUE SCAN          1

12-10-15 17         TABLE ACCESS   BY INDEX ROWID       1
12-10-15 17                        FULL                 2

12-10-15 18         INDEX          UNIQUE SCAN          1

12-10-15 18         TABLE ACCESS   BY INDEX ROWID       1
12-10-15 18                        FULL                 2

12-10-15 19         INDEX          UNIQUE SCAN          1
```

The following is a helpful script that will summarize index access by snapshot period.

💾 awr_sql_index_access.sql

```
col c1 heading 'Begin|Interval|Time'    format a20
col c2 heading 'Index|Range|Scans' format 999,999
col c3 heading 'Index|Unique|Scans' format 999,999
col c4 heading 'Index|Full|Scans' format 999,999
```

```
select
  r.c1   c1,
  r.c2   c2,
  u.c2   c3,
  f.c2   c4
from
(
select
  to_char(sn.begin_interval_time,'yy-mm-dd hh24')  c1,
  count(1)                                          c2
from
   dba_hist_sql_plan p,
   dba_hist_sqlstat  s,
   dba_hist_snapshot sn
where
   p.object_owner <> 'SYS'
and
   p.operation like '%INDEX%'
and
   p.options like '%RANGE%'
and
   p.sql_id = s.sql_id
and
   s.snap_id = sn.snap_id
group by
   to_char(sn.begin_interval_time,'yy-mm-dd hh24')
order by
1 ) r,
(
select
  to_char(sn.begin_interval_time,'yy-mm-dd hh24')  c1,
  count(1)                                          c2
from
   dba_hist_sql_plan p,
   dba_hist_sqlstat  s,
   dba_hist_snapshot sn
where
   p.object_owner <> 'SYS'
and
   p.operation like '%INDEX%'
and
   p.options like '%UNIQUE%'
and
   p.sql_id = s.sql_id
and
   s.snap_id = sn.snap_id
group by
   to_char(sn.begin_interval_time,'yy-mm-dd hh24')
order by
1 ) u,
(
select
  to_char(sn.begin_interval_time,'yy-mm-dd hh24')  c1,
  count(1)                                          c2
from
   dba_hist_sql_plan p,
   dba_hist_sqlstat  s,
   dba_hist_snapshot sn
where
```

SQL tuning with Regular Expression Indexes

```
   p.object_owner <> 'SYS'
and
   p.operation like '%INDEX%'
and
   p.options like '%FULL%'
and
   p.sql_id = s.sql_id
and
   s.snap_id = sn.snap_id
group by
  to_char(sn.begin_interval_time,'yy-mm-dd hh24')
order by
1 ) f
where
     r.c1 = u.c1
  and
     r.c1 = f.c1;
```

Here is the sample output showing those specific times when the database performs unique scans, index range scans and index fast full scans:

```
Begin                   Index    Index    Index
Interval                Range    Unique   Full
Time                    Scans    Scans    Scans
-------------------- -------- -------- --------
12-10-21 15                36       35        2
12-10-21 19                10        8        2
12-10-21 20                          8        2
12-10-21 21                          8        2
12-10-21 22                11        8        3
12-10-21 23                16       11        3


12-10-22 00                10        9        1
12-10-22 01                11        8        3
12-10-22 02                12        8        1
12-10-22 03                10        8        3
12-10-22 04                11        8        2
12-10-22 05                          8        3
12-10-22 06                          8        2
```

With a non-OLTP database that regularly performs large full-table and full-index scans, it is helpful to know those times when the full scan activity is high:

💾 awr_sql_full_scans.sql

```
col c1 heading 'Begin|Interval|Time'    format a20
col c2 heading 'Index|Table|Scans' format 999,999
col c3 heading 'Full|Table|Scans' format 999,999

select
  i.c1   c1,
  i.c2   c2,
  f.c2   c3
```

```
from
(
select
  to_char(sn.begin_interval_time,'yy-mm-dd hh24')  c1,
  count(1)                                 c2
from
  dba_hist_sql_plan p,
  dba_hist_sqlstat  s,
  dba_hist_snapshot sn
where
  p.object_owner <> 'SYS'
and
  p.operation like '%TABLE ACCESS%'
and
  p.options like '%INDEX%'
and
  p.sql_id = s.sql_id
and
  s.snap_id = sn.snap_id
group by
  to_char(sn.begin_interval_time,'yy-mm-dd hh24')
order by
1 ) i,
(
select
  to_char(sn.begin_interval_time,'yy-mm-dd hh24')  c1,
  count(1)                                 c2
from
  dba_hist_sql_plan p,
  dba_hist_sqlstat  s,
  dba_hist_snapshot sn
where
  p.object_owner <> 'SYS'
and
  p.operation like '%TABLE ACCESS%'
and
  p.options = 'FULL'
and
  p.sql_id = s.sql_id
and
  s.snap_id = sn.snap_id
group by
  to_char(sn.begin_interval_time,'yy-mm-dd hh24')
order by
1 ) f
where
    i.c1 = f.c1;
```

The output shows a comparison of index-full scans versus full-table scans:

Begin Interval Time	Index Table Scans	Full Table Scans
12-10-21 15	53	18
12-10-21 17	3	3
12-10-21 18	1	2

```
12-10-21 19          15          6
12-10-21 20                      6
12-10-21 21                      6
12-10-21 22          16          6
12-10-21 23          21          9
12-10-22 00          16          6
12-10-22 01                      6
12-10-22 02          17          6
12-10-22 03          15          6
12-10-22 04          16          6
12-10-22 05                      6
12-10-22 06                      6
12-10-22 07          15          6
12-10-22 08                      6
12-10-22 09                      6
12-10-22 10          18          8
12-10-22 11          16          6
12-10-22 12          14          6
12-10-22 13                      6
12-10-22 14                      6
12-10-22 15          15         11
12-10-22 16           1          7
12-10-22 17          15          6
12-10-22 18          16          6
12-10-22 19          15          6
```

Knowing the signature for large-table full-table scans can help in both SQL tuning and instance tuning. For SQL tuning, this report will indicate when to drill-down to verify that all of the large-table full-table scans are legitimate, and once verified, this same data can be used to dynamically reconfigure the Oracle instance to accommodate the large scans.

Monitoring SQL Workload Activity

The Ion for Oracle tool will instantly display SQL processing modality over time, quickly displaying any databases processing signature as illustrated in Figure 6.12:

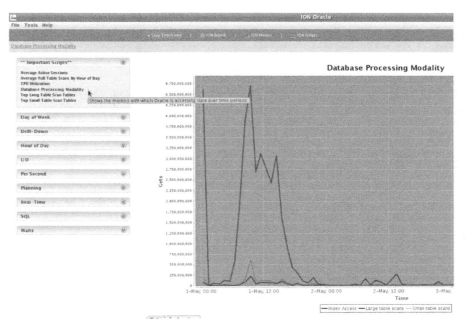

Figure 6.12: *Using Ion to display SQL workload processing modality*

Another tuning trick is to monitor SQL for optimal index usage.

Verifying Optimal Index Usage

Determining the index usage is especially important for improving the speed of queries with multiple *where* clause predicates. Oracle sometimes has a choice of indexes, and the tuning professional must examine each index and ensure that Oracle is using the best index, meaning the one that returns the result with the least consistent gets.

This problem occurs when the optimizer cannot find an index or when the most restrictive *where* clause in the SQL is not matched with an index.

When the optimizer cannot find an appropriate index to access table rows, the optimizer will always invoke a full-table scan, reading every row in the table. Hence, a large-table full-table scan might indicate a sub-optimal SQL statement that can be tuned by adding an index that matches the where clause of the query.

My tool, Ion for Oracle, instantly displays all tables and there predicate usage over time, very handy as shown in Figure 6.13:

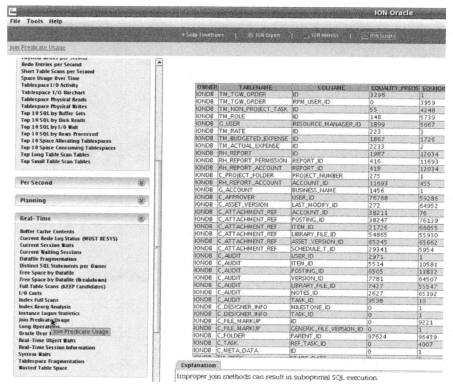

Figure 6.13: *Display SQL predicate usage in Ion for Oracle*

The next section will explore techniques for locating new indexing opportunities, removing superfluous indexes and deleting unused indexes.

Finding Indexing Opportunities

Clearly, one common symptom of a missing or invalidated index is that the SQL will perform an unnecessary large-table full-table scan. The *find_full_scans.sql* script can be used to show all full-table scans and indicates the table size in both number of rows and data blocks:

🖫 find_full_scans.sql

```
set echo off;
set feedback on

set pages 999;
column nbr_FTS   format 999,999
column num_rows  format 999,999,999
column blocks    format 999,999
```

```
column owner      format a14;
column name       format a24;
column ch         format a1;

column object_owner heading "Owner"              format a12;
column ct           heading "# of SQL selects" format 999,999;

select
   object_owner,
   count(*)     ct
from
   v$sql_plan
where
   object_owner is not null
group by
   object_owner
order by
   ct desc
;
--spool access.lst;

set heading off;
set feedback off;

set heading on;
set feedback on;
ttitle 'full table scans and counts|  |The "K" indicates that the table is
in the KEEP Pool (Oracle8).'
select
   p.owner,
   p.name,
   t.num_rows,
--   ltrim(t.cache) ch,
   decode(t.buffer_pool,'KEEP','Y','DEFAULT','N') K,
   s.blocks blocks,
   sum(a.executions) nbr_FTS
from
   dba_tables   t,
   dba_segments s,
   v$sqlarea a,
   (select distinct
     address,
     object_owner owner,
     object_name name
   from
     v$sql_plan
   where
     operation = 'TABLE ACCESS'
     and
     options = 'FULL') p
where
   a.address = p.address
   and
   t.owner = s.owner
   and
   t.table_name = s.segment_name
   and
   t.table_name = p.name
   and
```

SQL tuning with Regular Expression Indexes   **347**

```
      t.owner = p.owner
      and
      t.owner not in ('SYS','SYSTEM')
   having
      sum(a.executions) > 9
   group by
      p.owner, p.name, t.num_rows, t.cache, t.buffer_pool, s.blocks
   order by
      sum(a.executions) desc;

column nbr_RID  format 999,999,999
column num_rows format 999,999,999
column owner       format a15;
column name        format a25;

ttitle 'Table access by ROWID and counts'
select
   p.owner,
   p.name,
   t.num_rows,
   sum(s.executions) nbr_RID
from
   dba_tables t,
   v$sqlarea s,
   (select distinct
      address,
      object_owner owner,
      object_name name
   from
      v$sql_plan
   where
      operation = 'TABLE ACCESS'
      and
      options = 'BY ROWID') p
where
   s.address = p.address
   and
   t.table_name = p.name
   and
   t.owner = p.owner
having
   sum(s.executions) > 9
group by
   p.owner, p.name, t.num_rows
order by
   sum(s.executions) desc;

--*************************************************
--  Index Report Section
--*************************************************

column nbr_scans   format 999,999,999
column num_rows     format 999,999,999
column tbl_blocks format 999,999,999
column owner        format a9;
column table_name format a20;
column index_name format a20;

ttitle 'Index full scans and counts'
```

```
select
   p.owner,
   d.table_name,
   p.name index_name,
   seg.blocks tbl_blocks,
   sum(s.executions) nbr_scans
from
   dba_segments seg,
   v$sqlarea s,
   dba_indexes d,
   (select distinct
      address,
      object_owner owner,
      object_name name
   from
      v$sql_plan
   where
      operation = 'INDEX'
      and
      options = 'FULL SCAN') p
where
   d.index_name = p.name
   and
   s.address = p.address
   and
   d.table_name = seg.segment_name
   and
   seg.owner = p.owner
having
   sum(s.executions) > 9
group by
   p.owner, d.table_name, p.name, seg.blocks
order by
   sum(s.executions) desc;


ttitle 'Index range scans and counts'
select
   p.owner,
   d.table_name,
   p.name index_name,
   seg.blocks tbl_blocks,
   sum(s.executions) nbr_scans
from
   dba_segments seg,
   v$sqlarea s,
   dba_indexes d,
   (select distinct
      address,
      object_owner owner,
      object_name name
   from
      v$sql_plan
   where
      operation = 'INDEX'
      and
      options = 'RANGE SCAN') p
where
   d.index_name = p.name
```

```
   and
      s.address = p.address
   and
      d.table_name = seg.segment_name
   and
      seg.owner = p.owner
having
   sum(s.executions) > 9
group by
   p.owner, d.table_name, p.name, seg.blocks
order by
   sum(s.executions) desc;


ttitle 'Index unique scans and counts'
select
   p.owner,
   d.table_name,
   p.name index_name,
   sum(s.executions) nbr_scans
from
   v$sqlarean s,
   dba_indexes d,
   (select distinct
      address,
      object_owner owner,
      object_name name
   from
      v$sql_plan
   where
      operation = 'INDEX'
      and
      options = 'UNIQUE SCAN') p
where
   d.index_name = p.name
   and
   s.address = p.address
having
   sum(s.executions) > 9
group by
   p.owner, d.table_name, p.name
order by
   sum(s.executions) desc;
```

The results might look like the following:

```
                      Full table scans and counts
          Note that "K" indicates in the table is in the KEEP pool.

OWNER           NAME                          NUM_ROWS  C K   BLOCKS   NBR_FTS
-------------   -----------------------       --------- - -  --------  -------
SYS             DUAL                                    N          2   97,237
SYSTEM          SQLPLUS_PRODUCT_PROFILE                 N K        2   16,178
DONALD          PAGE                          3,450,209 N     932,120    9,091
DONALD          RWU_PAGE                            434 N          8    7,355
DONALD          PAGE_IMAGE                       18,067 N      1,104    5,368
```

This report shows that the *page* table is rather large at 932,000 data blocks and the *page* table has experienced 9,000 full-table scans. This should raise the suspicions of any good Oracle tuning professional, and the specific SQL should be examined to see if any of these scans are unnecessary, possible because of missing function-based indexes. The *get_sql.sql* script can be run to check for SQL that references the *page* table.

🖫 get_sql.sql

```
set lines 2000;

select
   sql_text,
   disk_reads,
   executions,
   parse_calls
from
   v$sqlarea
where
   lower(sql_text) like '% page %'
order by
   disk_reads desc
;
```

The following SQL statement is extracted from the output of the *get_sql.sql* script. After examination, it is obvious that the script is accessing customers by converting the customer name to uppercase using the *upper* BIF.

```
select
   p.page_name,
   o.order_date
from
   page       p,
   order      o
where
   upper(p.page_name) = upper(:v1)
and
   p.cust_nbr = o.cust_nbr
;
```

The *explain plan* utility can be now be run against this SQL, confirming that this query is performs a full-table scan:

```
OPTIONS                          OBJECT_NAME                       POSITION
-------------------------------- ------------------------------- ----------
SELECT STATEMENT
                                                                          4
  NESTED LOOPS
                                                                          1
    TABLE ACCESS
FULL                             PAGE                                     1
    TABLE ACCESS
BY INDEX ROWID                   ORDER                                    2
```

```
        INDEX
RANGE SCAN                    CUST_NBR_IDX                        1
```

A look at the *table access full page* option shows that the BIF is indeed responsible for the full-table scan.

A matching function-based index can be added on *upper(page_name)* to remedy this issue.

It is important to remember that is not 100% safe to add indexes to tables, as this can often change the execution plan for the query and slow-down insert and update times.

```
create index
   upper_page_name_idx
on
   page
      (upper(page_name))
  tablespace ts_page
  pctfree 10;
```

Next, the SQL is re-run and the results show that the full-table scan has been replaced with an index range scan on the new function-based index. The resulting execution time has been reduced from 45 seconds to less than 2 seconds.

```
OPERATION
- - - - - - - - - - - - - - - - - - - - - - - - - - - - - - - - - - - - - - - -
OPTIONS                       OBJECT_NAME                    POSITION
- - - - - - - - - - - - - - -  - - - - - - - - - - - - - - - - - - -  - - - - - - - - - -
SELECT STATEMENT
                                                                 5
  NESTED LOOPS
                                                                 1
    TABLE ACCESS
BY INDEX ROWID                PAGE                               1
      INDEX
RANGE SCAN                    PAGE_NBR_IDX                       1
    TABLE ACCESS
BY INDEX ROWID                ORDER                              2
      INDEX
RANGE SCAN                    UPPER_PAGE_NAME_IDX                1
```

In sum, it is relatively easy to detect missing function-based Oracle indexes and add them to tune the SQL.

Find SQL that Uses Sub-optimal ndexes

Oracle tuning experts advise never assuming that all optimal indexes, exist, especially function-based indexes. Remember, with rare exceptions, Oracle can only choose one index to access any given table in a SQL statement, and it is the human expert's job to ensure that the most restrictive index exists!

For beginners, Oracle has created several frameworks that will examine the access plans for SQL tuning sets and identify index and materialized view opportunities. These extra-cost tools include:

- **SQLAccess Advisor**: The Oracle SQLAccess advisor will examine workloads in an attempt to locate missing indexes and missing materialized views.

- **Real Application Testing**: The RAT framework allows the replaying of a SQL tuning set, seeking tuning opportunities. The RAT framework, in turn, works with the 11g SQL tuning advisor to locate missing indexes.

For complete details on using the extra-cost Oracle Real Application Testing (RAT) and the SQL Performance Analyzer (SPA), see chapter 19, *Oracle SQL Tuning Advisors*.

While these tools are getting better with each release of Oracle, a human SQL tuning expert can do a better job than any automated tool at finding missing indexes. While every expert has their own approach, locating missing indexes involves the following steps:

- **Locate high impact SQL**: Search for high impact SQL using several criteria (*disk reads, executions*) and historical SQL can be found in any of these three locations:

  - Search *v$sql* for frequently executed SQL (using the *executions* column)

  - Search the *stats$sql_plan* table in STATSPACK

  - Search the *dba_hist_sql_plan* in AWR (extra cost option)

- **Examine execution statistics**: For each high-impact SQL statement, compare the number of rows returned to the number of consistent gets required to fetch the rows. SQL with a missing index will use a sub-optimal index (or do a full table scan), showing too many buffer touches than are necessary to fetch the result row set.

- **Create a new index**: In a test or development environment, create the new index and re-run the SQL to see if the number of consistent gets is reduced. Remember, a new index may help more than just the SQL statement being tuned.

- **Implement the index:** Migrate the index into production and re-sample the workload to find the next high-impact SQL statement to tune.

- **Repeat as needed**: Finally, repeat the first step iteratively to tune the next SQL statement.

Finding SQL with Excessive I/O

The best way to search for SQL that might be used a less than optimal indexes is to compare the rows returned with the number of block fetches, all the while being conscious of aggregate queries that require full-scans (*min, max, sum, avg*, etc.).

In a situation where three queries return ten rows, but each has a very different numbers of data block reads, the following conditions might have contributed to the disparity:

- **Clustered data**: A SQL where the related rows are physically clustered together on the same data block using sorted hash cluster tables will fetch the ten rows with three data block reads.

- **Well tuned SQL**: With un-clustered data and a selective index, the ten rows can be fetched in less than 20 data block reads.

- **Sub-optimal index**: With a SQL with a missing index, fetching the ten rows might take hundreds of data block reads.

- **No indexes:** In a SQL without appropriate indexes, a full-table scan is required and fetching the ten rows might require thousands of data block reads.

Clearly, one hallmark of sub-optimal SQL execution is an unusually high number of data block reads for the number of rows being returned.

Hot Tip!

[oss out aggregations!

When fishing for sub-optimal SQL, you need to filter out aggregations (*min, max, avg, sum*) because they types of queries will need to perform full table scans of use query-rewrite for materialized views.

Now that the characteristics of sub-optimal index access have been presented, it is a good time to take a closer look at how to write scripts against the library cache, STATSPACK and AWR tables to identify queries with excessive I/O.

Finding sub-optimal SQL in the library cache

The following is a rough sample query that runs against *v$sqlarea* to locate queries with possible sub-optimal indexes. Of course, this SQL will have to be customized to match the SQL workloads being investigated. In this example, SQL that is currently in the library cache will be extracted, yet SQL is re-pinged to the front of the most-recently-used list each time that the SQL is executed:

🖫 get_sub_optimal_cached_sql.sql

```
set linesize 80 pagesize 80 trimspool on

ttitle "Top 10 Expensive SQL | Consistent Gets per Rows Fetched"

column sql_id heading "SQL ID"
column c2      heading "Avg Gets per Row"
column c3      heading "Total Gets"
column c4      heading "Total Rows"

select
   *
from
   (select
      sq.sql_id,
      round(sum(buffer_gets_delta) /
      decode(sum(rows_processed_delta), 0, 1,
      sum(rows_processed_delta))) c2,
      sum(buffer_gets_delta) c3,
      sum(rows_processed_delta) c4
   from
      dba_hist_snapshot sn,
      dba_hist_sqlstat sq,
      dba_hist_sqltext st
   where
      sn.snap_id = sq.snap_id
   and
      sn.dbid = sq.dbid
   and
      sn.instance_number = sq.instance_number
   and
      sn.dbid = st.dbid
   and
      sq.sql_id = st.sql_id
   and
      lower(sql_text) not like '%sum(%'
   and
      lower(sql_text) not like '%min(%'
   and
      lower(sql_text) not like '%max(%'
   and
      lower(sql_text) not like '%avg(%'
   and
      lower(sql_text) not like '%count(%'
   and
      sn.snap_id between &beginsnap and &endsnap
   and
      sq.parsing_schema_name not in ('SYS', 'SYSMAN', 'SYSTEM', 'MDSYS',
'WMSYS', 'TSMSYS', 'DBSNMP', 'OUTLN')
group by
   sq.sql_id
order by
   2 desc)
where
   rownum < 11;/
```

Here is a listing from this query:

```
@get_sub_optimal_cached_sql.sql

Enter value for beginsnap: 48810
Enter value for endsnap: 48913

old  11: and sn.snap_id between &beginsnap and &endsnap
new  11: and sn.snap_id between 48810 and 48913
```

```
Sun Jan 10                                               page     1
                     Top 10 Expensive SQL
              Consistent Gets per Rows Fetched

SQL ID           Avg Gets per Row     Total Gets Total Rows
-------------    ----------------     ---------- ----------
9m73y3n44dmgy         606,665,271    606,665,271          0
a5zs0psr0m2p9          24,997,386     49,994,772          2
a7m9jw016q6hf          17,280,238     17,280,238          0
5zzvgcvxcxtth           8,278,019      8,278,019          0
bc5kw9qc0v0dm           8,049,460      8,049,460          0
8nus8twjpc3r9           8,018,029    192,432,698         24
cg5rg1vzw5uaz           5,168,572      5,168,572          0
9ncywvmgtakg3           4,004,378      4,004,378          0
dj6bagqucttx9           2,199,463    892,982,149        406
7uv8ra7n7vdps           1,899,353      1,899,353          0
```

This query shows the most expensive SQL statements by average gets per row.

Finding Index Opportunities in AWR

The purchase of the extra-cost options required to use the Automatic Workload Repository (AWR) allows querying of AWR tables to locate SQL with indexing opportunities. The free STATSPACK utility will do exactly the same job of capturing historical SQL.

The following script shows expensive SQL statements by time period. Note that the list can be constrained to display the top-n most expensive queries and adjust the I/O threshold for the display:

💾 awr_expensive_sql.sql

```
set linesize 80 pagesize 80 trimspool on

ttitle "Top 10 Expensive SQL | Disk Reads per Rows Fetched"

column sql_id heading "SQL ID"
column c2 heading "Avg Reads per Row"
column c3 heading "Total Reads"
```

```
column c4 heading "Total Rows"

select
   *
from
   (select
      sq.sql_id,
      round(sum(disk_reads_delta) /
      decode(sum(rows_processed_delta),
      0,
      1,
      sum(rows_processed_delta))) c2,
   sum(disk_reads_delta) c3,
   sum(rows_processed_delta) c4
from
   dba_hist_snapshot sn,
   dba_hist_sqlstat  sq,
   dba_hist_sqltext  st
where
   sn.snap_id = sq.snap_id
and
   sn.dbid = sq.dbid
and
   sn.instance_number = sq.instance_number
and
   sn.dbid = st.dbid and sq.sql_id = st.sql_id
and
   lower(sql_text) not like '%sum(%'
and
   lower(sql_text) not like '%min(%'
and
   lower(sql_text) not like '%max(%'
and
   lower(sql_text) not like '%avg(%'
and
   lower(sql_text) not like '%count(%'
and
   sn.snap_id between &beginsnap and &endsnap
and
   sq.parsing_schema_name not in ('SYS', 'SYSMAN', 'SYSTEM', 'MDSYS',
'WMSYS', 'TSMSYS', 'DBSNMP', 'OUTLN')
group by
   sq.sql_id
order by
   2 desc)
where
   rownum < 11;
/
```

The output from this script shows the most expensive SQL based on disk I/O:

```
@awr_expensive_sql.sql

Enter value for beginsnap: 48810
Enter value for endsnap: 48913

old  11: and sn.snap_id between &beginsnap and &endsnap
```

```
new   11: and sn.snap_id between 48810 and 48913
```

                          Top 10 Expensive SQL
                       Disk Reads per Rows Fetched

SQL ID	Avg Reads per Row	Total Reads	Total Rows
a5zs0psr0m2p9	346,838	693,675	2
7uv8ra7n7vdps	217,933	217,933	0
cg5rg1vzw5uaz	139,402	139,402	0
5zzvgcvxcxtth	128,271	128,271	0
a7m9jw016q6hf	117,039	117,039	0
8nus8twjpc3r9	101,795	2,443,082	24
9m73y3n44dmgy	56,664	56,664	0
bc5kw9qc0v0dm	45,732	45,732	0
9ncywvmgtakg3	44,728	44,728	0
7181d5ckdz09m	22,864	1,188,947	52

It is important to remove unused and superfluous indexes from the production environment, but why?

Locating Un-used Indexes

It is critical to constantly monitor for unused indexes by examining the characteristics of the SQL workload to see how often the SQL is used. Unused indexes have several shortcomings:

- **Disk space waste**: Unused disks waste significant amounts of disk space. Disk is cheap, but indexes can still waste a significant amount of disk.

- **Slow inserts and updates**: With many indexes on a table, inserts can take large amounts of time, since all indexes must be updated at DML time.

It is impossible to know whether an index is used unless there is a way to track what SQL statements use the index.

The methods for identifying unused indexes are release specific, so the next few sections will examine techniques for locating unused indexes by release.

Finding Unused Indexes in Oracle 8i and Earlier

In Oracle releases 8i and earlier, this was a major undertaking since it was necessary to capture SQL directly from the library cache, generate an execution plan and save the indexes.

Over time, a list of used indexes was collected, and this list could be compared to the master index list in *dba_indexes* to find the unused indexes. For the script to locate unused indexes in unsupported releases, please Google for the query *access_index.sql* (available on www.dba-oracle .com).

Finding Unused Indexes in Oracle 9i

Starting in Oracle9i, the *v$object_usage* view is used to tell when an index is used. This is a primitive marker because it is a bit flag, only indicating if an index is used and not noting whether the index was used once or a million times. This simple command can be used to set the bit flag to monitor usage for an index:

```
alter index
   myindex
monitoring usage;
```

Once implemented, the *used* column of *v$object_usage* is simply queried as follows to see if the index was used:

```
select
   used
from
   v$object_usage
where
   index_name = 'MYINDEX';
```

Look Out!

Beware of index monitoring!

There is overhead to turning on index monitoring because all SQL statements in the library cache will be invalidated. Hence, it is best to turn on index monitoring immediately after starting the instance.

In order to use index monitoring to find unused indexes, it is important to leave index monitoring on long enough to ensure that all possible SQL statement have executed.

For example, a monthly job might use an index, so the monitoring must be turned on for a whole month in order to see it. Of course, in a case like this, it may be a better practice to create the index for the monthly job right before execution and then dropping the index.

While the index usage in a bit flag, it might be helpful to know the number of times that the index was invoked. In Oracle9i, STATSPACK for this by querying the *stats$sql_plan* table.

Finding Unused indexes in Oracle 10g and Beyond

In Oracle 10g and beyond, it is possible to more accurately count the number of times that an index was invoked by using the STATSPACK or AWR tables.

Without the add-on allowing quering against the AWR tables, the following query against the *stats$sql_plan* and *stats$sql_plan_usage* tables can be used:

🖫 statspack_unused_indexes.sql

```
ttitle "Unused Indexes by Time Period"

col owner heading "Index Owner" format a30
col index_name heading "Index Name" format a30

set linesize 95 trimspool on pagesize 80

select *
from
   (select
      owner,
      index_name
   from
      dba_indexes di
   where
      di.index_type != 'LOB'
   and
      owner not in ('SYS', 'SYSMAN', 'SYSTEM', 'MDSYS', 'WMSYS', 'TSMSYS',
'DBSNMP', 'OUTLN')
minus
select
   index_owner owner,
   index_name
from
   dba_constraints dc
where
   index_owner not in ('SYS', 'SYSMAN', 'SYSTEM', 'MDSYS', 'WMSYS',
'TSMSYS', 'DBSNMP', 'OUTLN')
minus
select
   p.object_owner owner,
   p.object_name   index_name
from
   stats$snapshot       sn,
   stats$sql_plan       p,
   stats$sql_summary    st,
   stats$sql_plan_usage spu
where
   st.sql_id = spu.sql_id
and
   spu.plan_hash_value = p.plan_hash_value
and
   st.hash_value = p.plan_hash_value
and
```

```
   sn.snap_id = st.snap_id
and
   sn.dbid = st.dbid
and
   sn.instance_number = st.instance_number
and
   sn.snap_id = spu.snap_id
and
   sn.dbid = spu.snap_id
and
   sn.instance_number = spu.instance_number
and
   sn.snap_id between &begin_snap and &end_snap
and
   p.object_type = 'INDEX'
)
where owner not in ('SYS', 'SYSMAN', 'SYSTEM', 'MDSYS', 'WMSYS', 'TSMSYS',
'DBSNMP', 'OUTLN')
order by 1, 2;/
```

The script above has a clause to ensure that the index is not used to enforce a primary key or foreign key relationship. Even though an index may appear to be used by SQL, it may be heavily used to enforce primary key and foreign key constraints.

```
Enter value for begin_snap: 48795

Enter value for end_snap: 48923

old  22:    sn.snap_id between &begin_snap and &end_snap
new  22:    sn.snap_id between 48795 and 48923
```

When dropping unused indexes, also watch out for any indexes that may be used internally to enforce primary key foreign key relationships.

Depending upon how the primary key or foreign key index is designed, the index may have a name or it may appear as a system owned index, beginning with SYS.

The Oracle performance pack and the Oracle Diagnostic pack are required to run the following query to see unused indexes:

🖫 awr_unused_indexes.sql

```
ttitle "Unused Indexes by Time Period"

col owner heading "Index Owner" format a30
col index_name heading "Index Name" format a30

set linesize 95 trimspool on pagesize 80

select * from
(select owner, index_name
```

```
from dba_indexes di
where
   di.index_type != 'LOB'
minus
select index_owner owner, index_name
from dba_constraints dc
minus
select
   p.object_owner owner,
   p.object_name index_name
from
   dba_hist_snapshot  sn,
   dba_hist_sql_plan   p,
   dba_hist_sqlstat   st
where
   st.sql_id = p.sql_id
and
   sn.snap_id = st.snap_id and sn.dbid = st.dbid and sn.instance_number =
st.instance_number
and
   sn.snap_id between &begin_snap and &end_snap
and
   p.object_type = 'INDEX'
)
where owner not in ('SYS', 'SYSMAN', 'SYSTEM', 'MDSYS', 'WMSYS', 'TSMSYS',
'DBSNMP', 'OUTLN')
order by 1, 2;
/
```

Dropping Un-used Indexes

Now that the unused indexes have been identified, being very careful to sample over a long enough time period to ensure that no queries have been missed, the final steps are simple:

- Take a backup of the index DDL using *dbms_metadata.*

- Drop the index

For taking a backup of an unused index, I recommend using the *dbms_metadata* package to punch-off a copy of the index DLL from the data dictionary:

```
set heading off;
set echo off;
Set pages 999;
set long 90000;

spool ddl_list.sql
select dbms_metadata.get_ddl('TABLE','DEPT','SCOTT') from dual;
select dbms_metadata.get_ddl('INDEX','DEPT_IDX','SCOTT') from dual;
spool off;
```

The next section will cover how to locate those indexes that can be considered infrequently-used.

Locating Infrequently Used Indexes

It is not uncommon for infrequently-used indexes to consume more resources than they save when they are used. For highly active tables, each and every DML statement requires Oracle to keep the index current, and the relative saving of the index on the infrequent SQL must be weighed against the continuous overhead of maintaining the index.

Disk space is cheap, so the cost of the disk required to store the index is usually negligible. Infrequently-used indexes do not impose a heavy overhead for static tables that are rarely updated, but they can wreak havoc on volatile tables, causing a measurable amount of operational overhead for very little benefit.

Remember, indexes always add overhead to DML operations, and it may often be a good practice for weekly and monthly jobs to drop the index and consider one of these alternative methods:

1.   Create the index, run the job and then drop the index.

2.   Allow the infrequent job to choose another plan that does not involve the index.

The *awr_infrequent_indexes.sql* query can be used to find infrequently-used indexes.

When using this query, the count should be adjusted to match the specific workload under investigation. The default for the example is 50 invocations. It is also possible to change the date format mask to change the aggregation period, which is set to monthly (*mon*) here:

🖫 awr_infrequent_indexes.sql

```
ttitle "Infrequently-used indexes by month"

col c1 heading "Month"             format a20
col c2 heading "Index Owner"       format a30
col c3 heading "Index Name"        format a30
col c4 heading "Invocation|Count"  format 99

set linesize 95 trimspool on pagesize 80

select
   to_char(sn.begin_interval_time,'Month') c1,
   p.object_owner c2,
   p.object_name c3,
   sum(executions_delta) c4
from
```

```
   dba_hist_snapshot    sn,
   dba_hist_sql_plan    p,
   dba_hist_sqlstat     st
where
   st.sql_id = p.sql_id
and
   sn.snap_id = st.snap_id
and
   sn.dbid = st.dbid
and
   sn.instance_number = st.instance_number
and
   p.object_type = 'INDEX'
and
   p.object_owner not in ('SYS', 'SYSMAN', 'SYSTEM', 'MDSYS', 'WMSYS',
'TSMSYS', 'DBSNMP')
group by
   to_char(sn.begin_interval_time, 'Month'),
   p.object_owner,
   p.object_name
having
   sum(executions_delta) < 50
order by
   1, 4 desc, 2, 3;
/
```

Again, it will be necessary to carefully perform a cost-benefit analysis against any infrequently-used indexes:

- **Benefit**: It is easy to see the benefit because the SQL is infrequently used. Simply run the query in the QA database once with the index and again without the index.

- **Cost:** As noted, the cost of an infrequently used index is directly proportional to the amount of updates to the target table. For each DML, the overhead to maintain the index may not be measurable, but it can add-up fast for highly active tables that perform thousands of updates per day.

This covers the issue of infrequently-used indexes, and the following section will address the issue of redundant indexes.

The Problem of Too Many Indexes

Over the years, it has not been uncommon for the busy DBA to create indexes and not notice when the jobs that use them are removed from the SQL workload.

For example, I once went onsite to a shop that was complaining that each tale insert was taking 45 seconds per row! Upon inspection, the table had 80 columns, but it had over 120 indexes! The DBA did not understand how to manage indexes, and after he was fired for inept work, there was a horrendous mess to be cleaned up.

It was not possible to simple delete all of the indexes because the system was live in production, and each index had to be carefully inspected and compared to historical SQL execution plans to locate those indexes that could be safely removed without impacting run-time performance.

One common misconception by developers is that every predicate in a SQL *where* clause should be indexed, but this is not true. Because Oracle supports multi-column indexes, it is easy to accidently create duplicate indexes, indexes that add overhead to DML and do not aid in speeding up SQL execution.

Aggressively remove duplicitous indexes!

Management commonly hires clandestine experts to review the technical ability of a DBA. One sure-fire way to get fired is to waste computing resources by allowing your database to have duplicate indexes.

Thus, it is important to remove duplicate indexes, but it will be helpful to get some insight into the common methods for finding indexes that can be safely dropped without effecting SQL execution.

The *dba_ind_columns* view can be queried to quickly locate indexes with duplicate columns, but the real challenge comes when deciding which index to drop.

This following script looks for indexes on tables with the same leading column then for indexes with the same two leading columns. This duplicate index column report provides a good starting point for trying to reduce redundancy in indexes:

💾 Find_duplicate_index_columns.sql

```
set linesize 150 trimspool on pagesize 80

column index_owner format a20
column column_name format a30
column position format 9
column nextcol format a18 heading "Next Column Match?"

select
   a.index_owner,
   a.column_name,
   a.index_name index_name1,
   b.index_name index_name2,
   a.column_position position,
  (select
      'YES'
   from
```

```
        dba_ind_columns x,
        dba_ind_columns y
   where
        x.index_owner = a.index_owner
   and
        y.index_owner = b.index_owner
   and
        x.index_name = a.index_name
   and
        y.index_name = b.index_name
   and
        x.column_position = 2
   and
        y.column_position = 2
   and
        x.column_name = y.column_name) nextcol
from
   dba_ind_columns a,
   dba_ind_columns b
where
   a.index_owner not in ('SYS', 'SYSMAN', 'SYSTEM', 'MDSYS', 'WMSYS',
'TSMSYS', 'DBSNMP')
and
   a.index_owner = b.index_owner
and
   a.column_name = b.column_name
and
   a.table_name = b.table_name
and
   a.index_name != b.index_name
and
   a.column_position = 1
and
   b.column_position = 1;
/
```

While this query does not provide every possible duplicate column, it does give a general idea on how to locate redundant index columns. It also serves as a good starting point for identifying index redundancy.

Some techniques for determining which redundant indexes to drop will be covered next.

Determining Which Index to Delete

If the optimizer mode is set to minimize SQL response time (*optimizer_mode=first_rows_n*), the cost-based optimizer chooses which index to satisfy a query. He examines the metadata statistics from *dbms_stats* to locate the index that he thinks will be the most selective, the index that will result in the least amount of data block reads:

1. First, the optimizer evaluates all of the predicates in the *where* clause and locates the predicate that is the most unique, the one that will return the smallest result set.

2. For that index column, Oracle then searches for a matching index, either a single column index or a multi-column index where the column is the leading column. Failing that, Oracle next tries to find an index on the next most restrictive column based on the optimizer's cardinality estimates. This might be an index on another column in the where clause or on a multi-column index that contains the restrictive item as a secondary key using the index skip scan method.

Remember, for any given table, Oracle will only choose one index to access the table unless there bitmap indexes, the bitmap merge plan, or in 9i and earlier, when the *and_equal* hint is used.

The following are some examples of redundant index columns. Consider this example below for a multi-column customer table. The *cust_id* column appears in three indexes and *cust_name* appears in several indexes. Which index is it safe to remove?

Index name	Index column
cust_id_idx	*cust_id (primary_key)*
cust_id_name_idx	*cust_id, cust_name*
cust_name_id_idx	*cust_name, cust_id*
cust_details_idx	*cust_id, cust_name, cust_type*

In this example, the *cust_name_id_idx* can safely be removed because all of its columns are completely contained in the *cust_details_idx*:

Index name	Index column
cust_id_idx	*cust_id (primary key)*
cust_id_name_idx	*cust_id, cust_name*
cust_name_id_idx	*cust_name, cust_id*
cust_details_idx	*cust_id, cust_name, cust_type*

Now, the index list has been pared down, but there are still two redundant *cust_id* columns:

Index name	Index column
cust_id_idx	*cust_id (primary key)*
cust_id_name_idx	*cust_id, cust_name*
cust_name_id_idx	*cust_name, cust_id*

In this example, the redundancy is necessary because the *cust_id_idx* is a primary key constraint. Also, the redundancy is acceptable in the *cust_name_id_idx* if there is a frequently executed SQL statement that required both of these columns in the *where* clause.

At this point, it may be tempting to examine the SQL workload and attempt to create a large multi-column index in an attempt to create a single index to service all of these queries.

The dynamics of multi-column indexes and how they are used for optimal SQL execution will be covered next.

Large Multi-column Indexes

Multi-column indexes with more than three columns may not provide more efficient access than a two-column index. The objective of the index is to reduce the amount of rows returned from a table access. Therefore each added column must substantially reduce the number of returned rows to be effective.

For example, assuming a large table, on a query with five or more *where (and)* clauses using a five-column index may return only one row. However, using a three-column index may return only 50 rows. A two-column index returns 200 rows. The time it takes to extract the one row from the 200 rows using nested-loops is negligible.

Thus the two-column index may be almost as efficient (fast) as the five-column index. The key is to index the most restrictive columns. Another tradeoff is a table with multiple column indexes where the leading columns are the same.

For instance, a table with four three-column indexes where the leading two columns are the same may work very efficiently on select statements but cause a heavy penalty on inserts and updates. Just one two-column index on the leading two columns may provide acceptable query performance while greatly improving DML.

Small tables with two or three columns may benefit by being rebuilt as an Index Organized Table (IOT). A two-column table with a primary key and a two-column index has one and one half times the data in indexes that are in the table. Making the table an IOT reduced the need for indexes because the table is the index. Also, IOTs can have indexes on non-leading columns if required. Again this has to be balanced with the overhead of maintaining the IOT.

Lastly, do not be afraid to use temporary indexes, creating and destroying the index when needed by a daily, weekly or monthly job.

For example, assume a nightly batch job that requires six hours to run. It will run in 30 minutes with an index, but this index in not needed for any other SQL. In this case, it might be more prudent to create the index before running the report and drop it upon completion.

I work with clients that drop certain indexes to expedite their bill run then recreate then for the normal application. They create indexes each night and drop them in the morning. There is nothing wrong with dynamically changing the database to respond to varying tasks if it results in efficiency.

The next section will cover tuning SQL queries by creating selective indexes to speed them up.

Row Clustering and SQL Performance

The CBO's decision to perform a full-table versus an index range scan is influenced by the *clustering_factor* column located inside the *dba_indexes* view, *db_block_size* and *avg_row_len*. It is important to understand how the CBO uses these statistics to determine the fastest way to deliver the desired rows.

Conversely, a high *clustering_factor*, where the value approaches the number of rows in the table (*num_rows*), indicates that the rows are not in the same sequence as the index, and additional I/O will be required for index range scans. As the *clustering_factor* approaches the number of rows in the table, the rows are out of sync with the index.

The *clustering_factor* column in the *dba_indexes* view is an important tuning tool.

By design, Oracle is a high-performance engine, and Oracle deliberately uses tricks to make Oracle run super-fast, like delaying index maintenance when rows are deleted. Similarly, Oracle tables can fragment, causing full-scan SQL operations to run far longer than necessary. For table reorganization, there are several utilities for returning a table to its pristine state:

- **Online reorganization**: Oracle uses the *dbms_redefinition* package to embed Create Table As Select statement (CTAS), such that a table can be reorganized while it is still accepting updates.

- **Deallocate unused space**: Oracle notes that the *deallocate unused space* clause is used to explicitly deallocate unused space at the end of a segment and makes that space available for other segments within the tablespace.

```
alter table xxx deallocate unused space;
alter index xxx deallocate unused space;
```

Internally, Oracle deallocates unused space beginning from the end of the objects, or allocated space, and moving downwards toward the beginning of the object, continuing until it reaches the high water mark (HWM). For indexes, *deallocate unused space* coalesces all leaf blocks within same branch of b-tree, and quickly frees up index leaf blocks for use.

The coalesce statement: Unlike the *deallocate unused space* syntax which removes space above the high-water mark, coalesce puts together discontiguous fragmented extents.

There are two type of space fragmentation in Oracle. First is the honeycomb fragmentation, when the free extents are side by side, and the Swiss Cheese fragmentation, when the extents are separated by live segments.

```
alter table xxx coalesce;

alter index xxx coalesce;
```

- **Shrink space**: Using the `alter table xxx shrink space compact` command also has the benefit of making full-table scans run faster, as less block accesses are required. With standard Oracle tables, space can be reclaimed with the *alter table shrink space* command:

```
SQL> alter table mytable enable row movement;
Table altered

SQL> alter table mytable shrink space;
Table altered
```

Row ordering matters!

Hot Tip!

In some systems where a table is always accessed by the same key sequence, re-ordering the table into the same order as the queries can dramatically reduce I/O and improve SQL performance.

With the introduction of these table reorg tools, the DBA gets a powerful tool for effective and easy database space management.

When reorganizing tables to improve SQL performance, keep this in mind:

- Only tables that experience multi-block reads (full-table scans) may see an appreciable SQL performance benefit.

- Some shops will use sorted hash cluster tables to maintain row sequence order (ie. in the same order as the most common indexed retrieval), and a table can be reorganized with an *order by* clause to make the rows in the same sequence as the index.

But it is not just tables that require periodic maintenance, it is also indexes.

Index Reorganization and SQL Performance

When an index is rebuilt, Oracle uses the current index to create the new index and read the existing index, front to back, building the new index in the target tablespace as temporary segments. Upon completion of reading the old index, the old index is dropped and the temporary segments become the fresh new index tree.

In general, index rebuilding greatly reduces index size in cases of indexes with lots of logically deleted entries, and this index size reduction, in turn, will improve the performance of SQL that does full-scan or index range scan operations.

Oracle has provided utilities for reorganizing indexes for quite some time now, and there is no dispute that SQL scan operations, such as index full scans, index fast-full scans and index range scans, will run longer against fragmented tables and indexes.

Production DBAs spend weekends reorganizing their data structures, returning them back into their original, pristine state, in preparation for the return of the end-users on Monday morning.

Rebuilding high-DML indexes in a schedule can be a DBA best practice under certain conditions:

- A job can be scheduled to rebuild, index and address errors in just a few minutes. Because most DBAs are salaried professionals, the DBA cost is negligible.

- During a weekly maintenance window the server sits idle. Because hardware depreciates rapidly, regardless of use, the cost of rebuilding indexes is essentially zero.

When Rebuilding Indexes May Help SQL Performance

It is quite true that rebuilding indexes does not always help performance, but there are many times when rebuilding an index does help, especially for indexes that experience high DML activity and have multiple freelists and experience index range scans or index fast-full scans.

Watch your SQL workload!

Indexes I/O matters alot! Only indexes that experience index range scans (*db file sequential reads*) will benefit from index rebuilding or coalescing.

Look Out!

The reason that SQL performance is improved after index maintenance is that the index is returned to its original pristine optimal state. Index performance suffers because many tasks compete from many freelists to get blocks as the index grows, and the physical structure of the index data blocks becomes scrambled.

In general, rebuilding an index may not improve SQL performance, especially when the SQL is performing index unique scans, dropping through the index tree to find a single ROWID. However, in rare cases index rebuilding has been shown to improve SQL performance:

- **Full table scans**: By reorganizing a fragmented index, the index becomes physically smaller, and less block reads are required to complete a full-table scan.

- **Index range scans**: For multi-block range scan operations, index rebuilding can reduce overall I/O.

In sum, it takes more than just an examination of the index, the SQL workload against the indexes must also be examined to find those indexes that experience frequent multi-block read operations.

In an index with a single freelist, index range scans need only perform a single movement of the read-write head on disk, and the contiguous data locks can be read as fast as the disk can spin. In a large multi-user environment, index blocks become discontiguous and the benefits of multiblock reads for index range scans are lost.

When Rebuilding Indexes Will Hurt Performance

While the pristine state of an index is generally optimal, there are rare cases where rebuilding indexes will cause *insert* DML to run more slowly.

For example, many systems achieve a steady state, whereby index blocks will move change sizes on a regularly basis. In such systems, batch delete operations may cause lots of dead index data blocks, but subsequent insert jobs will reuse these blocks.

Again, every application is different, and the DBA can carefully test index rebuilding performance by testing them against SQL workloads. For details on testing index performance, see the book Database Benchmarking by Bert Scalzo.

Choosing Candidates for Index Maintenance

For a shop without a scheduled downtime window to rebuild/coalesce indexes, it may be helpful to use an empirical approach to identify indexes that might benefit from a rebuild. As months pass, feedback is gathered on SQL performance for the specific indexes using STATSPACK or AWR, and the program has been successively refined to detect indexes that required maintenance.

Every SQL workload is different and no single rule set applies to every database. However, the propensity of an index becoming unbalanced is largely a function of these factors:

- **DML workload**: Databases with high batch delete jobs and frequent index key updates can fragment heavily.

- **Key length and blocksize:** Because Oracle indexes use block boundaries and index node boundaries, the index blocksize and key length factors into index fragmentation.

Oracle ACE Andrew Kerber notes this generic script to identify indexes that might benefit from index reorganization:

"I eventually wrote a simple query that generates a list of candidates for index rebuilds, and the commands necessary to rebuild the indexes once the tables reached a point where it was necessary.

The query reads a table we built called table_modifications that we loaded each night from dba_tab_modifications before we ran statistics. Monitoring must be turned on to use the dba_tab_modifications table."

🖫 find_sparse_indexes.sql

```
select
'exec analyzedb.reorg_a_table4('||""||rtrim(t.table_owner)||""||','||""||
rtrim(t.table_name)||""||');',
   t.table_owner||'.'||t.table_name name,
   a.num_rows,
   sum(t.inserts) ins,
   sum(t.updates) upd,
   sum(t.deletes) del,
   sum(t.updates)+sum(t.inserts)+sum(t.deletes) tot_chgs,
```

```
to_char((sum(t.deletes)/(decode(a.num_rows,0,1,a.num_rows)))*100.0,'999999.9
9') per_del,
round(((sum(t.updates)+sum(t.inserts)+sum(t.deletes))/(decode(a.num_rows,0,1
,a.num_rows)) *100.0),2) per_chg
from
   analyzedb.table_modifications t,
   all_tables a
where
   t.timestamp >= to_date('&from_date','dd-mon-yyyy')
and
   t.table_owner = a.owner and t.table_owner not in ('SYS','SYSTEM') and
t.table_name=a.table_name
having
   (sum(t.deletes)/(decode(a.num_rows,0,1,a.num_rows)))*100.0 >=5
group by
   t.table_owner, t.table_name, a.num_rows
order by
   num_rows desc, t.table_owner, t.table_name;
```

Again, not all indexes will benefit from periodic index rebuilding, and it is a good practice to test and re-test scripts to examine the index tree structure to find sparse indexes.

In sum, here are some DBA best practices for rebuilding indexes:

- Properly executed during scheduled downtime, index rebuilding/coalescing is a zero-cost, zero-risk activity.

- For databases without scheduled maintenance windows, it is necessary to write scripts to detect indexes that may benefit from a rebuild. This involves examining the index trees as well as historical SQL activity.

- An index will benefit from a rebuild/coalesce if it experiences a significant number of full scan operations (index fast-full scans, index range scans). Queries can be written against the AWR (*dba_hist_sql_plan*) or STATSPACK (*stats$sql_plan*) to see how often an index experiences multi-block scan activity.

- By definition, a freshly rebuilt index is in its pristine state. When a DBA rebuilds an index, they will examine historical workloads and adjust *pctfree* to accommodate future DML activity.

The next section will cover Oracle index hints.

Index Hints

Index hints are very helpful for tuning SQL. *index* hints help ensure that the most selective index is used. There are similar *index* hints that can be used in conjunction with the CBO as well to help tune SQL and improve index performance.

The *index* hint can also be used within subqueries. There are several hints that Oracle has developed to direct the optimizer's index use. These are: the *index* hint; the *and_equal* hint; the *index_asc* hint; the *index_desc* hint; the *index_combine* hint; and the *index_ffs* hint. The first hint covered is also the most commonly used, the *index* hint.

The Index Hint

The *index* hint is used to specify a table name and/or index name to be used. If only the table name is specified, the optimizer will choose the best index on the chosen table. If both the table and index names are specified, then the optimizer will use the chosen table and index. There are several conditions that must be met for the *index* hint to work properly:

- Table and index names must be spelled correctly. Here is an example of a query where the table name is misspelled:

```
select /*+ index(erp, dept_idx) */ * from emp;
```

- The table name must be specified for the hint to *index* hint to work. The following query does not meet this condition:

```
select /*+ index(dept_idx) */ * from emp;
```

- If the table is aliased in the query, the table alias must be used. The following query would ignore the *index* hint because the *emp* table is aliased with "e":

```
select /*+ index(emp,dept_idx) */ * from emp e;
```

- The index name is optional and does not need to be specified for the *index* hint to work. If the index name is not included, the optimizer will choose what it believes to be the best index on the table. This is not always the best decision and is not recommended for permanent tuning. The following query is an example of such a case:

```
select /*+ index(e) */ * from emp e;
```

As a general rule, it is always better to specify both the table and index when using the *index* hint. In some cases, a change in the CBO statistics can cause the optimizer to use a different index than what was used prior. It is best to play it safe and specify the index to be used.

The *index_join* Hint

The next hint is the *index_join* hint. This hint instructs the optimizer to use an index join as the access path. In order for this hint to be beneficial, there should be a small number of indexes that contain every columns needed to satisfy the query.

The *and_equal* Hint

The *and_equal* hint is used when you want to use two or more single column indexes to service a query. The *and_equal* hint accomplishes this by merging the indexes, allowing the separate non-unique indexes to act as if they were a concatenated index.

There are some conditions that must be met for the *and_equal* hint to work. First, the target table name must be specified. Second, at least two index names must be given. This hint allows up to five indexes to be included. The following example query demonstrates how this hint is used. In the example, the query is retrieving the names of all salespeople who report to manager number 7698. In this example, there are non-unique indexes for both the *job* and *mgr* tables:

```
select
   ename,
   job,
   deptno,
   mgr
from
   emp
where
   job = 'SALESMAN'
and
   mgr = 7698;
```

Here is the default CBO execution plan for the query. Pay careful attention to the row access method:

```
OPERATION
----------------------------------------------------------------
OPTIONS                      OBJECT_NAME              POSITION
----------------------------------------------------------------
SELECT STATEMENT
                                                         1
  TABLE ACCESS
  BY INDEX ROWID             EMP                         1
    INDEX
  RANGE SCAN                 JOB_IDX                     1
```

This execution plan shows that the optimizer chose to perform an index range scan on the *job_idx*, followed by a ROWID probe of the *emp* table to locate the employees of manager 7698.

This process can be streamlined using the *and_equal* hint. This hint tells Oracle to combine *mgr_idx* and *job_idx* so that the query can be resolved without the optimizer probing every *emp* row for manager 7698:

```
select /*+ and_equal(emp, job_idx, mgr_idx) */
   ename,
   job,
   deptno,
   mgr
from
   emp
where
   job = 'SALESMAN'
and
   mgr = 7698
;
```

Here is the execution plan. Note the AND-EQUAL plan step:

```
OPERATION
--------------------------------------------------------------------
OPTIONS                       OBJECT_NAME                POSITION
--------------------------    -------------------------  ----------
 SELECT STATEMENT
                                                            30
  TABLE ACCESS
BY INDEX ROWID                EMP                          1
     AND-EQUAL
        INDEX
RANGE SCAN                    JOB_IDX                      1
        INDEX
RANGE SCAN                    MGR_IDX                      2
```

The execution plan has definitely changed. Now the plan treats both indexes as if they were a single, concatenated index as illustrated in Figure 6.14.

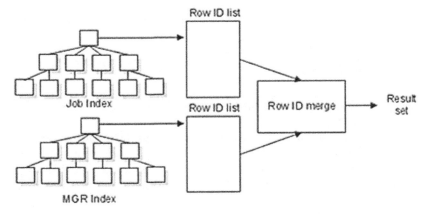

Figure 6.14: *Merging non-unique indexes with the and_equal hint*

The query now performs range scans on both the *mgr_inx* and *job_idx*, A ROWID intersection operation returns only the ROWIDS that match both conditions of the *where* clause. Because the query only checks the *emp* table when the rows are needed, there is significantly less table I/O.

The *index_asc* Hint

The next hint is the *index_asc* hint. This hint ensures that range scan operations use the ascending index. This is the default behavior, and has limited use when tuning SQL.

The *no_index* Hint

The *no_index* hint allows the optimizer to ignore an index. This hint is usually used when a parallel full-table scan would outperform an index range scan. In this case, the index is the same as the *full* hint.

The *index_desc* Hint

The *index_desc* hint is similar to the *index_asc* hint, only instead of specifying the ascending index, *index_desc* requires the descending index be used. This hint improves performance when using the *max* built-in function to calculate maximum values. See the query below:

```
select /*+ index_desc(emp, sal_idx) */
   ename,
   max(salary)
from
   emp
;
```

The *index_combine* Hint

The *index_combine* hint forces a bitmap access path for a table. In cases where no indexes are given as arguments in this hint, the optimizer will choose the best Boolean combination of bitmap indexes, based upon estimated table access cost. The *index_combine* hint tells the optimizer to do ROWID intersection operations on both bitmaps. Like with the *index* hint, it is usually best to specify both table and index names when using the *index_combine* hint.

Look at the following example using bitmap indexes on the *emp* table:

```
create bitmap index
```

```
   dept_bit
on
   emp
   (deptno);

create bitmap index
   job_bit
on
   emp
   (job);
```

Next examine the corresponding query. Notice that the results rows are filtered where *job=salesman* and *deptno=30:*

```
select
   ename,
   job,
   deptno,
   mgr
from
   emp
where
   job = 'SALESMAN'
and
   deptno = 30;
```

Below is the execution plan for the query. Notice that a bitmap index for *deptno* is being used to filter *job* rows:

```
OPERATION
-----------------------------------------------------------------------
OPTIONS                         OBJECT_NAME                   POSITION
------------------------------- ----------------------------- ----------
 SELECT STATEMENT
                                                                     1
  TABLE ACCESS
BY INDEX ROWID                  EMP                                  1
    BITMAP CONVERSION
TO ROWIDS                                                            1
     BITMAP INDEX
SINGLE VALUE                    DEPT_BIT                             1
```

Next, the *index_combine hint* is added to the query:

```
select /*+ index_combine(emp, dept_bit, job_bit) */
   ename,
   job,
   deptno,
   mgr
from
   emp
where
   job = 'SALESMAN'
and
   deptno = 30;
```

Here we see the execution plan.

Index Hints   **379**

```
OPERATION
-------------------------------------------------------------------------
OPTIONS                          OBJECT_NAME                    POSITION
----------------------------     -------------------------      ----------
 SELECT STATEMENT
                                                                       2
  TABLE ACCESS
BY INDEX ROWID                   EMP                                    1
    BITMAP CONVERSION
TO ROWIDS                                                              1
      BITMAP AND
        BITMAP INDEX
SINGLE VALUE                     DEPT_BIT                              1
        BITMAP INDEX
SINGLE VALUE                     JOB_BIT                               2
```

Notice that the bitmap indexes have merged together using a *bitmap conversion method*, reducing the execution time of the query. This is very helpful when querying large tables.

The *index_ffs* Hint

The next hint is the *index_ffs* hint. This hint is used to force the optimizer to scan all blocks in an index using multi-block reads when performing a fast full scan..

When this hint is used, the optimizer will also access the index in a non-sequential order. The *parallel* hint can be combined with the *index_ffs* hint to further increase the speed of the index fast full scan.

Fast full scans access the entire table. Depending upon the amount of parallelism, index fast full scans may be faster than index range scans. The SQL optimizer can be tricked with the *index_ffs* hint to select on the values of the second column in a concatenated index.

This can be useful when tables are huge and creating a new index would require too much disk space. In cases where there are no high-level index keys for the required search column in a large table, fast-full-index table scans will be faster than full-table scans.

The following example shows a concatenated index on two non-unique columns:

```
create index
  dept_job_idx
on
   emp
   (deptno, job);
```

Below is the corresponding SQL for the query. There is no index on the *job* column.

```
select
```

```
   ename,
   job,
   deptno,
   mgr
from
   emp
where
   job = 'SALESMAN'
;
```

Here is the execution plan. As expect, there is a full-table scan on the *emp* table:

```
OPERATION
-------------------------------------------------------------------
OPTIONS                        OBJECT_NAME                POSITION
------------------------------ -------------------------- ----------
 SELECT STATEMENT
                                                              1
  TABLE ACCESS
FULL                           EMP                            1
```

Now here is the same query using the *fast_ffs* hint. Notice that both the table name and index name are specified:

```
select  /*+ index_ffs(emp, dept_job_idx) */
   ename,
   job,
   deptno,
   mgr
from
   emp
where
   job = 'SALESMAN';
```

Because of the hint the full-table scan is replaced by a fast full-index scan:

```
OPERATION
-------------------------------------------------------------------
OPTIONS                        OBJECT_NAME                POSITION
------------------------------ -------------------------- ----------
 SELECT STATEMENT
                                                              34
  TABLE ACCESS
BY INDEX ROWID                 EMP                            1
    INDEX
FULL SCAN                      DEPT_JOB_IDX                   1
```

Notice that the index fast full scan execution plan is the mechanism responsible for fast index create and re-create.

Conclusion

Oracle indexes are a software tool that Oracle SQL can use to avoid expensive full-scan operations against tables and ensure that the desired rows are returned with a minimum of data file touches. The main points of this chapter include:

- Oracle has specialized indexes for specialized types of applications, such as the bitmap index and context indexes, but the b-tree index is far and away the most common type of index.

- Indexes consume system resources. Using an index can consume disk space and slow down DML, but that is the price to pay for getting rows back fast.

- Oracle indexes can retrieve rows in pre-sorted order, avoiding expensive back-end sort operations.

- Oracle optimizer parameters such as *optimizer_index_cost_adj* have a profound effect of the optimizer's propensity to invoke an index.

- Applying histogram statistics on indexes columns can improve the performance of SQL against columns that have heavily skewed values.

- Locating missing indexes is a powerful Oracle silver bullet. Adding a new index can change the entire landscape of SQL performance.

- The *first_rows_n* optimizer modes favor index access while the default *all_rows* optimizer mode favors full-scan operations because it tries to minimize computing resources.

- Function-based indexes are among the most powerful of all SQL tuning tools because anything in a SQL *where* clause can be matched with an index. Function-based indexes are a commonly overlooked feature.

- Oracle DBAs can examine the SQL workload with scripts to see exactly how tables are accessed via indexes.

- Heavily updated indexes can become sub-optimal for SQL that performs scan operations, and periodic rebuilding or coalescing can keep SQL performance at optimal levels,

The next chapter is dedicated to how Oracle SQL can use super-fast RAM storage to speed up SQL performance.

RAM and SQL Tuning

Don't get burned by disk I/O latency

RAM usage and SQL Tuning

Earlier chapters show disk I/O as the single slowest event in any Oracle database, and Oracle has many mechanisms to bypass disk I/O by using faster storage in RAM. The most common mechanism is the data buffer cache that is used to hold frequently referenced data blocks in RAM storage, for access hundreds of times faster than a disk read.

It is important to remember that disk access speed has not changed in 40 years. Fifty years after disks were introduced, disk speed is still measured in milliseconds (thousandths of a second) while RAM access speed is measured in nanoseconds (billionths of a second). In theory, RAM is 10,000 times faster than disk, but in Oracle RAM access can be expected to be hundreds of times faster than a disk read.

There is also an issue with RAM called volatility. When talking about RAM being volatile, it does not mean volatile as with gasoline. Rather, the term volatile means that the memory is completely erased when the power is turned off. Hence, the only way to utilize RAM for persistent data storage is to develop a mechanism to write the data from RAM to permanent disk storage.

In solid-state disk, persistence is achieved by special internal software that writes the RAM to disk backups, and within data buffer RAM in the SGA, Oracle has the database writer (DBWR) process to write data from volatile RAM to non-volatile disk storage. In order to achieve fast response time, these disk writes are performed asynchronously, sometime after the actual update has been completed.

Liar, liar! False ack liar!

When using a mass storage device, the disk arrays will sometimes lie to Oracle about completing a write request. This false acknowledgement (false ack) message to Oracle has been known to cause disk corruption!

Look Out!

Large disk arrays have RAM buffers too, and some of them tell Oracle that the data has been written to disk, when it's really still in the RAM buffer of the mass storage array.

In Oracle 11g, Oracle has leveraged on RAM-based storage by providing mechanisms for solid-state disk (SSD) with their flash cache feature, as well as with Oracle's Times Ten in-memory database. The ancient spinning platter disk are 1960's technology and disk will soon become obsolete within Oracle, serving only as backups for the initial data storage which is on SSD. See the book *"Oracle Solid-State Disk Tuning"* for more details on hypercharging Oracle I/O with fast RAM storage.

The next section will cover the internals of SQL processes and RAM usage.

SQL processing and RAM

When tuning SQL statements, it is important to remember that the RAM usage is transparent, controlled only by parameter settings. Oracle RAM usage is orchestrated on the DBA's behalf by the Oracle instance, but many internal operations can be hypercharged by directing Oracle SQL to use RAM for sorting and hash joins.

Just like a PL/SQL program, a SQL statement requires Oracle RAM memory for efficient performance and it is in these areas where RAM affects SQL execution speed:

- **Library cache RAM**: An optimal shared pool reduces SQL parsing and makes SQL run faster.

- **Data buffer RAM:** Fetching a data block from the RAM data buffers can be hundreds of times faster than disk access.

- **Hash join RAM:** The more RAM available for hash joins (via *pga_aggregate_target* or *hash_area_size)*, the greater the propensity for the Oracle SQL optimizer to choose a fast hash join.

- **Sorting RAM:** The more RAM available for row re-sequencing (via *pga_aggregate_target* or *sort_area_size*), the faster the processing of SQL *"order by"* and *"group by"* directives.

But there are times when there is need to override the Oracle defaults for hash joins and sorting. To prevent runaway tasks from hogging resources, Oracle has a built-in governor that prevents any individual session from consuming too many RAM resources. In the hands of a savvy DBA, these governors can be adjusted, resulting in more efficient processing for large batch jobs. This warrants a closer look.

Sizing the PGA

Almost every Oracle professional agrees that the old-fashioned *sort_area_size* and *hash_area_size* parameters imposed a cumbersome one-size-fits-all approach to sorting and hash joins. Different tasks require different RAM areas, and the trick has been to allow enough PGA RAM for sorting and hash joins without having any high-resource task hog all of the PGA, to the exclusion of other users.

As a review, remember that a hash join uses RAM from the PGA, and RAM resource are scarce, to be used wisely. Back in the days of Oracle8i, RAM was wasted every session in an amount equal to the RAM defined by the *hash_area_size* parameter, whether the session needed the RAM or not as shown in Figure 7.1:

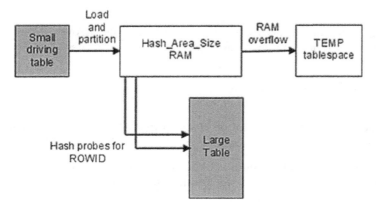

Figure 7.1: *RAM usage within an Oracle hash join*

Then, Oracle9i introduced the *pga_aggregate_target* parameter to fix this resource issue, and by-and-large, *pga_aggregate_target* works very well for most systems. Overall PGA usage can be checked with the *v$pga_target_advice* advisory utility or a STATSPACK or AWR report. High values for multi-pass executions, high disk sorts or low hash join invocation might indicate a low resource usage for PGA regions.

PGA management changes by release!

PGA management is very release specific. Methods used in 9i are very different from those used in 10g and 11g. Always carefully check real PGA use, especially when overriding the defaults for SQL queries.

Look Out!

There are important limitations of pga_aggregate_target, and some of these limitations are hidden. For example, the total work area cannot exceed 200 megabytes of RAM because of the default setting for *_pga_max_size*.

No RAM sort may use more than 5% of *pga_aggregate_target* or *_pga_max_size*, whichever is smaller. This means that no task may use more than 200 megabytes for sorting or hash joins. The algorithm further reduces this to (200/2) for sorts so the actual limit for pure sorts will be 100 megabytes.

These restrictions were made to insure that no large sorts or hash joins hog the PGA RAM area, but there are some secrets for optimizing the PGA. For example, the following set of parameters may be mutually-exclusive:

- **sort_area_size = 1048576** <-- sort_area_size is ignored when *pga_aggregate_target* is set and when *workarea_size_policy =auto*, unless you are using a specialized feature such as the shared server. If dedicated server connections are used, the *sort_area_size* parameter is ignored.

- **pga_aggregate_target = 500m** <-- The maximum default allowed value is 200 megabytes, this limits sorts to 25 megabytes (5% of 500m).

> *Note: there may be some cases where* sort_area_size *is used in Oracle utilities, but these have not been documented, even with* pga_aggregate_target.

The following section will provide a closer look why SQL tuning experts want to be able to control the RAM usage of their SQL statements.

SQL Tuning and Automatic Memory Management

When I first wrote my book "*Oracle Tuning: The Definitive Reference*", I noted that the future of Oracle is a proactive method whereby the major Oracle SGA RAM regions (shared pool, buffer caches) can be adjusted in anticipation of changes to processing needs.

When Oracle9i first allowed *alter system* commands to morph the SGA, Oracle 10g introduced Automatic Memory Management, a reactive tool to re-size the RAM regions.

Oracle Database 10g now has Automatic Memory Management (ASMM) in the form of the one-size-fits-all parameter called sga_target, which replaces many individual parameters and automates the allocation of RAM between the data buffers, shared pool and log buffers.

The tuning of these SGA memory regions used to be complex and time consuming, until ASMM automated the tuning. Using predictive models derived from *v$db_cache_advice* and *v$shared_pool_advice*, Oracle automatically monitors changing demands on the SGA regions and re-allocates RAM memory based on the existing workload.

It is a common misunderstanding that when using AMM by setting *sga_target* and *sga_memory_max*, the values for the traditional pool parameters, *db_cache_size*, *shared_pool_size*, etc., are not ignored. Rather, they will specify the minimum size that Oracle will always maintain for each sub-area in the SGA.

Beware of Automatic Memory Management!

Oracle's automatic memory management (AMM) is not appropriate for large mission-critical databases, where a human expert can always do a better job in optimizing RAM resources. AMM is designed for small databases.

Beware!

In sum, most shops continue to use self-created memory management tools because of the performance hits and the reactive nature of AMM, which does not anticipate upcoming changes in possessing, predictions which can now be made by analyzing STATSPACK and AWR data.

In 11g, Oracle automatic memory management is configured using the *memory_target* and *memory_max_target* initialization parameters. The memory_target parameter specifies the amount of shared memory available for Oracle to use when dynamically controlling the SGA and PGA. The *memory_max_target* AMM parameter specifies the max size that *memory_target* may take.

Manual RAM allocation vs. AMM

In an effort to complete with simple databases such as SQL Server, Oracle has undertaken the removal of much of the inherent complexity by building automated tools to manage storage, RAM and tuning.

This umbrella of simplicity is amazing and has allows the world's most flexible and robust database to be as simple to use as the lesser databases using this one-sized-fits-all technique of automation.

However, it is critical to understand that the Oracle automation tools were developed for hands-off, small departmental applications, and automation is not always the best approach for a large mission-critical database with thousands of concurrent users. Remember, with today's technology, no automated tool will ever be able to optimize the database as well as a human expert.

A competent Oracle professional will always be able to do a better job than an automated tool at forecasting and optimizing RAM resources for SQL statements. This is true for all automated tools, not just Oracle AMM, and there is no automated substitute for human intuition and experience.

Oracle designed AMM to simplify operations on small to midsize databases where it does an adequate job in managing the RAM pool in the absence of a DBA. However, in case after case on large systems, I have seen frequent AMM re-size operations cause performance problems on Oracle databases. As of Oracle 11g, I do not recommend using automatic memory management for large or for mission-critical databases.

The biggest issue with AMM is that it is a reactive tool. Unlike a proactive approach, AMM waits until it detects a problem before changing the SGA pool sizes. But on the other hand, developing a proactive approach is not easy either.

To be effective in proactive RAM tuning for an instance, it is necessary to understand basic statistical techniques such as linear and non-linear regression modeling and be able to analyze STATSPACK or AWR reports to identify RAM usage trends called signatures.

Once the repeating patterns of workload usage are identified, such as repeating in cycles of hour-of-the-day, day-of-the-week and day-of the-month, scripts can be automated to re-optimize the SGA pools immediately before the workload changes.

Never use MTS with AMM!

Hot Tip!

Using shared servers (MTS) with AMM and PL/SQL can hog all of the RAM on the Oracle instance!

This is especially true in cases when AMM is used with obsolete tools like shared servers, the multi-threaded server or MTS. Quest Software's Guy Harrison has this excellent warning about using the AMM with MTS:

> *"When you use MTS and AMM (or ASMM) together, PL/SQL programs that try to create large collections can effectively consume all available server memory with disastrous consequences.*
>
> *AMM allocates virtually all memory on the system to the large pool in order to accommodate the PL/SQL memory request. First it consumes the buffer cache, then it reduces the* pga_aggregate_target - *all the way to zero!"*

There are many pitfalls and perils to using automated tools, and it is critical that DBAs must always understand the limits of automation. To assist with this, the next section will cover some expert tricks for advanced PGA management.

Hidden parameters for Oracle PGA regions

With proper understanding, and knowing that these undocumented parameters are not supported by Oracle, the PGA regions can be adjusted to allow for system-specific sorting and hash joins:

- *_pga_max_size*: This hidden parameter defaults to 200 megabytes, regardless of the setting for pga_aggregate_target.

- *_smm_px_max_size*: This parameter is used for Oracle parallel query and defaults to 30% of the pga_aggregate_target setting, divided by degree of parallelism as set by a parallel hint, ALTER TABLE XXX PARALLEL command, or the parallel_automatic_tuning initialization parameter. For example, by default a degree=4 parallel query would have a maximum sort area value of 15 megabytes per session with a 200 megabyte pga_aggregate_target setting. Remember, parallel full-table scans bypass the data buffers and store the incoming data rows in the PGA region and not inside the data buffers, as defined by the db_cache_size parameter.

The following are additional undocumented parameters:

- *_smm_advice_enabled*: If TRUE, enable *v$pga_advice*.

- *_smm_advice_log_size*: This overwrites default size of the PGA advice workarea history log.

- *_smm_auto_cost_enabled*: If TRUE, use the AUTO size policy cost functions.

- *_smm_auto_max_io_size*: The maximum IO size (in KB) used by sort/hash-join in auto mode.

- *_smm_auto_min_io_size*: The minimum IO size (in KB) used by sort/hash-join in auto mode.

- *_smm_bound*: This overwrites memory manager automatically computed bound.

- *_smm_control*: This provides controls on the memory manager.

- *_smm_max_size*: This is the maximum work area size in auto mode (serial).

- *_smm_min_size*: The minimum work area size in auto mode.

- *_smm_px_max_size*: The maximum work area size in auto mode (global).

- *_smm_trace*: The on/off tracing for SQL memory manager

Sizing PGA for Fast SQL

For certain Oracle applications the Oracle professional will want to allow individual tasks to exceed the default limits imposed by Oracle. For example, PC-based, 64 bit Oracle servers (1 or 2 CPU's with 8 gigabytes of RAM) will often have unused RAM available.

For example, a fully-cached 5 gigabyte database on an 8 gigabyte dedicated Oracle server will have approximately 1 gigabyte available for the PGA, allowing 20% for the OS and other SGA regions:

Area	Size	
O/S	1.6	gig
SGA	5	gig
PGA Space	1	gig
Total	8	gig

The system has a *pga_aggregate_target* setting of 1 gigabyte and the undocumented parameters are at their default settings.

While it is unusual for an online system to require super-sized regions for sorting considering the result sets for online screens are normally small, there can be a benefit to having large RAM regions available for the Oracle optimizer.

The Oracle cost-based optimizer (CBO) will determine whether a hash join would be beneficial over a nested-loop join, so making more PGA available for hash joins will not have any detrimental effect since the optimizer will only invoke a super-sized hash join if it is better than a nested-loop join.

In a system like the example above, the following settings would increase the default sizes for large sorts and hash joins while limiting those for parallel sorts.

- *pga_aggregate_target = 4g*

- *_pga_max_size = 400m*

- *_smm_px_max_size = 333m*

With these hidden parameters set we see significant size increase for serial sorts and a throttling effect for parallel queries and sorts. However, bear in mind that it only valid for a specific release of Oracle10g, on a specific hardware and OS environment and not using any optional features such as the MTS.

A RAM sort or hash join may now have up to the full 200 megabytes, 5% of *pga_aggregate_target*, a 400% increase over a 1 gigabyte *pga_aggregate_target* setting. With the default settings, only a 200%, 100 megabyte size, increase would be possible.

Parallel queries are now limited to 333 megabytes of RAM (30% of *pga_aggegate_target* or *_smm_px_max_size*, such that a DEGREE=4 parallel query would have a maximum of 83 megabytes (333 meg/4) per slave which may actually be less due to internal sizing algorithms that set the memory increments used in setting sort areas. This throttling is used to prevent one parallel query using all available memory since *_smm_px_max_size* would default to 1.2 gigabytes with the setting for *pga_aggregate_target* at 4 gigabytes.

Great care must be taken with regard to setting the *pga_aggregate_target* to greater than the available memory. Calculate the maximum number of users who would be sorting/hashing and multiple that times the predicted size to get the actual limitations otherwise ORA-04030 errors or swapping may occur.

In conclusion, overriding the built-in safeguards of *pga_aggregate_target* can make more efficient use of RAM resources in cases where large RAM regions are available on the database server. When used with care, and the blessing of Oracle Technical Support, it can often make sense to override these default values to make better use of expensive RAM resources. There is also evidence that changing these parameters will have a positive effect of large, batch-oriented Oracle jobs, but be very careful to fully understand the limitations of the PGA parameters:

Important Caveats in PGA Management

Do not adjust any hidden parameters without opening a Service Request (SR) and getting the consent and advice of Oracle Technical Support. These are undocumented, hidden parameters, and anyone using them must be willing to accept full responsibility for any issues. Some hidden parameters have no effect when set at session level and ALTER SYSTEM commands must be issued for them to take effect.

These PGA rules do not apply to shared server environments using Oracle Shared Server (formerly known as MTS). However, the vast majority of Oracle shops do not use shared server sessions.

Each process, with one PGA area, may have multiple work areas. For example, a query might perform a parallel full-table scan followed by an *order by* sort, having one PGA and two workareas. The *_pga_max_size* controls the PGA size and *_smm_max_size* controls the size for each workarea.

Now that the basics of instance tuning have been presented, it is a good time to take a look at Oracle's new SQL tuning advisor functions.

Before Oracle10g, it was extremely difficult to track index usage and see how SQL statements behaved except when they were in the library cache. With Oracle10g and beyond, it is now possible to track SQL behavior over time and ensure that all SQL is using an optimal execution plan, and Oracle provides the ability to track SQL execution metrics with new dba_hist tables, most notably *dba_hist_sqlstat* and *dba_hist_sql_plan*.

It is important to track the relationship between database objects, such as tables, indexes and the SQL that accesses the objects.

Oracle SQL execution plans for any given statement may change if the system statistics change, dynamic sampling is used, materialized views are created or indexes are created or dropped.

Sizing PGA for Hash Joins

The rules are quite different depending on the Oracle release, and it is necessary to focus on the *hash_area_size* OR the *pga_aggregate_target* parameters.

Unfortunately, the Oracle hash join is more memory intensive than a nested loop join. To be faster than a nested loop join, the *hash_area_size* must be set large enough to hold the entire hash table in memory. This requires roughly 1.6 times the sum of the rows in the table.

If the Oracle hash join overflows the *hash_area_size* memory, the hash join will page into the TEMP tablespace, severely degrading the performance of the hash join. The following script can be used to dynamically allocate the proper *hash_area_size* for the SQL query in terms of the size of the hash join driving table.

```
select
   'alter session set hash_area_size='||trunc(sum(bytes)*1.6)||';'
```

```
from
   dba_segments
where
   segment_name = upper('&1');

spool off;

@run_hash
```

The following is the output from this script with the suggested hash area size calculation for the driving table. Pass the driving table name, and the script generates the appropriate ALTER SESSION command to ensure that there is enough space in *hash_area_size* RAM to hold the driving table.

```
SQL> @hash_area customer

alter session set hash_area_size=3774873;
```

In addition to seeing the *hash_area_size*, it is also necessary to be able to adjust the degree of parallelism in cases where a full-table scan is used to access the tables in a hash join.

Viewing RAM Usage for Hash Joins in SQL

Oracle has the ability to display RAM memory usage along with execution plan information. The following script was already included in Chapter 4, *Oracle SQL Join Internals*, but it bears repeating here since tracking RAM usage is a critical SQL tuning task.

To get this information, gather the address of the desired SQL statement from the *v$sql* view. For example, if there is a query that operates against the *customer* table, run the following query to get the address:

```
select
   address
from
   v$sql
where
   sql_text like '%CUSTOMER%';

88BB460C

1 row selected.
```

Now, with the address of the SQL statement in RAM, it can be plugged into the following script to get the execution plan details and the PGA memory usage for the SQL statement.

🖫 **show_ram_plan.sql**

```
select
   operation,
   options,
   object_name                      name,
   trunc(bytes/1024/1024)           "input(MB)",
   trunc(last_memory_used/1024)     last_mem,
   trunc(estimated_optimal_size/1024)  opt_mem,
   trunc(estimated_onepass_size/1024)  onepass_mem,
   decode(optimal_executions, null, null,
          optimal_executions||'/'||onepass_executions||'/'||
          multipasses_exections)        "O/1/M"
from
   v$sql_plan      p,
   v$sql_workarea  w
where
   p.address=w.address(+)
and
   p.hash_value=w.hash_value(+)
and
   p.id=w.operation_id(+)
and
   p.address='88BB460C';
```

The following is the results listing from this script. This is important because it reveals the RAM used for each step in the SQL.

```
OPERATION      OPTIONS   NAME  input(MB) LAST_MEM OPT_MEM ONEPASS_MEM O/1/M
-----------    --------  ----  --------- -------- ------- ----------- ----
SELECT STATE
SORT           GROUP BY    4582        8      16          16  26/0/0
HASH JOIN          SEMI    4582     5976    5194        2187  16/0/0
TABLE ACCESS FULL  ORDERS    51
TABLE ACCESS FULL  LINEITEM 1000
```

This shows the details about the execution plan along with specific memory usage details. This is an exciting new advance in Oracle and gives the Oracle DBA the ability to have a very high level of detail about the internal execution of any SQL statement.

A Case Study in Invoking Hash Joins

Oracle author Laurent Schneider notes that overriding the PGA defaults made a large batch processes run more than eight times faster when he used a *use_hash* hint. He set appropriate values for *pga_aggregate_target* and *_pga_max_size* as follows:

```
alter system set pga_aggregate_target=6G;

alter system set "_pga_max_size"=2000000000;
```

He then added this hint:

```
select /*+ norewrite full use_hash ordered */
```

He claims that it boosted his query performance from 12 hours down to only to 90 minutes.

Ah, if only it were that easy! Just change a setting and batch jobs run six times faster. Laurent Schneider goes on to note some perils and reliability issues relating to this parameter and says that setting the hidden parameter _pga_max_size often leads to a ORA-04030 error, even when plenty of memory was available.

There are other tricks for overcoming the built-in governor for PGA usage. Oracle has a 5% limit for any individual process, and by using parallel DML any single batch job can consume 30% of the PGA without touching any of the undocumented parameters. Oracle author Laurent Schneider noted a more stable solution for his hash join:

> *"I finally opted for a more maintainable solution.*
>
> *No more hints, no more undocumented parameter, but parallel processing up to 16 threads on a 4 CPU server.*
>
> *As discussed in metalink thread 460157.996, a supported way to increase the maximum PGA memory per single SQL query is to increase the degree of parallelism."*

While Laurent abandoned the undocumented approach, the promise of eight times faster execution speeds is very tempting. Once Oracle Technical Support grants permission to set an undocumented parameter, they can work to help resolve errors. While they may not address bugs, they may be able to provide alternatives and workarounds.

As Oracle sees that RAM costs are getting cheaper every day, there are more and more algorithms that use RAM to speed up I/O intensive processes. In Oracle 11g, there are two new internal methods using RAM, one for the hash join full and another for hash group by. The next section will provide a closer look.

The 11g Full Hash Join

The new Oracle 11g *hash join full* execution plan uses RAM to create results that use less than 50% of the logical I/O (consistent gets) than a traditional full join.

For more on the 11g *hash join full outer* execution plan, the full outer join was introduced with the SQL99 standard, but due to bugs it was not ready for production usage until Oracle 11g.

The Oracle 11g documentation includes the following notes on the hash join full outer execution plan and explains the internal machinations of the full hash join:

> *"The optimizer uses hash joins for processing an outer join if the data volume is high enough to make the hash join method efficient or if it is not possible to drive from the outer table to inner table.*
>
> *The order of tables is determined by the cost. The outer table, including preserved rows, may be used to build the hash table, or it may be used to probe one. . . "*

A full outer join retrieves rows from both tables, whether or not they have a matching row, and is used in cases where the goal is to get non-matching rows from both tables. There are many ways to formulate a full join, and the following is an example using the *with* clause.

In the example, due to lots of RAM defined in PGA, more than 5% of *pga_aggregate_target*, the standard full join is replaced by a *hash full join outer* operation:

```
with
    emp
as
(
    select
        'joel' ename,
        40 deptno
    from
        dual
    union all
    select
        'mary' ename,
        50 deptno
    from
        dual
)
select
    e.ename,
    d.dname
```

```
from
    emp e
full join
    dept d
using
(
    deptno
);
```

```
ENAM DNAME
---- --------------
JOEL OPERATIONS
MARY
     SALES
     RESEARCH
     ACCOUNTING
```

```
-----------------------------------------------------------------------
| Id | Operation             | Name     | Rows | Bytes | Cost (%CPU)| Time     |
-----------------------------------------------------------------------
|  0 | SELECT STATEMENT      |          |    8 |   120 |    8  (13)| 00:00:01 |
|  1 |  VIEW                 | VW_FOJ_0 |    8 |   120 |    8  (13)| 00:00:01 |
|* 2 |   HASH JOIN FULL OUTER|          |    8 |   176 |    8  (13)| 00:00:01 |
|  3 |    VIEW               |          |    2 |    18 |    4   (0)| 00:00:01 |
|  4 |     UNION-ALL         |          |      |       |           |          |
|  5 |      FAST DUAL        |          |    1 |       |    2   (0)| 00:00:01 |
|  6 |      FAST DUAL        |          |    1 |       |    2   (0)| 00:00:01 |
|  7 |    TABLE ACCESS FULL  | DEPT     |    4 |    52 |    3   (0)| 00:00:01 |
-----------------------------------------------------------------------
```

As previously noted, the *hash full outer join* is much faster (and safer!) than in release 10.2 because the optimizer uses a new operation called *hash join full outer* that scans each table only once instead of doing a union of two joins.

What follows are the results from 10gR2 showing the older *hash join outer* operator.

```
-----------------------------------------------------------------------
| Id | Operation                | Name                    | Rows | Bytes | Cost (%CPU)| Time     |
-----------------------------------------------------------------------
|  0 | SELECT STATEMENT         |                         |    5 |    75 |   13  (24)| 00:00:01 |
|  1 |  TEMP TABLE TRANSFORMATION|                        |      |       |           |          |
|  2 |   LOAD AS SELECT         |                         |      |       |           |          |
|  3 |    UNION-ALL             |                         |      |       |           |          |
|  4 |     FAST DUAL            |                         |    1 |       |    2   (0)| 00:00:01 |
|  5 |     FAST DUAL            |                         |    1 |       |    2   (0)| 00:00:01 |
|  6 |   VIEW                   |                         |    5 |    75 |    9  (12)| 00:00:01 |
|  7 |    UNION-ALL             |                         |      |       |           |          |
|* 8 |     HASH JOIN OUTER      |                         |    2 |    44 |    5  (20)| 00:00:01 |
|  9 |      VIEW                |                         |    2 |    18 |    2   (0)| 00:00:01 |
| 10 |       TABLE ACCESS FULL  | SYS_TEMP_0FD9D6601_2C2CE3|    2 |   38 |    2   (0)| 00:00:01 |
| 11 |      TABLE ACCESS FULL   | DEPT                    |    4 |    52 |    2   (0)| 00:00:01 |
-----------------------------------------------------------------------
```

```
|* 12 |      HASH JOIN ANTI        |                         |   3 |   48 |    5   (20)|
00:00:01 |
|  13 |        TABLE ACCESS FULL    | DEPT                    |   4 |   52 |    2    (0)|
00:00:01 |
|  14 |        VIEW                 |                         |   2 |    6 |    2    (0)|
00:00:01 |
|  15 |          TABLE ACCESS FULL  | SYS_TEMP_0FD9D6601_2C2CE3 |  2 |   38 |    2    (0)|
00:00:01 |
    8 - access("E"."DEPTNO"="D"."DEPTNO"(+))
   12 - access("E"."DEPTNO"="D"."DEPTNO")
```

Oracle must detect that there is enough PGA RAM to allow the optimizer to invoke the hash join, and it is up to the DBA to monitor PGA to ensure that SQL queries always have enough RAM for these faster internal operations.

For active queries, the following script can be used to watch the RAM memory consumption of a hash join full operation:

💾 **monitor_hash_join_ful_ram.sql**

```
select
   tempseg_size
from
   v$sql_workarea_active;
```

The *hash group by*, a SQL tuning feature that was new in Oracle release 10.2, is covered in the next section.

Using the *hash group by* Plan

Another new feature started in Oracle 11g is the ability to have SQL perform a *hash group by*, an alternative to traditional result set sorting (the *sort group by*) that uses an internal hash table in RAM. In truth, the hash group by was introduced in release 10.2 but it was too buggy to use.

Oracle will automatically replace a sort group by with a hash group by when there is enough RAM to handle the internal sort in RAM, defined via *pga_aggregate_target*. The following is an example of an 11g query that invokes a *hash group by* operation:

```
select
   cust_last_name,
   sum(nvl2(o.customer_id,0,1)) "Count"
from
   customers c,
   orders o
where
   c.credit_limit > 1000
and
   c.customer_id = o.customer_id(+)
GROUP BY cust_last_name;
```

```
---------------------------------------------------------------------------
| Id  | Operation            | Name           | Rows  | Bytes | Cost (%CPU)|
---------------------------------------------------------------------------
|   0 | SELECT STATEMENT     |                |   168 |  3192 |    6  (17) |
|   1 |  HASH GROUP BY       |                |   168 |  3192 |    6  (17) |
| *  2 |   NESTED LOOPS OUTER |                |   260 |  4940 |    5   (0) |
| *  3 |    TABLE ACCESS FULL | CUSTOMERS      |   260 |  3900 |    5   (0) |
| *  4 |    INDEX RANGE SCAN  | ORD_CUSTOMER_IX|   105 |   420 |    0   (0) |
---------------------------------------------------------------------------

Predicate Information (identified by operation id):
---------------------------------------------------

   3 - filter("C"."CREDIT_LIMIT">1000)
   4 - access("C"."CUSTOMER_ID"="0"."CUSTOMER_ID"(+))
       filter("O"."CUSTOMER_ID"(+)>0)
```

The syntax is exactly the same, but on 11g, the standard *sort group by* is replaced by *hash group by*.

Don't use *hash group by* in 10g!

In Oracle 10g, the *hash group by* has serious bugs that result in the wrong rows being returned from a query.

Look Out!

The following section covers special cases where hash joins fail and how to ensure that Oracle uses this powerful join tool.

When Hash Joins Fail

The hash join is very finicky, and there are many conditions that must be satisfied. It is not uncommon to find that a *use_hash* hint is ignored, and here are some common causes of this problem:

- **Check hash join parameters:** Make sure that you have the proper settings for *optimizer_index_cost_adj* and optimizer_max_permutations (Oracle9i and earlier) to limit the number of table join evaluations. Also check the values for *hash_area_size* and *hash_multiblock_io_count*. If using *pga_aggregate_target*, remember that it will not use more than 5% of the space for any hash join and it may need to be overridden.

- **Verify the hash join driving table:** Ensure that the smaller table is the driving table. This would be the first table in the *from* clause when using the *ordered* hint. This is because a *hash join* builds the memory array using the driving table.

- **Analyze CBO statistics:** Check that tables and/or columns of the join tables are appropriately analyzed with *dbms_stats*.

Advanced Oracle SQL Tuning

- **Check for skewed columns:** Histograms are recommended only for non-uniform column distributions. If necessary, the join order chosen by the cost-based optimizer using histograms or the ordered hint can be overridden.

- **Check RAM region:** Ensure that hash_area_size is large enough to hold the smaller table in memory. Otherwise, Oracle must write to the TEMP tablespace, slowing down the hash join. Oracle recommends that the hash_area_size for the driving table be set at 1.6 times the sum of bytes for the driving table.

By following these steps, it should be possible to add a *use_hash* hint to the SQL to invoke a *hash* join. Remember, it is always a good idea to run a explain plan on the SQL to ensure that the *hash* join is being invoked.

Monitoring RAM Operations for SQL

With each new release, Oracle enhances the *v$* views to include information about RAM memory utilization. Oracle has implemented RAM memory monitoring by enhancing the *v$process* view.

The new columns in the *v$process* view allows the DBA to show details about the program global area (PGA) regions for all current Oracle processes. The PGA is a dedicated area of RAM memory used by individual processes to perform RAM intensive functions, such as sorting.

The three new columns in the *v$process* view include *pga_used_memory*, *pga_allocated_memory* and *pga_max_memory*. From these metrics, it is possible to see the actual RAM utilization for individual background processes within the Oracle environment and also look at the RAM demands of individual connections to the database. To illustrate, consider the following query:

```
col c1 heading 'Program|Name'            format a30
col c2 heading 'PGA|Used|Memory'         format 999,999,999
col c3 heading 'PGA|Allocated|Memory'    format 999,999,999
col c4 heading 'PGA|Maximum|Memory'      format 999,999,999

select
   program        c1,
   pga_used_mem   c2,
   pga_alloc_mem  c3,
   pga_max_mem    c4
from
   v$process
order by
   c4 desc;
```

The following is the output, showing the RAM usage for each user on the database:

```
PROGRAM                 PGA_USED_MEM   PGA_ALLOC_MEM   PGA_MAX_MEM
```

```
----------------------------  ------------  --------------  -----------
oracle@janet  (PMON)               120,463         234,291         234,291
oracle@janet  (DBW0)             1,307,179       1,817,295       1,817,295
oracle@janet  (LGWR)             4,343,655       4,849,203       4,849,203
oracle@janet  (CKPT)               194,999         332,583         332,583
oracle@janet  (SMON)               179,923         775,311         775,323
oracle@janet  (RECO)               129,719         242,803         242,803
oracle@janet  (TNS V1-V3)        1,400,543       1,540,627       1,540,915
oracle@janet  (P000)               299,599         373,791         635,959
oracle@janet  (P001)               299,599         373,791         636,007
oracle@janet  (TNS V1-V3)        1,400,543       1,540,627       1,540,915
oracle@janet  (TNS V1-V3)           22,341       1,716,253       3,625,241
```

This example provides insight into the behavior of the Oracle database engine. For example, Oracle's log writer (LGWR) process is the highest consumer of PGA RAM memory, which makes sense because the Oracle Log Writer process must transfer redo log images from Oracle's Log Buffer (in RAM memory) to the online redo log filesystem.

High RAM memory utilization for Oracle's Database Writer (DBW0) process is also apparent. This also makes sense; because Oracle's asynchronous I/O process must make extensive use of RAM memory resources to ensure that all database changes are successfully written to the database.

Viewing RAM Usage for Individual Processes

The real value in viewing RAM usage in Oracle is to see RAM utilization for individual processes. Oracle uses a shared RAM region called *pga_aggregate_target*. When using the Oracle multithreaded server, the *pga_aggregate_target* parameter works similar to Oracle's large pool but with one important difference.

By having a shared RAM memory area, individual Oracle processes are free to use up to 5 percent of the total amount of memory within the pool when performing sorting and hash join activities. This is a huge improvement over the Oracle8*i* requirement that each PGA region be restricted according to the value of the *sort_area_size* initialization parameter.

Oracle also provides a useful *v$pgastat* view. The *v$pgastat* view shows the total amount of RAM memory utilization for every RAM memory region within the database. This information can reveal the high water mark of RAM utilization, and allows resizing of RAM memory demands according to the relative stress on the system. Here is a simple query against *v$pgastat*:

```
column name format a40
column value format 999,999,999

select
   name,
   value
from
```

```
   v$pgastat
order by
   value desc;
```

This listing will show the value of *pga_aggregate_target* and the high water marks for all RAM memory areas used by this instance. The next section provides a look at optimal, one pass and multipass RAM memory executions.

When an Oracle process requires an operation, such as a sort or a hash join, it goes to the shared RAM memory area within *pga_aggregate_target* region and attempts to obtain enough contiguous

RAM frames to perform the operation. If the process is able to acquire these RAM frames immediately, it is marked as an optimal RAM access.

If the RAM acquisition requires a single pass through *pga_aggregate_target*, the RAM memory allocation is marked as one pass. If all RAM is in use, Oracle may have to make multiple passes through *pga_aggregate_target* to acquire the RAM memory. This is called multipass.

Remember, RAM memory is extremely fast, and most sorts or hash joins are completed in microseconds. Oracle allows a single process to use up to 5 percent of the *pga_aggregate_target*, and parallel operations are allowed to consume up to 30 percent of the PGA RAM pool.

Multipass executions indicate a RAM shortage, and it is necessary to always allocate enough RAM to ensure that at least 95 percent of connected tasks can acquire their RAM memory optimally.

Information about workarea executions can be obtained by querying the *v$sysstat* view shown here:

```
col c1 heading 'Workarea|Profile' format a35
col c2 heading 'Count'             format 999,999,999
col c3 heading 'Percentage'        format 99

select
   name                                        c1,
   cnt                                         c2,
   decode(total, 0, 0, round(cnt*100/total))   c3
from
(
   select name,value cnt,(sum(value) over ()) total
   from
      v$sysstat
   where
   name like 'workarea exec%'
);
```

The output below shows the efficiency of RAM operations:

```
PROFILE                            CNT      PERCENTAGE
-------------------------------   ---------- ----------
workarea executions - optimal      5395          98
workarea executions - onepass       284           2
workarea executions - multipass       0           0
```

At least 95 percent of the tasks should have optimal workarea executions. The output above shows all workarea executions that were able to execute *optimal, onepass*, and *multipass* modes.

This listing provides valuable information regarding the appropriate size for the *pga_aggregate_target* region. It can also indicate an over-allocation of the RAM memory region. If the percentage of optimal workarea executions consistently stays at 98 to 100 percent, RAM frames can safely be stolen from *pga_aggregate_target* and reallocated to other areas of the Oracle SGA, such as *db_cache_size*, that may have a greater need for the RAM memory resources.

Viewing Individual RAM Work Areas

Oracle also provides data dictionary views that show the amount of RAM memory used by individual steps within the execution plan of SQL statements. This can be invaluable for the appropriate sizing of *hash_area_size, pga_aggregate_target* and other RAM-intensive parameters. The *v$sql_workarea_active* view shows the amount of RAM usage by each individual workarea within the Oracle database.

Also, Oracle provides several methods for joining tables, each with widely varying RAM memory usage. The Oracle SQL optimizer can choose *sort merge* joins, *nested loop* joins, *hash* joins and *star* joins methods. In some cases, the *hash* join can run faster than a *nested loop* join, but *hash* joins require RAM memory resources and a high setting for the *hash_area_size* and *pga_aggregate_target* parameter.

For a more comprehensive view of all tasks using RAM resources, the following query can be used to take advantage of the *v$sql_workarea_active* view:

🖫 show_pga_ram_details.sql

```
select
    to_number(decode(SID, 65535, NULL, SID))  sid,
    operation_type                            OPERATION,
    trunc(WORK_AREA_SIZE/1024)                WSIZE,
    trunc(EXPECTED_SIZE/1024)                 ESIZE,
    trunc(ACTUAL_MEM_USED/1024)               MEM,
```

```
   trunc(MAX_MEM_USED/1024)                "MAX MEM",
   number_passes                           PASS
from
   v$sql_workarea_active
order by 1,2;
```

The output below shows RAM usage for specific step of SQL execution plans:

```
SID OPERATION              WSIZE    ESIZE       MEM   MAX MEM PASS
--- --------------------- ------ --------- --------- --------- ----
 27 GROUP BY (SORT)           73        73        64        64    0
 44 HASH-JOIN              3148      3147      2437      6342    1
 71 HASH-JOIN             13241     19200     12884     34684    1
```

It also shows the amount of RAM used for each step of SQL execution. One SQL statement is performing a Group By sort using 73 KB of RAM memory. It includes the system ID (SID) for two SQL statements that are performing *hash* joins. These *hash* joins are using the 3 and 13 MB respectively to build their in-memory hash tables.

This is a good time to cover tracking RAM for hash joins.

Tracking Hash Joins

Because *hash* joins are so tightly controlled by available memory, the savvy DBA might track *hash* joins over time. The following SQL scripts can be used to track system-wide hash joins.

🖫 track_hash_joins.sql

```
select
  to_char(
    sn.begin_interval_time,
    'yy-mm-dd hh24'
  )                                 snap_time,
  count(*)                          ct,
  sum(st.rows_processed_delta)      row_ct,
  sum(st.disk_reads_delta)          disk,
  sum(st.cpu_time_delta)            cpu
from
  dba_hist_snapshot    sn,
  dba_hist_sqlstat     st,
  dba_hist_sql_plan    sp
where
  st.snap_id = sn.snap_id
and
  st.dbid = sn.dbid
and
  st.instance_number = sn.instance_number
```

```
and
   sp.sql_id = st.sql_id
and
   sp.dbid = st.dbid
and
   sp.plan_hash_value = st.plan_hash_value
and
   sp.operation = 'HASH JOIN'
group by
   to_char(sn.begin_interval_time,'yy-mm-dd hh24')
having
        count(*) > &hash_thr;
```

The sample output might look the following, showing the number of hash joins during the snapshot period along with the relative I/O and CPU associated with the processing.

The values for *rows_processed* are generally higher for hash joins which do full-table scans as opposed to nested loop joins with generally involved a very small set of returned rows.

Hash Join Thresholds by hour

Date	Hash Join Count	Rows Processed	Disk Reads	CPU Time
04-10-12 17	22	4,646	887	39,990,515
04-10-13 16	25	2,128	827	54,746,653
04-10-14 11	21	17,368	3,049	77,297,578
04-10-21 15	60	2,805	3,299	5,041,064
04-10-22 10	25	6,864	941	4,077,524
04-10-22 13	31	11,261	2,950	46,207,733
04-10-25 16	35	46,269	1,504	6,364,414

Oracle *hash* joins are dependent upon the system and session parameter settings.

Conclusion

This chapter has focused on the use of RAM to speed up SQL performance and how faster RAM storage can be leveraged to hypercharge SQL performance. The main points of this chapter include:

- RAM is especially useful in SQL sorting, and sorts can happen hundreds of times faster when Oracle is configured to avoid disk sort operations.

- RAM is used in Oracle hash joins, a type of join that is controlled by the Oracle DBA's settings for important PGA parameters.

- While the DBA control whether Oracle might invoke a hash join, the SQL optimizer makes the final decision based on the amount of RAM available to the SQL statement and the characteristics of the tables being joined.

- RAM usage can be monitored at the SQL level, the session level or for the whole database.

- Oracle PGA RAM has built-in defaults, such that no single user can hog too much RAM. When running batch jobs that need more than the defaults, Oracle can be adjusted to supersize the PGA.

The following chapter will provide a look at distributed SQL and cover how to tune SQL that runs over SQL*Net connections.

Tuning Distributed SQL

SQL can read tables from vastly different databases

Tuning Distributed SQL

Tuning distributed SQL is challenging because it involves two sets of optimizer data: one on the master database; and another whole set of metadata statistics on the remote database. Tuning distributed DML is also a challenge because of the requirement for a two-phase commit (2PC) to ensure transaction level recovery across geographical databases.

The best place to start learning about tuning distributed SQL is with an overview of distributed database technology.

Distributed Database Technology

Distributed databases are different from stand-alone databases in a variety of important ways. Foremost, the creation of a distributed Oracle database is sometimes the result of unplanned acquisitions. Whenever a new system enters the picture, the DBA may have no choice but to create a distributed system.

However, there are legitimate cases where the DBA will deliberately distribute the database across multiple instances:

1. **Geographical necessity**: A worldwide system often requires duplicated Oracle database in order to achieve fast response time. The Google Internet search engine is an excellent example of this type of distribution. Google achieves its super-fast response time by cloning the Oracle database server in many locations across the world.

2. **Local autonomy**: Often a company with numerous branch offices chooses to clone their schema and allow each branch to have an independent Oracle database.

3. **Privacy concerns**: Many distributed Oracle databases keep sensitive information, such as salaries, personal data, etc., on an isolated instance.

It is important to recognize that Oracle database distribution adds complexity to the overall system, both from a management and security perspective. For distributed systems that reproduce data in many locations, there is the additional problem of coordinating updates to many locations.

Coordinating Distributed Databases

Oracle has invested heavily in distributed database technology and the creation of a database link is very straightforward. The DBA has only to specify the database link name, the remote user to connect to, the password for the remote user and the TNS service name for the database link connection:

```
create public database link
  mylink
connect to
  remote_username
identified by
  mypassword
using 'tns_service_name';
```

By default, created database links are private, which means they are only accessible through the schema in which they are created. The following is an example of the creation of a database link, specifically a private database link:

```
create database link
   chicago
connect to
   admin
identified by
   administrator
using 'chicagodb';
```

Only those in the *scott* schema can access the created database link from above. But often, the goal will be to have all database schemas to be able to access the database link. In that case, the *public* clause of the *create database link* command can be used as shown in this example:

```
create public database link
   chicago
connect to
   admin
identified by
   administrator
using
   'chicagodb';
```

It is also possible to use synonyms to hide the fact that the table is remote over a database link. Assume that both Japan and Ohio have a customer table, identical in structure but containing different rows.

Oracle synonyms could be assigned as follows:

```
create synonym
   japan_customer
for
   customer@hq.sales.asia.japan;

create synonym
   ohio_customer
for
   customer@hq.mtfg.ohio;
```

Location independence means that the end users do not necessarily know about the physical location of each table. In a distributed database, rows can be retrieved without specifically referencing physical locations, making the database appear to end users as a unified whole. Because the underlying database links can be hidden, it will be necessary to view the execution plans to see if a distributed SQL query is being tuned.

Distributed SQL Table Joins

In today's networked world, it would not be uncommon to see a query join a table in New York with a table in San Francisco, all transparent to the end-user. However,

---

while this may be transparent to the end-user, it should not be transparent to the SQL developer since remote SQL table joins can be very challenging to tune.

There are two permutations of distributed joins, remote-to-remote and local-to-remote.

The remote-to-remote Distributed Join

In the remote-to-remote join, the local database serves only to initiate the SQL and collect the rowset while all of the work is done on the remote database. In the SQL below, note that the join work, usually accomplished with *nested loops*, and the sort of the result set should be done on the remote site:

```
select
    customer_name,
    order_nbr
from
    customer@chicago,
    order@chicago
where
    customer.customer_nbr = order.customer_nbr
and
    customer_nbr = :var1
order by
    customer_name,
    order_nbr;
```

A distributed query might be joining remote tables together, a case where a lot of the work is being done on the remote database as shown in Figure 8.1:

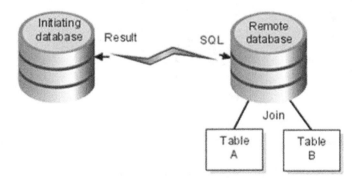

Figure 8.1: *A remote-to-remote distributed join*

In the above SQL it is important to note that the initiating database, the local database, is not aware of the optimization being done on the remote *chicago* database.

In these cases, it is important to go to the remote database and create a view that joins the tables together. This ensures that the remote site is always the driving site, so that the table joining is done in the same place as the data resides.

The local-to-remote distributed join

In the local-to-remote join, one table is local and one exists at a remote location:

```
select
    customer_name,
    order_nbr
from
    customer,
    order@chicago
where
    customer.customer_nbr = order.customer_nbr
and
    customer_nbr = :var1
order by
    customer_name,
    order_nbr;
```

It is also possible to join table across a database link, as in the case where local table is joined to a remote table as shown in Figure 8.2:

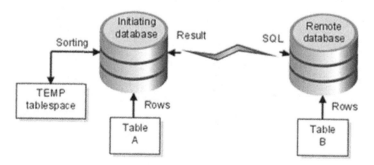

Figure 8.2: *A local-to-remote distributed join*

In the local-to-remote join, a common optimizer error is an unnecessary full-table scan on the remote table. It is important to ensure that the remote database has proper indexes and current *dbms_stats* metadata.

Additionally, when tuning local-to-remote table joins, the goal should always be to make the largest table the local table, to minimize network overhead.

Finally, the local-to-remote join presents the issue of result set sorting. By default, the local database will sort the result set. This may not be optimal in cases where the final rowset might be sorted on the remote server, before transmitting the final results across the network.

One solution for this sort issue is to specify an index hint on the remote table to force that data to be fetched in pre-sorted order.

Now that distributed joins have been explained a bit more, it is a good time to look into troubleshooting methods for tuning distributed SQL.

Troubleshooting Distributed Oracle SQL

Tuning distributed Oracle databases is fundamentally different than tuning a single Oracle database. Since a single SQL query may touch many Oracle database instances, the optimizer resolution becomes more complex. Tuning experts know that the first step in tuning an SQL statement involves extracting the execution plan for the SQL. This is a much more difficult task in distributed Oracle databases.

The main topics for troubleshooting and tuning distributed queries include these areas:

- Performance issues with distributed queries
- Creating cross-databases execution plans
- The problem of remote joins
- Determining the driving site and driving table for cross-database queries
- Tips for faster cross-database queries

The next section will cover the performance issues that happen when an SQL query spans several Oracle databases.

Performance Issues with Distributed Queries

The phenomenal challenge of optimizing SQL is made even harder when the query spans Oracle databases. The Oracle database is forced to break a distributed SQL statement up into several components and ship each query to the remote Oracle database for execution. The database must then gather the result set from each remote database and prepare a single result from the query.

The physical challenge for optimizing cross-database SQL is compounded by the following issues:

- **Unknown remote database characteristics**: The database involved in a distributed query may be vastly different from each other. For example, an EMP table on a giant IBM Mainframe can be joined with a SALARY table that resides on a tiny Windows server. The optimizer cannot always compute the relative expense of an operation on a remote server.

- **Hard to see the entire distributed execution plan**: A remote execution plan display will only show the SQL that was sent to the remote instance for execution. To see the execution plan for the remote instance, it is necessary to go to that instance and execute the sub-component to get the execution plan.

- **Oracle has no knowledge of network latency**: Oracle cannot factor in the costs of network transmission time between the instances. Hence, Oracle may choose a sub-optimal execution plan, resulting in excessive network traffic and slow results. However, Oracle has some safeguards against this problem. For example, if all the objects in a query are remote, and use the same database link, Oracle will attempt to send the complete query to the remote database for processing.

- **No cohesive SQL execution:** If some tables in an SQL query are remote and some are local, then Oracle will break up the query into individual SQL statements and pass the SQL to the remote database for independent execution. If one database is very slow, the whole query will wait.

Generally, the limiting factor in SQL performance of a distributed query over a database link is the speed of the network.

Where the speed of the network is a constraint, ensure there is a high-speed network with a proper Session Data Unit (SDU) setting and create a separate listener and a larger value for SDU to accommodate jumbo Ethernet frames.

By using a separate listener for the gigabit network with a larger SDU, jumbo Ethernet frames can be better exploited.

That covers most of the issues, and the next section will cover how to display cross-database execution plans and then how to tune distributed SQL.

Creating Cross-database Execution Plans

As every DBA knows, Oracle develops an execution plan for every SQL statement prior to starting the execution. In a single Oracle database, determining the execution plan is straightforward because a single Oracle data dictionary contains the object statistics.

Execution plan for distributed queries are different. The *set autotrace on* command does not work for distributed queries, and a special script must be run to display the remote execution plan.

🖫 remote_sql_execution_plan.sql

```
set long 2000
set arraysize 1

col operation format a22
col options format a8
col object_name format a10
col object_node format a5
col other format a20
col position format 99999
col optimizer format a10

select
   lpad(' ',2*(level-1))||operation operation,
   options,
   object_name,
   optimizer,
   object_node,
   other
from
   plan_table
start with id=0
connect by prior id=parent_id
;
```

Note that this differs from the standard SQL execution plan display because of the inclusion of the *other* column in the query.

For distributed queries, Oracle uses *plan_table.other* column to show the remote queries that were sent to the remote instance for execution.

```
connect pubs/pubs@pubs

truncate table plan_table;

explain plan for
select
   initcap(book.book_title)  c1,
   book_retail_price         c2,
   publishing_qty            c3
from
   book
natural join
   book_details@newpubs
```

```
order by
   book_title
;

@remote_plan
```

This yields an interesting execution plan. In this case, there is a remote hash join to the *book_details* table in the *newpubs* database. It is very important to note that Oracle has split this query.

Oracle sent the select statement for the *book_details* table over Oracle*Net to be executed on the remote instance (*newpubs*), and we the execution plan for this piece of the distributed query is not shown.

```
OPERATION              OPTIONS  OBJECT_NAM OPTIMIZER  OBJEC OTHER
---------------------- -------- ---------- ---------- ----- -----------
SELECT STATEMENT                           CHOOSE
   SORT                ORDER BY
      HASH JOIN
         TABLE ACCESS  FULL     BOOK       ANALYZED
         REMOTE                                        NEWPU SELECT
                                                       "BOOK_KEY","P
                                                       BS.US UBLISHING_QTY"
                                                       FROM
                                                       .ORAC "BOOK_DETAILS"
                                                       "BOOK
                                                       LE.CO _DETAILS" M
```

Now that we see how to get remote execution plans, let's look at how to control the site for the remote execution.

Determining the Driving Site and Driving Table for Cross-database Queries

Just like an SQL query has a driving table, a distributed query has a driving site. The choice of the driving site can be manipulated with the *driving_site* SQL hint. Here is an example of a remote query with a *driving_site* hint:

```
select /*+ driving_site(R1) */
   initcap(book.book_title) c1,
   book_retail_price        c2,
   publishing_qty           c3
from
   book@pubs                r1
natural join
   book_details@newpubs     r2
order by
   book_title
;
```

In this example, Oracle has been directed to make the r1 site (PUBS) the driving site for this query.

Next, let's explore the problems that we get when joining tables between geographically distributed tables.

The Problem of Remote Joins

Assume that we have a database link between two databases:

```
create public database link
   diogenes
connect to
   pubs
identified by
   pubs
using
   'diogenes';
```

It would be interesting to see the distributed execution plan for the following SQL. Note that three of the four database tables are remote, and only the *book_details* table is local to this instance.

```
connect pubs_remote/pubs_remote@newpubs

truncate table plan_table;

explain plan for
select
   initcap(book.book_title) c1,
   author_last_name,
   book_retail_price      c2,
   publishing_qty         c3
from
   book@pubs
natural join
   book_author@pubs
natural join
   author@pubs
natural join
   book_details
order by
   book_title
;

@remote_plan
```

The execution plan looks like the following.

The *remote* notation is easy to find in the output.

```
OPERATION              OPTIONS  OBJECT_NAM OPTIMIZER  OBJEC OTHER
---------------------  -------  ---------- ---------- ----- -------------------
SELECT STATEMENT
  SORT                 ORDER BY
    HASH JOIN
      HASH JOIN
        HASH JOIN
```

```
REMOTE                                    DIOGE SELECT"AUTHOR_KEY",
                                          NES.N "AUTHOR_LAST_NAME"
                                          F EWPUB ROM "AUTHOR"
                                          "AUTHORS"
REMOTE                                    DIOGE SELECT"AUTHOR_KEY",
                                          NES.N "BOOK_KEY" FROM
                                          "BOO EWPUB K_AUTHOR"
                                            S     OR"

REMOTE                                    DIOGE SELECT
                                          "BOOK_KEY","B NES.N
                                          BOOK_TITLE","BOOK_RET
                                          EWPUB AIL_PRICE" FROM
                                          "BOO S     K" "BOOK"
TABLE ACCESS    FULL    BOOK_DETAIL
                          LS
```

What is really happening inside a distributed SQL statement? Note that Oracle has broken the query up into many separate pieces:

1. Independent SQL is sent to each remote Oracle database

2. Result sets are sent back from each remote Oracle database. The query cannot continue until all remote Oracle databases have sent their results back over Oracle*Net.

3. The independent results from each remote request are collected inside the SGA RAM memory. Only after all results are collected can the SQL progress to join the tables.

4. Oracle performs hash joins on the remote result sets, creating a single result set for the query.

5. Oracle then sorts the result set for the *order by* clause in on the originating Oracle database.

6. Oracle passes the completed result back to the originating query.

With that look into the execution plan details for distributed queries, it is time to cover how to optimizer distributed SQL.

Overview of Distributed SQL Tuning

The goals for tuning a distributed SQL statement are just like tuning an ordinary SQL statement except for these important issues:

- **Metadata**: Two sets of metadata are involved, one on each database. Make sure to use the enhanced SQL explain plan script in this chapter when tuning distributed SQL.

- **Network**: The goal of tuning a distributed query is to minimize the amount of rows going over the network, carefully choosing what SQL work is done on the local vs. remote databases.

With these factors in mind, the following are some generalized tuning tips for distributed SQL. Given the challenges of distributed queries, there are several options available for improving the performance of cross-database queries:

- **Choose the right driving table**: Always execute the join remotely when the remote table is much larger than the local one!

- **Pull vs. Push**: In general, performance can be faster if you pull the data where the remote table is called from the master instance as opposed to a push where the join is performed on the remote table. This is especially true of there is a large sort, because the rows may be transferred to the remote host for sorting, and then back again afterwards.

- **Pre-join remote tables with views**: The best way to achieve joining the remote tables is by building a view of these tables on the remote site. Remote views allow join operations to happen on the remote Oracle database, thereby reducing the amount of Oracle*Net traffic. Note that the predicates do not have to be created within the view as they should be passed within the SQL statement sent from the local to remote node.

- **Use subqueries:** While correlated subqueries should be avoided in favor of standard joins, there are cases when a distributed SQL that only returns a small rowset from a remote database will run faster if a standard join s replaced with a correlated subquery. Using this technique, only the subquery is passed to the remote database and the remote database is not aware of the distributed join, making optimization easier to manage.

- **Make the largest table local to your SQL:** If possible, always try to make the largest table the local table, to minimize network overhead. The *driving_site* hint can be used for this purpose.

- **Use the ordered hint:** Joining tables across database links is always challenging, and a savvy developer will use the *ordered* hint to tip the optimizer off about the optimal table join order. This ensures fast SQL response time and also reduces the amount of work parsing the SQL statement.

- **Consider using views:** The ensure optimal performance; consider encapsulating a distributed join into a remote view. The view is defined on the remote database and is then referenced from the local database.

- **Replicate the tables locally**: If the tables are small and non-volatile, using Oracle replication to keep a local copy of the tables is the fastest alternative to distributed SQL. If it is possible to reduce network overhead by replicating a read-only table, it makes good sense to do so.

- **Remember sorting**: By default, all sorting imposed by *order by* and *group by* operations should be done on the local database to minimize network traffic.

The following section will provide a closer look at some of these issues.

Sorting and Distributed SQL

If the SQL performs a sort, it is necessary that the DBA be aware that the sort will be performed on the LOCAL database. This is one reason why it is a bad idea to use a push approach, because the rows will traverse back and forth.

When an Oracle database is accessed remotely by establishing an Oracle database link, Oracle*Net sometimes uses the temporary tablespace on the remote Oracle database, regardless of the Oracle database that invoked the SQL.

In other cases, applications on one instance that accessed another instance, with an Oracle database link, will use the temporary tablespaces on the originating Oracle database and not the processor that contains the link.

The moral is that Oracle*Net will sometimes use the temporary tablespaces on the remote Oracle database, and temporary tablespaces must be sized to accommodate remote data requests.

Parallelism and Distributed Queries

Parallel query across a database link can be quite complex. In a distributed environment, pieces of a table may reside on many remote servers. For example, assume that there is a distributed architecture where local customer tables are kept on each instance. All of the remote rows could be accessed in a single query using inter-instance parallel execution. In this example, the query is executed from the *north_carolina* instance, accessing two remote instances in-parallel:

```
select
   customer_name, sum(purchase_amount) from sales
union
select
   customer_name, sum(purchase_amount) from sales@chicago
union
select
   customer_name, sum(purchase_amount) from sales@new_york
group by
   customer_name;
```

In this case the *north_carolina* instance drives the distributed parallel query and it is the *north_carolina* instance that must gather and sort the result set.

Also, note that there are many hidden parameters that influence parallel query performance. It is critical to always consult Oracle technical support before changing an undocumented parameter.

```
NAME                                  VALUE
-----------------------------------   --------------------
_parallel_adaptive_max_users          1
_parallel_default_max_instances       1
_parallel_execution_message_align     FALSE
_parallel_fake_class_pct              0
_parallel_load_bal_unit               0
_parallel_load_balancing              TRUE
_parallel_min_message_pool            64560
_parallel_recovery_stopat             32767
_parallel_server_idle_time            5
_parallel_server_sleep_time           10
_parallel_txn_global                  FALSE
_parallelism_cost_fudge_factor        350
```

Monitoring parallel query for remote distributed queries is also challenging. SQL can be nested inside SQL and subqueries can be placed anywhere: in the *select* clause; in the *from* clause; and in the *where* clause.

Using Views for Distributed SQL

In some cases, I recommend creating a view on the remote site referencing the local tables and calling the remote table via the local view.

```
create view
   local_cust
as
   select * from cust@remote;
```

The same effect by can be achieved by using an inline view:

```
select /*+ driving_site(a) */
*
from (select stuff from emp@remote) a
```

Tuning with the *driving_site* Hint

In a true distributed query, the SQL optimization is done on the sending site. Because the local site may not have access to the CBO statistics on the remote site, Oracle punts and does a full-table scan.

The *driving_site* hint forces query execution to be done at a different site than the initiating instance. This is done when the remote table is much larger than the local table, and the desire is to have the work (join, sorting) done remotely to save the back-and-forth network traffic.

In the following example, the *driving_site* hint is used to force the work to be done on the site where the huge table resides:

```
select /*+ driving_site(h) */
   ename
from
  tiny_table        t,
  huge_table@remote h
where
   t.deptno = h.deptno;
```

The following section will broach the subject of forced partitioning on a distributed system.

Forcing Partition Pruning on Distributed SQL

Tuning distributed partitioned tables is especially tricky because the optimizer cannot recognize that a remote object is partitioned. Thus, the optimizer can generate less than optimal plans for remote partitioned objects, particularly when partition pruning would have been possible had the object been local.

If the explain plan lines shows a *partition range single* or *partition range iterator*, this indicates that Oracle is performing a Partition Prune. A distributed execution plan with *partition range all* indicates Oracle is scanning all partitions, which is not good for performance.

There are several conditions that can prevent partition pruning (partition range iterator):

- Putting a predicate on a function of a partition key column

- Using bind variables in partition key

- Not specifying the partition key in the query

The next section will cover the challenges of tuning distributed DDL.

Tuning distributed DDL

In general, Oracle requires that all DDL operations, such as *create table, create view, etc.,* occur on the original instance, and DDL is not available over a database link. This also applies to SQL tuning because the *driving_site* hint will not work in this type of DDL:

- CTAS (create table as select)

- Create materialized view

This is because CTAS and materialized view creation is DDL and DDL operations must take place on the original instance.

Metalink Note 825677.1 notes that a distributed DML statement must execute on the database where the DML target resides. Also, it says that the *driving_site* hint cannot override requirement for CTAS materialized view refreshes.

Conclusion

This chapter has covered some of the major points for tuning distributed SQL queries. The main point of this chapter is that tuning distributed SQL differs from ordinary SQL tuning because there are two sets of *dbms_stats* metadata involved and there are many factors that determine optimal execution of distributed SQL queries:

- **Tune to the network**: The goal of tuning distributed SQL often involves reducing network traffic.

- **Divide and conquer**: Always be aware of where the work is being done in a distributed query.

- **Push or pull data:** Do not be afraid to use the *driving_site* hint to optimizer a distributed SQL join to your specific environment.

Now it is time to move on and take a look at one of the most complex areas of Oracle SQL tuning, the use of Oracle parallel query to speed up SQL on SMP servers.

Tuning Parallel SQL Execution

Parallel query speeds up full-table scans

A Brief History of Parallel Query

One of the most exciting, yet most overlooked, features of Oracle databases is the ability to dedicate multiple processors to service an Oracle query. Each new release of Oracle brings new features, but it is important to remember that these features are driven by advances in hardware technology.

This chapter will cover how the benefits of parallel query are directly tied to the number of CPUs on the server, and it was not until the late 1990's when 16 and 32 CPU servers became widely used.

The Oracle database has implemented parallel query features that allow a query to effectively use both symmetric multiprocessors (SMP) and massively parallel processors (MPP). Using these features, it is possible to read a one-gigabyte table with sub-second response time. A review of these Oracle parallel architectures is a good place to begin, and then there will be follow up on tips for using parallel queries.

Beginning in the 1960s, IBM began to implement mainframe processors with multiple CPUs. These were known as dyadic (two processors) or quadratic (four processors). Once these processors were implemented, software and database developers struggled with developing products that could take advantage of the ability to use multiple processors to service a task.

These tools generally took the form of segmentation features that dedicated specific tasks to specific processors. They did not incorporate any ability to dynamically dedicate tasks to processors or to load-balance between CPUs.

Once the UNIX operating system became popular in the 1980s, hardware vendors (SUN, IBM, and Hewlett-Packard) began to offer computers with multiple CPUs and shared memory. These were known as SMP processors. On the other end of the spectrum, hardware vendors were experimenting with machines that contained hundreds, and even thousands, of individual CPUs. These became known as massively parallel processors.

As the Oracle database grew in popularity, the Oracle architects began to experiment with techniques that would allow the Oracle software to take advantage of these parallel features.

Parallelism can help even when *cpu_count=1*

It is not necessary to have many CPUs to see a benefit from parallel processing. Even on the same processor, multiple processes can speed up queries is the data is spread across many disk drives.

For parallel query to be most effective, the table should be partitioned onto separate disk devices, such that each process can do I/O against its segment of the table without interfering with the other simultaneous query processes.

However, the archaic client-server environment of the 1990s relied on RAID or a logical volume manager (LVM), which scrambles data files across disk packs in order to balance the I/O load. Consequently, full utilization of parallel query involves striping a table across numerous data files, each on a separate device.

Parallel query works best with symmetric multiprocessor (SMP) boxes. Also, it is important to configure the system to maximize the I/O bandwidth, either through disk striping or high-speed channels. Because of the parallel sorting feature, it is also a good idea to beef up the memory on the processor.

Parallel Sorting

Many people forget that while the parallel processes can read data simultaneously, these processes can also perform parallel sorting.

While sorting is no substitute for using a pre-sorted index, the parallel query manager will service requests sorting far faster than when using a single process. In addition to using multiple processes to retrieve the table, the query manager will also dedicate numerous processes to simultaneously sort the result set as illustrated in Figure 9.1:

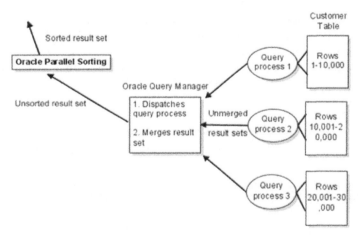

Figure 9.1: *Parallel sorting operations in Oracle*

The parallel sorting feature may increase the demands on the server RAM. Each parallel process can allocate *sort_area_size* in RAM to manage the sort.

The data retrieval itself will not be particularly fast, since all of the retrieval processes are competing for a channel on the same disk. But each sort process has its own sort area, as determined by the *sort_area_size* or *pga_aggregate_target* parameters, so the sorting of the result set will progress very quickly.

Parallel Query and I/O Buffering

One important fact about Oracle parallel query is that I/O is not always buffered. In traditional disk reads, Oracle places the data blocks in the data buffer caches (*db_cache_size*, *db_32k_cache_size*) in case a later SQL might need the block.

However, Oracle is intelligent and knows that a large table full-table scan is unlikely to retrieve rows that may be wanted by subsequent SQL statements.

While a huge data buffer might be right for an OLTP system, systems with SQL that does parallellized large-table full-table scans does not benefit from a large SGA. Instead, when Oracle performs a parallel full-table scan, the database blocks are read directly into the program global area (PGA), bypassing the data buffer RAM as shown in Figure 9.2:

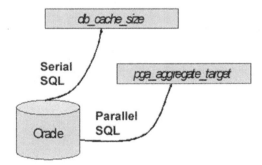

Figure 9.2: *Parallel full-table scans don't use the data buffer cache*

In addition to full-table scans and sorting, the parallel query option also allows for parallel processes for merge joins and hash join operations.

Tuning Parallel Join Operations

Parallel query will often improve the performance of large-table joins, but it is far from automatic and it is important to carefully experiment with the different join methods to determine the best join plan.

Only table joins that invoke full-table scans can benefit from parallelism, so the materials in this chapter will be limited to tuning parallel *nested loops* and *hash* joins.

Tuning Parallel Sort Merge Joins

As covered in Chapter 4, *Oracle SQL Join Internals,* the *sort merge* join is somewhat rare, and it is seen in cases where the SQL produces very large result sets such as daily reports and table detail summary queries.

The following example shows a simple parallel sort merge join. Note that the smaller driving table, the *customer* table, is specified with the *use_merge* hint, and then the parallel queries are specified on both tables, spawning 15 parallel query processes:

```
select /*+ use_merge(a,b) parallel(a, 15) parallel(b, 15) */
   a.cust_name,
   b.sales
from
   customer    a,
   ordor       b
where
   a.cust_key = b.cust_key;
```

The parallel execution plan looks like the following:

```
OPERATION
-------------------------------------------------------------------
OPTIONS                      OBJECT_NAME                  POSITION
-----------------------------  ---------------------------  ----------
OTHER_TAG
-------------------------------------------------------------------
SELECT STATEMENT
                                                              5
  MERGE JOIN
                                                              1
PARALLEL_TO_SERIAL
    SORT
JOIN                                                          1
PARALLEL_COMBINED_WITH_PARENT
      TABLE ACCESS
FULL                         EMP                             1
PARALLEL_TO_PARALLEL
    SORT
JOIN                                                          2
PARALLEL_COMBINED_WITH_PARENT
      TABLE ACCESS
FULL                         BONUS                           1
PARALLEL_TO_PARALLEL
```

In sum, a parallel *sort merge* join may be appropriate for a large tale join without a *where* clause, or in cases of missing indexes.

A far more common type of parallel join is the *hash join*, and the next section will provide a closer look at the internals of parallel hash joins.

Tuning Parallel Hash Joins

In review, the *hash* join is used when there is enough RAM, per *pga_aggregate_target*, and when joining a large table to a smaller table.

When the execution plans for a hash join are reviewed, it is clear that both tables experience a full-table scan, and it is beneficial to parallelize the largest table in the hash join as shown in Figure 9.3:

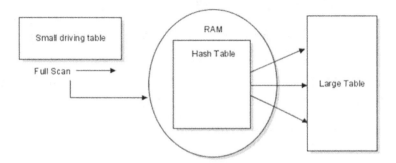

Figure 9.3: *The driving table in a hash join is the small table*

The following is an example of a parallelized hash join where the *smaltab* table has been set as the driving table with the *use_hash* hint. Once the driving table is defined, the *largetab* table can be parallelized:

```
select /*+ use_hash(e,b) parallel(b, 15) */
   e.ename,
   hiredate,
   b.comm
from
   smalltab e,
   largetab b
where
   e.ename = b.ename;
```

```
OPERATION
-----------------------------------------------------------------
OPTIONS                     OBJECT_NAME                 POSITION
-----------------------------------------------------------------
OTHER_TAG
-----------------------------------------------------------------
SELECT STATEMENT
                                                           3
   HASH JOIN
                                                           1
PARALLEL_TO_SERIAL
   TABLE ACCESS
FULL                        SMALLTAB                       1
PARALLEL_TO_PARALLEL
```

Remember, whoever writes the SQL controls whether a hash join occurs and the degree of parallelism for the large table.

The next section will cover the different ways that Oracle parallel query can be invoked.

How Oracle Parallel Query Works

When Oracle has to perform a legitimate, large, full-table scan, parallel query can make a dramatic difference in the response time.

The first step in a parallel full-table scan is to partition the table into equally-sized chunks. However, parallel query works best with symmetric multiprocessor (SMP) boxes. Also, it is important to configure the system to maximize the I/O bandwidth, either through disk striping or high-speed channels. Because of the parallel sorting feature, it is also a good idea to beef up the memory on the processor.

Remember, Oracle partitions an SQL query into sub-queries and dedicates separate processors to each one. At this time, parallel query is useful only for queries that perform full-table scans on long tables, but the performance improvements can be dramatic.

Here is how it works. Instead of having a single query server to manage the I/O against the table, parallel query allows the Oracle query server to dedicate many processes to simultaneously access the data. One of the latest trends is for systems to have more and more CPUs inside a single server. Using symmetric multiprocessing (SMP) servers, it is not uncommon for an Oracle server to have 8, 16 or 32 CPUs, along with many gigabytes of RAM for the Oracle SGA regions.

Oracle has kept pace with these changes and offers a wealth of tools to take advantage of the multiple CPUs on SMP servers.

Starting with Oracle8i, Oracle implemented parallelism in virtually every database function, including SQL access (full-table scans), parallel data manipulation (DML), and parallel recovery. The challenge for Oracle professionals is to configure their databases to use as many of the CPUs as possible.

Parallel query is not for index access!

Remember, parallel query only works on SQL that invokes a full-table scan. A *parallel* hint on a SQL that invokes an index access execution plan will be ignored by the optimizer.

Look Out!

Now, how exactly does parallel query work and how can it be used to improve response time on SQL that invokes large full-table scans?

In addition to full-table scans and sorting, the parallel query option also allows for parallel processes for merge joins and nested loops.

```
select /*+ full(customer) parallel(customer, 63) */
   cust_name,
   sum(sale_amount)
from
   customer
group by
   cust_name;
```

If there is an SMP with many CPUs in use, a parallel request can be issued. This will leave it up to each Oracle instance to use its default degree of parallelism. For example, note the *default* arguments in the parallel query hint below:

```
select /*+ parallel(employee_table, default, default) */
employee_name
from
employee_table
where
emp_type = 'SALARIED';
```

Oracle does a very good job in segmenting the table into equal chunks, and getting these sizes right is important because the SQL cannot complete until the very last parallel query process has completed.

Once the table has been partitioned into pieces, Oracle fires off parallel query slaves, sometimes called *factotum* processes, and each slave simultaneously reads a piece of the large table. Upon completion of all slave processes, Oracle passes the results back to a parallel query coordinator, which will reassemble the data, perform a sort if required, and return the results back to the end user.

Parallel query can deliver almost infinite scalability, so very large full-table scans that used to take many minutes can now be completed with sub-second response times as illustrated in Figure 9.4:

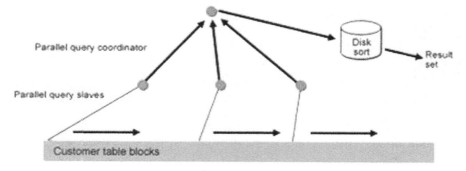

Figure 9.4: *Parallel query uses a divide and conquer approach*

Oracle parallel query is heavily influenced by the number of processors invoked, and full-table scans latency is reduced proportionally to the number of CPUs dedicated to reading the large table. The optimum degree of parallelism is N-1 parallel processes, where N=the number of CPUs on the dedicated Oracle server, as seen in Figure 9.5:

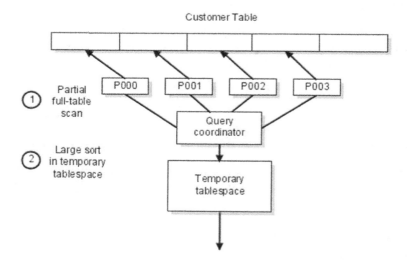

Figure 9.5: *Parallel query uses a divide and conquer approach*

It is also very important to note that Oracle can detect the server environment, including the specific number of CPUs on the server. At startup time, Oracle examines the number of CPUs on the server and sets a parameter called *cpu_count*, which is used in the computation of the default values of several other important parameters.

The next sections will provide a closer look at parallel hints and how they can be used to improve performance.

Parallel Hints

Parallel hints are used to improve the speed of queries that involve full-table scans. This section will cover three types of parallel hints; the *parallel* hint, the *pq_distribute* hint, and the *noparallel* hint.

The Parallel Hint

The *parallel* hint is used with full-table scans and ensures that the table name query is executed in parallel mode. The number of parallel query slaves is specified by the *degree* parameter. It is important to use the *parallel* hint in conjunction with the *full* hint so that full-table scans are used. If the *full* hint is not used, the optimizer might not choose a full-table scan, and thus will ignore the *parallel* hint.

The example below demonstrates the *parallel* hint on a database server with 36 CPUs:

```
select /*+ FULL(emp) PARALLEL(emp, 35) */
       ename
    from
       emp;
```

Next comes the *pq_distribute* hint.

The *pq_distribute* Hint

The *pq_distribute* hint is used to specify how rows of joined tables are distributed between producer and consumer parallel query servers. The hint uses three parameters: the table name; the outer distribution; and the inner distribution. The *pq_distribute* hint is generally used to improve parallel join operation performance when dealing with partitioned tables.

The *parallel_to_parallel* execution plan should be avoided when performing parallel query joins. When using this execution plan, the incoming and outgoing data streams are parallelized. This results in slow join performance. A better option is to use the *parallel_combined_with_parent* plan, which combines merge and sort operations together.

Before Oracle developed the *pq_distribute* hint, Oracle DBAs would have to force the *parallel_combined_with_parent* operation by deleting the CBO statistics on the inner table. The CBO statistics were removed because the SQL optimizer evaluates the size of potential broadcast tables based on CBO statistics. If the table was above the threshold value, the joining would be done using *parallel_to_parallel*, resulting in slow execution.

There are six possible variants of the *pq_distribute* hint, each resulting in a different table distribution. These examples are using the *emp* table. The parameters follow the syntax *pq_distribute(table, inner dist, outer dist)*:

- **pq_distribute(emp, hash, hash)**: This options routes the rows of each table to the consumer parallel query servers using hash functions on the join keys. When the mapping is concluded, the query servers perform the join between the resulting pair of partitions. This hint should be used when tables are of comparable size, and when the join operation is implemented using sort-merge join or hash join.

- **pq_distribute(emp, broadcast, none)**: This option guarantees that all outer table rows are broadcast to each parallel query server. While this is done, the inner table rows are randomly partitioned. This hint is useful when the outer table is small compared to the inner table. If the size of the inner table times the number of parallel query servers is greater than the size of the outer table, this hint should be used.

- **pq_distribute(emp, none, broadcast)**: This option broadcasts all rows of the inner table to each consumer parallel query server. While this is done, the outer table rows are randomly partitioned. This hint is useful when the inner table is smaller than the outer table. If the size of the inner table times the number of parallel query servers is less than the size of the outer table, this hint should be used.

- **Pq_distribute(emp, partition, none)**: This option maps the rows of the outer table using the partitioning of the inner table. For this to work, the inner table must be partitioned on the join keys. When the number of partitions of the outer table is equal or close to a multiple of the number of parallel query servers, this hint is useful.

- **pq_distribute(emp, none, partition)**: This options maps the rows of the outer table using the partitioning of the outer table. In this case, the outer table must be partitioned on the join keys. This hint is best used when the number of partitions of the outer table is divisible or nearly divisible by the number of query servers.

- **pq_(emp, none, none)**: This option requires that each parallel query server performs the join operation between the matching partition for each table. For this to work, each table must be partitioned equally on the join keys.

The *noparallel* Hint

In cases where parallelism is not wanted, the *noparallel* hint can be used. This hint is useful with queries that perform full-table scans on small tables. In this case, parallel query should be turned off for the table, and the table should be placed into the KEEP pool. In most cases, the CBO will recognize that small size of the table and not use a parallel query.

The next section will cover how to invoke parallel query from SQL.

Invoking Parallel Query

Oracle has several options for making SQL use parallel large-table full-table scans and you can implement parallel query.

- **Database-level parallelism**: For large data warehouse applications, automatic parallelism can be turned on for every full table scan in the entire database.

- **Table level parallelism**: Parallel query can be implemented at the table level with the *alter table tablename parallel nn* command. However, this command should only be used in systems that regularly perform full-table scans because issuing this command will make the optimizer see full-scans as less expensive than index access.

- **Session-level parallelism**: Parallelism can be turned on at the session level with the *alter session* command

- **Query level parallelism**: The preferred way to implement parallelism is at the SQL level using a parallel hint. In this fashion, the SQL developer controls the degree of parallelism.

Oracle also has an automatic parallelism feature using the *parallel_automatic_tuning* parameter.

Look Out!

Beware of table-level parallelism!

It can be very dangerous to turn on parallelism with the *alter table* command because the CBO may make system-wide changes to SQL's execution plans, changing index scans to full-table scans!

With parallelism in Oracle, there are several types of parallel query to consider:

- **Single-instance parallel query**: This is when a single instance fires off multiple processes to read sections of a large table at the same time. A parallel query coordinator then merges the results from each PQ factotum process.

- **RAC inter-instance parallel query**: In a clustered environment, Oracle RAC can perform large-table full-table scans in parallel using separate processes on each node.

- **Distributed parallel query**: In distributed databases when a table has been partitioned into separate instances, a parallel query can be invoked to read the remote tables simultaneously.

This section explores the differences between a monolithic server and a RAC cluster for parallelizing large-table full-table scans and exposes some of the differences between single instance and inter-instance parallelism.

For the examples below, assume two architectures with equal hardware resources of 16 CPUs and 32 gigabytes of RAM. There will be reads on a sales table that resides on 1,000,000 blocks. Each of these systems has the same total resources, 16 processors and 32 gig of RAM:

- **Monolithic SMP server**: 16 processors, 32 gig RAM

- **RAC servers**: Four nodes, each with 4 processors and 8 gigabytes of RAM

A common requirement of Oracle data warehouses are rollup and aggregation processes whereby super-large tables are read end-to-end, computing summary and average values. Some data warehouse queries also have *order by* or *group by* clauses, requiring Oracle to retrieve and sort a very-large result set.

The next section will include a review of single instance paralle query then it will delve into Oracle parallel query for RAC. There will also be an examination of a third type of inter-instance parallel query, Oracle Parallel Query in a distributed environment.

Single Instance Oracle Parallel Query

In a single instance environment, it is possible to dedicate as many resources as are desired. In the example below, there are 15 parallel query slave (factotum) processes and 16 gigabytes are allocated to sort the result set in RAM:

```
alter session set sort_area_size = 16384000000;

select /*+ full(sales) parallel(sales, 15) */
   customer_name,
   sum(purchase_amount)
from
   sales
group by
```

```
customer_name;
```

This type of parallel query is great, but what about a RAC database where there are many instances? In these cases, inter-instance parallelism can be created.

Oracle RAC and Inter-Instance Parallelism

The foundation of Oracle Real Application Clusters (RAC) revolves around parallelism, and long-term Oracle professionals remember that the original name for RAC was OPS, for Oracle Parallel Server.

With RAC, it is possible for an intra-parallel operation to utilize the processors across the nodes, using the second argument in the Oracle *parallel* hint. That gives an additional degree of parallelism while executing in parallel. For instance, a parallel query can be set up with *parallel* hint to utilize the CPUs from the many RAC instances as shown in Figure 9.6:

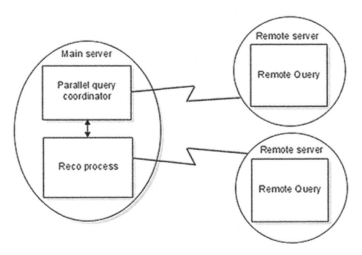

Figure 9.6: *Inter-instance parallel query*

In inter-instance parallel query, each instance requires a parallel query coordinator, many shops use n-1 parallelism, to reserve one CPU for the query coordinator. For example, if there are four instances, each with 4 CPUs, the SQL might use a degree of parallelism of three.

Hence, the query might look like this:

```
select /*+ full(sales) parallel(sales, 3,4) */
   customer_name,
```

```
    sum(purchase_amount)
from
    sales;
```

In this example, the degree of parallelism is three and all four instances are used. The query is executed with a total of 16 processes, 4 on each instance, and one parallel query coordinator on each instance as illustrated in Figure 9.7:

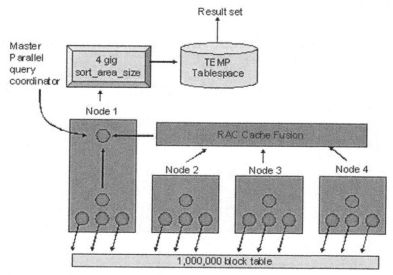

Figure 9.7: *Parallelism on Real Application Clusters*

From the illustration it becomes clear that the RAC implementation of the query might run slower than an equivalent query on a monolithic server with the same hardware. Note the differences between this RAC query and the vanilla Oracle parallel query on the monolithic server:

- **One-fourth fewer processes reading the table rows**: A process for the parallel query coordinator on each node must be reserved.

- **Overhead on the cache fusion layer**: As each node delivers the result set, the rows must be transferred to the master node that is controlling the query.

- **Slower sorting**: Because the master node only has 8 gig of RAM, the result set is too large to sort in-memory and a time consuming disk sort is required.

For more on using Oracle Real Application Clusters in a data warehouse, check out the book "*Oracle Real Application Clusters*" by Rampant TechPress.

Finding the Optimal Degree of Parallelism

Oracle is always improving, and the ability to detect the *cpu_count* and base parameters settings upon the external server environment is an important enhancement to Oracle software.

As more Oracle systems migrate to SMP, these derived Oracle parameters are even more important as Oracle customers undertake server consolidation and move dozens of databases onto giant servers with 32 or 64 CPUs.

The number of parallel query slave processes that service a table with the *degree* clause can be controlled. If the CPUs are available and the data is spread across many disks, the parallel *degree* is directly proportional to the SQL response time as illustrated in Figure 9.8:

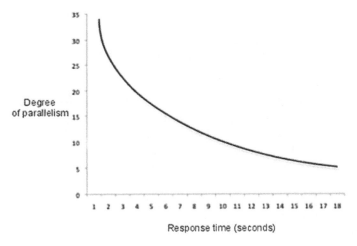

Figure 9.8: *More parallel processes means faster full-table scans*

The optimal *degree* of parallelism for a query is based on several factors. These factors are presented in their order of importance:

- **Processors**: The number of CPUs on the server are the most important factor, but this can be negated if the whole table resides on a single disk platter.

- **Disks:** The number of physical disks and the size of each disk are important for the optimal parallelism. When using SAME (Stripe and Mirror Everywhere, RAID-10) or ASM, the stripe size plays an important role in parallel query response time.

- **Partitioning**: For parallelizing queries by partition, the number of partitions that will be accessed, based upon partition pruning, if appropriate.

There are several formulas for computing the optimal degree of parallelism, and they are not perfect. The Oracle documentation provides a formula for computing the optimal degree of parallelism.

This is one possible formula for computing the optimal parallel degree:

```
P = ceil(D/max(floor(D/C), 1))
```

```
Where:
```

```
- P is based on the number of CPUs and the number of disks that the file is
striped onto.
```

```
- D is the number of disks  that the table is striped across (either
SQL*loader striping or OS striping).
```

```
- C is the number of CPUs available:
```

Before the age of super-large disks, the degree of parallelism could be optimized based on the number of disks that the table resides on, scaled down to be below *cpu_count*.

For example, if the server has 32 processors and the target table is striped across ten disks using ASM or RAID-10, a parallel degree higher than the disk stripe size might cause simultaneous requests from parallel processes on the same disk, causing enqueues. In this case, it would be necessary to start testing for the fastest degree using the number of disk stripes and increase to cpu_count-1, in this case testing from degree=10 up to degree=31.

However, this complex formula is not always suitable for the real world. A better rule for setting the degree of parallelism is to simply use the number of CPUs:

```
Optimal parallel degree = (number of CPUs)-1
```

As a general rule, the degree of parallelism can be set to the number of CPUs on the server, minus one, leaving the additional CPU for the parallel query coordinator. Remember, if when adopting this guideline, always be on the lookout for disk contention that will slow down the entire parallel query.

But it is not just the number of available processors that determines the optimal degree of parallelism. In many cases, disk enqueues can slow down parallel query. Today there is a plague of super-large disks devices, some with more than a terabyte on a single device. In a parallel query against a single disk drive, having many CPU processes may not matter since the disk will not be able to serve up simultaneous requests.

Find your optimal degree empirically!

Hot Tip!

There is no substitute for timing your parallel query. No amount of theory will be able to predict the optimal degree as well as you can by simply timing your parallel query with different degree values.

There has been a great deal of debate about what number of parallel processes results in the fastest response time. As a general rule, the optimal degree of parallelism can be safely set to N-1 where N is the number of processors in your SMP or MPP cluster. Remember, the proper degree of parallelism will always result in faster execution, provided you have a server with lots of CPUs.

When invoking parallel query, it is important to know the number of processors on the target server so that the optimal degree of parallelism can be set on the system. Here is how to check the CPUs on the Oracle server.

Checking CPU Count

Determining the number of processors is critical to determining the optimal parallelism, and there are commands for displaying the number of processors on the Oracle server.

Inside SQL*Plus, any of these other commands can be issued to see the *cpu_count*:

```
show parameter cpu

select
   value
from
   v$parameter
where
   name like 'cpu%;
```

There are also OS commands for revealing the number of CPUs on the server:

OS	Command
Linux	cat /proc/cpuinfo|grep processor|wc –l
Solaris	psrinfo -v|grep "Status of processor"|wc –l
AIX	lsdev -C|grep Process|wc –l
HP/UX	ioscan -C processor	grep processor	wc -l
Windows	Control panel → system

Table 9.1: *Display the number of CPU's for parallel query degree*

When using shell scripts for the SQL, the OS can be queried for *cpu_count* which can then be passed to the SQL:

```
#!/bin/ksh
# Get the CPU count:
num_cpu=`lsdev –C|grep mem|wc –l`

optimal_parallelism=`expr $num_cpu`-1

sqlplus system/manager<<!
select /*+ FULL(customer)
          PARALLEL(customer, $optimal_parallelism)*/
   cust__name
from
   customer;
exit
!
```

The next section will provide a closer look at the types of distributed parallelism that can be used in large Oracle environments.

Parallel Query for Distributed Instances

In a distributed environment, pieces of a table may reside on many remote servers. For example, assume there is a distributed architecture where local customer tables are kept on each instance. All of the remote rows could be accessed in a single query using inter-instance parallel execution. In this example, the query is executed from the *north_carolina* instance, accessing two remote instances in parallel:

```
select customer_name, sum(purchase_amount) from sales
union
select customer_name, sum(purchase_amount) from sales@san_francisco
union
select customer_name, sum(purchase_amount) from sales@new_york
group by
   customer_name;
```

In this case the *north_carolina* instance drives the distributed parallel query, and it is the *north_carolina* instance that must gather and sort the result set.

Oracle offers a wealth of distributed parallel query options, each with its own unique characteristics. The next section will explore the parallel query parameters and show how Oracle SQL can be configured for parallel execution.

Oracle Parallel Query Parameters

There are several initialization parameters that pertain to parallel query. The following are some of the parameters that Oracle sets at install time, based upon the *cpu_count*:

- *fast_start_parallel_rollback*
- *parallel_max_servers*
- *db_block_lru_latches*

There are also these parameters that control parallel query function:

- *parallel_adaptive_multi_user*
- *optimizer_percent_parallel*
- *fast_start_parallel_rollback*

Let's take a closer look at how the number of CPUs influences these parameters.

The *fast_start_parallel_rollback* Parameter

One exciting area of Oracle parallelism is the ability to invoke parallel rollbacks in cases of system crashes. In those rare cases when an Oracle database crashes, Oracle automatically detects in-flight transactions and rolls them back at startup time. This is called a parallel warmstart, and Oracle uses the *fast_start_parallel_rollback* parameter to govern the degree of parallelism for in-flight transactions based on the *cpu_count*.

Parallel data manipulation language (DML) recovery will dramatically speed up the time required to restart an Oracle database after an instance crash. The default value is two times the number of CPUs in the system, but some DBAs recommend setting this value to four times the *cpu_count*.

The *parallel_max_servers* Parameter

One significant enhancement within Oracle is the ability to automate the degree of parallelism for parallel query. Because Oracle is aware of the number of CPUs on the server, Oracle will automatically allocate the appropriate number of slave processes to maximize the response time of parallel queries.

Of course, there are other external factors, such as the use of table partitioning and the layout of your disk I/O subsystem, but setting the *parallel_max_servers* parameter will give Oracle a reasonable idea of the best degree of parallelism for your system, based on *cpu_count*.

Because Oracle parallel is heavily dependent on the number of CPUs on server, the default value for *parallel_max_servers* is set to the number of CPUs on the server. When running multiple instances on the same server, this default may be too high, in which case there will be excessive server paging and high CPU utilization.

The degree of parallelism is also dependent upon the number of partitions in the target table, so *parallel_max_servers* should be set high enough to allow Oracle to choose the best number of parallel query slaves for each query.

The *log_buffer* Parameter

Starting in Oracle 10g Release 2 and beyond, Oracle will automatically size the *log_buffer*, and *log_buffer* cannot be changed dynamically. The automatic *log_buffer* sizing is based on the granule size as determined by the *_ksmg_granule_size*.

The *db_block_lru_latches* Parameter

The number of LRU latches is used internally within the Oracle database to govern blocking within the Oracle database buffers, and this is heavily dependent upon the number of CPUs on the server.

Many savvy Oracle DBAs running multiple data buffers (e.g., *db_32k_cache_size*) recommend resetting this undocumented parameter to the recommended maximum value.

The default value for *db_block_lru_latches* is one-half the *cpu_count* on a dedicated server (e.g., only one Oracle database on the server). Oracle recommends that *db_block_lru_latches* never exceed *cpu_count* multiplied by 2 multiplied by 3, or *db_cache_size* divided by 50, whichever is higher.

There is a problem with this computation whenever there are multiple buffer pools (e.g., *keep*, *recycle*) because the number of latches assigned to each data buffer pool cannot be governed.

Each new release of Oracle brings exciting new improvements and features. Oracle 11g Release 2 is no exception.

Oracle 11g R2 Parallel Parameters

Newly introduced in Oracle 11g R2, there are several new parallel query parameters:

- The *parallel_degree_policy* parameter
- The *parallel_min_time_threshold* parameter
- The *parallel_degree_limit* parameter
- The *parallel_force_local* parameter

The next few sections will provide a closer look at these important enhancements to Oracle parallel query in 11g Release 2.

The *parallel_degree_policy* Parameter

The *parallel_degree_policy* parameter is related to the amount of table data residing in the data buffer cache. Using *parallel_degree_policy* allows Oracle to bypass direct path reads when Oracle determines that lots of the table data blocks already reside in the data buffer cache.

In traditional 32-bit systems, limited by only a few gig of RAM for the SGA, direct path reads, which bypass the SGA were always faster than reading a large table through the data buffer. However, with the advent of 64-bit servers with dozens of gigabytes for the *db_cache_size*, large tables are often be fully cached, negating the need to always perform direct path reads for parallel large-table full-table scans.

Some benchmark tests of *parallel_degree_policy* suggests that when *parallel_degree_policy=auto*, the optimizer will make the choice whether to use direct I/O vs. buffered I/O based on the size of the target table and the likelihood that table blocks might already exist within the data buffer caches.

The *parallel_min_time_threshold* Parameter

The *parallel_min_time_threshold* parameter only allows parallel query to be invoked against large tables or indexes, those where the *num_rows* suggests that it will take more than *nn* seconds to scan the table. The default for *parallel_min_time_threshold* is 30 (seconds), but this threshold can now be adjusted according to a judgment call about the optimal definition of what constitutes a large table. This parameter appears to be related to the deprecated *small_table_threshold* parameter.

The *parallel_degree_limit* Parameter

The *parallel_degree_limit* parameter sets a limit on the maximum degree of parallelism. The default is cpu_count*2.

The *parallel_force_local* Parameter

The *parallel_force_local* parameter prohibits parallel parallelism, a case where parallel queries on a RAC node are limited only to the local instance node.

Moving to take a closer look at parallel DML, the next section will show how large updates can be parallelized.

Parallel DML: *update, merge* and *delete*

SQL *updates, merges* and *deletes* can only be paralleled on partitioned tables. To specify parallel directives, follow one of the following methods:

- *alter session force parallel dml*

- Use an *update, merge* or *delete* parallel hint in the statement.

- Use a parallel clause in the definition of the table or reference object being updated or deleted.

The precedence rule in this category of operations is: Hint --> Session --> Parallel declaration specification of target table.

If the statement contains sub-queries or updatable views, they may have their own separate parallel hints or clauses. Remember, these parallel directives do not affect decisions to parallelize the *update, merge* or *delete* activities.

Once it is decided to use parallel processing, the maximum DOP that can be achieved in *delete, merge* and *update* is equal to the number of partitions or sub-partitions, in the case of composite sub-partitions, in the table.

Multiple partitions can be updated, merged into or deleted from by a single parallel execution, but each partition can only be updated or deleted by one parallel execution server at a time. Each parallel process transaction is a result of a different parallel execution server. Therefore, parallel DML requires multiple undo segments for performance.

However, there are some restrictions, quoting the Oracle documentation for accuracy, as shown below:

- A transaction can contain multiple parallel DML statements that modify different tables, but after a parallel DML statement modifies a table, no subsequent serial or parallel statement (DML or query) can access the same table again in that transaction.
  Parallel DML operations cannot be done on tables with triggers. Relevant triggers must be disabled in order to parallel DML on the table.

- A transaction involved in a parallel DML operation cannot be or become a distributed transaction.

- Clustered tables are not supported.

- Parallel DML: *insert .... select*

- An *insert ... select* statement parallels its *insert* and *select* operations independently, except for the DOP. The *insert* operation will be paralleled if at least one of the following is true:

  - The parallel hint is used in the *insert* in the DML statement.

  - The table being inserted into was specified with a parallel declaration specification.

  - The session is under the affect of an *alter session force parallel dml* statement.

The select statement follows its own set of rules, as specified in the query section. Only one parallel directive is picked for deciding the DOP of the whole statement. Then the chosen DOP is applied to both the *select* and *insert* operations using the precedence rule: Insert Hint directive --> Session --> Parallel declaration specification of the inserting table --> Maximum query directive.

Monitoring Oracle Parallel Query

Many Oracle professionals are not aware that Oracle provides system views to show the internal state of parallel queries.

To see how many parallel query servers are busy at any given time, the following query can be issued against the *v$pq_sysstat* view:

```
select
   statistic,
   value
from
   v$pq_sysstat
where
   statistic = 'Servers Busy';


STATISTIC          VALUE
---------          -----
```

In this case, there are 30 parallel servers busy at this moment. Do not be misled by this number. Parallel query servers are constantly accepting work or returning to idle status, so it is a good idea to issue the query many times over a one-hour period to get an accurate reading of parallel query activity. Only then will there be a realistic measure of how many parallel query servers are being used.

There is one other method for observing parallel query from inside Oracle. When running Oracle on UNIX, the ps command can be used to see the parallel query background processes in action:

```
ps -ef|grep "ora_p"
```

Oracle parallel query processes can be seen on the server because background processes will start when the query begins, and the processes can be watched through standard UNIX/Linux utilities.

These parallel query slave (factotum) processes are generally numbered from P000 through P*nnn*. The query below interrogates the *v$pq_tqstat* view to show execution details for each parallel query process:

🖫 parallel_tq_stats.sql

```
select
   tq_id,
   server_type,
   process,
   num_rows
from
   v$pq_tqstat
where
   dfo_number =
   (select max(dfo_number)
    from
       v$pq_tqstat)
order by
   tq_id,
   decode (substr(server_type,1,4),
     'Prod', 0, 'Cons', 1, 3)
;
```

TQ_ID	SERVER_TYP	PROCESS	NUM_ROWS
0	Producer	P003	173
0	Producer	P001	188
0	Producer	P004	219
0	Producer	P002	197
0	Producer	P000	777
0	Consumer	QC	796

The output shows five parallel query Producer processes, which correspond directly with the background processes P000 through P004.

Also, historical parallel queries can be monitoried using AWR and STATSPACK. Below, the *stats$sysstat* view is queried to reveal the number of parallel queries run over a specific time period:

🖫 statspack_opq.sql

```
set pages 9999;

column nbr_pq format 999,999,999
column mydate heading 'yr.  mo dy Hr.'

select
   to_char(snap_time,'yyyy-mm-dd HH24')        mydate,
   new.value  nbr_pq
from
   perfstat.stats$sysstat     old,
   perfstat.stats$sysstat     new,
   perfstat.stats$snapshot    sn
where
   new.name = old.name
and
   new.name = 'queries parallelized'
and
   new.snap_id = sn.snap_id
and
   old.snap_id = sn.snap_id-1
and
   new.value > 1
order by
   to_char(snap_time,'yyyy-mm-dd HH24')
;
```

```
yr.   mo dy      hr.        nbr_pq
------------   ------------------
2010-02-12      20          3,521
2010-02-12      21          2,082
2010-02-12      22          2,832
2010-02-13      20          5,152
2010-02-13      21          1,835
2010-02-13      22          2,623
2010-02-14      20          4,274
2010-02-14      21          1,429
2010-02-14      22          2,313
```

The *v$pq_sysstat* view can also be queried to see current parallel query activity:

```
select
   statistic,
   value
from
   v$pq_sysstat
where
```

```
   statistic = 'Servers Busy';
```

```
STATISTIC            VALUE
- - - - - - - - -    - - - - -
Servers Busy         43
```

At this instant in time, there are 43 parallel servers working. Remember, parallel query servers are constantly coming and going.

In sum, Oracle has several tools that can be used to watch the Oracle parallel query processes in action. This information is very useful when determining if parallelism is stressing the database server.

Bottlenecks in Oracle Parallel Query

The parallel query's divide and conquer approach clearly uses additional computing resources, and the performance of parallel query might be limited of external resources such as CPU, RAM and disk contention.

Remember, when 32 processes are assigned to service a query, system-wide resource consumption is created and if the 32 processes touch all of the disks on the system, the result could be massive disk waits.

Hence, it is important to examine the external environment when running large parallel queries.

Finding Disk Enqueues

The UNIX/Linux *iostat* utility can be used to see waits for individual disks, and when using disk arrays like EMC, the vendor has tools like EMC Symmetrix to look for waits on each disk spindle.

```
root> iostat 10
```

```
Disks:         % tm_act     Kbps      tps     Kb_read    Kb_wrtn

hdisk6           1.0         73.8      4.2     8999945    3314136
hdisk7           0.7         86.4      3.1    13790876     629660
hdisk8           0.0          0.6      0.0       90469       2176
hdisk9           0.8         74.4      3.1     9875281    2532636
hdisk10          0.5         54.6      1.7     9108228       3616
hdisk11          0.1         13.7      0.4     2279793        244
```

The following is a description of the key *iostat* output columns:

- **% tm_act:** The percentage of time that the disk was physically active.

- **Kbps:** The number of Kilobytes transferred per second.

- **tps:** the number of I/O requests to the disk. Note that multiple logical I/O requests may be merged into a single physical request.

- **Kb_read:** The number of Kilobytes read during the interval.

- **Kb_wrtn:** The number of Kilobytes written during the time interval.

In this example, the *iostat 10* command directs the OS to display one line of output for every disk, once every 10 seconds:

Also, disk-level enqueues can sometimes be seen in some dialects of UNIX, for example the wait column (*wa*) in the AIX *vmstat* utility.

Finding CPU Slowdowns

While there is variety of OS tools to look for CPU enqueues, it is important to remember that 100% CPU utilization is not a problem because processors are designed to throttle to 100%. In fact, it is considered normal.

Instead, the *runqueue* (*r*) column in the *vmstat* utility, the far-left column is where to look:

```
root> vmstat 5 5
```

```
kthr      memory              page                     faults          cpu
----- ----------- ------------------------ ------------- -----------
 r  b   avm    fre  re  pi  po  fr   sr  cy   in    sy   cs  us sy id wa
 7  5 220214   141   0   0   0   42   53   0 1724 12381 2206  19 46 28  7
 9  5 220933   195   0   0   1  216  290   0 1952 46118 2712  27 55 13  5
13  5 220646   452   0   0   1   33   54   0 2130 86185 3014  30 59  8  3
 6  5 220228   672   0   0   0    0    0   0 1929 25068 2485  25 49 16 10
```

The rule is simple. Whenever the *runqueue* exceeds the *cpu_count*, tasks are waiting on processing resources. In the listing above, CPU *runqueue* ranges from 6 to 13.

On a server where *cpu_count=8*, this would indicate CPU enqueues but on a server where *cpu_count=16*, there would be no CPU enqueue issues.

To add yet another set of tools to the toolbox, there are special scripts to see the internals of parallel queries.

Parallel Query Execution Plans

This chapter has shown that the parallel hint can be embedded into SQL to specify the number of parallel query slave processes. Inside parallel SQL plans it is important to see the *other_tag* in the execution plan.

🖫 parallel_plan.sql

```
set echo off
set long 2000
set pagesize 10000

column query       heading "Query Plan" format a80
column other       heading "PQO/Remote Query" format a60 word_wrap
column x           heading " " format a18

select distinct
   object_node "TQs / Remote DBs"
from
   plan_table
where
   object_node is not null
order by
   object_node;

select lpad(' ',2*(level-1))||operation||' '||options||' '
     ||object_name||' '
     ||decode(optimizer,'','','['||optimizer||'] ')
||decode(other_tag,'',decode(object_node,'','','['||object_node||']')
,'['||other_tag||' -> '||object_node||']')
     ||decode(id,0,'Cost = '||position) query
     ,null  x
     ,other
from
   plan_table
start with id = 0
connect by prior id = parent_id;
```

To see a parallel query execution plan, the different display formats for the execution plans for *parallel_plan.sql* should be examined.

```
select /*+ use_merge(e,b) parallel(e, 4) parallel(b, 4) */
   e.ename,
   hiredate,
   b.comm
from
   emp e,
   bonus b
where
   e.ename = b.ename
;
```

To see the difference between a standard explain plan and an enhanced parallel query execution plan, the following is a sample output from a standard execution plan:

```
OPERATION
----------------------------------------------------------------
OPTIONS                         OBJECT_NAME                POSITION
----------------------------    ------------------------   --------
OTHER_TAG
----------------------------------------------------------------
SELECT STATEMENT
                                                               5
  MERGE JOIN
                                                               1
PARALLEL_TO_SERIAL
    SORT
JOIN                                                           1
PARALLEL_COMBINED_WITH_PARENT
      TABLE ACCESS
FULL                            EMP                            1
PARALLEL_TO_PARALLEL
    SORT
JOIN                                                           2
PARALLEL_COMBINED_WITH_PARENT
      TABLE ACCESS
FULL                            BONUS                          1
PARALLEL_TO_PARALLEL
```

The following is the same execution plan displayed with parallel_plan.sql:

```
TQs / Remote DBs
----------------------------------------------------------------
:Q36000
:Q36001
:Q36002


Query Plan
----------------------------------------------------------------
                    PQO/Remote Query
------------------  --------------------------------------------
SELECT STATEMENT    [FIRST_ROWS] Cost = 5

  MERGE JOIN    [PARALLEL_TO_SERIAL -> :Q36002]
                SELECT /*+ ORDERED NO_EXPAND USE_MERGE(A2) */
                A1.C0,A1.C1,A2.C1 FROM :Q36000 A1,:Q36001 A2 WHERE
                A1.C0=A2.C0

    SORT JOIN   [PARALLEL_COMBINED_WITH_PARENT -> :Q36002]

      TABLE ACCESS FULL EMP [PARALLEL_TO_PARALLEL -> :Q36000]
                SELECT /*+ NO_EXPAND ROWID(A1) */ A1."ENAME"
                C0,A1."HIREDATE" C1 FROM "EMP" A1
                WHERE ROWID BETWEEN :B1
                AND :B2

    SORT JOIN   [PARALLEL_COMBINED_WITH_PARENT -> :Q36002]

      TABLE ACCESS FULL BONUS [PARALLEL_TO_PARALLEL -> :Q36001]
                SELECT /*+ NO_EXPAND ROWID(A1) */
                A1."ENAME" C0,A1."COMM" C1
                FROM "BONUS" A1 WHERE ROWID BETWEEN :B1 AND :B2
```

The enhanced explain plan shows considerable more detail about the internals of the execution plan, including details about the parallel query execution modes as noted in the *other_tag*.

The *other_tag* column is used by Oracle to provide additional detail about the type of parallel operation that is being performed during the execution of the query. Here are the possible values for *other_tag*:

- **Serial:** The *serial* tag indicates a linear operation such as an index scan.

- **Parallel_to_serial:** The *parallel_to_serial* tag is normally the first step in the execution plan, and it is where a parallel full-table scan is passed to the query coordinator for merging.

- **Parallel_from_serial:** The *parallel_from_serial* tag denotes a condition where the parallel processes must wait for a serial operation to complete. This could be a warning that a query may not be optimized, since the parallel processes are not allowed to begin immediately upon execution of the query.

- **Parallel_to_parallel:** The *parallel_to_parallel* tag is when a sort merge join doing a parallel full-table scan is immediately followed by a parallel disk sort in the *temp* tablespace.

- **Parallel_combined_with_parent:** This tag denotes a parallel full-table scan that is combined with an index lookup, such as a *nested loops* join.

- **Parallel_combined_with_child:** The *parallel_combined_with_child* tag denotes a case where a parallel full-table scan is combined with a child operation.

Look Out!

Beware of parallel_from_serial!

The parallel_from_serial tag might indicate a bottleneck as parallel query slave processes are waiting unnecessarily for a serial operation, such as an index range scan.

Conclusion

This chapter has explored the use of parallel query to speed up SQL that performs full-scan operations. The main points of this chapter include:

- Parallel query is only useful for full scan operations, and queries that access tables via indexes will see no benefit from parallel query.

- Parallel query can be set at the database level, the table level, the session level and the query level. Specialized scripts like *parallel_plan.sql* can be used to see the parallel details of parallelized queries.

- Table-level parallelism should only be enabled if the vast majority of SQL performs full scan operations. Altering a table to parallel changes the costing within the optimizer to make full scans appear cheaper.

- Parallel query is enabled with parameters that change radically between releases of Oracle.

- Use automatic parallelism only with data warehouse and decision support applications that are using *all_rows* optimization and the vast majority of queries perform full scans.

- While there are formulas for determining the optimal degree of parallelism, simple testing with different values is the fastest and most reliable method.

- The best way to enable parallelism is by using the *parallel* hint.

Now, it is time to move on to the next chapter and take a look at how views can be useful for SQL tuning.

SQL Tuning with Views

Using views mask the complexity of a query

Inside Oracle Views

Internally, an Oracle view is simply the representation of a SQL statement that is stored in the data dictionary so that it can easily be reused. Functionally, a view hides all of the tables from the end-user, and the view behaves as if it were a single table.

For example, if the following SQL query were frequently issued, it could be encapsulated into the data dictionary:

```
select
   empid
from
   emp;
```

For example purposes, it might make sense to make this a view. In reality, it is unlikely a view would never be created for a statement this simple, but it is important to start with an easy example.

To create a view use the create view command as seen in this example:

```
create view
   view_emp
as
select
   empid
from
   emp;
```

This command creates a new view called *view_emp*. This command does not result in anything being actually stored in the database at all except for a data dictionary entry that defines this view.

This means that every time the query is viewed, Oracle has to go out and execute the view and query the database data. The view can be queried like this:

```
select
   *
from
   view_emp
where
   empid between 500 and 1000;
```

And Oracle will transform the query into this:

```
select
   *
from
   (select empid from emp)
where
   empid between 500 and 1000;
```

An Oracle view can also be used to encapsulate a complex query into a single pseudo-table that behaves like a single table. For example, the following creates a view:

```
create or replace view
   cust_view
as
select
   customer_name,
   order_nbr,
   item_desc
from
   customer      c,
   order         o,
   item          i,
where
   c.cust_nbr = o.cust_nbr
```

```
and
   o_item_nbr = i.item_nbr;
```

The pseudotable in the following query hides the complexity of the underlying query and has no effect on the performance of the underlying SQL:

```
select
   *
from
   cust_view
where
   cust_nbr = 123;
```

In this example, every time the *cust_view* is queried, Oracle will join the three tables at runtime.

Since views do not improve performance, why use them? Most Oracle shops that employ views do so for end-user queries or for queries where they want to hide complexity and ensure uniform join methods.

Tuning SQL with Views

The relational database model brought with it the concept of views for the simplification of relational algebra, as it were. This provides a way to name a complex query and treat it as if it were a discrete table:

```
create view
   myview
as
select
   stuff
from
   tableA
natural join
   tableB
natiral join
   tableC;
```

Now, the query can be simplified logically, but physically, all of the SQL in the underlying view is executed at run-time:

```
select
   stuff
from
   myview
where
   xxx=yyy;
```

Oracle views provide a benefit in code reuse because the views ensure that everyone uses the exact same SQL to access their tables and column access security. Using the grant security model, views can be used for column-level security, such that some columns in a table may be hidden by not specifying them in a view.

All benefits come at a cost, and one downside to using views is that it adds complexity to the SQL and makes it harder for the optimizer to service a query with the minimum amount of resources, either I/O or CPU resources, depending on the optimizer goal.

Benefits of Oracle Views

Oracle views offer some compelling benefits. These include:

- **Commonality of code:** Since a view is based on one common set of SQL, this means that when it is called it's less likely to require parsing. This is because the basic underlying SQL that is called is always the same. However, since additional where clauses can be added when calling a view, it is still necessary to use bind variables. Additional *where* clauses without a bind variable can still cause a hard parse!

- **Security**: Views have long been used to hide the tables that actually contain the data being queried. Also, views can be used to restrict the columns that a given user has access to. Using views for security on less complex databases is probably not a bad thing. As databases become more complex, this solution becomes harder to scale and other solutions will be needed.

- **Predicate pushing**: Oracle supports pushing of predicates into a given view.

There are always costs to any tool that provides benefits, and the following sections will examine the drawbacks of tuning SQL with Oracle views.

Drawbacks in Tuning SQL that Contains Views

Some shops create complex views to represent large subsets of their schema and allow developers and end users to access these views. This approach often leads to poor performance. Here are some situations to avoid when working with complex views:

- **Querying subsets:** Developers will often query a subset of the complex view, not realizing that all tables in the view will be joined.

- **Adding complex *where* clauses:** Running SQL against views with complex *where* clauses will often override any tuning hints that are placed within the view, causing suboptimal execution plans.

- **Hinting the view:** A view cannot be treated as a real table, and adding SQL hints to view queries will often result in suboptimal execution plans. Remember, any time the optimizer gets confused, it will perform an unnecessary full-table scan. While hints can be used for specific SQL optimization, the use of views is strongly discouraged with hints because they can be invoked in many contexts.

While it is apparent that views are useful for end-user ad-hoc queries and cases where the goal is to simplify the syntax of complex SQL queries, there is a serious problem when queries contain views.

- **Predicate pushing:** The downside to reusable code is that *where* clause predicates must be pushed down the hierarchy of views, down to the base query. This adds processing overhead to the optimizer and increases the chances of a bad execution plan.

- **Non mergeable:** Because a view is an encapsulation of a complex query, it is used as if it were a discrete relational table. Hence, Oracle must pre-materialize a view whenever it is used in a query. This creates a hidden sub-plan that must be exposed for SQL tuning.

- **Unnecessary overhead:** Views are abused when they introduce unnecessary complexity. One example would be calling a view that is composed of 10 tables where the result set only requires data from two tables.

- **Excessive hard parsing:** Predicate pushing may result in a hard parse of the underlying SQL that is executed. Hence, it is important to make sure to use bind variables instead of literals in SQL code calling views. Thus, the SQL should look something like this instead for best performance:

```
select
    *
from
    vw_layer_two_dept_100
where
    empid=:b100;
```

To understand why views make it difficult to tune SQL, it would be helpful to look at what happens when a view is used with a *where* clause. To function, Oracle must push the *where* clause predicate to the underlying view.

Abusing Views in Oracle SQL

Views are very handy but they get badly abused, which is a shame. In my experience, I have seen views that return 50 columns and have 40 predicates used to return just two or three columns that could easily have been retrieved from a simple SQL query. This is clearly a case of view abuse and can lead to badly performing views.

Stacked views can also mask performance problems. Again, they can result in innumerable columns being returned when all that is really needed are a few of those columns. Also, predicate pushing tends to break down as views are stacked on top of more views.

Before stacking views, carefully review the rules for predicate pushing in the Oracle documentation. But beware, the predicate pushing rules are long and involved and may change between each release of Oracle!

Next, it is time to dive deeper and explore merging views and predicate pushing and then move on to examine complex SQL tuning with Oracle views.

Merging Views and SQL Tuning

At optimization time, the optimizer will attempt to flatten out the views by building and optimizing one large query against the base tables that comprise the view. This is known as merging views, and a merge is critical to avoid a hidden sub-plan from being introduced into the SQL.

When tuning SQL and there is the *view* notation in the explain plan, there may be a non-mergeable view:

```
select
    count(1) from(
    select distinct pat_id from
    (
        select
        p.pat_id,
        p.pat_last_name,
        p.pat_first_name,
        v.visit_id,
        v.arrive_dt_tm,
        v.depart_dt_tm,
        r.test_id,
        r.test_name,
        r.result_dt_tm,
        r.result_val
from
    patient p,
    pat_visit v,
    pat_result r
where
    p.pat_id=1
and
    p.pat_id=v.pat_id
and
    v.pat_id=r.pat_id)
);
```

The following is the view in the execution plan, indicating a sub-plan:

ID	PID	Operation Name	Rows	Bytes	Cost	CPU Cost	IO Cost
0		SELECT STATEMENT	1	2	8	25M	6
1	0	SORT AGGREGATE	1	2			

2	1	VIEW		1	2	8	25M	6
3	2	SORT UNIQUE NOSORT		1	24	8	25M	6
4	3	HASH JOIN		125	3000	7	8484914	6
5	4	NESTED LOOPS		5	90	3	42157	3
6	5	INDEX UNIQUE SCAN	XPKPATIENT	1	9	0	1050	0
7	5	TABLE ACCESS FULL	PAT_VISIT	5	45	3	41107	3
8	4	TABLE ACCESS FULL	PAT_RESULT	25	150	3	63107	3

Note that the *view* notation in an explain plan means that the view is not mergeable and Oracle must run a sub-plan, which is hidden.

Here are some more examples of the *view* generating a hidden sub-plan within the SQL:

Id	Operation	Name	Rows	Bytes	TempSpc	Cost (%CPU)	Time
0	SELECT STATEMENT					25382 (100)	
1	SORT ORDER BY		1371	404K		25382 (2)	00:02:30
2	NESTED LOOPS		1371	404K		25381 (2)	00:02:30
3	HASH JOIN		1366	368K		22646 (2)	00:02:14
4	HASH JOIN		8097	1866K		22270 (2)	00:02:12
5	HASH JOIN		9821	1707K	2064K	21475 (2)	00:02:07
6	VIEW		47886	1496K		794 (2)	00:00:05
7	HASH GROUP BY		47886	1683K	4904K	794 (2)	00:00:05
8	NESTED LOOPS		47886	1683K		333 (1)	00:00:02
9	VIEW		3	39		4 (0)	00:00:01
10	UNION-ALL						
11	FAST DUAL		1			2 (0)	00:00:01
12	INDEX RANGE SCAN	XRS_TAB_ORDERHIST_IDX	2	20		2 (0)	00:00:01
13	INDEX RANGE SCAN	PERF1_DECIND_APHCR	15962	358K		110 (1)	00:00:01
14	HASH JOIN		68374	9748K	8392K	20065 (2)	00:01:59
15	HASH JOIN		68153	7587K	7232K	10506 (2)	00:01:02
16	HASH JOIN		67921	6433K	5512K	1853 (2)	00:00:11
17	TABLE ACCESS FULL	TRAPPROVAL	67921	4709K		292 (2)	00:00:02
18	TABLE ACCESS FULL	TR_PLOTRVERSION	171K	4342K		979 (2)	00:00:06
19	TABLE ACCESS FULL	TRSPECAH	1196K	19M		6623 (2)	00:00:39
20	TABLE ACCESS FULL	TRSPECAH	1196K	36M		6623 (2)	00:00:39
21	VIEW		47886	2712K		794 (2)	00:00:05
22	HASH GROUP BY		47886	1683K	4904K	794 (2)	00:00:05
23	NESTED LOOPS		47886	1683K		333 (1)	00:00:02
24	VIEW		3	39		4 (0)	00:00:01
25	UNION-ALL						
26	FAST DUAL		1			2 (0)	00:00:01
27	INDEX RANGE SCAN	XRS_TAB_ORDERHIST_IDX	2	20		2 (0)	00:00:01
28	INDEX RANGE SCAN	PERF1_DECIND_APHCR	15962	358K		110 (1)	00:00:01
29	TABLE ACCESS FULL	TRAPPLROAM	113K	4439K		373 (2)	00:00:03
30	TABLE ACCESS BY INDEX ROWID	TRSPECAH	1	26		2 (0)	00:00:01
31	INDEX UNIQUE SCAN	TRKTRSPECAH	1			1 (0)	00:00:01

Id	Operation	Name	Rows	Bytes	TempSpc	Cost (%CPU)	Time
0	SELECT STATEMENT					21620 (100)	
1	SORT ORDER BY		79	27334		21620 (2)	00:02:08
2	HASH UNIQUE		79	27334		21619 (2)	00:02:08
3	HASH JOIN RIGHT OUTER		79	27334		21618 (2)	00:02:08
4	VIEW		1	19		2302 (1)	00:00:14
5	HASH GROUP BY		1	58		2302 (1)	00:00:14
6	VIEW		1	58		2302 (1)	00:00:14
7	FILTER						
8	HASH GROUP BY		1	189		2302 (1)	00:00:14
9	HASH JOIN		2	378		2301 (1)	00:00:14
10	NESTED LOOPS		310	50840		1876 (1)	00:00:12
11	NESTED LOOPS		310	43400		1255 (2)	00:00:08
12	HASH JOIN		305	35380		644 (3)	00:00:04
13	HASH JOIN		1359	84258		11 (10)	00:00:01
14	TABLE ACCESS FULL	XRTRATE	1359	38052		5 (0)	00:00:01
15	TABLE ACCESS FULL	XRTRATE	1359	46206		5 (0)	00:00:01
16	TABLE ACCESS FULL	XRTTIMECARD	153K	8086K		631 (2)	00:00:04
17	TABLE ACCESS BY INDEX ROWID	XRTTASK	1	24		2 (0)	00:00:01
18	INDEX UNIQUE SCAN	XRT_TASK	1			1 (0)	00:00:01
19	INDEX RANGE SCAN	XRT_FOLDER_APPLROAM	1	24		2 (0)	00:00:01
20	TABLE ACCESS BY INDEX ROWID	TRSPECAH	2062	51550		425 (1)	00:00:03
21	INDEX RANGE SCAN	XRT_FOLDER_APPLLOC	2065			8 (0)	00:00:01
22	HASH JOIN OUTER		79	25833		19315 (2)	00:01:54
23	NESTED LOOPS		79	24490		19309 (2)	00:01:54
24	HASH JOIN OUTER		79	17775		19298 (2)	00:01:54
25	HASH JOIN OUTER		79	16274		10343 (2)	00:01:01
26	HASH JOIN OUTER		79	14773		9908 (2)	00:00:59
27	HASH JOIN OUTER		79	13272		9453 (2)	00:00:56
28	HASH JOIN		79	10744		1129 (1)	00:00:07

```
|  29 |          NESTED LOOPS               |                     |    79 | 10270 |       |   259 | (0)| 00:00:02 |
|  30 |           NESTED LOOPS OUTER        |                     |    79 |  4187 |       |   101 | (0)| 00:00:01 |
|  31 |            NESTED LOOPS             |                     |    79 |  2765 |       |    43 | (0)| 00:00:01 |
|  32 |             TABLE ACCESS BY INDEX ROWID| X_COMPANY        |     1 |    14 |       |     2 | (0)| 00:00:01 |
|  33 |              INDEX UNIQUE SCAN      | XPKC_COMPANY        |     1 |       |       |     1 | (0)| 00:00:01 |
|  34 |             TABLE ACCESS BY INDEX ROWID| XRLOW_FOLDER     |    79 |  1659 |       |    41 | (0)| 00:00:01 |
|  35 |              INDEX RANGE SCAN       | XRT_FOLDER_PID      |    79 |       |       |     2 | (0)| 00:00:01 |
|  36 |            TABLE ACCESS BY INDEX ROWID | XRT_SRPRO_GROUP   |     1 |    18 |       |     1 | (0)| 00:00:01 |
|  37 |             INDEX UNIQUE SCAN       | XRTC_MASRPRO_GROUP  |     1 |       |       |     0 | (0)|          |
|  38 |           TABLE ACCESS BY INDEX ROWID | TRSPECAH          |     1 |    77 |       |     2 | (0)| 00:00:01 |
|  39 |            INDEX UNIQUE SCAN        | XRTTRSPECAH         |     1 |       |       |     1 | (0)| 00:00:01 |
|  40 |       VIEW                          |                     | 52536 |  307K |       |   868 | (2)| 00:00:06 |
|  41 |        HASH GROUP BY                |                     | 52536 | 1846K | 5368K |   868 | (2)| 00:00:06 |
|  42 |         NESTED LOOPS               |                     | 52536 | 1846K |       |   363 | (1)| 00:00:03 |
|  43 |          VIEW                       |                     |     3 |    39 |       |     4 | (0)| 00:00:01 |
|  44 |           UNION-ALL                 |                     |       |       |       |       |    |          |
|  45 |            FAST DUAL                |                     |     1 |       |       |     2 | (0)| 00:00:01 |
|  46 |            INDEX RANGE SCAN         | XRS_TAB_ORDERHIST_IDX |   2 |    20 |       |     2 | (0)| 00:00:01 |
|  47 |          INDEX RANGE SCAN          | XRSTR_TRSPECAH_SEC  | 17512 |  393K |       |   120 | (1)| 00:00:01 |
|  48 |       VIEW                          |                     |  2062 | 65984 |       |  8323 | (2)| 00:00:49 |
|  49 |        HASH GROUP BY                |                     |  2062 | 76294 |       |  8323 | (2)| 00:00:49 |
|  50 |         HASH JOIN                   |                     |  7188 |  259K |       |  8322 | (2)| 00:00:49 |
|  51 |          HASH JOIN                 |                     |  8454 |  206K |       |  1862 | (3)| 00:00:11 |
|  52 |           TABLE ACCESS BY INDEX ROWID | TRSPECAH          |  2062 | 26806 |       |   425 | (1)| 00:00:03 |
|  53 |            INDEX RANGE SCAN         | XRT_PROJECT_PROJID  |  2065 |       |       |     8 | (0)| 00:00:01 |
|  54 |           INDEX FAST FULL SCAN     | XRT_PROJECT_FID_PRNT| 1415K |   16M |       |  1417 | (3)| 00:00:09 |
|  55 |          TABLE ACCESS FULL         | XRTASK              | 1197K |   13M |       |  6441 | (2)| 00:00:38 |
|  56 |       VIEW                          |                     |  2062 | 39178 |       |   454 | (1)| 00:00:03 |
|  57 |        HASH GROUP BY                |                     |  2062 | 49488 |       |   454 | (1)| 00:00:03 |
|  58 |         HASH JOIN                   |                     |  4206 | 98K   |       |   453 | (1)| 00:00:03 |
|  59 |          TABLE ACCESS BY INDEX ROWID | TRSPECAH           |  2062 | 26806 |       |   425 | (1)| 00:00:03 |
|  60 |           INDEX RANGE SCAN         | XRT_PROJECT_PROJID  |  2065 |       |       |     8 | (0)| 00:00:01 |
|  61 |          TABLE ACCESS FULL         | XR_EXPENSES_PURCH   |  6431 | 70741 |       |    27 | (0)| 00:00:01 |
|  62 |       VIEW                          |                     |   852 | 16188 |       |   434 | (1)| 00:00:03 |
|  63 |        HASH GROUP BY                |                     |   852 | 19596 |       |   434 | (1)| 00:00:03 |
|  64 |         HASH JOIN                   |                     |  2380 | 54740 |       |   433 | (1)| 00:00:03 |
|  65 |          TABLE ACCESS BY INDEX ROWID | TRSPECAH           |  2062 | 26806 |       |   425 | (1)| 00:00:03 |
|  66 |           INDEX RANGE SCAN         | XRT_PROJECT_PROJID  |  2065 |       |       |     8 | (0)| 00:00:01 |
|  67 |          TABLE ACCESS FULL         | XR_EXPENSES_PURCH   |  2380 | 23800 |       |     8 | (0)| 00:00:01 |
|  68 |       VIEW                          |                     |  1148 | 21812 |       |  8955 | (2)| 00:00:53 |
|  69 |        HASH GROUP BY                |                     |  1148 | 57400 |       |  8955 | (2)| 00:00:53 |
|  70 |         HASH JOIN                   |                     |  1148 | 57400 |       |  8954 | (2)| 00:00:53 |
|  71 |          HASH JOIN                 |                     |  7188 |  259K |       |  8322 | (2)| 00:00:49 |
|  72 |           HASH JOIN               |                     |  8454 |  206K |       |  1862 | (3)| 00:00:11 |
|  73 |            TABLE ACCESS BY INDEX ROWID | TRSPECAH         |  2062 | 26806 |       |   425 | (1)| 00:00:03 |
|  74 |             INDEX RANGE SCAN      | XRT_PROJECT_PROJID  |  2065 |       |       |     8 | (0)| 00:00:01 |
|  75 |            INDEX FAST FULL SCAN   | XR_EXPENSES_PURCH   | 1415K |   16M |       |  1417 | (3)| 00:00:09 |
|  76 |           TABLE ACCESS FULL       | XRTASK              | 1197K |   13M |       |  6441 | (2)| 00:00:38 |
|  77 |          TABLE ACCESS FULL         | XRT_SRPRO_GROUP     |  184K | 2338K |       |   628 | (2)| 00:00:04 |
|  78 |         TABLE ACCESS BY INDEX ROWID | XR_EXPENSES_PURCH  |     1 |    85 |       |     1 | (0)| 00:00:01 |
|  79 |          INDEX UNIQUE SCAN         | XRT_PROJECT_PROJID  |     1 |       |       |     0 | (0)|          |
|  80 | TABLE ACCESS FULL                  | XRT_SRPRO_GROUP     |  1715 | 29155 |       |     6 | (0)| 00:00:01 |
```

Remember, seeing the *view* is expensive because the optimizer must stop processing until it can materialize the view for use by the main query execution plan.

But this is not the only issue with tuning SQL that uses views. There is also the issue of predicate pushing.

Predicate Pushing with Views

The Oracle SQL tuning problem becomes a nightmare when views are nested within other views. Oracle supports pushing of predicates into a given view. Assume there is a set of nested views, like this, where view 1 is referenced inside view 2. Also assume there is a set of layered views, like this:

```
-- *******************************************
-- view one
-- *******************************************
create view
   vw_layer_one
as
select
   *
from
   emp;
```

```
-- *********************************************
-- view two restricts the rows from view one
-- *********************************************
create view
   vw_layer_two_dept_100
as
select
   *
from
   vw_layer_one
where
   deptno=100;
```

Then this query is issued:

```
select *
from
   vw_layer_two_dept_100
where
   empid=100;
```

The predicate in this SQL is the *where empid=100* statement. There may be one or tens or even hundreds of predicates. The Oracle optimizer is written to push" predicates down into the views that are being referenced in the SQL. Thus, Oracle will transform the *vw_layer_one* view into a SQL statement that looks like this:

```
create view
   vw_layer_one
as
   select * from emp
where
   deptno=100
and
  empid=100;
```

Note that both the predicate from view two (*where deptno=100*) and the predicate from the SQL statement being executed (*where empid=100*) are pushed down into the final view that is executed. This can have significant performance benefits because now the bottom view can possibly use an index if one exists on *deptno* and/or *empid*.

Predicate pushing has a number of restrictions that are beyond the scope of this book, but more detailed information is available in the Oracle documentation.

Also, any predicate pushing may result in a hard parse of the underlying SQL that is executed. Hence, it is important to make sure bind variables are used instead of literals in SQL code calling views. Thus, the SQL should look something like the following instead for best performance:

```
select
   *
from
```

```
   vw_layer_two_dept_100
where
   empid=:b100;
```

Thus, predicate pushing can get very complex and predicate pushing presents the following gotchas:

- **Unnecessary overhead:** Calling views composed of many tables when data is only required from one or two.

- **Hard parsing**: Using literals in the SQL rather than bind variables when calling SQL code views. This source of predicate pushing can result in expensive hard parsing.

The next potential source of performance problems comes when hints are used against views.

Combining Hints and Views

Although it is important to be particularly careful when using hints against a view, the following are two ways they can be used without creating performance problems:

- Hints can be embedded inside the view definition. This is useful for cases where a view will be called without a where clause, but it can be quite damaging to performance when the view result set is altered by calling the view with a complex where clause.

- Hints can be added in the calling query. The danger with using hints in views is that the context of the query may change. When this happens, any existing hints within the view definition may be ignored, which can confuse the SQL optimizer and result in an unnecessary full-table scan.

When views are invoked with certain *where* clauses, the context of the view may change, as will the functionality of any SQL hints that may be embedded inside the view. This simple example shows how such a context change can occur:

```
select
   cust_name,
   cust_address
from
   cust_view
where
   cust_nbr = 123;
```

In this case, a view that performs a three-way table join on execution has been invoked, but the *where* clause in the SQL indicates that the user is interested only in data within a single table. Any SQL hints that might be embedded inside the view may be ignored.

Views and join elimination

Oracle join elimination was introduced in 10gr2 to prevent unnecessary joins of tables that reside inside views. In essence, join elimination is a part of the 11g tuning transformations.

In essence, Oracle join elimination is transparent and simple. Prior to 10gr2, a view that had a 10-way join would always join all ten tables together, regardless of the number of tables that were required to service the query. Rather than calling this unnecessary table joining a bug, Oracle fixed the problem and called it "join elimination".

Prior to executing a view, Oracle interrogates the original query, working backwards to see of all of the tables inside the view are required to deliver the result set. If not, Oracle will not join superfluous tables, thereby cutting-down on the number of joins and improving response time.

The new join elimination transformation has the JE abbreviation that is used within an optimizer trace file to indicate a join elimination. For example, an optimizer trace file might refer to a join elimination thusly:

```
JE: eliminate table: DEPARTMENTS
```

The next section will cover SQL tuning with in-line views.

Oracle In-line Views

Using in-line views, you are able to substitute a table name in an SQL from clause with a query. This extension allows for the formation of very unique and specific queries. For example, below are two simple SQL queries.

They both count the number of customers in the Southwestern region of the United States but go about doing so in two very different ways.
The first uses standard SQL:

```
select
    count(*)
from
    customer
where
    region= 'south';
```

The second query uses an in-line view:

```
select
```

```
   count(*)
from
   (select * from customer where region= 'south');
```

In-line views are often used in Oracle SQL to simplify complex queries. This is done by removing join operations and condensing several individual queries into one.

A good example of this consolidation is the script that shows the amount of free space within all Oracle tablespaces.

The *tsfree.sql* is an SQL script that queries the data dictionary to see the amount of free space within the database tablespace in Oracle. This script is routinely used as a tool for Oracle database administration.

In-line views are a powerful component of SQL because they allow the combination of several SQL queries into a single statement.

Note that the *from* clause in this SQL below specifies two sub-queries. These queries perform the summations and grouping of the *dba data flies* and *dba free space* views.

🖫 tsfree.sql

```
column "Tablespace" format a13
column "Used MB"    format 99,999,999
column "Free MB"    format 99,999,999
colimn "Total MB"   format 99,999,999

select
   fs.tablespace_name                          "Tablespace",
   (df.totalspace - fs.freespace)              "Used MB",
   fs.freespace                                "Free MB",
   df.totalspace                               "Total MB",
   round(100 * (fs.freespace / df.totalspace)) "Pct. Free"
from
   (select
      tablespace_name,
      round(sum(bytes) / 1048576) TotalSpace
   from
      dba_data_files
   group by
      tablespace_name
   ) df,
   (select
      tablespace_name,
      round(sum(bytes) / 1048576) FreeSpace
   from
      dba_free_space
   group by
      tablespace_name
   ) fs
where
   df.tablespace_name = fs.tablespace_name;
```

This SQL statement compares the amount of total space within each tablespace.

```
SQL> @tsfree
```

Tablespace	Used MB	Free MB	Total MB	Pct. Free
XANNOD	6	44	50	88
RBNNOX	5	45	50	90
RBLOKX	5	0	5	0
SGRLLPD	2	8	10	80
SGDOUPX	2	8	10	80
BRBS	68	32	100	32
RDVSSERD	2	18	20	90

This in-line view saves much time for the DBA. If using ANSI standard SQL, it would be necessary to write several SQL queries to compute this information, one to compute the sums for each view and another to compare the intermediate results.

It is important to remember that the *dba_free_space* and *dba_data_files* views are reliant on underlying internal Oracle structures. Despite this complexity, the *tsfree.sql* script runs very quickly when returning the tablespace report. The execution plan for this report is shown below. It is easy to appreciate the complexity of this listing.

The Oracle optimizer has a difficult job deciding which execution plan is best for this query. This speaks volumes for the power and efficacy of the Oracle analyzer:

```
OPERATION
-----------------------------------------------------------------------OPTIONS
OBJECT_NAME              POSITION
------------------------ ------------------------------- ----------
SELECT STATEMENT
                                                              819
  MERGE JOIN
                                                                1
    VIEW
                                                                1
      SORT
GROUP BY                                                        1
      VIEW
                        DBA_FREE_SPACE                           1
        UNION-ALL
                                                                1
          NESTED LOOPS
                                                                1
          NESTED LOOPS
                                                                1
            TABLE ACCESS
FULL                    TS$                                     1
            TABLE ACCESS
CLUSTER                 FET$                                    2
              INDEX
UNIQUE SCAN             I_FILE2                                 2
            NESTED LOOPS
                                                                2
          NESTED LOOPS
                                                                1
```

```
                  TABLE ACCESS
FULL                            TS$                        1
                  FIXED TABLE
FIXED INDEX #1                  X$KTFBFE                   2
                  INDEX
UNIQUE SCAN                     I_FILE2                    2
    SORT
JOIN                                                       2
       VIEW
                                                           1
          SORT
GROUP BY                                                   1
          VIEW
                                DBA_DATA_FILES             1
           UNION-ALL
                                                           1
              NESTED LOOPS
                                                           1
              NESTED LOOPS
                                                           1
                  FIXED TABLE
FULL                            X$KCCFN                    1
                  TABLE ACCESS
BY INDEX ROWID                  FILE$                      2
                  INDEX
UNIQUE SCAN                     I_FILE1                    1
                  TABLE ACCESS
CLUSTER                         TS$                        2
                  INDEX
UNIQUE SCAN                     I_TS#                      1
              NESTED LOOPS
                                                           2
              NESTED LOOPS
                                                           1
              NESTED LOOPS
                                                           1
                  FIXED TABLE
FULL                            X$KCCFN                    1
                  TABLE ACCESS
BY INDEX ROWID                  FILE$                      2
                  INDEX
UNIQUE SCAN                     I_FILE1                    1
                  FIXED TABLE
FIXED INDEX #1                  X$KTFBHC                   2
                  TABLE ACCESS
CLUSTER                         TS$                        2
                  INDEX
UNIQUE SCAN                     I_TS#                      1
```

Now, it is time to move on to some tips for ensuring the fastest possible execution time when using views.

Tips for Tuning SQL with Views

It is ironic that views make life simple for the developers but make life complex for the DBAs who must tune the execution! Here are some tricks for tuning SQL with views:

- **Use plan stability and SQL profiles**: SQL profiles and optimizer plan stability (stored outlines) can swap out a bad view plan with a correct plan using the base tables.

- **Use a stored procedure instead:** Instead of a view, encapsulate the complex SQL inside a stored procedure. This way, the SQL optimizer will not see any views because the SQL within the application.

- **Train the developers:** If possible, teach the developers to write SQL using the base tables instead of relying on the cosmetic simplicity of views.

- **Optimize to use views:** The all-powerful Oracle optimizer parameters can be used for holistic tuning of the entire workload. For example, using *optimizer_secure_view_merging* causes Oracle to materialize the view results, resulting in faster query performance.

In sum, Oracle views are a necessary evil, but nesting of views with complex queries is a frequent cause of poor SQL performance.

To summarize, Oracle views are an encapsulation of a complex query and must be used with care. Here are the key facts to remember:

- Views are not intended to improve SQL performance. When encapsulating SQL, it should be placed inside a stored procedure rather than using a view.

- Views hide the complexity of the underlying query, making it easier for inexperienced programmers and end users to formulate queries.

- Views can be used to tune queries with hints, provided that the view is always used in the proper context.

Now, it is time to move on and look at a special type of view, the materialized view.

SQL Tuning with Materialized Views

Many Oracle professionals misunderstand materialized views and how they differ from regular views. As covered earlier in this chapter, a view hides the complexity of an underlying SQL statement, but it still executes all of the underlying SQL whenever the SQL is executed.

On the other hand, a materialized view is actually executed at creation time, and the results from running the view are materialized into a actual table as shown in Figure 10.1:

Preaggregation of Oracle data

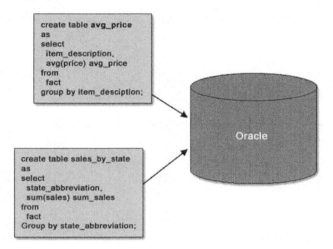

Figure 10.1: *Materialized views pre-summarize Oracle data*

Remember, the *create view* syntax only creates a definition in the data dictionary while the *create materialized view* syntax creates a real table!

Materialized views were first introduced with little fanfare and many Oracle professionals did not appreciate that materialized views would become a super-powerful SQL tuning tool. Since the view is executed at creation time, any SQL that references the SQL does not have to be re-executed and the results come back instantly!

Look Out!

A materialized view is a type of replication!

By stamping out a copy of a view at *create materialized view* time, we have created a redundant table that must be kept current. The refresh interval is determined by your tolerance for stale data.

In a sense, materialized views are used to replicate data, using a very similar mechanism as Oracle snapshot replication.

To see how snapshot replication and materialized view are related, the Oracle create snapshot syntax below gets a reply from Oracle stating *Materialized View Created.*

```
create snapshot
  cust_snap
```

```
on
  customer
refresh fast
  start with sysdate
  next sysdate + 1/1440
as
select * from customer@remote_db;
```

```
Materialized View Created.
```

Figure 10.2 shows that the Oracle SQL optimizer checks the Oracle data dictionary for the presence of a materialized view whenever a new SQL statement enters the Oracle library cache.

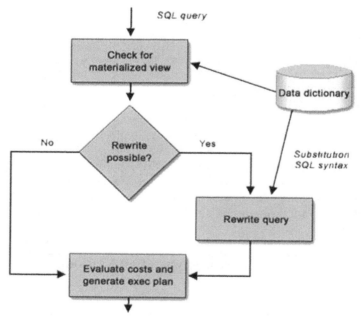

Figure 10.2: *Query re-write for materialized views*

Oracle automatically detects that a materialized view has been built and redirects the SQL to the pre-summarized data.

Materialized Views and Automatic SQL Query Rewrite

The query optimizer automatically recognizes when an existing materialized view can be used to satisfy a request. Next, it transparently rewrites the request to use the materialized view. Queries are then directed to the materialized view and not to the underlying detail tables, resulting in a significant performance gain.

The SQLAccess Advisor helps you tune SQL!

The extra-cost SQLAccess Advisor analyzes real-world SQL workloads and makes intelligent recommendations for creating materialized views.

The Oracle SQL optimizer now has other query rewrite capabilities. It often rewrites correlated subqueries into standard joins. For example, the Oracle 10g SQL optimizer automatically detects situations in which someone uses a *not exists* clause with an uncorrelated subquery and replaces the SQL with an equivalent query that runs much faster using a standard-order outer join with a not null criterion.

Here is the SQL query before rewrite:

```
select
   customer_name
from
   customer
where
   not exists
   (select
      customer_name
    from
     bad_credit);
```

Here is the same query after automatic query rewrite:

```
select
   customer_name
from
   customer c,
   bad_credit b
where
   b.customer_name(+) = c.customer_name
and
   b.customer_name is null;
```

In the next example, a materialized view has been created to determines the average salary for each job in the database.

Once the materialized view is created, queries can be run against the base table using the rewrite hint to direct the SQL optimizer to fetch the average salary from the materialized view rather than performing an expensive and time-consuming scan against the *emp* table as shown below.

```
create materialized view
   job_avg_sal
enable query rewrite
as
select
   job,
   avg(sal)avg_sal
from
   emp
group by
   job;


select /*+ rewrite(job_avg_sal) */
   avg(sal)
from
   emp
where
   job = 'CLERK';
```

Oracle is very sophisticated in SQL query rewrite capability. The Oracle DBA can control the propensity of the SQL optimizer to go to the materialized views to service the query. The options are as follows:

- **Full SQL text match**: In this method, the SQL text of the query's select statement clause is compared to the SQL text of the select clause in the materialized view's defining query.

- **Partial text match**: If a full SQL test match fails, the optimizer will attempt a partial SQL text match. The optimizer compares the remaining SQL text of the query (beginning with the *from* clause) to the remaining SQL text of the materialized view's defining query.

- **No match**: If the full and partial SQL text matches both fail, the optimizer uses general query rewrite methods that enable the use of a materialized view even if it contains only part of the data, more than the data, or data that can be converted.

When using query rewrite, materialized views satisfying the largest number of SQL queries are created. For example, if 20 queries commonly applied to the detail or fact tables have been identified, it might be possible to satisfy them with five or six well-written materialized views.

When unsure about which materialized views to create, rest assured that Oracle provides a set of advisory functions in the *dbms_olap* package to help in designing and evaluating materialized views for query rewrite. If a materialized view is to be used by query rewrite, it must be stored in the same database as its fact or detail tables.

A materialized view can also be partitioned, and a materialized view can be defined on a partitioned table and one or more indexes on the materialized view.

A Case Study in Materialized Views

A point-of-sale Oracle data warehouse had a system that was largely read-only with a short batch window for nightly updates. It soon became apparent that nearly every query in the system was performing a sum() or avg() function against several key tables.

The *v$sql_plan* view showed a considerable number of very-large-table full-table scans, and the system was virtually crippled by *db file scattered read waits*.

```
Top 5 Timed Events

                                                      % Total
Event                        Waits     Time (s) Ela Time
-------------------------- ------------ ----------- --------
db file scattered read       325,519      3,246     82.04
library cache load lock        4,673      1,363      9.26
db file sequential read      534,598      7,146      4.54
CPU time                       1,154        645      3.83
log file parallel write       19,157        837      1.68
```

Once the problem was identified as unnecessary disk reads, it was easily fixed by the creation of three materialized views and the employment of Oracle's automatic query rewrite. This reduced physical disk I/O by over 2,000 percent and improved performance by more than 30x — a real Silver Bullet!

Conclusions on Materialized Views for SQL Tuning

Oracle's introduction of materialized views significantly improved the performance of Oracle systems required to process complex SQL statements while delivering sub-second response time.

Knowing how to create materialized views can make any DBA the hero of any Oracle shop. I have created materialized views that made SQL run so fast that the end users did not trust the results!

For read-only tables, it is possible to take SQL that runs for 30 minutes and get sub-second response time. Materialized views are used to in read-only tables in cases where the same SQL, or permutation of the SQL, is run over-and-over. Materialized views are great for these types of read-only tables:

- **Pre-summarizing aggregations**: Systems that commonly compute averages and sums over millions of rows will be a giant benefit to materialized views since the aggregation is computed once, stored and the pre-fetched rows are available instantly to the SQL.

- **Pre-joining tables**: In legacy databases that were designed in 3rd normal form, back in the days when disk was expensive and databases were designed to be without any redundancy, materialized views are a Godsend. As disk prices fell, Oracle designers found that introducing redundancy dramatically improved SQL performance. Instead of a total redesign to introduce redundancy into the data model to improve SQL performance, a materialized view can be used to pre-join the tables for almost instantaneous SQL response time.

For systems with statistic tables or systems where the tables are updated at night in batch mode, a materialized view can be used to create a de-normalized schema by pre-joining tables, and commonly referenced tasks can be pre-aggregated to eliminate redundant queries.

Conclusion

This chapter has dealt with the use of Oracle views for SQL tuning as well as the view cousins, the in-line view and the materialized view. The main points of this chapter include:

- Views encapsulate complex SQL and store it in the data dictionary. While this helps manage SQL, it does not help SQL tuning.

- Oracle views have issues with predicate pushing and merging views.

- Oracle in-line views allow *select* statements to be placed in the *from* clause of a query, instead of a table name

- Materialized views are a great way to speed up SQL on read-only tables by pre-joining tables and pre-summarizing data.

The next chapter will explore how the state of the rows on the physical data blocks affects SQL performance and will emphasize those times when reorganizing table data can be used to speed up SQL performance.

Tuning SQL with Object Reorganization

Reorgs will remove garbage and make SQL run faster

Reorganizing Tables for High Performance

Oracle SQL does not exist in a vacuum, and the structure of the tables and indexes has a profound impact on SQL performance. Techniques like co-locating related rows, reducing row fragmentation and periodically reorganizing tables and indexes can help SQL run faster and with fewer disks I/O.

Like most other commercial databases, Oracle chose not to degrade runtime performance by keeping tables and indexes in a pristine state. Thus, Oracle indexes and tables will become increasingly disorganized after heavily DML activity. Hence, periodic reorganization may be required on tables and indexes to keep SQL performing at optimal levels.

Until Oracle10g brought the *dbms_redefinition* package, there was no easy way to compact tables without affecting end user activity. Figure 11.1 is an illustration of the concept of table fragmentation. The small squares indicate rows stored in the segment.

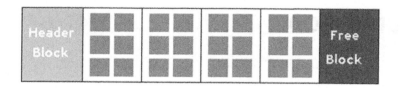

Figure 11.1: *A table segment illustration*

When end users insert rows into this table, Oracle fills-up all empty blocks that were defined with the initial parameter as shown in Figure 11.2.

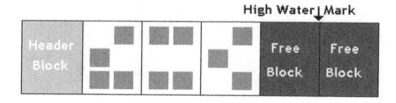

Figure 11.2: *After some rows have been deleted, the data segment wastes the space and HWM remains the same.*

The High Water Mark (HWM) for a table represents the highest data block used by a table. For performance reasons, Oracle does not reclaim free space below the High Water Mark. This is because Oracle reserves that free space for future row inserts and possible row growth after updates.

As a result, it is not uncommon to see excessive full-table scan times in tables where the High Water Mark has been raised and lots of rows are then deleted. Even though the table is now small in relative terms, full scans will go up to the HWM for the table.

Full scans read to the high water mark!

Remember that all full scan I/O will read to the table high water mark. After massive deletes, a full scan may read through many empty data blocks!

Also, when Oracle inserts rows through the *direct path* method (i.e. the *append* hint), new rows are always placed in data blocks above the HWM.

It is important for the DBA to know why, when and how to reorganize Oracle tables.

Faster SQL with Database Reorganizations

Ever since the earliest days of data processing, database experts have known that the physical layout of the data on disk can make queries run faster. Even in highly cached databases, clustering related data on adjacent data blocks can reduce logical I/O (*consistent gets*) and disk reads (*physical reads*) thereby making queries run far faster. Oracle also offers the cluster tables option to allow related row data to be clustered in the same data blocks.

> ⌂ **Note:** Cluster tables are not the same as cluster databases. Cluster database are RAC, Real Application Clusters.

Oracle provides table and index maintenance tools that allow re-optimization of data while the database continues to accept updates with the Oracle *dbms_redefinition* package. To keep the databases running super fast, Oracle chose not to incur the overhead of coalescing table rows and restructuring indexes during peak update times. The trick is to understand when a table or index will benefit from reorganization, so time is not wasted reorganizing table and indexes with no SQL performance benefits.

Oracle has offered some huge improvements in indexing, especially related to the detection of missing indexes and materialized views and the automation of index histogram detection for the SQL optimizer. There are also improvements to table maintenance in Oracle. Oracle Database 10g included the following online data reorganization enhancements:

- Online table redefinition enhancements
- Easy cloning of indexes, grants, constraints, etc.
- Conversion from LONG to LOB online
- Allowing unique index instead of primary key
- Changing tables without recompiling stored procedures
- Online segment shrink

Despite all of the great automated tools, routine table and index maintenance must still be performed in order to keep highly active databases performing at peak levels.

It has been proven that rebuilding tables and indexes improves the speed of queries, but dilettantes do not always understand the benefits of rebuilding Oracle indexes. There are two schools of thought on this important issue, and both sides make strong opposing arguments, sometimes leaving beginners confused about the real benefit of table and index reorganization. Neither of these statements is completely true, so the real answer is somewhere in-between:

- **Oracle Index Rebuilding is a waste of time:** Some claim that indexes are logically self-balancing and rarely need rebuilding. Even after an Oracle index rebuild, they claim that SQL query performance is rarely any faster.

- **Index Rebuilds improve performance:** Others note that indexes on tables with high DML, such as SQL inserts, updates and deletes will be heavily fragmented, with many empty blocks and a suboptimal access structure. They claim to witness huge performance improvements after rebuilding a busy Oracle index.

On the surface, both stances sound like good arguments, but digging a little deeper will help develop a more full understanding of index maintenance. The following is a logical approach to the issue of Oracle index rebuilding, and it starts with these assertions:

- **It is about I/O:** If SQL performance is faster after an index rebuild, it is because the query does fewer index block reads. This should be evident in the consistent gets, logical reads from the data buffer, and physical reads, which are calls to the disk spindle that may or may not result in a physical disk read depending on whether or not there is a RAM buffer on the disk.

- **Only some index access methods will benefit:** Index Fast Full scans and some Index Range Scans will run faster after a rebuild. Just like a full-table scan takes a long time when it reads a table with many empty blocks, reading a range of a sparse index will result in excessive logical reads, as empty index nodes are accessed by the SQL query execution. Index unique scans will not improve after a rebuild, since they only read their participating nodes.

- **Oracle Indexes can get clogged with empty and near empty index blocks:** As massive deletes take place, large chunks of an index are logically deleted, meaning that they are passed over by the pointers but still remain in the structure. Because the empty blocks remain, block-by-block scans, such as any scan affected by db_file_multiblock_read_count, and some index range scans will perform less reads; hence, the result is less I/O and faster performance.

The next section will reveal ways to tell just how synchronized an index is with a table column and how to use the powerful *clustering_factor* to tune SQL statements.

Tuning SQL Access with *clustering_factor*

With each new release of Oracle, the Cost Based Optimizer (CBO) improves. With Oracle9i, the enhancement was that when formulating an execution plan consideration was given to external influences such as CPU cost and I/O cost. As Oracle evolved into release Oracle11g, there have been even more improvements in the ability of the CBO to get the optimal execution plan for a query, but it is still important to understand this mechanism.

In order to understand how Oracle decides on an execution plan for a query, the first step is to learn the rules Oracle uses when it determines whether to use an index.

The most important characteristics of column data are the clustering factor for the column and the selectivity of column values, even though other important characteristics within tables are available to the CBO. A column called *clustering_factor* in the *dba_indexes* view offers information on how the table rows are synchronized with the index.

When the clustering factor is close to the number of data blocks and the column value is not row ordered when the *clustering_factor* approaches the number of rows in the table, the table rows are synchronized with the index.

To illustrate this concept, the following query will filter the result set using a column value:

```
select
    customer_name
from
    customer
where
    customer_state = 'North Carolina';
```

An index scan is faster for this query if the percentage of customers in North Carolina is small and the values are clustered on the data blocks. The decision to use an index versus a full-table scan is at least partially determined by the percentage of customers in North Carolina.

So, why would a CBO choose to perform a full-table scan when only a small number of rows are retrieved?

Four factors synchronize to help the CBO choose whether to use an index or a full-table scan: the selectivity of a column value; the *db_block_size*; the *avg_row_len*; and the cardinality. An index scan is usually faster if a data column has high selectivity and a low *clustering_factor* as shown in Figure 11.3:

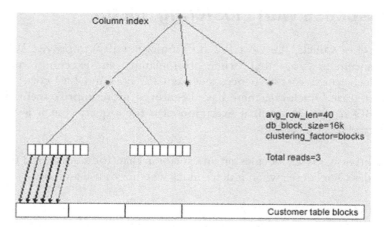

Figure 11.3: *A column with a low clustering factor, small rows and large blocks.*

If there is a frequent query that performs large index range scans, the table can be forced to be in the same order as the index. By maintaining row order and thereby removing suboptimal full-table scans, placing all adjacent rows in the same data block may allow some queries to run far faster.

Table row order can be forced with a single-table table cluster or by reorganizing the table with the *create table as select* syntax, using the SQL *order by* clause to force the row order. This is especially important when a majority of the SQL references a column with a high *clustering_factor*, a large *db_block_size*, and a small *avg_row_len*.

Even when a column has high selectivity, a high *clustering_factor*, and a small *avg_row_len*, there is still an indication that column values are randomly distributed in the table, and that an additional I/O will be required to obtain the rows.

On the other hand, as the *clustering_factor* nears the number of rows in the table, the rows fall out of sync with the index. This high *clustering_factor*, in which the value is close to the number of rows in the table (*num_rows*) indicates that the rows are out of sequence with the index and an additional I/O may be required for index range scans.

An index range scan would cause a huge amount of unnecessary I/O as shown in Figure 11.4, thus making a full-table scan more efficient.

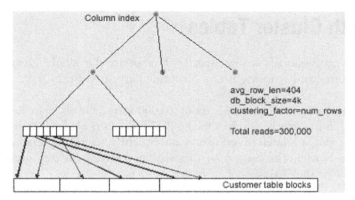

Figure 11.4: *A column with high clustering factor, small blocks and large rows.*

The CBO's choice to execute a full-table scan versus an index range scan is influenced by the *clustering_factor*, *db_block_size*, and *avg_row_len*.

Oracle developers have recognized that certain types of queries will run thousands of times faster when related data is placed together on disk. Oracle provides several tools for keeping an optimal *clustering_factor* for important queries:

- **Multi-table table clusters:** If the system always accesses related data together, using a multi-table cluster can greatly improve query performance. For example, if the system always displays customer row data with data from the orders table, the customer row and all of the orders can be placed on a single data block, requiring only a single consistent get to acquire all of the required data.

- **Single-table table clusters:** This technique allows Oracle to guarantee that data blocks are stored in column value order, allowing index range scans to run very quickly.

However, Oracle cluster tables have overhead, namely wasted disk space that must be reserved, using *pctfree*, for new rows to be placed on the proper block. There is also the overhead of maintaining overflow areas when it is impossible to store rows on their target block.

Many Oracle DBAs will choose to manually reorganize tables using the *dbms_redefinition* package, the *create table as select* or *alter table move* syntax using an *order by* and a *parallel* clause.

With this introduction to how the placement of data on disk affects SQL performance, it is time to take a closer look at changing the organization of the tables and indexes to speed up SQL execution speed.

Tuning SQL with Cluster Tables

All experienced Oracle professionals know that I/O is often the single greatest component of response time, and reducing I/O is a routine part of tuning SQL.

Disk operations are expressed in milliseconds, about 10,000 times slower than RAM speed which is expressed in nanoseconds. In Oracle, RAM access is about 100 times faster than a disk read, due to latch overhead. Consequently, anything that can minimize I/O or reduce bottlenecks caused by contention for files on disk-greatly improves the performance of the SQL.

For queries that access common rows with a table (e.g. get all items in order 123), unordered tables can experience huge I/O as the index retrieves a separate data block for each row requested.

If like rows are grouped together, as measured by the *clustering_factor* in *dba_indexes*, it is possible to get all of the rows with a single block read because the rows are together. To achieve this goal, 10g hash cluster tables, single table clusters or manual row re-sequencing (CTAS with *order by*) can be employed.

In high-volume online transaction processing (OLTP) environments, in which data is accessed via a primary index, re-sequencing table rows so that contiguous blocks follow the same order as their primary index can actually reduce physical I/O and improve response time during index-driven table queries.

This technique is useful only when the application selects multiple rows, when using index range scans or if the application issues multiple requests for consecutive keys. Databases with random primary-key unique accesses will not benefit from row re-sequencing.

Unlike the hash cluster where the symbolic key is hashed to the data block address, an index cluster uses an index to maintain row sequence.

A table cluster is a group of tables that share the same data blocks, since they share common columns and are often used together. When cluster tables are created, Oracle physically stores all rows for each table in the same data blocks. The cluster key value is the value of the cluster key columns for a particular row.

Index cluster tables can be either multi-table or single-table. Let's take a look at each method.

Multi-table Index Cluster Tables

In a multi-table index cluster, related table rows are grouped together to reduce disk I/O. Consider this SQL where all orders for a customer are fetched:

```
select
   customer_name,
   order_date
from
   customer
natural join
   orders
where
   cust_key = IBM;
```

If this customer has eight orders, each on a different data block, nine block fetches must be performed to return the query rows. Even if these blocks are already cached in the data buffers, there are still at least nine consistent gets as illustrated by Figure 11.5:

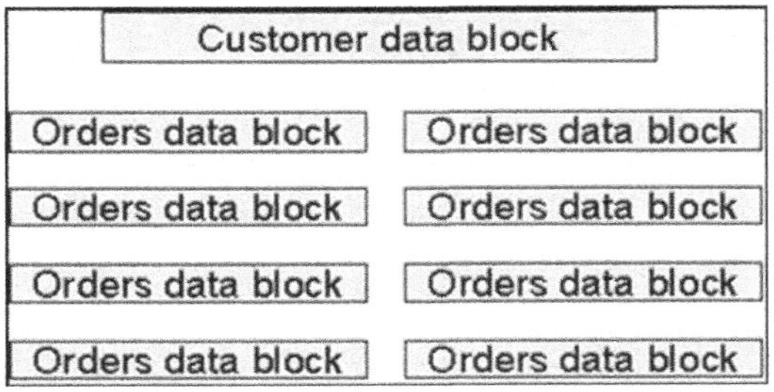

Customer data block	
Orders data block	Orders data block
Orders data block	Orders data block
Orders data block	Orders data block
Orders data block	Orders data block

Figure 11.5: *Unclustered data on many data blocks*

If the table is redefined as an index cluster table, Oracle will physically store the orders rows on the same data block as the parent customer row, thereby reducing I/O by a factor of eight per Figure 11.6:

Order	Order	Order	Customer row	Order	Order	Order

Figure 11.6: *Co-locating related rows on the same data block*

Remember, index clusters will only result in a reduction of I/O when the vast majority of data access is via the cluster index. Any row access via another index will still result in randomized block fetches.

Single-table Index Cluster Tables

A single-table index cluster table is a method whereby Oracle guarantees row sequence where *clustering_factor* in *dba_indexes* always approximates blocks in *dba_tables* as shown in Figure 11.7:

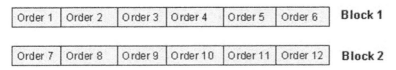

Figure 11.7: *Unclustered data on many data blocks*

Scans via an index range scan will always fetch as many rows as possible in a single I/O, depending on block size and average row length. Many shops that employ single-table index cluster tables use a *db_32k_cache_size* to ensure that they can fetch an index range scan in a single I/O (Figure 11.8).

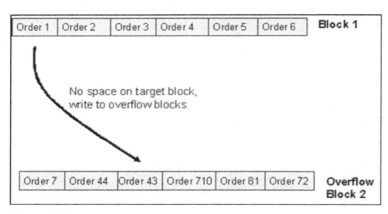

Figure 11.8: *Unclustered data on many data blocks*

To do this, Oracle must have an overflow area where new rows are placed if there is no room on the target block. Monitoring the overflow becomes an important task, and it may be necessary to periodically reorganize the single-table index cluster table to ensure that all row orders are maintained.

The value of *pctfree* for the table can be lowered to reserve space for new rows, but excessive row write to the overflow area will cause the *clustering_factor* to rise above the value for blocks in *dba_tables*.

Another way to improve SQL performance is by minimizing disk I/O on large rows by eliminating chained and fragmented rows.

Managing Row Chaining in Oracle

Improper settings for *pctfree* and *pctused* can also cause database fragmentation. Whenever a row in an Oracle database expands because of an update, there must be sufficient room on the data block to hold the expanded row. If a row spans several data blocks, the database must perform additional disk I/O to fetch the block into the SGA. This excessive disk I/O can cripple the performance of the database.

The space reserved for row expansion is controlled by the *pctfree* parameter. Row chaining is especially problematic in cases where a row with many *varchar* datatypes is stored with NULL values, and subsequent update operations populate the *varchar* columns with large values.

Fortunately, row chaining is relatively easy to detect. One important area of Oracle DBA work is tracking chained row fetches ('table fetch continued row' name in *v$sysstat* and *stats$sysstat*).

Watch out for chained rows!

Remember, migrated/chained rows always cause double the I/O for a row fetch. Hence, a primary goal of SQL tuning is to reduce unnecessary disk I/O by reducing rows fragmentation.

The "*table fetch continued row*" (chained row fetch) can result when any of the following conditions exist:

- **Raw long raw, BLOB or CLOB columns:** These may manifest as chained row fetches if the avg_row_len > db_block_size.

- **Tables with > 255 columns:** These are stored in 255 row-pieces, and show as migrated/chained rows.

- **pctfree too small:** Enough room on the data block was not allowed for the row to expand (via SQL Update statements), causing rows to chain onto adjacent blocks.

Migrated/chained rows can be reduced by reorganizing the table with the dbms_redefinition utility or CTAS. It is also possible to reduce large-object related row chaining by moving the object into a tablespace with a 32k blocksize. It is

---

Tuning SQL with Cluster Tables   **487**

tempting to gather the table fetch continued row statistic from *v$sysstat* or *stats$sysstat*. For example, consider the report generated by *statspack_find_chained_rows.sql*:

🖫 statspack_find_chained_rows.sql

```
column table_fetch_continued_row  format 999,999,999

select
   to_char(snap_time,'yyyy-mm-dd HH24'),
   avg(newmem.value-oldmem.value)table_fetch_continued_row
from
   perfstat.stats$sysstat oldmem,
   perfstat.stats$sysstat newmem,
   perfstat.stats$snapshot    sn
where
   snap_time > sysdate-&1
and
   newmem.snap_id = sn.snap_id
and
   oldmem.snap_id = sn.snap_id-1
and
   oldmem.name = 'table fetch continued row'
and
   newmem.name = 'table fetch continued row'
and
   newmem.value-oldmem.value > 0
having
   avg(newmem.value-oldmem.value) > 10000
group by
   to_char(snap_time,'yyyy-mm-dd HH24');
```

Note that the output below only reports total chained row fetches per hour, regardless of the amount of total rows read. The existing report is silly because it only reports the total chained row fetches per hour, a meaningless number because it is impossible to know from this information if it is 1% or 80% of the total row fetches:

```
yr.  mo dy Hr.    TABLE_FETCH_CONTINUED_ROW
---------------  -------------------------
2003-10-23 08                    4,462,409
2003-10-23 09                    2,962,667
2003-10-23 10                    7,178,844
```

In the example above, the 4 million chained row fetches would be fine if 10 trillion rows were read, but it would bad if only 5 million rows were read.

In Oracle, the total row fetches can be acquired by summing the *v$sysstat value* for *name* = *'table scan rows gotten'* plus *'table fetch by rowid'*. A more meaningful report is shown below, showing an alert only for those hours when total chained row fetches exceed 5% of total row fetches.

Continued	Row	Table Fetch	migrated/chained rows	
yr. mo dy Hr.	Fetched	Row	Percent	
---------------	----------	--------------	-----	
2003-10-23 08	53,372,282	4,462,409	6%	
2003-10-24 09	46,282,383	2,962,667	14%	
2003-10-28 10	14,373,264	7,178,844	50%	

The following *chained_row.sql* script will run against the Oracle data dictionary and produce a report showing those tables with excessive migrated/chained rows. Note that all of the tables in the Oracle database must be analyzed with the *dbms_stats* before running this script.

🖫 chained_row.sql

```
-- ************************************************************
-- WARNING:  This script relies on current CBO statistics
-- ************************************************************

spool chain.lst;
set pages 9999;

column c1 heading "Owner"   format a9;
column c2 heading "Table"   format a12;
column c3 heading "PCTFREE" format 99;
column c4 heading "PCTUSED" format 99;
column c5 heading "avg row" format 99,999;
column c6 heading "Rows"    format 999,999,999;
column c7 heading "Chains"  format 999,999,999;
column c8 heading "Pct"     format .99;

set heading off;
select 'Tables with migrated/chained rows and no BLOB columns.' from dual;
set heading on;

select
   owner             c1,
   table_name        c2,
   pct_free          c3,
   pct_used          c4,
   avg_row_len       c5,
   num_rows          c6,
   chain_cnt         c7,
   chain_cnt/num_rows c8
from dba_tables
where
owner not in ('SYS','SYSTEM')
and
table_name not in
 (select table_name from dba_tab_columns
   where
 data_type in ('RAW','LONG RAW', 'BLOB', 'CLOB')
 )
and
chain_cnt > 0
```

```
order by chain_cnt desc;
```

The resulting report includes important information on the table name and settings for *pctfree* and *pctused*, the average row length (*avg_row_len*) and a count of the chained rows at the time of the last analyze:

Owner	Table	PCTFREE	PCTUSED	avg row	Rows	Chains	Pct
SAPR3	ZG_TAB	10	40	80	5,003	1,487	.30
SAPR3	ZMM	10	40	422	18,309	509	.03
SAPR3	Z_Z_TBLS	10	40	43	458	53	.12
SAPR3	USR03	10	40	101	327	46	.14
SAPR3	Z_BURL	10	40	116	1,802	25	.01
SAPR3	ZGO_CITY	10	40	56	1,133	10	.01

Look Out!

Large objects will fragment!

You will see chaining fragmentation in tables that contain raw, BLOB, CLOB and long raw columns when the row length exceeds the db_block_size. In these cases, use a 32k blocksize with a db_32k_cache_size buffer.

Once the tables with migrated/chained rows have been identified, the *pctfree* for the table must be increased and the table reorganized, using data pump, *alter table xxx move*, *create table as select* or *dbms_redefinition*, to remove the chains. While there are several third-party products for reorganizing tables, table reorganization is most commonly done by running Oracle utilities such as *dbms_redefinition*.

Remember, for efficient space reuse, set a high value for *pctused*. A high value for *pctused* will effectively reuse space on data blocks but at the expense of additional I/O. A high *pctused* means that relatively full blocks are placed on the free list. Hence, these blocks will be able to accept only a few rows before becoming full again, leading to more I/O.

A low value for *pctused* will result in better performance. A low value for *pctused* means that Oracle will not place a data block onto the free list until it is nearly empty. The block will be able to accept many rows until it becomes full, thereby reducing I/O at insert time. Remember that it is always faster for Oracle to extend into new blocks than to reuse existing blocks. For superfast space acquisition on SQL *inserts*, free list link/unlinks can be turned off. It takes fewer resources for Oracle to extend a table than to manage free lists.

In effect, free lists can be turned off by setting *pctused* to 1. This will cause the free lists to be populated exclusively from new extents. Of course, this approach requires lots of extra disk space, and the table must be reorganized periodically to reclaim space within the table.

A Summary of Object Tuning Rules

The following rules govern the settings for the init.ora parameters *freelists*, *freelist groups*, *pctfree*, and *pctused*. The following are the general guidelines for setting object storage parameters.

- Always set pctused to allow enough room to accept a new row. There should never be free blocks that do not have enough room to accept a row. If they exist, this will cause a slowdown since Oracle will attempt to read five dead free blocks before extending the table to get an empty block.

- The presence of migrated/chained rows in a table means that pctfree is too low or that db_block_size is too small. In most cases within Oracle, RAW and LONG RAW columns make huge rows that exceed the maximum blocksize for Oracle, making migrated/chained rows unavoidable.

- If a table has simultaneous insert SQL processes, it needs to have simultaneous delete processes. Running a single purge job will place all of the free blocks on only one free list, and none of the other free lists will contain any free blocks from the purge.

- The freelists parameter should be set to the high-water mark of updates to a table. For example, if the customer table has up to 20 end users performing inserts at any time, then the customer table should have freelists=20.

- freelist groups should be set to the number of RAC nodes instances that access the table. For partitioned objects and cases of segment header contention, freelist_groups may be set for non-RAC systems.

The value of *pctused* and *pctfree* can easily be changed at any time with the *alter table* command, and the observant DBA should be able to develop a methodology for deciding the optimal settings for these parameters.

If a table has simultaneous *insert* dialog processes, it needs to have multiple *freelists* to reduce segment header contention, and the application should parallelize the *delete* processes to evenly repopulate each freelist. Running a single purge job will place all of the free blocks on only one freelist, and none of the other *freelists* will contain any free blocks from the purge job.

Multiple *freelists* can also waste disk. Tables with dozens of *freelists* may exhibit the sparse table phenomenon as the table grows and each *freelist* contains free blocks that are not known to the other *freelists*. If these tables consume too much space, the

---

Oracle DBA faces a tough decision. To maximize space reuse, the data block should be placed onto a *freelist* as soon as it is capable of receiving more than two new rows.

Therefore, a fairly high value for *pctused* is desired to maximize space reuse. On the other hand, this would result in slower runtime performance since Oracle will only be able to insert a few rows before having to perform an I/O to get another block.

This leads to the inevitable question of whether or not indexes benefit from routine maintenance.

Oracle Index Maintenance

Oracle deliberately allows indexes to leave their pristine state to keep DML performance high, allowing index trees to fragment as updates and deletes morph the physical tree structure.

Oracle leaves deleted leaf nodes within indexes after massive deletes, and when an index has lots of half-empty blocks, range scan activity can take longer and coalescing or rebuilding an index will indeed improve SQL performance.

As rows are added to an empty table, Oracle controls the addition of same level blocks, called splitting, until the higher level index node is unable to hold any more key pointer pairs. When the index can no longer split because the owner block is full, Oracle will spawn a whole new index level, keeping the index tree in perfect logical and physical balance.

However, *deletes* are a different story. Physically, Oracle indexes are always balanced because empty blocks stay inside the tree structure after a massive *delete*. Logically, Oracle indexes are not self-balancing because Oracle does not remove the dead blocks as they become empty. For example, Figure 11.9 shows an Oracle index before a massive delete.

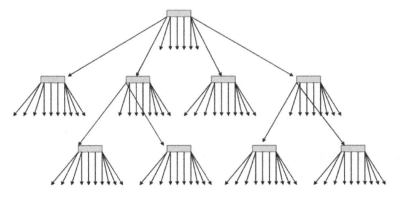

Figure 11.9: *A physical index before a massive row delete*

Now, after a massive delete, the physical representation of the index is exactly the same because the empty data blocks remain as illustrated in Figure 11.10. However, the logical internal pointer structure is quite unbalanced, because Oracle has routed around the deleted leaf nodes and has placed the empty index blocks back on the freelist, where they can be reused anywhere in the index tree structure

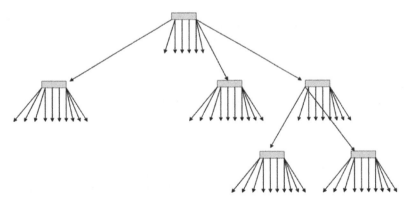

Figure 11.10: *The pointer structure of an index after a massive row delete*

This type of sparse index is sometimes called index browning, like a tree that has dead spots after being hit by lightening. Sparse indexes are typical for an index on highly active tables with large scale *insert*, *delete* and *update* activity. There may be thousands of empty (or near empty) index blocks in the tree, and the sparse data can cause excessive I/O. There are several types of Oracle SQL execution steps that will run longer against a sparse index:

- **Index Range Scans:** Index range scans that must access many near empty blocks will have excessive I/O compared to a rebuilt index.

- **Index Fast Full Scans:** Because 70% of an index can be deleted and the index will still have the same number of data blocks, a full index scan might run many times slower before it is rebuilt.

Since the SQL must visit the sparse blocks, the task will take longer to execute. At this point, it is important to remember that not all Oracle indexes will see a SQL performance boost after coalescing or rebuilding, and only those indexes are experience multi-block read will see a SQL performance boost after an index rebuild.

Not All Indexes Benefit from Rebuilding

When Oracle joins two tables with a nested loop, only one of the indexes may be accessed as a range. The optimizer always performs an index range scan on one index, gathers the *rowid* values, and does fetch by *rowid* on the matching rows in the other table. For example:

```
select
   customer_name,
   order_date
from
   customer
   orders
where
   customer.cust_key = orders.cust_key;
```

The Oracle documentation notes that a nested loop involves two loops:

> *"In a nested loop join, for every row in the outer row set, the inner row set is accessed to find all the matching rows to join.*
>
> *Therefore, in a nested loop join, the inner row set is accessed as many times as the number of rows in the outer row set."*

Oracle will only scan one index, build a set of keys, and then probe the rows from the other table as shown in Figure 11.11.

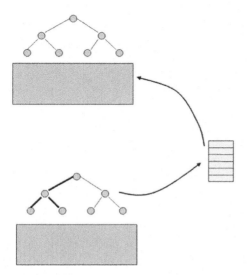

Figure 11.11: *Table joins include index range scans and index unique scans*

So, if this nested loop never uses the customer index, why is it there? The answer is, for index unique scans. In an index unique scan, a single row is accessed within the index, as seen in this query:

```
select
   customer_last_name,
   customer_address
from
   customer
where
   cust_key = 123;
```

In sum, the DBA must figure out how their indexes are being used by the SQL.

An index that never experiences range scans would not benefit from a larger blocksize. The question becomes one of finding those indexes that experience lots of range scans, and AWR can help.

It is possible to identify those indexes with the most index range scans with the following simple AWR script:

🖫 index_range_scans.sql

```
col c1 heading 'Object|Name'          format a30
col c2 heading 'Option'               format a15
col c3 heading 'Index|Usage|Count'    format 999,999

select
```

```
   p.object_name c1,
   p.options    c2,
   count(1)     c3
from
   dba_hist_sql_plan p,
   dba_hist_sqlstat  s
where
   p.object_owner <> 'SYS'
and
   p.options like '%RANGE SCAN%'
and

   p.operation like '%INDEX%'
and
   p.sql_id = s.sql_id
group by
   p.object_name,
   p.operation,
   p.options
order by
  1,2,3;
```

The following is the output showing overall total counts for each object and table access method.

Object Name	Option	Index Usage Count
CUSTOMER_CHECK	RANGE SCAN	4,232
AVAILABILITY_PRIMARY_KEY	RANGE SCAN	1,783
CON_UK	RANGE SCAN	473
CURRENT_SEVERITY	RANGE SCAN	323
CWM$CUBEDIMENSIONUSE_IDX	RANGE SCAN	72
ORDERS_FK	RANGE SCAN	20

So, when should an Oracle index be rebuilt? The following section will provide a closer look.

When Should Indexes Be Rebuilt?

From a software engineering perspective, it is impossible to make a database with physically self-balancing blocks. For example, take a database that has a bulk delete that removes 250,000 rows from a table, and each index block contains 1,000 pointers. Each index block may contain hundreds of pointers to other index nodes depending on the symbolic key size and the blocksize.

If the index software were written to rebalance the physical tree whenever an index block became empty, the bulk delete operation could take hundreds of times longer to execute. Oracle has made a deliberate decision not to coalesce near empty blocks and rebalance physical blocks solely for performance reasons.

In the example, to be physically self-balancing, the physical tree would have to be rebalanced 250 times during the bulk *delete*, and there would also be huge overhead when coalescing nearly empty blocks, shifting their pointers to nearly-full blocks. It is much more efficient to rebuild the index once, after the bulk *delete*. In fact, many shops that perform massive bulk operations in indexes tables will remove the indexes first, *delete* and *update* the rows and rebuild the indexes afterward.

When Oracle rebuilds an index, the index nodes are swept in order, chasing the pointer chains and placing the new index into the designated tablespace as temporary segments. The DBA controls the free space for node inserts with the *pctfree* parameter, which dictates how much room in the index block is reserved for future updates. For example, if the table will have 50% more rows added at a later time, *pctfree* could be set to 50 and half of each index would be left free to accept new entries without splitting or spawning.

The shape of the index tree can be controlled with two techniques:

- **pctfree:** Setting pctfree to a low value will leave space within each index block, creating a more vertical index tree as shown in Figure 11.12:

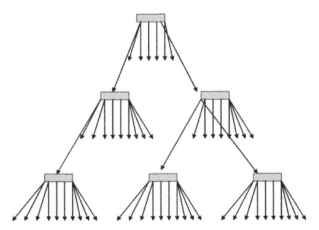

Figure 11.12: *A vertical Oracle index in a small blocksize*

- **Index Blocksize:** Because index splitting and spawning are controlled at the block level, a larger blocksize will result in a flatter index tree structure. This was demonstrated by Robin Schumacher in his book *Oracle Performance Troubleshooting* (2004, Rampant TechPress):

> "As you can see, the amount of logical reads has been reduced in half simply by using the new 16K tablespace and accompanying 16K data cache.
>
> Clearly, the benefits of properly using the new data caches and multi-block tablespace feature of Oracle9i and above are worth your investigation and trials in your own database."

Schumacher suggests using multiple blocksizes and putting all indexes and tables that experience full-table scans because of the requirements of *db_file_multiblock_read_count* into a 32k blocksize. This results in a flatter index tree with fewer levels as illustrated in Figure 11.13.

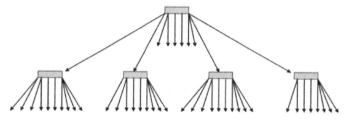

Figure 11.13: *A flat index tree with a large blocksize*

Many shops with downtime maintenance windows will schedule periodic rebuilding because it is a low risk operation such as the index will not be replaced unless it is successfully rebuilt.

All DBAs acknowledge that database maintenance of a part of the job, and they use tools such as the Oracle online redefinition utility, *dbms_redefinition* package, to periodically rebuild Oracle tables and indexes online, while the database continues to receive updates.

But how is maintenance to be performed on a 24x7 database? Oracle has the exciting online redefinition utility that uses Oracle replication techniques to allow the DBA to reorganize a table and its indexes while the database continues to accept updates. This structure is shown in Figure 11.14.

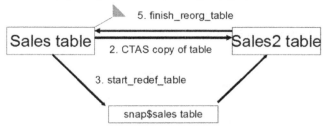

Figure 11.14: *Oracle online redefinition utility*

This will quickly identify indexes that will benefit the most from a 32k blocksize.

This index list can be double verified by using the AWR to identify indexes with high disk reads during each AWR snapshot period. The sample script below exposes the top five tables accessed mostly heavily by physical disk reads for every snapshot interval:

💾 **busy_table_io.sql**

```
col c0 heading 'Begin|Interval|time'  format a8
col c1 heading 'Table|Name'           format a20
col c2 heading 'Disk|Reads'           format 99,999,999
col c3 heading 'Rows|Processed'       format 99,999,999

select
*
from (
select
    to_char(s.begin_interval_time,'mm-dd hh24') c0,
    p.object_name c1,
    sum(t.disk_reads_total) c2,
    sum(t.rows_processed_total) c3,
    DENSE_RANK() OVER (PARTITION BY to_char(s.begin_interval_time,'mm-dd
hh24') ORDER BY SUM(t.disk_reads_total) desc) AS rnk
from
  dba_hist_sql_plan p,
  dba_hist_sqlstat t,
  dba_hist_snapshot s
where
  p.sql_id = t.sql_id
and
  t.snap_id = s.snap_id
and
  p.object_type like '%TABLE%'
group by
  to_char(s.begin_interval_time,'mm-dd hh24'),
  p.object_name
order by
c0 desc, rnk
)
```

```
where rnk <= 5;
```

The following is the sample output from the above script:

```
Begin
Interval  Table                     Disk        Rows
time      Name                      Reads     Processed        RNK
--------  --------------------    ---------   -----------   ----------
10-29 15  CUSTOMER_CHECK            55,732      498,056          1
10-29 15  CON_UK                    18,368      166,172          2
10-29 15  CURRENT_SEVERITY          11,727      102,545          3
10-29 15  ORDERS_FK                  5,876       86,671          4
10-29 15  SYN$                       2,624       23,674          5

10-29 14  CUSTOMER_CHECK            47,756      427,762          1
10-29 14  CON_UK                    15,939      142,878          2
10-29 14  CURRENT_SEVERITY           6,976      113,649          3
10-29 14  X$KZSRO                     4,772      119,417          4
10-29 14  ORDERS_FK                   2,274       20,292          5

10-29 13  CUSTOMER_CHECK            25,704      213,786          1
10-29 13  CON_UK                     8,568       71,382          2
10-29 13  OBJ$                       3,672       30,474          3
10-29 13  X$KZSRO                     2,448       20,328          4
10-29 13  SYN$                       1,224       10,146          5
```

This report shows the tables with the highest disk reads which is very important information for disk tuning.

The *dba_hist_sql_plan* table can also be used to gather counts about the frequency of participation of objects inside queries. This is a great query to quickly see what's going on between the tables and the SQL that accesses them.

🖫 count_table_access.sql

```
col c1 heading 'Object|Name'        format a30
col c2 heading 'Operation'          format a15
col c3 heading 'Option'             format a15
col c4 heading 'Object|Count'       format 999,999

break on c1 skip 2
break on c2 skip 2

select
  p.object_name c1,
  p.operation   c2,
  p.options     c3,
  count(1)      c4
from
  dba_hist_sql_plan p,
  dba_hist_sqlstat  s
where
  p.object_owner <> 'SYS'
```

```
and
   p.sql_id = s.sql_id
group by
   p.object_name,
   p.operation,
   p.options
order by
   1,2,3;
```

The following output shows overall total counts for each object and table access method.

Object Name	Operation	Option	Object Count
CUSTOMER	TABLE ACCESS	FULL	305
CUSTOMER _CHECK	INDEX	RANGE SCAN	2
CUSTOMER_ORDERS	TABLE ACCESS	BY INDEX ROWID	311
CUSTOMER_ORDERS		FULL	1
CUSTOMER_ORDERS_PRIMARY	INDEX	FULL SCAN	2
CUSTOMER_ORDERS_PRIMARY		UNIQUE SCAN	311
AVAILABILITY_PRIMARY_KEY		RANGE SCAN	4
CON_UK		RANGE SCAN	3
CURRENT_SEVERITY_PRIMARY_KEY		RANGE SCAN	1
CWM$CUBE	TABLE ACCESS	BY INDEX ROWID	2
CWM$CUBEDIMENSIONUSE		BY INDEX ROWID	2
CWM$CUBEDIMENSIONUSE_IDX	INDEX	RANGE SCAN	2
CWM$CUBE_PK		UNIQUE SCAN	2
CWM$DIMENSION_PK		FULL SCAN	2
MGMT_INV_VERSIONED_PATCH	TABLE ACCESS	BY INDEX ROWID	3
MGMT_JOB		BY INDEX ROWID	458
MGMT_JOB_EMD_STATUS_QUEUE		FULL	181
MGMT_JOB_EXECUTION		BY INDEX ROWID	456
MGMT_JOB_EXEC_IDX01	INDEX	RANGE SCAN	456
MGMT_JOB_EXEC_SUMMARY	TABLE ACCESS	BY INDEX ROWID	180
MGMT_JOB_EXEC_SUMM_IDX04	INDEX	RANGE SCAN	180
MGMT_JOB_HISTORY	TABLE ACCESS	BY INDEX ROWID	1
MGMT_JOB_HIST_IDX01	INDEX	RANGE SCAN	1
MGMT_JOB_PK		UNIQUE SCAN	458
MGMT_METRICS	TABLE ACCESS	BY INDEX ROWID	180

Using the output above, it is easy to monitor object participation, especially indexes, in the SQL queries and the mode with which an object was accessed by Oracle.

Why is it important to know how tables and indexes are accessed? It is all about performance. Objects that experience multi-block reads may perform faster in a larger blocksize and also reduce SGA overhead.

Conclusion

The focus of this chapter is for the SQL developer to understand more about how the placement of the rows on the data blocks can have an impact on SQL performance. The main points of this chapter include:

- Too much free space on each data block, as set by pctfree, can make full-scan operations take longer.

- A table high-water mark never goes down until the table is reorganized, and tables that experience frequent large-table full-table scans may see faster SQL after reorganizing the table to lower the high water mark.

With each new release and acquisition, Oracle adds new tuning tools to the tuning toolbox. As these tools continue to improve, it is still up the subjective judgment of the DBA to decide when or if it is necessary to reorganize Oracle tables and indexes. The tips in this chapter should help Oracle developers make that job a bit easier.

The next chapter will focus on Oracle sorting operations and how they influence SQL performance.

Tuning SQL Sort Operations

Oracle's sorting algorithms are a proprietary secret!

The History of Data Sorting

Oracle sorting is a very important component of Oracle tuning, yet sorting optimization is often overlooked because it is done automatically.

The process of sequencing database output goes back to the 1960's and in earlier databases the data was extracted in an unsorted fashion and sorted externally.
Here is a sample of MVS job control language (JCL) from the 1970's that performs a data extract, followed by a back-end sort:

```
//GOFORIT JOB (CLASS=A)
//STEP1  EXEC PGM=IDMSCOB
//SYSOUT DD DSN='ram_disk_dataset',DISP=(,DELETE,KEEP)
//STEP2 EXEC PGM=SORT
```

```
//SORTIN DD DSN='ram_disk_dataset',
// DISP=(OLD,DELETE, DELETE)
//SORTOUT DD DSN='new_sorted_dataset',
// DISP=(NEW,CATLG,DELETE),
// SPACE=(CYL,(100,100),RLSE),UNIT=SYSDA
```

Oracle SQL does far more than simply extract the row information from the tables, and the row data can be sorted and summarized in a number of ways. By using Oracle SQL in conjunction with SQL*Plus, row information can be sorted, transformed, formatted and displayed in a report format. In fact, SQL*Plus allows for sophisticated reports to be generated.

Many Oracle professionals fail to realize that the execution plan for Oracle SQL will often change when the data is sorted and transformed. To fully understand how Oracle SQL execution is affected, let's explore the different methods for sorting data. Oracle provides several SQL directives that cause sorting of row data.

- **Order by**: An operation that sorts a set of rows for a query with an *order by* clause.

- **Group by**: SQL that specifies a grouping will sorts a set of rows.

- **Join**: Some joins require row sorting (the *sort merge* join).

- **Aggregation**: A retrieval of a single row that is the result of applying a group function to a group of selected rows.

- **Select distinct**: This is an operation that forces SQL to eliminate duplicate rows from the result set. On Oracle 10gR2 and beyond, *distinct* often uses hashing instead of sorting to remove duplicate rows.

- **Select unique**: A *select unique* forces a sort to remove duplicate values from the result set.

- **Create Index**: DDL operation such as create index will need to sort the symbolic keys and ROWID values.

 ### Use select distinct only when necessary

Do not specify select distinct on a table where a unique index already exists on the column. If the column is already unique, using *distinct* causes an additional operation and slows SQL performance.

Sadly, sorting is a frequently overlooked aspect of Oracle tuning. In general, an Oracle database will automatically perform sorting operations, and the SQL tuning expert must understand all of the SQL directives that invoke Oracle sorting.

At the time a *SQL*Plus* session is established with Oracle, a private sort area is allocated in RAM memory for use by the session for sorting. If the connection is via a non-MTS dedicated connection, a program global area (PGA) is allocated according to the *sort_area_size or pga_aggregate_target* parameter. For connections via the multithreaded server, sort space is allocated in the *large_pool_size*.

Of course, sorts that cannot fit into the dedicated RAM area for the session will be paged out into the TEMP tablespaces for a disk sort, and disk sorts are thousands of times slower than memory sorts.

Disk sorts are expensive for several reasons. First, they are extremely slow when compared to in-memory sorts. Also, a disk sort consumes resources in the temporary tablespace. Oracle must also allocate buffer pool blocks to hold the blocks in the temporary tablespace.

In-memory sorts are always preferable to disk sorts, and disk sorts will surely slow down an individual task, as well as impact concurrent tasks on the Oracle instance. Also, excessive disk sorting will cause a high value for free buffer waits, paging other tasks' data blocks out of the buffer.   Hence, monitoring for disk sorts is an important task, and it is never desirable to have SQL invoke a disk sort unless there is a giant result set.

Sort at Query Time or Sort After Retrieval?

Oracle will always use the cheapest method for sequencing a result set, and the optimizer will use index retrieval, meaning it will extract the rows in sorted order, if it consumes fewer resources than a back-end sort. Remember, a sort that cannot fit into RAM will have to be done in the TEMP tablespace, which is very slow with lots of disk I/O.

Not all SQL will invoke a sorting operation. Here is an example of a query that uses an index to fetch the rows in pre-sorted order, using an index range scan:

```
select
   empno
from
   emp
where
   empno > 7876
order by
   empno;
```

```
Query Plan
--------------------------------------------------------------
SELECT STATEMENT    [CHOOSE] Cost=1
TABLE ACCESS BY ROWID EMP [ANALYZED]
  INDEX RANGE SCAN EMP_I1 [ANALYZED]
```

Retrieve your rows in pre-sorted order!

For testing your SQL sort performance, you can manually override the optimizer sorting and force Oracle to retrieve your rows in pre-sorted order with an /*+ *index */ hint.

The choice of pre-sorting or post-sorting depends on several factors:

- **The *optimizer_mode* parameter:** The *all_rows* optimizer mode favors non-index sorting while *first_rows* optimization favors index access and retrieval in index order.

- **The *_optimizer_cost_model* parameter:** The *cpu_cost* parameter favors indexes, while the *io_cost* setting favors sorting.

- **RAM region for the session:** The size of the *sort_area_size* or *pga_aggregate_target*, if used.

- **Pre-sorted index:** If there is an index with a low *clustering_factor* to the rows, near the value of *dba_tables blocks* column, the optimizer may choose to retrieve the rows in pre-sorted order.

- **Row size and block size:** The *db_block_size* and *avg_row_len* affects the optimizer's decision on how to perform sorting.

- **Rows returned:** The estimated size of the sorted result set factors heavily into the type of sort method used.

- **Statistics:** The quality of optimizer statistics, as computed by the *dbms_stats* package make a huge difference in making the right sorting choice, especially in cases where histograms may be needed to estimating the size of the final result set.

Oracle also has additional sorting parameters that can be revealed using SQL*Plus. These parameters are set by the DBA:

```
SQL> show parameters sort;
```

```
NAME                                TYPE     VALUE
---------------------------------   -------  ---------------
nls_sort                            string
sort_area_retained_size             integer  0
sort_area_size                      integer  10000
sort_multiblock_read_count          integer  2
```

For SQL gurus, it is also possible to see hidden Oracle sorting parameters, those that control the internal mechanisms of sorting, are only to be changed at the direction of Oracle technical support:

- **_newsort_enabled**: This is the new sort algorithm introduced in 10gR2 and beyond.

- **_sort_elimination_cost_ratio**: The cost ratio for sort elimination under *first_rows* mode.

- **_sort_multiblock_read_count**: The multi-block read count for sort.

- **_sort_space_for_write_buffers**: The tenths of *sort_area_size* devoted to direct write buffers.

- **_sortmerge_inequality_join_off**: This turns off sort-merge join on inequality.

- **_spin_count**: This is the amount to spin waiting for a latch.

- **_sql_connect_capability_override**: The SQL Connect Capability Table Override.

- **_sql_connect_capability_table**: The SQL Connect Capability Table (testing only).

- **_sqlexec_progression_cost**: The SQL execution progression monitoring cost threshold.

It is clear that Oracle sorting is very sophisticated. The following section will delve into external sorting and how it can be used to hypercharge SQL queries.

Tuning with External Sorts

In cases where the SQL retrieves giant result sets (over 100,000 rows), some shops define their TEMP tablespace with Flash disk (solid-state disk, or SSD), but that approach is limited by Oracle's internal sorting algorithms. For faster sorting and a choice of sort methods, it may be preferable to consider sorting outside of Oracle.

To perform an external sort with Oracle, just add a separate step for sorting after the SQL*Plus extraction of the unsorted rows. The following is a simple shell script that runs an unsorted Oracle SQL and pipes it into the UNIX *sort* utility:

```
#!/bin/ksh
sqlplus /nolog

@/u01/emp.sql > /u01/ssd/unsorted.txt 2>&1 |sort > /u01/ssd/sorted.txt
```

In external sorting, the *order by* clause is omitted and the unsorted result is redirected to a 3rd party sorting tool, such as the popular CoSort product which offers a variety of sorting method that can be used customize to the result set.

For sorting giant row sets, many shops use super-fast RAM disk (SSD) for sort storage where the SQL results can be sorted hundreds of times faster than platter disk. It is also possible for the TEMP tablespace to be in RAM disk.

The internal machinations of Oracle sorting are complex, but it is possible to control sorting within SQL.

Internals of Oracle Sorting

Oracle does not document how they do sorting because it is a highly proprietary secret. Under the covers, Oracle probably uses several sorting algorithms and the Oracle documentation notes that all sorts begin in the RAM defined by *pga_aggregate_target* or *sort_area_size*, and then spill-off onto disk (the TEMP tablespace), if the RAM is exhausted.

The secret sorting algorithms are a competitive advantage for Oracle and are a closely held secret, but their sorting changes by release. For example, Oracle introduced a new sorting algorithm in Oracle 10g release 2 governed by the hidden parameter *_newsort_enabled*. To test the speed of sorting, *_newsort_enabled=true* can be set in the test database.

For shops that have to sequence millions of rows of output on an hourly basis, external sort products can be faster than using Oracle to sort the data. Some shops purchase 3rd party vendor eternal sorting tools for Oracle, which employ specialized sorting algorithms for special data characteristics.

Managing Oracle Sorting

At the time a session is established with Oracle, a private sort area is allocated in memory for use by the session for sorting, based on the value of the *sort_area_size* (or *pga_aggregate_target*) initialization parameter.

Unfortunately, the amount of memory must be the same for all sessions, and it is not possible to add additional sort areas for tasks that are sort intensive. Therefore, the DBA must strike a balance between allocating enough sort area to avoid disk sorts for the large sorting tasks, keeping in mind that the extra sort area will be allocated and not used by tasks that do not require intensive sorting.

Whenever a sort cannot be completed within the assigned space, a disk sort is invoked using the temporary tablespace for the Oracle instance. A sort in the temporary tablespace is very I/O intensive and can slow down the entire database.

As a general rule, the *sort_area_size* should be large enough that only index creation and *order by* clauses using functions should be allowed to use a disk sort. However, operations on large tables will always perform disk sorts. For example, the following query will sort the salaries for all 100,000 employees at Oracle Corporation:

```
select
   salary
from
   employee
order by
   salary;
```

Oracle always tries to sort in the RAM space within *sort_area_size* and only goes to a disk sort when the RAM memory is exhausted. Fortunately, there are some techniques for avoiding disk sorts.

Avoiding Disk Sorts

Disk speed is measured in milliseconds (thousandths of a second) while RAM speed is expressed in nanoseconds (billionths of a second). Hence, disk operations are 10,000 times slower than RAM, and whenever a result set is too large to be sorted within our session RAM, the Oracle SQL will re-direct the sort out to disks, using the TEMP tablespace.

Using the SQL*Plus autotrace utility, it is easy to see if a SQL statement performed a disk sort. In the execution statistics, the row(s) are marked *sorts (disk):*

```
SQL> set autotrace on

SQL> select ename from emp where empno = 1122;


no rows selected

Execution Plan
----------------------------------------------------------
0 SELECT STATEMENT Optimizer=CHOOSE
1 0 TABLE ACCESS (BY INDEX ROWID) OF 'EMP'
```

```
2 1 INDEX (UNIQUE SCAN) OF 'PK_EMP' (UNIQUE)


Statistics
----------------------------------------------------------
    83  recursive calls
     0  db block gets
    21  consistent gets
     3  physical reads
     0  redo size
   221  bytes sent via SQL*Net to client
   368  bytes received via SQL*Net from client
     1  SQL*Net roundtrips to/from client
     0  sorts (memory)
     0  sorts (disk)
     0  rows processed
```

Disk sorts are expensive for several reasons. First, they consume resources in the temporary tablespaces. Oracle must also allocate buffer pool blocks to hold the blocks in the temporary tablespace.

Remember, in-memory sorts are always preferable to disk sorts, and disk sorts will surely slow down an individual SQL, as well as possibly slowing down other concurrent SQL as it take-up TEMP tablespace blocks.

Hypercharge your TEMP tablespace

One trick for making disk sorts super-fast is to define your TEMP tablespace onto super-fast solid-state (SSD) disk. See the book *Oracle solid-state Disk Tuning* for more details.

There are at some handy SQL tuning secrets for super-sizing the SQL RAM area for sorting.

Super Sizing SQL Sort areas

Many Oracle professionals do not know the important limitations of *pga_aggregate_target*, and they do not know that they can dedicate large amounts of RAM to avoid a time-consuming disk sort in the TEMP tablespace. Oracle imposes a limit to prevent any single SQL from "hogging" the shared RAM:

- The total work area cannot exceed 200 megabytes of RAM because of the default setting for *_pga_max_size*.

- No RAM sort may use more than 5% of *pga_aggregate_target* or *_pga_max_size*, whichever is smaller. This means that no task may use more than 10 megabytes for sorting.

While this arbitrary limit varies by release, it is set to about 1/20 of the available RAM, such that no task may have more than 5% of the RAM resources. But what about single threaded jobs in a nightly batch window?

How can this 5% limit be overridden? Essentially there are two choices for overriding the PGA governor:

- **Parallelization:** If the batch SQL is made to be parallel degree 15, each process will get RAM, and instead of a 5% the result will be 75% of the PGA RAM resources. This is preferable to adjusting hidden parameters and it provides a more sustainable solution for batch jobs that need giant sort areas in RAM.

- **Hints:** Staring in Oracle 10g release 2, Oracle introduced the *opt_param* SQL hint, very similar to the *alter session* method for changing parameters, but it is just for SQL. A ten megabyte *sort_area_size* for the SQL can easily be set as follows:

```
select /*+ opt_param('sort_area_size','10485760') */
    stuff
from
    hugetab
order by
    stuff;
```

- **Hidden parameters:** An honest discussion with Oracle technical support (My Oracle Support Community, or MOSC) might result in them allow the adjustment of the hidden parameters that control the governor on PGA RAM. The following settings would increase the default sizes for large sorts. With these hidden parameters set there is a 5 times larger size increase for sorts and a RAM sort may now have up to 50 megabytes (5% of *pga_aggregate_target*), which is a 5x increase.

```
pga_aggregate_target = 1000m

_pga_max_size = 1000m

_smm_px_max_size = 333m
```

Use parallel query to get more sort RAM!

Because each process in Oracle has its own RAM area, parallelizing a full-scan will allow for more RAM and you can often avoid disk sorts while avoiding the use of undocumented parameters.

Disk sorts can be expensive, so it is helpful to know how to monitor it in Oracle.

Monitoring Disk Sorts

For those who cannot afford to map their *temp* tablespace to SSD, the SQL must be carefully monitored to ensure that these expensive disk sorts are minimized.

The sort information can be captured in STATSPACK tables and plotted to determine the times when disk sorts are experienced by the instance. For visually-oriented people, the Ion for Oracle tool is a great way to quickly see average disk sorts by day of the week as shown in Figure 12.1:

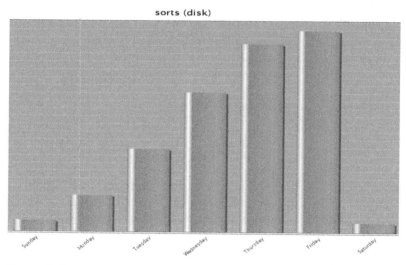

Figure 12.1: *Ion screenshot showing average disk sorts by day*

This is the STATSPACK script that will produce the numbers for the above graph.

💾 **statspack_plot_sorts_dow.sql**

```
set pages 9999;

column sorts_memory   format 999,999,999
column sorts_disk     format 999,999,999
column ratio          format .99999

select
   to_char(snap_time,'day')       DAY,
   avg(newmem.value-oldmem.value) sorts_memory,
   avg(newdsk.value-olddsk.value) sorts_disk
from
```

```
   perfstat.stats$sysstat oldmem,
   perfstat.stats$sysstat newmem,
   perfstat.stats$sysstat newdsk,
   perfstat.stats$sysstat olddsk,
   perfstat.stats$snapshot   sn
where
   newdsk.snap_id = sn.snap_id
and
   olddsk.snap_id = sn.snap_id-1
and
   newmem.snap_id = sn.snap_id
and
   oldmem.snap_id = sn.snap_id-1
and
   oldmem.name = 'sorts (memory)'
and
   newmem.name = 'sorts (memory)'
and
   olddsk.name = 'sorts (disk)'
and
   newdsk.name = 'sorts (disk)'
and
   newmem.value-oldmem.value > 0
group by
   to_char(snap_time,'day');
```

The listing below shows the number of disk sorts by day of the week. Clearly there is a spike in disk sorts on Thursday. This indicates a good starting point for investigating how to tune the SQL that does the Thursday sorts:

```
DAY         SORTS_MEMORY   SORTS_DISK
---------   ------------   ------------
friday            12,545          954
monday            14,352          223
saturday          12,430           33
sunday            13,807          445
thursday          17,042        1,234
tuesday           15,172          478
wednesday         14,650          143
```

With a minor change to the date format mask, this query will plot sorts by hours of the day:

🖫 statspack_plot_sorts_hod.sql

```
set pages 9999;

column sorts_memory   format 999,999,999
column sorts_disk         format 999,999,999
column ratio               format .99999

select
   to_char(snap_time,'HH24'),
```

```
    avg(newmem.value-oldmem.value) sorts_memory,
    avg(newdsk.value-olddsk.value) sorts_disk
from
    perfstat.stats$sysstat oldmem,
    perfstat.stats$sysstat newmem,
    perfstat.stats$sysstat newdsk,
    perfstat.stats$sysstat olddsk,
    perfstat.stats$snapshot   sn
where
    newdsk.snap_id = sn.snap_id
and
    olddsk.snap_id = sn.snap_id-1
and
    newmem.snap_id = sn.snap_id
and
    oldmem.snap_id = sn.snap_id-1
and
    oldmem.name = 'sorts (memory)'
and
    newmem.name = 'sorts (memory)'
and
    olddsk.name = 'sorts (disk)'
and
    newdsk.name = 'sorts (disk)'
and
    newmem.value-oldmem.value > 0
group by
    to_char(snap_time,'HH24')
;
```

```
TO  SORTS_MEMORY   SORTS_DISK
--  ------------   ------------
00        18,855           11
01        19,546           15
02        10,128            5
03         6,503            8
04        10,410            4
05         8,920            5
06         8,302            7
07         9,124           27
08        13,492           71
09        19,449           55
10        19,812          106
11        17,332           78
12        20,566           76
13        17,130           46
14        19,071           61
15        19,494           68
16        20,701           79
17        19,478           44
18        23,364           29
19        13,626           20
20        11,937           17
21         8,467            7
22         8,432           10
23        11,587           10
```

For shops that have purchased the AWR product via the Oracle Performance Pack and Oracle diagnostic pack licenses, the above queries can be modified to replace the *stats$sysstat* table with the *dba_hist_sysstat* view.

The *dba_hist_sysstat* view is one of the most valuable of the AWR history tables because it contains instance-wide summaries of many important performance metrics.

Here is another STATSPACK script to compare the percentage of disk sorts to RAM sorts:

🖫 statspack_sorts_alert.sql

```
set pages 9999;

column mydate      heading 'Yr.  Mo Dy  Hr.' format a16
column sorts_memory  format 999,999,999
column sorts_disk    format 999,999,999
column ratio         format .99999

select
   to_char(snap_time,'yyyy-mm-dd HH24') mydate,
   newmem.value-oldmem.value sorts_memory,
   newdsk.value-olddsk.value sorts_disk,
   ((newdsk.value-olddsk.value)/(newmem.value-oldmem.value)) ratio
from
   perfstat.stats$sysstat oldmem,
   perfstat.stats$sysstat newmem,
   perfstat.stats$sysstat newdsk,
   perfstat.stats$sysstat olddsk,
   perfstat.stats$snapshot   sn
where
   newdsk.snap_id = sn.snap_id
and
   olddsk.snap_id = sn.snap_id-1
and
   newmem.snap_id = sn.snap_id
and
   oldmem.snap_id = sn.snap_id-1
and
   oldmem.name = 'sorts (memory)'
and
   newmem.name = 'sorts (memory)'
and
   olddsk.name = 'sorts (disk)'
and
   newdsk.name = 'sorts (disk)'
and
   newmem.value-oldmem.value > 0
   and
   newdsk.value-olddsk.value > 100
;
```

Again the trends in this graph are not readily apparent, but once pasted into an excel spreadsheet and plotted with the chart wizard, a signature appears, showing disk sorts over time:

```
Yr.  Mo Dy  Hr.  SORTS_MEMORY    SORTS_DISK    RATIO
----------------  ------------  ------------  -------
2012-12-20  12          13,166           166   .01261
2012-12-20  16          25,694           223   .00868
2012-12-21  10          99,183           215   .00217
2012-12-21  15          13,662           130   .00952
2012-12-21  16          17,004           192   .01129
2012-12-22  10          18,900           141   .00746
2012-12-22  11          19,487           131   .00672
2012-12-26  12          12,502           147   .01176
2012-12-27  13          20,338           118   .00580
2012-12-27  18          11,032           119   .01079
2012-12-28  16          16,514           205   .01241
2012-12-29  10          17,327           242   .01397
2012-12-29  16          50,874           167   .00328
2013-01-02  08          15,574           108   .00693
2013-01-02  10          39,052           136   .00348
2013-01-03  11          13,193           153   .01160
2013-01-03  13          19,901           104   .00523
2013-01-03  15          19,929           130   .00652
```

Here is another handy script for monitoring sorting, showing average sorts, grouped by hour of the day:

🖫 statspack_avg_sorts_hod.sql

```
set pages 9999;

column sorts_memory   format 999,999,999
column sorts_disk     format 999,999,999
column ratio          format .99999

select
   to_char(snap_time,'HH24'),
   avg(newmem.value-oldmem.value) sorts_memory,
   avg(newdsk.value-olddsk.value) sorts_disk
from
   perfstat.stats$sysstat oldmem,
   perfstat.stats$sysstat newmem,
   perfstat.stats$sysstat newdsk,
   perfstat.stats$sysstat olddsk,
   perfstat.stats$snapshot    sn
where
   newdsk.snap_id = sn.snap_id
and
   olddsk.snap_id = sn.snap_id-1
and
   newmem.snap_id = sn.snap_id
and
   oldmem.snap_id = sn.snap_id-1
```

```
and
   oldmem.name = 'sorts (memory)'
and
   newmem.name = 'sorts (memory)'
and
   olddsk.name = 'sorts (disk)'
and
   newdsk.name = 'sorts (disk)'
and
   newmem.value-oldmem.value > 0
group by
   to_char(snap_time,'HH24');
```

```
TO  SORTS_MEMORY    SORTS_DISK
--  ------------    ------------
00        18,855           411
01        19,546           115
02        10,128            95
03         6,503            38
04        10,410           874
05         8,920           565
06         8,302            47
07         9,124           827
08        13,492           571
09        19,449           955
10        19,812           106
11        17,332           178
12        20,566           576
13        17,130           346
14        19,071           761
15        19,494           268
16        20,701           179
17        19,478           644
18        23,364           729
19        13,626           120
20        11,937           117
21         8,467            97
22         8,432           110
23        11,587           110
```

Some DBAs are just not not into managing scripts and want a comprehensive tool to monitor sorting within SQL and additional advice, I recommend my own tool *Ion for Oracle* at www.ion-dba.com. I spent a decade building her, and she contains all of the scripts in this book, and lots more, organized to make SQL tuning easy.

For visually-oriented people, using a GUI to monitoring sorting trends is very useful. Figure 12.2 is an Ion screenshot showing average disk sorts by hour of the day:

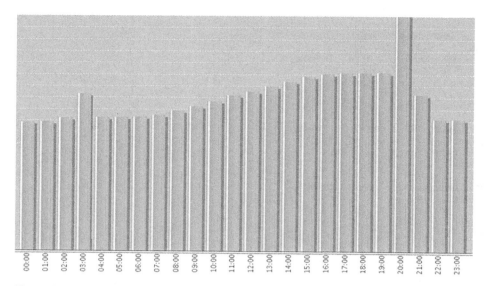

Figure 12.2: *Ion screenshot shows average sorts by hour of the day*

With the visual interface, it is possible to instantly see a spike in disk sorts at 8:00 PM each night, urging a trip to STATSPACK or AWR tables for further information.

Conclusion

This chapter has covered the internal behavior of sorting within Oracle SQL and shown how to adjust the ways that Oracle sorts SQL result sets. The main points of this chapter include:

- Sorts to disk are extremely expensive, as disk I/O is extremely slow. The goal of SQL tuning for sorting is to make the sort happen in RAM whenever feasible.

- Oracle will always begin sorting in RAM and will only spill over into disk when the result set is too large to hold in the PGA RAM.

- Oracle has a built-in RAM governor set to about 5% of total RAM. This limit can be overridden with parallel query, by adjusting hidden parameters only with Oracle's blessing or increasing the *sort_area_size* for any task that needs a large RAM sort area.

- SQL can be forced to retrieve rows in pre-sorted order.

- For batch SQL that returns hundreds of thousands of rows, an external sorting tool might be a viable option.

The next chapter will delve into the object extensions in Oracle and illustrate how the SQL for object-oriented constructs is tuned.

Tuning Object-oriented SQL

Oracle's object-oriented SQL extensions can be very mysterious

Over the years, Oracle has developed many useful SQL extensions that improve the productivity and effectiveness of Oracle SQL as a development language.

Object Oriented Oracle SQL

Starting in Oracle8, Oracle introduced object-orientation into their SQL. At one brief time, Oracle was re-named Oracle Universal Server (OUS), and Oracle touted their object-oriented extensions to be in line with the object-oriented craze of the 1990's. These included the following capabilities:

- **Modeling real-world objects:** It is no longer required for the relational database designer to model complex objects in their smallest components and rebuild them at run-time. Using Oracle's object-oriented constructs, real-world objects can have a concrete existence just like C++ objects. Oracle can use arrays of pointers to represent these complex objects and special SQL was designed to de-reference object pointers.

- **Coupling of data and behavior:** One of the important constructs of object orientation is the tight coupling of object behaviors with the objects themselves. In Oracle, a member method can be created upon the Oracle object, and all processes that manipulate the object are encapsulated inside Oracle's data dictionary.

This functionality has huge benefits for the development of all Oracle systems. Prior to the introduction of member methods, each Oracle developer was essentially a custom craftsman writing custom SQL to access Oracle information.

By using member methods, all interfaces to the Oracle database are performed using pre-tested methods with known interfaces. This way, the Oracle developer's role changes from custom craftsman to more of an assembly-line coder. All there is to do is simply choose from a list of prewritten member methods to access Oracle information.

The SQL Impedance Mismatch

Proponents of the object-oriented approach criticize SQL because it is not possible to directly model real-world objects and everything must be assembled from its components at query execution time. This is known as the SQL impedance mismatch as illustrated in Figure 13.1:

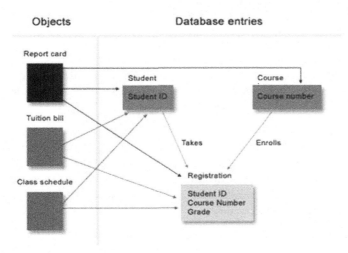

Figure 13.1: *The mapping of relational tables to objects*

While relational database SQL is very flexible, it does not match C++ structures which allow objects to be built and stored as arrays of pointers to sub-objects. Oracle implemented object-oriented constructs with pointers in the *nested* table which contained pointers to rows, and Oracle calls immutable rows pointers Object ID, or OID's for short. There are also built-in member methods, object inheritance and polymorphism, abstract data types and varray tables in the Oracle object-relational model, although these are rarely used in production databases.

The object-oriented purists complain that SQL is stupid, because it does not support complex objects!

Their argument is that you should not have to assemble your car every time that you want to drive your car.

Oracle offers numerous choices for the introduction of object-oriented data model constructs into relational database design. Oracle offers the ability to dereference table row pointers, abstract data types, and limited polymorphism and inheritance support.

There are several basic types of object-oriented extensions used in Oracle, namely abstract data types, *varray* tables and nested tables.

SQL Object Extension Performance

This section will focus on the SQL performance ramifications of using object-oriented extensions. The performance of an Abstract Data Type (ADT) table is much like that of any Oracle table. The differences primarily lie within the use of varray and nested tables. Here is a summary of the significant features of the Oracle SQL object extensions.

- **Varray tables:** The use of varray tables is beneficial because it lacks costly SQL joins and maintains the order of varray items, based upon the sequence in which they are stored. It is important to note that the longer row length of varray tables causes full-table scans to run longer. Another disadvantage is that items inside the varray cannot be indexed. Varrays cannot be used when the number of repeating items is unknown or excessively large.

- **Tables with Abstract Data Types:** There are several benefits to creating user-defined abstract datatypes within tables. These greatly simplify the design of the Oracle database and also provide uniform data definitions for common data items. While there is no downside concerning SQL performance, SQL syntax is affected in that all references to ADTs must be fully qualified.

- **Nested Tables:** Nested tables have the benefit of allowing for an infinite number of repeating groups. These repeating groups are sequestered into a separate table, which improves the performance of full-table scans. However, it can sometimes take longer to dereference the OID using nested tables that with a standard SQL table join. Because of this, many Oracle experts see no added benefit of using nested tables over traditional table joins.

These non-relational datatypes allow the Oracle DBA to create non-traditional table structures, un-normalized tables that require specialized object-oriented SQL.

Performance of Oracle Object-oriented SQL

To fully understand Oracle advanced design, it is necessary to take a look at the SQL performance ramifications of using object extensions. Overall, the performance of Abstract Data Type (ADT) tables is the same as any other Oracle table, but there are significant performance differences when implementing varray tables and nested tables:

- **ADT tables:** Creating user-defined datatypes simplifies Oracle database design. Doing ADTs also provides uniform data definitions for common data items. There is no downside for SQL performance, and the only downside for SQL syntax is the requirement that all references to ADTs be fully qualified.

- **Nested tables:** Nested tables have the advantage of being indexed, and the repeating groups are separated into another table so as not to degrade the performance of full-table scans. Nested tables allow for an infinite number of repeating groups. However, it sometimes takes longer to dereference the OID to access the nested table entries as opposed to ordinary SQL tables join operations. Most Oracle experts see no compelling benefit of using nested tables over traditional table joins.

- **Varray tables:** *Varray* tables have the benefit of avoiding costly SQL joins, and they can maintain the order of the varray items based upon the sequence when they were stored. However, the longer row length of varray tables causes full-table scans to run longer, and the items inside the varray cannot be indexed. More importantly, *varray* tables cannot be used when the number of repeating items is unknown or very large. Varray tables are also problematic because the non-standard SQL is very clumsy and hard to use:

```
SQL> SELECT * FROM person;

NAME   DOB
```

```
------------------------------- ---------
ADDRESS_V
-------------------------------------------
ADDRESS_N
-----------------------------------------------------

Jones 01-JAN-60
ADDRESSES_V('Line 1', 'Line 2', 'Line 3')
ADDRESSES_N('Line 1', 'Line 2', 'Line 3')
```

Now, it is time to move on to how changes to traditional table design impact Oracle SQL and see how Oracle SQL has extensions for extracting object-oriented data from relational tables.

Oracle offers a variety of data structures to help create robust database systems. Oracle supports the full use of binary large objects (BLOB), nested tables, non–first-normal-form table structures (VARRAY tables) and object-oriented table structures. It even treats flat data files as if they were tables within the Oracle database.

It is a challenge to many Oracle design professionals to know when to use these Oracle data model extensions. This section includes a brief review of advanced Oracle topics and how they are used to design high-performance Oracle databases.

The ability of Oracle to support object types, sometimes called user-defined datatypes, has profound implications for Oracle design and implementation. User-defined datatypes will enable the database designer to:

- **Create aggregate datatypes:** Aggregate datatypes are datatypes that contain other datatypes. For example, it is possible to create a type called *full_address* that contains all of the subfields necessary for a complete mailing address.

- **Nest user-defined datatypes:** Datatypes can be placed within other user-defined datatypes to create data structures that can be easily reused within Oracle tables and PL/SQL. For example, a datatype called *customer* could be created to contains a datatype called *customer_demographics*, which in turn contains a datatype called *job_history*, and so on.

One of the new user-defined data types in the Oracle object-relational model is a pointer data type. Essentially, a pointer is a unique reference to a row in a relational table. The ability to store these row IDs inside a relational table extends the traditional relational model and enhances the ability of an object-relational database to establish relationships between tables. The new abilities of pointer data types include:

- **Referencing sets of related rows in other tables**: It is now possible to violate first normal form and have a cell in a table that contains a pointer to repeating table values. For example, an *employee* table could contain a pointer called *job_history_set*, which in turn could contain pointers to all of the relevant rows in a *job_history* table. This technique also allows aggregate objects to be prebuilt, such that all of the specific rows that comprise the aggregate table could be preassembled.

- **Allow pointers to non-database objects in a flat file:** For example, a table cell could contain a pointer to a flat file that contains a non-database object such as a picture in *.gif* or *.jpeg* format.

- **The ability to establish one-to-many and many-to-many data relationships without relational foreign keys:** This would alleviate the need for relational join operations, because table columns could contain references to rows in other tables. By dereferencing these pointers, rows could be retrieved from other tables without ever using the time-consuming SQL join operator.

Repeating Data Items in Relational Tables

The idea of repeating data items within an object has long been repulsive to relational database designers. The common consensus among DBAs was that the removal of repeating data items was an important step towards a clean data model.

In traditional normalization, the removal of repeating and redundant groups is the first step when designing a relational database, leading to a database in the first-normal form (1NF).

The Origin of Normalization

I once asked Ted Codd how he came up with the term "normalization". Ted told me that at the time, President Nixon was "normalizing relations" with China. Codd said that if Nixon could normalize relations, then so could he!

The introduction of repeating groups changes this, leading to a table in the non-first-normal form (0NF). Oracle implemented this concept of repeating table groups by allowing for the *varray* datatype.

This adoption of the 0NF datatype in databases like Oracle led C. J. Date to change his definition of the relational database model. Date introduced the concept of a set into the relational database model. This allowed for 0NF relations to fit into the relational paradigm. There are some guidelines to consider when introducing repeating groups into an Oracle object table.

- Repeating data items should be small in size.

- Data should be static and seldom changed.

- Repeating data should never be queried as a "set."

It is important to note that Oracle has provided two methods to introduce repeating groups into a table design; nested tables, and the varray construct. Although these methods differ greatly concerning internal structure and SQL syntax, they serve the same purpose. Their differences include:

- **Element control:** Individual elements can be deleted from a nested table. This is not true of VARRAY tables.

- **Number of repeating groups:** Varrays have a maximum size, while nested tables can have an infinite number of subordinate rows. Instances with small numbers of repeating groups are usually use varray tables rather than nested tables.

- **Sequencing:** Varray rows will always retain their original sequences, while nested tables to do not necessarily do so.

- **Internal Storage:** Varray rows are stored in-line within Oracle using the same tablespace, while nested table data is stored in a store table out-of-line. This store table is generated by the system and is associated with the nested table.

- **Index capabilities:** Varray rows do not support indexes, while nested table entries do. Because of this, repeating items that require index-based SQL should be implemented using nested tables.

To help illustrate how repeating groups are implemented, an example of a simple employee database can be used. In this database, every employee has a history of previous employers. Because the employers' name is the only information needed, a subordinate table is not the most efficient way to represent this structure as shown in Figure 13.2.

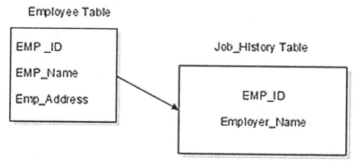

Figure 13.2: *First Normal Form (1NF) moves repeating groups into new tables*

This idea of removing repeating groups into a separate table is quite common and called first-normal form. However, using Oracle *varray* tables, the table structure can be simplified by rolling the repeating groups into a single table row.

Oracle has a construct that allows for the embedding of the *employer_name* into a single table row as shown in Figure 13.3.

Repeating VARRAY

Employee Table

EMP_ID	EMP_Name	Prev_EMP	Prev_EMP	Prev_EMP
123	James	IBM	ABC	General Mills
124	Kirk	Google	TNT	
126	Thomas	Apple	GE	Southwest

Figure 13.3: *A Non First Normal Form (0NF) table contains repeating groups*

One type of non-first-normal form table is the *varray* table.

Inside Varray Tables

The idea of non-first-normal form (0NF) tables originated in pre-relational databases when a data record needed to contain repeating groups of small, immutable redundant items. These might include:

- **Students and test scores:** A student may take the LSAT up to three times.
- **Employees and previous employers**: An employee database may store the names of an employees last ten employers.
- **Customers and credit scores:** A customer rows may contain the past 12 credit scores.

These are truly one-to-many data relationships that were traditionally normalized into separate tables. However, it makes no sense to create separate tables of test scores, previous employers and credit scores, and it would be nice to have a data model that allows us to keep these repeating items within the master tables and address them with a subscript number, just like an internal array.

Back before Oracle8 gave us *varray* tables, it would be necessary to represent repeating groups in a table in a very clumsy and non-elegant fashion, naming each repeating element.

Prior to the release of Oracle8, non-first normal form tables were created in a very messy and confused fashion. Below is an example of the syntax used to create a traditional Oracle table:

```
create table employee (
      full_name                  full_mailing_address_type,
      last_name                  varchar(40),
      previous_employer_one      varchar(40),
      previous_employer_two      varchar(40),
      previous_employer_three    varchar(40)
);
```

This is clumsy because the previous items within a loop cannot be referenced using a subscript. Ideally, the goal would to be able to loop through repeating items like in the pseudocode:

```
for i=1 to max_prev_emps
do
   select previous_employer(i)
done
```

It should be immediately apparent that this loop could be done in PL/SQL, but SQL does not support looping and special extensions are required to simulate a loop in Oracle SQL repeating groups. The following example will show how to define and query a repeating group in a *varray* table.

First create an Oracle type to hold the repeating group of previous employers.

```
create or replace type
   employer_name
as object
(e_name varchar(40))
;

create or replace type
   prior_employer_name_arr
as
   varray(10) of employer_name;
```

Next, the *employee* type is created. The create type command embeds the *varray* of prior employers into the table:

```
create or replace type
   employee
as object
(
   last_name                varchar(40),
   full_address             full_mailing_address_type,
   prior_employers          prior_employer_name_arr
);
```

Next, the *emp* table is created. This is done using the newly created *employee* type.

```
SQL> create table emp of employee;

Table Created.
```

The next step is to insert rows into the object table. Notice that repeating groups of previous employers are specified in addition to the use of *full_mailing_address_type* reference for the ADT.

```
insert into emp
values
(
   'Burleson',
   full_mailing_address_type('7474 Airplane Ave.','Rocky
Ford','NC','27445'),
   prior_employer_name_arr(
      employer_name('IBM'),
      employer_name('ATT'),
      employer_name('CNN')
   )
);
insert into emp
values
(
   'Lavender',
   full_mailing_address_type('7474 Bearpond Ave.','Big Lick','NC','17545'),
   prior_employer_name_arr(
      employer_name('Oracle'),
      employer_name('Sybase'),
      employer_name('Computer Associates')
   )
);
```

The next step is to perform the select SQL. All of the repeating groups with a single reference can be selected using the *prior_employers* column.

```
select
   p.prior_employers
from
   emp p
where
   p.last_name = 'Burleson';


PRIOR_EMPLOYERS(E_NAME)
-------------------------------------------------------------------------
----
PRIOR_EMPLOYER_NAME_ARR(EMPLOYER_NAME('IBM'), EMPLOYER_NAME('ATT'),
EMPLOYER_NAM
E('CNN'))
```

Look Out!

Object SQL has Display Issues!

In the SQL above, note the goofy display. If this SQL were embedded inside a program it would be very difficult to parse out the fetched SQL results.

Inside Varray Tables

The nature of these repeating groups can make the output difficult to interpret. In the following example, the SQL *table* keyword is used to flatten out the repeating groups, displaying the following information.

```
column l_name       heading "Last Name"       format a20;

select
   emp.last_name             l_name,
   prior_emps.*
from
   emp                       emp,
   table(p.prior_employers) prior_emps
where
   p.last_name = 'burleson';
```

Below is the newly flattened output. The single information is duplicated into each table row.

```
Last Name              E_NAME
-------------------    -----------------------------------------
Burleson               IBM
Burleson               ATT
Burleson               CNN
```

The overhead of writing non-standard SQL is not insignificant, plus there is the issue of parsing the SQL results. So, what about the performance of SQL against *varray* tables? The following section will provide a closer look.

Execution Plans for *varray* Tables

A look at the execution plans for the above query shows some of the new access methods added to Oracle SQL to help manage objects. The *collection iterator* and *pickler fetch* operations are two of these new features.

The *collection iterator* function is used to extract repeating groups that are embedded within a row. It is important to remember that the performance of tables with *varray* columns is similar to standard row select statements. Because *varray* data items are stored in-line, a fetch for the data block that contains the row will also contain the repeating groups.

```
OPERATION
-----------------------------------------------------------------OPTIONS
OBJECT_NAME                   POSITION
-----------------------    ------------------------------------ ----------
SELECT STATEMENT
                                                                    33

   NESTED LOOPS
                                                                    1

      TABLE ACCESS
FULL                          EMP                                   1
```

Clearly, varray tables do not have the overhead of joining into another table for the repeating group, but there are performance downsides:

- **Non-standard SQL:** Specialized orient-oriented SQL syntax is required to simulate looping through the repeating items.

- **High cost of sequencing:** The physical sequence of the items in the varray must be kept manually.

- **No indexes:** Items within a varray table cannot have an index.

- **No large groups:** It is not good to use varray tables when there are so many items that the rows fragment onto adjacent data blocks.

In sum, varray tables are rarely used for SQL performance reasons except in rare cases where the repeating group is small, non-volatile, pre-sequenced and never referenced independently of the master row within SQL because it cannot be indexed.

The next topic is the concept of nested tables and how they relate to Oracle SQL performance.

Oracle Nested tables

A nested table is another denormalization tool, a non-first normal form way of modeling a one-to-many relationship without creating subordinate tables.

Using the Oracle nested table structure, subordinate data items can be directly linked to the base table by using Oracle's newest construct: the object ID (OID). While it sounds innocuous, the ability to reference Oracle objects directly by using pointers, is a major departure from the relational model, a concept completely foreign to relational SQL.

Proponents of the object-oriented database model criticize SQL because of the requirement to reassemble an object every time it is used.

To address this legitimate concern about SQL normalization, Oracle introduced the concept of pointers, object ID (OID) address locators that violate the relational model and allow the creation of non-relational data structures with pointers to the rows.

Oracle has moved toward allowing complex objects to have a concrete existence. In order to support the concrete existence of complex objects, it will be necessary to

---

have the ability to build arrays of pointers with row references directly to Oracle tables.

Just as a C++ program can use the char** data structure to have a pointer to an array of pointers, Oracle allows similar constructs whereby the components of the complex objects reside in real tables with pointers to the subordinate objects. At runtime, Oracle simply needs to dereference the pointers, and the complex object can be quickly rebuilt from its component pieces.

A Nested Table Example

In the previous example, a *varray* table was used to represent a repeating group for previous employers. Another close example might include the idea of modeling previous addresses.

In today's mobile world, an employee commonly has a small number of previous employers, but most people move frequently. It is not uncommon to have over a dozen previous addresses, too many to place in a *varray* tables because the row length might exceed the physical blocksize.

It is time to try creating a nested table. First, a type using *full_mailing_address_type* is created:

```
create type
   prev_addrs
as object
   (prior_address full_mailing_address_type);
```

Next, the nested object is created:

```
create type
   nested_address
as table of
   prev_addrs;
```

Now, we create the parent table with the nested table.

```
create table
   emp1 (
   last_name           varchar2(40),
   current_address     full_mailing_address_type,
   prev_address        nested_address   )
   nested table
      prev_address
   store as
      nested_prev_address
   return as locator;
```

A nested table appears as a part of the master table. Internally, it is a separate table. The *store as* clause allows the DBA to give the nested table a specific name as shown in Figure 13.4:

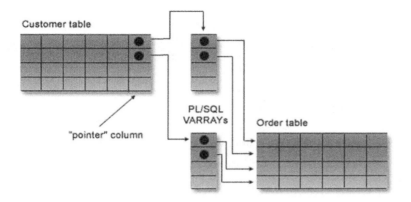

Figure 13.4: *Nested and varray tables use OID pointers*

The *nested_prev_address* subordinate table can be indexed just like any other Oracle table. Also, notice the use of the *return as locator* SQL syntax. In many cases, returning the entire nested table at query time can be time consuming.

The locator enables Oracle to use the pointer structures to dereference pointers to the location of the nested rows. A pointer dereference happens when a pointer is taken to an object and the program is asked to display the data to which the pointer is pointing.

In other words, if there is a pointer to a customer row, the OID can be referenced, thereby revealing the data for that customer. The link to the nested tables uses an Oracle OID instead of a traditional foreign key value.

This nested data structure allows for a new functionality within Oracle whereby tables could be nested within other tables. Nesting violates relational set theory, and specialized DDL and SQL are required to successfully manage this feature.

Unlike *varray* tables that contain embedded repeating groups, nested tables create subordinate tables that give the appearance of embedding.

Within the nested table structure, there are pointers that can be used to navigate between the nested tables and the master table.

Although the nested table appears to be part of the master table, it is however a separate table. Because of this, the *store as* clause can be used to give the nested table a unique name.

In this example, the *nested_prev_address* subordinate table can be indexed like any other Oracle table. In this example, the *return as locator* syntax is especially helpful. In many cases, the process of returning the entire nested table with a query can be time consuming. Using the locator enables Oracle to utilize the pointer structures to dereference the location of nested rows.

Nested Tables and SQL Performance

Nested tables are rarely used in high volume production databases for a variety of reasons:

- Unlike varray table where the repeating items cannot be indexed, nested tables allow indexing.

- The repeating groups are separated into another table so as not to degrade the performance of full-table scans.

- Nested tables allow for an infinite number of repeating groups.

However, there are some serious downsides to SQL performance with nested tables:

- It can take longer to dereference the OID than to join normal tables using a primary and foreign key.

- The non-standard SQL can make the code difficult to maintain.

In sum, most Oracle experts see no compelling benefit of using nested tables over traditional table joins.

The next section will provide a closer look at abstract data types in Oracle SQL.

ADTs and Oracle SQL

Also known as user-defined datatypes (UDTs), abstract datatypes can help you create less complex, easier to use database designs. These abstract datatypes are common in many programming languages and have been becoming more and more common within object-oriented databases.

Oracle implemented support for ADTs by extending Oracle SQL to include a *create type* definition. Figure 13.5 below shows an example of an abstract datatype, which can be seen as a collection of small basic datatypes treated as one entity :

Customer_Name		Customer_Address			
First_Name	Last_Name	Street	City	State	ZIP

Figure 13.5: *Customer_name and customer_address abstract datatypes*

There are many reasons that ADTs are useful when working within an Oracle database:

- **Encapsulation:** Using abstract datatypes within an Oracle design helps ensure that data definitions and default values are consistent throughout the database. Because abstract datatypes are treated as a complete entity, default values and value constraints remain consistent throughout the database.

- **Flexibility:** The second benefit of using ADTs is increased flexibility. Before the release of Oracle, DBAs were often inconvenienced by the inability to model grouped data columns. For instance, if you needed to select all address information for a particular customer, they had to go through the process of selecting and manipulating street address, city address and zip code as three separate columns.

This process has been streamlined using abstract datatypes. YOU can now create the datatype *full mailing address type* to the same effect. Those who can remember the dated COBOL programming language will likely find this familiar, as this construct was supported within COBOL's framework.

Programmers using COBOL could create data types that were composed of smaller subtypes, much in the same way ADTs are composed of smaller datatypes. For example, a COBOL programmer could define a full address like this:

```
05   CUSTOMER-ADDRESS.
       07 STREET-ADDRESS      PIC X(80).
       07 CITY-ADDRESS        PIC X(80).
       07 ZIP-CODE            PIC X(5).
```

Note that the customer address can be manipulated like an individual entity.

```
MOVE CUSTOMER-ADDRESS TO PRINT-REC.
```

```
MOVE SPACES TO CUSTOMER-ADDRESS.
```

This was how it has been done on COBOL since the 1950's, but now it is possible to do encapsulation with an Oracle abstract datatypes. First, the *create type* syntax can do the same type of grouping within Oracle.

```
create or replace type
   full_mailing_address_type
as object
( street        varchar2(80),
  city          varchar2(80),
  state         char(2),
  zip           varchar2(10) );
```

After it has been defined, you can use the *full mailing address type* to create tables.

```
CREATE TABLE
  customer
  (
    full_name             full_name_type,
    full_address          full_mailing_address_type,
  );
```

Once the table is defined, you can reference *full mailing address type* in the SQL, in the same manner as a primitive datatype.

```
insert into
   customer
values (
   full_name_type('ANDREW','S.','BURLESON'),
   full_mailing_address_type('123 1st st','Minot','ND','74635');
```

Once the table is selected, much different output is displayed than that of an ordinary *select* statement.

```
SQL> select * from customer;


FULL_NAME(FIRST_NAME, MI, LAST_NAME)
----------------------------------------
FULL_ADDRESS(STREET, CITY, STATE, ZIP)
----------------------------------------------------------------

FULL_NAME_TYPE('Andrew', 'S', 'Burleson')
FULL_MAILING_ADDRESS_TYPE('123 1st st', 'Minot', 'ND', '74635')
```

Although the syntax is different, the execution plans for these ADTs are the same as any intrinsic datatype. Note that the introduction of ADTs does not change SQL performance.

As common data structures are assembled into ADTs, they can often be used within many different definitions. This saves time coding and helps insure uniformity within the database.

For example, the datatype *full mailing address type* can be used in any table requiring an individual's full address.

In Oracle, data model constructs used in C++ or Smalltalk programming can be translated directly into an Oracle structure.

In addition, Oracle supports abstract data typing whereby customized data types are created with the strong typing inherent in any of the standard Oracle data types like *number*, *char*, *varchar2*, and *date*.

For example, below is an Oracle table created with abstract data types and a nested table.

```
create or replace type
   employee
as object  (
   last_name              varchar(40),
   full_address           full_mailing_address_type,
   prior_employers        prior_employer_name_arr
);
create table emp of employee;
```

Next, extensions to standard Oracle SQL are used to update these abstract data types.

```
insert into emp
values (
   'Burleson',
   full_mailing_address_type('7474 Airplane Ave.','Rocky
Ford','NC','27445'),
   prior_employer_name_arr(
      employer_name('IBM'),
      employer_name('ATT'),
      employer_name('CNN')
   ) );
```

Since the goal of this book is tuning, the overriding question at this point has to be how ADTs affect SQL Performance.

Abstract Datatypes and SQL Performance

Like any other Oracle features user-defined data types have distinct advantages and drawbacks:

- **Simplified referencing:** The ability to group-together many column values greatly improves programmer productivity and simplifies code because items do not have to be referenced at a granular level.

- **Unified naming:** Abstract datatypes make it easier to come up with unified names for groups and also support polymorphism. For example, a person_address *datatype* could be inherited as an employer_address datatype or a customer_address datatype.

On the downside, there is the issue of the non-standard SQL, but by and large, abstract datatypes have no negative impact on SQL performance.

Conclusion

Oracle provides a wealth of SQL extensions that can improve productivity and help to better model complex objects. These extensions can often change the execution plan for an SQL statement. Special consideration must be taken to index Oracle tables so that SQL with extensions can quickly access table rows.

The evolution of Oracle into an object-relational database has provided a huge number of extensions to the relational database model. It is the challenge of all Oracle design professionals to use these Oracle extensions to improve the performance and maintainability of Oracle databases. Relational professionals can no longer stay content with a basic understanding of relational algebra.

The successful Oracle designers must master all object-oriented concepts, including abstract data typing, nested tables, array tables, and those unique data structure extensions that make Oracle clearly one of the fastest and most robust databases in the marketplace.

The next chapter will delve deeper into Oracle subqueries and how to tune them.

Tuning SQL Subqueries

It looks like we have a Cartesian subquery. . .

Subquery Tuning and SQL

A subquery is a condition where an SQL query is nested or placed inside another SQL query. The ISO 99 SQL standard allows for SQL queries to be embedded inside other SQL statements in many different ways. SQL queries can be placed inside the *select* clause (scalar subqueries), inside the *from* clause (in-line views) and inside the *where* clause (basic subqueries).

The ability to nest SQL statements inside each other provides tremendous power to SQL and allows SQL statements to perform extremely complex processing without using a procedural language such as PL/SQL.

In relational terminology, the main query is called the outer query, and the subquery is often referred to as the inner query.

A nineteenth century philosophy professor named Augustus De Morgan created an interesting poem to demonstrate this fundamental truth about "nesting" of objects:

> Great fleas have little fleas
> upon their backs to bite 'em
>
> And little fleas have lesser fleas,
> and so ad-infinitum.
>
> The great fleas themselves, in turn
> have greater fleas to go on,
>
> While these again have greater still
> and greater still,
> and so on.

As a general rule, subqueries allow SQL to become much more than just a query language, and subqueries combined with analytic functions allow SQL to solve complex problems without using a procedural language. For more information on advanced SQL, see Laurent Schneider's book *Advanced SQL Programming*.

However, subqueries have several downsides, and the SQL optimizer will sometimes rewrite subqueries to replace them with standard joins when possible. The overhead of subqueries includes:

- **Hard to maintain SQL:** Nesting queries within queries makes the SQL difficult to understand and hard to maintain over time.

- **Hidden execution details:** Subquery execution plans are not easily displayed and the interface between the subquery and the outer query can be very complex.

Regardless of the shortcomings, subqueries are an important tuning tool with SQL, provided that the benefits and limitations are clearly understood.

It is also important to remember that because a subquery is a separate query embedded within a larger query, there can be many ways to rewrite a subquery for faster performance.

The best place to start tuning Oracle SQL subqueries is by reviewing the types of subqueries.

Types of SQL Subqueries

When a SQL statement specifies a subquery, the *where* clause should be checked carefully to determine if the subquery is a noncorrelated subquery or a correlated subquery.

As the world's most flexible database, Oracle SQL allows for subqueries to appear in many places in SQL:

- **Subqueries in the *select* clause:** Multiple queries can be placed within an outer query by placing subqueries in the *select* clause.

```
select
   select max(date) from sales,
   select min(date) from sales,
   select avg(price) from sales;
```

- **Subqueries *in the from* clause:** This is called an in-line view because the subquery assembles a table at runtime, just like a regular view.

```
select
   stuff,
from
   sales,
   select max(date) from sales,
where . . .
```

- **Subqueries in the *where* clause:** This is the most common type of subquery, and it includes the correlated and non-correlated subquery, depending on whether the subquery is independent of the outer query. There are these distinct types of *where* clause subqueries:

  - ***where equality subqueries:*** These subqueries apply Boolean conditions of the outer query to the subquery results.

```
select stuff from sales
where
sale_date > (select min(sale_date) from product);
```

  - ***where in/not in* subqueries:** These subqueries evaluate all matching rows in the outer query to each row returned in the subquery.

```
select stuff from sales
   stuff from sales
where sale_date in (select sale_date from product)
```

  - ***where exists/not exists* subqueries:** These subqueries.

```
select stuff from sales
where exists (select stuff from product);
```

With this familiarity with the types of subqueries, it is time to explore alternatives to subqueries. In Oracle SQL there are many ways to skin a cat, and there is a wide array of choices when optimizing SQL.

Tuning Guidelines for Subqueries

While entire books could be written about SQL subqueries, there are some general guidelines that can help achieve tuning success:

- **Flatten SQL to avoid subqueries:** Whenever possible, standard joins will perform faster than subqueries. Remember, simple SQL is fast SQL.

- **Tune subqueries separately:** Before plopping a subquery into the outer query, gather the execution plan and tune it before merging it into the parent query.

- **Don't try to do too much:** While Oracle SQL subqueries with analytics can solve complex problems, resist the temptation to write complex SQL. It is hard to read, hard to maintain and very difficult to optimize.

- **Never more than one subquery level:** Some advanced problems might require nested subqueries, a subquery within a subquery, but these are notorious for funky performance. In SQL there are always have options, and nesting subqueries can be asking for slow performance.

- **Test subqueries:** There are no equations to predict SQL speed, and it is important to always test while keeping the optimizer goal in mind. When tuning for response time, always *set timing on* and see the actual performance. When tuning for fast throughput, measure the row transfer rate.

While subqueries are a powerful tool, they come with their own baggage. if the required rows can be retrieved without a subquery, SQL performance will often be faster. The next section will cover more about how to avoid SQL subqueries.

Avoiding SQL Subqueries

At this point, it should be noted that all subqueries are optional, and for performance reasons, SQL can be reworked not to have any subqueries. Removing a subquery is called subquery factoring, a fancy name for removing subqueries into separate queries. This can be achieved in many ways:

- **Using the *with* clause:** Oracle allows for statements to begin with the *with* keyword, where multiple queries can be independently executed.

- **Create table as select (CTAS):** Subqueries can be pre-materialized by creating them as temporary tables using CTAS.

- **Global temporary tables (GTT):** Global temporary tables can also be used to materialize intermediate results.

- **PL/SQL:** It is not uncommon to break down subqueries into separate queries in PL/SQL and merge the results sets using PL/SQL.

- **Oracle analytic functions:** Oracle analytic functions can be used to replace subqueries. For example, an *exists* subquery can be sometimes be replaced using the analytic *rank* function.

The following sections will cover the types of subqueries.

Subqueries in the select Clause: The Scalar Subquery

A scalar subquery is sometimes called a single row subquery because there is a restriction that scalar subqueries may only return a single row.

If the scalar subquery returns multiple rows, a runtime error occurs, and if the scalar subquery returns no rows, the value NULL is passed to the main query:

```
select
    (
      select
          count(*)
      from
          emp
    )+(
      select
          count(*)
      from
          dept
    ) as "rows in dept + rows in emp"
from
    dual;
```

```
rows in dept + rows in emp
--------------------------
                        18
```

```
--------------------------------------------------------------------
| Id | Operation          | Name    | Rows | Cost (%CPU)| Time     |
--------------------------------------------------------------------
|  0 | SELECT STATEMENT   |         |    1 |     2   (0)| 00:00:01 |
|  1 |  SORT AGGREGATE    |         |    1 |            |          |
|  2 |   INDEX FULL SCAN  | PK_EMP  |   14 |     1   (0)| 00:00:01 |
|  3 |  SORT AGGREGATE    |         |    1 |            |          |
|  4 |   INDEX FULL SCAN  | PK_DEPT |    4 |     1   (0)| 00:00:01 |
|  5 |  FAST DUAL         |         |    1 |     2   (0)| 00:00:01 |
--------------------------------------------------------------------
```

Subquery in the from clause: The Inline View

In many cases an inline view can be tuned by removing it and substituting equivalent SQL syntax. In some cases, inline views with standard *sum* and *having* clauses, and in some cases an inline view, can be rewritten using the SQL99 *with* clause.

The following script shows a subquery in the *from* clause, filtering out all employees in the *accounting* department:

```
select
    ename
from
(
    select
        empno,
        ename,
        salary
    from
        emp
    where
        dept='ACCOUNTING'
)
where
    salary < 50000;
```

```
ENAME
----------
CLARK
MILLER
```

```
------------------------------------------------------------------------
| Id  | Operation         | Name | Rows | Bytes | Cost (%CPU)| Time     |
------------------------------------------------------------------------
|   0 | SELECT STATEMENT  |      |    1 |    13 |    3   (0)| 00:00:01 |
|*  1 |  TABLE ACCESS FULL| EMP  |    1 |    13 |    3   (0)| 00:00:01 |
------------------------------------------------------------------------
    1 - filter("DEPTNO"=ACCOUNTING AND "SALARY"<50000)
```

There are alternatives to any subquery, and here are two alternative ways to address the subquery in the *from* clause. The inline view can be removed and replaced with either CTAS or the SQL99 *with* clause:

```
--*****************************************
--  Use CTAS instead of a subquery
--*****************************************
create table
    accounting_dept
as
select
    empno,
    ename,
    sal
from
    emp
```

```
where
   dept='ACCOUNTING';

select
   ename
from
   accounting_dept
where
   salary <50000;

--*****************************************
-- Use the WITH clause instead of subquery
--*****************************************

with
   accounting_dept
as
(
   select
      empno,
      ename,
      salary
   from
      emp
   where
   dept='ACCOUNTING';
)
select
   ename
from
   accounting_dept
where
   salary <50000;
```

There are many ways to write an identical SQL query, each with vastly different performance.

Obviously, there are many cases where subqueries can be written in multiple, identical forms, and the same case holds true for Oracle analytic functions.

There are many cases where a simple sum grouping can be replaced with Oracle analytic functions as the following examples demonstrate. Here is a simple sum with the group by function:

```
select
   department_id,
   sum(salary) as total_salary
   from employees
group by
   department_id;
```

```
DEPARTMENT_ID TOTAL_SALARY
------------- ------------
           30        24900
```

```
   60        28800
   90        58000
   10         4400
  100        51608
   20        19000
   50       156400
   40         6500
   80       304500
   70        10000
  110        20308
               7000
```

Another equivalent approach to this query is to use the analytic *over* and *partition* syntax. This SQL is functionally identical to the above SQL that gives the same result with the sum clause:

```
select distinct
  department_id,
  sum(salary) over (partition by department_id) as total_salary
from employees;
```

This is another example of equivalent SQL syntax, yielding the same SQL results, but using an inline view subquery:

```
select *
from
(
  select distinct
    department_id,
    sum(salary) over (partition by department_id) as total_salary
  from employees
)
where total_salary > 100000
```

```
DEPARTMENT_ID TOTAL_SALARY
------------- ------------
           50       156400
           80       304500
```

The analytic functions *over* and *partition* are used to get the result set. This SQL can be rewritten in an equivalent form using the SQL *sum* with the *having* clause:

```
select
  department_id,
  sum(salary) as total_salary
from
  employees
group by
  department_id
having
  sum(salary) > 100000;
```

In conclusion, inline view subqueries can often be avoided by using *over* and *partition* with standard sum and *having* clauses. Which is best? In many cases these queries produce identical execution plans, so the choice should be governed by which ends up being easier to maintain. In almost every case, if the use of a subquery can be avoided, it should be!

The next sections will cover some more equivalent queries in order to provide a feel for the plethora of choices when writing SQL queries.

Subqueries in the *where* Clause

Subqueries can be used in a SQL *where* clause with many Boolean statements (*all, some, any, in, exists*), and it is maddening that many of these operators perform the same functionality, but with very different execution plans!

The following example includes three forms of an identical query:

```
select
   deptno
from
   dept
where
   deptno!=all
   (
      select
         emp.deptno
      from
         emp
      where
         emp.deptno is not null
   );
```

```
   DEPTNO
----------
       40
```

```
-----------------------------------------------------------------------------
| Id  | Operation          | Name    | Rows  | Bytes | Cost (%CPU)| Time     |
-----------------------------------------------------------------------------
|   0 | SELECT STATEMENT   |         |     3 |    18 |     5  (20)| 00:00:01 |
|*  1 |  HASH JOIN ANTI    |         |     3 |    18 |     5  (20)| 00:00:01 |
|   2 |   INDEX FULL SCAN  | PK_DEPT |     4 |    12 |     1   (0)| 00:00:01 |
|*  3 |   TABLE ACCESS FULL| EMP     |    14 |    42 |     3   (0)| 00:00:01 |
-----------------------------------------------------------------------------
   1 - access("DEPTNO"="EMP"."DEPTNO")
   3 - filter("EMP"."DEPTNO" IS NOT NULL)
```

This exact same query can be re-formatted as a *not in* subquery, with the same execution plan:

```
select
   deptno
from
   dept
```

```
where
   deptno not in
   (
      select
         emp.deptno
      from
         emp
      where
         emp.deptno is not null
   );


   DEPTNO
----------
       40
```

```
---------------------------------------------------------------------------
| Id | Operation          | Name     | Rows | Bytes | Cost (%CPU)| Time     |
---------------------------------------------------------------------------
|  0 | SELECT STATEMENT   |          |   3  |  18   |  5   (20)| 00:00:01 |
|* 1 |  HASH JOIN ANTI    |          |   3  |  18   |  5   (20)| 00:00:01 |
|  2 |   INDEX FULL SCAN  | PK_DEPT  |   4  |  12   |  1    (0)| 00:00:01 |
|* 3 |   TABLE ACCESS FULL| EMP      |  14  |  42   |  3    (0)| 00:00:01 |
---------------------------------------------------------------------------

   1 - access("DEPTNO"="EMP"."DEPTNO")
   3 - filter("EMP"."DEPTNO" IS NOT NULL)
```

A *not exists* subquery can alsoto get the same result set, again with the same results and an identical execution plan:

```
select
   deptno
from
   dept
where
   not exists
   (
      select
         *
      from
         emp
      where
         emp.deptno=dept.deptno
   );

   DEPTNO
----------
       40
```

```
---------------------------------------------------------------------------
| Id | Operation          | Name     | Rows | Bytes | Cost (%CPU)| Time     |
---------------------------------------------------------------------------
|  0 | SELECT STATEMENT   |          |   3  |  18   |  5   (20)| 00:00:01 |
|* 1 |  HASH JOIN ANTI    |          |   3  |  18   |  5   (20)| 00:00:01 |
|  2 |   INDEX FULL SCAN  | PK_DEPT  |   4  |  12   |  1    (0)| 00:00:01 |
|  3 |   TABLE ACCESS FULL| EMP      |  14  |  42   |  3    (0)| 00:00:01 |
---------------------------------------------------------------------------

   1 - access("EMP"."DEPTNO"="DEPT"."DEPTNO")
```

Here are some more examples of the wide array of choices in subquery formation. The example below includes a *same results, different syntax* issue using the *some* clause:

```
select
    deptno
from
    dept
where
    deptno=some
    (
        select
            emp.deptno
        from
            emp
    );
```

```
    DEPTNO
----------
        10
        20
        30
```

```
------------------------------------------------------------------------------
| Id  | Operation          | Name    | Rows | Bytes | Cost (%CPU)| Time     |
------------------------------------------------------------------------------
|   0 | SELECT STATEMENT   |         |    3 |    18 |    4  (25) | 00:00:01 |
|   1 |  NESTED LOOPS      |         |    3 |    18 |    4  (25) | 00:00:01 |
|   2 |   SORT UNIQUE      |         |   14 |    42 |    3   (0) | 00:00:01 |
|   3 |    TABLE ACCESS FULL| EMP    |   14 |    42 |    3   (0) | 00:00:01 |
|*  4 |    INDEX UNIQUE SCAN| PK_DEPT|    1 |     3 |    0   (0) | 00:00:01 |
------------------------------------------------------------------------------

    4 - access("DEPTNO"="EMP"."DEPTNO")
```

Here is the same query using the *in* clause:

```
select
    deptno
from
    dept
where
    deptno in
    (
        select
            emp.deptno
        from
            emp
    );
```

```
    DEPTNO
----------
        10
        20
        30
```

```
------------------------------------------------------------------------------
| Id  | Operation          | Name    | Rows | Bytes | Cost (%CPU)| Time     |
------------------------------------------------------------------------------
|   0 | SELECT STATEMENT   |         |    3 |    18 |    4  (25) | 00:00:01 |
|   1 |  NESTED LOOPS      |         |    3 |    18 |    4  (25) | 00:00:01 |
|   2 |   SORT UNIQUE      |         |   14 |    42 |    3   (0) | 00:00:01 |
|   3 |    TABLE ACCESS FULL| EMP    |   14 |    42 |    3   (0) | 00:00:01 |
|*  4 |    INDEX UNIQUE SCAN| PK_DEPT|    1 |     3 |    0   (0) | 00:00:01 |
```

```
   4 - access("DEPTNO"="EMP"."DEPTNO")
```

Here again, the same query using the *exists* clause:

```
select
   deptno
from
   dept
where
   exists
   (
      select
         *
      from
         emp
      where
         emp.deptno=dept.deptno
   );
```

```
      DEPTNO
   ----------
         10
         20
         30
```

Id	Operation	Name	Rows	Bytes	Cost (%CPU)	Time
0	SELECT STATEMENT		3	18	4 (25)	00:00:01
1	NESTED LOOPS		3	18	4 (25)	00:00:01
2	SORT UNIQUE		14	42	3 (0)	00:00:01
3	TABLE ACCESS FULL	EMP	14	42	3 (0)	00:00:01
* 4	INDEX UNIQUE SCAN	PK_DEPT	1	3	0 (0)	00:00:01

```
   4 - access("EMP"."DEPTNO"="DEPT"."DEPTNO")
```

Next, let's take a look at the difference between "IN" and "exists" in subqueries and see when to use each.

In vs. *exists* Subqueries

It should be clearer now that SQL is declarative, and there are many equivalent ways to write a query that gives the same results.

This is especially true for using the *in* vs. the *exists* clause. The Oracle documentation notes that:

> *"If the selective predicate is in the subquery, then use in.*
>
> *If the selective predicate is in the parent query, then use exists."*

Another rule of thumb was that if the subquery produced a relatively small result set, an *in* subquery should be used rather and an *exists* subquery.

Prior to Oracle 10g this was a big issue and a really bad execution plan would result if an *in* subquery were used instead of an *exists* subquery.

However, the Oracle optimizer has evolved, and as of Oracle 10g, the execution plans will be identical for both *in* and *exists* subqueries.

But there are subtle functional differences between the *in* and *exists* operators. For example, an *in* subquery may also contain literal values, and if too many values are specified in an *in* clause there is the risk getting the error:

```
ORA-01795: maximum number of expressions in a list is 1000
```

The following section will show some concrete examples of when different SQL gives identical results but with radically different response time.

Same Results, Different Syntax and Plans

Yes, there are many ways to formulate a SQL subquery, but it gets even stranger! There are many cases where an outer join and a correlated and non-correlated subquery can perform the same tasks!

If brain cramps have not already set it, it is time for a look at more complex examples of the *same results, different syntax* issue with subqueries.

The following example locates all authors who have not yet published a book.

```
select
   author_last_name
from
   author
where
   author_key not in
   (select
       author_key
    from
      book_author);
```

This type of query is called a non-correlated subquery because the subquery does not make any references to the outside query. To see how this works, this code should be run it against the pubs database database. The output should look like the following:

```
AUTHOR_LAST_NAME
----------------------------------------
```

```
clark
mee
```

In the next example, all authors who have not yet published their first book will be selected. Internally, this query reads all *author_key* values from the *book_author* table and then compares this result set with the *author_key* value in the author table.

The savvy Oracle SQL tuner is always on the lookout for both correlated and noncorrelated subqueries for several reasons. The foremost is to search for opportunities for replacing the subquery with a standard join, and the other is to examine the uniqueness of the indexes in the subquery to see if changing the index structure can change the table access method.

Non-correlated subquery:

Consider this example of a non-correlated subquery:

```
--*****************************************
-- Using non-correlated subquery
--*****************************************
select
  book_title
from
  book
where
  book_key not in (select book_key from sales);


Execution Plan
----------------------------------------------------------
   0       SELECT STATEMENT Optimizer=CHOOSE (Cost=1 Card=1 Bytes=64)
   1    0    FILTER
   2    1      TABLE ACCESS (FULL) OF 'BOOK' (Cost=1 Card=1 Bytes=64)
   3    1      TABLE ACCESS (FULL) OF 'SALES' (Cost=1 Card=5 Bytes=25)
```

Outer Join:

```
--*****************************************
-- Here is the same query using an outer join:
--*****************************************
select
  book_title
from
  book  b,
  sales  s
where
  b.book_key = s.book_key(+)
and
  quantity is null;
```

```
Execution Plan
----------------------------------------------------------
0    SELECT STATEMENT Optimizer=CHOOSE (Cost=3 Card=100 Bytes=8200)

1  0  FILTER
2  1    FILTER
3  2      HASH JOIN (OUTER)
4  3        TABLE ACCESS (FULL) OF 'BOOK' (Cost=1 Card=20 Bytes=1280)
5  3        TABLE ACCESS (FULL) OF 'SALES' (Cost=1 Card=100 Bytes=1800)
```

Correlated Subquery:

```
--*****************************************
-- The same data as a correlated subquery
--*****************************************
select
  book_title
from
  book
where
  book_title not in (
                select
                distinct
                  book_title
                from
                  book,
                  sales
                where
                  book.book_key = sales.book_key
                and
                  quantity > 0);
```

```
Execution Plan
----------------------------------------------------------
0    SELECT STATEMENT Optimizer=CHOOSE (Cost=1 Card=1 Bytes=59)
1  0  FILTER
2  1    TABLE ACCESS (FULL) OF 'BOOK' (Cost=1 Card=1 Bytes=59)
3  1    FILTER
4  3      NESTED LOOPS (Cost=6 Card=1 Bytes=82)
5  4        TABLE ACCESS (FULL) OF 'SALES' (Cost=1 Card=5 Bytes=90)
6  4        TABLE ACCESS (BY INDEX ROWID) OF 'BOOK' (Cost=1 Card=1)
7  6          INDEX (UNIQUE SCAN) OF 'PK_BOOK' (UNIQUE)
```

To be most effective when facing this bewildering choice of options for SQL tuning, it is important to must know these different ways to formulate queries and test the execution plans to see which provides the fastest response time or throughput. These issues are extremely complex, and to learn more, see the book *SQL Design Patterns*.

Tuning Scalar Subqueries

Scalar subqueries, first introduced in Oracle 9i SQL, were a powerful enhancement. They allow for executing multiple single row queries within the same outer SQL statement.

Oracle's introduction of scalar subquery support is another example of the company's commitment to keeping pace with the evolution of the SQL language, but it is a double-edged sword. Along with increased power comes increased complexity.

Oracle has long supported the notion of an inline view, whereby a subquery can be placed in the *from* clause, just as if it were a table name.

In the simple example below, the SQL subqueries are placed inside the *from* clause and assigned the aliases of *df* and *fs*. The *df* and *fs* subquery values are then referenced inside the *select* clause.

An examination of this query reveals that it sums and compares two ranges of values from two tables, all in a single query. For some readers, seeing SQL inside the *from* clause is probably quite strange, and the scalar subquery is even stranger! The scalar subquery is a take-off of the in-line view whereby SQL subqueries can be placed inside the *select* clause. The following section will give a closer look at a few examples.

Scalar Subquery Performance

Once the syntax becomes familiar, it does not take long to discover scalar subqueries to be very powerful. Scalar subqueries are especially useful for combining multiple queries into a single query. Scalar subqueries are used in the query below to compute several different types of aggregations (*max* and *avg*) in the same SQL statement. Note that this query uses both scalar subqueries and inline views.

```
select
    (select max(salary) from emp)            highest_salary,
    emp_name                                 employee_name,
    (select avg(bonus) from commission)  avg_comission,
    dept_name
from
    emp,
    (select dept_name from dept where dept = 'finance');
```

Scalar subqueries are also handy for inserting into tables, based on values from other tables. Below, a scalar subquery is used to compute the maximum credit for *bill* and insert this value into a *max_credit* table.

```
insert into
   max_credit
(
   name,
   max_credit
)
values
(
   'Bill',
   select max(credit) from credit_table where name = 'BILL'
);
```

The scalar subquery above is actually quite useful for Oracle data warehouse applications. In an Oracle data warehouse, it is common for the DBA to pre-aggregate values to speed up query execution, and scalar subqueries are a powerful helper in aggregation. Below, the *emp_salary_summary* table is populated with many types of aggregate values from the base tables.

```
insert into
   emp_salary_summary
(
   sum_salaries
   max_salary,
   min_salary,
   avg_salary,
values
(
   (select sum(salary) from emp),
   (select max(salary) from emp),
   (select min(salary) from emp),
   (select avg(salary) from emp);
```

Restrictions on Scalar Subqueries

Scalar subqueries are restricted to returning a single value because they select a finite value. Scalar subqueries could be used in previous versions of Oracle in some parts of a SQL statement, but Oracle extends their use to almost any place where an expression can be used, including:

- *case* expressions

- select statements

- *values* clauses of *insert* statements

- *where* clauses

- *order by* clauses

- Parameters to a function

There are also important restrictions on scalar subqueries. Scalar subqueries cannot be used for:

- Default values for columns

- *returning* clauses

- Hash expressions for clusters

- *start with* and *connect by* clauses

- Functional index expressions

    - *check* constraints on columns

    - *when* condition of triggers

    - *group by* and *having* clauses

Subqueries can often be rewritten to use a standard outer join, resulting in faster performance. An outer join uses the plus sign (+) operator to tell the database to return all non-matching rows with NULL values. Hence the outer join is combined with a NULL test in the *where* clause to reproduce the result set without using a subquery.

```
select
   b.book_key
from
   book   b,
   sales  s
where
   b.book_key = s.book_key(+)
and
   s.book_key IS NULL
;
```

The execution plans for these types of queries will be compared in more detail later, but for now, it is sufficient to be aware that subqueries can often be rewritten to improve the speed of the query and the resource demands on the database.

Removing Subqueries for Fast SQL Performance

Because SQL is a declarative language, equivalent queries can be formulated with numerous techniques. SQL is a state space query language where the desired rows are requested, but there are many ways to write the same query.

The examples below will show a simple two-way table query that can be written in these forms, each returning identical results but with vastly different performance:

- Outer join with NOT NULL test

- Non-correlated *not in* subquery

- Correlated NOT *exists* subquery

- *not in* subquery using the MINUS clause

- Standard correlated subquery

Complex SQL behaves in the same fashion, and SQL can be rewritten to improve performance. With the introduction of advanced analytical SQL functions such as the PIVOT operator in 11g, SQL coders can now solve complex programming problems without using PL/SQL.

SQL was never designed to perform complex process logic, and the performance of complex SQL will often be far worse than when the SQL is decomposed into manageable simple queries. Complex queries can be rewritten in many ways, all with the same results and different performance:

- **Complex subqueries:** Queries with nested subqueries, scalar subqueries and in-line views can often perform poorly.

- **Global temporary tables:** Global temporary tables allow a divide and conquer approach, allowing the SQL to be broken into many simple queries.

- **The *with* clause:** The SQL-99 *with* clause allows the execution of subqueries independently of the outer query.

Fortunately, there are some powerful SQL re-writing techniques.

Using Global Temporary Tables to Improve SQL Speed

The prudent use of temporary tables can dramatically improve Oracle SQL performance. Oracle SQL provides global temporary tables (GTT) and the SQL-99 *with* clause to improve the performance of complex queries that want to use permanent storage to hold intermediate results for a problem.

Before getting into the details, it is a good time to review the general properties of temporary tables, GTT and using subquery factoring, the SQL-99 standard *with* clause:

Great for SQL-only queries: One issue with SQL analytic functions is their poor performance, and decomposing a complex SQL problem into finite pieces is a proven divide-and-conquer method that makes the code faster and easier to maintain.

Not great for procedural language programs: The preferred method is not to use temporary table storage because it cannot be reused if the application aborts in mid-calculation because the temporary table is unique to the session. It is a programming best practice to have the application hold intermediate rowsets within a private array in RAM, but there are cases where temporary tables are appropriate.

Row persistence: Data in a GTT or *with* clause disappears when a session ends, and indexes on temporary tables are also temporary.

Indexing and Materialized Views: An index and a materialized view can be created on a GTT but an ad-hoc materialization cannot be indexed using the *with* clause:

```
create global temporary table
   tbl_temp
   (id number)
on commit preserve rows;

create index idx_tbl_temp on tbl_temp (id);

-- later, after some sample data exists, analyze the GTT:

exec dbms_stats.gather_table_stats('myowner, 'idx_tbl_temp');
exec dbms_stats.gather_index_stats('myowner, 'idx_tbl_temp');
```

Single, shared CBO statistics: A temporary table can be analyzed using *dbms_stats*, but every single session will share those statistics. If there exists one and only one optimal set of optimizer statistics, they can be kept with *dbms_stats* and it is important to make sure to never re-analyze the global temporary table:

If each global temporary table is different enough to warrant a different execution plans, the CBO statistics can be locked out forcing Oracle to use dynamic sampling:

```
exec dbms_stats.delete_table_stats('myowner', 'tbl_temp');
exec dbms_stats.lock_table_stats('myowner', 'tbl_temp);
select /*+ dynamic_sampling (tbl_temp 4) */ stuff from tbl_temp,  . . .
;
```

With the addition of temporary tables to hold the intermediate results, this query runs in less than three seconds, a 6x performance increase. Again, it is not easy to quantify the reason for this speed increase, since the DBA views do not map directly to Oracle tables; however, it is clear that temporary table show promise for improving the execution speed of certain types of Oracle SQL queries.

Removing Subqueries Using the *with* Clause

This same principle holds true for complex queries. Consider the following example of a query for listing all stores with above average sales.

To keep it simple, the example only references the aggregations once, where the SQL *with* clause is normally used when an aggregation is referenced multiple times in a query.

The following is an example of a request to see the names of all stores with above average sales. For each store, the average sales must be compared to the average sales for all store as illustrated in Figure 14.1:

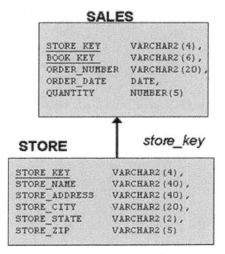

Figure 14.1: *Show all stores with above average sales*

Essentially, the query accesses the *store* and *sales* tables, comparing the sales for each store with the average sales for all stores. To answer this query, the following information must be available:

- The total sales for all stores.

- The number of stores.

- The sum of sales for each store.

To answer this in a single SQL statement, inline views will be employed along with a subquery inside a *having* clause:

```
select
   store_name,
   sum(quantity)    store_sales,
   (select sum(quantity) from sales)/(select count(*) from store) avg_sales
from
   store  s,
   sales  sl
where
   s.store_key = sl.store_key
having
   sum(quantity) > (select sum(quantity) from sales)/(select count(*) from
store)
group by
   store_name;
```

While this query provides the correct answer, it is difficult to read and complex to execute as it is recomputing the sum of sales multiple times. This query can also be specified using temporary tables:

```
create table t1 as
select sum(quantity) all_sales from stores;

create table t2 as
select count(*) nbr_stores from stores

create table t3 as
select store_name, sum(quantity) store_sales from store natural join sales;


select
   store_name
from
   t1,
   t2,
   t3
where
   store_sales > (all_sales / nbr_stores);
```

Next, this query can be rewritten yet again, using the SQL-99 *with* clause:

```
with
   number_stores as
      (select count(*) nbr_stores from store),
   total_sales as
      (select sum(quantity) all_sales from sales),
   store_sales as
      (select store_name, sum(quantity) sales from store natural join sales
       group by store_name)
select
   store_name
from
   number_stores,
   total_sales,
   store_sales
where
   sales > (all_sales / nbr_stores);
```

Again, each of these queries returns identical results but very different ways.

Oracle12c temporary table enhancements

Prior to Oracle12c, Oracle transactions used UNDO for temporary tables (*with* Clause materializations, global temporary tables) within the standard UNDO tablespace. Now, you can specify *"alter session set temp_undo_enabled=true"* to force the UNDO to be managed within the TEMP tablespace instead of within the UNDO tablespace.

This reduced the content of "regular" UNDO allowing for faster flashback operations. Oracle has also allowed "private optimizer statistics" for global temporary tables, instead of the Oracle 11g method in which everybody shared a single set of statistics.

Internals of Temporary Tables

There are several areas of internals for temporary tables such as how to see the internal execution plans and how to see the specific rows within the TEMP tablespace for an individual session.

How to See the Execution Plan for SQL Using Temporary Tables

TKPROF can be used to see the execution plans used by queries that involve global temporary tables. It should also be possible to see the execution plan for queries involving a global temporary tables using the SQL*Plus *autotrace* command.

How to Modify the Execution Plans for SQL Using Temporary Tables

Once created, a GTT behaves just like a real table, and hints can be embedded into the SQL to change the way that the GTT processes data. This is especially helpful for forcing an index.

If you have different sessions that need different execution plans due to the size and distribution of columns in a temporary table, it's not possible to adjust the CBO statistics for the temporary tables as they are generated by the users.

The Oracle documentation does suggest that an individual session can analyze statistics for a temporary table after creating it:

```
create global temporary table tbl_temp (id number) as . . . ;
create index idx_tbl_temp on tbl_temp (id);

exec dbms_stats.gather_index_stats('myowner, 'idx_tbl_temp');
exec dbms_stats.gather_table_stats('myowner, 'tbl_temp');
```

Internally, CBO statistics on a temporary table created by one session can also be used by other sessions. The problem arises when individual sessions create temporary tables with different characteristics to the level where it would change the execution plan.

For example, a small rowset might want a *nested loops* join while a large rowset might have a better execution plan with a *hash* join. If the statistics are still bad, it will be necessary to rely on dynamic sampling. To do this, bad statistics can be locked out and the optimizer forced to use dynamic sampling on the GTT:

```
exec dbms_stats.delete_table_stats('myowner', 'tbl_temp');
exec dbms_stats.lock_table_stats('myowner', 'tbl_temp);
```

This will force the CBO to use dynamic sampling to get information about the GTT or a with clause subquery factoring table.

Row Management of Temporary Tables

It is not easy, but it is possible to see the intermediate rows from a temporary table inside the PGA and/or TEMP tablespace

Both subquery factoring using the *with* clause and GTTs will write the intermediate results to the TEMP tablespace. Oracle stores GTT rows in the users temporary tablespace of the user, but this can be changed to a real tablespace by using the *tablespace* clause of the *create global temporary table* syntax.

The *v$sort_usage* view can be used to see how temp tablespace objects map to sessions:

```
select
    a.name,
    b.value
from
    v$statname     a,
    v$sesstat      b,
    v$session      s,
    v$sort_usage su
where
    a.statistic#=b.statistic#
and
    b.sid=s.sid
and
    s.saddr=su.session_addr;
```

Next, let's take a look at how Oracle has enhanced with clause in Oracle 11g and Oracle 12c

Oracle 11g Enhancements to the *with* Clause

Starting in 11g R2, there is a new SQL enhancement, recursive subquery factoring using the SQL *with* clause.

The *with* clause allows components of a complex query to be pre-materialized, making the entire query run faster. This same technique can also be used with GTTs.

If a *subquery_factoring_clause* refers to its own *query_name* in the subquery that defines it, then the *subquery_factoring_clause* is said to be recursive. A recursive *subquery_factoring_clause* must contain two query blocks: the first is the anchor member; and the second is the recursive member.

The anchor member must appear before the recursive member, and it cannot reference *query_name*. The anchor member can be composed of one or more query blocks combined by the set operators: union all; union; intersect; or minus.

The recursive member must follow the anchor member and must reference *query_name* exactly once. The recursive member must be combined with the anchor member using the union all set operator.

Here is an Oracle 11g hierarchical query:

```
col text format a40
col mgr format 9999

select
   rpad(' ',2*(level-1))||empno||': '||ename text,
   mgr
from
   scott.emp
connect by prior
   empno=mgr
start with
   job='PRESIDENT'
order siblings by
   ename;
```

```
TEXT                            MGR
------------------------------  -----
7839: KING
  7698: BLAKE                    7839
    7499: ALLEN                  7698
    7900: JAMES                  7698
    7654: MARTIN                 7698
    7844: TURNER                 7698
    7521: WARD                   7698
  7782: CLARK                    7839
    7934: MILLER                 7782
  7566: JONES                    7839
    7902: FORD                   7566
      7369: SMITH                7902
    7788: SCOTT                  7566
      7876: ADAMS                7788

Execution Plan
---------------------------------------------------------
Plan hash value: 763482334
```

```
-----------------------------------------------------------------| Id  |
Operation               | Name  | Rows  | Cost (%CPU)|
-----------------------------------------------------------------|  0  |
SELECT STATEMENT        |       |   14  |    4   (25)|
|*  1 |   CONNECT BY NO FILTERING WITH START-WITH
|   2 |     TABLE ACCESS FULL    | EMP   |   14  |   3    (0)|
-----------------------------------------------------------------

Predicate Information (identified by operation id):
---------------------------------------------------
   1 - access("MGR"=PRIOR "EMPNO")
       filter("JOB"='PRESIDENT')
```

The following is the equivalent query using the 11g R1 *with* clause recursive subquery factoring syntax:

```
col text format a40
col mgr format 9999

with
   empl (empno, ename, xlevel, mgr)
as
   (select empno, ename, 1, mgr
from
   scott.emp
where
   job='PRESIDENT'
union all
select
   e.empno,
   e.ename,
   empl.xlevel+1,
   e.mgr
from
   scott.emp e,
   empl
where
   e.mgr=empl.empno)
   search depth first by ename set ord
   select
     rpad(' ',2*xlevel)||empno||': '||ename text,
     mgr
   from
     empl;
```

Below is the hierarchical display of the results:

```
TEXT                        MGR
------------------------- -----
   7839: KING
     7698: BLAKE            7839
       7499: ALLEN          7698
       7900: JAMES          7698
       7654: MARTIN         7698
       7844: TURNER         7698
       7521: WARD           7698
     7782: CLARK            7839
```

```
      7934: MILLER          7782
     7566: JONES            7839
       7902: FORD           7566
     7369: SMITH            7902
       7788: SCOTT           7566
     7876: ADAMS            7788

14 rows selected.

Execution Plan
-------------------------------------------------------
Plan hash value: 3907725112

------------------------------------------------------------------------| Id  |
Operation                | Name | Rows | Cost (%CPU)|
------------------------------------------------------------------------|  0  | SELECT
STATEMENT              |      |  25 |   8   (25)|
|   1 |   VIEW             |      |      |  25 |   8   (25)|
|   2 |    UNION ALL (RECURSIVE WITH) DEPTH FIRST                        |*  3 |    TABLE
ACCESS FULL       | EMP  |   3 |   3   (0)|
|*  4 |      HASH JOIN         |      |      |  22 |   4   (25)|
|   5 |       RECURSIVE WITH PUMP  |      |      |      |
|*  6 |       TABLE ACCESS FULL     | EMP  |  13 |   3   (0)|
------------------------------------------------------------------------
Predicate Information (identified by operation id):
-------------------------------------------------
   3 - filter("JOB"='PRESIDENT')
   4 - access("E"."MGR"="EMPL"."EMPNO")
   6 - filter("E"."MGR" IS NOT NULL)
```

The next skill we will examine is how to remove subqueries with temporary tables.

Remove subqueries with global temporary tables

As an alternative to the *with* clause, create table as select (CTAS) can be used with global temporary tables to materialize intermediate results. For example, consider this complex query where a subquery has been removed:

```
drop table temp;

--**********************************************************
-- First, gather the maximum salary for each employee
--**********************************************************

create table
   temp
as
select
   empno,
   max(effective_date) max_date
from
   sal_hist
group by
   empno
;
```

```
-- *******************************************************
-- Next, select employees who got a raise in the past 90 days
-- *******************************************************

select
    ename
from
    emp e,
    temp t
where
    e.empno=t.empno
and
    t.max_date < sysdate-90;
```

Now there is a very fast execution plan with excellent response time:

```
OPERATION
----------------------------------------------------------------------
OPTIONS                     OBJECT_NAME                 POSITION
--------------------------- --------------------------- ----------
SELECT STATEMENT
                                                             19
  NESTED LOOPS
                                                              1
    TABLE ACCESS
FULL                        TEMP                              1
    TABLE ACCESS
BY INDEX ROWID              EMP                               2
      INDEX
RANGE SCAN                  EMP_EMPNO                         1
```

This is how SQL can be tuned by removing subqueries, but there is more information to follow about legitimate subqueries.

Correlated vs. Noncorrelated Subqueries

In a correlated subquery, the subquery references the outer table inside the subquery, while in a noncorrelated subquery the subquery is independent of the outer table.

Because a correlated subquery is tied with a Boolean to the outer query, the inner rowset must be compared, row-by-row to the parent query.

As a general rule, correlated queries should be avoided and there are example of where a correlated subquery can be rewritten as a non-correlated subquery.

Given a choice of correlated vs. non-correlated subqueries, it is necessary to consider that both types of subqueries have their own overhead:

- **Correlated subqueries:** Correlated subqueries require an index on the referenced column.

- **Non-correlated subqueries:** A non-correlated subquery must store the results of the subquery in TEMP storage.

Automatic rewrite of *exists* subqueries!

Whenever possible, Oracle will automatically transform correlated subqueries that use the *exists* clause.

Tuning Correlated Subqueries

A correlated subquery is a query whereby the key in the subquery is correlated, using the = operator, with a column that is selected in the outer query. On the other hand, a non-correlated subquery is a query where the subquery executes independently of the outer query, passing a result set to the outer query at the end of its execution.

```
select
   emp.ename,
   (
      select
         dept.dname
      from
         dept
      where
         dept.deptno=emp.deptno
   ) as dname
from
   emp;
```

```
ENAME       DNAME
----------  --------------
SMITH       RESEARCH
ALLEN       SALES
WARD        SALES
JONES       RESEARCH
MARTIN      SALES
BLAKE       SALES
CLARK       ACCOUNTING
SCOTT       RESEARCH
KING        ACCOUNTING
TURNER      SALES
ADAMS       RESEARCH
JAMES       SALES
FORD        RESEARCH
MILLER      ACCOUNTING
```

Id	Operation	Name	Rows	Bytes	Cost (%CPU)	Time
0	SELECT STATEMENT		14	126	3 (0)	00:00:01
1	TABLE ACCESS BY INDEX ROWID	DEPT	1	13	1 (0)	00:00:01
* 2	INDEX UNIQUE SCAN	PK_DEPT	1		0 (0)	00:00:01
3	TABLE ACCESS FULL	EMP	14	126	3 (0)	00:00:01

```
2 - access("DEPT"."DEPTNO"=:B1)
```

Here is another example of a correlated subquery where the *exists* clause is used:

```
select
   e1.ename,
   e1.job
from
   emp e1
where
   not exists
   (
      select
         *
      from
         emp e2
      where
         e1.job = e2.job
         and
         e1.empno != e2.empno
   );
```

```
ENAME        JOB
----------   ---------
KING         PRESIDENT
```

```
-------------------------------------------------------------------------
| Id  | Operation           | Name | Rows | Bytes | Cost (%CPU)| Time     |
-------------------------------------------------------------------------
|   0 | SELECT STATEMENT    |      |   14 |   420 |    7  (15)| 00:00:01 |
|*  1 |  HASH JOIN ANTI     |      |   14 |   420 |    7  (15)| 00:00:01 |
|   2 |   TABLE ACCESS FULL | EMP  |   14 |   252 |    3   (0)| 00:00:01 |
|   3 |   TABLE ACCESS FULL | EMP  |   14 |   168 |    3   (0)| 00:00:01 |
-------------------------------------------------------------------------
   1 - access("E1"."JOB"="E2"."JOB")
       filter("E1"."EMPNO"<>"E2"."EMPNO")
```

Rewriting Non-Correlated Subquery Using *not in*

Subqueries are not always evil to performance, and they are sometimes required to get the proper row set. For example, consider the following *not in* subquery to display employees who have not had a bad credit rating during the past year.

```
select
   ename
from
   emp
where
   empno NOT IN
   (select
      empno
   from
      bad_credit
   where
      bad_credit_date > sysdate-365
   );
```

Oracle will often transform a non-correlated subquery with a *not in* into a standard *nested loops* or *hash* join, and the default is to automatically rewrite anti-joins, as controlled by the init.ora parameter *always_anti_join* parameter.

```
OPERATION
--------------------------------------------------------------OPTIONS
OBJECT_NAME              POSITION
-----------------------  -------------------------  ----------
SELECT STATEMENT
                                                    1
   FILTER
                                                    1
     TABLE ACCESS
FULL                     EMP                        1
     TABLE ACCESS
FULL                     BAD_CREDIT                 2
```

But there are other cases where the SQL optimizer will automatically replace subqueries into a more efficient form. Below, Oracle will rewrite *not exists* queries.

Rewriting Non-Correlated Subquery Using *not exists*

Since SQL is a declarative language, the same query can be rewritten in many forms, each getting the same result but with vastly different execution plans and performance.

This example will select all books that do not have any sales. Note that this is a non-correlated sub-query, but it could be rewritten in several ways:

```
select
   book_key
from
   book
where
   book_key NOT IN (select book_key from sales);
```

There are serious problems with subqueries that may return NULL values. It is a good idea to discourage the use of the *not in* clause which invokes a sub-query and to prefer *not exists* which invokes a correlated sub-query, since the query returns no rows if any rows returned by the sub-query contain null values:

```
select
   book_key
from
   book
where
   NOT EXISTS (select book_key from sales);
```

Subqueries can often be rewritten to use a standard outer join, resulting in faster performance. An outer join uses the plus sign (+) operator to tell the database to return all non-matching rows with NULL values. Hence, the outer join is combined

---

with a NULL test in the *where* clause to reproduce the result set without using a sub-query:

```
select
   b.book_key
from
   book  b,
   sales s
where
   b.book_key = s.book_key(+)
and
   s.book_key IS NULL;
```

This execution plan will also be faster by eliminating the sub-query.

Additionally, the *minus* operator can be used to exclude results with better performance. For instance:

```
select book_key from book
minus
select book_key from sales;
```

Prior to Oracle10g there was a bug that caused a huge execution difference between *exists* and *in*. Starting in 10g R2 and beyond, Oracle will automatically rewrite an *in* subquery to use the *exists* clause.

Automatic Rewriting *not exists* Subqueries

Oracle will not automatically transform correlated subqueries that contain the *not exists* operator.

Consider this SQL to display employees who are not supporting their mother-in-law. Because this subquery is a correlated anti-join, Oracle will use an index to compare each row and filter out all rows except those where the employee has no inner table rows *where relation='mother in law'*.

```
select
   ename
from
   emp
where NOT EXISTS
   (select
      null
   from
      dependents
   where
      emp.empno = dependents.empno
   and
      relation='mother in law'
   );
```

As expected, the execution plan shows a full-table scan against the *emp* table because the subquery cannot use the *empno* index on the *emp* table. This full-table scan could be very time-consuming if the *emp* table had millions of rows.

```
OPERATION
------------------------------------------------------------------
OPTIONS                        OBJECT_NAME                 POSITION
------------------------------ -------------------------- ----------
SELECT STATEMENT
                                                              1
  FILTER
                                                              1
    TABLE ACCESS
FULL                           EMP                            1
    TABLE ACCESS
BY INDEX ROWID                 DEPENDENTS                     2
      INDEX
RANGE SCAN                     DEP_EMPNO                      1
```

This is a good example of how a *not exists* subquery can be written with an outer join and a NOT NULL test.

```
select distinct
    ename
from
    emp,
    dependents
where
    emp.empno = dependents.empno(+)
and
    relation(+)='mother in law'
and
    dependents.empno is null;
```

This produces the same results with a faster execution plan, especially since there is enough PGA RAM for the SQL optimizer to invoke a *hash join* access method.

```
OPERATION
------------------------------------------------------------------
OPTIONS                        OBJECT_NAME                 POSITION
------------------------------ -------------------------- ----------
SELECT STATEMENT
                                                              6
  SORT
UNIQUE                                                         1
    FILTER
                                                              1
      HASH JOIN
OUTER                                                          1
        TABLE ACCESS
FULL                           EMP                            1
        TABLE ACCESS
FULL                           DEPENDENTS                     2
```

Oracle can automatically rewrite *exists* subqueries.

Automatic Rewriting *exists* Subqueries

Oracle will sometime rewrite an *exists* subquery on your behalf. For example, consider this SQL to display all employees with bad credit:

```
select
   ename
from
   emp e
where EXISTS
   (select
      null
   from
      bad_credit b
   where
      e.empno=b.empno
   );
```

In the execution plan, the subquery is not shown. Instead, the optimizer was intelligent and replaced the subquery with the *view* access method and a full-table scan, avoiding the overhead of executing the subquery:

```
OPERATION
----------------------------------------------------------------------
OPTIONS                    OBJECT_NAME                POSITION
-------------------------- -------------------------- ----------
SELECT STATEMENT
                                                             1
   FILTER
                                                             1
      TABLE ACCESS
FULL                       EMP                               1
      INDEX
RANGE SCAN                  BAD_EMPNO                         2
```

The next tuning skill to be covered is how to rewrite non-equality subqueries.

Rewriting Non-equality Correlated Subqueries

Here is another case where Oracle will automatically flatten out a subquery and replace it with a one-pass scan. In this case, there is a correlated subquery using a less than condition:

```
select
   ename
from
   emp       e,
   sal_hist  s1
where
   e.empno = s1.empno
and
   effective_date <
   (select
      max(effective_date)
```

```
from
   sal_hist s2
where
   s1.empno=s2.empno
and
   s2.effective_date <= sysdate-90
);
```

Here, the subquery has been replaced automatically!

Instead of executing a separate query against the *sal_hist* table, Oracle rewrites the execution plan into a more efficient for as denoted by the *view* method:

```
OPERATION
-------------------------------------------------------------------------
OPTIONS                        OBJECT_NAME                 POSITION
-------------------------------------------------------------------------
OTHER_TAG
-------------------------------------------------------------------------
SELECT STATEMENT
                                                           1385
   NESTED LOOPS
                                                           1
      VIEW
                               VW_NSO_1                    1
         MINUS
                                                           1
            SORT
UNIQUE                                                     1
            TABLE ACCESS
FULL                           EMP                         1
            SORT
UNIQUE                                                     2
            TABLE ACCESS
FULL                           BAD_CREDIT                  1
         TABLE ACCESS
BY INDEX ROWID                 EMP                         2
            INDEX
RANGE SCAN                     EMP_EMPNO                   1
```

exists subqueries can be rewritten using SQL analytics, namely the *rank* function.

Rewriting *exists* Subqueries with the *rank* Function

The Oracle analytic functions present new ways to remove *exists* subqueries, and an *exists* subquery can be rewritten with the analytic *rank* and *partition* clauses. The example below will show how the *exists* subquery can be replaced with a rank function, but more importantly it will illustrate how there is a tradeoff between I/O and CPU overhead:

- **Exists subquery:** The exists query has far more logical reads but little internal computational overhead.

- **Rank. . . over. . . partition**: The analytic form of the SQL greatly reduces I/O, but at the expense of higher internal processing for the SQL statement.

Consider this simple SQL by Oracle ACE Laurent Schneider. The goal is to find out the best paid employees in each department:

```
create table
   lsc_emp
as
   select * from emp;

create index lsc_i on lsc_emp(deptno,sal);

exec dbms_stats.gather_table_stats(user,'LSC_EMP',cascade=>true)
```

Before Oracle introduced analytic functions, one way to find the highest paid employees in a department is to use an exists subquery. The subquery would compute the max salary and serve it as the value against which the outer query measured salaries:

```
select
    *
from
   lsc_emp e1
where
   exists (
       select
          1
       from
          lsc_emp e2
       where
          e1.deptno=e2.deptno
       having
          e1.sal=max(e2.sal)
);
```

Notice that the following subquery causes the invocation of multiple index range scans inside of the full table scan of the emp table:

```
Execution Plan
----------------------------------------------------------
Plan hash value: 2224773357

---------------------------------------------------------------------------
| Id  | Operation          | Name    | Rows | Bytes | Cost (%CPU)| Time     |
---------------------------------------------------------------------------
|   0 | SELECT STATEMENT   |         |    1 |    68 |    56   (0)| 00:00:01 |
|*  1 |  FILTER            |         |      |       |            |          |
|   2 |   TABLE ACCESS FULL| LSC_EMP |  107 |  7276 |     2   (0)| 00:00:01 |
|*  3 |   FILTER           |         |      |       |            |          |
|   4 |    SORT AGGREGATE  |         |    1 |     7 |            |          |
|*  5 |     INDEX RANGE SCAN| LSC_I  |   10 |    70 |     1   (0)| 00:00:01 |
---------------------------------------------------------------------------

Predicate Information (identified by operation id):
----------------------------------------------------

   1 - filter( EXISTS (SELECT MAX("E2"."SALARY") FROM "LSC_EMP" "E2"
              WHERE "E2"."DEPARTMENT_ID"=:B1 HAVING MAX("E2"."SALARY")=:B2))
   3 - filter(MAX("E2"."SALARY")=:B1)
   5 - access("E2"."DEPARTMENT_ID"=:B1)
```

Finally, note that this query required 79 consistent gets:

```
Statistics
```

```
------------------------------------------------------------
         1   recursive calls
         0   db block gets
        79   consistent gets
         0   physical reads
         0   redo size
      1991   bytes sent via SQL*Net to client
       520   bytes received via SQL*Net from client
         2   SQL*Net roundtrips to/from client
         0   sorts (memory)
         0   sorts (disk)
        11   rows processed
```

Now, the same can be run for the query using the Oracle analytic functions. In this example, the exists subquery is replaced with an inline view, a select inside the from clause, and the rank analytic function is used to determine the highest salaried employees:

```
select
    *
from
    (
    select
        e.*,
        rank()
    over
        (partition by deptno order by sal desc) r
    from
        lsc_emp e)
where
    r=1
and
    deptno is NOT NULL;
```

Readability is important!

While the above query runs much faster than the original *exists* subquery, it is much harder to understand, and consequently, much harder to maintain!

Note that the Statistics below show only four consistent gets, as opposed to 78 consistent gets in the original query. While a reduction in consistent gets does not always correlate to faster execution time, it is fair to say that this form of the query does 19 times less I/O to retrieve the desired rows!

```
Statistics
------------------------------------------------------------
         1   recursive calls
         0   db block gets
         4   consistent gets
         0   physical reads
         0   redo size
```

Rewriting Non-equality Correlated Subqueries

```
2151  bytes sent via SQL*Net to client
 520  bytes received via SQL*Net from client
   2  SQL*Net roundtrips to/from client
   1  sorts (memory)
   0  sorts (disk)
  12  rows processed
```

On a slightly different note, hints can be used to tune Oracle subqueries.

Subquery Hint Tuning

While hints are rarely a permanent solution to a SQL tuning problems, they are useful in cases where the goal is to test the performance of different execution plans. In general, subquery hints fall into these categories:

- **Index hints:** Index hints within subqueries can be effective in certain situations.

- **Subquery isolation hints:** Subqueries that are not merged into the outer query are sometimes executed as the last step in the execution plan. To change this, the push_subq and precompute_subquery hints causes all subqueries in the query block to be executed at the earliest possible place in the execution plan, often before the outer query is executed.

- **Anti-join hints:** The merge_aj and hash_aj hints are used in cases of a not in subquery when full-table access is faster than index access.

If the subquery is relatively inexpensive and reduces the number of rows significantly, then it improves the overall performance to evaluate the subquery as soon as possible. Note that the *push_subq* hint has no effect if the subquery is using a sort merge join or when the subquery references a remote table.

	Global temporary tables and the *with* clause!
Hot Tip!	Remember that global temporary tables and the *with* clause and the *materialize* hint are great alternative to the *push_subq* and *precompute_subquery* hints.

Oracle has several hints to isolate the execution of subqueries such as the *push_subq* as well as some undocumented hints like the *materialize* hint and *precompute_subquery* hints.

These hints can have the same effect as removing the subquery into a separate query with global temporary tables or using the *with* clause to separate out the subquery. The *precompute_subquery* hint directs the optimizer to execute the subquery first, before the outer query.

The following section will delve into tuning subqueries with index hints.

Subquery Tuning with Index Hints

Note that if a table specific hint is placed in the outer query, it is not recognized in the subquery. An *index* hint requires both the table name and the index name. If the query specifies a table name alias, "a" in this case, the optimizer is directed to choose the best index:

```
select /*+ index(a emp_idx) */
   a.empno
from
   dept      b,
   emp       a,
   salgrade c
where
   EXISTS (
      select
         a.empno
      from
         dept b,
         emp a,
         salgrade c
      where
         a.deptno=b.deptno
      and
         a.job <> 'clerk'
      and
         a.sal between c.losal and c.hisal
      )
and
   a.deptno=b.deptno
and
   a.job <> 'clerk'
and
   a.sal between losal and hisal;
```

This execution plan is very inefficient, using the slow and cumbersome Cartesian merge scan. In this case, every row in the inner query is executed multiple times, once for every row in the outer query. This query can be made more efficient by using an index for the subquery.

A *cartesian* join method is seldom the best option for an execution plan. When a *cartesian* table access method is found, ensure that all tables have the proper join clauses in the *where* clause. For example, if eight tables are being joined, there should be seven equality conditions in the *where* clause specifying the join keys for the tables:

```
OPERATION
------------------------------------------------------------------
OPTIONS                    OBJECT_NAME                 POSITION
------------------------    ------------------------    ----------
```

```
SELECT STATEMENT                                                      538344
   FILTER
      NESTED LOOPS
         MERGE JOIN
CARTESIAN                                                                  1
            INDEX
FULL SCAN                        DEPT_DEPT                                  1
            SORT
JOIN                                                                       2
               TABLE ACCESS
FULL                             SALGRADE                                  1
            TABLE ACCESS
BY INDEX ROWID                   EMP                                       2
               INDEX
RANGE SCAN                       DEPT_EMP                                   1
      NESTED LOOPS
         MERGE JOIN
CARTESIAN                                                                  1
            INDEX
FULL SCAN                        DEPT_DEPT                                  1
            SORT
JOIN                                                                       2
               TABLE ACCESS
FULL                             SALGRADE                                  1
            TABLE ACCESS
BY INDEX ROWID                   EMP                                       2
               INDEX
RANGE SCAN                       DEPT_EMP                                   1
```

In the next example, the hint is moved from the outer query to the subquery.

Notice that the *index* hint is now used in the *exists* clause:

```
select
   a.empno
from
   dept b,
   emp a,
   salgrade c
where
   EXISTS (
      select /*+ index(a emp_idx) */
         a.empno
      from
         dept b,
         emp a,
         salgrade c
      where
         a.deptno=b.deptno
      and
         a.job <> 'clerk'
      and
         a.sal between c.losal and c.hisal
      )
and
   a.deptno=b.deptno
and
   a.job <> 'clerk'
and
```

```
a.sal between losal and hisal;
```

The following execution plan has changed, eliminating the Cartesian merge-join.

```
OPERATION
-------------------------------------------------------------------
OPTIONS                       OBJECT_NAME               POSITION
-----------------------       -------------------       ---------
 SELECT STATEMENT
                                                         108281
  FILTER
                                                         1
   NESTED LOOPS
                                                         1
    NESTED LOOPS
     TABLE ACCESS
FULL                          SALGRADE                  1
     TABLE ACCESS
BY INDEX ROWID                EMP                       2
      INDEX
FULL SCAN                     JOB_IDX                   1
      INDEX
RANGE SCAN                    DEPT_DEPT                 2
    NESTED LOOPS
     NESTED LOOPS
      TABLE ACCESS
FULL                          SALGRADE                  1
      TABLE ACCESS
BY INDEX ROWID                EMP                       2
       INDEX
FULL SCAN                     JOB_IDX                   1
       INDEX
RANGE SCAN                    DEPT_DEPT                 2
```

Hints in a subquery affect the execution plan for the subquery but do not affect the execution plan for the outer query.

While the appendix of this book shows usage notes for many SQL hints, there are several hints that are specifically designed for use in tuning SQL subqueries.

- **The *push_subq* and *precompute_subquery* hint:** Sometime it is faster for Oracle to execute a subquery before the outer query. The *push_subq* and *precompute_subquery* hints are one of the most powerful of the subquery hints because it operates on the sequence that subqueries are executed. Using a *push_subq* or *precompute_subquery* hint directs the optimizer to run the subquery at the earliest possible time in the execution plan.

- **The *merge_aj* hint:** The *merge_aj* hint is a merge anti-join directive that is placed in a *not in* subquery to perform an anti-join where full-table access is faster than index access.

- **The *hash_aj* hint:** The *hash_aj* hint is can be used in a *not in* subquery to perform a hash anti-join in lieu of the *nested loops* access method.

But far and away, the most useful of these hints is the *push_subq* hint.

Tuning Subqueries With the *push_subq* Hint

The *push_subq* hint is commonly used in legitimate subqueries to force the subquery to execute sooner in the execution plan. The *push_subq* hint forces the execution plan to execute subqueries at the earliest possible location in the query block. Under normal circumstances, unmerged subqueries are executed as the last step in an execution plan.

In circumstances where the subquery is inexpensive and beneficial, it is best for the subquery to be evaluated early in the execution plan. Note that the *push_subq* hint does not affect subqueries that use sort merge joins or those that reference remote tables.

The next step is to look at the anti-join hints.

Table Anti-Join Hints

In addition to table joins, there is also the SQL anti-join. A SQL anti-join is a function that is used when SQL includes a *not exists* or *not in* clause. The following query locates customers who do not have bad credit, and is an example of an anti-clause.

```
select
   customer_name
from
   customer
where
   customer_number NOT IN
   (
    select
       customer_number
    from
       bad_credit_history
   );
```

When given the choice between *not exists* and *not in*, most DBAs prefer to use the *not exists* clause. It is worth noting that when SQL includes a *not in* clause, a subquery is used, while with *not exists* a correlated subquery is used.

This can be beneficial as a *not exists* query will not return any rows if the subquery contains null values. There are many reasons why you would need to use the non-existence of rows in one table to query rows of another table, and Oracle has developed several hints to this end.

The *merge_aj* Hint

The first hint that will be covered is the *merge_aj* hint. This hint is used within a *not in* subquery to perform an anti-join in cases when full-table access is preferred over index access. Consider the following example query that displays department names that do not have any salesmen:

```
select
   dname
from
   dept
where
   deptno NOT IN
   (select
      deptno
    from
      emp
    where
      job = 'SALESMAN');
```

This performance of this type of query is generally poor when the data column of the subquery contains null values. This is because the subquery executes for each and every row in the outer query block. Below is the execution plan for the query:

```
OPERATION
- - - - - - - - - - - - - - - - - - - - - - - - - - - - - - - - - - - - - - - - - -
OPTIONS                       OBJECT_NAME                  POSITION
- - - - - - - - - - - - - - - - - - - - - - - - - - - - - - - - - - - - - - - - - -
 SELECT STATEMENT
                                                                 1
  FILTER
                                                                 1
    TABLE ACCESS
FULL                          DEPT                           1
    TABLE ACCESS
BY INDEX ROWID                EMP                            2
      INDEX
RANGE SCAN                    JOB_IDX                        1
```

An alternative method exists for evaluating *not in* subqueries that avoids the inefficiency of reevaluating the subquery for every row in the outer query block. In order to use this method, three conditions must be met. First, a hint must be used in the subquery query block. This hint can either be *hash_aj* or *merge_aj*, depending upon the type of join type wanted. Second, the column requested in the *not in* clause must have a *not null* constraint.

Lastly, the *not null* must predicate exist in the subquery column. When these conditions are met, this method can be used. It is especially useful in cases when the outer query block has produced an excessive number of rows.

Below is an example of a query with the *merge_aj* hint added to the subquery. Notice that the *not null* constraint is on the deptno column:

```
select
   dname
from
   dept
where
   deptno NOT IN
   (select /*+ merge_aj */
      deptno
   from
      emp
   where
      job = 'SALESMAN');
```

The method has caused the execution plan to change. Notice how the *merge anti-join* is used in place of the filter operation:

```
OPERATION
--------------------------------------------------------------------
OPTIONS                    OBJECT_NAME                POSITION
--------------------------- --------------------------- ----------
  SELECT STATEMENT
                                                            5
  MERGE JOIN
ANTI                                                        1
    SORT
JOIN                                                        1
      TABLE ACCESS
FULL                       DEPT                            1
    SORT
UNIQUE                                                     2
      VIEW
                           VW_NSO_1                        1
        TABLE ACCESS
BY INDEX ROWID             EMP                             1
          INDEX
RANGE SCAN                 JOB_IDX                         1
```

The next hint to examine is the *hash_aj* hint.

SQL Tuning With the *hash_aj* Hint

The *hash_aj* hint is useful in cases when a hash join is desired. In order to do this, the *hash_aj* hint should be placed in a *not in* subquery, as demonstrated in the query below:

```
select
   dname
from
   dept
where
   deptno NOT IN
   (select /*+ hash_aj */
```

```
      deptno
 from
    emp
 where
    job = 'SALESMAN');
```

Below is the corresponding execution plan. Notice that the plan specifies a hash join and includes a full-table of the dept table.

```
OPERATION¶-------------------------------------------------------------------¶
OPTIONS                     OBJECT_NAME                 POSITION¶----------------------------
--------------------------- ----------
  SELECT STATEMENT
                                                            3
  HASH JOIN
ANTI                                                        1
    TABLE ACCESS
FULL                        DEPT                            1
    VIEW
                            VW_NSO_1                        2
      TABLE ACCESS
BY INDEX ROWID              EMP                             1
        INDEX
RANGE SCAN                  JOB_IDX                         1
```

In conclusion, The *merge_aj* and *hash_aj* hints are very useful and can improve the performance of *not in* subqueries, as long as the subquery column is set to not null.

Conclusion

Subqueries are the most complex component of SQL tuning and nested SQL is especially difficult to tune. The main points of this chapter include:

- **Subqueries are everywhere:** Oracle allows subqueries to be placed in the *select* clause, the *from* clause and the *where* clause.

- **Rewrite SQL:** For optimal SQL performance, techniques such as the *with* clause or PL/SQL should be used in order to remove subqueries.

- **Divide and conquer:** Always get the execution plan and tune a subquery before adding it into the master SQL query.

- **Do not use SQL to replace a program:** Complex problems are for programming languages like PL/SQL, and it is important to use the right tool for the job. For fast performance, use SQL to fetch the rows and a computer program to analyze the data.

- **Use real-world testing:** SQL tuning is not a science and only empirical timing will reveal the execution plan with the fastest response time.

For more details on tuning SQL subqueries, see the books *Advanced Coracle SQL Programming* and *SQL Design Patterns*.

The next chapter will provide a closer look at troubleshooting techniques for finding and tuning sub-optimal SQL.

Troubleshooting SQL

You are judged by their SQL troubleshooting skills

Troubleshooting Problem SQL

This chapter will examine various tools and techniques that can be used to identify sub-optimal SQL. It will also and explore the 11g holistic tuning tools whereby the entire SQL workload, rather than tuning specific SQL statements, is tuned.

Defining the characteristics of sub-optimal SQL execution and looking at dictionary queries that can be used for fishing for problematic SQL statements is a great place to start. Holistic SQL troubleshooting is an interesting process that will be described in more detail in this chapter.

The Holistic Approach to SQL Tuning

All Oracle professionals use scripts to quickly find and fix problem SQL. Fortunately, Oracle is better than most database vendors at providing information in the data dictionary, STATSPACK and AWR to help with the localization and analyses of problematic SQL. With the techniques and scripts presented in this chapter, it should be easy to quickly pinpoint bad SQL.

In fact, learning to quickly pinpoint resource-intensive SQL code that is causing undo strain on the database is an indispensible skill. Combining that skill with an understanding of current and historical SQL execution patterns will enable the performance of highly successful workload analysis.

STATSPACK and AWR reports make it easy to find bad SQL, but the process of optimizing a SQL workload can be quite complicated. Optimizing individual SQL statements will produce some of the best performance enhancements, but it is important to always remember that global SQL tuning must happen first.

While there are third-party software products that can help in rewriting SQL queries, there are no tools that will tell whether or not a particular SQL statement has a poor execution plan.

Some experts zealously advocate a singular diagnostic approach, but the real way to success is to use all of the troubleshooting approaches, borrowing the best from ratio-based, bottleneck analysis and workload analysis techniques.

Before just jumping in, it is critical to understand how to separate the SQL from the application. When a complaint comes in, the end-user is simply reporting that their transactions are slow. At this point, a performance problem could have many causes:

Environment problem:

- Disk contention
- Network latency
- CPU enqueues

Application problems:

- Poorly designed application
- Application server software problem
- Application Server hardware bottleneck

Database problem:

- Oracle instance contention (lock/latch, buffer busy waits)

- Sub-optimal SQL optimization

This chapter is devoted to troubleshooting SQL. For those yearning for a more complete treatment of Oracle troubleshooting, see the *Oracle Troubleshooting* book by Robin Schumacher.

The easiest way to know if there is a SQL problem is to isolate the SQL and test it independently of the environment. The SQL can be lifted from the application source code or from the *v$sql* view, and then it can be executed in both QA and production SQL*Plus.

It is not all that difficult to tell if the SQL optimizer has been misconfigured. In the past, the Oracle optimizer has gotten a bad rap due to configuration issues. This is one of the reasons that cost-based optimizer (CBO) statistics are automatically collected as of Oracle 10g.

Regardless, there are often SQL bugs and configuration problems that are the root cause of sub-optimal SQL executions. Troubleshooting for SQL bugs is a good place to start the investigation into SQL problems.

Troubleshooting Oracle SQL Bugs

The Oracle SQL optimizer is one of the world's most complex software programs, and it is a phenomenal challenge to always generate the best execution plan for any query.

Due to the inherent complexity of their software, Oracle has introduced *v$system_fix_control* and *v$session_fix_control* in 10g release 2 and beyond. These views display the status of optimizer bug patches and show whether specific features and fixes are enabled or disabled.

The *v$system_fix_control* view can be used to display the SQL features of the optimizer by release. The relevant columns in *v$system_fix_control* are *optimizer_feature_enable*, *bugno*, *value*, *sql_feature* and *description*.

The maddening difference between the *v$system_fix_control* column of *optimizer_feature_enable*, which is the anchor that lists the specific details by release of Oracle, and the Oracle parameter *optimizer_features_enable*, is just one little letter, yet it can enough to drive a troubleshooter crazy!

For example, to see all of the new SQL optimizer features and bugs in Oracle 11g, try the following command:

💾 display_optimizer_features_by_release.sql

```
set trimspool on

col c1 heading "Release"                format a8
col c2 heading "Feature|Description" format a50

select
   optimizer_feature_enable,
   description
from
   v$system_fix_control
where
   substr(optimizer_feature_enable,1,2) = '11'
order by
   to_number(optimizer_feature_enable),
   description;
```

See MOSC note 5483301.8, which has details on using *v$system_fix_control*.

The *v$session_fix_control* view is designed ONLY FOR TESTING, and it allows specific optimizer features to be enabled and disabled. This SQL optimization fix control feature is enabled via a hidden parameter called *_fix_control*.

Remember, hidden parameters like the *_fix_control* parameter should only be adjusted with the knowledge and consent of Oracle technical support. Failure to collaborate with Oracle technical support on changes to hidden parameters can have dire consequences.

```
alter session set "_fix_control"='5483301:off';
```

The following section will cover an important initial aspect of SQL troubleshooting by defining what constitutes bad SQL.

What is Bad SQL?

Before problem SQL can be identified in the database, it is necessary to define the problem by answering the question: "What is bad SQL?" What criteria should be used when starting the hunt for problem SQL?

Everyone has their own approach and experts disagree on what constitutes inefficient SQL, so there is no standard answer. The following are some general criteria that can be used when evaluating SQL execution factors:

- **Slow Response Time (Elapsed time):** This is how much time the query took to parse, execute, and fetch the rows.

- **High CPU Time:** This is how much CPU resources used run the query.

- **Excessive Physical I/O:** Disk reads are the single slowest operation in Oracle, and any excessive disk reads on the database might be due to a system wide problem with SQL optimization. Remember, Oracle maintenance activities such as re-analyzing statistics with *dbms_stats* can cause thousands of SQL statements to change their execution plans.

- **High Logical I/O:** As many Oracle databases are fully-cached, disk reads become less of an issue than logical buffer touches, the *consistent gets* metric. Excessive logical I/O from poorly optimized SQL statements will drive up CPU consumption and slow down system-wide response time.

- **Low SQL reentrancy:** Oracle is designed to reuse SQL statements, and any database where all of the SQL has *v$sql* executions=1 may have a problem with SQL being reentrant.

- **High SQL executions:** Conversely, the *v$sql* executions columns for SQL statements that are executed hundreds of times per second must always be examined. A query that takes a fraction of a second to execute may still be causing a headache on the system if it is executed erroneously. One example would be, a query that executes in a runaway PL/SQL loop over and over again

- **Suspicious execution plans:** Scripts can be used to quickly examine the STATSPACK/AWR tables to search for expensive execution plans steps such as Cartesian joins and large-table full-table scans, indicators of sub-optimal SQL. I have seen cases where a DBA dropped an index from a production database causing thousands of SQL statements to change from index access to full-scan access, causing a major performance bottleneck.

- **Low PGA:** There are also scripts for detecting sorts: disk and low values for hash joins, indicators that low PGA RAM is causing the SQL optimizer to choose sub-optimal execution plans.

This is just a taste of the things a tuning expert will examine in a SQL workload, and there are more details later in this chapter. Fortunately Oracle keeps a wealth of data in STATSPACK and AWR, and time-series SQL workload tuning is quite easy once the principles are clear and the SQL troubleshooting scripts in this chapter are properly applied.

For a full collection of Oracle diagnostic scripts, see the *BC Oracle scripts download* at www.oracle-script.com a collection of over 600 scripts to help quickly pinpoint any performance problem.

The next section will provide a closer look at pinpointing the origin of sub-optimal SQL execution.

Identifying Problem SQL

When beginning the search for inefficient SQL in the library cache, it is necessary to first define what constitutes inefficient SQL. Remember, Oracle has several optimizer goals, each with different definitions of the best execution plan:

- **First rows:** The *first_rows_n optimizer_mode* is designed to fetch the desired rows with the goal of minimizing response time. The *first_rows_n* modes favor index access.

- **All rows:** The default *optimizer_mode of all_rows* is designed to maximize data throughput and minimize server resources. Commonly used in decision support systems and data warehouses, the *all_rows* optimization favors parallelism and full-scan tables access.

Look Out!

Customize your SQL optimizer parameters!
The single most common mistake in SQL optimization is forgetting to change the default *optimizer_mode=all_rows* for online transaction processing systems!

Far and away, most Oracle OLTP systems will want to optimize their SQL using *first_rows* optimization (e.g. *first_rows_10, first_rows_100, first_rows_1000*). A simple change of *optimizer_mode* will instantly tell Oracle to start making full use of index access. But remember, everything is a tradeoff, and using indexes to fetch results as quickly as possible improves response time at the expense of additional I/O resources for the index access.

When I look for sub-optimal SQL workloads, I use the following steps:

1. Find the sessions responsible for hogging the most computing resources (I/O, CPU, and network latency).

2. Identify the SQL that is associated with these sessions.

3. For each session, evaluate each SQL statement, successively discarding the fully-optimized SQL.

4. Highlight the worst SQL and then tune it for faster performance.

The following sections go through these four steps and yield a working roadmap for finding sub-optimal SQL in a real-world SQL workload. Included some great scripts for locating problem session SQL.

Finding Problem Sessions

It is not necessary to buy a database monitor to see the top sessions. At the OS level, the *sar*, *top* or *glance* utilities can be used to see top sessions, and within Oracle *v$sesstat* can be queried to see the top session hogs.

It might sound complicated, but it is really quite easy. Some experts say to examine the sum total of physical I/O, some approaches advocate examining CPU, while others still advocate a combination of physical and logical I/O.

Whatever the preference, the script in *top_20_sessions.sql* can be used to quickly focus in on the top twenty sessions in an Oracle database. NOTE: In this example, the initial sort is on physical I/O but can be changed to any other column desired:

🖫 top_20_sessions.sql

```
select * from
(select b.sid sid,
    decode (b.username,null,e.name,b.username) user_name,
    d.spid os_id,
    b.machine machine_name,
    to_char(logon_time,'dd-mon-yy hh:mi:ss pm') logon_time,
    (sum(decode(c.name,'physical reads',value,0)) +
    sum(decode(c.name,'physical writes',value,0)) +
    sum(decode(c.name,'physical writes direct',value,0)) +
    sum(decode(c.name,'physical writes direct (lob)',value,0))+
    sum(decode(c.name,'physical reads direct (lob)',value,0)) +
    sum(decode(c.name,'physical reads direct',value,0)))
    total_physical_io,
    (sum(decode(c.name,'db block gets',value,0)) +
    sum(decode(c.name,'db block changes',value,0)) +
    sum(decode(c.name,'consistent changes',value,0)) +
    sum(decode(c.name,'consistent gets',value,0)) )
    total_logical_io,
    (sum(decode(c.name,'session pga memory',value,0))+
    sum(decode(c.name,'session uga memory',value,0)) )
    total_memory_usage,
    sum(decode(c.name,'parse count (total)',value,0)) parses,
    sum(decode(c.name,'cpu used by this session',value,0))
    total_cpu,
    sum(decode(c.name,'parse time cpu',value,0)) parse_cpu,
    sum(decode(c.name,'recursive cpu usage',value,0))
       recursive_cpu,
    sum(decode(c.name,'cpu used by this session',value,0)) -
    sum(decode(c.name,'parse time cpu',value,0)) -
    sum(decode(c.name,'recursive cpu usage',value,0))
       other_cpu,
```

```
        sum(decode(c.name,'sorts (disk)',value,0)) disk_sorts,
        sum(decode(c.name,'sorts (memory)',value,0)) memory_sorts,
        sum(decode(c.name,'sorts (rows)',value,0)) rows_sorted,
        sum(decode(c.name,'user commits',value,0)) commits,
        sum(decode(c.name,'user rollbacks',value,0)) rollbacks,
        sum(decode(c.name,'execute count',value,0)) executions
from sys.v_$sesstat a,
     sys.v_$session b,
     sys.v_$statname c,
     sys.v_$process d,
     sys.v_$bgprocess e
where a.statistic#=c.statistic# and
      b.sid=a.sid and
      d.addr = b.paddr and
      e.paddr (+) = b.paddr and
      c.NAME in ('physical reads',
                 'physical writes',
                 'physical writes direct',
                 'physical reads direct',
                 'physical writes direct (lob)',
                 'physical reads direct (lob)',
                 'db block gets',
                 'db block changes',
                 'consistent changes',
                 'consistent gets',
                 'session pga memory',
                 'session uga memory',
                 'parse count (total)',
                 'CPU used by this session',
                 'parse time cpu',
                 'recursive cpu usage',
                 'sorts (disk)',
                 'sorts (memory)',
                 'sorts (rows)',
                 'user commits',
                 'user rollbacks',
                 'execute count'
)
group by b.sid,
         d.spid,
         decode (b.username,null,e.name,b.username),
         b.machine,
         to_char(logon_time,'dd-mon-yy hh:mi:ss pm')
order by 6 desc)
where rownum < 21;
```

The above query can also be modified to exclude Oracle background processes, the
SYS and SYSTEM user, etc. The end result should be a current list of top offending
sessions in the database as ranked by various performance metrics, which is the
normal way to rank problem user accounts.

SID	USER...	OS_ID	MACHINE...	LOGON_TIME	TOTAL_PH...	TOTAL_L...	TOTAL_MEM...	PAR...	TOT...	PAR...	RECUR...
152	SYSM...	2040	lstcha2003	01-dec-04 ...	3.00	1134191.00	955168.00	406...	0.00	13.00	221490...
146	SYSM...	1396	lstcha2003	03-dec-04 ...	35.00	21789.00	1045600.00	283...	0.00	245.00	361.00
162	SYSM...	1396	lstcha2003	03-dec-04 ...	16.00	1769.00	700800.00	339.00	0.00	2.00	23.00
144	SYSM...	1396	lstcha2003	01-dec-04 ...	6.00	1333527.00	768180.00	231...	0.00	15.00	419.00
140	SYSM...	1396	lstcha2003	01-dec-04 ...	439.00	3223273...	1586080.00	544...	0.00	333...	55798.00
149	SYSM...	1396	lstcha2003	01-dec-04 ...	46.00	3062974.00	1004972.00	777.00	0.00	7.00	733.00
142	SYSM...	1396	lstcha2003	01-dec-04 ...	37.00	228448.00	1110892.00	257...	0.00	113.00	667.00
133	SYSM...	1396	lstcha2003	01-dec-04 ...	21.00	299.00	602468.00	80.00	0.00	0.00	2.00
131	SYSM...	1396	lstcha2003	01-dec-04 ...	15.00	527.00	783800.00	124.00	0.00	0.00	0.00
134	SYSM...	1396	lstcha2003	01-dec-04 ...	189.00	8359.00	1069060.00	714.00	0.00	14.00	86.00
151	SPV	688	LEAVES\LS...	17-dec-04 ...	80.00	7154.00	584972.00	304.00	0.00	6.00	6.00
165	SMON	992	LSTCHA2003	23-nov-04 ...	1210.00	4144932.00	978188.00	277...	0.00	517.00	0.00
164	RECO	1004	LSTCHA2003	23-nov-04 ...	1.00	3425.00	519436.00	112...	0.00	0.00	0.00
158	MMON	412	LSTCHA2003	23-nov-04 ...	402.00	3157815.00	5563116.00	646...	0.00	601...	0.00
167	LGWR	1704	LSTCHA2003	23-nov-04 ...	18.00	0.00	5106956.00	0.00	0.00	0.00	0.00
168	DBW0	556	LSTCHA2003	23-nov-04 ...	1775674.00	6.00	2272588.00	0.00	0.00	0.00	0.00
141	DBSN...	1632	LEAVES\LS...	23-nov-04 ...	220.00	3679438.00	1144416.00	499...	0.00	11.00	80.00
166	CJPT	996	LSTCHA2003	23-nov-04 ...	2048.00	0.00	985708.00	0.00	0.00	0.00	0.00
163	CXQ0	1284	LSTCHA2003	23-nov-04 ...	65.00	1649981.00	912508.00	114...	0.00	10.00	0.00
137		1268	LSTCHA2003	23-nov-04 ...	53.00	6436456.00	781436.00	783...	0.00	165...	8741.00

This method is a good starting point, but it lacks depth, specifically the details within each session.

Fortunately, Oracle has provided a powerful performance view that can be used to derive such data. The *v$sql_plan* view contains execution plan data for all submitted SQL statements, and *v$sql_plan* gives us a wealth of information regarding the performance and efficiency of all of the SQL statements within a session. The *v$sql* has these troubleshooting columns:

- **sharable_mem:** Amount of shared memory used by the child cursor (in bytes).

- **persistent_mem:** Fixed amount of memory used for the lifetime of the child cursor (in bytes).

- **invalidations:** Number of times this child cursor has been invalidated.

- **parse_calls:** Number of parse calls for this child cursor.

- **disk_reads:** Number of disk reads for this child cursor.

- **direct_writes:** Number of direct writes for this child cursor.

- **buffer_gets:** Number of buffer gets for this child cursor.

- **parsing_user_id:** User ID of the user who originally built this child cursor.

- **parsing_schema_id:** Schema ID that was used to originally build this child cursor.

- **parsing_schema_name:** Schema name that was used to originally build this child cursor.

- **kept_versions:** Indicates whether this child cursor has been marked to be kept pinned in the cache using the *dbms_shared_pool* package.

- **address:** Address of the handle to the parent for this cursor.

- **type_chk_heap:** Descriptor of the type check heap for this child cursor.

- **child_address:** Address of the child cursor.

For example, assume that the interest is in finding sessions that have large-table full-table scans, which is a possible symptom of sub-optimal SQL. Assuming that a large table is any table over 1 MB, the following query will display large-table full-table scans by user:

🖫 high_scan_sql.sql

```
select
    c.username username,
    count(a.hash_value) scan_count
from
    sys.v_$sql_plan   a,
    sys.dba_segments  b,
    sys.dba_users     c,
    sys.v_$sql        d
where
    a.object_owner (+) = b.owner
and
    a.object_name (+) = b.segment_name
and
    b.segment_type IN ('TABLE', 'TABLE PARTITION')
and
    a.operation like '%TABLE%'
and
    a.options = 'FULL'
and
    c.user_id = d.parsing_user_id
and
    d.hash_value = a.hash_value
and
    b.bytes / 1024 > 1024
group by
    c.username
order by
    2 desc;
```

The output from the above query might look something like the following:

```
USERNAME      SCAN_COUNT
----------    ----------
SYSTEM               14
SYS                  11
ERADMIN               6
ORA_MONITOR           3
```

In a similar fashion, it is possible uncover those users who have executed expensive Cartesian joins with the *find_cartesian_joins.sql* query:

🖫 find_cartesian_joins.sql

```
select
    username,
    count(distinct c.hash_value) nbr_stmts
from
    sys.v_$sql a,
    sys.dba_users b,
    sys.v_$sql_plan c
where
    a.parsing_user_id = b.user_id
and
    options = 'CARTESIAN'
and
    operation like '%JOIN%'
and
    a.hash_value = c.hash_value
group by
    username
order by
    2 desc;
```

A result set from this query could look similar to the following:

```
USERNAME    NBR_STMTS
---------   ---------
SYS                 2
SYSMAN              2
ORA_MONITOR         1
```

The *v$sql_plan* view has complete execution plan details and statistics, and the top SQL is written from *v$sql* plan into the STATSPACK *stats$sql_plan* table for long-term analysis, and it is also in the AWR *dba_hist_sql_plan* if the extra-cost performance and diagnostic packs have been purchased from Oracle.

The next challenge will be how to identify high resource SQL statements.

Identify the Resource-Intensive SQL

Now that the top resource hog session and users in the database have been examined, the focus can be turned to the top SQL hogs. This *high_resource_sql.sql* script uses the *v$sqlarea* view to locate high resource SQL:

🖫 high_resource_sql.sql

```
select sql_text,
       username,
       disk_reads_per_exec,
       buffer_gets,
```

```
             disk_reads,
             parse_calls,
             sorts,
             executions,
             rows_processed,
             hit_ratio,
             first_load_time,
             sharable_mem,
             persistent_mem,
             runtime_mem,
             cpu_time,
             elapsed_time,
             address,
             hash_value
from
(select sql_text ,
        b.username ,
 round((a.disk_reads/decode(a.executions,0,1,
 a.executions)),2)
             disk_reads_per_exec,
             a.disk_reads ,
             a.buffer_gets ,
             a.parse_calls ,
             a.sorts ,
             a.executions ,
             a.rows_processed ,
             100 - round(100 *
             a.disk_reads/greatest(a.buffer_gets,1),2) hit_ratio,
             a.first_load_time ,
             sharable_mem ,
             persistent_mem ,
             runtime_mem,
             cpu_time,
             elapsed_time,
             address,
             hash_value
from
   sys.v_$sqlarea a,
   sys.all_users  b
where
   a.parsing_user_id=b.user_id and
   b.username not in ('sys','system')
order by 3 desc)
where rownum < 21;
```

The code above will pull the top twenty SQL statements as ranked by disk reads per execution

Note that the *rownum* filter at the end of this script can be changed to show more or all SQL that has executed in a database. Also note that *where* predicates can be added to only show the SQL for one or more of the previously identified top sessions.

Starting in Oracle9i, the *cpu_time* and *elapsed_time* columns were added, which provided more data that could be used to determine the overall efficiency of an SQL statement.

It is important to examine the output of this query and see how it uses the criteria set forth at the beginning of this chapter to pinpoint problematic SQL.

The query to sort by any of these timed statistics can be changed depending on the criteria needed to bubble the worst running SQL to the top of the result set.

The full output of the above script will show the I/O characteristics of each SQL statement, including the number of disk reads (physical I/O) and buffer gets (logical I/O) are shown along with numbers that display the average I/O consumption of each SQL statement.

Look Out!

Watch out for single execution SQL!

Queries that have only been executed once may have misleading statistics with respect to disk reads as the data needed for the first run of the query was likely read from disk into data buffer RAM memory (*db_cache_size*).

The executions column of the top SQL's result set will also give clues to the repetition for a SQL statement. When troubleshooting a slow SQL workload, look out for any query that shows an execution count that is significantly larger than any other SQL in the listing.

Remember, disk reads are the single slowest component of any SQL execution, and there are many things that can be done to reduce disk reads, such as employing the KEEP pool and using fast solid-state disks.

The *v$sql_plan* view can also be used to locate troublesome SQL.

Troubleshooting with *v$sql_plan*

The *v$sql_plan* view can also help with identification of problem SQL. For example, you may want to know how many total SQL statements are causing Cartesian joins on a system. The following query can answer that question:

💾 cartesian_sum.sql

```
select
   count(distinct hash_value) carteisan_statements,
   count(*)                   total_cartesian_joins
from
   sys.v_$sql_plan
```

```
where
   options = 'CARTESIAN'
and
   operation like '%JOIN%'
```

The output from this query will resemble the following, and note that it is possible for a single SQL statement to contain more than one Cartesian join:

```
CARTESIAN_STATEMENTS    TOTAL_CARTESIAN_JOINS
----------------------  ----------------------
                    3                        3
```

Once Cartesian joins have been located, the actual SQL statements containing the Cartesian joins, along with their performance metrics, can be viewed by using a query against *v$sql_plan*:

🖫 sql_cartesian.sql

```
select *
from
   sys.v_$sql
where
   hash_value in
      (select hash_value
       from
          sys.v_$sql_plan
       where
          options = 'CARTESIAN'
          and
          operation LIKE '%JOIN%' )
order by
   hash_value;
```

Another area of interest is large-table full-table scan activity. Remember, large-table full-table scans may be legitimate, but they are also a common symptom of missing indexes and other SQL optimization problems.

Small-table full-table scans are not a worry because Oracle can access small tables via *db file scattered read* operations more efficiency than using an index.

Using the *v$sql_plan* view, any SQL statement that contains one or more large-table full-table scans can be identified. The following query shows any SQL statement containing a large table scan, defined in the query as any table over 1 MB, along with a count of how many large scans it causes for each execution, the total number of times the statement has been executed, and the sum total of all scans it has caused on the system:

🖫 large_scan_count.sql

```sql
select
     sql_text,
     total_large_scans,
       executions,
       executions * total_large_scans sum_large_scans
from
(select
       sql_text,
       count(*) total_large_scans,
       executions
 from
       sys.v_$sql_plan    a,
       sys.dba_segments  b,
       sys.v_$sql          c
 where
       a.object_owner  (+) = b.owner
   and
       a.object_name  (+) = b.segment_name
   and
       b.segment_type IN ('TABLE', 'TABLE PARTITION')
   and
       a.operation LIKE '%TABLE%'
   and
       a.options = 'FULL'
   and
       c.hash_value = a.hash_value
   and
       b.bytes / 1024 > 1024
   group by
     sql_text, executions)
order by
   4 desc;
```

This query produces output like that shown below. The output shows executions and the number of scans for each SQL statement:

This type of query can also be run for partitioned tables. For example, assume that the goal is to investigate better use of partitioning. It would first be necessary to

---

locate large tables that get frequent full table scans. The *tabscan.sql* query below will identify the actual objects that are the target of such scans:

🖫 **tabscan.sql**

```
select
    table_owner,
    table_name,
    table_type,
    size_kb,
    statement_count,
    reference_count,
    executions,
    executions * reference_count total_scans
from
    (select
    a.object_owner table_owner,
    a.object_name table_name,
    b.segment_type table_type,
    b.bytes / 1024 size_kb,
    sum(c.executions ) executions,
    count( distinct a.hash_value ) statement_count,
    count( * ) reference_count
from
    sys.v_$sql_plan   a,
    sys.dba_segments b,
    sys.v_$sql        c
where
    a.object_owner (+) = b.owner
    and a.object_name (+) = b.segment_name
    and b.segment_type in ('TABLE', 'TABLE PARTITION')
    and a.operation like '%TABLE%'
    and a.options = 'FULL'
    and a.hash_value = c.hash_value
    and b.bytes / 1024 > 1024
group by
    a.object_owner, a.object_name, a.operation,
    b.bytes / 1024, b.segment_type
order by
    4 desc, 1, 2 );
```

This script displays the table name, the table type (standard, partitioned), the table size, the number of SQL statements that cause a scan to be performed, the number of total scans for the table each time the statement is executed, the number of SQL executions to date, and the total number of scans that the table has experienced (total single scans * executions):

	TABLE_OWNER	TABLE_NAME	TABLE_TYPE	SIZE_KB	STATEMENT_COUNT	REFERENCE_COUNT	EXECUTIONS	TOTAL_SCANS
1	ERADMIN	EMP	TABLE	19456	2	2	2	4
2	ERADMIN	PATIENT	TABLE	3496	1	1	1	1
3	ERADMIN	ADMISSION	TABLE	3136	4	7	31	217

The query will help determine what tables might benefit from better indexing or partitioning. When reviewing such output, the clever DBA might begin to wonder if the tables being scanned have indexes, and if so, why are the queries that are scanning the tables not making use of them?

The real question is whether a SQL statement that has only one large table scan but is executed 1,000 times or a SQL statement that has ten large-table full-table scans but has only been executed a few times should be more worrisome?

The answer is *"It depends"*, but it should be apparent how such a query can assist in identifying SQL statements that have the potential to cause system slowdowns.

As previously noted, the best way to tune the database is by tuning the workload as a whole, examining historical SQL execution patterns. The easiest way to perform historical SQL analysis is to use STATSPACK or AWR, and set the SQL collection thresholds to capture exceptional SQL, based on specific workload characteristics.

While STATSPACK and AWR reports can easily show the top SQL that has the most disk reads, the following dictionary query can be used to reveal the SQL with the most disk reads:

🖫 display_top_sql_disk_reads.sql

```
select
   sql_id,
   child_number,
   sql_text,
   disk_reads
from
   (select
      sql_id_child_number,
      sql_text,
      elaped_time,
      cpu_time,
      disk_reads,
    rank () over
      (order by disk_reads desc)
    as
      sql_rank
    from
      v$sql)
where
   sql_rank < 10;
```

The following is another variant of this SQL to display the top SQL by elapsed time:

🗄 display_top_sql_elspsed_time.sql

```
select
   sql_id,
   child_number,
   sql_text,
   elapsed_time
from
   (select
      sql_id_child_number,
      sql_text,
      elaped_time,
      cpu_time,
      disk_reads,
   rank ()
   over
      (order by elapsed_time desc)
   as
      sql_rank
   from
      v$sql)
where
   sql_rank < 10;
```

Once the SQL statements are found from *v$sql* and *v$sql_plan*, the entire SQL text for any SQL that appear inefficient can be retrieved. Note that the *hash_value* values for each SQL statement can be plugged it into the *fullsql.sql* script below to obtain the full SQL statement:

🗄 fullsql.sql

```
select
   sql_text
from
   sys.v_$sqltext
where
   hash_value = <enter hash value for sql statement>
order by
   piece;
```

Remember, one of the first steps in Oracle troubleshooting is to quickly check to see what SQL is currently executing, so that it can be determined whether or not any resource intensive SQL is dragging down the database's overall performance levels.

This is very easy to do and only involves making one change to the *high_resource_sql.sql* query by adding the following filter to the main query's *where* clause:

```
where
   a.parsing_user_id=b.user_id
```

```
and
    b.username not in ('SYS','SYSTEM')
and
    a.users_executing > 0
order by
    3 desc;
```

This query change will display the worst SQL that is currently running in the database so any queries are causing a dip in database performance can be quickly identified. This is a fairly traditional approach, but there are plenty of other tricks for SQL troubleshooting.

SQL Troubleshooting with *v$sql_plan_statistics*

The troubleshooting techniques that have been shown so far are indeed traditional ways of pinpointing problem SQL in Oracle. However, there are some new methods that can be used to get a handle on how well SQL is executing.

Oracle has the *v$sql_plan_statistics* view that yields even more statistical data about the execution of inefficient SQL statements. This view can tell how many *buffer gets*, *disk reads* and other metrics and even shows the *cumulative* and *last executed* counts of all the SQL metrics.

This view can be referenced to get an idea which exact step within in a SQL execution plan is responsible for most of the resource consumption. Note that to enable the collection of data for this view, *statistics_level-all* must be set.

The following *planstats.sql* is an example query that uses the *v$sql_plan_statistics* view to display the statistics for a specific SQL statement.

The DBA simply has to supply the *hash_value* as determine previously in this chapter:

🖫 planstats.sql
```
select
        operation,
        options,
        object_owner,
        object_name,
        executions,
        last_output_rows,
        last_cr_buffer_gets,
        last_cu_buffer_gets,
        last_disk_reads,
        last_disk_writes,
        last_elapsed_time
from
        sys.v_$sql_plan a,
```

```
        sys.v_$sql_plan_statistics b
where
        a.hash_value = b.hash_value and
        a.id = b.operation_id and
        a.hash_value = <enter hash value>
order by a.id;
```

Every single detail about a SQL statement can be displayed, right down to the resources used for each execution plan step.

For shops who have purchased the AWR, the *dba_hist_sql_plan* view can be used to see workload level SQL execution details as shown below:

🖫 awr_dba_hist_sql_plan.sql

```
select
   p.object_owner      c1,
   p.object_type       c2,
   p.object_name       c3,
   avg(p.cpu_cost)     c4,
   avg(p.io_cost)      c5
from
   dba_hist_sql_plan p
group by
   p.object_owner,
   p.object_type,
   p.object_name
order by  1,2,4 desc;
```

This shows each table and index and the CPU and I/O costs associated with each table or index.

Owner	Average Object Type	Object Name	Average CPU Cost	IO Cost
OLAPSYS	INDEX	CWM$CUBEDIMENSIONUSE_IDX	200	0
OLAPSYS	INDEX (UNIQUE)	CWM$DIMENSION_PK		
OLAPSYS		CWM$CUBE_PK	7,321	0
OLAPSYS		CWM$MODEL_PK	7,321	0
OLAPSYS	TABLE	CWM$CUBE	7,911	0
OLAPSYS		CWM$MODEL	7,321	0
OLAPSYS		CWM2$CUBE	7,121	2
OLAPSYS		CWM$CUBEDIMENSIONUSE	730	0

The next topic will be how to determine opportunities for the use of indexes that have been missed or overlooked.

Finding indexing opportunities

Expensive tools like the Oracle SQLAccess advisor are not necessary for finding missing indexes, as this can be accomplished with vanilla data dictionary scripts.

For example, it is necessary to find unindexed foreign keys and other columns that are used over-and-over again as tables are joined.

The SQL *where* clause must also be examined in order to find high-cardinality conditions that might benefit from SQL.

SQL must be examined to identify those queries that will benefit from new indexes. There is no science, and nor secret formulas to help with this, so real-world techniques must be applied.

Traditionally, missing indexes are identified with empirical SQL workload testing. This consists of gathering a representative workload, running it and examining the results to locate index and materialized view opportunities.

While only examination of the actual SQL statements can answer the second part of that question, the first part can be answered through the following *unused_indx.sql* query.

This is an important query. Please take a minute to examine how this query reads from *v$sql_plan*, *dba_segments* and *dba_indexes*:

🖫 unused_indx.sql

```
select distinct
    a.object_owner    table_owner,
    a.object_name     table_name,
    b.segment_type    table_type,
    b.bytes / 1024    size_kb,
    d.index_name      index_name
from
    sys.v_$sql_plan  a,
    sys.dba_segments b,
    sys.dba_indexes  d
where
    a.object_owner (+) = b.owner
    and a.object_name (+) = b.segment_name
    and b.segment_type in ('TABLE', 'TABLE PARTITION')
    and a.operation like '%TABLE%'
    and a.options = 'FULL'
    and b.bytes / 1024 > 1024
    and b.segment_name = d.table_name
    and b.owner = d.table_owner
order by
```

```
1, 2;
```

The results below show all full-table scans and all candidate indexes that might be used to service the query. This output is important because there are times when the optimizer parameters are sub-optimal for the system goals, such as when using *optimizer_mode=all_rows* for an online transaction database, and even though an index exists, the optimizer will bypass the index access:

	TABLE_OWNER	TABLE_NAME	TABLE_TYPE	SIZE_KB	INDEX_NAME
1	ERADMIN	ADMISSION	TABLE	2048	I_ADMISSION1
2	ERADMIN	ADMISSION	TABLE	2048	I_ADMISSION2
3	ERADMIN	PATIENT	TABLE	3072	I_PATIENT1
4	ERADMIN	PATIENT	TABLE	3072	I_PATIENT2
5	ERADMIN	PATIENT	TABLE	3072	I_PATIENT3

Again, this is only a primitive start, but it can be enhanced iteratively to meet specific needs. These types of queries are commonly used to ensure that any large tables being scanned are legitimate and all indexes are being used by the SQL optimizer.

Conclusion

All Oracle professionals need to understand what to do when the end-users complain about slow Oracle response time. Oracle provides numerous *v$* views to show what the SQL is doing. Historical SQL execution details are also available via STATSPACK and AWR. The main points of this chapter include:

- The first step in troubleshooting is to isolate and test the SQL to ensure that the SQL, and not the application, is responsible for the slowdown.

- The *v$sql* view gives details about the major metrics such as disk reads, executions, buffer gets and other important metrics.

- The *v$sql_plan* view tells about the plan details, and the *v$sql_plan_statistics* tells details on every step in the plans.

- Historical SQL troubleshooting is accomplished via the *stats$sql_plan* table and the AWR *dba_hist_sql_plan* tables.

- Common troubleshooting queries look for symptoms of bad execution plans, seeking Cartesian joins and large-table full-table scans.

- For databases where minimizing response time is the optimizer goal, the approach would be to run queries to see if all indexes exists and if all of indexes are being used effectively.

The next chapter will provide a closer look at SQL tuning within the library cache.

SQL Tuning & the Library Cache

The Oracle Library Cache is quite complex!

The Library Cache and Oracle SQL Performance

Just as data buffers cache rows for faster subsequent access, the Oracle library cache is designed to hold SQL statements for faster subsequent reuse.

Data only has two states: it is in the cache; or it isn't. In contrast, a SQL statement can have many states. Even after the executable has been created, there are multiple incarnations of the SQL statement to allow for different variables. Hence, the library cache within the shared pool must accommodate multiple versions of the same SQL statement.

The goal of the library cache is to make a SQL statement reentrant such that it is not necessary to incur the overhead to parse and determine the optimal plan for each SQL statement. With reentrant SQL, it is simply a load and go process, by using a previously prepared execution plan from a prior incarnation of the SQL statement.

Until RAM because cheap enough to fully cache all incoming SQL in perpetuity, the library cache is a limited resource and only the most popular SQL statements should reside in RAM where they are available for fast reuse. When a SQL statement is finished executing and the rows are delivered, the session cursor in closed and the SQL begins the process of ageing out of the library cache.

Just as unused data blocks age out of the data buffers, unused SQL statements will age out of the library cache, based on a least recently used algorithm. Whenever a SQL statement is reused, it is pinged to the head of the shared pool LRU list, thereby keeping the SQL for a longer period of time.

Just as a computer program must be compiled into an executable, a similar process happens with SQL inside the library cache, and there are discrete steps for transforming SQL source code into executable object code. A lot of work happens inside the library cache RAM as a SQL statement is prepared and executed:

1. **Parse phase:** During parsing we load the SQL into the RAM heap of the library cache. Oracle then searches for an identical statement in library cache, and if not found, it checks the SQL syntax.

2. **Semantic phase:** Once the SQL statement has been validated for syntax, all table and column names are checked against the data dictionary to ensure that they are valid.

3. **Security phase:** This phase validates the security rules to ensure that the requestor is authorized to view the data. This involves comparing the privileges of the user against the names of the tables in the SQL.

4. **Query rewrite phase:** The optimizer may decide to rewrite a query into an equivalent, but faster, form or a materialized view.

5. **Costing phase:** In the costing phase, Oracle determines all possible ways to service the query and generates a decision tree, adding costs to each leaf and choosing the plan with the best cost.

6. **Generate phase:** Oracle takes its best plan and translates it into native calls to access the Oracle data files.

7. **Bind phase:** The executable is now bound to the Oracle database, and all variable values are assigned real values for execution.

8. **Execution phase:** The executable code is now run against the Oracle data files.

9. **Transform phase:** After execution the SQL query, Oracle may sort the result set and apply function-based transformations to the rowset.

10. **Fetch phase:** After completion of the query, the result rows are fetched back into the calling program. (e.g. PL/SQL, C program, SQL*Plus).

SQL statement go through several phases in being prepared for execution. Figure 16.1 is a repeat of the steps presented in Chapter 2 on how Oracle creates an executable for a SQL statement:

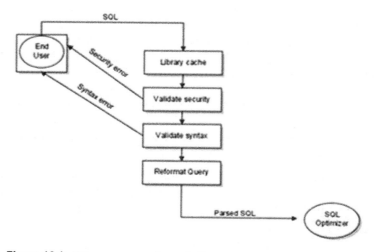

Figure 16.1: *The steps to transform a SQL statement into executable code*

This is a lot of processing and a SQL statement can be at any of these stages at any given time.

Before delving into details on tuning SQL for optimal reuse, the next section will provide a review on parsing and cursors, and then move into the major tuning knobs for optimizing the library cache.

All About Parsing

Oracle must parse a SQL statement, and any given SQL statement may have many parse calls. A parse call can happen under several conditions:

- **Load and go:** This is the ideal condition, where a matching SQL has been found, and it is read to execute.

- **New SQL:** When a brand new SQL statement enters Oracle, it is parsed.

- **Aged out SQL:** A parsed SQL statement once existed in the library cache, but it has aged out to make room for new SQL.

- **Session cursor cache:** When *session_cached_cursors* is implemented, popular SQL, that with more than three parse calls, is moved into the session cache. Hence, subsequent parse calls are very fast because the address of the cursor in the cache is already known and Oracle does not have to run a hash to find the address.

- **PL/SQL cursor cache:** In a similar fashion, cached PL/SQL cursors issue parse calls very quickly.

The next section will examine Oracle cursors.

All About Cursors

To the uninitiated, the term cursor refers to sailor with a nasty vocabulary. However in Oracle a cursor is a record keeper, marking a position with the result set of SQL rows.

Oracle is written in the C language and the library cache is essentially a C array allocated in the RAM heap inside the SGA. Internally, session cursors are handles or pointers into the library cache private areas which are established for individual Oracle sessions as illustrated in Figure 16.2:

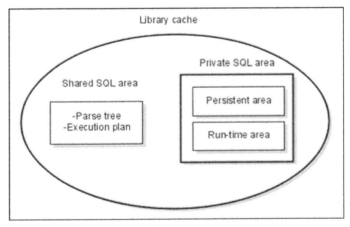

Figure 16.2: *The Components inside the Library Cache*

Managing Multiple Child Cursors

SQL can have multiple children cursors. It is a good time to look at the multiple cursor structure within the shared pool library cache.

First, it is important to remember that for every single SQL statement there is one single parent cursor. Internally, a parent cursor is simply a pointer to an object", and the object is, in turn, a RAM structure that contains all of the child cursors for the statement. In other words, a parent cursor is a pointer to an array of pointers very similar to a C programming object array using the *char*** C language operator,

Each child cursor also has this structure, but the structure is different because the child object contains two heaps as shown in Figure 16.3:

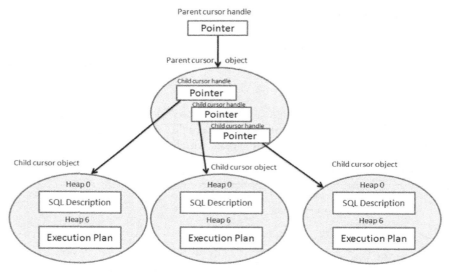

Figure 16.3: *The pointer and object structures for parent and child cursors*

Within the child cursor, there are two RAM heaps, numbered zero and six respectively.

- **Heap 0:** This contains identifying information for the SQL statement

- **Heap 6:** This contains the execution plan for the child SQL

Even when a SQL statement has only one version, there is still a parent and child cursor. The parent cursor has a pointer to its object. The parent object, in turn, contains a pointer to the child cursor, which has a pointer to information in heap 0 and heap 6 as shown in Figure 16.4:

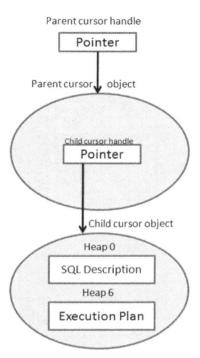

Parent cursor handle

Pointer

Parent cursor object

Child cursor handle

Pointer

Child cursor object

Heap 0

SQL Description

Heap 6

Execution Plan

Figure 16.4: *SQL with only version will still have a child cursor*

Viewing Oracle Cursors

While these internal cursor structures are hidden from view, details about parent and child cursors found in the *x$* structures.

Many of the *v$* views, such as *v$sql, v$sql_plan* and *v$open_cursor,* contain columns that refer to the cursors.

Remember, when a SQL statement is executed with multiple child cursors, multiple versions are created within the library cache of the shared pool.

The *v$sqlarea* view can be queried for details on child cursors using the *sharable_mem* and *persistent_mem* columns as follows:

v$sqlarea cursor details:

```
select
   sql_id,
   address,
```

```
    hash_value,
    sharable_mem,
    persistent_mem,
    runtime_mem,
    version_count,
    loaded_versions,
    open_versions,
    invalidations,
    parse_calls,
    kept_versions,
    last_active_child_address,
    bind_data
from
v$sqlarea;
```

v$sql cursor details:

```
select
    sql_id,
    loaded_versions,
    open_versions,
    parse_calls,
    kept_versions,
    plan_hash_value,
    child_number,
    child_address,
    literal_hash_value
from
    v$sql;
```

v$open_cursor details:

```
select
    sql_id,
    sql_text,
    saddr,
    address,
    hash_value,
    sql_exec_id
from
    v$open_cursor;
```

Finding the Reason for Multiple Child Cursors

See MOSC note Note:296377.1 for instructions on finding mismatch values in the *v$sql_shared_cursor view.*

One technique it suggests is to search *v$sql* with the SQL statement, to get the parent and child addresses to see if they are to see if multiple child cursors exist:

🖫 display_parent_n_child_cursors.sql

```
select
   address         parent_cursor,
   child_address  child_cursor,
   sql_text
from
   v$sql
where
   lower(sql_text) like 'insert_start_of_your_sql_statement_here%';
```

If the above SQL returns multiple rows, then the SQL has child cursors.

```
ADDRESS   CHILD_AD SQL_TEXT
--------  -------- -------------------------------------
7A3B1920 7A38F464 Select * from mystuff where . . .
7A3B1920 7A38ECB8 Select * from mystuff where . . .
```

Once two SQL statements that have identical *v$sql address* and *hash_value* and multiple child cursors have been identified, it is clear that the SQL was not shared, but the reason why the SQL was not shared is not so clear.

v$sql_shared_cursor can also be queried. The *v$sql_shared_cursor* has a bunch of Boolean (Y/N) flags to indicate the status of cursors. These states can include:

- unbound_cursor
- explain_plan_cursor
- bind_mismatch
- describe_mismatch
- language_mismatch
- translation_mismatch
- row_level_sec_mismatch
- remote_trans_mismatch
- incomp_ltrl_mismatch
- overlap_time_mismatch
- sql_redirect_mismatch
- mv_query_gen_mismatch

- user_bind_peek_mismatch

- typchk_dep_mismatch

- no_trigger_mismatch

- incomplete_cursor

- cursor_parts_mismatch

- stb_object_mismatch

- row_ship_mismatch

- pq_slave_mismatch

- top_level_ddl_mismatch

- multi_px_mismatch

- bind_peeked_pq_mismatch

- mv_rewrite_mismatch

- optimizer_mode_mismatch

Watch the *bind_mismatch*!

The most common reason for a SQL statement not to be shared is when we have a reentrant SQL that has been executed multiple times with different bind variable values. This is the *bind_mismatch* column in *v$sql_shared_cursor*!

Look Out!

In the SQL below, the *bind_mismatch* column has been marked. To run this against any other SQL, it is simply a matter of replacing the *kglhdpar* with the appropriate *v$sql address* value:

```
select *
from
   v$sql_shared_cursor
where
   kglhdpar = 'child_address_value';


ADDRESS   KGLHDPAR U S O O S L S E B P I S T A B D L T R I I R L I O S M U T N F
-------- -------- - - - - - - - - - - - - - - - - - - - - - - - - - - - - - - -
7A38F464 7A3B1920 N N N N N N N N N N N N N N N N N N N N N N N N N N N N N N N N
7A38ECB8 7A3B1920 N N N N N N N N N N N N N Y N N N N N N N N N N N N N N N N N N
                                          ^
                   That B is Bind_Mismatch.
```

For a more sophisticated example, here is an interesting script that is intended to be run right after an SQL is executed, using *v$session.prev_sql_addr*. Based on MOSC note 120655.1, this script queries *v$sql_shared_cursor* to show the reason why a SQL statement cannot be shared.

sql_shared_cursor.sql

```
select version_count,address,hash_value,parsing_schema_name,reason,sql_text
from (
select
 address,''
 ||decode(max(                  UNBOUND_CURSOR),'Y',                    '
UNBOUND_CURSOR')
 ||decode(max(             SQL_TYPE_MISMATCH),'Y',               '
SQL_TYPE_MISMATCH')
 ||decode(max(            OPTIMIZER_MISMATCH),'Y',              '
OPTIMIZER_MISMATCH')
 ||decode(max(              OUTLINE_MISMATCH),'Y',                '
OUTLINE_MISMATCH')
 ||decode(max(            STATS_ROW_MISMATCH),'Y',              '
STATS_ROW_MISMATCH')
 ||decode(max(              LITERAL_MISMATCH),'Y',                '
LITERAL_MISMATCH')
 ||decode(max(             SEC_DEPTH_MISMATCH),'Y',               '
SEC_DEPTH_MISMATCH')
 ||decode(max(           EXPLAIN_PLAN_CURSOR),'Y',             '
EXPLAIN_PLAN_CURSOR')
 ||decode(max(          BUFFERED_DML_MISMATCH),'Y',            '
BUFFERED_DML_MISMATCH')
 ||decode(max(             PDML_ENV_MISMATCH),'Y',               '
PDML_ENV_MISMATCH')
 ||decode(max(            INST_DRTLD_MISMATCH),'Y',              '
INST_DRTLD_MISMATCH')
 ||decode(max(             SLAVE_QC_MISMATCH),'Y',               '
SLAVE_QC_MISMATCH')
 ||decode(max(            TYPECHECK_MISMATCH),'Y',              '
TYPECHECK_MISMATCH')
 ||decode(max(           AUTH_CHECK_MISMATCH),'Y',             '
AUTH_CHECK_MISMATCH')
 ||decode(max(                  BIND_MISMATCH),'Y',                    '
BIND_MISMATCH')
 ||decode(max(              DESCRIBE_MISMATCH),'Y',                '
DESCRIBE_MISMATCH')
 ||decode(max(              LANGUAGE_MISMATCH),'Y',                '
LANGUAGE_MISMATCH')
 ||decode(max(           TRANSLATION_MISMATCH),'Y',             '
TRANSLATION_MISMATCH')
 ||decode(max(          ROW_LEVEL_SEC_MISMATCH),'Y',            '
ROW_LEVEL_SEC_MISMATCH')
 ||decode(max(                  INSUFF_PRIVS),'Y',                     '
INSUFF_PRIVS')
 ||decode(max(              INSUFF_PRIVS_REM),'Y',                 '
INSUFF_PRIVS_REM')
 ||decode(max(          REMOTE_TRANS_MISMATCH),'Y',             '
REMOTE_TRANS_MISMATCH')
```

```
 ||decode(max(     LOGMINER_SESSION_MISMATCH),'Y',     '
LOGMINER_SESSION_MISMATCH')
 ||decode(max(          INCOMP_LTRL_MISMATCH),'Y',     '
INCOMP_LTRL_MISMATCH')
 ||decode(max(          OVERLAP_TIME_MISMATCH),'Y',    '
OVERLAP_TIME_MISMATCH')
 ||decode(max(         SQL_REDIRECT_MISMATCH),'Y',     '
SQL_REDIRECT_MISMATCH')
 ||decode(max(          MV_QUERY_GEN_MISMATCH),'Y',    '
MV_QUERY_GEN_MISMATCH')
 ||decode(max(       USER_BIND_PEEK_MISMATCH),'Y',     '
USER_BIND_PEEK_MISMATCH')
 ||decode(max(          TYPCHK_DEP_MISMATCH),'Y',      '
TYPCHK_DEP_MISMATCH')
 ||decode(max(          NO_TRIGGER_MISMATCH),'Y',      '
NO_TRIGGER_MISMATCH')
 ||decode(max(            FLASHBACK_CURSOR),'Y',       '
FLASHBACK_CURSOR')
 ||decode(max(      ANYDATA_TRANSFORMATION),'Y',       '
ANYDATA_TRANSFORMATION')
 ||decode(max(           INCOMPLETE_CURSOR),'Y',       '
INCOMPLETE_CURSOR')
 ||decode(max(        TOP_LEVEL_RPI_CURSOR),'Y',       '
TOP_LEVEL_RPI_CURSOR')
 ||decode(max(        DIFFERENT_LONG_LENGTH),'Y',      '
DIFFERENT_LONG_LENGTH')
 ||decode(max(        LOGICAL_STANDBY_APPLY),'Y',      '
LOGICAL_STANDBY_APPLY')
 ||decode(max(             DIFF_CALL_DURN),'Y',        '
DIFF_CALL_DURN')
 ||decode(max(             BIND_UACS_DIFF),'Y',        '
BIND_UACS_DIFF')
 ||decode(max(      PLSQL_CMP_SWITCHS_DIFF),'Y',       '
PLSQL_CMP_SWITCHS_DIFF')
 ||decode(max(       CURSOR_PARTS_MISMATCH),'Y',       '
CURSOR_PARTS_MISMATCH')
 ||decode(max(         STB_OBJECT_MISMATCH),'Y',       '
STB_OBJECT_MISMATCH')
 ||decode(max(          ROW_SHIP_MISMATCH),'Y',        '
ROW_SHIP_MISMATCH')
 ||decode(max(          PQ_SLAVE_MISMATCH),'Y',        '
PQ_SLAVE_MISMATCH')
 ||decode(max(       TOP_LEVEL_DDL_MISMATCH),'Y',      '
TOP_LEVEL_DDL_MISMATCH')
 ||decode(max(           MULTI_PX_MISMATCH),'Y',       '
MULTI_PX_MISMATCH')
 ||decode(max(       BIND_PEEKED_PQ_MISMATCH),'Y',     '
BIND_PEEKED_PQ_MISMATCH')
 ||decode(max(         MV_REWRITE_MISMATCH),'Y',       '
MV_REWRITE_MISMATCH')
 ||decode(max(         ROLL_INVALID_MISMATCH),'Y',     '
ROLL_INVALID_MISMATCH')
 ||decode(max(        OPTIMIZER_MODE_MISMATCH),'Y',    '
OPTIMIZER_MODE_MISMATCH')
 ||decode(max(                PX_MISMATCH),'Y',        '
PX_MISMATCH')
 ||decode(max(        MV_STALEOBJ_MISMATCH),'Y',       '
MV_STALEOBJ_MISMATCH')
```

```
  ||decode(max(        FLASHBACK_TABLE_MISMATCH),'Y',        '
FLASHBACK_TABLE_MISMATCH')
  ||decode(max(         LITREP_COMP_MISMATCH),'Y',          '
LITREP_COMP_MISMATCH')
 reason
from
  v$sql_shared_cursor
group by
  address
) join v$sqlarea using(address) where version_count>&versions
order by version_count desc,address;
```

The output from this query is important because it displays the specific reasons for the multiple child cursors from the parent SQL query:

```
VERSION_COUNT ADDRESS           HASH_VALUE PARSING_SCHEMA_NAME
------------- ----------------  ---------- -------------------------
REASON
------------------------------------------------------------------------
SQL_TEXT
------------------------------------------------------------------------
         3284 0000000BDDB2B058 3120008336
 OPTIMIZER_MISMATCH AUTH_CHECK_MISMATCH BIND_MISMATCH LANGUAGE_MISMATCH ROLL_INVALID_MISMATCH
PX_MISMATCH
INSERT INTO RSART.LOG( LOG_NO, LOG_TIME, USER_INFO, COMMAND, ERROR_CODE, ERROR_MESSAGE, NOTES,
CALL_STACK, ERROR_STACK ) VALUES( :B8 , SYSDATE, :B7 , :B6 , :B5 , :B4 , :B3 , :B2 , :B1 )
```

Now that parsing and cursors are a little less mysterious, the next section will cover techniques for making SQL reusable within the library cache.

Reusing SQL Inside the Library Cache

Just as the data buffer is used to cache block for reuse, the goal for the library cache is to make SQL cached and ready for reuse.

When Oracle recognizes an incoming SQL statement, it starts by seeing if a stored outline or a SQL profile exists.

```
-- *********************************************************
-- These are seen as the same SQL statements by Oracle:
-- *********************************************************

SELECT * FROM customer;
Select * From Customer;
Select * from CUSTOMER;
```

If there is a bunch of SQL where *executions=1*, then there may be excessive overhead from hard parsing. So, is there a way to ensure that all forms of a SQL statement are identical and thereby reduce the expensive hard parsing? Here are few common techniques:

- **Place all SQL inside stored procedures:** This encapsulation of SQL has several major benefits. In addition to ensuring that all forms of the SQL are identical to reduce hard parsing, it also has the benefit of allowing the stored procedure to be cached in the shared pool using *dbms_shared_pool.keep*.

- **Use host variables:** It always a good idea to use host variables inside SQL and avoid literal values. For example, the SQL in the form (*select stuff from emp where emp_name= ':var1*) can be reused, where SQL with literal values (*select stuff from emp where emp_name='JONES'*) is unlikely to ever be reused by another statement. For end-user query tools that generate ad-hoc SQL with literal values embedded inside the SQL (e.g. Crystal Reports), Oracle gives us the *cursor_sharing=force* and *cursor_sharing=similar* features to make SQL reentrant.

Place All SQL Inside Stored Procedures

To ensure identical SQL, the best approach is to create an application that contains no ad-hoc SQL. Instead, all SQL is placed inside stored procedures and functions, and the application calls these procedures to retrieve the data. This approach also has these additional benefits:

- **Reentrant SQL:** Because the SQL is tightly controlled, there should be no non-reentrant SQL statements.

- **Easy Management:** The DBA has access to the source code for all SQL.

- **Centralized source code:** The Oracle data dictionary is a great place to store SQL statements where they can be backed up and protected.

- **Portable Applications:** Because the application layer issues no SQL, the application becomes portable.

Use Host Variables

It is an Oracle best practice to have all SQL within an application avoid the use of literal values in the *where* clause and to replace all literals with host variables:

```
select stuff from mytab where region = :myvar1;
```

In this fashion SQL becomes reentrant which is the primary job of the library cache. In cases where ad-hoc end-user generated SQL makes host variable impossible, there is the *cursor_sharing=force* will make the SQL reentrant.

With that basic information in hand, it is time to dive in and examine specific techniques for tuning the library cache for fast SQL execution.

Tuning the Library Cache

The internal machinations of the shared pool and library cache are highly-guarded proprietary secrets, but users do have some control over how SQL is stored for reusability.

These parameters affect the behavior of the library cache:

- *shared_pool_size*: The most important tuning knob of all, it is important to give the instance enough shared_pool_size to accommodate all frequently re-executed SQL.

- *open_cursors:* This parameter is a governor that restricts the maximum number of cursors that any given session may allocate within the library cache.

- *session_cached_cursors:* The session_cached_cursors can be used to pin the cursors for the most popular SQL.

- *cursor_space_for_time:* The cursor_space_for_time parameter is being deprecated starting in Oracle 10g release 2.

- *cursor_sharing:* This is one of the most powerful parameters of all for system that cannot have SQL with embedded host variables.

The most important library cache parameter is the *shared_pool_size*.

Tuning *shared_pool_size*

The shared pool contains several key Oracle performance-related memory areas, and providing enough RAM in *shared_pool_size* is critical to optimal SQL performance.

The shared pool has many residents besides SQL. PL/SQL packages, stored procedures, functions and cursor information all share resources within this RAM region of the SGA.

Hot Tip!

Less can be more!

Remember, databases where SQL can never be re-used do not benefit from a library cache, and there are cases where a tiny *shared_pool_size* will improve system-wide SQL performance.

Later in this chapter, there will be information and scripts to be used to increase the *shared_pool_size* region, but the most important thing to remember about shared pool sizing is to watch for reloads and invalidations.

There are some other things that can be done to help relieve shared pool contention and improve SQL execution speed:

- **Bind the SQL:** Use bind variables, PL/SQL procedures or functions and views to reduce the size of large SQL statements to prevent hashing problems.

- **Find popular SQL and PL/SQL:** Use the scripts from this book to examine the usage patterns of SQL, packages, procedures, functions and cursors.

- **Size *shared_pool* incrementally:** If gross usage of the shared pool in a non-ad-hoc environment exceeds 95%, or rises to 95% or greater and stays there, establish a shared pool size large enough to hold the fixed size portions and pin all reentrant packages and procedures. Gradually increase shared pool by 20% increments until usage drops below 90% on the average.

- **Re-size for different workloads:** If the shared pool shows a mixed ad-hoc and reuse environment, establish a shared pool size large enough to hold the fixed size portions, pin reusable packages and establish a comfort level above this required level of pool fill. Establish a routine flush cycle to filter non-reusable code from the pool.

- With ad-hoc SQL, small is better: If the shared pool shows that no reusable SQL is being used establish a shared pool large enough to hold the fixed size portions plus a few megabytes, usually not more than 40, and allow the shared pool modified least recently used (LRU) algorithm to manage the pool.

- **Dictionary cache miss ratio:** In any shared pool, if the overall data dictionary cache miss ratio exceeds 1 percent, increase the size of the shared pool.

For sizing the shared pool, I recommend increasing the shared pool size in 20% increments to reduce *reloads* and *invalidations* and to increase object cache hit ratios. While these metrics are in all STATSPACK and AWR reports, this data is also available via custom scripts.

Trend Reporting on the Library Cache

The only way to monitor the shared pool for proper sizing is to measure *invalidations* and *reloads* over time, and STATSPACK or AWR is a great way to do this.

The STATSPACK report scripts *sprepsql.sql* and *sprsqins.sql scripts* are used to generate the STATSPACK report for SQL statements, statistics and plan usage. The STATSPACK SQL report shows the shareable memory used by a SQL cursor, and it is the sum of all memory used by the SQL, including child cursors.

In STATSPACK, the collection threshold, *p_def_version_count_th*, can be used to govern the threshold for the SQL child cursors. The following is a good report on usage within the library cache using STATSPACK historical data:

🖫 rpt_lib.sql

```
set lines 80;
set pages 999;

column mydate      heading 'Yr.  Mo Dy  Hr.' format a16
column reloads           format 999,999,999
column hit_ratio         format 999.99
column pin_hit_ratio format 999.99

break on mydate skip 2;
select
   to_char(snap_time,'yyyy-mm-dd HH24')  mydate,
   new.namespace,
   (new.gethits-old.gethits)/(new.gets-old.gets) hit_ratio,
   (new.pinhits-old.pinhits)/(new.pins-old.pins) pin_hit_ratio,
   new.reloads
from
   stats$librarycache old,
   stats$librarycache new,
   stats$snapshot      sn
where
   new.snap_id = sn.snap_id
and
   old.snap_id = new.snap_id-1
and
   old.namespace = new.namespace
and
   new.gets-old.gets > 0
and
   new.pins-old.pins > 0;
```

The following output show changes to the important library cache metrics over time:

```
Yr.  Mo Dy  Hr.  NAMESPACE        HIT_RATIO PIN_HIT_RATIO    RELOADS
----------------- ---------------- --------- ------------- ------------
2012-12-20 10     BODY                 1.00          1.00            5
                  PIPE                 1.00          1.00            0
                  SQL AREA              .99           .96        2,957
                  TABLE/PROCEDURE      1.00           .91          212
                  TRIGGER              1.00          1.00            0
                  BODY                 1.00          1.00            5
                  INDEX                1.00          1.00            0

2012-12-20 11     BODY                  .99           .99            5
                  CLUSTER              1.00          1.00            1
                  INDEX                1.00          1.00            0
                  PIPE                 1.00          1.00            0
                  SQL AREA              .98           .99        2,999
                  TABLE/PROCEDURE       .99          1.00          221
                  TRIGGER              1.00          1.00            0
```

The Library Cache Miss Ratio

Library cache misses occur during the parsing and preparation of the execution plans for SQL statements.

The library cache miss ratio is the ratio of the sum of library cache reloads to the sum of pins and is a great sizing indicator for the shared pool. In general, if the library cache ratio is over 1, consideration should be given to adding RAM to the *shared_pool_size*.

While it is not an exact science, high library cache misses are an indication that the shared pool is not big enough to hold the shared SQL for all currently running programs. Remember, library cache misses during the execute phase occur when the parsed representation exists in the library cache but has been bounced out of the shared pool.

Because shared pool sizing is an iterative process, a time-based proactive approach is best and the following script will track the library cache miss ration over time:

🖫 library_cache_miss.sql

```
set lines 80;
set pages 999;

column mydate heading 'Yr.  Mo Dy  Hr.'                     format a16
column c1      heading    "execs"                           format 9,999,999
column c2      heading    "Cache Misses|While Executing"    format 9,999,999
column c3      heading    "Library Cache|Miss Ratio"        format 999.99999

break on mydate skip 2;

select
   to_char(snap_time,'yyyy-mm-dd HH24')   mydate,
   sum(new.pins-old.pins)                 c1,
   sum(new.reloads-old.reloads)           c2,
   sum(new.reloads-old.reloads)/
   sum(new.pins-old.pins)                 c3
from
   stats$librarycache old,
   stats$librarycache new,
   stats$snapshot      sn
where
   new.snap_id = sn.snap_id
and
   old.snap_id = new.snap_id-1
and
   old.namespace = new.namespace
group by
   to_char(snap_time,'yyyy-mm-dd HH24');
```

Here is the output showing the library cache miss ration by hour of the day.

```
                    Cache Misses       Library Cache
Yr.  Mo Dy  Hr.     execs While Executing    Miss Ratio
---------------- ---------- --------------- --------------------
2012-12-20 10      10,338         3             .00029
2012-12-20 11     182,477       134             .00073
2012-12-20 12     190,707       202             .00106
2012-12-20 13       2,803        11             .00392
```

The next section will cover monitoring of the library cache hit ratio, which is a general measure of the effectiveness of the library cache.

The Library Cache Hit Ratio

The library cache hit ratio is an Oracle metric that monitors the percentage of entries in the library cache that were parsed more than once (reloads) over the lifetime of the instance.

Since it is not possible to know in advance just how many SQL statements need to be cached, the Oracle DBA must set *shared_pool_size* large enough to prevent excessive re-parsing of SQL.

Here is a script for measuring the library cache hit ratio:

🖫 library_cache_hit_ratio.sql

```sql
select
   'Buffer Cache' name,
   round ( (congets.value + dbgets.value - physreads.value) * 100
   / (congets.value + dbgets.value), 2
) value
from
   v$sysstat congets,
   v$sysstat dbgets,
   v$sysstat physreads
where
   congets.name = 'consistent gets'
and
   dbgets.name = 'db block gets'
and
   physreads.name = 'physical reads'
union all
select
   'execute/noparse',
   decode (sign (round ( (ec.value - pc.value)
* 100
/ decode (ec.value, 0, 1, ec.value), 2)), -1, 0, round ( (ec.value -
pc.value) * 100 / decode (ec.value, 0, 1, ec.value), 2))
```

```
from
   v$sysstat ec,
   v$sysstat pc
where
   ec.name = 'execute count'
and
   pc.name in ('parse count', 'parse count (total)')
union all
select
   'Memory Sort',
   round ( ms.value / decode ((ds.value + ms.value), 0, 1, (ds.value +
ms.value)) * 100, 2
)
from
   v$sysstat ds,
   v$sysstat ms
where
   ms.name = 'sorts (memory)'
and
   ds.name = 'sorts (disk)'
union all
select
   'sql area get hitrate', round (gethitratio * 100, 2)
from
   v$librarycache
where
   namespace = 'SQL AREA'
union all
select
   'avg latch hit (no miss)',
   round ((sum (gets) - sum (misses)) * 100 / sum (gets), 2)
from
   v$latch
union all
select
   'avg latch hit (no sleep)',
   round ((sum (gets) - sum (sleeps)) * 100 / sum (gets), 2)
from
   v$latch;
```

```
NAME                         VALUE
------------------------     ----------
Buffer Cache                 97.31
execute/noparse              91.18
Memory Sort                  99.99
sql area get hitrate         92.08
avg latch hit (no miss)      97.70
avg latch hit (no sleep)     99.93
```

Again, additional and more sophisticated scripts will be presented later in this chapter, but these are the major tuning guidelines for optimizing the shared pool.

The next section covers more about the *open_cursors* parameter.

Using *open_cursors*

The *open_cursors* parameter is a governor, a block to prevent runaway tasks from consuming too much library cache RAM.

Any session may execute many SQL statements and the *open_cursors* parameter governs the total number of open cursors for any given session.

For example, if *open_cursors=100*, Oracle will be allowed to allocate up to 100 cursor slots in the library cache. Because the slots are only allocated as they are requested, there is no added overhead to setting this value higher than actually needed.

The starting value is set by Oracle at instance creation time.

Just like the *sessions* and *processes* parameters, application usage determines the value for *open_cursors*. If the *open_cursors* value is set too high, there is risk having a task abort with the ORA-01000 error:

```
ORA-01000 maximum open cursors exceeded
```

Whenever an ORA-01000 error is returned, it will be necessary to determine if the session has a bug or whether the cursor requests are legitimate. The *open_cursors* parameter can be changed dynamically while the database is running using an *alter system* statement:

```
alter system set open_cursors = 400 scope=both;
```

A high water mark for open cursors can be monitored with a query like this:

🖫 hwm_open_cursors.sql

```
set trimspool on
set linesize 180

col hwm_open_cur format 99,999
col max_open_cur format 99,999

select
   max(a.value)  as hwm_open_cur,
   p.value       as max_open_cur
from
   v$sesstat a,
   v$statname b,
   v$parameter p
where
   a.statistic# = b.statistic#
and
```

```
    b.name = 'opened cursors current'
and
    p.name= 'open_cursors'
group by p.value;
```

HWM_OPEN_CUR MAX_OPEN_CUR
------------ ------------
      106   900

In sum, the *open_cursors* parameter default value is usually enough for any application, and it can be increased as needed, depending upon the application.

Monitoring Open Cursors

There are a couple of good views for monitoring open cursors:

- *v$open_cursor*
- *v$sesstat*

The following scripts show the values for open cursors:

🖫 monitor_open_cursors.sql

```
select
   stat.value,
   sess.username,
   sess.sid,
   sess.serial#
from
   v$sesstat   stat,
   v$statname b,
   v$session   sess
where
   stat.statistic# = b.statistic#
and
   sess.sid=stat.sid
and
   b.name = 'opened cursors current';
```

```
    VALUE USERNAME                                    SID     SERIAL#
---------- -------------------------------------- ---------- ----------
       52 REPLAD                                      618       44142
       52 REPLAD                                      621       26877
        1 REPLAD                                      624       42421
       52 DBTOOLS                                     629        7689
       52 APP_ADMIN                                   633       58834
       61 APPDBVIEWX                                  634       56637
```

```
        1  RSART                              640       53861
        1  REPLAD                             642       27221
       52  REPLAD                             643       55454
        1  REPLAD                             645       11886
        1  REPLAD                             651       56666
```

💾 user_open_cursors.sql

```
select
   sum(stat.value)
   total_cur,
   avg(stat.value)  avg_cur,
   max(stat.value)  max_cur,
   sess.username,
   sess.machine
from
   v$sesstat    stat,
   v$statname       b,
   v$session    sess
where
   stat.statistic# = b.statistic#
and
   sess.sid=stat.sid
and
   b.name = 'opened cursors current'
group by
   sess.username,
   sess.machine
order by 1 desc;
```

```
TOTAL_CUR    AVG_CUR    MAX_CUR USERNAME                                 MACHINE
---------- ---------- ---------- -------------------------------------- ------------
       300         50         53 APP_ADMIN                              APTEST1
       196         49         51 REPLAD                                 APTEST1
       143      35.75         54 SYS                                    APTEST1
       106        106        106 APPDBVIEWX                             APTEST1
       102         51         51 APP_USRMANAGER                         APTEST1
       100         10         52 REPLAD                                 APTEST1
```

The next section will cover the *session_cached_cursors* parameter.

Using *session_cached_cursors*

As new SQL enters the database, Oracle checks the library cache for parsed SQL statements, and the *session_cached_cursors* can be used to pin the cursors for the most popular SQL.

When *session_cached_cursors* is implemented, popular SQL, that with more than three parse calls, is moved into the session cache. It is important to remember that the session cursor cache is not permanent, and SQL cursors will age out, using the same Least Recently Used (LRU) algorithm that is used for data blocks.

Pinning SQL with *session_cached_cursors* is especially useful for reentrant SQL that contains host variables, and there are many incarnations of the SQL, each with a different host variable value. The *session_cached_cursors* parameter is used to reduce the amount of parsing with SQL statements that use host variables and with PL/SQL cursors.

The *session_cached_cursors* parameter has a default value of 50, and increasing the value of *session_cached_cursors* will requires a larger *shared_pool_size* to cache the cursors.

Many shops double the default value for *session_cached_cursors* to 100, and some use values as high as 1,000, depending on the application.

Oracle notes that the *session_cached_cursors* is related to the *open_cursors* parameter, and if there are concerns that cursors are being paged-out of the library cache, increasing *session_cached_cursors* up to the value of *open_cursors* can improve performance.

The *session cursor cache hits* value in STATSPACK or AWR reports is used to monitor the benefit of increasing *session_cached_cursors*. This metric is also visible with data dictionary scripts:

🖫 monitor_session_cached_cursors.sql

```
col c1 heading "SID"
col c2 heading "Cache|Hits"
col c3 heading "All Parsing"
col c4 heading "Un-used Session|Cached Cursors"

select
   stat1.sid       c1,
   stat1.value c2,
   stat2.value c3,
   stat2.value c4
from
   v$sesstat   stat1,
   v$sesstat   stat2,
   v$statname  name1,
   v$statname  name2
where
   stat1.statistic# = name1.statistic#
and
   stat2.statistic#=name2.statistic#
and
   name1.name = 'session cursor cache hits'
and
   name2.name= 'parse count (total)'
and
   stat2.sid= stat1.sid;
```

Cache   Un-used Session

SID	Hits	All Parsing	Cached Cursors
618	2127	1244	1244
621	1181	1155	1155
624	0	1	1
629	698	754	754
633	17407	35105	35105
634	4853	5863	5863
640	0	1	1
642	0	1	1
643	2689	1630	1630
645	0	1	1

Using *cursor_space_for_time*

The *cursor_space_for_time* parameter is a tuning knob allowing SQL to stay pinned inside the library cache shared pool area, making all SQL ineligible for the aging out process until the cursor for the SQL statement is closed.

The default for *cursor_space_for_time=false* which means that it is OK for a SQL statement to age out before the cursor is closed.

Setting *cursor_space_for_time=true* allows the use of more space for cursors in order to save time. Oracle recommends only setting *cursor_space_for_time=true* in databases where the *shared_pool_size* is large enough to hold all open cursors simultaneously.

With *cursor_space_for_time=true*, Oracle will not bother to check the library cache on subsequent SQL execution calls because the SQL has already been pinned in the library cache. This technique can improve the performance in very rare cases where the *shared_pool_size* is huge and all SQL can be fully cached, but *cursor_space_for_time* should not be set to *true* if there are cache misses on execution calls. Remember, library cache misses indicate that the *shared_pool_size* is already too small, and forcing the pinning of shared SQL areas with *cursor_space_for_time=true* will only aggravate an existing problem.

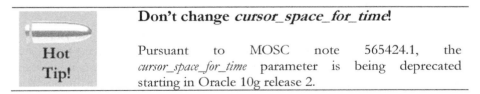

Don't change *cursor_space_for_time*!

Hot Tip! Pursuant to MOSC note 565424.1, the *cursor_space_for_time* parameter is being deprecated starting in Oracle 10g release 2.

In sum, this can be a very dangerous parameter, and *cursor_space_for_time* should never be changed from its default value of *false* except with the advice and consent of Oracle Technical Support.

The next section covers the powerful *cursor_sharing* parameter and how it can be used to minimize SQL processing overhead.

Using *cursor_sharing*

Some Oracle databases with high ad-hoc query activity (Crystal Reports, Business Objects) cannot avoid inline literals inside the SQL, and that is why Oracle introduced the *cursor_sharing* parameter. This use of *cursor_sharing=force* has be a huge benefit for database plagued with literals (i.e. non-reentrant SQL) in their library cache.

The dynamic shop often has SQL that is generated by ad-hoc query tools with hard-coded literal values embedded within the SQL. Hard-coded literal values make the SQL statements non-reusable unless *cursor_sharing=force* is set in the Oracle initialization file.

Shops that are plagued with non-reusable SQL can adopt either the persistent or the dynamic execution plan philosophy. To use optimizer plan stability with non-reusable SQL, the DBA will set *cursor_sharing=force* and then extract the transformed SQL from the library cache and use optimizer plan stability to make the execution plan persistent.

Historically, the *cursor_sharing* initialization parameter seemed like a great idea initially. However, several false starts, multiple bugs and performance that did not quite meet expectations caused most users to shelve the idea of *cursor_sharing* until a more stable release.

Essentially there are two options for the *cursor_sharing* parameter; *exact*, which means that the cursors have to be exact in order to be shared, and *force* which means every literal was replaced with a bind variable. Many Oracle shops that use purchased packages are stuck with poorly implemented applications from third-parties that could not have the source code altered except by an act of God, so the ability to force bind variables is a good idea.

But it is not always a good idea to force bind variables for 100% of statements. When a bind variable is volatile, such that the value of the bind variable affects the execution plan for the SQL, it is not a good idea to replace the literals in a statement with a bind variable. Fortunately, there is the *similar* option which will only substitute when the bind variable will not affect the execution plan.

The following simple case study will give an idea how cursor sharing improves SQL execution:

A Case Study in Cursor Sharing

An Oracle 11g database had experienced poor performance immediately after a new manufacturing plant was added to the existing database. A standard STATSPACK report was used to isolate the top five wait events which looked similar to this:

```
Top 5 Wait Events
~~~~~~~~~~~~~~~~~~                          Wait      % Total
Event                          Waits   Time (cs)   Wt Time
--------------------------- ----------- ----------- -------
enqueue                         25,901     479,654   46.71
db file scattered read      10,579,442     197,205   29.20
db file sequential read        724,325     196,583    9.14
latch free                   1,150,979      51,084    4.97
log file parallel write        148,932      39,822    3.88
```

A review of the SQL section of the STATSPACK report revealed that almost all of the SQL used literals in the *where* clause of all queries.

```
where
   customer_state = 'Alabama'
and
   customer_type = 'LAWYER';
```

The *cursor_sharing* parameter was the only fast solution because the application was a vendor package with dynamically generated SQL and it could not easily be changed without using Optimizer Plan Stability (Stored Outlines), a very time-consuming task.

Setting *cursor_sharing=force* greatly reduced the contention on the library cache and reduced CPU consumption. The end users reported a 75 percent improvement in overall performance.

Oracle Cursor Sharing Enhancements

An exciting internal feature of Oracle 11g allows the cost-based SQL optimizer to change execution plans even when optimizer plan stability is used. This is called peeking and allows the cost-based SQL optimizer to change execution plans when the value of a bind variable would cause a significant change to the execution plan for the SQL.

Use cursor_sharing=similar only in 11g!

While *cursor_sharing=similar* has been around since Oracle 9i, it had a few bugs and it has only become useable as of Oracle 11g.

Hot Tip!

Cursor sharing has a processing overhead at optimization time, and it should only be used if an application generates dynamic SQL or with applications that must embed literal values. PL/SQL applications should be written for the SQL to use bind variables, and these systems will not benefit from cursor sharing.

To illustrate with a simple example, consider a simple example where our *cursor_sharing* parameter is set to *force*. This will change all SQL literal values to host variables inside the library cache.

Now, assume that there an index on a region column of a customer table. The region column has four values; north, south, east, and west. The data values for the region column are highly skewed with 90% of the values in the south region.

Hence, the cost-based SQL optimizer would be faster performing a full-table scan when south is specified and an index range scan when east, west or north is specified. When using cursor sharing, the cost-based SQL optimizer changes any literal values in the SQL to bind variables. Hence, this statement would be changed as follows:

```
select
   customer_stuff
from
   customer
where
   region = 'west';
```

The transformation replaces the literal west with a host variable:

```
select
   customer_stuff
from
   customer
where
   region = ':var1';
```

In Oracle 11g with *cursor_sharing=similar*, the cost-based SQL optimizer peeks at the values of user-defined bind variables on the first invocation of a cursor. This lets the optimizer determine the selectivity of the *where* clause operator and change the execution plan whenever the south value appears in the SQL.

This enhancement greatly improves the performance of cursor sharing when a bind variable is used against a highly skewed column.

With *cursor_sharing=similar*, Oracle will switch in the bind variables if doing so makes no difference to the outcome but will use literal values if using bind variables would make a significant difference to the outcome.

Hot Tip!

The view *v$sql_shared_cursor* has an important column called *user_bind_peek_mismatch* which is defined as a cursor that is not shared because value of one or more user binds is different and this has a potential to change the execution plan.

Here is a query where the user supplies the SQL ID, and Oracle will display of there is a bind mismatch:

```
select
   sql_id,
   bind_mismatch
from
   v$sql_shared_cursor
where
   sql_id = '&my_sql_id';
```

Remember, Oracle's bind peeking is only useful for highly skewed column distributions. Peeking is only useful when Oracle detects that the value of a column literal will affect the execution plan. For index columns without excessive skew, peeking is a wasted step.

Using 11g Adaptive Cursor Sharing

Oracle has improved *cursor_sharing* several times over the years. Remember, 11g adaptive cursor sharing is only deployed in rare cases where a skewed column distribution indicates that a different execution plan would be faster. For example, a query with a popular bind variable value would be best served with a full table scan while an unpopular bind variable value would benefit from an index access plan.

Disabling Adaptive Cursor Sharing

Remember, the need for adaptive cursor sharing can be a rare occurrence in many systems. In many OLTP databases there exists one, and only one, optimal SQL execution plan for a query, regardless of the value of a bind variable. For these types of databases, the overhead of adaptive cursor sharing may be bypassed by disabling the adaptive cursor sharing feature:

```
-- ****************************************
-- Turn off adaptive cursor sharing:
-- ****************************************
alter system set "cursor_sharing"=exact scope=both;

alter system set "_optimizer_extended_cursor_sharing_rel"=none scope=both;

alter system set "_optimizer_extended_cursor_sharing"=none scope= both;

alter system set "_optimizer_adaptive_cursor_sharing"=false scope= both;
```

In my experience at BC, about 80% of shops have uniformly distributed data. Large tables remain large, and the distribution of values within a column remains unchanged.

For testing purposes, it may be desirable to turn off optimizer bind variable peeking and this can be done in a couple of ways:

- Re-set the _optim_peek_user_binds_ hidden parameter.

- Re-analyze using dbms_stats with the argument: `method_opt=> 'for all columns size 1';`

Effectively Using Adaptive Cursor Sharing

Of course, it is quite rare to find a real-world system where the value of a bind variable is going to make a significant difference in the SQL execution plan.

On the other hand, roughly 20% of databases experience highly volatile data loads, where tables are small on one day and huge the next, or cases where there is a "difference that makes a difference".

In these databases, huge changes in the tables data, usually associated with high DML, changes the distribution of data values, necessitating a re-analysis of column histograms.

Histograms are critical to the CBO decision to choose an index rather than a full scan, and also for determining the optimal table join order. For testing, Oracle can be forced to invoke adaptive cursor sharing with the adaptive cursor sharing hint (*acs_1*):

```
select /* ACS_1 */
   count(c1)
from
   mytab
where
   shewed_column = :HOSTVAR1;
```

The *v$sql* view has a column named *is_bind_sensitive* that is set to 'Y', to indicate that different bind variable values may result in different execution plans. The following SQL can be used to check the status:

🖫 check_bind_sensitive_sql.sql

```
select
   sql_id,
   child_number,
   is_bind_sensitive,
   is_bind_aware
from
   v$sql
where
   sql_text =
   'select
      max(id)
    from
      acs_test_tab
    where
      record_type = :l_record_type';
```

```
9bmm6cmwa8saf              0 Y N
```

The following are additional sample queries for 11g adaptive cursor sharing:

```
select
   hash_value,
   sql_id,
   child_number,
   range_id,
   low,
   high,
   predicate
from
   v$sql_cs_selectivity;
```

And:

```
select
   hash_value,
   sql_id,
   child_number,
   bucket_id,
   count
from
   v$sql_cs_histogram;
```

And:

```
select
  sql_id,
```

Oracle Cursor Sharing Enhancements

```
   hash_value,
   plan_hash_value,
   is_bind_sensitive,
   is_bind_aware,
   sql_text
from
   v$sql;
```

And:

```
select
   hash_value,
   sql_id,
   child_number,
   bind_set_hash_value,
   peeked,
   executions,
   rows_processed,
   buffer_gets
   cpu_time
from
   v$sql_cs_statistics;
```

Clearly, the library cache is a very sophisticated method for making SQL re-entrant with the goal of reducing processing overhead and making SQL run quickly in a busy environment. The main points of this section include:

- The library cache serves to cache SQL in much the same way as the data buffers cache data blocks.

- Oracle has only a few tuning knobs, and the main tuning activity for the library cache is the proper sizing of the shared pool.

- Monitoring the library cache involved tracking several metrics over time, normally the library cache miss ration, pins, reloads and invalidations.

- Oracle provides *cursor_sharing=force* for ad-hoc SQL system where the SQL cannot be written to use host variables.

- Non-reentrant SQL is characterized by a *v$sql* value where executions=1, and these systems are candidates for the *cursor_sharing* parameter.

The next chapter will explore how to do proactive time-series SQL tuning with the STATSPACK and AWR utilities.

Time Series SQL Tuning

Time-Series SQL tuning gives you valuable feedback.

Proactive Time-Series SQL Tuning

Oracle has codified a holistic approach to SQL tuning starting in Oracle 11g, and the accepted method for system-wide SQL tuning now involves testing real-world workloads consisting of real-world SQL, and applying global tuning methods, such as adjusting CBO statistics and optimizing SQL parameters, before tuning individual SQL statements.

Just as the *v$sql_plan* view revolutionized Oracle tuning, the Oracle STATSPACK and extra-cost AWR tables have revolutionized SQL tuning.

Most Oracle experts note that SQL optimization is one of the most important factors in database tuning, yet the transient nature of SQL execution has made it difficult to see the impact of SQL execution over time.

The AWR tables contain useful information about the time-series execution plans for SQL statements, and this repository can be used to display details about the frequency of usage for table and indexes:

- **Each SQL statement may generate many access plans:** From the information on dynamic sampling and dbms_stats, the execution plans for SQL statements will change over time to accommodate changes in the data they access. It is important to understand how and when a frequently executed SQL statement changes its access plan.

- **Each object is access by many access plans:** In most OLTP systems, tables and indexes show repeating patterns of usage and clear patterns can be detected when averaging object access of day-of-the-week and hour-of-the-day.

The following basic relationships, illustrated in Figure 17.1, between database objects and SQL statements are important:

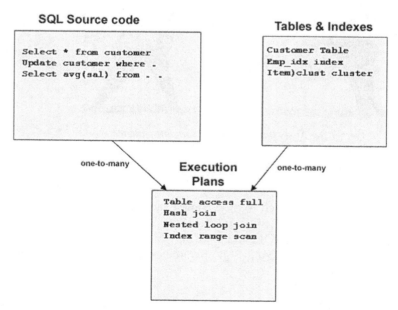

Figure 17.1: *Time-series relationships between SQL and database objects*

Figure 17.1 shows that there is a many-to-many relationship between any given SQL statement and the tables it accesses. Once this fundamental relationship is clear, the AWR tables can be used to perform time-based SQL tuning.

For example, tracking a SQL workload over time involves looking at the transactions per second and disk I/O per second.

It will be necessary to define transactions per second (TPS) and investigate how it is different for different server components. To Oracle, a transaction is a SQL statement:

- **Oracle transactions per second:** The Oracle documentation has the "Transactions/Sec" defined as the number of commits (successful SQL) and rollbacks (aborted SQL) per second. In sum, it is the SQL statements per second being measured.

- **Disk transactions per second:** To a disk, the number of transactions per second is the number of I/O requests, usually a block.

- **OS transactions per second:** To the Operating system, a transaction is the creation and destruction of a process in UNIX/Linux or a thread in Windows. Note that a database transaction, a SQL statement, may have many associated OS processes or Oracle background processes.

For example, Oracle indirectly measures I/O per second for a SQL workload by measuring database block reads, a measure of physical disk I/O. This can be seen in any STATSPACK or AWR report, or the Ion tool can be used to quickly plot disk I/O trends over time as shown in Figure 17.2:

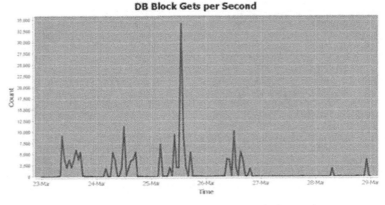

Figure 17.2: *A plot of DB block gets per second in the Ion tool*

For Oracle transactions, the transactions per second can be found in the load profile section of any AWR or STATSPACK report:

```
STATSPACK
Load Profile
~~~~~~~~~~~~                         Per Second          Per Transaction
                                     ---------------      ---------------
              Redo size:             2,189.01             2,376.67
          Logical reads:             5,467.24             5,935.95
          Block changes:                10.59                11.50
         Physical reads:             1,953.94             2,121.45
        Physical writes:                20.35                22.10
             User calls:               131.08               142.32
                 Parses:                28.80                31.27
            Hard parses:                 0.30                 0.33
                  Sorts:                 3.98                 4.32
                 Logons:                 0.21                 0.22
               Executes:                28.60                31.05
           Transactions:                 0.92
```

Oracle transactions per second can also be plotted interactively using the Ion tool as shown in Figure 17.3:

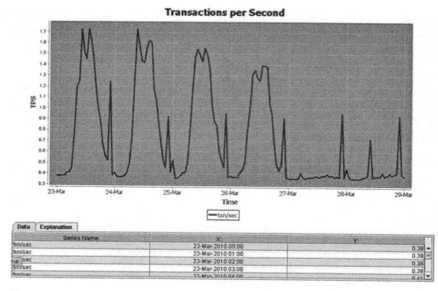

Figure 17.3: *A plot of transactions per second in the Ion tool*

Now that the concepts of SQL workload trend analysis have been covered, it is a good time to take a closer look at using STATSPACK and AWR to tune SQL workloads.

SQL Trending with STATSPACK and AWR

In general, there are two approaches to Oracle proactive tuning, running scripts against STATSPACK or AWR, versus using a tool to display the salient metrics over time.

The script-based approach is infinitely more flexible, but the output must be collected and charted in order to see the trends.

STATSPACK vs. AWR

Instead of AWR, we can also use STATSPACK for time-series SQL tuning, remembering that STATSPACK does not require the purchase of the extra-cost performance pack and diagnostic pack.

Table 17.1 below shows the important SQL tuning tables. Remember, STATSPACK has 90% of the functionality of AWR and it is not necessary to spend thousands of dollars extra to purchase a license, as is required to use the *dba_hist* tables.

v$ View	STATSPACK table	AWR Table
v$sqlstat	stats$sql_statistics	dba_hist_sqlstat
v$sql	stats$sql_summary	dba_hist_sql_summary
v$sql_workarea		dba_hist_sql_workarea
v$sql_plan	stats$sql_plan_usage	dba_hist_sql_workarea
v$sql_workarea	stats$sql_workarea_histogram	dba_hist_sql_workarea_histogram

Table 17.1: *V$ STATSPACK vs. AWR SQL tuning tables*

If these tables are graphed into an entity relation diagram, it is easy to see the relationships between the time-series SQL tuning tables as shown in Figure 17.4:

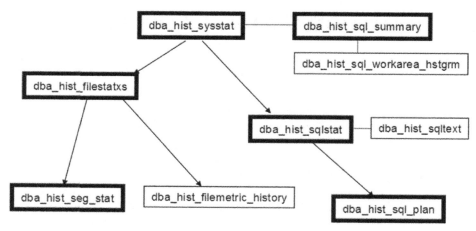

Figure 17.4: *The dba_hist views for SQL tuning*

These simple tables represent a revolution in Oracle SQL tuning, and time-series techniques can be employed to optimize SQL with better results than ever before.

The following section provides a closer look at these AWR tables and the amazing details that they can provide about SQL execution over time.

The *dba_hist_sqlstat* Table

The *dba_hist_sqlstat* table is very similar to the *v$sql* view, but it contains important delta metrics, showing changes in SQL tuning metrics between each snapshot. These include important change information on disk reads and buffer gets, as well as time-series delta information on application, I/O and concurrency wait times. For example, consider the query:

🖫 sqlstat_deltas.sql

```
col c1 heading 'Begin|Interval|time'       format a8
col c2 heading 'SQL|ID'                     format a13
col c3 heading 'Exec|Delta'                 format 9,999
col c4 heading 'Buffer|Gets|Delta'          format 9,999
col c5 heading 'Disk|Reads|Delta'           format 9,999
col c6 heading 'IO Wait|Delta'              format 9,999
col c7 heading 'Application|Wait|Delta'     format 9,999
col c8 heading 'Concurrency|Wait|Delta'     format 9,999

break on c1

select
  to_char(s.begin_interval_time,'mm-dd hh24')  c1,
```

```
   sql.sql_id                 c2,
   sql.executions_delta       c3,
   sql.buffer_gets_delta      c4,
   sql.disk_reads_delta       c5,
   sql.iowait_delta           c6,
   sql.apwait_delta           c7,
   sql.ccwait_delta           c8
from
   dba_hist_sqlstat           sql,
   dba_hist_snapshot            s
where
   s.snap_id = sql.snap_id
order by
   c1,
   c2;
```

The following is a sample of the output. This is very important because the changes in SQL execution over time periods can be visualized.

For each snapshot period, it is possible to see the change in the number of times that the SQL was executed as well as important performance information about the performance of the statement.

Begin Interval time	SQL ID	Exec Delta	Buffer Gets Delta	Disk Reads Delta	IO Wait Delta	Application Wait Delta	Concurrency Wait Delta
10-10 16	0sfgqjz5cs52w	24	72	12	0	3	0
	1784a4705pt01	1	685	6	0	17	0
	19rkm1wsf9axx	10	61	4	0	0	0
	1d5d88cnwxcw4	52	193	4	6	0	0
	1fvsn5j51ugz3	4	0	0	0	0	0
	1uym1vta995yb	1	102	0	0	0	0
	23yu0nncnp8m9	24	72	0	0	6	0
	298ppdduqr7wm	1	3	0	0	0	0
	2cpffmjm98pcm	4	12	0	0	0	0
	2prbzh4qfms7u	1	4,956	19	1	34	5
10-10 17	0sfgqjz5cs52w	30	90	1	0	0	0
	19rkm1wsf9axx	14	88	0	0	0	0
	1fvsn5j51ugz3	4	0	0	0	0	0
	1zcdwkknwdpgh	4	4	0	0	0	0
	23yu0nncnp8m9	30	91	0	0	0	5
	298ppdduqr7wm	1	3	0	0	0	0
	2cpffmjm98pcm	4	12	0	0	0	0
	2prbzh4qfms7u	1	4,940	20	0	0	0
	2ysccdanw72pv	30	60	0	0	0	0
	3505vtqmvvf40	2	321	5	1	0	0

This report is especially useful because it is possible to track the logical I/O (buffer gets) versus physical I/O for each statement over time, thereby yielding important information about the behavior of the SQL statement. Ion can also be used to locate the Top 10 SQL by disk reads as shown in Figure 17.5:

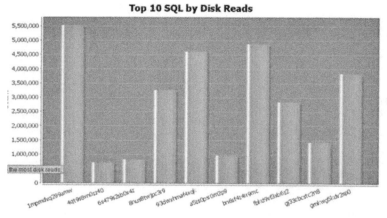

Figure 17.5: *The top-10 SQL statements by disk reads*

This output gives a quick overview of the top SQL during any AWR snapshot period and shows how their behavior has changed since the last snapshot period.

While this trends physical I/O, it might also be desirable to track logical I/O. The above script can be changed slightly in order to examine logical reads (consistent gets) averages for any given SQL statement as shown in Figure 17.6:

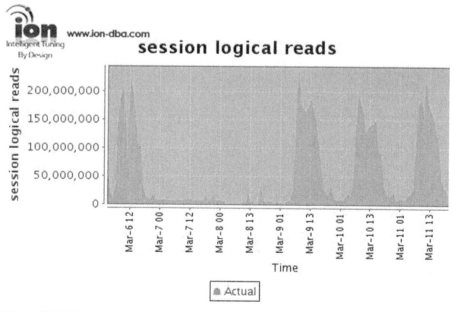

Figure 17.6: *Daily logical vs. physical I/O in Ion.*

Remember, detecting changes in the behavior of commonly executed SQL statements is the key to time-series SQL tuning.

Plot Exceptional Conditions!

A *where* clause can easily be added to the above script to create a threshold report, showing exceptions over time.

Next, the query can be altered to give time-series changes for a specific SQL statement. This is important to seeing how a SQL statement changes over time:

🖫 sqlstat_deltas_detail.sql

```
col c1 heading 'Begin|Interval|time'      format a8
col c2 heading 'Exec|Delta'               format 999,999
col c3 heading 'Buffer|Gets|Delta'        format 999,999
col c4 heading 'Disk|Reads|Delta'         format 9,999
col c5 heading 'IO Wait|Delta'            format 9,999
col c6 heading 'App|Wait|Delta'           format 9,999
col c7 heading 'Cncr|Wait|Delta'          format 9,999
col c8 heading 'CPU|Time|Delta'           format 999,999
col c9 heading 'Elpsd|Time|Delta'         format 999,999

accept sqlid prompt 'Enter SQL ID: '

ttitle 'time series execution for|&sqlid'

break on c1

select
  to_char(s.begin_interval_time,'mm-dd hh24')  c1,
  sql.executions_delta      c2,
  sql.buffer_gets_delta     c3,
  sql.disk_reads_delta      c4,
  sql.iowait_delta          c5,
  sql.apwait_delta          c6,
  sql.ccwait_delta          c7,
  sql.cpu_time_delta        c8,
  sql.elapsed_time_delta    c9
from
  dba_hist_sqlstat          sql,
  dba_hist_snapshot         s
where
  s.snap_id = sql.snap_id
and
  sql_id = '&sqlid'
order by    c1;
```

The following output shows changes to the execution of a specific SQL statement and how its behavior changes over time:

```
SQL> @ sqlstat_deltas_detail

Enter SQL ID: 19rkm1wsf9axx
```

Begin Interval time	Exec Delta	Buffer Gets Delta	Disk Reads Delta	IO Wait Delta	App Wait Delta	Cncr Wait Delta	CPU Time Delta	Elpsd Time Delta
10-14 10	709	2,127	0	0	0	0	398,899	423,014
10-14 11	696	2,088	0	0	0	0	374,502	437,614
10-14 12	710	2,130	0	0	0	0	384,579	385,388
10-14 13	693	2,079	0	0	0	0	363,648	378,252
10-14 14	708	2,124	0	0	0	0	373,902	373,902
10-14 15	697	2,091	0	0	0	0	388,047	410,605
10-14 16	707	2,121	0	0	0	0	386,542	491,830
10-14 17	698	2,094	0	0	0	0	378,087	587,544
10-14 18	708	2,124	0	0	0	0	376,491	385,816
10-14 19	695	2,085	0	0	0	0	361,850	361,850
10-14 20	708	2,124	0	0	0	0	368,889	368,889
10-14 21	696	2,088	0	0	0	0	363,111	412,521
10-14 22	709	2,127	0	0	0	0	369,015	369,015
10-14 23	695	2,085	0	0	0	0	362,480	362,480
10-15 00	709	2,127	0	0	0	0	368,554	368,554
10-15 01	697	2,091	0	0	0	0	362,987	362,987
10-15 02	696	2,088	0	0	0	2	361,445	380,944
10-15 03	708	2,124	0	0	0	0	367,292	367,292
10-15 04	697	2,091	0	0	0	0	362,279	362,279
10-15 05	708	2,124	0	0	0	0	367,697	367,697
10-15 06	696	2,088	0	0	0	0	361,423	361,423
10-15 07	709	2,127	0	0	0	0	374,766	577,559
10-15 08	697	2,091	0	0	0	0	364,879	410,328

In the listing above, it is evident how the number of executions varies over time. Ion can be used to plot the top-10 SQL by wait times as shown in Figure 17.7:

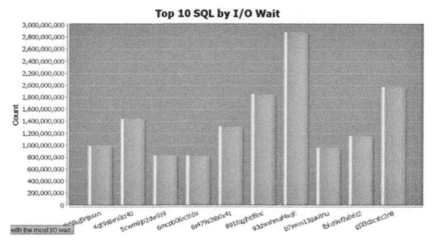

Figure 17.7: *The top-10 SQL by I/O wait times*

The above example shows the average waits for the SQL workload over time. Of course, the execution speed may change due to any number of factors:

- Different bind variables

- Database resource shortage

- High physical reads from data buffer shortage

With this information, it is possible to drill down into those specific times when SQL statements performed badly and see exactly why its execution time was slow.

The following section provides a look at another exciting table, the *dba_hist_sql_plan* table, which stores time-series execution details for those who have purchased the extra-cost packs required to view this table.

The *dba_hist_sql_plan* Table

The *dba_hist_sql_plan* table contains time-series data about each object, table, index or view involved in the query. The important columns include the *cost, cardinality, cpu_cost, io_cost* and *temp_space* required for the object.

The sample query below retrieves SQL statements which have high query execution cost identified by Oracle optimizer.

🖫 high_cost_sql.sql

```
col c1  heading 'SQL|ID'                    format a13
```

```
col c2 heading 'Cost'                   format 9,999,999
col c3 heading 'SQL Text'               format a200

select
  p.sql_id          c1,
  p.cost            c2,
  to_char(s.sql_text) c3
from
  dba_hist_sql_plan    p,
  dba_hist_sqltext     s
where
      p.id = 0
  and
      p.sql_id = s.sql_id
  and
      p.cost is not null
order by
  p.cost desc;
```

The output of the above query might look like this, showing the high cost SQL statements over time:

```
SQL
ID                    Cost SQL Text
------------- ---------- -------------------------------------------
847ahztscj4xw    358,456 select
                             s.begin_interval_time   c1,
                             pl.sql_id               c2,
                             pl.object_name          c3,
                             pl.search_columns       c4,
                             pl.cardinality          c5,
                             pl.access_predicates    c6,
                             pl.filter_predicates    c7
                         from
                             dba_hist_sql_plan pl,
                             dba_hist_snapshot s
                         order by
                             c1, c2

58du2p8phcznu      5,110 select
                             begin_interval_time   c1,
                             search_columns        c2,
                             count(*)              c3
                         from
                             dba_hist_sqltext
                         natural join
                             dba_hist_snapshot
                         natural join
                             dba_hist_sql_plan
                         where
                             lower(sql_text) like lower('%idx%')
                         group by
                             begin_interval_time,search_columns
```

There is much more information in *dba_hist_sql_plan* that is useful. The query below will extract important costing information for all objects involved in each query. Note that in the script below, SYS objects are not counted:

🖫 sql_object_char.sql

```
col c1 heading 'Owner'              format a13
col c2 heading 'Object|Type'        format a15

col c3 heading 'Object|Name'        format a25
col c4 heading 'Average|CPU|Cost'   format 9,999,999
col c5 heading 'Average|IO|Cost'    format 9,999,999


break on c1 skip 2
break on c2 skip 2


select
  p.object_owner    c1,
  p.object_type     c2,
  p.object_name     c3,
  avg(p.cpu_cost)   c4,
  avg(p.io_cost)    c5
from
  dba_hist_sql_plan p
where
       p.object_name is not null
   and
       p.object_owner <> 'SYS'
group by
  p.object_owner,
  p.object_type,
  p.object_name
order by
  1,2,4 desc;
```

The following is a sample of the output. The results show the average CPU and I/O costs for all objects that participate in queries, over time periods.

Owner	Object Type	Object Name	Average CPU Cost	Average IO Cost
OLAPSYS	INDEX	CWM$CUBEDIMENSIONUSE_IDX	200	0
OLAPSYS	INDEX (UNIQUE)	CWM$DIMENSION_PK		
OLAPSYS		CWM$CUBE_PK	7,321	0
OLAPSYS		CWM$MODEL_PK	7,321	0
OLAPSYS	TABLE	CWM$CUBE	7,911	0
OLAPSYS		CWM$MODEL	7,321	0
OLAPSYS		CWM2$CUBE	7,121	2
OLAPSYS		CWM$CUBEDIMENSIONUSE	730	0

MYSCHEMA		CUSTOMER_DETS_PK	21,564	2
MYSCHEMA		STATS$SGASTAT_U	21,442	2
MYSCHEMA		STATS$SQL_SUMMARY_PK	16,842	2
MYSCHEMA		STATS$SQLTEXT_PK	14,442	1
MYSCHEMA		STATS$IDLE_EVENT_PK	8,171	0
SPV	INDEX (UNIQUE)	WSPV_REP_PK	7,321	0
SPV		SPV_ALERT_DEF_PK	7,321	0
SPV	TABLE	WSPV_REPORTS	789,052	28
SPV		SPV_MONITOR	54,092	3
SPV		SPV_SAVED_CHARTS	38,337	3
SPV		SPV_DB_LIST	37,487	3
SPV		SPV_SCHED	35,607	3
SPV		SPV_FV_STAT	35,607	3

This script can now be changed to allow the user to enter a table name and see changes in access details over time:

💾 sql_object_char_detail.sql

```
accept tabname prompt 'Enter Table Name:'

col c0 heading 'Begin|Interval|time'  format a8
col c1 heading 'Owner'                format a10
col c2 heading 'Object|Type'          format a10
col c3 heading 'Object|Name'          format a15
col c4 heading 'Average|CPU|Cost'     format 9,999,999
col c5 heading 'Average|IO|Cost'      format 9,999,999

break on c1 skip 2
break on c2 skip 2

select
  to_char(sn.begin_interval_time,'mm-dd hh24')  c0,
  p.object_owner                                c1,
  p.object_type                                 c2,
  p.object_name                                 c3,
  avg(p.cpu_cost)                               c4,
  avg(p.io_cost)                                c5
from
  dba_hist_sql_plan  p,
  dba_hist_sqlstat   st,
  dba_hist_snapshot  sn
where
  p.object_name is not null
and
  p.object_owner <> 'SYS'
and
  p.object_name = 'CUSTOMER_DETS'
and
  p.sql_id = st.sql_id
and
  st.snap_id = sn.snap_id
group by
```

```
 to_char(sn.begin_interval_time,'mm-dd hh24'),
 p.object_owner,
 p.object_type,
 p.object_name
order by
 1,2,3 desc;
```

This script is great because it is possible to see changes to the table's access patterns over time, which is a very useful feature:

```
Begin                                       Average     Average
Interval            Object    Object            CPU          IO
time      Owner     Type      Name             Cost        Cost
--------  --------- --------- ---------------  ---------  ---------
10-25 17  MYSCHEMA  TABLE     CUSTOMER_DETS      28,935           3
10-26 15  MYSCHEMA            CUSTOMER_DETS      28,935           3
10-27 18  MYSCHEMA            CUSTOMER_DETS   5,571,375          24
10-28 12  MYSCHEMA            CUSTOMER_DETS      28,935           3
```

Now that the DBA has access to the important table structures, it would be appropriate to examine how spectacular reports can be retrieved from the AWR data to reveal hidden bottlenecks and show exactly how the database is performing.

Viewing Table and Index Access with AWR

One of the problems in Oracle9i was the single bit-flag that was used to monitor index usage. The flag was set with the *alter index xxx monitoring usage* command, and then it was possible to see if the index was accessed by querying the *v$object_usage* view.

The goal of any index access is to use the most selective index for a query, the index that fetches the rows with the least I/O's. The Oracle data dictionary is usually quite good at this, but it is up to the DBA to define the index. Missing function-based indexes are a common source of suboptimal SQL execution because Oracle will not use an indexed column unless the *where* clause matches the index column exactly.

For example, the average executions by day-of-the-week can be charted as shown in Figure 17.8:

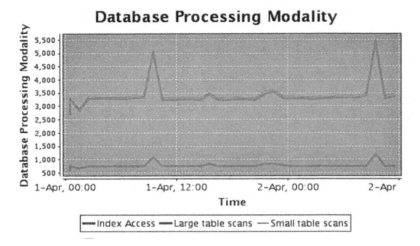

Figure 17.8: *Signature for a specific SQL statement in Ion tool*

The next section will cover some methods for tracking SQL operations over time and begin with a script to track the *nested loops* join.

Tracking SQL nested loop joins

As a review, nested loop joins are the most common method for Oracle to match rows in multiple tables. Nested loop joins always invoke an index and they are never parallelized. The following *nested_join_alert. sql* script to count nested loop joins per hour:

Look Out!

These scripts will only track the SQL that you have directed Oracle to capture via your SQL collection settings in AWR or STATSPACK. It will not collect "transient SQL" that did not appear in *v$sql* at snapshot time, and not all SQL will appear in these reports.

🖫 nested_join_alert.sql

```
col c1 heading 'Date'              format a20
col c2 heading 'Nested|Loops|Count'  format 99,999,999
col c3 heading 'Rows|Processed'     format 99,999,999
col c4 heading 'Disk|Reads'         format 99,999,999
col c5 heading 'CPU|Time'           format 99,999,999
```

```
accept nested_thr char prompt 'Enter Nested Join Threshold: '

ttitle 'Nested Join Threshold|&nested_thr'

select
   to_char(sn.begin_interval_time,'yy-mm-dd hh24')   c1,
   count(*)                                          c2,
   sum(st.rows_processed_delta)                      c3,
   sum(st.disk_reads_delta)                          c4,
   sum(st.cpu_time_delta)                            c5
from
   dba_hist_snapshot  sn,
   dba_hist_sql_plan  p,
   dba_hist_sqlstat   st
where
   st.sql_id = p.sql_id
and
   sn.snap_id = st.snap_id
and
   p.operation = 'NESTED LOOPS'
having
   count(*) > &hash_thr
group by
   begin_interval_time;
```

The output below shows the number of total nested loop joins during the snapshot period along with a count of the rows processed and the associated disk I/O. This report is useful where the DBA wants to know if increasing *pga_aggregate_target* will improve performance.

Nested Loop Join Thresholds

Date	Nested Loops Count	Rows Processed	Disk Reads	CPU Time
04-10-10 16	22	750	796	4,017,301
04-10-10 17	25	846	6	3,903,560
04-10-10 19	26	751	1,430	4,165,270
04-10-10 20	24	920	3	3,940,002
04-10-10 21	25	782	5	3,816,152
04-10-11 02	26	905	0	3,935,547
04-10-11 03	22	1,001	0	3,918,891
04-10-11 04	29	757	8	3,939,071
04-10-11 05	28	757	745	4,395,197
04-10-11 06	24	839	4	4,010,775

In the report above, nested loops are favored by SQL that returns a small number of *rows_processed* than hash joins, which tend to return largest result sets.

The following *sql_index.sql* script exposes the cumulative usage of database indexes:

🖫 sql_index.sql

```
col c0  heading 'Begin|Interval|time'  format a8
col c1  heading 'Index|Name'           format a20
col c2  heading 'Disk|Reads'           format 99,999,999
col c3  heading 'Rows|Processed'       format 99,999,999

select
  to_char(s.begin_interval_time,'mm-dd hh24')  c0,
  p.object_name              c1,
  sum(t.disk_reads_total)    c2,
  sum(t.rows_processed_total) c3
from
      dba_hist_sql_plan p,
      dba_hist_sqlstat  t,
      dba_hist_snapshot s
where
      p.sql_id = t.sql_id
   and
      t.snap_id = s.snap_id
   and
      p.object_type like '%INDEX%'
group by
      to_char(s.begin_interval_time,'mm-dd hh24'),
      p.object_name
order by
      c0,c1,c2 desc;
```

The following is a sample of the output where the stress on every important index is shown over time. This information is important for placing index blocks into the KEEP pool to reduce disk reads and for determining the optimal setting for the important *optimizer_index_caching* parameter.

Begin Interval time	Index Name	Disk Reads	Rows Processed
10-14 12	I_CACHE_STATS_1		114
10-14 12	I_COL_USAGE$	201	8,984
10-14 12	I_FILE1	2	0
10-14 12	I_IND1	93	604
10-14 12	I_JOB_NEXT	1	247,816
10-14 11	I_KOPM1	4	2,935
10-14 11	I_MON_MODS$_OBJ	12	28,498
10-14 11	I_OBJ1	72,852	604
10-14 11	I_PARTOBJ$	93	604
10-14 11	I_SCHEDULER_JOB2	4	0
10-14 11	SYS_C002433	302	4,629
10-14 11	SYS_IOT_TOP_8540	0	75,544
10-14 11	SYS_IOT_TOP_8542	1	4,629
10-14 11	WRH$_DATAFILE_PK	2	0
10-14 10	WRH$_SEG_STAT_OBJ_PK	93	604
10-14 10	WRH$_TEMPFILE_PK		0
10-14 10	WRI$_ADV_ACTIONS_PK	38	1,760

The above report shows the highest impact tables. The following *sql_index_access.sql* script will summarize index access by snapshot period.

💾 sql_index_access.sql

```
col c1 heading 'Begin|Interval|Time'    format a20
col c2 heading 'Index|Range|Scans' format 999,999
col c3 heading 'Index|Unique|Scans' format 999,999
col c4 heading 'Index|Full|Scans' format 999,999

select
  r.c1   c1,
  r.c2   c2,
  u.c2   c3,
  f.c2   c4
from
(
select
  to_char(sn.begin_interval_time,'yy-mm-dd hh24')   c1,
  count(1)                          c2
from
   dba_hist_sql_plan p,
   dba_hist_sqlstat  s,
   dba_hist_snapshot sn
where
   p.object_owner <> 'SYS'
and
   p.operation like '%INDEX%'
and
   p.options like '%RANGE%'
and
   p.sql_id = s.sql_id
and
   s.snap_id = sn.snap_id
group by
   to_char(sn.begin_interval_time,'yy-mm-dd hh24')
order by
1 ) r,
(
select
   to_char(sn.begin_interval_time,'yy-mm-dd hh24')   c1,
   count(1)                          c2
from
   dba_hist_sql_plan p,
   dba_hist_sqlstat  s,
   dba_hist_snapshot sn
where
   p.object_owner <> 'SYS'
and
   p.operation like '%INDEX%'
and
   p.options like '%UNIQUE%'
and
   p.sql_id = s.sql_id
and
```

```
     s.snap_id = sn.snap_id
group by
  to_char(sn.begin_interval_time,'yy-mm-dd hh24')
order by
1 ) u,
(
select
  to_char(sn.begin_interval_time,'yy-mm-dd hh24')  c1,
  count(1)                          c2
from
  dba_hist_sql_plan p,
  dba_hist_sqlstat  s,
  dba_hist_snapshot sn
where
  p.object_owner <> 'SYS'
and
  p.operation like '%INDEX%'
and
  p.options like '%FULL%'
and
  p.sql_id = s.sql_id
and
  s.snap_id = sn.snap_id
group by
  to_char(sn.begin_interval_time,'yy-mm-dd hh24')
order by
1 ) f
where
    r.c1 = u.c1
  and
    r.c1 = f.c1;
```

The sample output below shows those specific times when the database performs unique scans, index range scans and index fast full scans:

Begin Interval Time	Index Range Scans	Index Unique Scans	Index Full Scans
04-10-21 15	36	35	2
04-10-21 19	10	8	2
04-10-21 20		8	2
04-10-21 21		8	2
04-10-21 22	11	8	3
04-10-21 23	16	11	3
04-10-22 00	10	9	1
04-10-22 01	11	8	3
04-10-22 02	12	8	1
04-10-22 03	10	8	3
04-10-22 04	11	8	2
04-10-22 05		8	3
04-10-22 06		8	2
04-10-22 07	10	8	3
04-10-22 08		8	2

SQL object usage can also be summarized by day-of-the-week:

💾 sql_object_avg_dy.sql

```
col c1 heading 'Object|Name'        format a30
col c2 heading 'Week Day'           format a15
col c3 heading 'Invocation|Count'   format 99,999,999

break on c1 skip 2
break on c2 skip 2

select

decode(c2,1,'Monday',2,'Tuesday',3,'Wednesday',4,'Thursday',5,'Friday',6,'Sa
turday',7,'Sunday') c2,
  c1,
  c3
from
(
select
   p.object_name                         c1,
   to_char(sn.end_interval_time,'d')     c2,
   count(1)                              c3
from
  dba_hist_sql_plan    p,
  dba_hist_sqlstat     s,
  dba_hist_snapshot    sn
where
  p.object_owner <> 'SYS'
and
  p.sql_id = s.sql_id
and
  s.snap_id = sn.snap_id
group by
   p.object_name,
   to_char(sn.end_interval_time,'d')
order by
  c2,c1
);
```

The output below shows the top objects within the database during each snapshot period.

Week Day	Object Name	Invocation Count
Monday	CUSTOMER	44
	CUSTOMER_ORDERS	44
	CUSTOMER_ORDERS_PRIMARY	44
	MGMT_CURRENT_METRICS_PK	43
	MGMT_FAILOVER_TABLE	47
	MGMT_JOB	235
	MGMT_JOB_EMD_STATUS_QUEUE	91

	MGMT_JOB_EXECUTION	235
	MGMT_JOB_EXEC_IDX01	235
	MGMT_JOB_EXEC_SUMMARY	94
	MGMT_JOB_EXEC_SUMM_IDX04	94
	MGMT_JOB_PK	235
	MGMT_METRICS	65
	MGMT_METRICS_1HOUR_PK	43
Tuesday	CUSTOMER	40
	CUSTOMER _CHECK	2
	CUSTOMER _PRIMARY	1
	CUSTOMER_ORDERS	46
	CUSTOMER_ORDERS_PRIMARY	46
	LOGMNR_LOG$	3
	LOGMNR_LOG$_PK	3
	LOGSTDBY$PARAMETERS	2
	MGMT_CURRENT_METRICS_PK	31
	MGMT_FAILOVER_TABLE	42
	MGMT_JOB	200
	MGMT_JOB_EMD_STATUS_QUEUE	78
	MGMT_JOB_EXECUTION	200
	MGMT_JOB_EXEC_IDX01	200
	MGMT_JOB_EXEC_SUMMARY	80
	MGMT_JOB_EXEC_SUMM_IDX04	80
	MGMT_JOB_PK	200
	MGMT_METRICS	48
Wednesday	CURRENT_SEVERITY_PRIMARY_KEY	1
	MGMT_CURRENT_METRICS_PK	17
	MGMT_CURRENT_SEVERITY	1
	MGMT_FAILOVER_TABLE	24
	MGMT_JOB	120
	MGMT_JOB_EMD_STATUS_QUEUE	46
	MGMT_JOB_EXECUTION	120
	MGMT_JOB_EXEC_IDX01	120
	MGMT_JOB_EXEC_SUMMARY	48
	MGMT_JOB_EXEC_SUMM_IDX04	48
	MGMT_JOB_PK	120
	MGMT_METRICS	36
	MGMT_METRICS_1HOUR_PK	14
	MGMT_METRICS_IDX_01	24
	MGMT_METRICS_IDX_03	1
	MGMT_METRICS_PK	11

When these results are posted, a well-defined signature emerges for particular tables, access plans and SQL statements.

Most Oracle databases are remarkably predictable, with the exception of Decision Support and ad-hoc query systems, and the the usage of all SQL components can be quickly tracked.

Understanding the SQL signature can be extremely useful for determining what objects to place in the KEEP pool and to determining the most active tables and indexes in the database.

Once a particular SQL statement for which details are desired has been identified, it is possible to view its execution plan used by optimizer to actually execute the statement. The query below retrieves an execution plan for a particular SQL statement of interest:

💾 sql_details.sql

```
accept sqlid prompt 'Please enter SQL ID: '

col c1 heading 'Operation'          format a20
col c2 heading 'Options'            format a20
col c3 heading 'Object|Name'        format a25
col c4 heading 'Search Columns'     format 999,999
col c5 heading 'Cardinality'        format 999,999

select
   operation              c1,
   options                c2,
   object_name            c3,
   search_columns         c4,
   cardinality            c5
from
   dba_hist_sql_plan p
where
       p.sql_id = '&sqlid'
order by
   p.id;
```

This is one of the most important of all of the SQL tuning tools. Here is a sample of the output from this script:

Operation	Options	Name	Search Cols	Cardinality
SELECT STATEMENT			0	
VIEW			3	4
SORT	ORDER BY		4	4
VIEW			2	4
UNION-ALL			0	
FILTER			6	
NESTED LOOPS	OUTER		0	3
NESTED LOOPS	ANTI		0	3
TABLE ACCESS	BY INDEX ROWID	STATS$SYSTEM_EVENT	0	70
INDEX	RANGE SCAN	STATS$SYSTEM_EVENT_PK	3	70
INDEX	UNIQUE SCAN	STATS$IDLE_EVENT_PK	1	46
TABLE ACCESS	BY INDEX ROWID	STATS$SYSTEM_EVENT	0	1
INDEX	UNIQUE SCAN	STATS$SYSTEM_EVENT_PK	4	1
FILTER			0	
FAST DUAL			1	1

If there is a non-OLTP database that regularly performs large full-table and full-index scans, it is helpful to know those times when the full scan activity is high. The following query will yield that information:

💾 sql_full_scans.sql

```
col c1   heading   'Begin|Interval|Time'     format a20
col c2   heading   'Index|Table|Scans'       format 999,999
col c3   heading   'Full|Table|Scans'        format 999,999
select
  i.c1   c1,
  i.c2   c2,
  f.c2   c3
from
(
select
  to_char(sn.begin_interval_time,'yy-mm-dd hh24')   c1,
  count(1)                                 c2
from
   dba_hist_sql_plan p,
   dba_hist_sqlstat  s,
   dba_hist_snapshot sn
where
   p.object_owner <> 'SYS'
and
   p.operation like '%TABLE ACCESS%'
and
   p.options like '%INDEX%'
and
   p.sql_id = s.sql_id
and
   s.snap_id = sn.snap_id
group by
   to_char(sn.begin_interval_time,'yy-mm-dd hh24')
order by
1 ) i,
(
select
  to_char(sn.begin_interval_time,'yy-mm-dd hh24')   c1,
  count(1)                                 c2
from
   dba_hist_sql_plan p,
   dba_hist_sqlstat  s,
   dba_hist_snapshot sn
where
   p.object_owner <> 'SYS'
and
   p.operation like '%TABLE ACCESS%'
and
   p.options = 'FULL'
and
   p.sql_id = s.sql_id
and
   s.snap_id = sn.snap_id
group by
   to_char(sn.begin_interval_time,'yy-mm-dd hh24')
order by
```

```
1 ) f
where
     i.cl = f.cl;
```

The output below shows a comparison of index-full scans versus full-table scans.

```
Begin                   Index    Full
Interval                Table    Table
Time                    Scans    Scans
------------------      --------  -------
04-10-21 15                53       18
04-10-21 17                 3        3
04-10-21 18                 1        2
04-10-21 19                15        6
04-10-21 20                         6
04-10-21 21                         6
04-10-21 22                16        6
04-10-21 23                21        9
04-10-22 00                16        6
04-10-22 01                         6
04-10-22 02                17        6
04-10-22 03                15        6
```

Knowing the signature for large-table full-table scans can help in both SQL tuning and instance tuning. For SQL tuning, this report will tell when to drill down to verify that all of the large-table full-table scans are legitimate. Once verified, this same data can be used to dynamically reconfigure the Oracle instance to accommodate the large scans.

With that introduction to the indexing component, it will be useful to learn how to use the AWR data to track full-scan behavior over time.

Tracking Full-Scan SQL Over Time

All of the specific SQL access methods can be counted and their behavior tracked over time. This is especially important for large-table full-table scans because they are a common symptom of suboptimal execution plans (i.e. missing indexes).

Once it has been determined that the large-table full-table scans are legitimate, the DBA must know those times when they are executed so that a selective parallel query can be implemented, depending on the existing CPU consumption on the server. Oracle Parallel Query (OPQ) drives up CPU consumption and should be invoked when the server can handle the additional load.

full_table_scans.sql

```
ttile 'Large Full-table scans|Per Snapshot Period'

col c1 heading 'Begin|Interval|time' format a20
col c4 heading 'FTS|Count'            format 999,999

break on c1 skip 2
break on c2 skip 2

select
  to_char(sn.begin_interval_time,'yy-mm-dd hh24')  c1,
  count(1)                                          c4
from
  dba_hist_sql_plan p,
  dba_hist_sqlstat  s,
  dba_hist_snapshot sn,
  dba_segments      o
where
  p.object_owner <> 'SYS'
and
  p.object_owner = o.owner
and
  p.object_name = o.segment_name
and
  o.blocks > 1000
and
  p.operation like '%TABLE ACCESS%'
and
  p.options like '%FULL%'
and
  p.sql_id = s.sql_id
and
  s.snap_id = sn.snap_id
group by
  to_char(sn.begin_interval_time,'yy-mm-dd hh24')
order by
  1;
```

The output below shows the overall total counts for tables that experience large-table full-table scans because the scans may be due to a missing index.

```
     Large Full-table scans
       Per Snapshot Period

Begin
Interval                 FTS
time                     Count
--------------------    --------
04-10-18 11                  4
04-10-21 17                  1
04-10-21 23                  2
04-10-22 15                  2
04-10-22 16                  2
04-10-22 23                  2
04-10-24 00                  2
04-10-25 00                  2
04-10-25 10                  2
```

```
04-10-25 17                    9
04-10-25 18                    1
04-10-25 21                    1
04-10-26 12                    1
04-10-26 13                    3
04-10-26 14                    3
04-10-26 15                   11
04-10-26 16                    4
04-10-26 17                    4
04-10-26 18                    3
04-10-26 23                    2
04-10-27 13                    2
04-10-27 14                    3
04-10-27 15                    4
04-10-27 16                    4
04-10-27 17                    3
04-10-27 18                   17
04-10-27 19                    1
04-10-28 12                   22
04-10-28 13                    2
04-10-29 13                    9
```

This data can be easily plotted to see the trend for a database as shown in Figure 17.9:

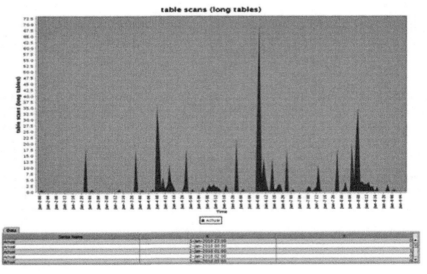

Figure 17.9: *Linear trends of large-table full-table scans*

This data can also be aggregated and rolled up into daily averages to see the signature for full-table scans as shown in Figure 17.10:

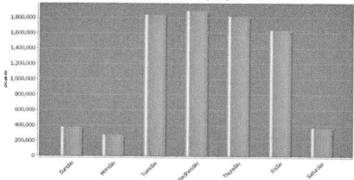

Figure 17.10: *Trends of large-table full-table scans*

Search for Bad SQL Symptoms!

Hot Tip!

One of the most common manifestations of suboptimal SQL is a large-table full-table scan. Whenever an index is missing, Oracle may be forced to read every row in the table.

Remember, large-table full-table scans are not always inappropriate and if the large-table full-table scans are legitimate, information about the the periods in which they are invoked is important, so OPQ can be invoked to speed up the scans as shown in the *sql_access_hr.sql* script that follows:

💾 sql_access_hr.sql

```
ttitle 'Large Table Full-table scans|Averages per Hour'

col c1 heading 'Day|Hour'                   format a20
col c2 heading 'FTS|Count'                  format 999,999

break on c1 skip 2
break on c2 skip 2

select
  to_char(sn.begin_interval_time,'hh24')   c1,
  count(1)                                  c2
from
  dba_hist_sql_plan   p,
  dba_hist_sqlstat    s,
  dba_hist_snapshot   sn,
  dba_segments        o
```

```
where
   p.object_owner <> 'SYS'
and
   p.object_owner = o.owner
and
   p.object_name = o.segment_name
and
   o.blocks > 1000
and
   p.operation like '%TABLE ACCESS%'
and
   p.options like '%FULL%'
and
   p.sql_id = s.sql_id
and
   s.snap_id = sn.snap_id
group by
  to_char(sn.begin_interval_time,'hh24')
order by 1;
```

The following output shows the average number of large-table full-table scans per hour.

```
Large Table Full-table scans
Averages per Hour

Day                       FTS
Hour                    Count
-------------------- --------
00                          4
10                          2
11                          4
12                         23
13                         16
14                          6
15                         17
16                         10
17                         17
18                         21
19                          1
23                          6
```

The script below shows the same data for day of the week:

💾 sql_access_day.sql

```
ttitle 'Large Table Full-table scans|Averages per Week Day'

col c1 heading 'Week|Day'           format a20
col c2 heading 'FTS|Count'          format 999,999

break on c1 skip 2
break on c2 skip 2

select
```

```
   to_char(sn.begin_interval_time,'day')   c1,
   count(1)                                 c2
from
   dba_hist_sql_plan p,
   dba_hist_sqlstat  s,
   dba_hist_snapshot sn,
   dba_segments      o
where
   p.object_owner <> 'SYS'
and
   p.object_owner = o.owner
and
   p.object_name = o.segment_name
and
   o.blocks > 1000
and
   p.operation like '%TABLE ACCESS%'
and
   p.options like '%FULL%'
and
   p.sql_id = s.sql_id
and
   s.snap_id = sn.snap_id
group by
   to_char(sn.begin_interval_time,'day')
order by
1;
```

The following sample query output shows specific times the database experienced large table scans.

```
Large Table Full-table scans
Averages per Week Day


Week                      FTS
Day                      Count
-------------------- --------
sunday                     2
monday                    19
tuesday                   31
wednesday                 34
thursday                  27
friday                    15
Saturday                   2
```

The *sql_scan_sums.sql* script will show the access patterns of usage over time. If a DBA is really driven to know their system, all they need to do is understand how SQL accesses the tables and indexes in the database to provide amazing insight. The optimal instance configuration for large-table full-table scans is quite different than the configuration for an OLTP databases, and the report generated by the *sql_scan_sums.sql* script will quickly identify changes in table access patterns.

🖫 sql_scan_sums.sql

```
col c1 heading 'Begin|Interval|Time'          format a20
col c2 heading 'Large|Table|Full Table|Scans' format 999,999
col c3 heading 'Small|Table|Full Table|Scans' format 999,999
col c4 heading 'Total|Index|Scans'            format 999,999


select
  f.c1   c1,
  f.c2   c2,
  s.c2   c3,
  i.c2   c4
from
(
select
  to_char(sn.begin_interval_time,'yy-mm-dd hh24')  c1,
  count(1)                          c2
from
   dba_hist_sql_plan p,
   dba_hist_sqlstat  s,
   dba_hist_snapshot sn,
   dba_segments      o
where
  p.object_owner <> 'SYS'
and
   p.object_owner = o.owner
and
   p.object_name = o.segment_name
and
   o.blocks > 1000
and
   p.operation like '%TABLE ACCESS%'
and
   p.options like '%FULL%'
and
   p.sql_id = s.sql_id
and
   s.snap_id = sn.snap_id
group by
  to_char(sn.begin_interval_time,'yy-mm-dd hh24')
order by
1 ) f,
(
select
  to_char(sn.begin_interval_time,'yy-mm-dd hh24')  c1,
  count(1)                              c2
from
   dba_hist_sql_plan p,
   dba_hist_sqlstat  s,
   dba_hist_snapshot sn,
   dba_segments       o
where
   p.object_owner <> 'SYS'
and
   p.object_owner = o.owner
and
   p.object_name = o.segment_name
```

```
and
   o.blocks < 1000
and
   p.operation like '%INDEX%'
and
   p.sql_id = s.sql_id
and
   s.snap_id = sn.snap_id
group by
   to_char(sn.begin_interval_time,'yy-mm-dd hh24')
order by
1 ) s,
(
select
   to_char(sn.begin_interval_time,'yy-mm-dd hh24')   c1,
   count(1)                                  c2
from
   dba_hist_sql_plan p,
   dba_hist_sqlstat  s,
   dba_hist_snapshot sn
where
   p.object_owner <> 'SYS'
and
   p.operation like '%INDEX%'
and
   p.sql_id = s.sql_id
and
   s.snap_id = sn.snap_id
group by
   to_char(sn.begin_interval_time,'yy-mm-dd hh24')
order by
1 ) i
where
      f.c1 = s.c1
   and
      f.c1 = i.c1;
```

The sample output looks like the following, where there is a comparison of index versus table scan access. This is a very important signature for any database because it shows, at a glance, the balance between index (OLTP) and data warehouse type access.

Begin Interval Time	Large Table Full Table Scans	Small Table Full Table Scans	Total Index Scans
04-10-22 15	2	19	21
04-10-22 16		1	1
04-10-25 10		18	20
04-10-25 17	9	15	17
04-10-25 18	1	19	22
04-10-25 21		19	24
04-10-26 12		23	28
04-10-26 13	3	17	19
04-10-26 14		18	19

```
04-10-26 15                   11            4            7
04-10-26 16                    4           18           18
04-10-26 17                                17           19
04-10-26 18                    3           17           17
04-10-27 13                    2           17           19
04-10-27 14                    3           17           19
04-10-27 15                    4           17           18
04-10-27 16                                17           17
04-10-27 17                    3           17           20
04-10-27 18                   17           20           22
04-10-27 19                    1           20           26
04-10-28 12                   22           17           20
04-10-28 13                    2           17           17
04-10-29 13                    9           18           19
```

This is an important report because it shows the method with which Oracle is accessing data over time periods. This is especially important because it shows when the database processing modality shifts between OLTP (*first_rows* index access) to a batch reporting mode (*all_rows* full scans) as shown in Figure 17.11.

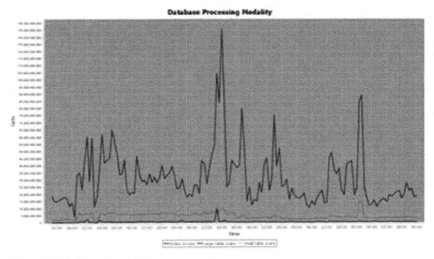

Figure 17.11: *Ion plot of full scans vs. index access*

The example in Figure 17.11 is typical of an OLTP database with the majority of access being via small-table full-table scans and index access. In this case, the large-table full-table scans must be carefully checked, their legitimacy verified for such things as missing indexes, and then they should be adjusted to maximize their throughput.

Of course, in a really busy database, there may be concurrent OLTP index access and full-table scans for reports and it is the DBA's job to know the specific times when the system shifts table access modes as well as the identity of those tables that experience the changes.

The following *sql_full_scans_avg_dy.sql* script can be used to roll-up average scans into daily averages.

💾 sql_full_scans_avg_dy.sql

```
col c1 heading 'Begin|Interval|Time'   format a20
col c2 heading 'Index|Table|Scans' format 999,999
col c3 heading 'Full|Table|Scans' format 999,999

select
  i.c1  c1,
  i.c2  c2,
  f.c2  c3
from
(
select
  to_char(sn.begin_interval_time,'day')   c1,
  count(1)                                 c2
from
  dba_hist_sql_plan p,
  dba_hist_sqlstat  s,
  dba_hist_snapshot sn
where
  p.object_owner <> 'SYS'
and
  p.operation like '%TABLE ACCESS%'
and
  p.options like '%INDEX%'
and
  p.sql_id = s.sql_id
and
  s.snap_id = sn.snap_id
group by
  to_char(sn.begin_interval_time,'day')
order by
1 ) i,
(
select
  to_char(sn.begin_interval_time,'day')   c1,
  count(1)                                 c2
from
  dba_hist_sql_plan p,
  dba_hist_sqlstat  s,
  dba_hist_snapshot sn
where
  p.object_owner <> 'SYS'
and
  p.operation like '%TABLE ACCESS%'
and
  p.options = 'FULL'
and
  p.sql_id = s.sql_id
and
```

```
    s.snap_id = sn.snap_id
group by
  to_char(sn.begin_interval_time,'day')
order by
1 ) f
where
    i.c1 = f.c1;
```

The sample output is shown below:

```
Begin                   Index     Full
Interval                Table     Table
Time                    Scans     Scans
--------------------   --------  --------
sunday                     393       189
monday                     383       216
tuesday                    353       206
wednesday                  357       178
thursday                   488       219
friday                     618       285
saturday                   400       189
```

For example, the signature shown above indicates that Fridays are very high in full-table scans, probably as the result of weekly reporting.

With this knowledge, the DBA can anticipate the changes in processing from index access to LTFTS access by adjusting instance configurations.

Whenever the database changes into a mode dominated by LTFTS, the data buffer sizes, such as *db_cache_size* and *db_nk_cache_size*, can be decreased. Since parallel LTFTS bypass the data buffers, the intermediate rows are kept in the *pga_aggregate_target* region. Hence, it may be desirable to use *dbms_scheduler* to anticipate this change and resize the SGA just in time to accommodate the regularly repeating change in access patterns.

Because indexes are important components of SQL tuning, it is necessary to see how to count the frequency that indexes are used within Oracle.

Counting Index Usage Inside SQL

Prior to Oracle9i, it was very difficult to see if an index was being used by the SQL in the database. It required explaining all of the SQL in the library cache into a holding area and then parsing through the execution plans for the index name. Things were simplified slightly in Oracle 9i when the primitive *alter index xxx monitoring* command and the ability to see if the index was invoked were introduced.

One problem has always been that it is very difficult to know what indexes are the most popular. In Oracle10g and beyond, it is easy to see what indexes are used, when they are used and the context in which they are used. The following is a simple AWR query that can be used to plot index usage:

🖫 index_usage_hr.sql

```
col c1 heading 'Begin|Interval|time'  format a20
col c2 heading 'Search Columns'       format 999
col c3 heading 'Invocation|Count'     format 99,999,999


break on c1 skip 2

accept idxname char prompt 'Enter Index Name: '

ttitle 'Invocation Counts for index|&idxname'

select
   to_char(sn.begin_interval_time,'yy-mm-dd hh24')  c1,
   p.search_columns                                  c2,
   count(*)                                          c3
from
   dba_hist_snapshot    sn,
   dba_hist_sql_plan    p,
   dba_hist_sqlstat     st
where
   st.sql_id = p.sql_id
and
   sn.snap_id = st.snap_id
and
   p.object_name = '&idxname'
group by
   begin_interval_time,search_columns;
```

The query will produce an output showing a summary count of the index specified during the snapshot interval.

```
SQL> @index_usage_hr

Enter Index Name: cust_index
```

This can be compared to the number of times that a table was invoked from SQL. Here is a sample of the output from the script:

```
Invocation Counts for cust_index


Begin
Interval                              Invocation
time                Search Columns      Count
```

```
--------------------  -------------  -----------
04-10-21 15                       1            3
04-10-10 16                       0            1
04-10-10 19                       1            1
04-10-11 02                       0            2
04-10-11 04                       2            1
04-10-11 06                       3            1
04-10-11 11                       0            1
04-10-11 12                       0            2
04-10-11 13                       2            1
04-10-11 15                       0            3
04-10-11 17                       0           14
04-10-11 18                       4            1
04-10-11 19                       0            1
04-10-11 20                       3            7
04-10-11 21                       0            1
```

The AWR SQL tuning tables offer a wealth of important time metrics. This data can also be summed up by snapshot period giving an overall view of how Oracle is accessing the table data.

💾 access_counts.sql

```
ttile 'Table Access|Operation Counts|Per Snapshot Period'

col c1 heading 'Begin|Interval|time'  format a20
col c2 heading 'Operation'            format a15
col c3 heading 'Option'               format a15
col c4 heading 'Object|Count'         format 999,999

break on c1 skip 2
break on c2 skip 2

select
  to_char(sn.begin_interval_time,'yy-mm-dd hh24')  c1,
  p.operation    c2,
  p.options      c3,
  count(1)       c4
from
  dba_hist_sql_plan p,
  dba_hist_sqlstat  s,
  dba_hist_snapshot sn
where
  p.object_owner <> 'SYS'
and
  p.sql_id = s.sql_id
and
  s.snap_id = sn.snap_id
group by
  to_char(sn.begin_interval_time,'yy-mm-dd hh24'),
  p.operation,
  p.options
order by
  1,2,3;
```

The output of the query is shown below, and it includes overall total counts for each object and table access method.

```
Begin
Interval                                              Object
time              Operation         Option            Count
----------------  ----------------  ----------------  --------
04-10-15 16       INDEX             UNIQUE SCAN              1

04-10-15 16       TABLE ACCESS      BY INDEX ROWID          1
04-10-15 16                         FULL                    2

04-10-15 17       INDEX             UNIQUE SCAN              1

04-10-15 17       TABLE ACCESS      BY INDEX ROWID          1
04-10-15 17                         FULL                    2

04-10-15 18       INDEX             UNIQUE SCAN              1

04-10-15 18       TABLE ACCESS      BY INDEX ROWID          1
04-10-15 18                         FULL                    2

04-10-15 19       INDEX             UNIQUE SCAN              1

04-10-15 19       TABLE ACCESS      BY INDEX ROWID          1
04-10-15 19                         FULL                    2

04-10-15 20       INDEX             UNIQUE SCAN              1
```

It is also possible to track how often tables and indexes are accessed over time, showing how often the SQL requested rows from specific tables as illustrated in Figure 17.12:

OWNER	TABLENAME	COLNAME	EQUALITY...	EQUIJOIN...
SH	CUSTOMERS	CUST_TOTAL_ID	0	1
SH	COUNTRIES	COUNTRY_ID	0	1
SH	COUNTRIES	COUNTRY_SU...	0	1
SH	COUNTRIES	COUNTRY_RE...	0	1
SH	COUNTRIES	COUNTRY_TO...	0	1
SYS	OBJ$	NAME	418	117
PERFSTAT	STATS$SNAPSHOT	SNAP_ID	2	2
PERFSTAT	STATS$SYSTEM_EVENT	SNAP_ID	0	2
PERFSTAT	STATS$TIME_MODEL...	STAT_ID	0	1
PERFSTAT	STATS$IOSTAT_FUNC...	FUNCTION_ID	0	1
ION	CUSTOMERS	CUSTOMER_ID	4	6
ION	ORDER_ITEMS	ORDER_ID	8	5
ION	ORDER_ITEMS	PRODUCT_ID	0	1

Figure 17.12: *The Ion Tool time-series plot for particular SQL statement*

The next section will provide a look into how to track SQL sorting activity over time.

Tracking SQL Sort Activity

Sorting occurs when a SQL statement processes a large order by or group by clause where the result set is too small to fit into the PGA RAM, as per *sort_area_size* or *pga_aggregate_target*. Because PGA RAM availability varies according to the system workload it is important to track SQL sorting over time and see if there are any repeating signatures by day of the week or hour of the day.

Figure 17.13 below shows how the Ion for Oracle tool can track average disk sort activity over time:

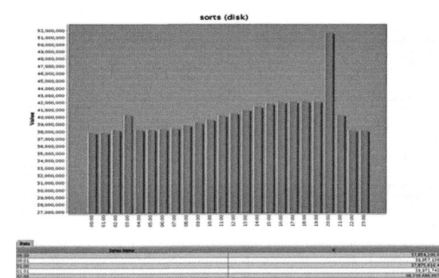

Figure 17.13: *Linear average disk sorts for a SQL workload in the Ion tool*

It is also possible to see the signature of average disk sorts by day in Figure 17.14:

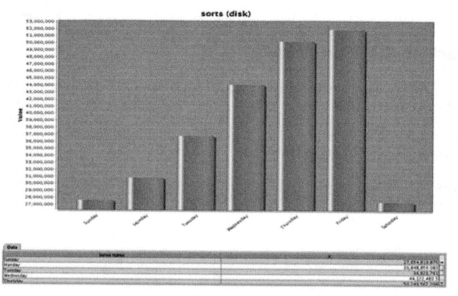

Figure 17.14: *Daily average disk sorts for a SQL workload in the Ion tool*

This makes it easy to track sort activity over time and adjust the PGA regions during times of high stress to relieve excessive disk sorting. The next section will cover how to track SQL hard parses over time.

Tracking SQL Library Cache Hard Parses

Monitoring the library cache behavior and the fact that Oracle provides several views to allow the tracking of important metrics such as total hard parses over time was covered in Chapter 16 of this text. Tuning individual SQL within the library cache is tricky, and a holistic approach to library cache tuning will track all SQL statements as a whole.

The *v$librarycache* view as well as the *stats$librarycache* and the *dba_hist_librarycache* can be queried to see hard parses over time. Figure 17.15 is a screenshot of the Ion tool showing the tracking of hard parses over time:

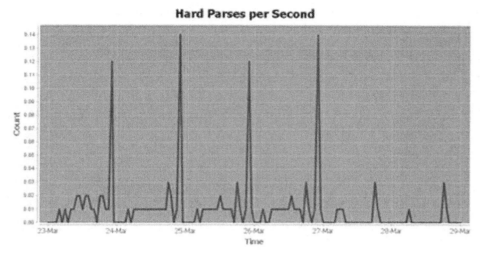

Figure 17.15: *The time-series plot for particular SQL statement*

Conclusion

This chapter has shown that holistic SQL tuning is the best way to optimize any Oracle database, and tracking SQL execution resources over time is the best was to ensure overall tuning success for SQL workloads. This chapter has concentrated on proactive SQL tuning techniques using proven time-series analysis tools.

The main points of this chapter include:

- SQL tuning is fluid, and effective SQL tuning acknowledges that SQL execution workloads and plans change over time.

- The workload as a whole should always be tuned before tuning individual SQL statements.

- SQL workloads are optimized by adjusting SGA and PGA regions, the optimizer parameters and CBO statistics.

- Most system develop signatures, which are repeating trends of execution, when metrics are averaged by day of the week or hour of the day.

- Some systems have multiple SQL workloads, and scheduled reconfigurations need to be scheduled when the workloads change.

- Holistic SQL monitoring includes general workload metrics such as transactions per second, disk I/O per second and logical reads per second.

- It is important to track SQL execution patterns over time, and there are scripts to track nested loops and hash joins over time.

- Sorting is an important SQL tuning area, and disk sorts can be tracked over time.

- Hard parses can be tracked over time to measure the effectiveness of library cache optimization.

The next chapter will delve into DML tuning and cover how to optimize *insert*, *update* and *delete* SQL.

Oracle DML Tuning

DML Tuning is not for neophytes

Oracle DML tuning

Oracle DML tuning is challenging because the SQL data manipulation language (DML) syntax for *insert, update* and *delete* offer very few syntax options.

However, there are many tricks that can be used within Oracle to speed up DML, and this chapter is devoted to real-world techniques that are used in large shops to manage Oracle database while they accepts millions of changes every hour.

Oracle has many ways to tune DML based on the type of DML statement:

- **Tune the DML subquery:** Many Oracle DML statements use a where clause subquery and optimizing the subquery will improve the DML performance.

- **Use bulking:** Oracle PL/SQL has a bulk operator that often is faster than a standard SQL DML.

- **Drop indexes & constraints:** For batch DML, dropping and re-creating indexes and constraints will improve overall performance.

- **Parallel DML:** Parallelizing DML that performs full-scan dramatically improves DML performance.

- **Use fast storage:** In many shops, using super-fast SSD instead of disks can greatly improve DML performance. After the DML is complete, the tablespace can be moved to slower, platter-style disks.

- **Segregate data buffers:** In some cases, using a small data buffer for the high DML objects will improve DML performance by making writes to disk more efficient.

- **Use utilities:** Replacing DML with Oracle utilities such as SQL*Loader and PL/SQL bulking operations can be faster than vanilla DML.

However, each type of DML has its own specific tuning techniques.

Let's start my examining Oracle *insert* performance and examine the tools that we can use to optimize row inserts.

Optimizing Oracle SQL insert performance

Every shop is different, but there are some *insert* tuning techniques that can work in a multitude of workloads. Remember, you can have choices for doing table inserts including the Data Pump and SQL*Loader utilities, as well as PL/SQL bulk load tools such as the *forall* operator (Figure 19.1):

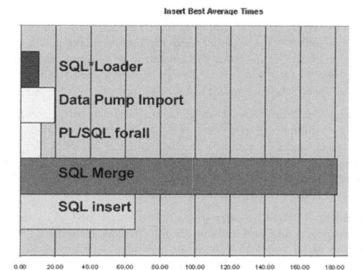

Figure 19.1: *A comparison of insert speeds*

As we see above, the fastest way to slam rows into an Oracle table is to use bulk inserts like the PL/SQL *forall* operator, inserting with super-fast solid-state media. Using these techniques you can insert over 500,000 rows per second when using fast SSD storage.

In the chart in Figure 19.1 we also see Oracle Utilities like SQL*Loader and Oracle Data Pump, alternative options for inserting rows into Oracle tables.

When we use standard SQL *insert* statements to load Oracle data tables, there are several tuning approaches. Some applications require PL/SQL to issues the inserts, other system issue massive batch loads, while other shops process selective inserts.

High Impact *insert* Tuning Techniques

Some insert tuning is more effective than others and these are the biggest "bang for the buck" approaches. Here are some techniques which can increase insert speed by more than double:

- **Tune your indexes:** Using specialized techniques such as reverse key indexes and bitmap indexes can greatly improve insert performance of specialized DML.

- **Using SSD for the *insert* table tablespaces**: For databases that require high-speed loads, some shops define the insert table partition on solid-state RAM disk.

These shops do their real-time inserts to SSD in order to maintain fast consistent response time, and transfer the data to traditional disk at a later time. Oracle with SSD can support over 500,000 rows per second for inserts, making it a great solution for shops that must "drink from the garden hose" during ETL insert feeds. The book *Oracle Solid-State Disk Tuning*, notes a respectable 30% improvement in insert speed when using SSD.

- **Parallelize the load**: You can invoke parallel DML (i.e. using the *parallel* and *append* hint) to have multiple inserts into the same table. For this *insert* optimization, make sure to define multiple freelists and use the SQL "*append*" option. Mark Bobak notes that if you submit parallel jobs to insert against the table at the same time, using the *append* hint may cause serialization, removing the benefit of parallel jobstreams.

- **Use PL/SQL bulking**: PL/SQL often out-performs standard SQL inserts because of the array processing and bulking in the "forall" statement. Kent Crotty shows examples where forall provides a 30x performance improvement on inserts, making PL/SQL as fast as SQL*Loader, one of the fastest ways to load Oracle data.

Tips for batch inserts

If you are loading data in a single-threaded batch window and you can perform a backup before and after the load job, these methods can be used to greatly improve performance of *insert* statements:

- **Disable/drop indexes and constraints**: It's far faster to rebuild indexes after the data load, all at-once. Also indexes will rebuild cleaner, and with less I/O if they reside in a tablespace with a large block size.

- *Use the append* **method**: By using the *append* hint, you ensure that Oracle always grabs "fresh" data blocks by raising the high-water-mark for the table. If you are doing parallel insert DML, the *append* mode is the default and you don't need to specify any *append* hint.

```
insert /*+ append */ into customer values ('hello',';there');
```

- *Use Nologging*: If you are taking full backups before and after a batch insert, also consider putting the table into *nologging* mode, which will allow Oracle to avoid almost all redo logging. Remember, if your database is in *noarchivelog* mode and you are no using the *append* hint for inserts, you WILL STILL generate redo logs!

```
alter table customer nologging;

-- a zillion insert statements

alter table customer logging;
```

Low-impact *insert* techniques (5% and 20% faster)

There are other insert tuning techniques where marginal performance improvements can be seen under special circumstances:

- **Use a large blocksize**: Heavy insert/update tables can see faster performance when segregated into another blocksize which is mapped to a small data buffer cache. Smaller data buffer caches often see faster throughput performance. By defining large (i.e. 32k) blocksizes for the target table, you reduce I/O because more rows fit onto a block before a "block full" condition (as set by PCTFREE) unlinks the block from the freelist.

- **Manage segment header contention for parallel inserts**: Make sure to define multiple freelist (or freelist groups) to remove contention for the table header. Multiple freelists add additional segment header blocks, removing the bottleneck. You can also use Automatic Segment Space Management (bitmap freelists) to support parallel DML, but ASSM has some limitations.

Now let's move on and take a closer look at some specialized techniques for improving SQL insert performance.

Tuning insert speed with the nologging option

The *nologging* option is a great way to speed-up inserts and index creation. It bypasses the writing of the redo log, significantly improving performance. However, this approach is quite dangerous if you need to roll-forward through this time period during a database recovery.

In nologging mode you are running without a safety net when you run nologging operations and you must make a "backup sandwich" with the *nologging* operations as the filler:

- **Backup before and after nologging operations:** You must take a backup, both before and after all nologging operations.

- **Only nologging operations during the nologging window:** Between the backups (the nologging processing window), ONLY *nologging* operations should be run in the middle of this "backup sandwich".

The nologging clause is quite convoluted and dependent on several factors.

- **Database in *noarchivelog* mode:** If your database is in "noarchivelog" mode and you are no using the *append* hint for inserts, you will still generate redo logs!

- **Database in *archivelog* mode:** If you are in *archivelog* mode, the table must be altered to nologging mode (*alter table customer nologging*) and the SQL must be using the *append* hint. Otherwise, redo logs will be generated for the *insert* statements.

You can use *nologging* for batch inserts into tables and for a variety of DBA maintenance tasks, normally performed inside a backup sandwich:

- **Insert into tables with nologging:** If you use the *append* hint and place the table in nologging mode, redo will be bypassed.

```
alter table customer nologging;

insert /*+ append */ into customer values ('hello',';there');
```

- **You can create indexes with nologging:** The only danger with using nologging is that you must re-run the create index syntax if you perform a roll-forward database recovery. Using nologging with create index can speed index creation by up to 30%.

```
create index newidx . . . nologging;
```

- **Other nologging options:** Only the following operations can make use of the *nologging* option:

    o   alter table...move partition

    o   alter table...split partition

    o   alter index...split partition

    o   alter index...rebuild

    o   alter index...rebuild partition

    o   create table...as select (CTAS)

    o   create index

    o   direct load with SQL*Loader

    o   direct load insert (using append)

Next, let's look at reverse key indexing and insert performance.

Reverse key indexes and insert performance

Using reverse-key indexes will speed-up Oracle *insert* statements, especially with an increasing key, like an index on an Oracle sequence (which is used for the primary key of the target table).

In large mission-critical systems, reverse key indexes (often created in small 2k blocksizes), are also important for tuning inserts on RAC systems because the internal key reversal reduced segment contention and buffer busy waits.

For large batch inserts, many shops will drop and rebuild the indexes after the batch insert, but using a Oracle reverse key index will greatly speed-up data loads because the high-order index key has been reversed.

Reverse key indexes looks like a regular index

A reverse key index does not change the functionality of the index, and it's not the same thing as reversing the index key values.

In general, an Oracle reverse key index relieve data block contention (buffer busy waits) when inserting into any index where the index key is a monotonically increasing value which must be duplicated in the higher-level index nodes.

With the index key reversal, only the lowest-level index node is changed, and not all of the high-order index nodes, resulting in far faster insert speed. For updates, Oracle updates the index nodes with each update statement.

Depending on the size of your update batch, it's often faster to drop, update and then re-build the index. If you have more than one CPU, you might consider doing a parallel index rebuild for faster speed. It splits-up the full-table scan:

The Oracle documentation says that a reverse key index reverses the bytes of each column indexed (except the ROWID) while keeping the column order intact.

By reversing the keys of the index, the insertions become distributed across all leaf keys in the index. Reverse-key indexes reduce "hot spots" in indexes, especially primary key indexes, by reversing the bytes of the leaf blocks and thus eliminating the contention for leaf blocks across instances.

Next, let's look at marginal techniques for improving SQL insert performance, placing the table into a larger blocksize to reduce I/O.

Blocksize and insert performance

While there is lots of empirical evidence of faster *insert* performance in non-standard blocksizes, this is an advanced technique that should only be attempted by an experienced DBA.

Here is a small single-CPU, single-user benchmark showing the performance of loads into a larger blocksize:

```
alter system set db_2k_cache_size=64m scope=spfile;
alter system set db_16k_cache_size=64m scope=spfile;

startup force

create tablespace twok blocksize 2k; <-- using ASM defaults to 100m
create tablespace sixteenk blocksize 16k;
create table load2k tablespace twok as select * from dba_objects; < creates
8k rows

drop table load2k; <- first create was to preload buffers


set timing on;

create table load2k tablespace twok as select * from dba_objects;
create table load16k tablespace sixteenk as select * from dba_objects;
```

Even with this super-tiny sample on Linux using Oracle10g (with ASM) the results were impressive, with a 5% - 10% performance improvement using larger blocksizes.

	2k blksze	16k blksze
8k table size	4.33 secs	4.16 secs
80k table size	8.74 secs	8.31 secs

Again, re-working blocksizes for a 10% speed improvement may not be right for your database because there are many other factors to consider. For example, a larger blocksize may improve SQL inserts, but it may have undesirable side effects. For example, changing blocksizes for inserts on a RAC databases is not recommended because the increased overhead of shipping large blocks through the cache fusion layer offsets any performance improvement.

Multiple blocksizes are not for dilettantes!

Using multiple blocksizes to improve SQL insert performance is a very tricky operation that is only done in very large Oracle shops where a 5%-10% improvement equates to millions of I/O operations.

Look Out!

Next, let's take a look at how to configure our database to maximize SQL delete speed.

Oracle Delete Tuning

A delete is like any other DML (data manipulation language) statement, and Oracle provides several techniques for doing large batch deletes at a faster speed:

High impact techniques (over 20% faster):

- **Tune the delete subquery:** Many Oracle deletes use a *where* clause subquery and optimizing the subquery will improve the SQL delete speed. Subquery optimization techniques are discussed in great detail in chapter 14 and may include the *push_subq* and *precompute_subquery* hints.

- **Implement partitioning:** Removing large volumes of adjunct data is a related partition is faster. If you can segregate the data to be deleted into a separate partition, super fast deletes become easy with the "alter tablespace xxx drop partition" syntax. If you are not licensed for Oracle partitioning, and you load your rows in-order, you could roll-your-own partitioning, using different tables names for each partition.

- **Parallelize deletes**: For large delete statements that require full-table scans, Oracle parallel DML includes *delete* statements and you can parallelize large deletes for faster performance. You can also submit multiple, simultaneous delete statements against the same table, just make sure that you have enough freelists (or ASSM) to handle the concurrency.

- **Drop indexes and constraints**: Dropping indexes before a mass *delete* and rebuilding them afterwards can improve delete performance because each individual delete would have to remove itself from the index, causing slowdowns. Oracle removes index entries without re-balancing the index tree (a "logical delete"), but this is still time-consuming, especially if you have lots of indexes on the target table.

Low-impact techniques (between 5% and 20% faster)

These specialized cases where marginal performance improvements can be seen under special circumstances:

- **Use a larger blocksize**: Heavy *insert/update/delete* tables can see faster performance when segregated into another blocksize which is mapped to a small data buffer cache.

- **Segregated small data buffer cache**: Smaller data buffer caches often see faster delete throughput performance by reducing the time required to locate and write dirty blocks to disk. The time delay in an Oracle delete is largely the time spent writing the new blocks to disk, and placing the table into a 32k blocksize will marginally speed-up delete DML because there will be more rows deleted before a physical write. This speed difference can range from zero up to ten percent, depending on the type of delete and the sequencing of the rows.

- **Use bulk bind deletes**: In certain cases using *bulk collect/forall* can improve delete performance. Bulk Binds are a PL/SQL technique where, instead of multiple individual delete statements, all of the operations are carried out at once, in bulk. This avoids the context-switching you get when the PL/SQL engine has to pass over to the SQL engine.

- **Use a small *pctused***: For tuning mass deletes you can reduce freelist overhead by setting Oracle to only re-add a block to the freelists when the block is dead empty by setting a low value for *pctused.*

Let's take a closer look at these *delete* tuning techniques.

Using bulk deletes

The bulk delete operation is the same regardless of server version. Using the *forall_test* table, a single predicate is needed in the *where* clause, but for this example both the *id* and *code* columns are included as if they represented a concatenated key.

The *delete_forall.sql* script listed below is used for this test. The script contains rollback statements, which are necessary to make sure the bulk operation has something to delete. Since the script uses separate collections for each bind, it is suitable for all versions of Oracle that support bulk operations.

🖫 delete_forall.sql

```
SET SERVEROUTPUT ON

DECLARE
  TYPE t_id_tab IS TABLE OF forall_test.id%TYPE;
  TYPE t_code_tab IS TABLE OF forall_test.code%TYPE;
```

```
  l_id_tab     t_id_tab    := t_id_tab();
  l_code_tab   t_code_tab  := t_code_tab();
  l_start      NUMBER;
  l_size       NUMBER      := 10000;
BEGIN
  -- Populate collections.
  FOR i IN 1 .. l_size LOOP
    l_id_tab.extend;
    l_code_tab.extend;
    l_id_tab(l_id_tab.last)      := i;
    l_code_tab(l_code_tab.last) := TO_CHAR(i);
  END LOOP;

-- Time regular updates.
  l_start := DBMS_UTILITY.get_time;
  FOR i IN l_id_tab.first .. l_id_tab.last LOOP
    DELETE FROM forall_test
    WHERE  id   = l_id_tab(i)
    AND    code = l_code_tab(i);
  END LOOP;

  ROLLBACK;
  DBMS_OUTPUT.put_line('Normal Deletes : ' ||
                       (DBMS_UTILITY.get_time - l_start));
  l_start := DBMS_UTILITY.get_time;
  -- Time bulk updates.
  FORALL i IN l_id_tab.first .. l_id_tab.last
    DELETE FROM forall_test
    WHERE  id   = l_id_tab(i)
    AND    code = l_code_tab(i);
  DBMS_OUTPUT.put_line('Bulk Deletes   : ' ||
                       (DBMS_UTILITY.get_time - l_start));
  ROLLBACK;
END;
/
```

Before running the *delete_forall.sql* script make sure the *forall_test* table is populated using the *insert_forall.sql* script or there will be no records to delete.

```
SQL> @delete_forall.sql
```

Here we see a count of the number of normal deletes and bulk deletes:

```
Normal Deletes : 416
Bulk Deletes   : 204
```

The performance of the bulk delete is similar to the performance of the bulk update; the bulk operation is approximately twice the speed of the conventional operation.

Next, let's look at Oracle *update* tuning.

Oracle Update Tuning

The SQL standard for DML *update* statements can be complex and convoluted and there are best practices that can help you to write efficient *update* statements.

High impact *update* techniques (over 20% faster):

- **Tune the update subquery:** Updates that query from other tables can be optimized using the subquery tuning techniques that we learned in Chapter 14.

- **Use CTAS in lieu of large updates:** Copying a table with a *where* clause is often faster than doing a massive update. **Simplify the *where* predicates**: This can result in faster update execution plans.

- **Use a small, separate data cache for high DML tables:** Research suggests that heavy *insert* tables can see faster performance when the table is mapped to a small RAM data buffer. In a small buffer, Oracle is able to quickly identify and write dirty blocks back to disk.

- **Use SSD:** Benchmark tests suggest that SSD can do updates more than 100 times faster than platter disks. If you are still using traditional platter disks, you can buy small amounts of SSD and apply them directly to your problematic I/O areas. You can segregate your high-updates objects (tables & indexes) into a separate blocksize so that they can have a separate, small data buffer. Remember, because SSD appears to the OS as a standard storage device, it can be mapped to those tables that experience a high DML rate and later transferred (via transportable tablespaces) to a platter disk data file.

Low-impact techniques (between 5% and 20% faster)

- **Use a larger blocksize**: Heavy insert/update tables can see faster performance when segregated into another blocksize which is mapped to a small data buffer cache.

- **Use bulk PL/SQL operators**: In some cases, using PL/SQL for bulk deletes is faster than native SQL.

- **Redundant set in where clause**: In some cases you can repeat the *set* condition of an *update* statement in the *where* clause. This technique exploits an issue within the optimizer and it may not work on your specific release. For example, assume that we are giving a bonus to all DBA staff members:

```
update emp set bonus='Y' where dept='DBA';
```

In some cases, negating the condition will make the insert run faster:

```
update emp set bonus='Y' where dept='DBA' and bonus!='Y';
```

Next, let's take a closer look at these techniques and see where they might apply to your tuning situation. We will start by showing those cases where using CTAS can be faster than a vanilla SQL *update*.

CTAS versus SQL Updates

This is a secret that is not taught at Oracle University, a trick known to all DBA's who spend late nights, weekends and holidays performing database maintenance during tight windows of opportunity.

When you are updating the majority of rows in a table, using Create Table as Select (CTAS) is often more efficient performance than a standard update. The CTAS method employs this technique:

- The database is offline and a full backup will be done after the table is modified.

- All indexes and constraints are dropped and rebuilt after the table update.

- The decode clause is used to change the data when the table is copied. (e.g. *select decode (status,'new','old',status from mytab;)*

- The CTAS method uses the *nologging* and *parallel* method to speed up the table copy.

- After the table is copied and re-named, all indexes and constraints are re-created in *nologging* and *parallel* mode.

The CTAS method is designed for massive updates, and it is used by DBA's during batch windows when the database is in maintenance mode and no other operations are being done against the target table.

The CTAS method is fastest when the vast majority of the table rows are effected. As a general rule of thumb, any update that effects more than half the table rows may see faster performance with a CTAS update.

For example, assume that the following update changes 75% of our table rows:

```
update
   mytab
```

```
set
   status = 'new'
where
   status = 'old';
```

In this case, a parallelized CTAS may perform far faster (Note: Make sure that you have an SMP server before using the *parallel* degree option):

```
create table
   new_mytab
NOLOGGING as
select  /*+ full parallel(mytab,35)*/
   decode (status,'new','old',status,
   col2, col3, col4
from mytab;

-- rebuild indexes, triggers and constraints to new_mytab

rename mytab      to bkup_mytab;

rename new_mytab to mytab;
```

In cases where the updates are part of a scheduled weekend batch, this technique can reduce a large table update dramatically saving precious hours during scheduled maintenance windows.

Now let's look at another technique to improve insert performance.

Include the *set* condition in the update's *where* clause

This technique is somewhat counterintuitive but it's a best practice to include the opposite condition of an *update* clause in the *where* clause. This technique exploits an issue within the optimizer and it may not work on your specific release.

Below is another case where the developer forgot to include the *set* condition in the *update where* clause. This update causes a full-table scan and the associated high redo waits (*log file parallel write* waits and *log file sync* waits).

Simply including the existing state of the *set* clause can result in a huge performance improvement for *update* statements because the negative where clause allows an index to be used for the update:

```
-- *****************************
-- full scan update
-- *****************************
```

```
update history set flag=0 where class='x'

-- *****************************
-- indexed update
-- *****************************
update history set flag=0 where class='x' and flag!=0
```

Don't use this for large updates!

This technique is for updates that change a relatively small amount of table rows. Because an index is used for the update, the *parallel* hint cannot be used to tune this type of update.

Now let's explore how a small data buffer can give us a marginal performance boost for high-update tables.

Consider a small, separate data cache for high DML tables

As more people adopt the new mainframe computers, 64-bit servers with giant data buffers, we see a delay caused by the database writer process having to scan through giant data buffers seeking dirty blocks.

By segregating high activity tables into a separate, smaller data buffer, Oracle has far less RAM frames to scan for dirty block, improving the throughput and also reducing CPU consumption. This is especially important for high update tables with more than 100 row changes per second.

MOSC Note: 223299.1 also embraces the importance of multiple blocksizes, listing the multiple buffer regions as among the most powerful tuning techniques.

Simplifying the *where* clause predicates

The most common issue with updates is the requirement to have a complex *select* statement is the where clause to identify the rows to be updated. The best techniques for simplifying *update* where clauses include:

- Predicate pushing

- Rewriting subqueries as outer joins (if possible)

- Oracle SQL subquery un-nesting

- Partitioning Pruning: Oracle partitioning is a divide and conquer approach where the data is organized such that the SQL statements can access the data faster than with a non-partitioned table.

- Avoid *in* and *not in:* It is a good idea to discourage the use of the *not in* clause (which invokes a sub-query) and to prefer *not exists* (which invokes a correlated sub-query).

While partitioning is dine primarily to improve the manageability of a very large table, there are also performance improvements associated with partitioned tables.

- **Partition-wise joins:** Oracle offers partition-wise table joins, where Oracle takes a large table join and breaks it down into several smaller joins that can be executed against each partition. Partition-wise joins only apply to merge joins and hash joins, not nested loop joins. Table joins with a low cardinality (just a few matching rows as a percentage of the original table rows) will not benefit from partition-wise joins.

- **Partition pruning:** Oracle partition pruning is a divided and conquer approach where Oracle is Partition Aware, excluding any partitions that do not contain blocks that are needed to satisfy the query result set. Partition pruning can make SQL run at blistering speeds.

Partition Pruning has huge benefits!

Some DBA's report that partition pruning can take a SQL query down from hours to minutes, an 18,000 times performance improvement!

Using bulk binds for PL/SQL updates

This quick test demonstrates the impact of using bulk binds as an alternative to a SQL Update statement. Whenever you have a PL/SQL based application, you can greatly improve the speed of updates with "bulk binding" (the use of the *bulk collect* and *forall* operators).

In this simple test, a *forall_test* table is used to compare the performance of individual updates against bulk updates. The script using forall is called *update_forall.sql*.

Notice the use of the *row* keyword in the bulk operation *(SET   ROW = l_tab(i))* below. This *row* keyword allows updates using the whole record definition and you won't need to reference each-and-every individual elements of the record!

Let's take a close look and see the exact differences in runtime performance. Here is the test script that does SQL updates with the *forall* operator:

🖫 update_forall.sql

```
SET SERVEROUTPUT ON

DECLARE
  TYPE t_id_tab IS TABLE OF forall_test.id%TYPE;
  TYPE t_forall_test_tab IS TABLE OF forall_test%ROWTYPE;
  l_id_tab  t_id_tab             := t_id_tab();
  l_tab     t_forall_test_tab := t_forall_test_tab ();
  l_start   NUMBER;
  l_size    NUMBER               := 10000;
BEGIN
  -- Populate collections.
  FOR i IN 1 .. l_size LOOP
    l_id_tab.extend;
    l_tab.extend;
    l_id_tab(l_id_tab.last)      := i;
    l_tab(l_tab.last).id         := i;
    l_tab(l_tab.last).code       := TO_CHAR(i);
    l_tab(l_tab.last).description := 'Description: ' || TO_CHAR(i);
  END LOOP;

  -- Time regular updates.
  l_start := DBMS_UTILITY.get_time;
  FOR i IN l_tab.first .. l_tab.last LOOP
    UPDATE forall_test
    SET    ROW = l_tab(i)
    WHERE  id  = l_tab(i).id;
  END LOOP;

  DBMS_OUTPUT.put_line('Normal Updates : ' ||
                       (DBMS_UTILITY.get_time - l_start));
  l_start := DBMS_UTILITY.get_time;
  -- Time bulk updates.

  -- ****************************************************
  -- ***   Here is the forall
  -- ****************************************************
  FORALL i IN l_tab.first .. l_tab.last
    UPDATE forall_test
    SET    ROW = l_tab(i)
    WHERE  id  = l_id_tab(i);
```

```
  DBMS_OUTPUT.put_line('Bulk Updates  : ' ||
                      (DBMS_UTILITY.get_time - l_start));
  COMMIT;
END;/
```

Using PL/SQL for high speed SQL updates

The *update_forall.sql* script has a similar internal structure to the insert_forall.sql script described earlier. The main difference is the update statement requires a *where* clause that references the tables ID column allowing individual rows to be targeted. If the bulk operation was altered to reference the ID column within the collection, the following compilation error would be produced.

```
-- ***************************
-- Incorrect bulk operation.
-- ***************************

  FORALL i IN l_tab.first .. l_tab.last
    UPDATE forall_test
    SET    ROW = l_tab(i)
    WHERE  id  = l_tab(i).id;
```

```
Errors for PROCEDURE UPDATE_FORALL:

LINE/COL ERROR
-------- -----------------------------------------------------------
36/5     PL/SQL: SQL Statement ignored
38/18    PL/SQL: ORA-22806: not an object or REF
38/18    PLS-00382: expression is of wrong type
38/18    PLS-00436: implementation restriction: cannot reference
         fields of BULK In-BIND table of records
```

Before running the script make sure the *forall_test* table is populated using the *insert_forall.sql* script or there will be no records to update. The results from the *update_forall.sql* script are listed below.

```
SQL> @update_forall.sql
```

Here we see counts of regular vs. bulk updates:

```
Normal Updates : 202
Bulk Updates   : 104

PL/SQL procedure successfully completed.
```

In this example, the use of *forall* creates approximately twice the speed of the conventional PL/SQL update method.

Now let's look at how *subquery factoring* (the *with* clause) can be used in Oracle DML statements.

Oracle subquery factoring (*with* clause) for DML

In Chapter 14 we discussed cases where pre-materializing a subquery can lead to simpler, faster and easier to maintain SQL. We can also use subquery factoring in DML statements, replacing the subquery using the *with* clause.

Here is the syntax for using subquery factoring in DML:

```
-- ********************************************
-- Using the with clause for inserts:
-- ********************************************

insert into
   table_name
select
   stuff
from
   mytab;

insert into
   table_name
with
   subquery_name
as (select stuff from mytab)
select
   stuff
from
   subquery_name;

-- ********************************************
-- Using the with clause for updates:
-- ********************************************

update
   table_name
set
   column_name =
   select
      stuff
   from
      mytab);

update
   table_name
set
   column_name =
   (with
      subquery_name
   as (select stuff from mytab)
```

```
  select
     stuff
  from
     subquery_name);

-- **********************************************
-- Using the with clause for deletes:
-- **********************************************

delete from
   table_name
where
   column_name in
   select
      stuff
   from
      subquery_name);

delete from
   table_name
where
   column_name in
   (with
      subquery_name
   as (select stuff from mytab)
   select
      stuff
   from
      subquery_name);
```

While your mileage may vary, there may not be a performance boost from using the *with* clause in DML, and you may wish to consider other subquery tuning options such as the *push_subq* and *precompute_subquery* hints.

Conclusion

This chapter has provided an overview of SQL tuning in Oracle, with a focus on the new 10g SQL tuning features. The main points of this chapter include:

- The goals of SQL tuning involve verifying the best execution plan for any statements.

- The best execution plan is either the plan that starts returning rows the fastest or the plan that executes the query with the smallest resource consumption.

- Oracle10g and beyond now automatically collects and refreshes schema statistics using the *dbms_stats* package.

- Histogram collection can now be easily automated, and some of these databases choose to put histograms on all key columns to improve the accuracy of table join order.

- One common cause of suboptimal SQL is missing materialized view and indexes, especially function-based indexes.

- Oracle provides a wealth of hints to change the optimizer execution plans.

- SQL Profiles are a great improvement over the stored outlines of the Optimizer Plan Stability.

- The new *dba_hist* tables contain a wealth of historical information about historical SQL execution statistics.

- Time-series analysis of object usage within SQL can yield important insights into holistic tuning for SQL statements.

The SQLTuning Advisor and SQLAccess Advisor provide an easy method for identifying and tuning SQL with suboptimal execution plans. Next, let's move on and see how the extra-cost SQL advisors can help us optimizer our SQL.

Oracle SQL
Tuning Advisors

Oracle SQL Tuning Advisors will give you tuning tips

Towards Automated SQL Tuning

Until the advent of the Oracle 10g intelligent SQL tuning advisors (The SQL Access advisor and SQL Tuning Advisor), SQL tuning was time-consuming and required a complete understanding of SQL execution.

That all started to change in Oracle 10g, and in Oracle 11g, where Oracle has advertised "fully automated" SQL tuning, claiming that their automated SQL Performance tools would make SQL tuning so easy that anyone could do it.

In reality, Oracle has a spotty history of implementing intelligent tools. Their first attempt was called "Oracle Expert" a tool that would commonly cause performance problems, and often delivered unhelpful tuning suggestions. In the industry, the tool was not popular and Oracle dropped the product before 10g was released.

The idea behind the intelligent SQL tuning advisor is good. SQL tuning is a semi-structured task with some well-structured decision rules that can be fully automated.

As such, automated tools can be created to perform the well-defined and tedious tasks in SQL tuning, jobs like running workloads and making basic suggestions.

In sum, while Oracle is making great progress with automation of SQL tuning, their tools are nowhere near as good as a human expert. Because SQL tuning requires human intuition, the technology does not yet exist that would allow Oracle (or any other database vendor) to completely mimic decades of human expertise.

However, these tools do a reasonable job for finding obvious SQL tuning problems such as missing indexes, and with each new release, Oracle gets closer to automating SQL optimization.

Now that we understand the limitations of the SQL tuning advisors, let's start with an overview of their architecture.

Oracle's Automatic SQL Tuning Approach

Oracle uses a reasonable approach to SQL tuning, running pre-defined real-world SQL against real databases, measuring metrics, and re-executing alternatives and measuring the response time, only recommending changes that run at least 3 times faster than the original SQL.
SQL tuning is an art, not a science, and only empirical testing will prove which tuning suggestions result in the fastest performance.

The Oracle automatic SQL tuning advisor allowed us to implement tuning suggestions in the form of SQL profiles that will improve performance. Now with Oracle 11g, the DBA can tell Oracle to automatically apply SQL profiles for statements whenever the suggested profile gives 3-times better performance than that of the existing statement.

These performance comparisons are done by a new 11g administrative task that is executed during a user-specified maintenance window. In a nutshell, the 11g fully automated SQL tuning works like this:

Step 1 - Define the SQL workload: The DBA defines a "set" of problematic SQL statements using exception thresholds (e.g. all SQL with > 100,000 disk reads), select from the cursor cache or the AWR. This is called the SQL Tuning set, or STS.

Step 2 - Set-up a changed environment: Here you can choose to change your initialization parameters, test your performance against a previous release of the CBO (a very useful feature when testing upgrades) or conduct "custom experiments" on the effect of environmental changes on your SQL tuning set.

Step 3 - Schedule & run your tests: The workload is scheduled for execution during "low usage" periods, so that an empirical sample of real-world execution times can be collected and compared, using different execution plans.

Step 4 - Implement the changes: You can flag SQL statements for changes and tune them with the SQL Tuning Advisor.

Before we examine the nuances of the 11g fully automated SQL tuning features, let's briefly review the goals of SQL tuning.

The Goals of Holistic SQL Tuning

As a review, holistic tuning in Oracle 11g is a broad-brush approach that can save thousands of hours of tedious manual SQL tuning. By applying global changes, the DBA can tune hundreds of queries at once, and implement them via SQL profiles.

DBAs who fail to do holistic SQL tuning first (especially those who tune SQL with optimizer directives), may find that subsequent global changes (e.g. optimizer parameter change) may un-tune the SQL. By starting with system-level tuning, the DBA can establish an "optimal baseline", before diving into the tuning of individual SQL statements:

- **Optimize the server kernel:** You must always tune your disk and network I/O subsystem (RAID, DASD bandwidth, network) to optimize the I/O time, network packet size and dispatching frequency. Kernel settings have an indirect effect on SQL performance. For example, a kernel setting may speed-up I/O, a change which is noted by the CBO workload statistics (using *dbms_stats.gather_workload_stats*). This, in turn, directly influences the optimizer's access decisions.

- **Adjusting your optimizer statistics**: You must always collect and store optimizer statistics to allow the optimizer to learn more about the distribution of your data to take more intelligent execution plans.

- **Adjust optimizer parameters**: *Optimizer optimizer_mode, optimizer_index_caching, optimizer_index_cost_adj.*

- **Optimize your instance**: Your choice of *db_block_size, db_cache_size*, and OS parameters (*db_file_multiblock_read_count, cpu_count*, &c), can influence SQL performance.

- **Tune your SQL Access workload with physical indexes and materialized views**: Just as the 10g SQLAccess advisor recommends missing indexes and missing materialized views, you should always optimize your SQL workload with indexes, especially function-based indexes, a Godsend for SQL tuning.

Now, Oracle 11g does not have all of the intelligence of a human SQL tuning expert, but the 11g SQL Performance Analyzer (SPA) is a great way to test for the effect of environmental changes to your Oracle environment. Next, let's take a closer look at how Oracle has automated the SQL tuning process with SPA.

Decision Support and Expert Systems Technology

Oracle made a commitment to Decision Support Systems (DSS) Technology starting in Oracle 9i when they started to publish "advisory" utilities, the result of monitoring the Oracle instance and coming up with estimated benefits for making a change to the database configuration. In the world of applied artificial intelligence, an expert system (e.g. AMM, ASM) solves a well-structured problem for the DBA, while a decision support system solves a semi-structured problem with the DBA, who supplies the human intuition required to solve a complex problem.

Oracle's commitment to earning a distinguished reputation in the database marketplace is one of the major reasons that Oracle commands a major market share. One of the most exciting areas of Oracle technology is automation, especially the self-management features. Oracle has now automated many critical components, including memory advisors (AMM), automated storage management (ASM), and Oracle is now working to enhance more intelligent utilities including ADDM, the Automated Database Diagnostic Monitor, and the new 11g SQL Performance Analyzer (SPA).

The Oracle 11g SPA functions as a DSS, by automating the well-structured components of a complex tuning task, such as hypothesis testing. In SPA, the DBA defines a representative workload and then tests this workload empirically, running the actual queries against the database and collecting performance metrics. SPA allows the DBA to obtain real-world performance results for several types of environmental changes:

- **Optimizer software levels**: Compare SQL execution between different releases of the cost-based optimizer (CBO).

- **Initialization parameters**: Pre-test changes to global parameters, most often the Oracle optimizer parameters (*optimizer_mode*, *optimizer_index_cost_adj*, *optimizer_index_caching*). Prior to Oracle 10g, adjusting these optimizer parameters was the only way to compensate for sample size issues with *dbms_stats*.

- **Guided workflow:** This is a hypothesis testing option that allows the DBA to create customized experiments and validate their hypotheses using empirical methods.

As of Oracle10g and beyond, the use of *dbms_stats.gather_system_stats* and improved sampling within *dbms_stats* had made adjustments to these parameters far less important. Ceteris Parabus, always adjust CBO statistics before adjusting optimizer parms.

Instead of using theory and mathematical calculations, Oracle SPA tests the SQL Tuning Set (STS) workload in a real-world environment, running the workload repeatedly while using heuristic methods to tally the optimal execution plan for the SQL. The DBA can then review the changes to execution plans and tune the SQL (using the SQL Tuning Advisor) to lock-in the execution plans using SQL profiles.

Let's take a closer look at SPA and see how holistic SQL tuning can remove the tedium of tuning SQL statements.

The Oracle 11g SQL Performance Analyzer is a step in the direction of fully automated SQL tuning, allowing the database administrator to create a STS "workload", a unified set of SQL which comes from either the cursor cache (Shared Pool) or from the AWR (the Automated Workload Repository).

The DBA can use exception thresholds to select the SQL for each STS, based on execution criteria such as disk reads, consistent gets, executions, etc. Once the DBA has chosen their STS, SPA allows them to run the workload while changing Oracle environmental factors, namely the CBO release level, init.ora parameters and customized hypothesis testing using the guided workflow option.

The central question becomes which Oracle initialization parameters would be the most appropriate within the SQL performance analyzer? Because the SPA is used to measure changes in SQL execution plans, it only makes sense that we would want to choose those Oracle parameters which will influence the behavior of the Oracle optimizer.

These would include the basic Oracle optimizer parameters (including *optimizer_index_cost_adj*, *optimizer_mode*, *optimizer_index_caching*), as well as other important initialization parameters. We also have non-optimizer parameters which effect SQL execution plan decisions.

- **db_file_multiblock_read_count**. When this parameter is set to a high value the Oracle cost based optimizer recognizes that scattered multiblock reads may be less expensive than sequential reads. (i.e. full table scans and full index scans). **10gr2 Note:** Starting in Oracle 10g release 2, Oracle recommends not setting the *db_file_multiblock_read_count* parameter, allowing Oracle to empirically determine the optimal setting.

- **parallel_automatic_tuning**. When *parallel_automatic_tuning* is set to "on" the Oracle optimizer will parallelize legitimate full table scans. Because we have told Oracle that parallel full table scans can be done very quickly using parallel query Oracle's cost based optimizer will assign a higher cost index access, making the optimizer friendlier to full table scans.

- **hash_area_size** (if not overridden by *pga_aggregate_target*): The setting for *hash_area_size* governs the propensity of Oracle's optimizer to favor hash joins over nested loop and for merge joins. This makes it an ideal testing parameter for changes to Oracle memory regions so that you can see how they would be affected within a production environment.

- **pga_aggregate_target:** The settings for *pga_aggregate_target* have a profound impact on the behavior of Oracle SQL statements, making this an interesting test case for the SQL performance analyzer, especially with regard of the propensity of the Oracle optimizer to do in memory sorts, and hash joins.

- **sort_area_size** (if not overridden by *pga_aggregate_target*): The *sort_area_size* parameter influences the cost based optimizer when deciding whether or not to perform index access, or to perform a sort of the ultimate results set from the SQL query. The higher the value for *sort_area_size* the more likely it will be that the Oracle 11g optimizer will invoke a backend sort, because it knows that the sort can be performed in memory. Of course, this depends upon the Oracle optimizers estimated cardinality for the results set of the SQL query.

Of course, we can change any parameters we like. Let's now see how the SPA captures changes in SQL execution plans.

The SQL performance analyzer allows the DBA to define the SQL Tuning set (the STS), as a source for the test (usually using historical SQL from the AWR tables).

The SPA receives one or more SQL statements as input (via the SPA), and provides advice on which tuning conditions have the best execution plans, gives the proof for the advice, shows an estimated performance benefit, and allegedly has a facility to automatically implement changes that are more than 3x faster than the "before" condition".

Inside the 11g SQL Performance Analyzer

The declarative nature of the SQL syntax has always made it difficult to perform SQL tuning. The basic tenet of cost-based SQL optimization is that the person who writes a SQL query simply "declares" what columns they want to see (the *select* clause), the tables where the columns reside (the *from* clause), and the filtering conditions (the *where* clause). It's up to the SQL optimizer to always determine the optimal execution plan. This is a formidable challenge, especially in a dynamic environment, which is why Oracle introduced the 10g new feature of CBO dynamic sampling.

Oracle tuning consultants have know for many years that the best way to tune an Oracle system is to take a top-down approach, finding the optimal configuration for external factors (i.e. OS kernel settings, disk I/O subsystem), and determining the best overall setting for the Oracle instance (i.e. init.ora parameters).

Holistic tuning involves tuning a representative workload, adjusting global parameters in order to optimize as much SQL as possible. Only then, is it prudent to start tuning individual SQL statements. Many Oracle professional who adopt a bottom-up approach (tune the SQL first), find all of their hard-work un-done when a change is made to a global setting, such as one of the SQL optimizer parameters or re-computing optimizer statistics.

Oracle's holistic SQL tuning approach is new, and given the misleading marketing name "fully automated SQL tuning". Holistic tuning is well-known to working DBA's who have been doing manual workload-based optimization since Oracle6. Now in 11g, Oracle gives us an automated method.

The Oracle 11g SQL Performance Analyzer (SPA), is primarily designed to speed up the holistic SQL tuning process, automating much of the tedium. Once you create a workload (called a SQL Tuning Set, or STS), Oracle will repeatedly execute the workload, using sophisticated predictive models (using a regression testing approach) to accurately identify the salient changes to execution plans, based on your environmental changes.

Using SPA, we can predict the impact of system changes on a workload, and we can forecast changes in response times for SQL after making any change, like parameter changes, schema changes, hardware changes, OS changes, or Oracle upgrades; any change that influence SQL plans is a good candidate for SPA.

Comparing the SPA Results

The final step in SPA allows the DBA to quickly isolate sub-optimal SQL statement and tune them with the 11g SQL Tuning Advisor. When viewing the results, you can use OEM for a visually display of all delta values between the execution run, but most important, you can do a side-by-side comparison of the before-and-after execution plans.

Oracle has always been ahead of the curve in automating well-structured DBA tasks, and the SPA is just the latest incarnation in real-world SQL tuning tools. Tools such as SPA free-up the DBA to pursue other important DBA tasks, relieving them of the tedium of individually tuning SQL statements.

Gathering the SQL Tuning set

The SQL workload (the STS) can be thought of as a container for conducting and analyzing many SQL statements. The STS is fed to the SPA for real-world execution with before-and-after comparisons of changes to holistic "environmental" conditions, specifically CBO levels or changed init.ora parameters.

Internally, the SPA is stored as a database object that contains one or more SQL statements combined with their execution statistics and context such as particular schema, application module name, list of bind variables, etc. The STS also includes a set of basic execution statistics such as CPU and elapsed times, disk reads and buffer gets, number of executions, etc.

When creating a STS, the SQL statements can be filtered by different patterns such as application module name or execution statistics, such as high disk reads. Once created, STS can be an input source for the SQL Tuning Advisor.

Typically, the following steps are used to define the STS using the *dbms_sqltune* package. The steps within the new 11g OEM screen for "guided workflow" are simple and straightforward, and serve as an online interface to the *dbms_sqltune.create_sqlset* procedure:

Step 1: **Options:** Choose a name for your SQL tuning set (STS). This encapsulated SQL workload is created using the *dbms_sqltune.create_sqlset* procedure. For example, the following script can be used to create a STS called SQLSET1:

```
exec dbms_sqltune.create_sqlset ('MYSET1');
```

Step 2: **Load methods:** Here is where you can choose the source for your SQL workload, and to take historical SQL statements from AWR.

Step 3: **Filter options:** You can choose "filtering" conditions, based on your specific tuning needs. For example, if your database is disk I/O bound, you might choose only SQL statements that have more than 100k disk reads.

Step 4: **Schedule:** This is an interface to the *dbms_scheduler* package, allowing you to define and schedule a job.

Step 5: **Review:** Here you can see the actual source calls to *dbms_sqltune.create_sqlset* and the *dbms_scheduler.create_job* procedure call syntax.

There is an interface to the SQL Performance Analyzer in the enterprise manager in the OEM Advisor Central area, and a number of new to *dba_advisor* views have been added in 11g which will display information from the SQL Performance Advisor.

The technology behind SPA is encapsulated inside a new package called *dbms_sqlpa*. Here is an overview for the procedures of the *dbms_sqlpa* package:

- *cancel_analysis_task:* This procedure cancels the currently executing task analysis of one or more SQL statements.

- *create_analysis_task* : This function Creates an advisor task to process and analyze one or more SQL statements.

- *drop_analysis_task*: This procedure drops a SQL analysis task.

- *execute_analysis_task:* This function & procedure executes a previously created analysis task.

- *interrupt_analysis_task* : This procedure interrupts the currently executing analysis task.

- *report_analysis_task*: This function displays the results of an analysis task.

- *reset_analysis_task*: This procedure resets the currently executing analysis task to its initial state.

- *resume_analysis_task:* This procedure resumes a previously interrupted analysis task that was created to process a SQL tuning set.

- *set_analysis_task_parameter:* This procedure sets the SQL analysis task parameter value.

- *set_analysis_default_parameter:* This procedure Sets the SQL analysis task parameter default value

In sum, the new 11g SQL Performance Analyzer is a great way to test for holistic tuning changes. Remember, the savvy Oracle DBA will always adjust their Oracle initialization parameters to optimizer as much of the workload as possible before diving into the tuning of specific SQL statements.

Oracle 11g guided workflow screen

The OEM screen for the SPA "guided workflow" contains a pre-defined set of steps for holistic SQL workload tuning:

Step 1: Create SQL Performance Analyzer Task, based on SQL Tuning Set.
Step 2: Replay SQL Tuning Set in Initial Environment.
Step 3: Create replay Trial using changed environment.
Step 4: Create Replay trial comparison (using trials from step 2 and step 3).
Step 5: View trial comparison report.

Using the guided workflow functionality, we can take our SQL tuning set and execute it twice (before and after), saving the SQL execution results (disk reads, buffer gets) using some of the common SQL execution metrics found in the *dba_hist_sqlstat* table:

dba_hist_sqlstat Columns:

fetches_total , end_of_fetch_count_total, sorts_total, executions_total, loads_total, invalidations_total, parse_calls_total, disk_reads_total, buffer_gets_total, rows_processed_total, cpu_time_total, elapsed_time_total

Guided Workflow Items

execute_elapsed_time, elapsed_time, parse_time, execute_elapsed_time, execute_cpu_time, buffer_gets, disk_reads, direct_writes, optimizer_cost

Here it's important to note that the guided workflow does not measure these important SQL execution metrics such as sorts and fetches.

Next, let's explore the Oracle SQLTuning advisor.

Using the Oracle SQLTuning Advisor

The extra-cost SQLTuning Advisor (STA) works with the Automatic Tuning Optimizer (ATO) to analyze historical SQL workload using data from the AWR, and

---

it generates recommendations for new indexes and materialized views that will reduce the disk I/O associated with troublesome SQL statements.

The STA is primarily designed to replace the manual tuning of SQL statements and speed up the overall SQL tuning process. The SQL Tuning Advisor studies poorly executing SQL statements and evaluates resource consumption in terms of CPU, I/O, and temporary space.

The advisor receives one or more SQL statements as input and provides advice on how to optimize their execution plans, gives the rationale for the advice, the estimated performance benefit, and the actual command to implement the advice.

The STA can be thought of as a container for conducting and analyzing many tuning tasks. It calls the optimizer internally and performs the analysis as follows:

1. Executes the stale or missing statistics analysis and makes a recommendation to collect, if necessary.

2. Plans the tuning analysis and creates a SQL Profile. The SQL Profile is a collection of the historical information of prior runs of the SQL statement, comparison details of the actual and estimated cardinality, and predicate selectivity, etc. SQL Profile is stored persistently in the data dictionary, so it does not require any application code changes.

3. Performs the access path analysis. The Optimizer recommends new indexes that produce a significantly faster execution path.

4. Restructure the SQL statement. Optimizer identifies SQL statements that have bad plans and makes relevant suggestions to restructure them.

The plan analysis mode, which creates the SQL Profiles, is a significant stage where additional information for the query is collected by the optimizer. This analysis is not possible in the normal mode.

Such a SQL profile helps generate a better execution plan than the normal optimization. Additional tasks like checking for advanced predicate selectivity, correlation between columns, join skews, and complex predicates such as functions, help in profiling the SQL statement. Once a statement is profiled and stored, it can be used at will.

Let's look at a specific SQLTuning advisor session.

Using SQLTuning Advisor Session

This method has many stages. In the first stage, the SQL Advisor task can be created by taking SQL statement input from a variety of sources. They are as follows:

- High Load SQL statements, identified by ADDM.

- SQL statements that are currently in cursor cache from the *v$sql_plan* view.

- SQL statements based on the range of snapshot IDs from the Automatic Workload Repository (AWR). By default, the AWR maintains data for up to seven days.

- Simple SQL Statement Text. A user can define a custom workload consisting of statements of interest to the user. These may be statements that are either in cursor cache or high-load, to be captured by ADDM or AWR.

- SQL Tuning Set (STS). A SQL Tuning Set is a named set of SQL statements with their associated execution context and basic execution statistics.

The following is an example of a SQL Tuning session, using this new functionality:

Step 1: Create a tuning task

There is a SQL statement, perhaps from a packaged application, and the DBA may not be able to change the code.

```
create_tuning_task (
sql_text => 'select * from emp_history
where empid_id = :bnd_var',f
bind_list =>
sql_binds(anydata.ConvertNumber(100)),
usern_name => 'scott',
scope => 'comprehensive',
time_limit => 60,
task_name => 'bad_sql',
description => 'sql that performs poorly');
```

The time limit is set to 60, so the optimizer will spend up to 60 seconds analyzing this SQL statement. The comprehensive setting indicated that the optimizer should perform its additional analysis. Instead of using the above SQL, the *sql_id* out of OEM or other catalog tables such as *sql_advisor_%* can be used.

```
create_tuning_task (sql_id =>
'abc123456xyz');
```

Step 2: Execute the tuning task.

```
execute_tuning_task (
task_name => 'bad_sql');
```

The results of this execution have been put into the new catalog tables, and can be seen by querying dba_advisor_% views such as *dba_advisor_findings*, *dba_advisor_recommendations*, etc.

Step 3: See the results.

```
set long 10000;

select report_tuning_task (task_name => 'bad_sql') from dual;
```

This will return a complete report of the results, including findings and recommendations. This report can also be run via OEM.

Step 4: Determine what is to be implemented, and execute accordingly.

```
accept_sql_profile (tastk_name => 'bad_sql',
name => 'use_this_profile');
```

This will store the profile in the catalog, which is similar to a stored outline in previous releases of Oracle. So, when using the optimizer in normal mode, when the bad SQL comes along, instead of using the original access path, this new profile will be used instead.

Next, let's investigate the Automatic Database Diagnostic Monitor (ADDM) in more detail.

Oracle Automatic Database Diagnostics Monitor

If you purchase the extra-cost Oracle Performance pack and Diagnostic pack, you get access to an automated tool called ADDM, the automatic database diagnostic monitor. Prior to Oracle10g, SQL tuning could not be automated and the DBA spent much of their time adding indexes, managing materialized views, changing *init.ora* parameters, testing hints, reading TKPROF output, examining explain plans, and so on.

Oracle offers more automatic mechanisms for rudimentary SQL tuning. The AWR tables allow Oracle to collect and maintain detailed SQL execution statistics, and this stored data is then used by the Advanced Database Diagnostic Monitor (ADDM, pronounced 'Adam').

ADDM attempts to supply a root cause analysis along with recommendations on what to do to fix the problem. An ADDM output might contain information that there is read/write contention, a freelist problem, or the need to use locally managed tablespaces.

The ADDM tool can be accessed either via the command line interface or through the Oracle Enterprise Manager (OEM), but most DBAs prefer the command line interface.

Oracle also has the new SQL Tuning Advisor to assist with tuning SQL. This use of this tool is based on changes to the optimizer. The optimizer now has a tuning mode that is used when tuning SQL. The tuning mode causes the optimizer to go through four checks:

- **Analyze SQL Statistics**: Check for missing or stale CBO statistics.

- **SQL Profiling:** Determine additional information that will make a statement run better and save it off for use later, similar to a stored outline.

- **SQL Access Analysis:** Verify that the access path is the most optimal or make recommendations for a better one.

- **SQL Structure Analysis:** Determine if tweaking the SQL will make it run better such as changing a not in to a not exists, for example.

ADDM can identify high load SQL statements, which can, in turn, be fed into the SQL Tuning Advisor below. ADDM automatically detects common performance problems, including these conditions:

- Excessive I/O

- CPU Bottlenecks

- Contention Issues

- High Parsing

- Lock Contention

- Buffer Sizing Issues

- RAC Tuning Issues

ADDM is invoked every 30 minutes or whenever the DBA specifies. The DBA can begin with ADDM by creating a new snapshot with information populated in *dba_hist_snapshot*:

```
exec dbms_workload_repository.create_snapshot();
```

The *addm_rpt.sql* script can be used to view the output of the snapshot, including recommendations:

💾 addm_rpt.sql

```
set long 1000000
set pagesize 50000

column get_clob format a80

select dbms_advisor.get_task_report(task_name, 'TEXT', 'ALL') as
first_ADDM_report
from
   dba_advisor_tasks
where
   task_id=(
      select max(t.task_id)
      from
         dba_advisor_tasks t,
         dba_advisor_log l
      where
         t.task_id = l.task_id
      and
         t.advisor_name='ADDM'
      and
         l.status= 'COMPLETED'
   );
```

The following is an example of output that ADDM might generate. This result shows that the ADDM detected excessive physical reads and used the *v$db_cache_advice* method to determine that this instance would benefit from a larger data buffer cache::

```
FINDING 3: 5.2% impact (147 seconds)
------------------------------------
The buffer cache was undersized causing significant additional read I/O.

RECOMMENDATION 1: DB Configuration, 5.2% benefit (147 seconds)
ACTION: Increase SGA target size by increasing the value of parameter
"sga_target" by 24 M.

SYMPTOMS THAT LED TO THE FINDING:
Wait class "User I/O" was consuming significant database time. (5.3%  impact
[150 seconds])
```

Conclusion

This chapter shows how Oracle automation strategy is being applied to SQL tuning activities. As we have seen, the SQL advisors are great for systems without a DBA but they are nowhere near as sophisticated as a human tuning expert.

There will always be room for a human SQL tuning expert because SQL tuning is a semi-structured task where on completely definable set of well structures rules can be applied to all situations.

Book Conclusion

In this book I have applied my 25 years of accumulated knowledge about SQL tuning onto a pragmatic approach, geared for the practicing Oracle tuning professionals. While the Oracle SQL optimizer will continue to evolve, there is no optimizer that will always choose the best execution plan for every SQL statement and SQL tuning will always be an advanced area of Oracle database administration.

The main points of this book include:

- The Oracle SQL optimizer is one of the world's most sophisticated software packages and the internals are a tightly-held competitive secret.

- Oracle has adopted a SQL tuning best practice of holistic tuning whereby we optimize the instance for our SQL workload before tuning individual SQL statements.

- An Oracle database may have several workloads, and it's our job to identify these workloads and deploy parameter and statistics change just-in-time to accommodate the new SQL.

- The key to successful proactive SQL tuning is to monitor your SQL workload for exceptional conditions using STATSPACK or AWR data.

- Oracle has many global tuning tools that effect all SQL within the instance, namely the SGA sizing parameters, the SQL optimizer parameters and the collection of optimal optimizer statistics.

- Every release of Oracle is unique, and there are few SQL tuning rules that apply to all versions and release of Oracle.

- Oracle SQL tuning is an art, not a science. There are no formulas to predict what SQL statement will run faster and the only way to test SQL performance is to time the query.

Oracle technology is constantly changing, so please visit the book details page on www.rampant-books.com for the latest updates and errata.

Oracle SQL Advanced Analytics

Advanced Analytics requires an advanced analyst

Inside SQL Analytics

As SQL progressed over the decades, a movement began to extend the capabilities of SQL to make it less of a query-only tool and more of a full-blown programming environment.

Oracle began adding advanced functions that allow SQL to do some very powerful things, like performing complete data analysis, tasks that used to require a PL/SQL program.

However, these advanced analytics are not for everyone. Trying to do too much in SQL can make your SQL hard to understand and maintain, and in some cases, the execution plans are horrible, far worse than using "vanilla" SQL inside PL/SQL.

In general, there are cases where using SQL analytics will not help achieve optimal performance. Some analytics are helpful as they can do several things with only one pass through a table.

Although SQL analytics is very useful, a major point of this chapter is to not over-extend the use of SQL to solve complex programming problems. In order to achieve the fastest possible performance, super-complex SQL statements can be re-written into smaller pieces, as explained earlier in the discussion of the *with* clause.

Oracle has many helpful built-in SQL functions, and it's possible to create custom built-in functions, making SQL infinitely extensible. This chapter will cover the basics of these functions and will provide several examples demonstrating the use within a working SQL environment.

Creating Custom SQL Extensions

As previously noted, SQL is infinitely extensible, and if you cannot find a BIF that suits your needs, you can create your own custom SQL function. Once compiled, it becomes a part of your SQL dialect.

Building functions directly into your SQL language has many important features:

- **Tight Integration**: Because you can create custom analytic functions, they are tightly-coupled with Oracle, making it easy to maintain complex code.

- **No Code Hunts**: Because the functions are part-and-parcel of the SQL, there is no need to go on a code hunt to locate a function.

- **Easy Changes:** Because the function is in the data dictionary, one quick change to the function and all SQL will immediately adopt the new behavior, avoiding expensive code changes.

For example, assume that there is an application that computes sales tax on book purchases five million times each day.

We can create a custom SQL built-in function in a PL/SQL function named *plus_tax* that accepts a book price and returns the price plus 7% tax.

Below is the code to create a custom SQL BIF. Note that the *deterministic* clause is required for a SQL BIF. This is necessary to tell the database that the function will always return the same output value when given the same input value.

```
create or replace function
  plus_tax(p_book_retail_price number)
return number deterministic
as
  price_plus_tax number(5,2);
begin
  -- tax is set at 7%
  price_plus_tax := p_book_retail_price +  p_book_retail_price*.07;

  return price_plus_tax;
end;
/
```

Now that we have created this function, it becomes a part of your SQL dialect and it can be used right inside your SQL, like this example:

```
select
   price,
   plus_tax(price),
   price + plus_tax(price) total_amount
from
   sales_table;
```

So, let's assume that the tax rate changes from 7% to 8%. In a traditional system, the procedural code would have to be located and the program re-compiled and unit tested. But because it's an integrated part of SQL, simply change the *plus_tax* PL/SQL function, and viola, the code changes are complete.

Now, with an understanding of the concept of SQL extensibility, let's take a closer look at creating our own SQL analytic functions with PL/SQL.

Extending SQL with PL/SQL Functions

We can build PL/SQL functions that can become integrated with SQL, thereby extending SQL to do whatever we desire.

A function is a PL/SQL named block that returns a value. It is commonly used to convert or assign values. Whereas a procedure is executed, a function is called, as in the example below:

```
begin
  …
  get_area(10,20,n_area);
  n_area := calc_area(10,20);
  …
end;
```

In the code fragment above, the area is calculated by a procedure named *get_area* and a function names *calc_area*. The procedure was passed three values and it copied the calculated area into the *n_area* variable when the procedure exited.

The next line uses a function that is passed two values, calculates the area, and returns that value, which is assigned to the *n_area* variable. Notice that the function is used directly in the assignment operation. A function is defined in the format below.

```
create or replace function
   <Name>
   (<variable list>)
return
   <datatype>
as (or is)
  local variable declaration
begin
  code section
exceptions
end;
```

This is similar to the procedure definition except that it uses the return definition. A function returns a datatype, not a variable.

```
create or replace function
   calc_area
   (n_length in number,
    n_width  in number)
  return number
as
begin
  return n_length*n_width;
end;/

Function created.
```

Above the function *calc_area* is defined so that it returns a number. In the function body there must be a *return* statement defining what is returned. In the example above, the *return* statement is in line 4.

A function name can be very descriptive with up to 32 characters and the function is always created in the schema of the user that creates the function. As with the procedure, a function can declare any number of values in the declaration section, limited only by the usability of the function.

However, unlike a procedure, a function cannot be passed variables in mode *out* or *inout*. A function can only return a datatype. If a function is defined with an *out* or *inout* variable, the function will compile but will raise an exception when executed.

```
ORA-06572: Function <name> has out arguments
```

An example used earlier in the book converted a temperature in Fahrenheit to Celsius. This is a perfect example of a function, which takes a value and returns a number.

```
create or replace function
   f2c
(n_faren IN number)
  return number
as
  n_cel number := 0;
begin
  n_cel := (5/9)*(n_faren -32);
  return n_cel;
end;
/
```

In this example, the function *f2c* takes a number in mode *in*, calculates the values in Celsius and returns the Celsius value.

Now, that we see how SQL can be extended, let's review some of the hundreds of built-in SQL functions, and start with some basic mathematic functions.

Mathematic Functions in SQL

Oracle has many functions that can be used to transform data. The following example will explore the *sin, cos,* and *tan* trigonometric functions. Take for example the following query:

```
select
   sin(4),
   cos(4),
   tan(4)
from
   dual;
```

```
SIN(4) COS(4) TAN(4)
------ ------ ------
-.7568 -.6536 1.1578
```

With this expression, the sine, cosine and the tangent for an angle of four radians is returned.

For these trigonometric functions, both *binary_double* and *number* data types are supported. If the argument is *binary_float*, the expression will be converted to *binary_double*. It is important to remember that mathematic functions perform much faster with a *binary_double* data type rather than the *number* data type, as shown below:

```
set timing on

declare
   x number := 1;
begin
   for i in 1 .. 1000000
   loop
      x := sin(x);
   end loop;
end;
/
```

```
PL/SQL procedure successfully completed.
```

```
Elapsed: 00:00:25.58
```

```
set timing on
declare
   x binary_double := 1d;
begin
   for i in 1 .. 1000000
   loop
      x := sin(x);
   end loop;
end;
/
```

```
PL/SQL procedure successfully completed.
```

```
Elapsed: 00:00:00.76
```

Binary Functions in SQL

Oracle has handy binary functions that can be used when dealing with binary data types. Two of the most common are the *bin_to_num* and *bitand* functions.

The *bin_to_num* function converts a binary list of 0 and 1 to decimal integer. For example (1,1,0,1) is converted to $1*8+1*4+0*2+1$, or 13_{10}. The *bitand* function selects the bits that are sets in both arguments. For example 1101_2 & 1011_2 share 1001_2, which is 9_{10}. Look at the example below:

```
select
   bitand
   (
      bin_to_num(1,1,0,1),
      bin_to_num(1,0,1,1)
   )
from
   dual;
```

```
BITAND(BIN_TO_NUM(1,1,0,1),BIN_TO_NUM(1,0,1,1))
-----------------------------------------------
                                              9
```

Sign Functions

The *sign* function will return a -1, 0, or 1 based on the value of the data. For example, -10 will return a -1, while 10 will return a 1. The *abs* function returns the absolute value of the data. The following query demonstrates these functions:

```
select
   sign(-10), sign(0), sign(+10),
   abs(-10), abs(0), abs(-10)
from
   dual;
```

```
SIGN(-10)    SIGN(0)  SIGN(+10)    ABS(-10)     ABS(0)    ABS(-10)
---------- ---------- ---------- ---------- ---------- ----------
       -1          0          1         10          0         10
```

Note that each of these functions accept *number*, *binary_float* and *binary_double* data types.

Rounding and Truncating Functions

There are several functions that can be used to round and truncate data values. The *trunc* function removes any digits beyond the decimal point for both positive and negative values. Therefore, *trunc(-x)* has the same function as *-trunc(x)*.

The *round* function rounds a value to a specified number of decimal places.

The *floor(x)* function returns the highest integer that is not greater than x, while the *ceil(x)* does the opposite and returns the lowest integer that is not less than x. An example of these expressions in use is shown below:

```
select
   x.column_value x,
   round(x.column_value) "round(x)",
   trunc(x.column_value) "trunc(x)",
   floor(x.column_value) "floor(x)",
   ceil(x.column_value) "ceil(x)"
from
   table(sys.odcinumberlist(-9.9,-1.1,-0.5,0.5,1.1,9.9)) x;
```

X	ROUND(X)	TRUNC(X)	FLOOR(X)	CEIL(X)
-9.9	-10	-9	-10	-9
-1.1	-1	-1	-2	-1
-.5	-1	0	-1	0
.5	1	0	0	1
1.1	1	1	1	2
9.9	10	9	9	10

The *trunc* and *round* functions have the following syntax consisting of two arguments.

- trunc(column_name, decimals)
- round(column_name, decimals)

The first argument specifies the column name, and the second is an integer that specifies the number of decimal places the rounding or truncating will be enforced. For example, specifying *round(x, 2)* will round a value to the hundredth decimal place. The following query demonstrates both functions using several different decimal values:

```
select
   x.column_value x,
   round(x.column_value, -2) "round(x,-2)",
   trunc(x.column_value, -2) "trunc(x,-2)",
   round(x.column_value, 0)  "round(x)",
   trunc(x.column_value, 0)  "trunc(x)",
   round(x.column_value, 2)  "round(x,2)",
   trunc(x.column_value, 2)  "trunc(x,2)",
from
   table(sys.odcinumberlist(1234.4321,-9876.6789)) x;
```

X	ROUND(X,-2)	TRUNC(X,-2)	ROUND(X)	TRUNC(X)	ROUND(X,2)	TRUNC(X,2)
1200	1200	1200	1234	1234	1234.43	1234.43
-9900	-9800	-9800	-9877	-9876	-9876.68	-9876.67

Note that the *round* and *trunc* functions can also be used with *date* data types, as shown below:

```
select
   sysdate,
   round(sysdate),
   trunc(sysdate)
from
   dual;
```

```
SYSDATE              ROUND(SYSDATE)       TRUNC(SYSDATE)
-------------------- -------------------- --------------------
25.01.2008 21:08:26  26.01.2008 00:00:00  25.01.2008 00:00:00
```

It is important to note that *timestamp* is converted to *date* when using the *trunc* and *round* functions.

Both *trunc* and *round* accept a second argument to truncate or round to a specific period of time. MI truncates to the minute, HH to the hour, DD to the day, MM to the month, Q to the quarter, Y to the year and CC to the century. When rounding, MM rounds up from the 16th day and Q from the 16th day of the second month. IW is fairly useful as it truncates to Monday regardless of session parameters.

D is the first day of the week, which is Sunday when the territory is set to America. W is the week of the month and WW is the week of year. The following query demonstrates these different date options:

```
select
   d.column_value "d",
   fmt.column_value "fmt",
   round(d.column_value, fmt.column_value) "round(d,fmt)",
   trunc(d.column_value, fmt.column_value) "trunc(d,fmt)"
from
   table(sys.odcidatelist(timestamp '1994-08-18 12:30:30.00')) d,
   table
   (
      sys.odcivarchar2list
      (
         'MI', 'HH', 'DD', 'D', 'W', 'WW', 'IW',
         'MM', 'Q', 'Y', 'IY', 'CC'
      )
```

```
   ) fmt;
```

```
D                       FMT ROUND(D,FMT)         TRUNC(D,FMT)
----------------------- --- ------------------- -------------------
18.08.1994 12:30:30 MI  18.08.1994 12:31:00 18.08.1994 12:30:00
18.08.1994 12:30:30 HH  18.08.1994 13:00:00 18.08.1994 12:00:00
18.08.1994 12:30:30 DD  19.08.1994 00:00:00 18.08.1994 00:00:00
18.08.1994 12:30:30 D   21.08.1994 00:00:00 14.08.1994 00:00:00
18.08.1994 12:30:30 W   22.08.1994 00:00:00 15.08.1994 00:00:00
18.08.1994 12:30:30 WW  20.08.1994 00:00:00 13.08.1994 00:00:00
18.08.1994 12:30:30 IW  22.08.1994 00:00:00 15.08.1994 00:00:00
18.08.1994 12:30:30 MM  01.09.1994 00:00:00 01.08.1994 00:00:00
18.08.1994 12:30:30 Q   01.10.1994 00:00:00 01.07.1994 00:00:00
18.08.1994 12:30:30 Y   01.01.1995 00:00:00 01.01.1994 00:00:00
18.08.1994 12:30:30 IY  02.01.1995 00:00:00 03.01.1994 00:00:00
18.08.1994 12:30:30 CC  01.01.2001 00:00:00 01.01.1901 00:00:00
```

The following query demonstrates the trunc function using the date data type:

```
select
   trunc(date '2008-02-14','IW') IW,
   trunc(date '2008-02-14','W')  W,
   TRUNC(DATE '2008-02-14','WW') WW,
   TRUNC(DATE '2008-02-14','D')  D
from
   dual;
```

```
IW         W          WW         D
---------- ---------- ---------- ----------
Mon 11 Feb Fri 8 Feb  Tue 12 Feb Sun 10 Feb
```

- IW always truncates to Monday.
- W truncates to Friday (1st day of Feb, 2008).
- WW truncates to Tuesday (1st day of 2008).
- D truncates to Sunday (in America).

It is possible to use *trunc* to get the day of the week rather than using *to_number(to_char(d, 'D'))*.

```
select
   trunc(sysdate)-trunc(sysdate,'iw') "day"
from
   dual;
```

```
TRUNC(SYSDATE)-TRUNC(SYSDATE,'IW')
----------------------------------
                4
```

Creating Custom SQL Extensions

With this method, Monday is 0 and Sunday is 6. The main advantage of this technique is that it can be used in materialized views, function-based indexes, and session-independent views and procedures:

```
select
    column_value n,
    round(column_value*20)/20 "round(n)"
from
    table(sys.odcinumberlist(1.12, 2.53, 5.25));
```

```
         N    ROUND(N)
---------- -------------
      1.12        1.10
      2.53        2.55
      5.25        5.25
```

The value is multiplied by 20 before rounding. After rounding, the value is divided by 20. This functionally rounds at a five-hundredths granularity.

```
select
    column_value d,
    date '2000-01-01'+
        trunc((column_value - date '2000-01-01')*96)/96 "trunc(d)"
from
    table(sys.odcidatelist(
        timestamp '2009-02-21 05:25:45',
        timestamp '2009-02-25 06:31:30'
));
```

```
D                   TRUNC(D)
------------------- -------------------
2009-02-21 05:25:45 2009-02-21 05:15:00
2009-02-25 06:31:30 2009-02-25 06:30:00
```

The difference with an arbitrary date is multiplied by 96 to split the day in 96 periods of 15 minutes (24 hours times 4 quarters = 96 periods).

Some periods could be switched to default calendar periods by adding a period before the *trunc*:

```
select
    column_value d,
    to_char(trunc(add_months(column_value, 3), 'y'), '"fy"yy') "fy"
from
    table
    (
        sys.odcidatelist(
            date '2008-09-30',
```

```
        date '2008-12-21',
        date '2009-02-25'
    )
);
```

```
D          FY
---------- ----
2008-09-30 FY08
2008-12-21 FY09
2009-02-25 FY09
```

The fiscal year starts in October, three months before the calendar year. This three-month period is added before truncating the date.

SQL Modulo Functions

Both the *mod* and *remainder* functions return the remainder of x divided by y. For example, consider this SQL:

```
select
    x.column_value                              x,
    y.column_value                              y,
    mod(x.column_value, y.column_value)         "mod(x,y)",
    remainder(x.column_value, y.column_value) "remainder(x,y)"
from
    table(sys.odcinumberlist(-30,-20,20,30)) x,
    table(sys.odcinumberlist(-7,7))           y;
```

```
         X          Y MOD(X,Y) REMAINDER(X,Y)
---------- ---------- ---------- --------------
       -30         -7         -2             -2
       -30          7         -2             -2
       -20         -7         -6              1
       -20          7         -6              1
        20         -7          6             -1
        20          7          6             -1
        30         -7          2              2
        30          7          2              2
```

The *mod* and *remainder* functions will both return the same absolute remainder value, only in two different forms. This difference stems from the formulas used by these functions to calculate the remainder. The *mod* function uses the *floor* function in its formula, while *remainder* used *round*.

The key difference between these functions is the way in which the remainder is expressed. Because of the built-in *floor* function, *mod* will always express the

---

remainder relative to the next lowest integer.   For example, the function *mod*(20,7) = 3 6/7 and will return a 6 as the remainder.

The *remainder* function on the other hand will report the remainder relative to the closest whole integer. Using the same values as before, *remainder*(20,7) will report 3 6/7 as having a remainder of -1. Because 3.857 is closer to 4 than 3, the remainder is expressed as a negative value relative to 4. When dealing with negative numbers, the sign of the x argument will determine the sign of the modulo and the remainder.

A special case exists for modulo functions containing a 0. In Perl or in C, modulo 0 is illegal. This is not however the case in SQL. *remainder* returns an error for modulo 0 but *mod* simply returns the first argument.

```
select
   mod(5, 0)
from
   dual;
```

```
  MOD(5,0)
----------
         5
```

SQL Functions to Search and Modify Strings

The *substr* function extracts a substring from a string using the following syntax:

```
substr(string, starting_position, length)
```

In the following query, *substr* returns a substring of the employee name, starting at the beginning of the string, which is position 1. The third parameter is the maximum length; by default, the rest of the string is returned.

```
select
   ename,
   substr(ename, 1, 2)
from
   emp;
```

```
ENAME       SU
----------  --
SMITH       SM
ALLEN       AL
WARD        WA
JONES       JO
```

```
MARTIN    MA
BLAKE     BL
CLARK     CL
SCOTT     SC
KING      KI
TURNER    TU
ADAMS     AD
JAMES     JA
FORD      FO
MILLER    MI
```

In a similar fashion, the *instr* function returns the location of a substring from within a string using the following syntax:

```
instr( string, substring, starting_position, occurrence of string)
```

The following example returns the second occurrence of substring 'ra' from string 'Advanced Oracle SQL Programming,' starting at the beginning (position 1).

```
select
   instr
   (
      'Advanced Oracle SQL Programming',
      'ra',1,2) RA
from
   dual;
```

```
  RA
----------
        25
```

We can also use *substr* and *instr* together. This example extracts the second word from the string 'Advanced Oracle SQL Programming' using both the *substr* and *instr* functions.

Note that this SQL query defines the second word as the substring starting right after the first space. The length of the word is equal to the difference between the position of the first space and the position of the second space.

```
select
   substr
   (column_value,instr(column_value ' ')+1,
      instr(column_value,' ',1,2)-
      instr(column_value,' ')-1) "word2"
from
```

```
      table(sys.odcivarchar2list('Advanced Oracle SQL Programming'));

WORD2
----------
Oracle
```

There are several functions that can change the length of Strings. The *lpad* and *rpad* functions can be used to pad a string, adding characters to either side.

By default, the padding character is a space, but any character can be used. The *lpad* function adds the defined character to the left of the string and *rpad* does the same to the right. In order to get a center effect, the string should can be padded to 10 + half of the length of the string, and then padded to 20, as shown below:

```
select
   lpad(dname, 20, '.') left,
   rpad(dname, 20, '.') right,
   rpad(lpad(dname, 10+length(dname)/2, '.'), 20, '.') middle
from
   dept;


LEFT                 RIGHT                MIDDLE
-------------------- -------------------- --------------------
..........ACCOUNTING ACCOUNTING.......... .....ACCOUNTING.....
...........RESEARCH  RESEARCH............ ......RESEARCH......
..............SALES  SALES............... .......SALES........
..........OPERATIONS OPERATIONS.......... .....OPERATIONS.....
```

The opposite of the pad functions are the trim functions. These can be used to remove characters from the leading and trailing edges of a string. There are three main trim functions: *trim*, *ltrim* and *rtrim*. The *trim* function defaults to trimming the leading and trailing spaces from a string, but other characters can be selected as well. Below is an example of the three *trim* functions in use. Note that the function is set to remove the 's' character:

```
select
   ename,
   trim(leading  's' from ename),
   trim(trailing 's' from ename),
   trim(both     's' from ename)
from
   emp
where
   ename like '%S%';


ENAME      TRIM(LEADI TRIM(TRAIL TRIM(BOTH'
---------- ---------- ---------- ----------
```

```
SMITH      MITH        SMITH      MITH
JONES      JONES       JONE       JONE
SCOTT      COTT        SCOTT      COTT
ADAMS      ADAMS       ADAM       ADAM
JAMES      JAMES       JAME       JAME
```

While the *trim* function does not support the removal of more than one character, *ltrim* and *rtrim* support removing multiple characters from a string. For example, these functions can be used to remove leading or trailing consonants from a string using a query like one below. Note that the trim stops at the first vowel:

```
select
    ename,
    ltrim(ename, 'BCDFGHJKLMNPQRSTVWXZ'),
    rtrim(ename, 'BCDFGHJKLMNPQRSTVWXZ')
from
    emp
where
    rownum < 6;
```

```
ENAME      LTRIM(ENAM RTRIM(ENAM
---------- ---------- ----------
SMITH      ITH        SMI
ALLEN      ALLEN      ALLE
WARD       ARD        WA
JONES      ONES       JONE
MARTIN     ARTIN      MARTI
```

```
select
    *
from
    table(sys.odcivarchar2list('123','ABC456','789GHI','JKL'))
where
    ltrim(column_value,'0123456789') is null;
```

```
COL
---
123
```

Note that the *ltrim* functions returns an empty string where the string contains only digits.

There are two functions that are helpful for replacing characters or groups of characters from a string. The *translate* function substitutes one character for another, and the *replace* function substitutes a string for another string, as shown below:

```
select
    loc,
```

```
   replace(loc,'YORK','ORLEANS'),
   translate(loc,'AOIEY ','@013')
from
   dept;
```

```
LOC             REPLACE(LOC,'YO  TRANSLATE(LOC
-------------   ---------------  -------------
NEW YORK        NEW ORLEANS      N3W0RK
DALLAS          DALLAS           D@LL@S
CHICAGO         CHICAGO          CH1C@G0
BOSTON          BOSTON           B0ST0N
```

The string 'YORK' is searched and replaced by the string 'ORLEANS'. If the last argument is omitted, the searched string is omitted as well, deleting the string.

In the above example, *translate* substitutes the 'A', 'O', 'E', 'I', 'Y' and ' ' characters with '@', '0', '3', '1', *null* and *null*, respectively. When the third argument is shorter than the second, the characters from the first string that have no correspondence to the second string are removed. The third argument is not optional and if it is *null*, *translate* returns *null*.

There are several functions that can be used to change the case of a string. These functions are *upper*, *lower* and *initcap*. The *upper* function returns everything in uppercase, *lower* in lowercase and *initcap* capitalizes the first letter of each word and sets the other letters to lowercase.

```
select
   upper(column_value),
   lower(column_value),
   initcap(column_value)
from
   table(sys.odcivarchar2list('JoHn sMiTh'));
```

```
UPPER(COLU  LOWER(COLU  INITCAP(CO
----------  ----------  ----------
JOHN SMITH  john smith  John Smith
```

Regular Expression Functions

Oracle 10g first introduced regular expression functions in SQL with the functions *regexp_substr*, *regexp_replace*, *regexp_instr* and *regexp_like*. Oracle 11g has extended the set of available expressions by adding *regexp_count*.

```
select
   ename,
   regexp_substr(ename,'dam')      substr,
```

```
    regexp_instr(ename, 't')          instr,
    regexp_replace(ename,'AM','@')     replace,
    regexp_count(ename, 'A')           count
from
    emp
where
    regexp_like(ename,'S');
```

ENAME	SUBSTR	INSTR	REPLACE	COUNT
SMITH		4	SMITH	0
JONES		0	JONES	0
SCOTT		4	SCOTT	0
ADAMS	DAM	0	AD@S	2
JAMES		0	J@ES	1

The *regexp_substr* function allows you to search a string for a regular expression, and then returns the expression if available. *regexp_instr* returns the position of the defined substring, in this example the first 'T', and *regexp_replace* replaces a substring with an expression. Notice that in the above example the 'AM' string has been replaced with an "@." The *regexp_count* function counts the occurrences of an expression, in this case an "A". The *regexp_like* function returns all strings that contain a defined pattern, in this case an "S."

The *regexp_substr* function uses the following syntax to search for a pattern in a substring.

```
regexp_substr (string, pattern, position, occurrence)
```

Regular expressions support the use of *posix* operators, like [[:alnum:]] and [[:alpha:]]. '[[:alpha:]]' is the *posix* regular expression that matches any letter, as shown in the example above. The second set of consecutive word characters is returned.

There are several operators that can be used within the pattern operator to help filter results:

- '.' returns any character except NULL.

- '^' matches the first character of a substring.

- '$' matches the last character of a substring.

- '+' specifies that the number of characters to be matched is one or more.

- '?' returns zero or one occurrence or a substring.

- '*' matches zero or more occurrences of a substring.

- {a} matches exactly *a* number of occurrences.

Creating Custom SQL Extensions

- {a,} matches *a* or more occurrences.

- {a,b} matches at least *a* number of occurrences but no more than *b*.

The third argument is the starting position. This argument defaults to 1, meaning the pattern will be searched from the beginning of the substring.

The fourth argument in 11g represents the occurrence of the substring.

Below is an example of the *regexp_substr* function in use. Notice the use of the '[[:alpha:]]+' expression. The starting position is set to 1, and the query will search for the second occurrence of one or more alphabetic characters:

```
select
    regexp_substr('Advanced Oracle SQL Programming','[[:alpha:]]+',1,2)
from
    dual;


REGEXP
------
Oracle
```

```
select
    regexp_substr('Advanced Oracle SQL Programming','\w+',1,2)
from
    dual;


REGEXP
------
Oracle
```

Oracle 10gR2 introduced Perl-influenced regular expressions. '\w' represents any letter, number and the underscore. Unfortunately, in comparison to the old-style approach with *instr* and *substr*, the 10g regular expressions perform poorly, as shown in the query below:

```
set timing on

declare
    x varchar2(40);
begin
    for i in 1..10000000 loop
        x := 'Advanced Oracle SQL Programming';
        x := substr(x,
            instr(x, ' ')+1,
            instr(x, ' ', 1,2)-instr(x, ' ')-1);
    end loop;
end;
```

```
/

PL/SQL procedure successfully completed.

Elapsed: 00:00:20.40

set timing on

declare
   x varchar2(40);
begin
   for i in 1..10000000 loop
      X := 'Advanced Oracle SQL Programming';
      x := regexp_substr(x,'\w+',1,2);
   end loop;
end;
/

PL/SQL procedure successfully completed.

Elapsed: 00:02:10.82
```

The *replace* function replaces all occurrences of a string. *regexp_replace* has the same behavior by default, but when the fifth parameter, *occurrence*, is set to a value greater than zero, the substitution is not global.

```
select
   regexp_replace
   ('Advanced Oracle SQL Programming',
      '([[:alpha:]]+)[[:space:]]([[:alpha:]]+)',
      '\2: \1',1,1)
from
   dual;

REGEXP_REPLACE('ADVANCEDORACLESQ
--------------------------------
Oracle: Advanced SQL Programming
```

The search pattern contains a group of one or more alphabetic characters, followed by a space, then followed by a group of one or more alphabetic characters. This pattern is present more than once in the string, but only the first occurrence is affected. The replace pattern contains a reference to the second word, followed by a column and a space, followed by the first string.

```
select
   regexp_substr
   ('Advanced Oracle SQL Programming','(\w).*?\1',1,1,'i')
from
   dual;

REGE
----
Adva
```

The search pattern contains any alphabetic character followed by a non-greedy number of characters followed by the same character as in the group. The search starts at the character one and looks for the first match of the pattern. The modifier 'i' indicates a case insensitive search.

Non-greedy expressions appeared in 10gR2. The difference between a non-greedy expression like '.*?', '.+?', '.??', '.{2}?', '.{3,5}?' or '.{6,}?' and a greedy expression like '.*', '.+', '.?', '.{2}', '.{3,5}' or '.{6,}' is that the non-greedy searches for the smallest possible string and the greedy for the largest possible string:

```
select
   regexp_substr('Oracle','.{2,4}?') non_greedy,
   regexp_substr('Oracle','.{2,4}')  greedy
from
   dual;
```

```
NON_GREEDY GREEDY
---------- ------
Or         Orac
```

Both patterns select from two to four characters. In this case, it could be 'Or', 'Ora' or 'Orac'. The non-greedy pattern returns two characters, and the greedy returns four.

The function *regexp_substr* matches *ename* to a pattern and returns the matched string. Here are some examples.

- '^K' checks if the name starts with 'K.'

- 'T$' checks if it ends with 'T.'

- '^[ABC]' checks if it starts with A, B or C.

- '^.?M' checks if the string start with one or zero characters followed by M, which means the first or second character is a 'M.'

- '(RD|ES)$' checks if it ends with either ES or RD.

- '(..R) {2}$' checks if the pattern "one character + one character + the letter R" is found twice consecutively.

- '^.{4}[A-E]' checks if the fifth character (the character following 4 characters at the beginning of the string) is not in the range A-E.

```
SELECT
   ENAME,
   REGEXP_SUBSTR(ENAME,'^K') "^K",
   REGEXP_SUBSTR(ENAME,'T$') "T$",
   REGEXP_SUBSTR(ENAME,'^[ABC]') "^[ABC]",
   REGEXP_SUBSTR(ENAME,'^.?M') "^.?M",
```

```
   REGEXP_SUBSTR(ENAME,'(RD|ES)$') "(RD|ES)$",
   REGEXP_SUBSTR(ENAME,'(..R){2}') "(..R){2}",
   REGEXP_SUBSTR(ENAME,'^.{4}[^A-E]') "^.{4}[^A-E]"
FROM
   EMP;


ENAME      ^K T$ ^[ABC] ^.?M (RD|ES)$ (..R){2} ^.{4}[^A-E
---------- -- -- ------ ---- -------- -------- ----------
SMITH                    SM                     SMITH
ALLEN            A                              ALLEN
WARD                          RD
JONES                    ES                     JONES
MARTIN                   M                      MARTI
BLAKE         B
CLARK            C                              CLARK
SCOTT      T                                    SCOTT
KING       K
TURNER                                 TURNER
ADAMS            A                              ADAMS
JAMES                         ES                JAMES
FORD                          RD
MILLER                   M
```

Note that *king* is not matched because the fifth character is not a character different from A-E. To test a string less than five characters, the pattern ^.{1,4}$ could be used.

SQL Conversion Functions

Implicit conversion exists between numeric, date-time and character data types.

The *length* function returns the number of bytes in a character string. For example, the length function will return '3' for number 999. The *sinh* function will return the hyperbolic sin of an argument. In the following example, the *sinh* function converts string '000' to a number.

The *last_day* function will return the last day of the month based upon the *date* value. In the following example, the last day of month converts string '01-FEB-2008' to a the date '29-FEB-08.'

```
select
   length(999),
   sinh('000'),
   last_day('01-feb-2008')
from
   dual;


LENGTH(999) SINH('000') LAST_DAY(
----------- ----------- ---------
```

A number can be converted to a character using the *chr* and *ascii* functions.

The *chr* function converts a number to the corresponding ASCII character and the *ascii* function converts a character to its corresponding ASCII value:

```
select
    chr(65),
    ascii('z')
from
    dual;


C ASCII('Z')
- ----------
A         90
```

The *hextoraw* function converts a hexadecimal string to a *raw* data type. The *hextoraw* function is useful when comparing a raw value from a table or a function to a literal value. The *dump* function provides octal (8), decimal (10), hexadecimal (16) or character (17) dump.

Look at the following example. The type 23 represents the *raw* data type. The length is 6 bytes. The function *vsize* returns the length in bytes:

```
select
    dump
    (hextoraw('4f5241434c45'),17)
dump,vsize
    (hextoraw('4f5241434c45')) vsize
from
    dual;


DUMP                          VSIZE
------------------------      -----
Typ=23 Len=6: O,R,A,C,L,E      6
```

The *rawtohex* function does the opposite and converts raw data to a string containing hexadecimals. The *sys_guid* function generates 32 bytes of raw data. The globally unique identifier is transformed to a hexadecimal string by *rawtohex* and then to an integer by *to_number*:

```
select
    to_number
    (rawtohex(sys_guid()),'XXXXXXXXXXXXXXXXXXXXXXXXXXXXXXXX')
from
```

```
   dual;
```

```
TO_NUMBER(RAWTOHEX(SYS_GUID()),'XXXXXXXXXXXXXXXXXXXXXXXXXXXXXXXX')
-----------------------------------------------------------------
                         94677074495605736132992199838641691196
```

The *extract* function with a date data type will return numeric values for the year, month or the day. It is not possible to extract the time out of the date data type with this function:

```
select
   sysdate,
   extract(year  from sysdate) yyyy,
   extract(month from sysdate) mm,
   extract(day   from sysdate) dd
from
   dual;
```

```
SYSDATE      YYYY  MM  DD
----------  -----  --- ---
2008-02-08   2008   2   8
```

The *extract* function with a timestamp returns numeric values for the year, the month, the day and also the hour, the minute and the second. The second may contain fractions of a second. The hour and minute are extracted at GMT+00:00 and the offset, if applicable, is retrieved from the time zone. The region and abbreviation are returned as strings:

```
select
   current_timestamp,
   extract(hour            from current_timestamp) hh,
   extract(minute          from current_timestamp) mi,
   extract(second          from current_timestamp) ss,
   extract(timezone_hour   from current_timestamp) tzh,
   extract(timezone_minute from current_timestamp) tzm,
   extract(timezone_region from current_timestamp) tzr,
   extract(timezone_abbr   from current_timestamp) tza
from
   dual;
```

```
CURRENT_TIMESTAMP              HH  MI         SS TZH TZM TZR            TZA
----------------------------  --- --- ---------- --- --- ------------- ---
2008-02-08 13:25:13 EUROPE/ZURICH 12  25  13.103363   1   0 Europe/Zurich CET
```

The *extract* function with a year-to-month interval returns numeric values for the year or the month:

```
with t as
```

```
(select(current_timestamp - timestamp '1970-01-01 00:00:00 +00:00')
        year(2) to month y2m
  from
    dual
)
select
  y2m,
  extract(year from y2m) yyyy,
  extract(month from y2m) mm
from
  t;
```

```
Y2M     YYYY  MM
------  ----- ---
+38-01    38   1
```

Using *extract* with a day-to-second interval returns numeric values for the day, hour, minute and second. The interval between January 1st, 1970 and the current time is used to calculate a number of seconds that represents the UNIX time.

```
with t as
(
  select
    (current_timestamp - timestamp '1970-01-01 00:00:00 +00:00')
        day(6) to second(6) d2s
  from
    dual
)
select
  d2s,
  86400*extract(day from d2s) +
  3600*extract(hour from d2s) +
  60*extract(minute from d2s) +
  extract(second from d2s)
    unixtime
from
  t;
```

```
D2S                          UNIXTIME
----------------------- ------------------
+013917 12:25:13.247043  1202473513.247043
```

The function *numtodsinterval* converts a number of *day, hour, minute* or *second* to a day-to-second interval. Adding a number of seconds to January 1st, 1970 is useful for converting UNIX timestamps to Oracle timestamps.

The function *numtoyminterval* returns an interval from a number of *year* or *month*:

```
select
  (timestamp '1970-01-01 00:00:00 +00:00'+
```

```
    numtodsinterval(1202473513.247043,'second')
    ) at time zone sessiontimezone timestamp
from
    dual;
```

```
TIMESTAMP
-----------------------------------------
2008-02-08 13:25:13.247043 Europe/Zurich
```

The *to_dsinterval* and *to_yminterval* functions create an interval from a string. The string format cannot be changed. The two possible notations are listed. A large number of possible formats for dates and numbers exist.

```
select
    to_dsinterval('+1 2:3:4.5')    d2s_sql,
    to_dsinterval('p1dt2h3m4.5s')  d2s_iso,
    to_yminterval('1-2')           y2m_sql,
    to_yminterval('p1y2m')         y2m_iso
from
    dual;
```

```
D2S_SQL          D2S_ISO          Y2M_SQL Y2M_ISO
---------------- ---------------- ------- -------
+01 02:03:04.50  +01 02:03:04.50  +01-02  +01-02
```

The *to_char* function converts a date or a timestamp to a string. Note the FM formatter: by default, words like Day or Month are padded. In English, the longest month is September, so all months will be right-padded with spaces to nine characters.

The numeric values are left-padded with zero. FM provides a nicer output by removing extra spaces and leading zeroes. For hours, however, 05:01:02 looks better than 5:1:2. So the second FM formatting switches back to the default padding behavior. Note the capitalization of the format elements: Day returns Friday, *day* returns *friday* and day returns Friday.

```
select
    to_char
    (current_timestamp,'FMDay ddth Month, YYYY B.C., FMHH:MI:SSXFF AM
TZH:TZM') today
from
    dual;
```

```
TODAY
-----------------------------------------------------------
Friday 1st February, 2008 A.D., 05:01:02.560225 PM +01:00
```

Creating Custom SQL Extensions   **743**

Also note the difference between HH and HH24. HH is often used together with AM to display the time in 12 hours format (from 1 to 12), and HH24 is the 24 hours format (from 0 to 23).

A fancy option to observe is the SP suffix, which spells the element. Unfortunately, it is not possible to choose a language other than English. The TH suffix is used for ordinal numbers.

```
select
    to_char
    (
        to_timestamp
        (
            to_char
            (
                42e-9
            ),
            '.ff9'
        ),
        'ff9sp ff9spth'
    ) "42"
from
    dual;
```

```
42
---------------------
forty-two forty-second
```

The number is expressed in nanoseconds (10^{-9} seconds) and spelled as a cardinal and an ordinal number.

The inverse functions to_date, to_timestamp and *to_timestamp_tz* convert a string to a date, a timestamp, and a timestamp with time zone:

```
SELECT

to_date('1-viii-1291 ad','dd-rm-yyyy bc') "date",
    to_timestamp('3000000 20000 100000000','j sssss ff') "timestamp",
    to_timestamp_tz('4 02','dd hh24') "timestamp_tz"
from
    dual;
```

```
DATE       TIMESTAMP                     TIMESTAMP_TZ
---------- ----------------------------- -----------------------------
1291-08-01 3501-08-15 05:33:20.100000000 2008-02-04 02:00 EUROPE/ZURICH
```

The *rm* function is a Roman month from I to XII, J is the Julian day, where day 1 is January 1st, 4712 BC, day 60 is March 1st, 4712 BC. Day 1 is the first supported day of the Oracle Calendar and day 5373484 is the last supported day of the Oracle Calendar, December 31st, 9999 AD.

The *sssss* argument is the number of seconds since midnight (0-86399). FF is a fraction of seconds. It is not mandatory to specify all fields. The third expression returns the 4th of the current month, at 02:00:00.00 at session time zone.

```
select
    to_date('2 FEB. 08','DD-MONTH-RRRR')   dd_month_rr,
    to_date('2-JAN-1994','DD/MM/YY')       dd_mm_yy,
    to_date('06-06-2007', 'FXDD-MM-YYYY')  fxdd_mm_yyyy,
    to_date('1/1/08','FXFMDD/MM/RR')       fxfmdd_mm_rr
from
    dual;
```

```
DD_MONTH_RR DD_MM_YY   FXDD_MM_YY FXFMDD_MM_RR
----------- ---------- ---------- ------------
2008-02-02  1994-01-02 2007-06-06 2008-01-01
```

By default, Oracle tolerates fairly different formats such as the number of spaces, the characters used as separators and the leading zeroes. RR and YY accept two digits years, where "99" represents 1999 with the RR mask and 2099 with the YY mask. RR has been used to fix the year 2000 issues at the end of the 20th century.

Until the year 2049, RR will return dates from 1950 to 2049. As of 2050, it will return dates from 2050 to 2149. FX is the strict format checker. The separator must be identical, the format of the day and month must include a leading zero when smaller than 10, and the year must be 4 characters long. It is a good practice to always enter the year with four digits, and using the default format DD-MON-RR is a not advisable as it introduces the year 2050 bug.

```
select
    to_date('19-apr-03') date_of_birth,
    to_date('18-apr-68') date_of_retirement,
    (to_date('18-apr-68')-to_date('19-apr-03')) year to month
    age_of_retirement
from
    dual;
```

```
DATE_OF_B DATE_OF_R AGE_OF
--------- --------- ------
19-APR-03 18-APR-68 -35-00
```

The query above shows the date of birth and date of retirement and the difference between those. The age of -35 years is due to the missing century information, which is probably the next century issue after 2000.

The *to_char* function is used with numbers for various formatting and calculation tasks:

```
select
    to_char(column_value,'fms99,999.00$')   "fms99,999.00$",
    to_char(column_value,'l9g990d00mi')     "l9g990d00mi",
    to_char(column_value,'fmxxxxxx')        "fmxxxxxx",
    to_char(column_value,'rm')              "rm",
    to_char(column_value,'0.99eeee')        "0.99999eeee ",
    to_char(column_value,'9999v99')         "9999v99"
from
    table(sys.odcinumberlist(-1.234, 1899, 1234*5678));
```

```
FMS99,999.0 L9G990D00MI    FMXXXX RM          0.99999EEE 9999V99
----------- -------------- ------ ----------- ---------- -------
-$1.23            SFr.1.23- ###### ########## -1.23E+00     -123
+$1,899.00  SFr.1'899.00   76B        MDCCCXCIX  1.90E+03  189900
########### ############## 6AE9BC ########## 7.01E+06 #######
```

By default, a number is left padded up to the maximum length. The maximum length of '99' is 3, as it may contain numbers from -99 to 99. The FM formatter removes the leading spaces. '$', ',' and '.' represent the dollar currency symbol, the comma thousand separator and the decimal point. 'L', 'G' and 'D' is the locale equivalency to '$', ',' and '.'. X is a hexadecimal digit from 0 to F.

As we know, the *rm* is the Roman representation of integers from 1 to 3999. Its maximum length of 15 is reached by MMMDCCCLXXXVIII. EEEE forces scientific notation. V is an invisible dot. Any number longer than the output pattern is returned as a chain of hashes.

The inverse functions are *to_number*, *to_binary_float* and *to_binary_double*:

```
select
    to_number('2008+','9999s') "9999s",
    to_binary_float('inf') "inf",
    to_binary_double('9.876543e+210','9.999999eeee') "9.99999eeee"
from
    dual;
```

```
     9999S     Inf 9.99999EEEE
---------- ---------- -----------
      2008     Inf  9.877E+210
```

The S is a trailing positive or negative sign. The *inf* function is the positive infinity when using *binary_float* or *binary_double*. NaN is an undefined number (Not A Number), like SQRT(-1). Note the infinity symbol that represents the infinity for a number datatype is '~'. It is, however, not possible to convert a string to positive infinity with *to_number*.

Numbers very close to 1E126 are displayed with '~'.

```
select
   to_char(9.9999999999999999999999999999999999999e125)
from
   dual;
```

```
T
-
~
```

The functions *to_char, to_date, to_number, to_binary_double, to_binary_float, to_timestamp* and *to_timestamp_tz* all support a third parameter that can override the default locale behavior:

```
select
   to_char
   (
      -1e5/81,
      '9g999d99',
      'nls_numeric_characters='','''''''
   ) "9g999d99",
   to_number
   (
      '1,20sfr.',
      '999d991',
      'nls_currency=''sfr.'' nls_numeric_characters='',.'''
   ) "999d991",
   to_char
   (
      to_date('avril','month','nls_date_language=french'),
      'month',
      'nls_date_language=''latin uzbek'''
   ) "month"
from
   dual;
```

```
9G999D99    999D99L MONTH
--------- ---------- --------
-1'234,57      1.2 APREL
```

The formatting also depends on the territory; there is no *nls_date_territory* yet, which means the setting must be changed at the session level. It is not possible to have two functions within the same statements using different territories.

```
select
   to_char
   (
     sysdate,
     'dl'
   ) "dl",
   to_char
   (
     sysdate,
     'day=d'
   ) "d",
   value "nls_territory"
from
   nls_session_parameters
where
   parameter='nls_territory';
```

```
DL                           D             NLS_TERRITORY
---------------------------- ------------- -------------
wednesday, 20 february 2008  WEDNESDAY=6   BANGLADESH
```

Many parameters, like currencies or numeric characters, are derived from *nls_territory* when not explicitly set. Settings like 'DL' (long date, 10g), 'TS' (short time, 10g) or 'D' (day of week) depend on the territory.

It is possible to convert to large objects. The *to_blob* function converts raw data to blob and *to_clob* converts character data to *clob*:

```
select
   to_blob
   (hextoraw('42')) blob,
   to_clob
   ('42') clob
from
   dual;
```

```
BLOB CLOB
---- ----
42   42
```

Note that only the 11g SQL*Plus client can display blob.

The final conversion function is *cast*. The *cast* function enables conversion from any type. It is useful in statements like *create table as select* (CTAS) to specify the length and the data type of a column.

```
select
   cast
   (
```

```
      'inf'
      as
      binary_float
   ),
   cast
   (
      binary_double_nan
      as
      varchar2(3)
   ),
   cast
   (
      null
      as
      number(6,2)
   )
from
   dual;
```

```
CAST('INF'ASBINARY_FLOAT) CAS CAST(NULLASNUMBER(6,2))
------------------------ --- ----------------------
                        Inf Nan <NULL>
```

SQL NLS Functions

The *nls_upper*, *nls_lower* and *nls_initcap* functions use the setting *nls_sort* to define what is the uppercase of a specific character.

```
select
   nls_upper
   (
      'Ich weiß es nicht',
      'NLS_SORT=XSWISS'
   ),
   nls_initcap
   (
      'éléphant',
      'NLS_SORT=XFRENCH'
   )
from
   dual;
```

```
NLS_UPPER('ICHWEIß NLS_INIT
------------------ --------
ICH WEISZ ES NICHT Éléphant
```

The locale uppercase of a Swiss-German sentence and initial capitalization of a French word are returned. It is possible to modify an existing linguistic sort or add a new one using the Oracle Locale Builder graphical tool:

```
select
    *
from
    table
    (
        sys.odcivarchar2list
        (
            'privé',
            'priver',
            'privation'
        )
    )
order by
    nlssort(column_value,'nls_sort=xfrench');
```

```
COLUMN_VALUE
------------
privation
privé
priver
```

In French, the sort is accent insensitive:

```
create index
    ename_ci
on
    emp(nlssort(ename,'nls_sort=binary_ci'));
alter session
set
    nls_comp=linguistic
    nls_sort=binary_ci;
select
    empno,
    ename
from
    emp
where
    ename='scott';
```

```
    EMPNO ENAME
---------- ----------
     7788 SCOTT
-------------------------------------------------------------------------------
| Id | Operation                   | Name     | Rows | Bytes | Cost (%CPU)| Time     |
-------------------------------------------------------------------------------
|  0 | SELECT STATEMENT            |          |    1 |    37 |    2   (0)| 00:00:01 |
|  1 |  TABLE ACCESS BY INDEX ROWID| EMP      |    1 |    37 |    2   (0)| 00:00:01 |
|* 2 |   INDEX RANGE SCAN          | ENAME_CI |    1 |       |    1   (0)| 00:00:01 |
-------------------------------------------------------------------------------

Predicate Information (identified by operation id):
---------------------------------------------------

   2 - access(NLSSORT("ENAME",'nls_sort=''BINARY_CI''')=HEXTORAW('73636F747400'))
```

The comparison is done linguistically and the sort is binary case insensitive (10g). The function-based index is scanned to find the appropriate rows that match the sorting pattern.

National Character Set and SQL Tuning

Unicode and multi-byte functions are available to do conversions and use different length semantics. As *instr*, *length* and *substr* work best with single-byte character sets, a multi-byte character may use bytes or char semantics.

```
select
   lengthb(unistr('x')) lengthb,
   lengthc(unistr('x')) lengthc
from
   dual;


  LENGTHB    LENGTHC
---------- ----------
         2          1
```

The *unistr* function returns a Unicode string and is the inverse function of *asciistr*. The *lengthb* function returns the length in bytes, where *lengthc* returns the length in characters. The *length2* and *length4* are for fixed width character sets. *length*, *instr* and *substr* also have Unicode variations *instrb*, *instrc*, *instr2*, *instr4* and *substrb*, *substrc*, *substr2* and *substr4*.

```
select
   convert(upper('chryséléphantin'),'us7ascii')
from
   dual;

CONVERT(UPPER('
---------------
CHRYSELEPHANTIN
```

The string is converted to a non-accentuated string.

The *nchr* function is similar to *chr*, but it returns a national character (*nchar*). The *to_char* and *to_nchar* functions convert characters to and from the national character set.

The *to_nclob* function converts LOB or strings to Unicode large objects.

Logical Functions with True or False Values

There is no support for the Boolean data type in Oracle. Nevertheless, Oracle has implemented a few functions to perform logical operations.

The *case* function uses if/then/else logic to compare data values. *case* can also be used to change the presentation of data without manipulating raw table data. For example, The *case* function can be used with an inventory table to return "on-hand" or "reorder" based upon a desired stock levels, as demonstrated below:

```
select
   product,
'stock' = case
when qty > 20
then 'on-hand'
else 're-order'
end from inv;
```

```
PRODUCT          Stock
----------   ----------
Pencil           On-hand
Desk             On-hand
Pen              re-order
Mouse            On-hand
```

The *decode* function is used for checking equivalency between two arguments, the first and second in the query below. The *greatest* function returns the greatest of the arguments and *least* the returns smallest. Here is an example of *decode* and *case* used together:

```
select
   ename,
   sal,
   decode
   (
      greatest(sal,2800),
      sal,
      decode
      (
         job,
         'PRESIDENT',
         TO_NUMBER(NULL),
         1
      )
   ) decode,
   case
      when sal>=2800 and job!='PRESIDENT'
      then 1
```

```
    end case
from
    emp;
```

```
ENAME           SAL    DECODE        CASE
----------  ----------  ----------  ----------
SMITH           800
ALLEN          1600
WARD           1250
JONES          2975        1            1
MARTIN         1250
BLAKE          2850        1            1
CLARK          2450
SCOTT          3000        1            1
KING           5000
TURNER         1500
ADAMS          1100
JAMES           950
FORD           3000        1            1
MILLER         1300
```

Nevertheless, *case* has an additional interesting property regarding indexing. The *case* SQL expression could be used in a function-based index; therefore, any condition could be indexed.

```
create index
    clerk_or_lowsal
on
    emp
    (
        case when job='CLERK' or sal<1260 then 1 end
    );
select
    ename,
    job,
    sal
from
    emp
where
    case when job='CLERK' or sal<1260 then 1 end = 1;
```

```
ENAME       JOB             SAL
----------  ----------  ----------
SMITH       CLERK           800
WARD        SALESMAN       1250
MARTIN      SALESMAN       1250
ADAMS       CLERK          1100
JAMES       CLERK           950
MILLER      CLERK          1300
```

```
--------------------------------------------------------------------------------
| Id | Operation                   | Name | Rows | Bytes | Cost (%CPU)| Time     |
--------------------------------------------------------------------------------
|  0 | SELECT STATEMENT            |      |    5 |   100 |    2   (0)| 00:00:01 |
|  1 |  TABLE ACCESS BY INDEX ROWID| EMP  |    5 |   100 |    2   (0)| 00:00:01 |
```

Creating Custom SQL Extensions

```
|*  2  |   INDEX RANGE SCAN          | CLERK_OR_LOWSAL |    5 |       |    1   (0)| 00:00:01 |
-----------------------------------------------------------------------------------------
Predicate Information (identified by operation id):
---------------------------------------------------

   2 - access(CASE  WHEN ("JOB"='CLERK' OR "SAL"<1260) THEN 1 END =1)
```

The clerks and employees with a salary lower than 1260 are returned. The condition is integrated in a case statement and indexed.

SQL Null Functions

Null functions can translate *null* into a value and a value into *null*. Any type can contain *null*: numbers, dates, or strings.

The *nvl* function returns Y when X is null and X when X is not null. NVL2 returns Y when X is not null and Z when X is null. The *coalesce* function returns the first non-null expression:

```
with
    x
as
(
    select
        column_value x
    from
        table(sys.odcivarchar2list('x',null))
),
    y
as
(
    select
        column_value y
    from
        table(sys.odcivarchar2list('y',null))
),
    z
as
(
    select
        column_value z
    from
        table(sys.odcivarchar2list('z',null))
)
select
    x,
    y,
    z,
    nvl(x,y),
    nvl2(x,y,z),
    coalesce(x,y,z)
from
```

```
  x,y,z;
```

```
X        Y        Z      NVL(X,Y)  NVL2(X,Y,Z)  COALESCE(X,Y,Z)
------   ------   ------  --------  -----------  ---------------
X        Y        Z       X         Y            X
X        Y        <NULL>  X         Y            X
X        <NULL>   Z       X         <NULL>       X
X        <NULL>   <NULL>  X         <NULL>       X
<NULL>   Y        Z       Y         Z            Y
<NULL>   Y        <NULL>  Y         <NULL>       Y
<NULL>   <NULL>   Z       <NULL>    Z            Z
<NULL>   <NULL>   <NULL>  <NULL>    <NULL>       <NULL>
```

The *nullif* function returns *null* if both arguments are equal; otherwise, it returns the first argument.

```
select
    ename,
    comm,
    nullif(comm,0)
from
    emp
where
    deptno=30;
```

```
ENAME           COMM NULLIF(COMM,0)
----------   ---------- --------------
ALLEN            300            300
WARD             500            500
MARTIN          1400           1400
BLAKE         <NULL>       <NULL>
TURNER             0   <NULL>
JAMES         <NULL>       <NULL>
```

The *lnnvl* function returns *true* when the condition passed as parameter is either *false* or *null*.

```
select
    ename,
    sal,
    comm
from
    emp
where
    sal<=1550
    and
    lnnvl(comm!=0);
```

```
ENAME           SAL        COMM
----------   ---------- ----------
SMITH           800 <NULL>
```

```
TURNER        1500         0
ADAMS         1100  <NULL>
JAMES          950  <NULL>
MILLER        1300  <NULL>
```

Conclusion

This appendix covered many SQL functions available in Oracle including mathematic, binary, and modulo functions. A brief description of each function was provided as well as examples of use. This appendix also noted where Oracle 11g introduced improvements to various functions.

Index

Made in the USA
Monee, IL
14 August 2023

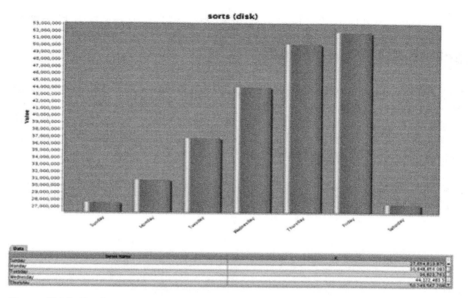

Figure 17.14: *Daily average disk sorts for a SQL workload in the Ion tool*

This makes it easy to track sort activity over time and adjust the PGA regions during times of high stress to relieve excessive disk sorting. The next section will cover how to track SQL hard parses over time.

Tracking SQL Library Cache Hard Parses

Monitoring the library cache behavior and the fact that Oracle provides several views to allow the tracking of important metrics such as total hard parses over time was covered in Chapter 16 of this text. Tuning individual SQL within the library cache is tricky, and a holistic approach to library cache tuning will track all SQL statements as a whole.

The *v$librarycache* view as well as the *stats$librarycache* and the *dba_hist_librarycache* can be queried to see hard parses over time. Figure 17.15 is a screenshot of the Ion tool showing the tracking of hard parses over time: